STUDIES IN WORLD HISTORY

THE SLAVS

Roger Portal

THE SLAVS

*A Cultural and Historical Survey of the
Slavonic Peoples*

Translated from the French by Patrick Evans

1817

HARPER & ROW, PUBLISHERS
New York and Evanston

Contents

BOOK TWO: THE BALKANS IN TURKISH
HANDS. RUSSIA: A CONTINENTAL EMPIRE
(16th AND 17th CENTURIES)

BOOK THREE: MODERN STATES (1700–1860)

1*

BOOK FIVE: THE SLAVS DRAW CLOSER TOGETHER (1917–1960)

Plates

ACKNOWLEDGEMENTS

The publishers wish to thank the following for providing illustrations for this volume: Novosti Press Agency, Paris, plates 1a, 13, 22d, 27a, b, c; Academy of Sciences, Moscow, plate 1b; Polish Embassy, Paris, plates 2, 3, 19a, c, d, e, 24; Georges Viollon-Rapho, plate 4; Exportprojekt, Ljubljana, plate 5; T.Dabac, plates 6, 7; National Gallery, Sofia, plate 8; Collection Dominique Aronson, Paris (photo Jean-Abel Lavaud), plate 9; André Michel and Librairie Armand Colin, plate 10; Pic, plate 11; Sabena, Brussels, plate 12; Prints Department, Bibliothèque Nationale, Paris, plates 14, 15 (photo Giraudon); Roger Viollet, plate 16; Giraudon, plate 17; *La Pologne* and Eustachy Kossakowski, plate 18; Polska Academia Nauk, plate 19b; Librairie Armand Colin, plate 20 (photo Jean-Abel Lavaud); J.Dupaquier, plates 22a, b; Morin, plate 22c; Tolstoy Museum, Institut d'Etudes Slaves, Paris, plate 23; M.Sebak and Editions Orbis, plate 25; Graficki Zavod Hrvtske, Zagreb, plate 26. The jacket photograph is a detail from the painting 'Collective Farm Threshing' by the Russian artist A.A.Plastov in the Russian Museum of Art, Kiev (photo Novosti Press Agency).

Illustrations in Text

Maps

Tables

Introduction

The Essential Background

THE GREAT family of Slav peoples, which occupies most of eastern and south-eastern Europe and the northern portion of the continent of Asia, is composed of East Slavs (Great Russians, Ukrainians, Byelorussians); West Slavs (Poles, Czechs, Lusations); and South Slavs (Slovenes, Croats, Serbs, Bosnians and Montenegrins, Macedonians and Bulgars).

Divided today into five states (of which three are federal, namely the USSR and the Republics of Yugoslavia and Czechoslovakia, and two non-federal: Poland and Bulgaria), the mass of approximately 250,000,000 Slavs is particularly dense and homogeneous from the Oder to the Ural River, and from the Adriatic to the Black Sea. To the west and the south the limits of the Slav territories have varied little since the tenth century; only to the eastward has there been any marked extension, beginning in the sixteenth century, to reach the Pacific in the seventeenth and Central Asia in the nineteenth.

Do their history and the characteristic features of their civilization justify us in attempting a comprehensive study, devoted to the Slavs exclusively?

Have they a common culture? Is there such a thing as 'Slav solidarity'? Truth compels us to quote the following statement by the famous specialist in the Polish language, Baudoin de Courtenay (d. 1929), commenting on the appearance of a new Polish periodical entitled *Slav Civilization* (*Kultura slowianska*): 'There is at the present time no specifically Slav civilization, common to all the Slavs and to none of the other peoples; and in all probability there never has been and never will be.'[1]

The geographical situation of the Slav peoples is sufficient to explain the fact that, in the course of a history which emerges with increasing clarity from the tenth century onwards, they achieved some degree of political fusion here and there, and from time to time. Prior to the Turkish conquest, the Poles and Czechs, and the Poles, Ukrainians and Byelorussians,

[1] In the spelling of Slav names and other words the same principle has been followed as in the original: simplicity has been the aim, and the system used varies from country to country, thus: USSR – The most usually accepted English transliterations have been followed; Poland, Czechoslovakia – the peculiarities of the national alphabet in each case have been retained; Yugoslavia, Bulgaria – the customary international transcription has been employed, with Latin characters in place of Cyrillic. (*Tr.*)

Approximate pronunciation of the chief signs used:

c	=	ts	š =	sh
č, ć	=	tch	ž =	'zh' (as in leisure)

and the South Slavs, all experienced brief phases of solidarity in the form
of ephemeral kingdoms.

The study of the Slavs nevertheless presents different civilizations and
destinies which have grown divergently from a common source. This
source, it should be noted, is little more than a convenient fiction with
which to veil our ignorance of what was actually going on in the centuries
immediately prior to the Christian era. The earliest stirrings of Slav history
are visible between the sixth and ninth centuries AD, on the eastern flank
of a Europe which already had a good deal of recorded history behind it;
by that time the Slav peoples had acquired their respective individualities,
and these were subsequently moulded by circumstances in different and
sometimes diametrically opposite ways.

Why then, in this Europe – or rather Eurasia – of which they were and
are an integral part, should we make a distinct entity out of the Slavs,
whose origins are European; who have no anthropological homogeneity
which would set them apart from their western neighbours; who do not
constitute a race in any meaningful sense of the term; and who have been
deeply involved in European history for the last ten centuries?

FIGURE 1 Bronze plaque
with animal mask.
Final period of the La
Tène civilization, second
century; found in a
graveyard at
Malomerice, near Brno
(Czechoslovakia).

The Slavs Are Europeans

We must start by rejecting the view which isolates the Eastern Slavs from Europe and invests them with an Asiatic character. True, there was the Mongol conquest; but its influence on Russian society between the thirteenth and fifteenth centuries was very restricted. Again, there have been Turkish minorities in European Russia; but they were submerged by waves of Slav colonization. And in the sixteenth and seventeenth centuries there was the occupation of Siberia, a continent which had remained almost uninhabited until the arrival of the Russians. None of these factors justifies us in describing the Eastern Slavs as Asiatics. They came from central Europe in the first place and did not become any less European when they extended their civilization eastwards to the Pacific. (It should be noted in passing that the Ural River has never constituted a barrier; any attempt to make it the frontier of Europe is quite artificial.) Even during the period when they were largely subjected to Mongol overlordship and out of touch with the West, their essentially European civilization, the heir to the traditions of both Kiev and Byzantium, remained essentially intact.

It was Byzantium which enabled the South Slavs to survive five centuries of Ottoman occupation. In that part of the Slav world the interpenetration of cultures, though extensive, was superficial. Conversion to Islam was widespread among the Slavs of Bosnia, but never became a vehicle of pan-Turkism. The Greek church and the Slav language together constituted a wall between the Turks and the Bulgars, who were strengthened by the presence of near-by Constantinople.

The South Slavs, then, must also be accounted Europeans, or a southern type and temperament (figure 2).

Linguistic and Religious Diversity

The languages spoken by the Slavs are all Indo-European, forming a single related group distinguished from the Romance and Teutonic languages by characteristic differences in morphology, and more especially in phonetics and syntax. But this linguistic kinship would not by itself make the Slavs and their world a proper subject for exclusive study, for it has done little to create any effective Slav solidarity. It is true that a majority of them (namely the Eastern Slavs and the Serbs and Bulgars) use a script (the so-called 'Cyrillic': figure 3) which has had some effect as an isolating factor. But the other Slav peoples never adopted it.

The religious factor has been more important, but here again there is no unity. The most that can be said is that a preponderance of the Slavs (the East Slavs, Serbs, Montenegrins, Macedonians and Bulgars) have belonged to the Orthodox Church, and that until the eighteenth century this common ground provided them with a potential unity and profoundly influenced their respective civilizations.

The conversion of the Slavs to Christianity was undertaken by the

SLAV POPULATION FIGURES, TWENTIETH CENTURY	
TOTAL POPULATION	DISTRIBUTION
Soviet Union (1959): 208,827,000	Russians 114,588,000 Ukrainians 36,981,000 Byelorussians 7,829,000
Poland (1946): 23,900,000 (1961): 30,500,000	
Czechoslovakia (1961): 13,742,000 (*National minorities:* 6%)	Bohemia-Moravia 9,567,000 Slovakia 4,175,000
Yugoslavia (1953): 16,937,000	Serbia 6,979,000 Croatia 3,919,000 Slovenia 1,466,000 Bosnia-Herzegovina 2,848,000 Macedonia 1,305,000 Montenegro 420,000
(1959 *estimate*): 18,448,000	Serbia 7,504,000 Croatia 4,182,000 Slovenia 1,585,000 Bosnia-Herzegovina 3,283,000 Macedonia 1,481,000 Montenegro 479,000
Bulgaria (1963): 8,000,000	

Byzantine Church. Bishops Cyril and Methodius spread the Greek rite as far north as Bohemia, but the Western Church soon recaptured these outlying positions, and Roman Catholicism prevailed in consequence among the Czechs and Slovaks and also the Poles, who were converted in 966, in the time of Mieszko, the Duke of Bohemia's brother-in-law. The Slovenes and Croats were also won over to the Roman Church.

Although the wave of conversion originated in the Balkans it is the Russians, not the Serbs, Montenegrins, Macedonians and Bulgars, who constitute the main mass of Orthodox believers. Russia was Byzantium's greatest spiritual conquest; when Byzantium decayed, her heritage was taken over by Kiev, and subsequently by Moscow. The cleavage between the eastern and western Churches, which showed itself first in the schism of 1054, became final with the capture of Constantinople by the Turks in 1453. Despite the projects for reunion which crop up so frequently – notably in the writings of priests who travelled in Russia, such as Krijanitch in the seventeenth century – there was profound hostility between the Roman and Orthodox communities; one result of this was a heightening of the tension already created between Russia and Poland by political rivalry. Thus religion, which was a link between Russia and the Balkan Slavs – who, however, were too far away to benefit directly from Russian religious sympathy – drove a wedge between neighbours.

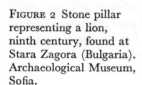

FIGURE 2 Stone pillar representing a lion, ninth century, found at Stara Zagora (Bulgaria). Archaeological Museum, Sofia.

In addition, a relatively small proportion of the East Slavs, in the Ukraine, broke away from the Orthodox Church, and, while retaining its ritual, placed themselves under papal authority; this 'United Church' (hence the name Uniates) of Greek Catholics was dominant in the region of Kiev from 1596, and in the western Ukraine (with Lviv and Przemysl as focal points) from the end of the seventeenth century. But Orthodox reconquest under the Tsarist regime, followed by the religious policy of the Soviet government, reduced their numbers virtually to zero in that part of Ukraine which is included in the basin of the Dnieper. They remained numerically strong in the western Ukraine, which belonged to Poland until the partitions began and thereafter formed part of Austrian Galicia until the outbreak of the First World War. The Uniates have been regarded with suspicion by Orthodox and Catholics alike; and the simultaneous existence, in a Galicia dominated by a Polish majority, of two forms of religion, has been a divisive influence.

Nor have Catholicism and Orthodoxy been the only religious forces promoting division among the Slavs. Islam entered the Balkans with the Ottomans, and though few religions can have been imbued less strongly with proselytizing zeal, large numbers of Slavs who had become Turkish subjects by force of conquest became Muslims of their own volition. Bosnia presents the curious case of a population partly Roman Catholic, partly Orthodox and partly Muslim. In the Balkans, where Franciscan missionary labours had somewhat extended the sway of Roman Catholicism at the expense of Orthodoxy, the Muslims constituted an inert, impervious mass which only national feeling was capable of stirring into activity, and uniting with the Orthodox, against the Austrian invasion of 1878.

Another disruptive force, stronger than that exerted by Islam, was the shock of the Reformation. Its first manifestation among the Slavs was the heretical Hussite movement in fourteenth-century Bohemia. Despite its national and social aspects this was essentially a religious uprising; it overflowed into Poland and its influence on the mentality of the Czechs was deep and enduring. Crushed but never extirpated, it was reborn as Lutheranism in the sixteenth century. Most of Bohemia went over to Protestantism, but was recaptured by Roman Catholicism as a result of the Thirty Years War. Thereafter the Reformation was represented in Bohemia by the non-Slav section of the population, the German minority. These vicissitudes are perhaps a clue to the pragmatic attitude and relative religious indifference, which are typical of the Czech mentality and in which the Czechs would seem to differ from the other Slav peoples.

Finally, an error to avoid is that of overestimating the ties of feeling among the Orthodox. Whatever spiritual cohesion may once have existed was soon dispelled by the rise of nationalism in the nineteenth century; it had in any case been rendered precarious long before by historical development and linguistic differences. The Serbs and Bulgars were united in their opposition to the Greek clergy in Macedonia, but in nothing else.

Dependence and Independence

What has made the Slav peoples into a distinct entity is their geographical situation and its consequences. Because they live in the eastern territories of the European peninsula they have been in continuous contact with the peoples of Asia, and as soon as they had settled permanently – from the Baltic to the Adriatic, and from the plains of the Vistula to those of the Upper Volga – they found themselves engaged in a struggle, destined to endure for centuries, both against conquerors from the East and against the older and more efficiently organized states of the West. Only two of the Slav peoples were able to achieve independence and maintain it for any length of time. One was the Poles, whose population included the Byelorussians and Ukrainians for a considerable period, but who suffered a century and a half of eclipse from the middle of the eighteenth century. The other was the Russians, who, after throwing off the Mongol occupation in the fifteenth century and thereafter repressing and partially absorbing the pockets of Turkish-descended population east of the Volga, gradually built up the immense empire, at once European and Asiatic, which has constituted a permanent bastion of the Slav world and which no external power has succeeded in destroying. The Czechs and Slovaks, and the Slovenes, Croats, Serbs and Bulgars, were less fortunate, succumbing to foreign domination at an early stage. The crucial factor was the Turkish invasion in the sixteenth century, which drew a wavering line of demarcation between, on the one hand, those of the Slavs who remained inside Christendom and came either under German influence (the Czechs, Slovaks, Croats and a few of the Serbs) or Hungarian influence (Slovaks); and, on the other, those who became subjects of the Crescent (the Bosnians, Montenegrins, Macedonians, Bulgars and most of the Serbs). From then until the movements of national awakening in the nineteenth century – and with the exception of the Czechs of Bohemia, who experienced a short-lived autonomy within the framework of the Hapsburg empire, an autonomy terminated by the Battle of the White Mountain (1620) – all these were subject peoples, whose development and progress were correspondingly inhibited and who, well into the nineteenth century, preserved some of their most archaic characteristics amid the modernity of the rest of Europe. Whereas the influence of Teutonic civilization on the Slovenes and Croats was of a progressive kind, Turkish domination, which simply by force of circumstance also radiated its influence among the Christian peoples of the Balkans, acted as a narcotic, producing inertia; only the territories along the Adriatic shore remained partially immune to Turkish stagnation, thanks to the progressive impetus imparted by Venetian influence. The Germans were more dynamic than the Venetians, both materially and in their religion, but the progress stimulated by their rule was accompanied by oppression, territorial encroachment and ethnic assimilation, with the result that the areas occupied by the Czechs, Croats and Slovenes were gradually reduced in size.

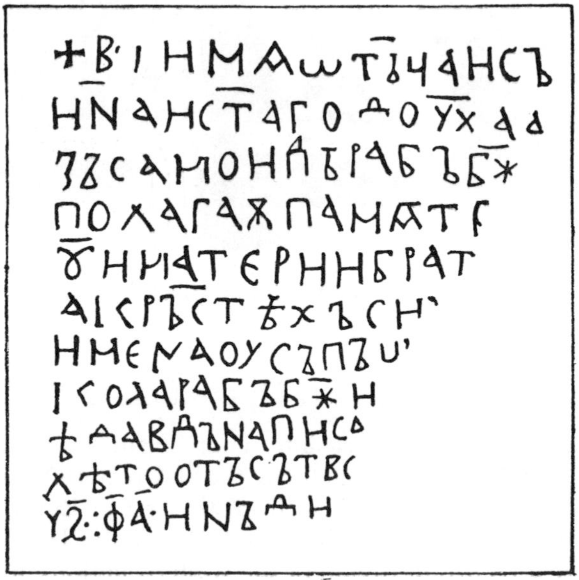

FIGURE 3 Earliest known inscription in Cyrillic letters (AD 993), on a tombstone in Macedonia.

Thus it came about that some of the Slav peoples were in a state of continual change and expansion, while others were on the retreat and the defensive. Those in the first category were free to develop within a political and social framework which they established early and were able to strengthen as the centuries rolled on, but which might be temporarily shattered (as was the case with Poland, subjected to partition by three foreign powers at the end of the eighteenth century). Those in the second category were embodied in alien political complexes, in a state of suspended animation which might be temporarily exchanged for a period of glorious awakening such as the reign of Charles IV of Bohemia.

It follows that we must break our material down in order to build it up, and that we must take account of the historical factors peculiar to the development of each of the Slav peoples. The East Slavs, the Poles and the South Slavs are the main groups, and must be studied separately.

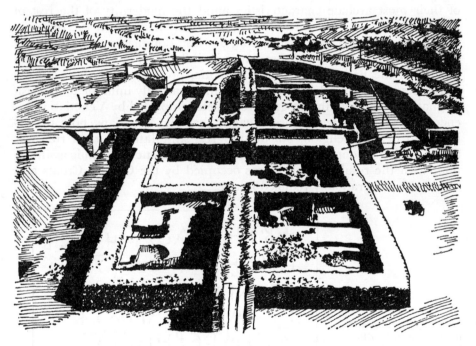

FIGURE 4 Foundations of a basilica at Mikulcice, from the time of the empire of Great Moravia.

A Common Interest: Opposition to the Turks

Despite having evolved into separate entities, and despite the many conflicts of interest between them, the Slav peoples possess one common feature which differentiates them from the rest of Europe. They were for many centuries in constant, direct contact with the Turks, crusades against whom were a recurrent dream of the western nations, a dream translated from time to time into action. Only the Austrians and Hungarians were like the Slavs in having to sustain a protracted struggle with the Ottoman Empire along their own frontiers; and, even so, Austria performed this protective role – that of a military borderland, a march – for only a short time, and it was the king of Poland who saved Vienna in 1683. The Croats and the Serbs of Slavonia, Syrmia and the Banat, interposed between the Austrians and Hungarians on one hand and the Turks on the other, constituted a Slavonic fringe throughout whose length the 'military confines' were organized in the eighteenth century. To the south of this *limes* or human rampart the Slav peoples of the Balkans were forever struggling to snatch their freedom from the occupying Turks. The Poles and Russians were in frequent conflict with the enemy from without, a conflict interrupted at times on the Polish side by anti-Russian alliances born of the standing animosity between the two countries and the perpetual ambition of each to capture territory from the other. Military engagement between the Poles and Turks was moreover considerably reduced at an early stage, after the Russians had regained possession of the territories on the right bank of the Dnieper which had once formed part of the state of Kiev and were subsequently divided between Lithuania and the Polish-Lithuanian kingdom. A lengthier conflict was that of Muscovy against the Tartars, whose forward positions were not far distant from Moscow itself even as late as the sixteenth century (map 9). This was not merely a matter of disengaging the capital by freeing it from the threat of marauding bands of cavalry; it was a major necessity, involving as it did the Russian colonial drive southwards towards the Black Sea and the re-creation of the political unity of the Slav peoples in Russia, a unity the Mongols had shattered. What the Russians were carrying out was in fact a crusade, whose culmination was the conquest of the Crimea at the end of the eighteenth century.

This Orthodox crusade was less prominent in Western eyes than the efforts of the Poles, and the Austrian and Hungarian campaigns on the Danube naturally drew more attention than either; the Russian enterprise bore the disfiguring stamp of heresy and was in any case of little or no practical consequence to Catholic Christendom. The fact remains that it produced an intermittent solidarity between the Poles and Russians and the co-operation of the East and South Slavs against the common enemy.

Danger from Germany and Austria

Another common obstacle produced a similar effect. The Germanic peoples' *Drang nach Osten* was executed at the expense of the Poles, who lost the lands lying between the Elbe and the Oder (map 5) and were cut off from the Baltic for a long time to come. Continued by the German knightly orders in the Baltic countries, this 'drive to the east' came to a head-on clash with the East Slavs on the Estonian border.

The 'Battle of the Ice', fought in 1242 on Lake Peipus by Alexander Nevskv, Prince of Suzdal, who stemmed the tide of invasion, has remained,

like the victory over the Tartars at Kulikovo (1380), one of the great
dates in Russian national history. The Poles, for their part, celebrate
Grünenwald (Tannenberg), the battle in which the Polish-Lithuanian
kingdom broke the power of the Teutonic Knights in 1410.

It is true that by the time Poland had become a powerful state with considerable access to the Baltic, a position she held in the sixteenth and
seventeenth centuries, the German danger had largely diminished; to the
Russians, the Poles during this period were enemies and invaders whose
cavalry even succeeded in reaching Moscow (1609). The partitions of
Poland, mainly benefiting her Russian neighbour, reversed the situation
and increased the enmity between the two peoples. But Russian oppression
was less ominous to the Poles than German colonization, which threatened
a real loss of national identity.

The German danger, which reappeared during the First World War,
had been masked in the interim by several developments; the Russian
reaction in the eighteenth century against the 'reign of the Germans', who
had become powerful at court and in the administration about 1740; the
glorious campaigns of the imperial armies, which camped in Berlin in the
course of the Seven Years War, and later, after contributing to the downfall of Napoleon, enabled Nicholas 1 to become 'the arbiter of Europe';
and, finally, the stabilization of Russia's frontier with Prussia, at the expense of Poland. Between the world wars, Nazi imperialism included
among its objectives both the Ukraine and the territory of the reconstituted
Polish state.

An equally deep-rooted antagonism has divided the Germans and the
Czechs; the latter have suffered from German colonization which, while
based on the towns, also nibbled persistently at the edges of the Bohemian
plateau. The Slovenes were subjected to similar pressures. Nineteenth-
century nationalism in both peoples was fortified by anti-German feeling.
Further south the situation was of course different, since it was by Christian
armies advancing from Austria that the Slavs under Turkish rule expected
to be liberated. But the Austro-Hungarian Empire's policy of penetration
in the Balkans, and the occupation (1878) and annexation (1908) of
Herzegovina, made the Teutonic threat felt here as elsewhere, and fostered
a sense of unity between the South Slavs and the dominions of the Tsar.
Inevitably there have been *rapprochements* from time to time, and much
influence in both directions; but neither of these, nor dynastic relationships, have done much in the long term to end the fundamental conflict
between the Germans and Slavs. Present-day concord between Poland and
Russia is in fact based on a vivid awareness of possible future aggression
from the west.

Dubious Collective Spirit

The agrarian community known as the *obchtchina* was an autochthonous
creation, found only among the Eastern Slavs. It combined collective

ownership of the land with individual cultivation; produce was periodically shared out; and the whole was managed by a peasant committee, the *mir*. The origins of the institution are obscure.

Some historians have regarded the *obchtchina* as an economic and social necessity, a defensive reaction to difficult natural conditions, a spontaneous and very ancient form of the struggle for existence. It must be admitted, however, that there is virtually no documentary mention of the *obchtchina* before the sixteenth century. Other writers consider it to have been a governmental creation, a framework imposed on the peasantry by the central power for administrative and fiscal reasons; it is argued that it originated in the sixteenth century at the earliest, and that its emergence depended on that of a centralized state.

Neither explanation necessarily excludes the other. The *mir* may have been a very ancient institution; and it was certainly consolidated and more widely imposed in Russia during the reign of Ivan the Terrible. But it is not the general property of the Slavs. It is unknown among the Poles, Czechs and Slovaks. It is completely different from the patriarchal forms of agrarian organization formerly found in one part of the Balkans under the general name of *zadruga*. And even in Russia it is typical only of Great Russia, not of Southern Russia or Siberia.

We therefore cannot regard this institution as reflecting a putative, inherently Russian mentality. It undoubtedly fostered the growth of a new mentality among the peasants, so that in the nineteenth century, when Russia was achieving self-awareness and measuring herself against western countries, the *obchtchina* figured as an original inheritance from the past, in which the mentality of the Russian peasant was characteristically expressed. But this does not alter the fact that the *obchtchina* was born of environmental and historical circumstances. Attempts have been made to link the *mir* and the *kolkhoz*; it is claimed that the *kolkhoz* system was all the easier to instal because of the rural community which had existed before it. There is little to support this view. As we shall see, the rural community was crumbling on the eve of the First World War and would indeed have declined much earlier had it not received an injection of new life from the agrarian reforms of 1861.

Strength of Foreign Traditions and Influences

The geographical situation of the Slav peoples, exposing them to pressure first from Asia and then from the west, has rendered them highly susceptible to foreign influences. Direct domination by the Turks, Germans or Hungarians, which placed a single alien civilization in the ascendant and produced either straightforward adoption of alien ways, or an intermingling with effects on both sides, restricted the number and variety of influences entering the country from outside but thereby drove its own effects all the deeper into the lives of the people. Things were different in the two independent states, Russia and Poland, which were more accessible to trends from abroad; only the upper classes, in a fever of modernistic plagiarism, adopted western clothes and behaviour. Bosnian monks in the nineteenth century still wore Turkish headgear and stuck pistols in their belts; whereas in Russia at the same period German clothes were worn only by the nobles and some of their servants, and a few rich merchants.

One of the key factors was religion. Western influences were naturally stronger in Catholic countries; elsewhere they came up against the stubborn conservatism of Orthodoxy and the hold of the Orthodox clergy on popular life. Hence the superficial nature of western influence, confined to a small and wealthy minority for whom the adoption of Western fashions and attitudes constituted at once an increase in material comfort and a badge of social superiority.

But the preservation of the time-honoured features of the Slav civilizations was due above all to the fact that until very recent times the countries concerned were still essentially agricultural. The Slav peoples were peasant peoples, largely immune to urban, extraneous influences (to a peasant, change is something which goes on in towns), and endowed with passive resistance with which to thwart any attempt at assimilation by a foreign power; thus the permanence of Slav national characteristics has been guaranteed by economic backwardness. The Slav territories lay too far to the east, on the borders of empty Asia, remote from the arteries of world travel and communication through which the life-blood of Europe flowed from the fifteenth century onwards. The rise and growth of industry, which modified the entire structure of western society, occurred much later in the Slav world. Moreover, the one Slav country which was caught up in the general movement and experienced a precocious industrial and urban development was also that which was subjected most heavily to foreign pressure: the civilization of the Czechs was brought to the verge of extinction by the advance of German colonists in town and city. But the Croats and Slovenes – the latter especially – remained immune, protected by their rugged environment.

Slav 'backwardness' is a relative term; it does not apply equally to all the Slav peoples. Those who came under Byzantium and subsequently the Turks – the Bosnians, Montenegrins, and Bulgars, and the Serbs south of the Danube and the Sava – developed at the same relaxed pace as their rulers and lingered in stagnation from the fifteenth until the nineteenth century, when the national liberation movement jolted them out of it. Things fared otherwise with those who came under the Holy Roman Emperors and their successors the Hapsburgs: thus the Czechs escaped the retardation which has been a slur on the East Slavs. But the Slovaks on one hand, and on the other the Slovenes and Croats, inhabiting opposite ends of the Pannonian basin, with the Hungarians between, fell victims to it – a fact to be explained both by the physical nature of the terrain and by its position as a border region next to the Turks. A different phenomenon altogether is presented by the Poles and East Slavs, whose destiny was

Map 1 The Slavs in the Tenth Century

under their own control Poland was in close communication with the West but her easterly position created conditions that hampered her development. Russia, being more isolated, was further handicapped, and it was not until the sixteenth century that her connections with western European life were definitely established.

'National' Civilizations

Even in early periods, before the development of conscious nationhood, what we have to consider is national rather than specifically Slav civilizations.

For despite their common origin and related languages, the Slav peoples exhibit more differences than resemblances. Each of them has its own history, which has shaped its traditions, outlook and way of life. The justification for bringing these peoples together in a single study must be sought not so much in the past as in the present; each of them now has its own state framework, federal in most cases, through which to preserve its own individuality, and all these states have the same type of regime. The resulting uniformity should not be summarily explained by invoking the 'Slav' past; the real reasons for the triumph of new political and social forms in this sector of Europe, a triumph which includes some non-Slavic peoples (Rumanians, Hungarians, Albanians), lie in economic and social conditions, in historical circumstances, and in the sheer weight of the largest and most powerful of the Slav peoples, the one which had its revolution before any of the others. But in so far as these new forms are progressively transforming every aspect of life, they are tending to produce a unified civilization on that part of the earth's surface where the Slavs are overwhelmingly in the majority. The paradox is that just when this new, common civilization is coming to birth among the Slav peoples, the technological revolution of the twentieth century is approximating it to the civilization of the United States.

Some Over-Simplifications Corrected

The expression 'Slav civilizations' or 'Slav cultures' does none the less imply certain shared characteristics which have been emphasized time and again in literature; such are mysticism, instinctive taste in the arts (with the possible exception of painting) and a fondness for singing and dancing. These are the supposed ingredients of the 'Slav soul'.

But it is odd to reflect that the peoples to whom these attractive qualities are imputed are simultaneously criticized for their itch to ape foreign ways, and for backwardness and ignorance – for their barbarism, in short; a verdict which some of the most highly educated Slavs have not infrequently reinforced by their contemptuous attitude towards their own national cultures.

It is only during the last hundred years, at most, that the Slavs have begun to rise in the estimation of the world. And quite apart from any question of esteem, it is an undoubted fact that material progress was much slower to get under way among those of them who lived under foreign domination than it was for the peoples of the West; independent political existence and state organization – the precondition of progress – are a relatively new experience for them. It should be noted in this connection that the charge of backwardness has been levelled chiefly at the Orthodox countries, especially those which are geographically closest to the Turks.

Parallelism, Not Congruence

It is not to be forgotten that Slav society, while needing to be studied in relation to its respective national settings, developed against a background which is common to all the European peoples. Like the Teutons and the Latins, the Slavs underwent the economic and social phases whose characteristics are denoted by 'feudalism' and 'capitalism'; but they did it more slowly and in their own way. It is true that the word 'feudalism' does not mean quite the same thing to Marxist historians as to the 'bourgeois' historians of the West. But in so far as it defines, for example, the interdependent relationship between peasants and landed overlords, it dominated western Slav life until the eighteenth century and eastern until the middle of the nineteenth, a nascent or embryonic form of capitalism meanwhile growing up in its midst at a time when, in the West, powerful banking houses were already in existence and the tremendous forces of the industrial revolution were about to be unleashed.

The result was that society in the Slav countries (with the exception of Bohemia, whose development was bound up with that of her Germanic neighbours) remained archaic for much longer; in those countries, the flow of historical time had slowed down.

The countries in question display astonishing contrasts not only with the West, but with each other. Whereas in western Europe the peasants were serfs in the later days of the Empire and gradually shed their feudal bonds to become independent property-owners, in Russia and Poland the free peasantry which had evolved from the break-up of the tribal system did just the opposite, falling little by little into a servitude which was crystallized by legislation and not dissolved until the nineteenth century. The Middle Ages, in fact, were projected into the contemporary world. This is the reason for the abrupt contrasts typical of the Slav countries. Capitalism made its appearance much later than in the West: in Russia, the merchant class was numerically weak in the seventeenth century and non-existent prior to that period; industry (with sporadic exceptions in the eighteenth century) sprang up under Peter the Great; and there was no banking system until after 1860. In the Russian economy, modern and in many cases ultra-modern forms existed side by side with the most archaic. The same is true of the Balkans, where pre-capitalist economic life continued until the twentieth century. Bohemia excepted, the condition of the Slav countries when the decisive change of régime swept over them – 1917 in Russia, 1945 in the others – was characterized by lack of industrial development (even in Russia, in relation to her human and natural resources), insignificance of the middle classes, the predominance of an agricultural economy and the peasant spirit.

The combination of industrialization and conservative nationalism, typical of the nineteenth-century West, has become, in a new social context, a vital necessity for the socialist states of today.

The Case of Russia

We have very little information about the Slavs prior to the tenth century, and there has therefore been much conflict of opinion concerning of civilizations of the earliest Slav communities. It was long assumed that the tribes inhabiting the regions between the Baltic and the Black Sea were still mainly dependent on hunting and food-fathering at the beginning of the Christian era, and that by the ninth and tenth centuries, when the first rudimentary Russian states were formed, they had not developed beyond the stage of simple agriculture. Really, however, they had progressed a good deal further; various crafts were vigorously pursued, and in addition to purely agricultural settlements there were townships on the waterways linking one region to another. When the warlike Varangians penetrated Russia from the north, and while their ships were scouring the coasts of the Baltic and the Channel and making their way up the rivers of the West, they encountered along the Volkhov and the Dnieper a type of society which, though less highly developed than that of western Europe, had achieved some degree of political organization in the form of transient military confederations. And although the Varangians, after an initial period as mercenary adventurers based on Novgorod, were to supply the Slavs of the Dnieper basin with a long line of dynastic rulers, it was not properly speaking from them that the Slavs acquired the idea of a state. The state of Kiev was not a creation of the Norsemen; it was the result of a long process of prior social development among the East Slavs, to which was added the energetic leadership of these foreign but rapidly Russianized warriors. Receiving its religion from Byzantium during the ninth and tenth centuries, Kiev created a brilliant civilization in no way inferior to that of the small Capetian states of the West. And the recent archaeological finds of birchbark inscriptions at Novgorod prove that, by the eleventh century, the ability to read and write was not confined to the clergy; education had spread to some at least of the townspeople (plate 1).

The Mongol conquest in the thirteenth century placed a brutal check on a course of development which might have parallelled that of the western countries. The long, grim struggle for deliverance drew Russia's forces not westward but eastward, confronting her with huge tracts of empty territory which it was an easy matter for her subsequently to conquer and occupy, but which had nothing to offer in the way of civilization and culture. The advantages of colonization and wider markets were like a cheque drawn on the future; the benefits were extremely slow to materialize. Russia's strongest and most fruitful contact was still that with the West. Fierce struggles with the Prussians and the Poles concentrated much of her dynamism in this quarter; and peaceful relations with the Hanseatic cities, through the trading communities of Pskov and Novgorod, maintained a link, albeit tenuous, with the western world, whose economy was expanding and whose towns were multiplying. But these connections did nothing to relieve her acutely isolated, excessively continental position, and the fact that she had no ports.

It was at this juncture in her history that Russia became backward by comparison with the West, and with the passage of time her backwardness was increasingly flagrant. In effect she had suffered no more than a passing severance from the European sphere. But by the time when the youthful state of Muscovy, having gradually won its way to a centralized, orderly condition, had established solid and permanent connections with the West in the sixteenth century, Russia's image abroad was that of a barbarous Asiatic country whose progress, such as it was, could be attributed only to contact with the West. This false perspective – an optical illusion in which the unique qualities and hard-won advances of Russian civilization, and even its most brilliant and striking characteristics (which emerged in the artistic field), were undervalued and largely ignored – lasted almost to the present day; and the great reforms of the eighteenth century, unjustly interpreted as an imitative 'westernization' of Russia, merely served to reinforce it. Even in the early twentieth century the West found it impossible to believe that the works of such an artist as Rublev, whose fame had been recognized by the Council of Moscow in 1551 but who was completely unknown to western scholars, had been painted by a Russian; at least one expert ascribed his *Trinity* to an Italian.

Clearly, then, the reader will constantly be called upon to adapt and adjust his attitude as the story unfolds. Modern Russia, struggling from the time of Peter the Great onwards to overcome a handicap of such long standing, did not emerge in the twinkling of an eye, but grew gradually from roots developed in the preceding periods: it was fifteenth and sixteenth century Russia, neither barbarous nor Asiatic, which rendered possible the country's entry into the concert of European powers.

Both the manner and the tempo of the advance which began in the eighteenth century are undoubtedly surprising to contemplate. Progress was spasmodic and inconsistent, shot through with contrasts. Social organization and material conditions remained unaltered for nearly all Russians until the 1861 reforms abolished serfdom, whose stranglehold embraced something like half the peasantry and which the rest of Europe legitimately regarded as a freakish survival. But on the economic side Russia was so advanced that in the eighteenth century her metallurgical industry was the main European producer of pig-iron, which she supplied to English foundries; this situation continued until coke supplanted wood as a fuel and the English ironmasters became independent of Russian supplies. The scope and modernity of this industry are in striking contrast with others, such as textiles, which remained underdeveloped for want of adequate markets.

It was as late as 1880–90 that the industrial revolution really took hold of Russia, creating yet further disparities between regions, such as the Urals, where antiquated methods of production remained in force, and those whose factories were the equal of anything in the industrial West, such as the Ukraine, where, it must be admitted, foreign initiative played

the leading part. Another contrast was that between the general backwardness of industry, and the advanced state of scientific research associated
with such names as Mendeleyev and Pavlov.

The October Revolution – a revolution in the fullest sense of the term,
to which history affords no parallel – abruptly transformed the whole
political, economic and social structure and also modified artistic output
of every kind. But radical though the change undoubtedly was – an abrupt
break in the history of Russia and her civilization – it must not be forgotten
how large a legacy from the past the revolution subsequently gathered up,
absorbed and put to new uses. This novel advance was in fact rather the
sudden acceleration of a development already in progress; and though it
has assumed new and original forms and is gradually fashioning a new
civilization, it has had far too brief a space of time, a mere half-century, in
which to effect a corresponding transformation of Russian minds and attitudes; faced by the enormous tasks involved in the active metamorphosis
of every department of life, tasks which have been pursued through the
civil wars and two foreign wars, it has left some corners as yet unillumin-
ated, untouched. These gaps are being gradually dealt with by a leadership
which, while systematic, rational, and intent on levelling out differences,
is on the whole extremely supple and versatile in its approach. It can at
least be said that the disparities, economic, social and political, which have
been typical of Russia during all her previous history, are now tending to
disappear in favour of some degree of unity and harmony.

Nationalism in Ferment: Pan-Slavism

Among intellectuals in eastern and south-eastern Europe, one of the
forms taken by the upsurge of nationalism in the nineteenth century was
the notion of a community of Slav peoples at once ethnically distinct from
the Anglo-Saxons, Teutons and Latins, and superior to all three. Russian
devotees of Slavism were impelled by a sense of pride; during the reign of
Alexander I the Tsarist empire had acquired a new importance on the
international scene, and it appeared to have a mission of civilization and
protection to fulfil towards the other Slav peoples, who had as yet not regained independence. The latter, thirsty for liberty and unable to secure it
without external help, were moved by self-preservation. With the exception of Poland, whose national characteristics had been clearly and consciously established for centuries and which was suffering from Russian
oppression at the time, all these peoples were still struggling to take possession of the primary instrument of their future existence as nations – their
own language. At such a moment, there was naturally a great temptation
for them to picture a victorious onward march ending in the promised
land, a linguistic and cultural commonwealth under the guidance and
production of the most powerful of all the Slav peoples.

In reality, however, political interest was at the bottom of the Pan-
Slav movement, which was an expression of Russian imperialism and

which, from the subject peoples' point of view, contained a concealed but basic contradiction; namely that the increasing growth of national consciousness, based on each nation's study of its own past, was inconceivable without the maintenance of the individual languages and the accentuation of the differences already existing between the Slavs.

The Pan-Slav Congress at Prague in 1848, and that at Moscow in 1867, produced nothing. As soon as it was thought of as a political possibility the proposed unity of the Slav peoples foundered on the rocks of practical reality. Each people was looking for its own path, its own future, and by the eighteen-seventies the Pan-Slavism of such a statesman as Danilevski (1822–85) was merely a pretext for the policy of the Russian government in the Balkans and central Asia. It was no longer defined in reference to the other Slav peoples and 'national' civilizations, but solely in reference to the western powers and their civilization, whose decline it predicted with comfortable assurance. It was the opinion of a restricted circle of intellectuals and carried no weight.

The increasing probability of world war endowed a peaceful, conciliatory version of Pan-Slavism with a renewed topical appeal; but the Prague Congress of 1908, at which the term 'Neo-Slavism' was launched, was regarded with deep suspicion by the Czechs, Slovaks and Austrian Ukrainians and succeeded only in exposing more clearly than before the discordant Slav nationalisms within the reigning empires.

What Nationalism Divided, Socialism Must Unite

For all that, the Pan-Slavism of 1848 had been the point of confluence for profounder tendencies which contained the germ of a fertile idea, that of unity between peoples labouring to bring freedom and justice to birth. A fugitive and premature hope, but one which was written into the programme of every socialist party, every workers' syndicate and every trade union for the next half-century or more, and which became increasingly substantial and convincing as economic development swelled the numbers of the proleteriat, engendered closer communication between the most intelligent working class elements in all industrial countries, and transposed the problem of relations between peoples to the social plane, making it independent of linguistic and cultural differences.

Poland having been dismembered by partition, a section of her people was impatiently enduring Russian imperial tyranny. And the Slav peoples beyond the Russian frontiers, all of whom were subjects of the German, Austro-Hungarian or Ottoman empires, had been caught up in the great tide of nationalism which had been tearing at Europe since the end of the eighteenth century. The ancient nations of Poland and Bohemia had a long experience behind them of organic existence as independent states; nationlities with less historical confirmation to lean upon, like those of Slovakia, Croatia, Serbia and Bulgaria, could remember the rudimentary beginnings of such existence, which they had enjoyed in the distant past; the potential nationalities of Slovenia and, inside the Russian empire, those of Ukraine and White Russia, were rapidly developing national self-awareness; and each of these, led and stimulated by its own intellectual élite, aspired to independence or autonomy, and, in either event, to the untrammelled affirmation of its own way of life.

Nationalities, and states too, in some instances, were being reborn. Serbia (1815–29) and Bulgaria (1878–85) became beacons of hope to those Slavs who were still under Turkish dominion (or Austro-Hungarian, after the occupation of Bosnia in 1878); concurrently the Croats and Slovenes, the Czechs and Slovaks, and to a lesser extent the Ukrainians, were conducting an ever sharper struggle against the centralizing or assimilative policies of Austria, Hungary, Prussia and Russia. The First World War liberated the Czechs, Slovaks and Poles, and brought most of the South Slavs together in the new state of Yugoslavia. The Second World War made it possible to re-draw the frontiers in greater conformity with the actual distribution of the Slav peoples.

But the nationalistic drive was a divisive factor. The brief 'springtime of the peoples' (1848), lit up so brightly with hopes and illusions, was followed by a long period during which the Slav nationalisms went their separate ways, with occasional tactical *rapprochements*. There was little hope of agreement between the Serbs and Bulgars, both of whom claimed Macedonia; or between the Croats and the Serbs, competing for Bosnia and the Dalmatian coast; or between the Poles and the Ukrainians in Galicia, the former looking to Warsaw and the latter to Kiev. Interpretation of historical traditions, and of the not infrequently ambiguous characteristics of regional lauguages, were used as arguments in claims and counter-claims which lent an aggressive sting to nationalistic rivalries. War and the all-powerful will of the victors created Slav states which turned the formerly oppressed into oppressors, with minorities of their own – in some cases Slav minorities; examples are Poland, Czechoslovakia and Yugoslavia between the two world wars. To this situation the Second World War appears to have brought a satisfactory remedy: the rearrangement of frontiers, and, still more pertinent, the adoption of a federal system by states with different Slav cultures and languages to accommodate.

The present-day cohesion of the Slav peoples depends primarily on their all having the same type of government and similar forms of social organization. Except in the case of Yugoslavia it depends also on a common external policy, which at present is highly flexible, much debated, and not so much imposed as suggested by the leading Slav power. To this extent, the success of the Bolshevik Revolution (1917) and the subsequent spread of socialist government in Europe (1945–7) have enabled the Slav peoples to realize the hope entertained by the élite of the workers' movement in earlier days, that of an international of the common people.

The classes comprising the common people were the very foundation on which the national movement depended in the countries concerned, not only because of the support they gave the insurrectionary leaders on specific occasions but also through their uninterrupted tradition of resistance. It is true that when national awareness was still vague and inchoate, the feelings of the oppressed populations were roused by immediate causes and directed towards immediate objectives, mostly originating in burdensome social conditions; yet larger, national aspirations crept in everywhere. Even religious conflict was permeated by them. The Hussite rising in Bohemia, despite all the efforts of Jan Hus himself, was tinged with opposition to the Germans. The Serbian and Bulgarian peasants, led by their *haiduks,* maintained a protracted struggle against the Turks both in the name of Orthodoxy and in protest against oppressive taxation. Foreign rule, appropriating not only political power but the soil and the means of production, frequently also involved two peoples in conflict on a class-war level; an example is the poorer Czech peasants exploited by German landowners.

But the class struggle was never identified with the fight for independence; the former cut across the latter and made the issues more complicated. It created solidarity across frontiers – the fraternization in the nineteenth century, for instance, between Czech and Austrian workers, and between Polish and Russian workers, despite unfriendly relations between these peoples on the national plane. But it also created tension between Slavs, like that between Ukrainian peasants in Galicia and the Polish owners of the estates on which they worked. Only a uniform solution to workers' and peasants' problems, applied regardless of country, was sufficient to bring about a real *rapprochement* between peoples whose nationalistic feelings ran high, and which had been unable to achieve independence save by passing through a phase of capitalistic state organization.

This *rapprochement* is the result of the evolution, accompanied by a series of revolutions, of the various Slav nationalisms during the last hundred years. It is a unity at once spontaneous and imposed and, appearances notwithstanding, still precarious. The minds of those participating in it have been moulded by many centuries of frontier conflict, and are consequently slow to adjust themselves to a new and all-embracing structure whose economies and peoples, under identical regimes, are united in close solidarity despite past divergences.

Origins of the Slavs

It seems probable that the Slavs originally came from the northern Carpathians (map 1), and that the Veneti, whom Roman and Greek sources describe as inhabiting the region between the Oder (*Odra*) and Vistula (*Visla*) in the first and second centuries of the Christian era, were a Slav people. It has to be admitted that we know little about the Slavs before the eighth century; and the question of their original habitat, of their expansion during the thousand years before Christianity, and of their fate during the first few centuries thereafter, is still much debated. Controversy on these problems between Slav and German historians has

2*

sometimes overstepped the bounds of pure scholarship; a Germanic
pedigree has been claimed for the Veneti, to try to prove that the first
settlers in the lands along the Vistula were ancestors of the present-day
Germans.

For the next four centuries there is no mention of the Slavs, who re-
appear in the sixth century in Gothic and Byzantine sources. Jordanes, the
Gothic historian and bishop of that century, alludes to the Veneti as the
Sclavenes and Antae, inhabiting a vast tract of territory on the upper
Vistula. And the historian Procopius of Caesarea (d. 562) mentions the
Antae as an enormously numerous people living north of the Sea of Azov,
in present-day Ukraine. It is supposed that these two groups are the
originals of the Western and Eastern Slavs respectively, though the fact
that from the seventh century the historical sources make no mention of
the Antae raises a delicate problem of filiation between them and the Slavs
whom we find settled in the Dnieper basin in the eighth century. As for the
Western Slavs, their territory extended from the shores of the Baltic to cover
what we now know as Poland, Bohemia, Moravia, Slovakia, and Pannonia.

The sixth century marks the Slavs' entry into history and, in particular,
the beginning of an expansion which enabled them in the course of three

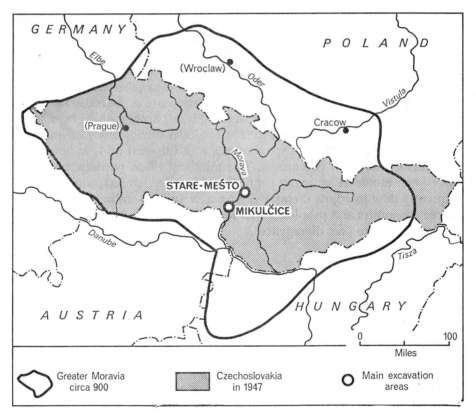

Map 2 Great Moravia in the Tenth Century

centuries to occupy positions which on the whole they have retained to the present day; their only later expansion was eastwards, towards Asia. It was in the sixth century that the Lombards and Gepidae, who had settled in the Danube basin, moved towards Italy and thereby temporarily cleared the way to the south, with the result that the Slavs occupied the whole Balkan peninsula. The end of the eighth century, which was the time of their greatest westward and southward expansion, has been justly called the 'heroic age' of Slav history.

What military confederations (if any) did they set up, and how far did they progress towards anything like state organization? We know that in the ninth century, in what is now Czechoslovakia, there was an 'empire' of Greater Moravia; an interesting light has been thrown on it by excavations recently carried out at Stare Mešto, Modra, Sady and Mikulčice, revealing the existence of small, very ancient towns (possibly going back to the eighth and seventh centuries BC) which had reached a notably advanced stage by the time of the mission of Cyril and Methodius. The large ramparts, the stone churches and other buildings which have emerged at Mikulčice, on the Morava, where excavation began in 1954, seem to indicate military government and a non-agricultural population estimated at 2,000, and bear witness to the progress achieved by the Slavs of Moravia on the borders of the Frankish and Saxon empires (map 2 and figure 4).

Further south, however, the Slavs mingled with the existing inhabitants, whose distribution was sparse in the middle Danube basin – a corridor periodically devastated by invasion from the east – and comparatively dense beyond it, in territories which had once been Roman possessions and which Byzantium was to defend and administer as far as she could. Between the Black Sea and the Adriatic, the pattern is a mosaic of peoples in which the Slav element predominates only in the area now covered by the republics of Yugoslavia and Bulgaria. It is important to note the peculiar conditions under which the Slavs settled in this part of Europe, south of the eastern Alps and the line formed by the Drave and Danube valleys. This area, into which the South Slavs made their way, had already experienced the benefits of life under an organized state and was still, at least in principle, under the authority of the most highly civilized empire in the world, the influence of whose nearby capital, Byzantium, extended throughout the Balkans. After the Hunnish invasion and the occupation of the middle Danube basin by the Hungarians in the tenth century, had finally cut off the Eastern and Western Slavs from the Southern Slavs the development of the latter began to assume an entirely different style, a distinctive complexity blended together from the most diverse cultural influences.

In the west, where they faced the Germans, the expansion of the Slavs was quickly frustrated by the Frankish empire of Charlemagne; his *limes sorabicus* (established in 805) and *limes saxonicus* (808) constituted a military defence line but seem not to have corresponded to ethnographic demarcations, since they included a certain number of Slavs. Meanwhile the

Germanic peoples pressing east from the Elbe were forcing the Slavs back
towards the Oder and the Vistula. Ethnic homogeneity, dynamic energy
and a fairly high level of development on both sides exacerbated a struggle
to which time as yet has brought no term. But in the east the prospect was
very different: the marshes and forests of the upper basins of the Volga and
Dnieper, scantily peopled by settlers of Finnish stock, presented no barriers
to an expansion which soon began feeling its way to the most favourable
regions and swerved south-east towards the Black Sea, coming up against
the nomad tribes of the Steppe in the process. The only territory on which
the Slavs were unable to lay their hands was the north-east coast of the
Baltic, strongly occupied by the Balts and Finns.

FIGURE 5 Reconstruction of the town of Biskupin (Poland).

By the time the Slavs had spread and settled over much of central,
eastern and southern Europe they had accumulated a lengthy past, on
which we unfortunately possess no information save from archaeological
sources; these are not easy to interpret. Their civilization is connected, by
Slav historians who are themselves Slavs, with another, of great antiquity,
the so-called Lusatian civilization, dating from the third millennium BC
and covering an extensive area bounded by the Baltic and the Carpathians,
the Oder and the upper reaches of the Volga and Oka; these historians
maintain that the subsequent impact of neither the Germans nor the Balts
was capable of destroying a continuity which, in these proto-Slavic dominions, led from the Lusatians to the Veneti and so to the Slavs of the sixth
century. This continuity is of no concern to us here, except in so far as it

may help to explain certain features of Slav civilization between the sixth and eighth centuries: between, that is, the first use of the word 'Slav' by the historians, and the period at which the linguistic unity of the Slav tribes, represented by 'common Slavonic', began gradually disintegrating into three groups of Slav languages all of which rapidly developed into national idioms.

The Lusatian Civilization and Poland

Excavations in Poland, at Biskupin (90 kilometres north-east of Poznań, not far from Gniezno), begun in 1934, have brought to light inhabited sites of great antiquity (third and second millennia BC). This discovery is of special interest for the valuable information it yields on the 'Lusatian' civilization of the proto-Slavs, the pre-Christian ancestors of the Slavs (figure 5).

At Biskupin there have been found the remains of a fortified town, surrounded by timber ramparts and comprising a system of streets paved with logs, along which stood approximately a hundred houses. The inhabitants were engaged in farming and stock-raising; hunting and food-gathering were merely supplementary forms of livelihood.

This substantial town of about one thousand inhabitants, which was organized on typical primitive community lines, eventually declined but was succeeded by others on the same site; continuous occupation, in changing form, can be traced down to the earliest period of Poland's existence as a unified state.

Book One

FROM 'RUS' TO RUSSIA

8th–15th Centuries

1

The East Slavs

A NEW state came into being on the banks of the Dnieper in the tenth century: a Russia which had made itself part of Christendom and whose civilization, inspired and coloured by that of Byzantium, was fully European in stature. This new creation was short-lived. The brilliant state of Kiev was submerged and wiped out by Asiatic invasions; the East Slavs were compelled to build up, slowly and painfully, a new political entity farther to the north, in the forests of the upper Volga – Moscow.

I THE FIRST RUSSIAN STATE

Obscure Beginnings: The Age of the Primitive Community

The great Slav majority, to which four-fifths of the population of the Soviet Union belongs, consists of a single group, the East Slavs. Originally concentrated in a relatively small area, this group spread out to populate the forests of the upper Dnieper and upper Volga, and the Ukrainian steppe on both sides of the middle Dnieper. In the north-east, they mingled with the sparse Finnish population round Moscow and the middle Volga. In the south-east, they entered a corridor-zone continually traversed from east to west by invaders from Asia, and even briefly occupied on one occasion by Goths from the west. But here too, keeping close to the rivers and expanding both northward and southward to wherever the forest met the steppe, they soon began to constitute a permanent population capable of assimilating and Slavicising any invading minority. It was in the early centuries of the Christian era that the Eastern Slav peoples took up their historic positions in this way. Very little is known about this obscure period.

The *Chronicle* of Nestor (1377) – which we shall be meeting again – alludes to Slav peoples living between the Baltic and the Black Sea and bearing a wide variety of names:

> ... And these Slavs, too, settled along the Dnieper and were called the Polyane; others, the Drevlyane, because they lived in the depths of the forests; others, again, settled between the Pripet and the Duna and were called Dregovitches; others settled along the Desna and were called Polotchane, after the Polota, a stream which joins the Duna. And the Slavs who settled round Lake Ilmen kept

their own name of Slavs and built a city which they called Novgorod. And others settled along the Desna, the Sem and the Sula and were called Severyane. Thus did the Slavonic people spread, and its writing was called 'Slavonic' accordingly.

. . . These are they who, in the 'Rus', speak Slavonic: the Polyane, Drevlyane, Novgorodians, Polotchane, Dregovitches, Severyane, and the Buzhane, who are so called because they settled along the Bug, and who later came to be known as the Volhynians.

What are the realities behind these names? Is it possible to form a clear picture of the organization and way of life of these peoples? And what was their inheritance from the past? In the south, the extensive plains on which they took up their abode had been affected by ancient civilizations of high quality. From the eighth century BC to the second century AD, these southern regions, occupied first by the Scythians (from the eighth to the first century BC) and then by the Sarmatians, had known a civilization which was impregnated with Hellenism and Asiatic influence and which was destroyed by the Goths in the third century AD. At this juncture appeared the Antae, who, according to the latest research, form a link between the Helleno-Scythian-Sarmatian civilization and that of ninth-century Kiev.

It is practically certain that the Antae were Slavs; but they are unlikely to have inherited very much from their predecessors, who had been swept away in the welter of successive invasions. There seems every reason to believe that there was a general decline in the level of civilization round the shores of the Black Sea in the first centuries of our era, even if it be conceded that the Slav peoples in the ninth century were not in so rudimentary and backward a condition as used to be thought. It is generally agreed today that, by the eighth century, Slav society in eastern Europe was agricultural; agriculture, as the basic occupation, determined the nature of society. Honey-gathering, fishing and hunting (concerned in particular with fur-bearing animals) were rarely the sole means of subsistence; they were extras, making it possible to amass wealth and causing a certain limited degree of social differentiation. Agriculture was still primitive, confined to clearings on which the underbrush had been burnt, and entailing a kind of nomadism of the fields; even so, it indicates a settled state of society, attached to the local soil and of necessity possessing the rudiments of political organization.

In the ninth century, the names of the Slav peoples still stood for no more than groups of tribes organized on a partiarchal basis. This basis, however, had already begun breaking up, to be superseded by groups of families connected not by kinship but by their constituting a land-owning community. In northern and central Russia, the existence of autonomous communities was the direct result of natural conditions; the families belonging to the community divided up the arable land in the clearings, which were surrounded by woods and pastures held in common, presenting an almost impregnable barrier-zone to any outsider unfamiliar with the tracks and paths. Farther south, on the wooded steppe, easier communications rendered local autonomy less viable and gave an impetus to organization on a large scale; it is therefore in this region that the beginnings of something like a state can first be seen appearing.

Family communities had effectively shed any egalitarian features by the ninth century. The families which owned most land supplied chiefs or princes for the community in time of war; and by recruiting on their own demesnes they formed armed detachments under their command, *druzhinas*, which grew into a permanent institution and strengthened the leaders' authority in time of peace. Thus there arose among the East Slavs a feudal type of organization, superimposed on the old communal ways. The latter survived in the form of the *veche*, a general assembly of the families of the community which was convened when important decisions impended, and which continued to play a significant role in the northern half of Russia. But fortified towns, surrounded by palisades, became the accepted centres of local power, each with its own prince in command; Kiev, Smolensk and Novgorod are the most prominent examples.

The comparative isolation of the Slav communities, keeping government fragmented into a large number of small-scale units, did not preclude active relations either between the Slav towns themselves or between the Slav peoples and their neighbours. The river systems of the gigantic plain bounded by the shores of the Black Sea and the Baltic, with portages over the watersheds, provided convenient communication all the year round. The rise in the number of 'towns', or rather of small fortified centres, should consequently be attributed less to progress in the technique of government than to the growth of trade. The Slav '*birgs*' were essentially markets; Slav society in the ninth century did not consist of two classes only, the military and the peasants, but already included a middle class of traders.

The flow of trade did not end on the fluctuating borders of the Slav-held territories; it was connected to the commercial life of neighbouring peoples, communication with whom was effected along three main diagonals. The western Duna, the Volkhov, Lake Ladoga and the Neva put the Slavs into close contact with the Scandinavian world. To the south, trade was carried on with the Byzantine empire by way of the Dnieper, and with the Khazar kingdom – between the Black Sea and the Sea of Aral – along the Oka and the lower Volga. And to the east, the Bulgars were accessible via the middle Volga and the Kama. But the territory of the Bulgars was only a staging-post on the route to the markets of Central Asia; and the Khazar kingdom was a crossroads for the commerce and civilization of the Arab and Byzantine countries. So the East Slav world was by no means cut off from international trade routes. But the volume of trade was small, affecting only a tiny fraction of the population, and making no substantial difference to the majority's characteristic way of life. Trade accentuated social inequalities, which became most marked wherever trade was most active. But the chief importance of the major trade routes through the Slav lands lay in their facilitating the entry of foreigners, and of foreign political and religious factors.

The First Russian State; A Significant Controversy

In the eighth and ninth centuries, colonial dependence, more or less complete, was the lot of the Slavs in the vicinity of the major natural waterways which intersected the Slav territories, and which allowed outside influences to enter those territories. The Slavs of the steppe paid tribute to the Khazars. And in the north the Slavs found themselves being invaded by Scandinavians – Norsemen, like those who made their presence felt so forcibly in western Europe. These adventurous seafarers, who were warriors or traders as occasion prompted, pushed their way into all Europe's estuaries and round into the Mediterranean. Entering the Duna or the Volkhov from the Baltic, they crossed the watershed between the Duna and the Dnieper and re-embarked on the latter to reach the Black Sea. On their way they established settlements of their own people; they imposed their presence on the country, intervening in the affairs of the Slav towns, laying them under tribute or serving them as mercenaries, and rapidly becoming an integral part of the Slavs' political development. These Norsemen were the Varangians and the route they followed was 'the way of the Varangians to the Greeks', connecting the Baltic with the Black Sea. The route had several variants but the objective of all was the same: Kiev, and beyond it, Byzantium (figure 6).

It was the Varangians who, settling in the ninth century in Novgorod and Kiev, gained command of a large portion of the territory of the East Slavs and provided the latter with their first line of kings. A panegyric for the dynasty was supplied by the *Chronicle* of Nestor, the *Tale of Past Times* (*Povest vremenykh let*), composed in the fourteenth century and covering three centuries of history, from the ninth to the twelfth.

The *Chronicle* is a monument to the glory of the Scandinavian-descended sovereigns of Kiev, the founders of the first Russian state, who acted as leaven on the hitherto unorganized mass of the Slav population. It tells how towards the middle of the ninth century (in 862 according to the *Chronicle*, but probably in 856) certain towns in the north – Novgorod, Byeloozero and Izborsk – having refused to pay tribute to the Varangians and driven them out, dissipated their strength by making war on one another and eventually decided to invite them back: 'Our country is large and rich but lacks order. Come and be our prince.' This was the 'appeal to the Varangians', which placed Novgorod in the hands of the Viking leader Rurik, and made his successor, Oleg, prince of Kiev, which was henceforward capital of the first Russian state.

The *Tale of Past Times* is almost the only documentary record of Rurik and his descendants. Being written to celebrate the valour and achievements of a dynasty, it must be regarded with some reserve. Moreover the problem it poses, that of the part played by the Varangians in the history of the East Slavs, is a delicate one; it has divided historians into two camps, the pro-Scandinavians and anti-Scandinavians, the former declaring that the Varangians did in fact create a Russian state, the latter that they merely transplanted themselves into a society sufficiently advanced to have created an adequate political structure already. This is by no means an empty dispute, since by preferring either position we predetermine our ideas on the quality and progress of civilization among the East Slavs. Most Slav historians are unable to stomach the notion that the state of Kiev was created by foreign invaders; German and Scandinavian historians, on the other hand, remain firmly pro-Scandinavian.

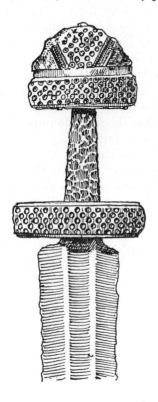

FIGURE 6 Sword-hilt, tenth century, found in 1949 in a *kurgan* at Gnezdovo (USSR).

The documentary and graphic evidence is indecisive. But a neo-Scandinavian theory will enable us to reconcile the rival viewpoints, and moreover has good sense on its side. It is probable and indeed almost certain that, before the coming of the Varangians, political organization was centred round fortified trading towns such as Novgorod, Smolensk and Kiev; within these small areas there doubtless existed, embryonically, the essentials of statehood – central authority, armed force and fiscal arrange-ments. The Viking conquerors made no great changes in the structure of government and social life. Moreover they were few in number and were rapidly Slavicised, speaking the language of the country and worshipping in it, surrounded to an ever greater extent by non-Varangian subordinates, and, finally, pursuing a policy which furthered Slav national interests.

Under Rurik and his successors they undoubtedly succeeded in temporarily uniting the Slav peoples and in harnessing their own undeniable energy and drive to the service of the new state thus brought into being. However true it be that the tasks confronting the East Slavs – already conscious of constituting a political entity but divided as yet into scattered groups, and therefore weak – existed before the Varangians' arrival, the latter provided the catalyst hastening the emergence of the first Russian state.

The interest of our controversy is wider than that of the origins of the state of Kiev. It centres about two polar opposites: on the one hand, the long, slow development of societies which, driven by a kind of ineluctable necessity, at last evolve their own form and technique of government; on the other, the effect of external factors and in particular the arrival of those providential individuals who come as a revelation to the formless, unconscious masses, and determine their history. The controversy also raises the traditional but highly questionable notion of a basically anarchic Slav spirit – intolerant of official control, and requiring the forcible imposition of the order and discipline implicit in the notion of a state.

It is in this period that we first meet the word 'Russian' (*Rus*, *Ros*), whose origin is obscure and which eventually came to denote the East Slavs as a whole. Did it apply initially only to the Varangian minority, as most of the 'pro-Scandinavian' school believe, or to a small section of the East Slavs, as is maintained by some Soviet historians? And was its meaning primarily ethnic, social or geographical? The most recent hypotheses (and they are no more than that) posit the existence of a people called the Rus, inhabiting the valleys of the Desna and Sejm in the early ninth century, and powerful enough to have welded the East Slavs into a unity; the Varangians are supposed to have been merely accessories to the process. But however it came about, the fact remains that there was a Russian state around Kiev in the ninth century, and that in the tenth it extended northwards to the region of Lake Ilmen – a state whose story is the history of a brilliant civilization.

Russia as Kiev (9th–13th Centuries)

Achievements of the Scandinavian Princes
The provision of a dynasty was not the only service rendered by the Norsemen. For although they were very few by comparison with the Slavs they constituted a dynamic, forward-looking element, whose influence was not effective merely at the top, in the person of the ruler and his immediate subordinates, but at every level of society. The hundreds of Russo-Scandinavian graves found scattered in the country round Yaroslav, and particularly round Rostov, testify to the importance of this contribution, which contemporary Russian historians tend to minimize.

Furthermore, and this above all is why they are so important, the Varangians, through their military expeditions, established close contact with the Byzantine empire. Conflict between the Slavs and Byzantium had of course been going on for a long time in the Danube area; the Antae were attacking Byzantium in 518. But after the Antae disappeared from the scene (which may mean no more than that contact was broken off between them and the Byzantines, to whom we owe the knowledge of their existence) the aggressive power of the Slavs disappeared too. They regained their military dynamism under Varangian leadership in the ninth century. The Norsemen were only moderately attracted by the 'land of towns' (Gardarik) of the East Slavs round Lake Ilmen; far away in the south, beyond the forests and marshes of the Volkhov and the upper Dnieper, lay the city of Byzantium, the only city in the world they absolutely coveted; to them, indeed, the only real city in the world.

Originally, they had regarded the home of the East Slavs merely as a place of transit; it was Byzantine resistance which forced them to settle there. An abortive conquest turned a staging-area into an organized state. But the preconditions were already in being; the Varangians found an advanced society and gave it a framework which soon extended to embrace all the East Slavs. And it was thanks to them that the *Rus* ceased henceforward to be a centre of colonization or of foreign exploitation. For four centuries, until they succumbed to Mongol invasion, the Russians victoriously defended their country against their Asiatic neighbours and asserted their political existence *vis-à-vis* the Byzantine empire. It was the relations they established with the latter which proved fruitful; through warfare and peaceful intercourse – an alternation reflected in a series of treaties in the tenth century – culture (in the religious form which was natural to it in that age), and religion itself, made their way into Russia from Byzantium. The state of Kiev was a raw military power; the graces of civilization came to it from the south. But the influence was cultural and religious only. The Grand Prince of Kiev treated with the Byzantine emperor on an equal footing. It is moreover very probable that the Russians' new-found dynamism was not due solely to the Norsemen, but was in part a matter of demography; it was connected with a population-growth still represented in our own day by the gradual expansion of the Russian people towards the north-east and south-east. The Varangians gave this swarming mass a structure which made it aware of its own strength (map 3).

Political Discord, Unified Civilization, Linguistic Divergences
The history of the princes of Kiev makes an eventful and at times tragic story. Theoretically, the unity of the Slav state was ensured by the subordination of younger brothers to the eldest, each son inheriting a part of his father's domains; in practice, the country was shaken by fratricidal struggle and bloody battles. There were times when the state of Kiev was dangerously weak in relation to its neighbours, and other times when unity was achieved by a process of elimination – as, for example, under Vladimir from 980 to 1015, and under Yaroslav the Wise from 1034 to

1054. The state reached its heyday in the middle of the eleventh century, when its territory included Novgorod, Byeloozero, Tchernigov, Murom, Pereyaslav, Riazan, Suzdal, Viatcheslav, Smolensk, Kiev and Volhynia. But the princes' internecine struggles exposed the realm to invasion – not, as before, by the Poles and Scandinavians, but by the Asiatics of the steppe: the Pechenegs, followed by the dreaded Polovtsians, under whose blows the state of Kiev gradually broke up. The only figure who stands out from the confused background is Vladimir Monomakh (1113–25), whose

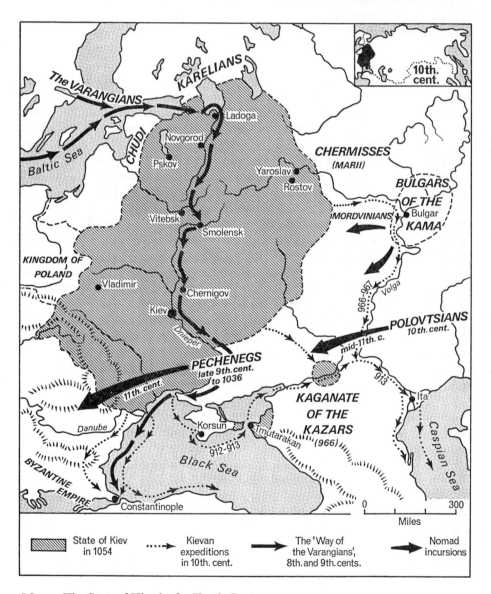

Map 3 The State of Kiev in the Tenth Century

reign represents the last period of comparative peace in the history of the state of Kiev.

The looting of Kiev, 'mother of Russian cities', by the reigning prince of Suzdal in 1169, closed one of the great chapters in Russian history. The sun had set on the realm of Kiev; to the east, behind the Polovtsians, the Mongols were advancing. When the latter captured the city in 1240, the kingdom they subjugated was already littered with ruins and its population decimated. The history of the Russians was continued farther north, in the forests of the central regions; Kiev was succeeded by Moscow.

The political unity of the areas inhabited by the East Slavs had always been precarious. But there is no doubt about the unity of their culture and civilization. From the Baltic to the Black Sea, differences in dialect were no barrier to comprehension between the East Slavs, and the only contrasts between their ways of life were those dictated by natural conditions. Nevertheless there began in the twelfth century a process of linguistic differentiation which gradually centred itself round three dialects, the Great Russian, Byelorussian and Ukrainian. Historical circumstances made the cleavage permanent by determining the respective development of each of these three population groups, of which the first took refuge from the Mongol invasions in central and northern Russia, while the others were in contact with the peoples of Poland in the west, and, in the south, at grips with the incursion from Asia. On the other hand, the written and literary language, which was that of the Church, was used by an infinitesimal clerical minority and was universally the same.

Kiev and the Outside World

Politically, the state of Kiev was made up of ill-assorted units which the grand princes found themselves periodically compelled to reconquer. But internal difficulties did not stop them from launching out beyond the East Slav territories. Sviatoslav, by attacking the Bulgars of the Danube and setting up his throne in their capital, achieved a partial and somewhat precarious union between the Eastern and Southern Slavs which lasted until the terrible defeat inflicted on him in 970 by the Byzantine emperor, John Tzimisces, which forced him to fall back into southern Russia. In 968, this same Sviatoslav had taken Itil, the capital of the Khazars, dealing the final blow to a kingdom which was already on its last legs and had been much infiltrated by Russian colonists, and which might have formed part of a vast Russian empire, stretching from the Urals to the Danube, but for a sudden attack by the Pechenegs who swept across Khazar territory, making towards Kiev, just when Sviatoslav was fighting the Danubian Bulgars. After his defeat by John Tzimisces, Sviatoslav encountered the Pecheneg hordes on the bank of the Dnieper about 972; he was killed, and the victors used his skull for a drinking-cup.

Prior to these momentous events, Russian expeditions had been crossing the Black Sea and the Caspian and attacking the coasts of the Caucasus and Asia Minor. To visualize the state of Kiev as exclusively continental,

and active only on an axis from south-east to north-west, would be to mis-
conceive both the power at its disposal and the orientation of its policy. In
reality, until the Pechenegs cut off access to the south, Kiev was an intensely active maritime power, whose fleets were continually in evidence
on the Black Sea. It was they which maintained relations with Byzantium,
and were therefore in effect responsible for the most important chapter in
the history of Kiev.

Byzantium and Kiev. Conversion to Christianity
The links connecting the civilized empire of Byzantium with the semi-
barbarous state of Kiev and Novgorod were of more than one kind. Their
importance has sometimes been overestimated by historians; the Byzantine
influence, which was considerable, operated essentially on the cultural
plane, and it is from Byzantine records and pro-Byzantine Russian chronicles that we are able to piece together a picture of relations between
Byzantium and Kiev.

Affairs between the state of Kiev and the Scandinavians and Poles are
rather more obscure; there seem to have been episodes of intervention by
Norwegian chieftains in the internal discords of the Kiev régime; these do
at any rate testify to a tradition of solidarity between the Rurikovitch
dynasty – despite their having become Slavicised and pursuing a Russian
policy – and their original home. But Scandinavia's real contribution to
the Slavs had been made by the Viking invasions of the ninth century, and
the settling of Varangian leaders on Slav soil.

In the south it was different: the close contact established with Byzantium affected the whole history of the Kiev territories, their economy,
social structure and cultural and religious development. It is true that the
Byzantine influence was often exercised through intermediary channels
and that it came sweeping in triumphantly only after many setbacks; it is
in this sense that certain adjustments must be made in the traditional
account, which ascribed all progress in Kiev to the Byzantines.

Kiev and its dominations were converted to the Greek form of Christianity. This was a slow process; there was nothing easy about it, no tidal wave
of baptism. Christianity's earliest advance, through various channels, into
the region of Kiev in the ninth century, and its triumph in the form of the
official acceptance of the Byzantine hierarchy in that city in 1039, are
separated by a lapse of two centuries – centuries characterized by periods
of war between Byzantium and the Slavs, and periods of peace in which
commercial and cultural relationships were close. It is in fact a gross over-
simplification to give Vladimir all the credit for the conversion of Kiev and
its dominions to the Christian faith. Most of the Varangian leaders who
gradually subdued the country round Kiev and Novgorod were pagans,
like the Slavs themselves. There are nevertheless grounds for supposing
that those of them who had made their way into the middle Dnieper region
by the most westerly route, namely along the Niemen, were converted to
Christianity in its western, Roman form. This may have been the case

with Askold, the conqueror of Kiev. Moreover, whereas northern Russia was slower to be reached by Christian influences, southern Russia, being closer to cultural centres in the Balkans, Asia Minor and the Caucasus, was more accessible to such currents. As a result, Christianity in both forms entered the Kiev lands during the ninth century, affecting individuals or small groups who were a tiny minority among their pagan contemporaries. The religion of the people was of course bound to be that of their rulers, and the latter wavered for a long time between Byzantium and Rome. Indeed, it is not quite possible to say that Byzantium won: for when, after 987, Vladimir gave orders for the idols to be destroyed and imposed Greek Christianity on his people, it was to the Bulgarians on the Danube that he applied for a clergy and the Scriptures.

Kiev's conversion to Christianity was in effect a political measure; which is why it came only after mature reflection and was carried through with some difficulty. Court circles, and the princes themselves until the accession of Vladimir – that second Constantine – were divided between pagan and Christian influence. It is fairly certain that paganism was strongly upheld by the indigenous tribal chieftains and that it was an aspect of resistance to the authority of the princes, whose tendency was naturally towards centralization; to be pagan was to defend local liberty and tradition. The princes were not slow to realize that Christianity was a progressive force politically as well as morally, on account of its hierarchical organization and its authority over the faithful. Nevertheless the power of tradition was such that the state of Kiev, into which Christianity had been slowly infiltrating, long remained officially pagan; until the time of Vladimir its princes alternately favoured Christianity (the regent Olga was baptized in 955) or provided a spearhead for the anti-Christian reaction (Sviatoslav, for example, remained an uncompromising pagan). Under Vladimir's rule Christianity won the day. Even so, it was that prince's conviction that the clergy should be subservient to the royal power and independent of any external authority. This is the reason why Kiev received its new religion neither from Rome nor, properly speaking, from Byzantium. Northern Bulgaria was the necessary intermediary. Vladimir had no intention of recognizing the authority of the patriarchate of Constantinople over his newly-appointed clergy; moreover he needed priests who could speak to the Slavs in their own language, and these Byzantium could not provide. But in the second half of the ninth century, Bishops Cyril and Methodius, wishing to take the gospel to the Slavs in the Khazar domains, had created an alphabet based on the Greek but adjusted to the sounds of Slavonic, thus enabling themselves to translate the Bible into the Bulgarian dialect of Salonika, their native city. This Cyrillic alphabet (figure 3) was the forerunner of the present Russian alphabet; Church Slavonic, the language of the Biblical translation, was the Russians' literary language until the eighteenth century, and is still the liturgical language of Orthodox Slavs.

Kiev, Western Europe and Rome

It must not be thought, however, that the state of Kiev sealed itself off from the West by adopting Greek Christianity in its most narrowly national form. On the contrary, the conversion of southern Russia, followed gradually by that of northern Russia, introduced Kiev into the Christian world, and brought it closer to the western nations by hoisting it out of semi-barbarism. In its advance the new religion was of course obliged to accommodate itself to popular traditions and superstitions, and did not become effective in the countryside till much later; for years the towns and market-villages, the centre of gravity of whose life was the city of Kiev, their religious metropolis, were isolated Christian outposts. They received a large influx of Bulgarian priests when the Bulgarian kingdom was eliminated in 1018. It was only from 1039 that Greek priests began appearing in Kiev; from then to the end of the century, the cultural influence of Byzantium was supreme.

The main event of the middle of the eleventh century was the last major military expedition launched by Kiev against Byzantium. Between the first big attack by the Varangians, under Askold's leadership, in 860–1, and this final abortive attempt, relations between Kiev and Byzantium had gradually tended towards a sometimes unsteady equilibrium. The capture of Constantinople soon became no more than a fugitive ideal. Kiev's military and naval strength, even at its height, was frustrated by superior methods of defence. Byzantine diplomacy created permanent enemies for Kiev by inciting the peoples of the steppe; and Greek fire, which had scattered and destroyed Igor's fleet off Constantinople in 941, was a searing memory to the would-be invaders. Moreover, as we shall see, peaceful relations with Byzantium were dictated by the very nature of Kiev's economy. And finally, the Byzantine empire sometimes needed the support of the princes of Kiev. As early as 911, after an expedition against Constantinople, Oleg concluded a commercial treaty with the emperor. In 944, after the failure of Igor's attack, this treaty was combined with a military alliance. Sviatoslav's ambitions in the Danube basin had an adverse effect on relations between the two states, but John Tzimisces' victory forced Sviatoslav to sign the peace treaty of 971. In 997 there was a swing in the opposite direction: the Byzantine empire, threatened by internal dissension, was obliged to ask for assistance from the Grand Prince of Kiev. The treaty of 988, by which the emperors Basil and Constantine obtained the services of Slav mercenaries, also provided for the subsequent marriage of the princess Anna, the emperor's sister, to Vladimir.

The exchanges of diplomatic missions between Kiev and Rome, and the visit of St Boniface in 1007, may give the impression that Kiev's relations with the West were at least as active as with Byzantium. In reality, however, social and economic necessity, as well as geography, made for close links between the Byzantine empire and the East Slavs. To Byzantium, Kiev was a market for the purchase of men and merchandise, a source of mercenaries and slaves, furs, wax and honey. To the princes of Kiev,

Byzantium was an indispensable trade outlet through which human beings and agricultural produce could be exchanged for sumptuous woven stuffs and other luxuries, such as goldsmiths' and silversmiths' work, without which the Grand Prince's court would have been little better than the home of a country squire.

Kiev's Economy, etc.

The economy of the state of Kiev was essentially agricultural; the Russians' chief occupations were cereal farming and stock-raising, supplemented by hunting, fishing and bee-keeping. Archaeological excavations have established the fact that in the middle Dnieper and upper Volga region, the food-gathering stage was outgrown at an early period and that a fixed society dependent on agriculture existed even on the outer fringe of Kiev's dominions, in the 'Mesopotamia' bounded by the Volga and Oka, which at that time was the most advanced position occupied by the East Slavs. Documentary evidence confirms this: for example, the *Russkaya Pravda*, an edict of Vladimir and Yaroslav concerning the church, alludes to the cultivation of wheat, barley, rye, spelt, millet, flax, hemp and also cabbages, turnips and garlic. Cows, sheep and pigs were raised, and horses and oxen were used as draught animals (figure 7).

FIGURE 7 Ancient plough at Novoselsky, on the Desna (Russia).

Itinerant agriculture (*perelog*) was a traditional practice; in the forests and on the wooded steppe, where the soil was poor, it was carried out in burnt clearings. It was less primitive than has often been supposed; the trees were felled carefully and the trimmings, etc., spread evenly over the soil, which was enriched with their ashes and abandoned after five years' cultivation. Yields were high for the first two years but thereafter fell steeply. But this 'nomadism of the fields' was so well suited to natural conditions that in some regions it lasted on into the nineteenth century, side by side with the most up-to-date agriculture; it was still a paying proposition, partly because results could be got with relatively little work. On the steppes of southern Russia, where itinerant cultivation was also the rule, the peasant had merely to burn the grass in order to clear the ground, causing the 'seas of flame' mentioned in the chronicles. The average yield over a period of time was rather low; the peasant, with his primitive implements and inefficient Mediterranean plough, the use of which began in the south and spread northwards, was often on the verge of famine.

Landlord and Peasant

This agricultural society had already developed certain differentiations of level. At this period almost all the peasants were still free. They were the *smerdy* ('the stinking ones'), hereditary owners of the soil on condition that they begot sons to cultivate it after them – for it was expressly laid down even in the first enactments which were drawn up on Yaroslav's orders to apply to the whole country, and which were completed during the next two centuries to form the *Russkaya Pravda (Russian Right)*, that the primary owner of all land in Russia was the Grand Prince. But there were also indebted peasants (the *zakupy*, conditional serfs), who were only half-free, and depended on their creditors; and others less free still, who were almost slaves, the *kholopy*, former prisoners of war or peasants with a heavy load of debt. Insolvency and large estates were the two factors which gradually transformed the free peasantry of small landowners into a mass of serfs.

In the Kiev period, however, large-scale landownership was still in its infancy. The ruling prince had an entourage of boyars who constituted both his *druzhina* and his council, and executed a very wide assortment of administrative functions. The boyars were attached to the prince of their own free will and could leave him at any time if they wished. Russia never developed a feudal hierarchy in the western sense. Moreover the boyars were not originally landlords; they were a mobile armed force maintained by the prince and not bound to the soil in any way, though instances occurred in which a prominent boyar recruited a *druzhina* of his own from the *smerdy* of the district he administered. Economically, therefore, the survival of the régime depended on levying the various kinds of tribute which the rural population was required to pay. Each year the prince 'invited his people' together and collected the prescribed payments in kind – grain, furs, honey, beeswax, etc. – and also assembled the prisoners of war captured from the peoples he had conquered. Summer, when it was easy to feed the horses, was the time for military campaigning; winter was a time of peace, when transport on the frozen tracks was convenient and the tax-gatherers went out on circuit.

The Towns

The princes also raised revenues from the towns. Perhaps historians have been guilty of a misnomer in applying the word 'town' to those numerous villages-cum-market-places whose inhabitants included not only soldiers, craftsmen and traders but also a high proportion of peasants. According to the Russian historian I.I.Sreznevsky, Kievan Russia during the reign of Prince Igor had over twenty towns: Byeloozero, Vititchev, Vrutchev, Vyshgorod, Izborsk, Kiev, Korosten, Ladoga, Lyubetch, Murom, Novgorod, Ovrutch, Peremyshl, Peresetchen, Polotsk, Pskov, Rodnia, Smolensk, Turov, Tcherven and Tchernigov. But except for Novgorod, Pskov, Tchernigov and above all Kiev, it seems dubious to call them towns.

According to Tikhomirov (*The Ancient Towns of Russia*, 1940), the number of these urban centres had risen to approximately three hundred by the time of the Mongol invasion. It is safe to say that, despite the internal and external difficulties of the state of Kiev, there was a definite development of urban life between the ninth and thirteenth centuries. These 'towns' undoubtedly included a considerable rustic element, such as agricultural day-labourers, and peasants who had run away from their home districts because they were in debt to a landowner. In most cases the 'town' was a *kreml*, a fortified place guarding a river-crossing or a road. But it also became increasingly a centre for an artisan population living in houses clustered round the outside of the *kreml* – a kind of embryonic suburb – and protected by it.

A thoroughly rural economy was of course the keynote of Russian life in the Kiev period, and indeed the more backward regions remained largely self-supporting even as late as the nineteenth century. Nevertheless specialization and the division of labour (according to Rybakov there were as many as sixty different trades in the city of Kiev) had progressed enough to create commercial dealings in the immediate neighbourhood of villages, and more especially within and between towns.

The distinctive, specific features of these early Russian urban centres were the community council or *veche*, responsible for town administration in collaboration with the prince's officials; and trade, which was shaped not only by the economy of the surrounding district but also by the fact that the towns were situated on the great trade routes by land or water to Scandinavia, Baghdad and Byzantium. The larger communities had German, Jewish and Armenian quarters in addition to a Varangian quarter, and Russian traders were to be found in the most distant countries. But we must not be misled by the variety and value of the goods circulating, and the motley of nationalities living together, in the principality of Kiev; the volume of trade was small and so was the number of traders. Until the end of the tenth century the currencies circulating in the principality were all foreign; no Russian coinage was minted before Vladimir's reign. If the Kiev territories look like a land of cities and substantial commerce, despite their agricultural and largely closed economy, they do so only in comparison with the period of their decline and fall – the economic retrogression caused by the Polovtsians' repeated attacks, and the internal collapse of the state of Kiev, beginning in the second quarter of the twelfth century.

Caravan Routes to Byzantium

Taxes paid in cash by the towns, and in kind by the country-folk, filled the prince's treasury and supplied him with stocks for sale abroad. Most of them were despatched in the spring, as soon as the rivers were ice-free, to the greatest city in the civilized world, Byzantium, or Tsargrad as the Slavs called it. A large official convoy, strongly protected, made its way down the Dnieper; its flat-bottomed boats were carried on men's backs wherever there were rapids to be by-passed. Attacks by the nomadic Pechenegs or Polovtsians had sometimes to be beaten off before the shore of the Black Sea was reached and the cargo of slaves, furs and beeswax could be conveyed, not without difficulty, to the gates of Tsargrad, where goods and money changed hands. The strangers from the north were regarded with some trepidation and were admitted on conducted visits to the great city only after being carefully disarmed. The state of Kiev also traded with the western countries and with Central Asia, but the annual caravan to Byzantium was clearly of greater importance: it filled the prince's coffers and was significant politically as well as economically.

The Origins of Serfdom

The prince's officers soon tended to become landowners, with estates to support them and, more especially, tracts of forest whose produce of furs and honey was a substantial source of income. The Church was also given lands of its own. And the prince's domains were growing. Concurrently, the number of free peasants in districts already permanently settled was shrinking. Fiscal burdens, and indebtedness aggravated by the prince's frequent wars, tied the small proprietor ever more closely to the soil, the ownership of which was slipping from his hands. Any hitherto uncultivated area presented to an official of the prince was populated by half-free *zakupy* who were given small plots and the use of ploughs and other instruments, for which they were charged rent, and also had to work periodically on the portion of the estate which the owner was exploiting directly himself. The full-time labourers on the latter were *kholopy*, who had no personal freedom and were entirely in their master's hands.

This situation was nevertheless only the embryonic stage of serfdom. The population-density was low and was kept so by frequent warfare. The consequent difficulty of securing regular workers and tax-payers was what made the princes and boyars so anxious to attach the hitherto free peasantry to their estates. But at the same time there were still vast, inviting expanses of country which had never been cleared. Neither the princes nor the boyars possessed the administrative arrangements they would have needed to bring about the general enslavement of the peasant population. War itself, and its attendant disorganization, retarded the subjection of the peasants, the first signs of which appeared in the eleventh century.

A fairly clear picture of the structure of Russian society is provided by the *Russkaya Pravda*, which decrees the fines payable for various offences and determines the rights of large landowners. It was largely inspired by Germanic law.

A Golden Age ?

Commercial activity and the freedom of the peasants have combined to throw a legendary aura round the state of Kiev. It has sometimes been said that the Russian peasant was never happier, and – on flimsy evidence – that general health and wellbeing were never higher than under Vladimir; comparison with the later stages of the state's history has caused its peak to be regarded as a golden age. This view places overmuch reliance on the official writings, whose purpose was to commemorate the glories of Rurik's dynasty, and tends to overlook our knowledge of what was really going on in town and countryside. The fact remains, however, that Kiev was a great power, as is shown by its influence abroad, its commercial and political relations with the countries of both West and East; and that it created a setting whose splendour matched that greatness.

Signposts of a Civilization and Its Culture

Byzantine architecture was preponderant at the court but was even more in evidence in church-building; and in both cases there was an admixture of Asiatic influences. The two cathedrals of Sancta Sophia, one at Kiev – the Byzantium of the Dnieper – and the other at Novgorod, both decorated with mosaics, were built in the first half of the eleventh century, a period which also saw the erection of monasteries, such as that of the Crypts (1051).

Sancta Sophia of Kiev, the marble for which was imported from the region of Constantinople, and which was completed in 1049 in the reign of Yaroslav, was much admired by travellers; so was the Tithe Church (another Sancta Sophia, now no longer standing), which was even bigger and more sumptuous. The Great Cathedral of Sancta Sophia at Novgorod, built between 1045 and 1052, the Sancta Sophia of Polotsk, and Saint Saviour of Tchernigov bear striking witness to the civilization of Kiev and show that the highest forms of artistic achievement had spread through eastern Europe. Nor was this entirely a matter of importation, either in conception or in workmanship. Working expertly alongside Greek architects and craftsmen were their local counterparts, the product of centuries of tradition and skill, without whom such projects could never have been carried out. And everything which has come down to us from the day-to-day life of that period, such as household utensils, ornaments of various kinds, and weapons, speaks of a society whose level of attainment was as high as that of the western European countries; evidently there was a burgeoning of activity combining native crafts with that imitation of Greek art which the princes considered indispensable for fulfilling their desire to make their leading cities, or at least Kiev, as fine as Constantinople itself. As elsewhere, and indeed as in the West, the intellectual curiosity of the

3

rulers led to looting: when Charlemagne was embellishing Aix-la-
Chapelle with art treasures plundered from Italy, Vladimir was collecting
ancient statues and altars in Korsun, which his troops occupied in 989.

Conscious National Spirit

In Yaroslav's reign copyists and translators were attached to the court;
the literary models they encouraged the native annalists to follow were
Byzantine. But the individuality of the local spirit influenced architectural

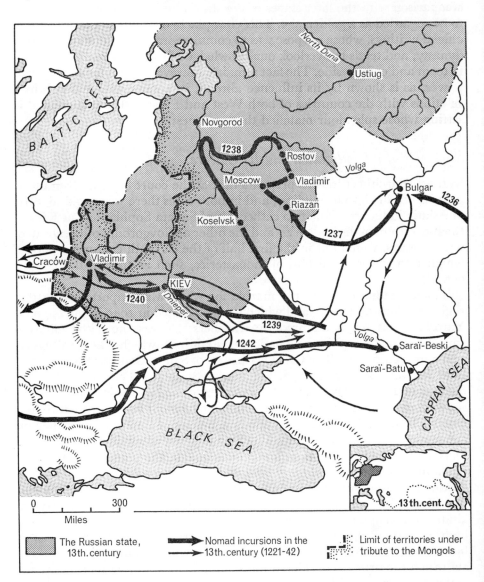

Map 4 Mongol Invasions in the Thirteenth Century

decoration and came out still more strongly in literary composition, which displayed a markedly national character. The annals written at this time begin to show a preoccupation with the history of the 'Russian land'; the *Tale of Past Times,* already mentioned, records the notable deeds of Rurik's dynasty; the *Lay (Slovo) of Igor's Campaign,* narrating the expedition of a prince of Novgorod against the Polovtsians in 1185 or 1186, is a patriotic memorial whose authenticity has been questioned but which, even if composed later, recreates a highly convincing historical atmosphere. Culture was naturally the province of the monks, but they had no monopoly of it. In the succession of more or less uncultivated rulers who spent their lives on horseback there were exceptions, notably Vladimir Monomakh (1113–25), who wrote for his son's benefit a book of *Instruction (Putchenie),* some passages of which strike a decidedly personal note.

The civilized splendour of Kiev was short-lived. From the second half of the twelfth century onwards, the increasing insecurity of the southern regions weakened the position of the grand princes of Kiev compared with the rulers of the central regions, where the forests formed a shield against the invading nomads. In the triangle formed by the upper Volga, the Oka and the Moskva, where Russian colonists began ousting the local Finnish tribes in the tenth century, particularly round Suzdal, Rostov, Vladimir, and Moscow (founded in 1147), there grew up a principality which dealt the fatal blow to an enfeebled Kiev well before the Mongols came in. It was in fact Andrey Bogoliubsky, prince of Suzdal, who sacked and destroyed Kiev in 1169. The title of grand prince was thereafter only an empty word. Andrey Bogoliubsky, and his brother Vselevod (1176–1212), who succeeded him and whose numerous progeny earned him the name of 'Vselevod-with-the-large-brood', took up their residence at Vladimir.

Thus when the wave of Mongol invasion, having overthrown the principality of Suzdal, set out again from the Caucasus to reach Kiev in 1240, the latter was already a dead city. The ravages inflicted by the nomads for the previous hundred years, aggravated by quarrels between the princes and the total cessation of commerce with Byzantium, which had been sacked by the Crusaders in 1204, had ruined Kiev's prosperity. By a curious paradox, the Christians of the West had unwittingly aided the Asiatic hordes, and played a part in obliterating from the map a state which had been Christianity's outpost in the East.

Contrasts and Continuity

The cultural axis of the first Russian state ran through Kiev and Novgorod; but the central regions on the upper Volga, still in process of being colonized, which received an influx of settlers fleeing from the Mongol invasions in the south, also had their urban centres, such as Vladimir and Suzdal, where a few stone churches, inspired by the architecture of Kiev, were built towards the end of the twelfth century. (Moscow, whose existence is attested as early as 1147, was still a village.) In these churches Armenian and Caucasian influence, travelling up the Volga, made itself felt by the addition of sculpture. These unusual artistic creations were laid in ruins by the Mongol invasions of the next century.

Despite these monuments to a brilliant state of culture, primitive Russia bore a rather different look from the western Christian countries, whose walled settlements dominated by numerous stone buildings had acquired the stature of genuine towns by the thirteenth century. The Russian churches, with their splendid stone architecture, were sumptuous exceptions, and in the north their massive whiteness contrasted powerfully with the grey *isbas* clustering round them. The majority of churches were built of timber, in a pyramidal shape imposed by the material, and in a style matching that of dwelling-houses. Ramparts and houses were built of plain logs which were left showing; most of the country being forest or wooded steppe, timber was the almost universal material. Towards the south, the *isba* was replaced by the Ukrainian *khata* with its whitewashed beams. In this period were fashioned the main features of a way of life which was to remain unaltered for centuries: linen and woollen clothing, furs, knee-boots, the very food and drink (for whereas mead, which as in the West was brewed for people in easy circumstances, disappeared almost entirely, *kvas*, fermented from rye and acidulated fruits, has held its own) – everything typical of the Russian peasant's daily life in the nineteenth century goes back at least as far as the Kiev period.

II PEACE UNDER THE MONGOLS

The Tatar or Mongol invasion did not include the Slav population in the region of Novgorod; it submerged only that of south-western Russia, at the foot of the Carpathians, and the swift flow of its tide was followed soon after by the ebb. In the latter region, round the towns of Galitch and Vladimir (a different Vladimir, on the upper reaches of the River Bug), and Kholm and subsequently Lvov, which rose to capital status, there had arisen the principality of Galicia-Volhynia, whose history is closely involved with that of Hungary and Poland, and which reached a high level of civilization in the thirteenth century. This outpost of the East Slavs towards the West – which western Europe, however, regarded as an outlying bulwark against the peril from Asia – found itself incapable, despite the courage and ability of its king Daniel Romanovitch (1205–64), of sustaining its independence; constantly under attack from the Mongols of the east, it fell under Polish domination in the fourteenth century and for a long time to come played no further part in the history of Russia.

Novgorod: A Free Commercial City

It was otherwise with the 'land of Novgorod'. Novgorod is one of the oldest Russian towns but nevertheless goes back no further than the tenth century (the most ancient town in the region was Ladoga, towards the mouth of the Volkhov; Novgorod means 'new town'). Recent excavations, and the discovery, between 1951 and 1958, of over two hundred inscriptions on birchbark, have given us a much altered picture of its past (plate 1). Maintaining close relations with the German towns of the Baltic, drawing wealth from a colonial territory which stretched beyond the Ural river, exporting furs and flax and importing fabrics and metal tools, Novgorod not only supplied an economic link between the vast and almost uninhabited forest regions of northern Russia and the populous, active towns of central Europe; it also connected the latter with the markets of the Orient, via the Volga basin.

FIGURE 8 Handle of a dipper. Woodcarving, Novgorod, eleventh century.

To the east and north-east – into the Pomorye, the coastal regions of the Arctic Ocean – the boyars of Novgorod sent out semi-military, semi-commercial expeditions which had no difficulty in levying a tribute of furs from the native population (the Nenets or Samoyeds, the Komi Zyriany, the Voguls and the Ostiaks). Novgorod inaugurated the policy of colonial conquest which in a few centuries was to take the Russians to the Pacific.

This merchant town was not, as used to be believed, a merchant state. It was dominated by its military leaders and an oligarchy of large land-owners. Its life was, moreover, interdependent with that of central Russia, where the land was more fertile and which supplied Novgorod with grain. The boyars of Novgorod had as their ruler a prince who lived elsewhere, and whose powers were much curbed by the communal council (veche). Though the town had to treat with the prince, usually the prince of Suzdal or, in some cases, of Vladimir (in Muscovy), and though it made use of his druzhina, its steady income from trade, and its ability to raise an armed force locally with which to oppose the prince if he became overbearing, guaranteed the de facto independence of this community which was something like a republic but never became a democracy.

Excavation has uncovered an extensive network of streets; in their houses were found the remains of fabrics, fruit, grain and, most important of all, documents showing that education had spread well beyond clerical circles. The birchbark inscriptions discovered are short private notes or letters, most of which did not require the services of a professional scrivener. Among the discoveries made in 1956 were the remains of a pupil's birch-bark exercise book, dating from the end of the twelfth century, and a child's primer of the alphabet from the end of the thirteenth.

As for the layout of the town, it remained unaltered from the tenth century till the changes ordered by Catherine II in the eighteenth. Novgorod was surrounded by fortifications inside which, in a position commanding the Volkhov, stood the Kreml, half of whose area was taken up by the Cathedral of Sancta Sophia, built about the middle of the eleventh century. The streets were very narrow (hardly more than six yards in width) and were 'paved' with planks from the tenth century onwards; they were flanked by the gardens of houses or in some cases the houses themselves, whose ground floor was used for storing tools and provisions; the first floor was for living in and was reached by a ladder. Rooms were lighted by narrow windows, each of which could be closed with a single plank; glass panes made their appearance in the wealthiest houses in the fourteenth century (plate 1).

It was from the west that Novgorod's independence was threatened. In the twelfth century Germanic expansion in its dual form, commercial and religious, reached Livonian territory, on the south-eastern shore of the Baltic. This conquest, a victory for the Cross over paganism, was accompanied by compulsory conversion and by massacres of the local population; it was financed by the urban merchants and led to the foundation of Riga (1201) and the spread of the Knights of the Sword to Livonia. The knights created a number of settlements which were at once strongholds and market centres and put German merchants to live in their suburbs. The domains of the Order now marched with Russian territory a little to the west of Lake Peipus (Lake of the Tchudi) and along the middle Duna (west Duna). In 1224 the Knights seized Yurief, despite the heroic resistance of Viatchko, prince of Polotsk, and re-named it Derpt (Dorpat, the present-day Tartu).

This was the start of the continual struggle between the Slavs and Teutons for possession of the Baltic coast, a struggle complicated by the intervention of Sweden from the north. In northern Russia, indeed, the Varangians had been assimilated and their victorious hold over the country was now only a memory. It was the powerful trading town of Novgorod which, in the twelfth century, took the offensive with a view to extending its influence beyond the Gulf of Finland, and employed Karelian mercenaries to launch raids against Swedish towns (expedition against Sigtun, 1187). But in the next century Novgorod had to fight off attacks from Swedish armies, and did it with complete success. In 1240 the prince of Novgorod, Alexander Yaroslavitch, routed the Swedes on the Neva and became the first national hero in Russian history (Alexander Nevsky). Two years later he defended Novgorod from destruction by the Knights of the Sword, who had meanwhile taken possession of Pskov; overcoming the Germans on the ice of Lake Peipus (Battle of the Ice, 5 April 1242), he compelled the Order to relinquish Pskov and by this memorable victory established an ethnic frontier which has lasted from the twelfth century to the twentieth. At the same time, by defeating an expedition which had been plotted in Rome as well as in the back-shops of the German towns of the north, and which had assumed the character of a crusade against the eastern church, he became in Russian eyes at once the defender of nationality and of orthodoxy.

Novgorod was not only a flourishing trading centre. Part of its population (15 per cent) was engaged in agriculture; and, what was more important, it had a well developed artisan class (making, among other things, clothes and knee-boots) and was thus a centre of production, supplying the neighbouring regions and especially Moscow. These artisans were organized in guilds and corporations which continued in existence for some time after the town's capture by the Muscovites. This was a 'western' legacy to a Russia whose other communities possessed no such craft organizations.

During its period of greatness Novgorod covered itself with monasteries and churches; their style shows a perceptible evolution, passing from the pure Byzantine tradition to an architecture whose details are typically Russian and even Novgorodian. As elsewhere, flattish cupolas were succeeded by onion-domes, in groups of three or five; proportions grew simpler and more modest. In the merchant quarter, the 'Court of Yaroslav' was dominated by several fourteenth and fifteenth century churches, dedicated to the patron saints of the corporations. And the whole town was dotted with places of worship whose interior walls are covered with murals; one such is the Church of the Saviour (1378), whose murals are the work of the Byzantine artist Theophanes the Greek, Rublev's master. Novgorod had cultural links with the whole Slav world; the painters who in the fourteenth century decorated the Church of the Nativity, adjoining the town cemetery, came from Serbia.

The Rise of the Second Russian State

Trade, and conflict with the Germans and the Swedes, had rendered the merchant city and *de facto* republic of Novgorod both wealthy and powerful. But Novgorod lay on the further edge of the Rus and looked largely eastwards. Hence it was not Novgorod which took over the heritage of Kiev but the principality of Suzdal-Vladimir, a recently colonized territory governed by military leaders who were also landowners, and who ruled their boyars as well as their peasants with a heavy hand. The superiority of Suzdal-Vladimir was due to a number of causes, the chief of which was the effectiveness of its fighting forces, or rather the drive of such outstanding individuals as Andrey Bogoliubsky (1157–74), who sacked Kiev, Vsevolod Yurevitch (1176–1212), who assumed the title of Grand Prince of Vladimir, and Ivan Vsyevolodovitch (d. 1238), the builder of Nijni Novgorod.

The principality's geographical position was another factor making for power. Until the Mongols came in, the princes of Vladimir had less to fear from nomad raids and foreign intervention in general than had their cousins of Kiev. To the west lay the protecting forests of White Russia, with the Pripet Marshes beyond them; to the north and east lay other forest-clad solitudes whose small, scattered population constituted no threat, despite their frequent refusal to pay the tribute of furs imposed by the princes of Vladimir and the boyars of Novgorod.

It was thus in Suzdal-Vladimir, a comparatively fertile region whose clearings produced flax and grain, that the heart of future Russia was located. This was the setting in which the princes of the Rurikovitch family, starting with Andrey Bogoliubsky, succeeded in bringing their boyars to heel, became territorial sovereigns in more than name, and carried on the tradition of the national crusade which had been initiated by the grand princes of Kiev.

Mongols and Russians

Vladimir-Suzdal was none the less unable to escape being overrun by the Mongols. In his westward march, Baty, one of Genghis Khan's successors, ravaged Moscow in 1237 and crushed the Grand Prince of Vladimir in 1238 before swooping on Kiev in 1240. Henceforward the princes of Muscovy were subjects of the power of the Golden Horde, whose seat of government, Saraï ('the Palace'), the general headquarters of the Mongol armies in Europe, was at the mouth of the Volga. The princes held their authority from the Mongols' khan (chief) and had to journey to his court to present their humble respects; they also paid tribute and supplied military contingents. To the Tatars, Muscovy was a frontier zone and a field for exploitation; but it was only a tiny fraction of the Mongol empire, situated on its remotest fringe, and bordered to the north and east by sparsely inhabited, almost inaccessible areas; never therefore a crucial or sensitive sector in the Golden Horde's defences.

From their new situation the grand princes of Vladimir derived a real though restricted freedom, and an increase in power. The tribute was based on a population count; the task of levying it enabled them to impose their own authority more firmly; and a policy of submission to the conqueror – of collaboration with the khan – assured them of external support in the event of disturbance or insurrection. Under the protective shadow of the Saraï the grand princes of Vladimir prepared to reconquer what they had lost.

It is, of course, undeniable that the Mongols sowed ruin and destruction. Pushkin made the celebrated accusation: 'The Tatars were nothing like the Moors: having conquered Russia, they did not acquaint her with algebra and Aristotle.' Devastated landscapes, towns laid in ashes, massacres – these were the fruits of war in the second half of the thirteenth century. But, as we have seen, the Mongols cannot be held solely responsible for the decline of the Russia of Kiev. Moreover, what is known by common consent as 'the Mongol yoke' seems in reality to have been a period of gradual rehabilitation. It is true that the conquerors' exactions were a heavy burden on the people, made heavier, as was the custom of the time, in proportion as the prince's agents were dishonest; and the forced levy of soldiers must have been more burdensome still in a country whose level of population was not high and where the average expectation of life, given harsh natural conditions and the hardships of war and occupation, was inevitably short. The political interests of the Golden Horde involved campaigns in Asia and the Caucasus, in which contingents from all the empire's provinces were obliged to take part; and Russia was one of those provinces. It is true, again, that the Mongol invasion decisively separated Russia from the western world and the Mediterranean, though relations between Kiev and Byzantium had become tenuous and uncertain some time before the Mongols came in.

FIGURE 9 Church of the Trinity, Pskov (USSR), reconstruction.

In the other scale of the balance must be set the fact that Suzdal and the other Russian territories found themselves suddenly connected with the continent of Asia, and took part in the caravan trade whose trains of pack animals threaded their way without let or hindrance between the Dnieper and the frontiers of India and China. Mongol rule was not concerned with assimilation; even where they were converted to Islam, the Tatars did not persecute the Orthodox Church; nor did they tamper in any way with the political and administrative structure of their Russian territories, contenting themselves merely with installing *bashaks* (governors) in the most important towns. What the Tatars cared about was raising money and men from their subject peoples, expeditiously and indirectly, through the local rulers; and they wanted the flow of trade, and the chain of military power, to be maintained unbroken from one end of the empire to the other. It was the Tatars who introduced into Russia the system of relays of horses

3*

– a burdensome organization, no doubt, for the population which had to provide it, but one which was indispensable to the prosperity, and the very existence, of so vast a state.

In fact, the Mongol yoke gave the Russian lands two centuries of peace which are in striking contrast with their immediately previous history, and lead one to bring in a milder verdict on the Tatars and their effects on Russia than most Russian historians do. Moreover, the Mongols had remained nomadic and their cultural level was lower than that of the farming Russians; hence the princes' and big landowners' adoption and adaptation of the conquerors' ways of dressing, and the infiltration of Tatar words into some sections of the Russian vocabulary – war, trade, money and clothes – were without influence on the way of life of the Russian people, who, indeed, absorbed into their own culture a number of Mongols who had been converted to Christianity.

There remains the question of how far Mongol rule was responsible for Russia's economic and political backwardness. The Mongols did not cause the decline of the state of Kiev. Nor is it certain that the new principality of Suzdal-Vladimir would have fared any better without them. And by occupying the steppe regions the Mongols forced part of the Russian people, augmented by refugees, to occupy a smaller living-space, and thus produced favourable conditions for the growth of a state by increasing the population density. Finally, the khan's authority upheld that of the princes of Vladimir and consequently reduced the disruptive effect of internecine conflict between princely rivals. As can be seen from the whole of Russian history, the handicap of geographical conditions, combined with Russia's easterly position, is quite enough to account for her slow, difficult progress.

Russians versus Poles in Lithuania

It should also be remembered that Mongol domination extended to less than the whole of Russian territory. The regions north of the Duna and the upper Volga (north of Tver) remained intact. To the west, the rise of the firmly established kingdom of Lithuania caused the Tatars progressively to abandon, during the fourteenth century, all their territory lying along, and to the west of, the Dnieper. Vitebsk and Minsk in the reign of King Gedimin of Lithuania (1316–41), Kiev and Tchernigov under his successor Olgerd (1345–77), and, at a later period, Smolensk, all became Lithuanian towns. This was an important development precisely because it took place in the fourteenth century, during which the distinction between the three branches of the East Slavs became more definite than hitherto. These branches were the Byelorussians (White Russians) between the River Pripet and the western reaches of the River Duna, who were then under Lithuanian rule; the Great Russian peoples of Novgorod and Vladimir-Suzdal, ruled by the Golden Horde (by remote control in the case of Novgorod); and finally, in the south, in the region divided between the Lithuanian kingdom and the Tatars, the Little Russian or Ukrainian people, which was only sparsely represented in the devastated country east of the river but was slightly more numerous to the west of it, and which was the nucleus of the future Ukrainian nation.

Lithuania's existence as a separate kingdom was short; in 1385 it was united with Poland, Olgerd's son Jagellon (1377–92) becoming at once king of Poland and prince of Lithuania. The rulers of this new Polish-Lithuanian state were Lithuanians. Lithuania nevertheless survived as a protected principality under Vitovt, Jagellon's cousin. When, in 1410, the principality was faced with the danger of conquest by the Teutonic Knights who had settled in Prussia, Byelorussian and Ukrainian contingents formed part of the Polish-Lithuanian army which defeated the Germans at the memorable battle of Tannenberg. This, coming after the Battle on the Ice, put an end of Germanic expansion in the east.

While the Lithuanian kingdom lasted, the Russian element in its population was a preponderant influence; Russian law spread from Russian territory into Lithuania, and Orthodoxy gained ground at the expense of both Catholicism and paganism. This position was reversed by the union of 1385, which made the Poles predominant in the new, enlarged state. Lithuanian lords, and subsequently Russian lords as well, became converts to Catholicism and adopted Polish manners and customs, while the main body of the Russian population clung to its national language and religion. Persecuted as a minority in Lithuania proper, the Russian population along the whole of the Dnieper and to a considerable depth westward from it (since in the fifteenth century the principality of Lithuania included the whole of the upper Dnieper basin) withstood every attempt to convert it to Catholicism. Nevertheless Vitovt eventually, in 1418, declared Lithuania to be officially Roman Catholic, though the Orthodox inhabitants were allowed to retain the eastern rite. From this time onwards the western borders of Russian territory were disputed between Russia and Poland; the latter regarded the great Polish landowners as the pillars of her cause, while the Russian population seems to have looked to the grand princes of Vladimir, and later of Moscow, as the authentic upholders of its national and religous traditions.

The Emergence of Moscow
The principality of Suzdal, viewed as a whole, presented favourable preconditions for the birth of a new state; but the fact that Moscow, rather than some other town, became the capital was, historically speaking, largely a matter of chance. In the early days of Mongol domination there was no state of Suzdal in any real sense of the term; the country was divided among the descendants of Vselovod 'of-the-large-brood', who had become hereditary landlords; one of them purchased from the Mongols the title of grand prince of Vladimir and, with it, an authority over the others which was at first only nominal.

Alexander Nevsky (1252–63) was the Grand Prince of Vladimir during whose reign Moscow began to emerge from obscurity. In 1260 Alexander settled one of his sons, Daniel, there, and the miniature principality, under Mongol protection in the early stages, gradually grew in power. Alexander, who had beaten the Swedes and the Knights of the Sword, established the policy which Muscovy followed for the next half-century and more: he collaborated closely with the Golden Horde, and buttressed the collaboration with matrimonial alliances. Daniel's successor, George (1303-25), married Khan Uzbek's sister, and with his father-in-law's support wrested the title of Grand Prince from Michael of Tver. The protracted conflict which ensued between Tver and Moscow is mainly significant for the fact that with the help of Mongol troops George's successor, Ivan I, nicknamed Kalita (the 'purse', i.e. the charitable), reduced to submission not only the principality of Tver but the greater part of Suzdal as well. During his reign, in 1326, the Metropolitan of Vladimir – hitherto the capital of Orthodoxy – moved to Moscow. This was an essential complement to the grand princes' policy of centralization: their authority over the lesser princes was now supported by an ecclesiastical hierarchy whose leader had his residence in the capital. Not that the Metropolitan took his orders from the Grand Prince – on the contrary, it was often he who gave them, and there were even critical moments at which he held the future of the principality in his hands. But the united influence of a clergy which at that time was the only educated class in the country, and which supplied diplomatic agents and envoys, was henceforward at the service of the Grand Prince; and a policy of political unification under Moscow was in the interest of the Church, which stood to gain in power and influence thereby.

Danger from Lithuania Repulsed

The active part played by the Metropolitan quickly became apparent when, under the successors of Ivan Kalita (d.1341), the principality of Moscow was simultaneously deprived of Mongol protection and threatened by Lithuania. Neither Simeon the Proud (1341-52) nor Ivan II (1352-9) was able to arrest the advance of Olgerd, under whom Lithuania reached the summit of its power. The title of grand prince had already passed to Suzdal at the death of Ivan II; and when Olgerd captured Kiev in 1361 he secured Byzantium's consent that Kiev should once more become a metropolitan see. It looked as if this western-based initiative would recapture the Russian territories held by the Mongols (and thus indirectly deprive the princes of Suzdal of their lands), and restore the state of Kiev to its former greatness. But the Khan of the Golden Horde, whose power had begun to wane, negotiated with the Metropolitan Alexis of Moscow and restored the title of grand prince of Dmitri, Ivan II's son, who was thus enabled to recover his authority over the princes of Suzdal. Meanwhile the threat presented from the west by Lithuania was dissipated by the death of Olgerd in 1377 – which, as we have indicated, was the signal for disputes concerning the succession.

The Rise of Moscow

The principality was as yet very small: some one hundred and fifty miles to the north, Yaroslav, on the Volga, was independent of it (Rostov, thirty miles south of Yaroslav, came under Muscovite rule in 1374); Suzdal to the north-east, and Murom to the east, less than one hundred and twenty-five miles away, were independent; so was Riazan, the centre of a small but powerful state to the south-east. A hundred and fifty miles to the north-west, Tver was an enemy town. Mojaisk, sixty miles west of Moscow, was already a satellite of the principality but lay beyond its borders.

But in throwing its weight behind Ivan II's son, the Church of Moscow had not been lacking in foresight. Dmitri (1359–89) has come down in history as a man of outstanding intelligence and resolute character. His principal achievement was to initiate resistance to the Mongols and constitute himself the champion of national independence. His grandfather had beaten back the Swedish and German invaders; Dmitri was the first to organize a vast crusade, in which religious and political ends were combined. Jagellon, king of Poland, and the principality of Tver, had both contracted an alliance with the Mongols; the remaining towns preserved a prudent neutrality. Dmitri confronted Khan Mamaï's army at Kulikovo (the Field of the Woodcock) on 8 September 1380 and defeated it with overwhelming slaughter. It is true the victory was short-lived; two years later the new Khan, Toktamysh, sacked Moscow, captured the citadel (Kremlin) and made Dmitri start paying tribute again. Nevertheless the first major defeat of the Mongols at Kulikovo, which earned Dmitri the title of Donskoi, marked the beginning of a long struggle for independence in which Moscow was to play a leading part.

The period from the death of Dmitri in 1389 to the accession of Ivan III in 1462, consisting of the lengthy reigns of Vassily (1389–1425) and Vassily the Blind (1425–62), saw the Muscovite princes' power extended and consolidated considerably, in virtual freedom from Mongol control. Vassily rendered homage to the khan and, by purchase from him, obtained suzerainty over Murom, Nijni-Novgorod and Suzdal. But Moscovy's subordination to the Golden Horde was becoming more and more nominal. When

Изъ Евангелія XIV. в, находящагося въ библіотекѣ Импер Академіи Наукъ

FIGURE 10 Anthropomorphic letters, initials in a fourteenth-century Russian MS of the Gospels. Library of the Academy of Sciences, Leningrad.

the second Mongol empire was set up and Timur (Tamerlane) moved into the steppes of southern Russia to impose his authority on the Horde, Mongol power did not come rolling northwards to swamp Muscovy, as it had done a hundred and fifty years earlier. Timur's army halted in 1395 at the Oka, which was firmly held by Vassily's forces. The tribute had still to be paid; the time was not quite ripe for snapping that link, and, by refusing payment a few years later, Vassily provoked the Mongols to the sack of Moscow by a punitive expedition (1408). His successor, Vassily the Blind, had an easier task, quarrels within the Horde enabling him to play off one Mongol faction against another, to the principality's advantage. It was with the support of Mongol princes that, in 1450, he put down a palace revolution which had temporarily lost him his throne; and during the last twelve years of his reign he added Novgorod, Pskov and Riazan to his dominions.

At his death in 1462, Muscovy covered 270,270 square miles and was the most powerful principality in Russia; its hegemony was recognized by the neighbouring towns, such as Tver. It was for all practical purposes independent of the Mongols, and the fall of Constantinople to the Turks in 1453 rendered Moscow the only large independent centre of the eastern rite. The dynasty of Vselovod, shining with the glory of Alexander Nevsky and Dmitri Donskoi, was associated henceforth with the cause of Orthodoxy and independence.

A Society on the Move. Internal Colonization

In the twelfth century, great changes had begun in the economic and social structure of Russian life. The incursions of the Polovtsians triggered the process; the Mongol invasion continued it, depopulating the steppes to the east of the Dnieper and causing a northward migration to the Oka and Volga, which had already been impinged on by voluntary colonization from Novgorod. Demographically, the axis of Russia shifted from the north-south line of the Dnieper to the east-west line of the upper Volga. Though the population density cannot be ascertained at all exactly, it was undoubtedly low; nevertheless the clearings in the forests multiplied, villages sprang up in the vacant expanses between towns, and in the loneliest regions the monks were admirably productive pioneers winning new ground for civilization. In the fourteenth century Sergei of Radonezh (d. 1390) founded the monastery of St Sergius (twenty-eight miles northeast of Moscow), which was destined to play a tremendous role in national history. Sergei, who started the work of clearing the northern forests which carried the official church as far as the Solovki Islands in the White Sea, is one of old Russia's most popular saints.

Colonization created new economic and social situations. Bigger harvests were required; less land was therefore periodically left fallow, and more careful methods of cultivation were adopted; the second half of the fifteenth century saw the introduction of manuring and a three- or four-yearly rotation of crops, with a fallow period. Rye and barley were still the chief cereals, but flax and hops became more prominent than before.

Freedom and the Peasantry

The peasants, generally speaking, lived on the estates of princes or boyars or their underlings, or on church lands. These properties had been given by the sovereign prince to his counsellors and friends or, in the second case, were intended to support the monasteries and clergy; as time went on, inheritance crept in and they became patrimonies (*votchina*). A peasant on an estate was subject to taxation and the *corvée*, but at this period was still free to leave his lord's service; a freedom which, however, had more of the shadow than the substance, since if he did go he left all his belongings behind, and the feudal owners did everything possible to keep their indispensable labour-force tied to the land. Thus there gradually grew up a system which has been called 'manorial exploitation', and which was increasingly based on forced labour. This was the start of a long course of development leading, by the seventeenth century, to total serfdom.

Outside the estates, on tracts of land which, in districts which had been settled for a long time, steadily shrank in size, there existed a peasant class which was free not just in name but in fact: the 'black' peasants, who were of course subject to the sovereign's control (he being the owner of all land in his dominions) and who had to render taxes and *corvée*. But these impositions were less onerous than on the estates, and the peasants kept their communal organization and their freedom. The further we go from the central areas, into the largely uncleared forests of the north and north-east, the greater the proportion of these free peasants in the local population. Their numbers were increased by fugitives from the feudal estates and also by voluntary colonists (and in a few instances by colonists sent out by the feudal lords) from the central regions, where, despite the scanty population, production and consumption in a still primitive economy were constantly threatening to become unbalanced.

Overpopulation has been a recurrent phenomenon throughout Russia's agrarian history. Every hamlet in Muscovy produced its emigrants, especially in years of bad harvest. So whereas the peasant population of the Oka and upper Volga regions were oppressed ever more heavily by the yoke of Muscovite feudalism, Russian colonization to the northward perpetuated the existence of a class of free peasants down to the nineteenth century and the abolition of serfdom.

The liberty of the 'black' peasants was continually threatened, as might be expected, by the endeavours of the feudal lords and the monasteries to include them within the boundaries of the existing estates. But local geography was a counterforce to be reckoned with. In the central districts, the network of towns and villages, and the tracks and footpaths connecting them, were sufficiently developed for the authority of the princes and lords as sovereign proprietors to be respected by, or imposed on, the free peasants. But farther north, beyond the Volga, it was another matter. Remote hamlets in the depths of the forest, defended by natural obstacles which snow in the winter, and floods and slush in the spring thaw, rendered

almost impassable, and which were accessible only by tracks known sometimes only to the local inhabitants – in such conditions it is not surprising
that many inhabited localities were left to their own devices for years at a
stretch by the prince's agents, who ventured into them on tax-gathering
expeditions neither without fear nor without danger.

Russians and non-Russian Natives: New Contacts

The Russians' colonial expansion to the east brought them into contact
with various peoples of Finnish and Turkish stock. This type of expansion
should be distinguished from the military expeditions dispatched by
Novgorod, and later by Moscow, to subject these peoples to the *jassak*, a
tribute of furs. As early as the twelfth century, the Nenets or Samoyeds of
the tundra, the Komi-Zyriany and Permians of the taïga, and, a little later,
the Voguls and Ostiaks of the Ural region, had been forced to submit to
this tax; and in 1220, Vselvod's son founded Nijni Novgorod in the heart
of Mordvinian territory. The Russian colonies dotted about in these new
areas were small, and the indigenous population, mainly nomadic, was
sparse. The successful levying of tribute demanded a certain degree of
organization, consisting of fortified posts (*ostrogi*) to which the natives delivered their packages of furs, and which were surrounded by small cleared
areas inhabited and farmed by the settlers. These posts, which were strung
out along the routes used by the invaders to make their way in, were sited
at strategic points, such as the confluence of rivers. But though they had
been set up in the first place to enforce respect from the natives, they soon
served also to extend the prince's authority to the Russian settlers: a transition all the more easily effected in that the latter were frequently under
attack by the resentful local population and were compelled to seek the
authorities' protection from time to time.

To the east, then, the picture we must keep in mind is one of vast thinly-
populated expanses which were a field for exploitation as well as settlement; and also a place of refuge and liberty for peasants threatened with
serfdom, at least in so far as the indigenous population were willing to put
up with newcomers. This dual drive to the east, in which the government's
political aims and the people's elementary needs were inextricably mixed,
caused a gradual development of agriculture in regions where hunting and
food-gathering had been the only means of life; it also brought about the
forcible conversion and partial assimilation of the pagan inhabitants, in
particular the Voguls.

Rural Economy: Trade with the Outside World

In Russia generally, the economy was still agricultural and every town
tended to be a self-contained, self-supporting unit of production and consumption. This almost closed economy represents a retrograde step by comparison with that of Kiev. Nevertheless, not all the towns were destroyed by
the invasions; and a certain amount of inter-urban, and even inter-

continental, trade managed to survive. Still, if such centres as Tver, Moscow and Riazan were actively connected with the trade routes which, under the Mongol Empire, led to central Asia and China, their population was too small to support more than an insignificant volume of trade; the barter of small quantities of fabrics and luxury articles was an occupation which concerned a few merchants and nobles and no one else. The amount of money in circulation was minute.

Birth of the Rouble

The decline of the state of Kiev and its decomposition into separate principalities, beginning in the twelfth century, were the outward and visible signs of an economic retrogression characterized by a total absence of Russian currency; the period from the twelfth to the second half of the fourteenth century is known as the *bezmonetni* period (period without money). The biggest transactions were carried out by means of silver ingots; smaller ones, on the rare occasions when barter was not employed, with coinage struck by the Horde, or with *groschi* from Prague.

The minting of currency was resumed in Russia during the second half of the fourteenth century; the *den'ga* (a coin not of Tatar but of Russian origin, whose value was calculated from that of the rouble, the word used in Novgorod to denote a silver ingot, and which became a unit of accountancy, though not of currency, in fourteenth-century Moscow) was struck in the larger principalities – Moscow, Suzdal, Nijni Novgorod and Riazan, followed by Tver after 1400. Yaroslav and Rostov also had currencies of their own, and Smolensk created one in the fifteenth century. Novgorod and Pskov, as the inlets through which foreign money reached Russia, did not start minting their own coins until the fourteen-twenties. The activities of these various mints bear witness to the development of a silver economy; it was also found necessary to issue a copper coinage of low value, but its relationship to the *den'ga* has not been precisely ascertained.

The unification of the Russian territories under the aegis of Moscow caused a number of mints to become less active, and finally to cease operating altogether. By the time a single monetary system was introduced under the reform of 1534, the only mints still functioning were those of Moscow, Novgorod and Pskov; the last two were closed in the seventeenth century. Meanwhile Russian coinage had spread beyond the frontiers of the principalities during the fifteenth century and was replacing Tatar currency in the Volga region a hundred years before the conquest of that region by Ivan IV.

Urban Liberties on the Wane

In the central districts, the weakness of the town as an autonomous entity was evinced by the decline in the power of the communal assembly (*veche*) in the older towns; and the new towns created or fostered by the princes – Moscow, for example – were not autonomous.

Only in the north-west, in Pskov and more especially Novgorod, did the

time-honoured forms of municipal liberty continue to obtain. Although
these two towns lost the privilege of choosing their ruling princes at the end
of the thirteenth century, and became tribute-paying dependencies of the
Grand Prince of Vladimir, that sovereign's authority over them was nominal. He was represented by a governor in each, but was under oath to respect their autonomy. The reason for this situation was that Novgorod and
Pskov, unlike the central towns, each still had a powerful oligarchy which,
owing to the geographical position of the two towns, had been able to
maintain an almost uninterrupted commercial relationship with the
Hanseatic communities. Furs, of which a steady supply was collected from
the subject peoples, were not the only commodity on offer. Both towns
traded principally with the West, for whose goods they themselves represented an attractive market; theirs was by no means a mere transit economy; and since Muscovy was to a certain extent the granary of both,
there was trade in that direction too. It is not surprising that a merchant
class developed which in both cases was closely linked with the boyars,
that is, with those who financed military affairs and who, in Pskov, ensured
the power of the city council, and, in Novgorod, of the archbishop, elected
by the *veche* as the head of that *de facto* republic. The social inequalities resulting from the economic development of these two great communities
were a cause of frequent unrest, especially in the fifteenth century, when
general economic conditions, combined with external pressure, were undermining the position of Novgorod. The insurrection there, in 1418, was one
symptom of such unrest.

New Life in the Arts. Icon Painters: Theophanes and Rublev
The commercial towns of the north-west were the focal points of civilization during this period. It was, indeed, largely thanks to them that in and
around Moscow itself there was a notable development of literature and
art towards the end of the fourteenth century. The problem of Mongol
domination and its consequences comes up again in this context. The
period of conquest – during which the centre and south of the country were
sown with ruins and the centres of Russian cultural life sank into decadence
– was followed by a period of recovery to which some historians refer as a
renaissance, a renaissance springing at once from Russian tradition and
from Byzantine influence. For the Mongols, contrary to what is sometimes
imagined, in no way debarred contact between Russia and the western
world. The cessation of overland trade with Constantinople, via what had
previously been the state of Kiev, should be regarded chiefly as the final
stage of a lengthy period of decline; when in addition the country was
ravaged and depopulated and lost its last remnants of political importance,
it became, economically speaking, a spent force. But literary and artistic
influences, though carried by individuals, not groups, and by a single work
of art here and there, not a steady stream of imports, continued to make
their way into Russia – travelling, indeed, by a slightly more easterly route
after the Mongols, about 1266, had ceded to the Genovese the port of

Kaffa, in the Crimea. The trading towns' prosperity, one of whose consequences was the building of more churches and monasteries, attracted Serbian and Greek artists (such as Theophanes, who reached Novgorod by way of Kaffa in 1370).

The decline of the state of Kiev made hardly any difference to the influence of Byzantine civilization on Pskov and Novgorod. The influence was still strong even in the fourteenth century; the frescoes of the Church of the Transfiguration at Volotovo (1352) are an imitation of Byzantine work, with Italian renaissance elements transmitted through Byzantium. The growth of trade relations with the West never resulted in any strong German influence on the arts in Russia, except as regards a few architectural details; the 'doors of Korsun' in the Cathedral of Sancta Sophia at Novgorod, which were cast in Magdeburg in the second half of the twelfth century, are quite untypical. At a time when culture and art were bound to be exclusively religious in character, religion was a barrier, not a link, between the West and Russia.

In the south-west, on the other hand, Russia remained as receptive as ever to influences from the Mediterranean Near East, which came to her either directly, or by way of Greater Serbia, the channel of transmission in either case being the new trade route opened up by the Genovese from Constantinople to the Crimea.

Russia's Mesopotamia: A New Artistic Centre

Nearer than Kiev to the old-established towns of Novgorod and Pskov, where the development of the arts continued against a background of political disturbance, there appeared in the twelfth century a new centre of culture in the triangle formed by the Rivers Oka and Volga, that Russian Mesopotamia intersected by the River Kliasma, which was to form the nucleus of the Muscovite state.

Vladimir and Suzdal were its earliest important towns; other prominent places were Yaroslav, Rostov and Pereyaslav-Zaleski. Vladimir originated as a fortified post set up in 1108 by Vladimir Monomakh; the prince's palace and the Cathedral of St George were built in 1157. When Moscow was still a little market town of no special importance, Vladimir was not only a capital but an architectural jewel (plate 10).

Stretching from west to east on a cliff one hundred and fifty feet above the Kliasma, Vladimir was resplendent with white stone buildings: the Golden Gate barring the road from the south, the Eastern Gate that from Suzdal; the Church of the Saviour (1164); Andrey Bogoliubsky's palace; the Cathedral of the Dormition (i.e. the death of Our Lady, a brief sleep followed by her ascension into heaven); and, most impressive of all, the Cathedral of St Dimitri (1194–7), so memorable for its elegant design and its exterior decoration of lions, griffons and fantastic animals and an ascension of Alexander the Great, who was regarded as symbolic of the princely power. A few miles away rose the charming Church of the Intercession, on a small island in the Nerl, in a landscape of green meadows and wooded horizons.

Suzdal, twenty-five miles off to the north-east, became the religious centre of the region in the fourteenth century, but rapidly lost its vitality and dwindled to a shadow of its former self; meanwhile rising activity was the keynote in Vladimir, and Yaroslav and other riverside towns, particularly those on the upper Volga, whose economic importance emerged more and more prominently from the thirteenth century onwards.

It was in the same period that Moscow, the unifier of Russia, and somewhat less exposed than the other principalities to Mongol aggression, began building, and attracted artists from Novgorod, Vladimir, and Vladimir's neighbour, Suzdal. But the fourteenth century was none the less a great period for Novgorodian art, especially in painting, the dominating figure being Theophanes the Greek, who painted the frescoes in the Church of the Saviour in Ilina Street (1378). He then moved to Moscow in about 1390 and collaborated with the young Rublev in decorating the Cathedral of the Archangel and the Annunciation, in the Kremlin.

The influence of a Greek artist like Theophanes consisted not only in his adherence to Byzantine models, which were austere in the main, but into which her personal sensibility, and that of his Russian colleagues, infused a greater sense of life. It lay also in his daily contact with the admirers who gathered round to watch him at work (unlike most Russian icon painters, he did not paint in solitude). In discussion and argument with them he dilated on his memories of the only great and beautiful city in the world – Tsargrad, Constantinople, to which all eyes were turned.

Rublev's entire output is bound up with the life and development of Moscow. He was born between 1360 and 1370; in his childhood he must have heard tales of Prince Dmitri's victory on the Field of the Woodcock (1380), and, on the other hand, of the sufferings endured in Moscow when the city was destroyed by the Tatars, in 1382. He was not a foreigner like Theophanes, but a Russian whose sensibility seems to have been tutored as much by ordinary life and its sorrows as by the contemplation of divine realities. At the present time the works attributed to him are some forty icons, some of which – such as the famous 'Trinity', the three icons of the iconostasis in the Cathedral of the Trinity and St Sergius at Zagorsk – are the direct creations of his personal genius, while others bear its stamp but are the collective work of the studio he directed. He thus stands at the dividing line between the Middle Ages, when art was anonymous, and a new period, in which the artist's personality takes a leading place.

The icons were works inspired by a living faith, aiming directly at the admiration and feelings of the people. But the literature of the period had a much smaller public; it circulated in church and court circles only. Religious works, translated from Greek into Serbian or Bulgarian, were copied in the monasteries, where learned monks composed lives of the saints and continued the task begun by the chroniclers of Kiev. We should beware of exaggerating the importance of this Russian renaissance; it affected a few key cities, the distances between which were great. It was a real renaissance – the high quality of its creations, and the emergence of new art-forms, such as the miniature, earn it that title; but what was really typical of it was an upsurge of building activity, encouraged by the comparatively peaceful conditions of the fourteenth century. It was never a broad movement, testifying to an underlying psychological and spiritual change and involving considerable strata of the population. Few original literary works, except in the religious field, have been bequeathed to us by the fourteenth and fifteenth centuries. Mention should be made, however, of the patriotic narratives inspired by the struggle against the Tatars: the *Lay of the Massacre at Mamaï*, and the *Tale from Beyond the River Don* (*Zadontchina*) (late fourteenth – early fifteenth century); and also the work of Nikitin, a merchant of Tver, who wrote an account of his travels in Persia and India, the *Journey of the Merchant Nikitin beyond the Three Seas* (1465).

FIGURE 11 The monks of St Sergius writing the chronicle of their abbey. Miniature from the MS *Life of St Sergius*.

This account is less important for its literary value than for its implications. Russia in the fourteenth century both welcomed foreigners in and had its own colonies abroad – not only in the cosmopolitan port of Kaffa but also in Constantinople, and the towns of the Caucasus, and Persia. And while Russia was still open to Greek influences entering the country from the south-west, she herself exerted some degree of artistic influence beyond her borders; frescoes inspired by the art of Novgorod have been discovered in Gothland. Russian dynamism expressed itself in a great many different ways during this period; it extended to every side of life. But her general economic level was too low to support an ample burgeoning of civilized life at home and a corresponding degree of cultural intercourse with her neighbours. Stone churches in the cities, and monasteries which were centres of artistic and literary activity, buried in the vast expanses of the forests – these, as in the preceding period, were exceptions; isolated jewels in a country dotted with wooden villages, in which an unlettered folk lived out a laborious existence.

A Despotic State: The Great Reign of Ivan III

The reign of Ivan III was a significant phase in the development of the state of Muscovy. By the end of the fifteenth century the unification of central Russia under the Grand Prince of Moscow was complete; feudal separatism had had its day. Novgorod, which was inclined by its commercial interests rather towards Poland and Lithuania, surrendered after a victorious campaign by Ivan; it lost the last of its liberties in 1478. Political domination, manifested by the arrival of a lieutenant (*namestnik*) of the Grand Prince, was emphasized by the deportation of numerous boyars and merchants, and a redistribution of estates in favour of the Muscovite nobility. Novgorod – the only part of the ancient *Rus* in which, despite the city's aristocratic character, a powerful middle class had existed – was now like the rest of Russia: its rulers were landed nobles, over whom the Grand Prince's power was becoming unchallengeable.

Decline of an Ancient Aristocracy; Rise of the New Men
The boyars, who on their huge estates had been monarchs of all they surveyed, now began to be replaced by a different kind of servant of the Grand Prince; and, as we shall see, this development was accelerated under Ivan the Terrible. The faithful henchmen with whom the Grand Prince surrounded himself were recruited from the stubborn, hard-headed class of small landowners; to reward them for services rendered, and also to support them during the military campaigns which were his main activity, he gave them lands on precarious tenure (*pomestie*). The whole atmosphere was one of war and violence. In the highly important social changes taking place, men's arbitrary wills, the abuse of power, and the actions, both individual and collective, of men-at-arms, made at least as much difference as the gradual modifications going on underneath, to which those actions gave such dramatic visible expression.

A larger internal market than hitherto was developing as a result of unification, and the country's closed, rural economy was breaking up in consequence. The owners of the large estates (*votchina*) had difficulty in adapting themselves to the change, and their economic superiority began declining. Their participation in military affairs became more and more of a burden, and lured them into debt. Meanwhile the profits of agriculture were finding their way into the hands of the non-combatant merchants, and also of the monasteries, whose estates were managed more astutely. The same hands, moreover, attracted the small amount of currency in circulation, in sums augmented by usury. This nascent concentration of capital, though of insignificant dimensions at the time, heralded the coming of a different species of economy.

In the immediate situation, the break-up of the big estates produced other and more important effects. As the Grand Prince's authority extended, taking in more land and enabling him to strengthen his hand by the simple method of confiscation, the number of faithful servants to be rewarded with estates increased accordingly. Thus a new aristocracy was arising, strongly attached to the central power, and not so much displacing the old aristocracy of powerful boyars as being superimposed on it. The boyars still had many privileges, but found their freedom of action slipping away; they could no longer use their troops for effective resistance to the supreme authority. They yielded to the Grand Prince's sway, entered his council (the *duma* of the boyars), and accepted positions in the organized administration which was beginning to take shape.

The division of the task of government into its various components was still rudimentary. The central services were given the form of *prikazes*, some of which dealt with affairs considered to be of general importance, such as finance and the army, while others had charge of particular territories. A corps of bureaucrats (the *diaki*) was built up; and the Sudebnik, the administrative and judicial code drawn up by order of the Grand Prince in 1497, bears witness to the progress made by centralization.

FIGURE 12
State seal from
the time of
Ivan III
(Russia).

The apparatus of state organization became a reality under Ivan III. He was a grand prince whose ambition had already begun to look further than his own territories. Not content with dubbing himself tsar on occasion, he regarded himself as the successor of the rulers of Byzantium, adopting the two-headed eagle as his coat of arms. His crown was the 'hat of Monomakh', which according to legend was an heirloom from the emperor of that name. All this pomp and circumstance was designed to impress people at home; foreign diplomats had no great opinion of it, but were compelled to submit to humiliating ceremonies at times, as when the tsar would wash the hand he had extended to greet them.

In the country at large, the sovereign's power was vested in lieutenants (*namestniki*), who lived at the expense of the regions in which they were responsible for executing justice and collecting taxes; the amount of the latter was beginning to be laid down systematically. These representatives of the royal authority were virtually isolated from the capital; distance and poor communications gave them a high degree of arbitrary power. But their situation was precarious – they might be recalled without notice, or subjected to penalties which were often appallingly severe. No official could feel sure of the conditions or duration of his appointment; the administration was given to sudden changes of mind. Indeed, it had to be, for it operated in military style, in a barely pacified country, and the tsar's functionaries, both of the old and the new generation, and even in his immediate retinue, were always competing intensely for precedence. The coteries which grew up among the leading aristocratic families required careful handling by the sovereign.

Architecture for Monarchs

The old, timber-built citadel (Kremlin) was an incongruous setting for the new splendour of the grand princes. It was replaced, in the last years of the fifteenth century and the beginning of the sixteenth, by stone buildings of monumental dignity which are still the city of Moscow's most powerful attraction. The churches, palaces and ring-wall constituting the Kremlin, built between 1475 and 1509 by order of Ivan Kalita and Ivan III, were the work of Russian mastermasons and craftsmen, mostly from Pskov, under the direction of north Italian architects: Ridolfo Fioraventi of Bologna, Pietro Antonio Solario of Milan, Marco Ruffo and Alevisio Novi.

One route by which Italian influence had entered Muscovy was the Don and the Genovese port of Kaffa – 'the port of Moscow', to borrow Louis Réau's expression – at least until Kaffa was taken by the Turks in 1474. But it came in more abundantly from the adjacent states of Hungary and Poland, the Italian renaissance having taken root fairly substantially in Craców and Buda. In 1472 the Grand Prince Ivan III married Zoë (Sophia) Paleologou, who was the niece of the last Byzantine emperor and had taken refuge in Rome after the fall of Constantinople; when he decided to reconstruct the Kremlin, it was to Italy that he turned in his search for architectural talent. This was lacking in Muscovy, though not entirely so; it would be a gross exaggeration to describe the Kremlin as an Italian achievement.

Neither as regards the actual work, which was carried out almost exclusively by Russians, nor as regards the style of its three famous domed churches, is the Kremlin Italian. The churches in question are the Cathedral of the Dormition (*Uspensky sobor*), in which the tsars were crowned, and which was built by Fioraventi; the Cathedral of the Annunciation (*Blagovetchenski sobor*), by architects from Pskov; and the Cathedral of the Archangel Michael (*Arkhangelsky sobor*), by Alevisio Novi, which contains the tombs of the tsars down to Peter the Great.

What the Friazins (Franks – Latins), as these architects were called, were in fact called upon to do was to subordinate themselves to the traditions of Muscovite architecture. Direct Italian influence can, however, be seen in the Granite Palace (*Granitovaïa Palata*), whose façade, with its facets and bosses, recalls the Palazzo Bevilacqua in Bologna; perhaps also in the crenellated walls of the Kremlin; and, more definitely, in the Cathedral of the Archangel, which (as Réau says) conforms to the taste of the early Italian renaissance. Where western influence made itself chiefly felt most was not in stylistic imitation but in giving Russian participants a fresh grounding, or an enhanced perfection, in building technique, the practical realization of monumental plans.

Icon painting continued in undiminished brilliance until the early sixteenth century. Its chief representative was the master-painter Denis; he was probably born about 1440, but that is almost all we know about him except that his reputation was great, comparable to that of Rublev; that his studio was a family affair, with his sons working under him; that he was commissioned to paint important personages such as the Metropolitans Peter and Alexis, defenders of the faith; and that he decorated monasteries and churches – the monastery of Therapont at Byeloozero (the frescoes of which are still in existence), that of Joseph at Volokolamsk, and the Cathedral of the Dormition in the Kremlin.

He belongs to the Rublev tradition; his works are full of tenderness and human dignity. But he lived at a time when the art of the icon was sinking into a fossilized condition, conforming to rigidly prescribed models and completely losing its originality. Historically speaking he is none the less of great importance, both because he worked in a consistently fourteenth-century style and because his inspiration was partially drawn from recent national history, from Moscow's rising greatness in all its aspects, and from the struggle against the Tatars – a characteristic instance is the border of little pictures surrounding his portrait of the Metropolitan Alexis.

In contrast to the rising power of Moscow, Novgorod, though still very active commercially, was in a permanent state of crisis as a result of having been incorporated into Muscovy. Novgorod's artistic output in this period expresses nostalgia for past splendour; its architecture shows a swing back to archaic forms, and its graphic art evokes victories over the princes of central Russia in times gone by; in the icon of the 'Battle of the Suzdalians and Novgorodians', for example, the army of Suzdal is shown being put to flight when the archbishop John erects the image of the Virgin on the ramparts.

Icon painting in Pskov was freer, more receptive towards western influence, and was regarded with some disapproval by the Muscovites.

2

The West Slavs

BOTH THE the Poles and the Czechs had to struggle against Germanic pressure in order to maintain their identity. The first built up a greater Poland whose axis was the Vistula and which, though its frontiers varied, extended to the Baltic coast. The second fashioned a small feudal state which was more influenced by the West, and more civilized, than any of the other Slav countries, and hammered out their national unity on the anvil of harsh religious conflict.

I THE POLES

The Polish People

The Polish people originated from the Slav tribes who spread northwards from the Carpathians to occupy, in the early centuries of the Christian era, the basins of the Odra (Oder) and Wisla (Vistula). But the term Polska is not recorded prior to the tenth century, when, the Poles having already a lengthy though obscure history, one of their leaders, Mieszko I, ruling in Poznan (one of the most ancient Polish towns, like Craców and Gniezno), extended his authority to the whole country, and having married a Christian (the duke of Bohemia's sister) was himself baptized in 966. Mieszko's reign was the start of Poland's history as a country.

The Poles are the 'people of the plain' – the plain which slopes away gently to the northward from the Carpathians and the mountains of Bohemia. The mouths of the large rivers draining it (the Odra and Wisla) provide the outlets on the Baltic which are indispensable to the country's economy. Beyond the Odra the Poles' Teutonic neighbours, pushing aggressively eastwards and spreading along the Baltic coast, forced them to vacate the area between the Elbe and the Odra and, subsequently, much of the coastal region. The entire course of Polish history is interwoven with German-Polish rivalry, whereas Russia, Poland's neighbour to the east, presented no danger till much later. In direct contact with the West, whence came the Franciscan and Dominican monks who gradually converted her people to Christianity in the twelfth and thirteenth centuries, Poland underwent a religious history and general development which parallel those of Russia, or rather Kiev, under Byzantine influence.

She was equally well provided with natural resources, and the first Polish chronicle, that of Gallus Anonymus (early thirteenth century), depicts her as 'a country where the air is healthy and the earth fruitful, where the forests abound with honey and the rivers with fish, where the knights are full of valour and the peasants work hard, where the horses have staying-power and the oxen are willing, where the cows give much milk and the sheep much wool'. But, unlike Kiev and Russia generally, Poland never came under the Mongols, who attacked Craców without success in 1241; her development proceeded unhindered.

The plain of the Vistula is not uniform. The plateaux of the south – Little Poland and the region of Craców – which are particularly fertile and have abundant mineral resources, are of a different character from central Poland and were for some time politically separate from it, becoming a dependency first of the Moravian and later of the Czech kingdom. Polish territorial unity spread outwards from Great Poland. It was achieved by the efforts of the Piasts, a dynasty descended from Mieszko, and was rendered easier by a common language whose dialectal variations were not great, and by a gradually extending network of *castra* – strategic focal points which enabled local market-places to function undisturbed, and whose interdependence rapidly broke up the isolation of the flat country-side. In the eleventh century, however, the country's centre of gravity shifted to the south, controlled at that time by the Piasts, and Craców became the capital.

Poland as a state was not yet firmly on its feet; the powers of its rulers, most of whom were not crowned, were disputed by the feudal landowners, who were building up big estates and who merely strengthened their own privileges by recognizing a sovereign. Nevertheless, under the auspices of a political authority which reached its peak under Boleslas the Bold, who

FIGURE 13
Metal drinking-bowl, Wroclaw (Poland).

was crowned in 1076, Polish territory underwent a gradual transformation. The growth of trade, and relations with the West, Rome and even Byzantium, created a complex of influences, all of which left their mark on Polish civilization. Alongside the palaces in the 'cities' (or rather fortified towns, such as Poznań, Wroclav, Cracóv, Gniezno, Kruszwica and Kalisz) Romanesque churches were built; nearly all of these have now gone, leaving only a little masonry and stained glass and a few frescoes, such as those at Leczyca and the twelfth-century examples discovered in 1959 at Wislica. Byzantine influence is evident in mosaics (Church of St Andrew, Cracóv). A small number of curious stone monuments, mostly in western Pomerania, can be seen in the primitive countryside, whose inhabitants took three centuries to convert to Christianity and retained a good many heathen customs. Surviving traces of fine craft work (ladles, painted egg-shells, utensils made of horn, and carvings of animals) indicate that the peasants had risen some way above subsistence level.

In proportion as Christianity became the religion of the country, Latin replaced the vernacular; from the reign of Mieszko onwards it was the official administrative language.

Polish Agriculture
It was thought at one time that tenth-century Poland consisted entirely of forests and marshes and that the population lived by hunting and food-gathering, with very little agriculture; but this view has long been exploded. The introduction of winter wheat, and the progress of stock-breeding (which, incidentally, remained the chief rural occupation until the thirteenth century), had already started yielding marketable surpluses which were exchanged by barter. The small towns of western Poland and the coastal areas (Gdańsk, Wolin, Opole, Gniezno) traded over great distances; excavation has turned up Arab money and a few Polish coins. A rapid diversification of agriculture began in the tenth century. The Cistercian monks introduced the cultivation of high-quality fruit and even, despite the climate, planted vineyards, though these eventually disappeared when Hungarian wines started to be imported. The crops grown included flax, hemp and hops. Hunting certainly remained important, less for fur than for food; but the need to preserve useful species had already caused the establishment of game preserves (Zaseki). Nature's bounty could no longer be squandered. Though there were huge uncleared expanses, dwindling slowly as cultivation advanced, the numerous restrictions typical of an agricultural society were already in existence.

Rural Government. Nobles and Peasants
As tribal organization broke up, leaving only its basic unit, the family, the ownership of land followed suit; and among the peasantry thus created there grew up a prosperous minority in whose hands an increasing amount of real property was concentrated. Events followed exactly the same pattern as in the West. The king conferred privileges on the Church and his

leading vassals; the result was a class of wealthy aristocrats living on the estates they had acquired or been presented with, as the case might be, and pressing the helpless peasantry into line with their own interests in every available way. Slavery still existed, but slowly died out; meanwhile most of the peasants were sinking into serfdom.

Their subjection was in line with the general trend of Polish agriculture, which was becoming increasingly orientated towards the export of cereals. Small units were still the rule in the twelfth and thirteenth centuries. But large holdings – sometimes as large as 1,250 acres – were beginning to emerge in the form of feudal 'reserves' (*folwarki*), worked by agricultural retainers and producing wheat. In the fourteenth century these units began to predominate over the peasant smallholdings, multiplying especially along the navigable rivers leading to the Baltic; access to the sea, after the treaty of Torun (1466), hastened their development. Whereas the *corvée* had been almost unknown in the fourteenth century, it now weighed oppressively on the peasants, who were compelled both to work on the reserves and to help transport the crop; the number of days on which they had to do so depended on whether they could supply haulage themselves or not. The next step arose from the need to keep the requisite numbers of workers on the land; legislation was introduced to limit removals and finally to forbid them altogether. By the early sixteenth century the tenant-farmer and his family had become bound to the estate. Thus Poland, despite its very different political system, followed the same evolution as Muscovy and Bohemia.

There was, however, in this moderately diversified society consisting mainly of the great landowners and the peasant masses, an intermediate class of small freehold landowners whose property had not been absorbed

FIGURE 14 Romanesque tombstone, twelfth century, at Wislica (Poland)

Map 5 Poland in the Year 1000

into the big estates; and within this class there was a category of military knights whose social rank was below that of the feudal lords. These knights became the *szlachta*, an aristocratic body under the patronage of the great families, who thus had considerable room for manoeuvre in their dealings with the sovereign. The fertility of the soil and the exploitation of the peasants gave the power to a landowning nobility which the king never succeeded in bringing under complete control.

Towns under German Law

In Poland as in Bohemia, German colonization stimulated the development of towns; though in neither country can the town as such be regarded as a German creation. More than half the towns in medieval Poland had developed from markets existing in the shadow of the forts (*grod, gorod, castra*) which kept the roads and river-crossings secure. Some of these towns had a sizeable population by the tenth century, such as Gdańsk (2,000 inhabitants), Poznań and Gniezno (5,000). German colonization made the towns grow faster, bringing with it a German system of laws (the so-called 'right of Magdeburg') which prevailed because it facilitated that growth. It should be noted, however, that Poland had its own burgher class before the German colonists arrived, especially in the larger centres such as Poznań and Craców, on which German law was conferred in 1253 and 1257 respectively. Enjoying a considerable degree of self-government in administrative and judicial matters, and endowed with commercial privileges which largely made up for municipal expenses (keeping the ramparts in good order, providing a contingent of troops, and paying revenue in cash), the Polish towns made great strides in the thirteenth century and after. Warsaw, then only a village, was granted urban status in 1289.

As Poland's towns developed, her artisan class became more numerous and diverse, and in her sawmills and forges she possessed the primitive prototypes of modern industry. The rich saltpans of Wieliczka (producing the so-called Craców salt) and those in Ruthenia, the argentiferous lead mines of Olkusz and Chenciny, copper mining at Kielce, open-cast iron workings – all these were busily exploited and made money for the sovereign, who owned the rights. The trade routes through Poland, parallel to the Vistula (at that time not used for navigation above Torun), the Oder and their tributaries, connected Hungary with the Baltic. Poland traded with Flanders, Germany, Prussia and Muscovy; as well as supplying transit facilities she had her own import and export trade, in which the main commodities were Polish wheat and timber passing in one direction and Flemish and English cloth in the other. The principal commercial centres were Craców, Lwow and the port of Danzig; Craców was particularly important as the outlet for Little Poland, exporting yew for bows and oak for shipbuilding.

Poland as a Baltic Power
Subjected in the thirteenth century to an intensive wave of German settlement from the west, the Polish territories were also influenced by the pull of Bohemia in the south. Bohemia was like Poland in having a great number of German settlers, but was economically more advanced. In 1300, the mercantile burgher class of Craców sent an appeal to Wenceslas II, king of Bohemia, and he was crowned as king of Poland at Gniezno. The Piasts lost the sovereign power for twenty years.

But the real decision about Poland's future was being fought out on the Baltic coast; the Teutonic Knights, who established themselves strongly in Pomerania and Prussia between 1233 and 1466, cut off the Poles' access to the sea. It took Poland over a century to recapture her maritime outlets. Casimir III, ruling the interior (1333–70), enlarged his realm towards the south-east by imposing his authority on Galicia (Lwow and the country round) but achieved nothing against the Knights. The capital event was the marriage of one of his grand-nieces, Hedwiga, to Jagellon, Grand Duke of Lithuania, who became King of Poland (1386–1434); the kingdom was strengthened by the addition of the 'lands of Lithuania and Russia' and by an accretion of military force resulting in the victory of Grünwald (Tannenberg) over the Teutonic Knights (1410). Nevertheless thirty years of fighting under Casimir Jagellon (1447–92), ending in the treaty of Torun (1466), were necessary before Poland could recover an outlet to the Baltic in the form of Danzig and part of Pomerania.

FIGURE 15 The Polish eagle. Left, seal of Przemysl II, prince of Great Poland (1291). National Museum, Cracow. – Right, scutcheon on the monument of Henryk IV, prince of Silesia (thirteenth century). Church of the Holy Cross, Wroclaw.

Russo-Polish Rivalry; and a Permanent Crusade

The *de facto* union of Poland and Lithuania, whose grand dukes supplied Poland with her new dynasty, had the effect of suddenly widening the Poles' field of action, extending it far beyond the limits of Polish territory in the direction of Muscovy and the Black Sea. The grand duchy of Lithuania comprised not only the region of Vilna, with its population of heathen Balts, but stretched far to the south, in consequence of the Jagellons' having liberated Kiev, and the right bank of the Dnieper almost to its mouth, from the Tatars. Having been converted to Christianity at the time of the union, the dynasty transmitted to the Poles a crusading tradition which was transferred later to the struggle against the Turks. The liberated territories became a colonial area in which the Polish aristocracy carved out huge estates. The Polish horizon expanded to the shore of the Mediterranean – a novel and tempting prospect but an uncertain one, not without danger for a state whose real interests lay on the Vistula, and whose gaze needed to be directed constantly towards the north.

Even in the fifteenth century, however, as we shall see, the struggle against the Teutons distracted the Poles from their southern leanings. Meanwhile a more pressing problem was the discontent of the Orthodox population who were in a majority in the Lithuanian-held territories; for these new possessions were Russian lands which the Jagellons had acquired, and which now found themselves under Catholic rule. Through union with Lithuania, Poland was henceforward in contact with the grand principality of Moscow, which was in process of transforming itself into the state of Russia and was eager to claim the whole former *Rus*, lately delivered from the Tatars. The maintenance of Polish-Lithuanian sovereignty to some distance beyond Smolensk depended on a combination of forces which, from the fourteenth century to the seventeenth, was to work in favour of Poland.

A great state territorially speaking, whose boundaries enclosed a patchwork of nationalities, in the fifteenth century the *Regnum Poloniae* displayed, after a temporary setback, an expansive force which can be attributed only to the inherent vitality of the Polish people. In the fourteenth century the German settlers had managed to become the leading element in the towns and had entered the clergy and administration in considerable numbers, though they never affected the character of the rural districts. The fifteenth century was characterized by a re-Polonization of the towns, including those where German influence was strongest. In Craców, the proportion of Poles among the artisan classes increased from 13 per cent in 1401 to 41 per cent at the end of the century. The same phenomenon can be traced in Poznań and Gniezno.

Population pressure, which was felt in town and country alike, manifested itself in Lithuania's southern territory – Ukraine – as elsewhere. Polish lords and peasants began settling there. But they were under constant threat from the Tatars; and despite the protection of a line of forts from Kamienec Podolsk to the vicinity of Kiev, colonization remained sparse. Only a few isolated groups ventured beyond this bastion on to the steppe, rapidly adopted military organization in self-defence, and eventually joined the ranks of the Cossacks.

Poland's Latin Culture

Poland grew up as a member of Catholic Christendom. The country was closely involved in the intellectual and artistic life of the West; by the end of the fifteenth century it had become – in the words of the Florentine humanist Buonaccorsi (Callimachus), tutor to the sons of Casimir Jagellon (d. 1492) – *terra latina*.

The language of learning and literature was Latin, which was also the official language. Very few texts in Polish have come down to us from this period. They consist of sermons and psalters, such as the fourteenth-century psalter of St Florian, a translation of the Psalms of David into – significantly! – three languages, Latin, German and Polish. To these can be added the fifteenth-century psalter of Pulawy and the Bible of Queen Sophia.

4

The fourteenth century, during which Polish economic life made great progress under Casimir the Great (1333–70), was also marked by rapid growth in cultural matters. The event of the greatest significance for the future was the foundation in 1364 of the University of Craców, where teaching began in 1400 and which quickly acquired a European reputation for mathematics and agronomics. It was also a centre of theological and political discussion reflecting the vital intellectual interests of the day.

The sciences, law and religion were represented by Polish scholars who had studied at the recently founded university of Prague or the Italian universities. When, after Grünwald, the future of the Teutonic Order was debated at the Council of Constance, the defender of the rights of the people of Prussia against their German conquerors was a theologian from Craców. The Hussite movement, which, for social reasons, aroused much sympathy among the Polish middle classes and minor nobility, was not without echoes in Craców. But the Polish church was strong and triumphantly overcame the threat of heresy.

FIGURE 16 Highly characteristic milestone and boundary stone, near Kalisz (Poland), an ancient town fortified by Boleslas the Great.

Artistic, as well as intellectual, influences reached Poland continually from the West. Gothic art and architecture had made their way in from France during the twelfth and thirteenth centuries, both indirectly, from the abbeys of the Rhineland, and, in Little Poland, directly, with the Cistercians. Gothic predominated throughout the Polish Middle Ages and lived on through the fifteenth century; its decorative spirit was drawn from popular life, regaling the piety of the faithful with those polychromed statues of the Virgin whose charming faces radiate a celestial smile, calculated to delight the beholder's sensibility rather than to kindle his devotion. Stone was the only building material at first, but the introduction of brick in the thirteenth century enabled even the smallest town to have its own religious buildings. In some cases the decoration shows that Byzantine influence had flowed in from the East; the murals, such as those at Sandomierz and Lublin, inspired by the Russian school of Wolyn, imply an urge for church unity which was still very much alive, at least towards Orthodoxy.

II CZECHS AND SLOVAKS

Great Moravia went under to the Magyars in the early tenth century. The Hungarians, who settled on the Pannonian plain and were soon converted to Christianity, were like a wedge driven between the West and South Slavs, separating them permanently. They also disrupted the political harmony between Bohemia, Moravia and Slovakia by taking over the whole of the Slovaks' territory. Though intellectual ties between the Czechs and Slovaks still obtained, the latter's future was now tied to the Hungarians', and the cultural divergences between the two branches of the Czechoslovaks were accentuated.

The Nation and the State

The Slavs of Bohemia, for the first two centuries of their history, are still wrapped in obscurity. The union gradually achieved by the tribes who colonized the Vltava basin has left traces in the historical legends compiled by Cosmas, the earliest Czech chronicler (figure 19). According to one of these a certain Přemysl (who may be an apocryphal figure) was the original representative of a dynasty which was destined to reign until 1306, and the early monarchs of which were baptized in the time of Methodius and built churches but were obliged to make large concessions to the Germanic clergy, against whom there was a strong tide of national feeling. Wenceslas (924–9) lost his throne through difficulties of this kind, but has nevertheless been immortalized as the 'good king' of legend and the carol, invoked as Bohemia's patron saint.

Bohemia enjoyed a period of greatness under his successor, Boleslas I, extending her authority into Polish territory, towards Craców, and affording some degree of tutelage to the newly created Poland ruled by Mieszko. Subsequently, however, after savage battles with the kings of Saxony, Bohemia was compelled to become a fief of the Holy Roman Empire, retaining an autonomy under which her nobles elected her king from the Přemyslid house. In 873 Prague became a bishopric, under the archbishopric of Mainz.

But the country's Christianity was still only skin-deep; the civilizing influence of the new religion clashed with traditional customs and pagan law. In 992 the new bishop of Prague, Adalbert, of the Slavnikovci family (who at the time still possessed eastern Bohemia as a duchy independent of Prague), brought in Benedictine monks, who founded the country's first monastery at Brevnov; the bishop's action caused a popular uprising, supported by Boleslas, who availed himself of the opportunity to kill off most of the Slavnikovci family and complete the unification of Bohemia (995). At the end of the eleventh century Vratislav assumed the royal title (figure 20), but Bohemia remained faithful to the empire and the new sovereign even received the double title of king of Bohemia and Poland. Paganism had been finally suppressed during that century and an attempt had been made to introduce the Slavonic liturgy, but Pope Gregory VIII refused his permission. Bohemia's religious future was thereby sealed; and when in 1099, while the sovereign was still alive, an imperial edict announced that in future the nobles would not be consulted in choosing the new king, the country's subordination to the Empire appeared to be complete.

But as things turned out, the relationship varied with circumstances. The conflicts surrounding the imperial succession in the twelfth century enabled King Přemysl I to declare his kingdom hereditary; the emperor would merely confirm the title of his vassal the king of Bohemia, who would in theory still be elected by the nobles but would in practice be independent of their choice. The concept of a Czech state of Bohemia gained a stronger hold under this ambiguous arrangement, which was thus a source of support to a nation whose future was threatened by the presence of foreign settlers.

The Czech Nation and the German Influx
In addition to being associated politically with the Holy Roman Empire, the Czech people lived at a commercial crossroads which was a meeting-place for the merchants of other countries. The Czechs were therefore little able to resist German penetration, a favourable field for which was provided by the presence of a German colony in Prague and by the activities of German priests and monks, whose influence was increasing. A still more important factor in the Germanization of the country was the task of clearing and populating the outlying regions, a task undertaken in the twelfth and subsequent centuries by the Czech nobility, who invited German settlers to their new villages. German merchants and peasants had already begun to move south along the trade routes leading down from the Baltic and North Sea ports; the Bohemian landowners' encouragement coincided with a more pressing motive – their own country was overcrowded; and they came flooding into Bohemia, absorbing the Slav element in the border districts and becoming an important minority everywhere else. They were not the creators of the urban accumulations which the gradual division of labour and growth of trade had engendered round the forts erected by local rulers; but the first development of town and city life in the modern sense was due to them, and so was the introduction of a foreign legal system. The communes of Bohemia, many of which sprang up in the thirteenth century and which were both fortified towns and centres of trade,

owed their constitution to the 'right of Magdeburg', not to the laws obtaining in the old Czech villages. They were inhabited by a mixed population, and though the Czechs soon grew to be the majority, the leading circles in town society were German. Much time was to elapse, however, before the towns attained any political influence; this was entirely in the hands of the Czech landed nobility.

FIGURE 17 Czech coins of the eleventh and twelfth centuries. Left, silver shilling of Vratislav II (1061–92), reverse. – Right, silver shilling of Borivoj (who reigned 1100–7 and 1109–10), obverse.

The whole subsequent course of Bohemian history was affected by this ethnic duality, which appeared on the social and economic plane as well but whose effects, at least during this period, must not be overestimated. Bohemia's astonishing internal progress in the fourteenth century, which brought town and countryside together and created common interests between the Czech nobles and German burghers, gave the country a temporary unity under Charles IV.

Nor was the environment, into which the German settlers came, so 'underdeveloped' that they can be credited with having introduced all the qualities which made that progress possible. The Czechs' agricultural methods were not antiquated; the parts of the country most affected by colonization were neither backward nor barbarous. Bohemian progress, running parallel to that of the Germans in their own country, had created townships with a busy artisan class. What the immigrants did was to accelerate the country's progress by augmenting its productive capacity, by introducing a form of urban organization which favoured the expansion of trade, and by establishing stronger commercial links with their country of origin. But though Bohemia's towns and cities were dominated by the German burgher class, their development – as can be seen from that of Prague, for example – would have been impossible without the participation of the Czech people and the collaboration of the two elements. Rivalry between them was for long confined to the social plane. And, since education was still essentially Latin and religious, the German contribution on the cultural plane was minimal.

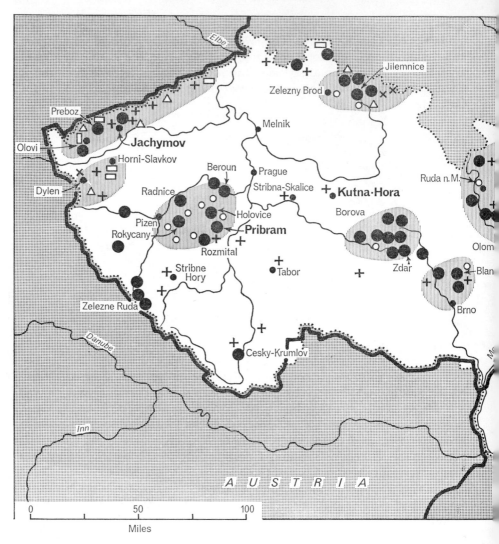

Map 6 Industry in Bohemia and Slovakia in the Fifteenth Century

Bohemia's 'Golden Age'

Bohemia was the most advanced Slav country in the fourteenth century. Her many silver mines were run on a model system of mining law; an outstanding example is the mine at Kutná Hora (figure 18), where a mint was set up in 1300. The mines were one of the king's sources of income and enabled him to issue the 'groat of Prague', which circulated far beyond Bohemia itself. Money was tending to replace barter. Much trade passed between the towns; many of them were of recent foundation, and the most important were royal possessions. And though he had to defend his power and lands against the great aristocratic families, his position and prospects resembled those of sovereigns in the West (map 6).

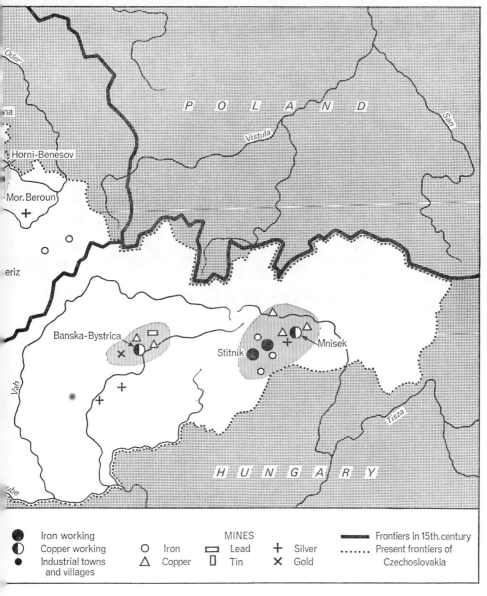

Iron working
Copper working
Industrial towns and villages

MINES
Iron · Lead · Silver
Copper · Tin · Gold

Frontiers in 15th. century
Present frontiers of Czechoslovakia

This position of power and respect was due to Charles IV (son of John of Luxemburg [1347–78] who died gallantly on the field of Crécy). Despite his assumption of the imperial crown in 1355, Charles elected to reside mainly in Prague. He transformed the city, building a new quarter (*Nove Mesto*) and, in 1348, with the Pope's consent, founded the university, 'so that the kingdom's faithful inhabitants, eager to acquire the fruits of the arts, should not be obliged to beg them abroad but should find a well-supplied table at home'. Modelled on Paris and Bologna, this was the first university in central Europe. Prague, whose population was 100,000,

attracted large numbers of students, who were divided into 'nations'
(Czechs, Saxons, Bavarians and Poles). The bulk of the population were
Czech shopkeepers and craftsmen, of whom there was an increasing influx
from the countryside. City government was discharged by an aristocracy
and bourgeoisie of German descent. Prague, in communication with the
other great European cities, and responsive to every contemporary trend
in thought and art, enjoyed in the late fourteenth century a brilliant,
turbulent life and was a leading centre of civilization.

FIGURE 18 Royal Mint, Kutna Hora (Bohemia): the Courtyard of the Italians,
fourteenth century, reconstruction.

Life had become comparatively secure all over Bohemia. The acreage of
cultivated land continued to increase. Fish-farming, in numerous ponds
constructed for the purpose, was being developed. Charles introduced viti-
culture; vinestocks from Burgundy and Alsace were acclimatized round
Prague. But Bohemia's distinctive features, as before, were her mining
industry, her craftsmen and her urban development.

A land of towns both large and small, whose human climate was progressive and where churches, and some secular buildings too, were erected
in the Gothic style, initially by foreign architects and later by their Czech
pupils; a land very receptive to French influences, which can be traced in
Bohemian music; a land excited by the religious controversies issuing from
the university of Prague – such was Bohemia, whose intellectual life was at
once cosmopolitan and intense. Most of the literary works of the time were
in Latin; so were the royal charters which were preserved in the castle of
Karlstejn, near Prague, recently built at the king's command by Mathieu
d'Arras. It was under the title *Majestas Carolina* that Charles IV caused a
legal code to be drawn up, limiting the power of the nobles. But already a
Czech national literature, in the language of the country, was shyly putting
out its first buds; the *Chronicle of Dolimil*, for example – one of the scanty
signs of a nascent anti-German reaction – and later, at the end of the
century, the works of Tomas Štítny.

The Hussite Movement; Social and National Overtones

At the beginning of the fifteenth century the kingdom of Bohemia, which included Silesia and Lusatia as well as Bohemia and Moravia, was still among the most active and prosperous of European states, but had reached a pitch of social tension which eventually gave birth to the Hussite movement.

The growth of a feudalism at once secular and ecclesiastic had been accompanied by peasant resistance and occasional disturbances; but it was the development of two urban classes, the craftsmen and merchants, which was to give these popular stirrings weight and significance. At a time when powerful currents of religious reform were on the move in Europe, the opulent Bohemian church, owning one third of the cultivable land, and numerous urban sites and buildings which, in the nature of things, never came on the market, attracted the hostility both of the aristocratic laity and of the mercantile class. The sale of indulgences, and the transfer of large sums to the papal court in Rome whenever ecclesiastical benefices were about to change hands, involved such outpourings of precious metal that the currency was adversely affected. Meanwhile the people, burdened with taxes, tithes and the fees charged by the priests for the various religious ministrations of a lifetime, from birth to death, were very ready to listen to projects for a return to a Church vowed to poverty, disinterested in its motives, independent of Rome, easier on the individual's purse and more concerned for the welfare of his soul.

The Hussite movement, though deriving its impetus from social injustice, was originally a religious movement; the clergy's moral degeneration had aroused an urgent desire for reform within the Church itself. The traffic in benefices, the scandalous life of many of Prague's priests, and the wealth of the great prelates, caused indignation in a minority of clerics, among whom emerged the figure of Jan Hus.

Jan Hus: Patriot, Christian, Reformer

Jan Hus, who was born about 1370, became dean, and afterwards rector, of the University of Prague. He had thoroughly absorbed Wycliffe's writings, and in 1402 began preaching in the Chapel of Bethlehem, in Prague, against clerical abuses. His sermons attracted large, passionately interested congregations, and he fell foul of the archbishop of Prague in connection with the sale of indulgences. Compelled to take refuge for a while in southern Bohemia, where unrest was stronger than elsewhere and he could preach with less danger, he agreed to defend his ideas at the Council of Constance. Despite holding a safe-conduct he was arrested and died a martyr to the faith, being burnt at the stake as a heretic on 6 July 1415. In the following year his friend Master Jerome of Prague suffered the same fate.

Jan Hus, whose preaching and tragic death started a train of events which proved decisive for the development of Czech national consciousness, combined the customary regional patriotism of his age with a sense of

4*

universal Christianity: 'I prefer', he said, 'good English priests to cowardly Czech priests, and a decent German to my wicked brother.' But the setting in which he worked was a Bohemia whose economic development had increased the proportion of Czechs both in the urban population and among the professors and students of the University of Prague. Under Hus, control of the university passed to the Czech 'nation' (student community), which had hitherto yielded precedence to the foreign 'nations': German, Saxon and Polish (royal decree of Kutná-Hora, 1409). Latin was of course still the university language, and Hus employed it for some of his own writings. But his most moving works, including the admirable *Letters to the Czech Faithful*, written in prison at Constance while under sentence of death, are in the national language, which he had used whenever possible during his public life. To him, moreover, is due the first simplification of the highly idiosyncratic Czech spelling.

The Hussite Wars

After Hus's death, popular unrest took a more radical turn. Public hostility was aimed at the Church and, in the towns, at the German patricians (because they supported the higher clergy); not, however, at the Germans as such. Some of the reforming preachers were German, such as Peter and Nicholas of Dresden, both of whom were active in Prague. Widespread disturbances broke out, and in Plzen, Klatovy, Žatec and Domažlice the town administration was taken over by the insurgent middle class. In Prague, a sermon preached in the Church of our Lady of the Snows by a disciple of Hus, John of Želiv, on 30 July 1419, was the signal for a successful revolt. The lower middle classes assumed the governing power and confiscated ecclesiastical property, but later sought an alliance with the nobles to suppress the insurgent mob and also negotiated with the new emperor, Sigismund, in the hope of retaining the advantages they had won.

An Extraordinary Experiment: Tabor

In the countryside all over Bohemia, popular assemblies were being set up whose members were drawn from various classes; communion in both kinds, and the religious ideals of Jan Hus, held these assemblies together in an apparent unity masking the diversity of interests involved. A meeting held by one such assembly in July 1419, at the instigation of Nicholas of Hus, a minor noble, on a hill known as Mount Tabor, was the origin of an amazing attempt by the extremist wing of Jan Hus's disciples to found an egalitarian city of God on earth. In 1420 there was created a new community called Tabor, the citizens of which came from a broad spectrum of social backgrounds – craftsmen, peasants and ruined noblemen, and a foreign element consisting of Austrian and Polish landworkers. The end of the world was thought to be at hand, so all goods were held in common; the town was democratically organized; ramparts were built; an army was raised, with a stiffening of chariots. Tabor found itself being joined by fighting detachments from every part of Bohemia; that from Plzen was headed by Jan Žižka of Trocnov, who had been one of the earliest organizers of Hussite troops.

Meanwhile in Prague negotiations with Sigismund had broken down, and the crusade declared by Pope Martin v against the Hussite heretics had made self-defence urgently necessary; moderates and radicals united in a religious policy defined by the Four Articles, or Articles of Prague (freedom of speech in the pulpit, communion in both kinds, punishment of mortal sin, and transfer of church property to civil ownership). Prague appealed to the armies of Tabor for protection, and on two occasions in 1420 the crusaders of Sigismund and the papal legate were defeated before its walls.

What appeared to be a movement of religious reform was in fact, under the surface, something else besides: a conflict of social aims. The burghers and the urban petty nobility wanted nothing more than municipal control and a profitable secularization of church property, and they were anxious not to exceed these objectives. The peasantry, on the other hand, was fighting for the suppression of serfdom and for a social programme which was not clearly formulated but which undoubtedly implied destruction of the existing order. It was in Prague that Taborite influence was eliminated first. But in Tabor itself, where the original community conception had soon begun to look impossibly utopian, the death of Nicholas of Hus in December 1420 placed Jan Žižka in supreme command of the Taborite armed forces; the tendency to realism and moderation, represented by Žižka, gained the ascendancy, and Tabor became a municipal republic governed by an aristocracy of minor nobles, burghers and craftsmen.

This was bound to happen; the utopian bubble had burst, as it always does. The control of town government throughout Bohemia was in process of transfer to a new category of administrative leaders, based on the corporations and the minor nobility. Two urban federations arose: the Prague Federation, numbering twenty-one municipalities and virtually ruling the country; and the Taborite Federation in southern and western Bohemia, which carried less weight but had Žižka's powerful army at its disposal. Twice more, in 1421, the Taborites repulsed the crusaders, and Žižka, who was received in triumph in the capital, took command of the Prague Federation's troops. By this time the Hussite movement's prospects had come to depend irremediably on its military strength. After the assassination in 1422 of John of Želiv, who had tried to impose a dictatorship of the people on Prague, the city notables in control of the urban federation began negotiating to place the king of Poland's nephew on the throne of Bohemia, and allied themselves with the Catholic nobility against Jan Žižka. The latter, who had parted company with Tabor but not quarrelled with it and had founded a Little Tabor (1422–33) at Hradec Kralove, crushed an army raised by Prague and the Catholic nobles at the battle of Malešov (June 1424) and brought the federation to heel. But in October 1424 he died.

The Taborite forces found a new leader in the person of Procopius the

Tall, nicknamed the Shaven, who inflicted two defeats on the crusaders in 1426, held his ground firmly against the emperor Sigismund at the conference of Pressburg (1429) and launched the famous expeditions beyond Bohemia's borders known as his 'magnificent raids'. This was the Hussite movement's period of glory, when it drove into Slovakia, Austria, Saxony (1429) and even made its way to Nuremberg, in Franconia. The Utraquist heresy, symbolized by the chalice, had filled Europe with disquiet. A last major crusade, organized by the legate Juliano Cesarini, quickly fizzled out: Procopius's army, reinforced by Polish Hussite troops under the command of Sigismund Korybut; the king of Poland's nephew, who had been offered the Bohemian throne), scattered the crusaders near Domažlice in August 1431.

Defeat

The moment had now come for negotiation; and, ironically, for the break-up of the Hussite movement. Ten years of war had weighed cruelly on Bohemia, where rising prices, particularly of food, had made life progressively harder for the poor. Business dealings were impeded by the Church's ban on trading with the heretics. The cost of maintaining troops was heavy, and despite the cessation of payments to the Church the people's lot had become no easier. The town-dwelling middle classes were ready to abandon hostilities if the advantages they had won could be guaranteed for the future. The conciliatory policy adopted towards the Utraquists by the legate Cesarini and the Council of Basel resulted in the Convention of Cheb (1432), which permitted a delegation led by Procopius to appear before the Council and defend the Four Articles of Prague.

At Basel nothing was achieved; negotiations were continued in Prague, where the nobility, the university and the burghers detached themselves from Procopius and agreed to reinstate the Church provided they were given a guarantee of the right to communicate in both kinds. This concession was embodied in the *Compacta* of Hussite Bohemia in 1436.

Meanwhile the war was still going on, and Procopius, with most of the country in his power, saw many of his subordinate commanders going over to the emperor; he laid siege unsuccessfully to Plzen (1433–4), was forced to abandon the new quarter of Prague, and was eventually overwhelmed at Lipany (near Česky Brod) on 30 November 1434, by a force of mercenaries raised by the nobles. One by one, all the towns in Bohemia offered their submission to Sigismund, who was accepted as the country's sovereign in 1436. The surviving Taborite troops, and their commander Jan Roháč of Dubá, were all hanged or put to the sword in the autumn of 1437.

The Hussite Heritage

By dispossessing the Church, the Hussite movement brought about such a transfer of property to the nobles and middle classes as can be paralleled in the history of no other country. Not till two centuries later, after the disasters of the Thirty Years War, was it possible to reconstitute the Church's estates in Bohemia. The diminution of the Church's economic power, and the radical nature of the Hussite movement, despite its eventual collapse, caused modifications in Bohemia's religious life which demonstrate the movement's kinship with the Reformation.

But the movement's essential content was social and national. The Hussite armies united in their ranks the middle stratum of the urban bourgeoisie, the fighting members of the lesser nobility, and a poverty-stricken multitude from the villages and countryside who were imbued with a very real revolutionary enthusiasm. The Hussites' 'magnificent raids' outside Bohemia, in Silesia, Poland, Saxony and Bavaria, struck a sympathetic chord in the subject populations, independently of nationality. In that context, the movement was essentially an anti-feudal insurrection under the mask of religion. In Bohemia itself, however, its complexion was distinctly national. It had to contend with foreign intervention which was supported by the privileged classes (the urban patricians, and the *grands seigneurs* both lay and ecclesiastic); those classes were largely German. And the movement's popular character rendered it a source of strength for Czech customs and culture.

It was in fact in the fifteenth century that Czech began to rank as the national language. The language of the people threw off its lowly status to become the language of religion and even, briefly, of diplomacy (at the king of Poland's court). A literature emerged: the *Epistles* of Žižka, patriotic poems, songs and hymns, translations of the Scriptures, sermons, religious treatises from Tabor – a treasury of themes and expressions from which the Czech literary renaissance in the nineteenth century, after the centuries of darkness, was to draw its inspiration.

It is of course also true that, in their hatred of Catholicism, the Hussites were destroyers of churches, statues and paintings. But their moral rigour had no quarrel with the traditional arts of the country, and signs are not wanting of the creative output with which they enriched the national heritage. Examples are the illuminated Bible attributed to Philip of Paderov, and that of 'the Miller's Wife of Tabor'.

But their greatest achievement was in the field of popular education. Wherever they held power – notably in Prague and at Tabor – they founded schools in which Czech was used for all teaching purposes, and the result was a rise in the cultural level of large sections of the population. Hussite education, though intended as a weapon for the defence of heresy, also helped to strengthen the people's sense of the national language, culture and way of life. And conflict both military and bloodless – the Hussite wars, and the controversies of the Czech preachers and the Catholic clergy – bequeathed to posterity the dazzling names of those leaders and martyrs who became the key figures in the mystique of Czech patriotism.

3

The South Slavs - Fledgeling States and Their Vicissitudes

In the sixth and seventh centuries the Southern Slav peoples – Slovenes, Croats and Serbs – spread out over the eastern Alps, the Danube basin and the Balkans, and penetrated southward into the Peloponnesus. Occupying mainly the plains, they clashed with various Romanized Greco-Illyrian peoples; the mountain-dwelling, stock-raising element among the latter gradually adopted Slav customs and became the Vlachs or Wallachians. The more civilized elements, in the Roman towns and along the Dalmatian coast, held out longer against the process of Slavicisation. In the south, the Slavs were assimilated into the Greek population; in the east, where their numbers included a high proportion of Turco-Tatar elements, they formed the Bulgarian people.

Having settled in territories which were the hinge between the western world and Byzantium, the newcomers soon found themselves exposed to the competing influences of the Franks in the north and the Greeks in the south.

Alphabets at War
Greater Moravia at the end of the ninth century was an apple of contention between Rome and Byzantium. The Germanic Frankish clergy had already started converting the country to Christianity when, in 863, Prince Rostislav sent for two monks from Thessalonica, Cyril and Methodius, whose mission was to have momentous consequences for the religious future of south-eastern Europe. By creating for the Slavs a written language for literary and liturgical use, a language which had its own alphabet and was based on the Slavonic idiom of Thessalonica, and into which they translated the Gospels, Cyril and Methodius provided them at once with a common instrument of civilization and a weapon of defence against Germanic influence (figure 19).

The translations of Cyril and Methodius were written in Glagolitic, an ecclesiastical script of Cyril's invention which, unlike the Latin alphabet, was capable of representing all the sounds in the language. At that time (the ninth century) the Western and Southern Slav dialects were still fairly like one another, and the peoples of Greater Moravia, for whom

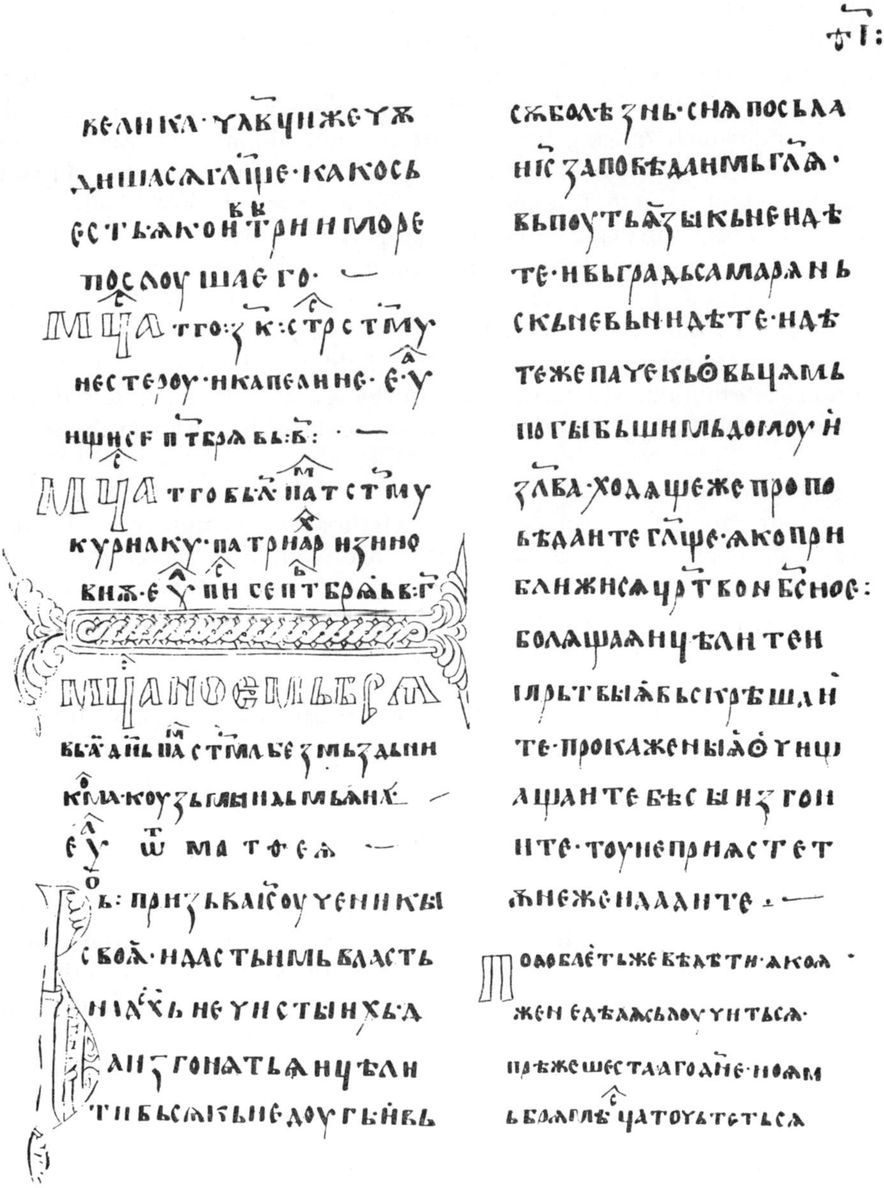

FIGURE 19 Example of Cyrillic script (1030). Slav Gospel, known as the *Text of the Coronation of the Library of Rheims*, facsimile of 1862, Paris. The MS may have been presented by Anne of Russia to the bishop of Châlons when he came to conduct her to her future husband, Henri I; or it may have been seized in the pillage of Constantinople by the Crusaders in 1204.

Latin was a foreign language, had no difficulty in understanding the Scriptures as translated by Cyril and Methodius.

But Glagolitic, which spread to every region where the South Slavs had settled, soon found itself being ousted by a powerful competitor. In the eleventh century, Russian and Bulgarian translators began using a new script, the so-called 'Cyrillic', which was more convenient to the Greek clergy and which quickly pushed out the old alphabet in Serbia and Macedonia. Glagolitic held on in Croatia until the sixteenth century, and to some extent after that. There was even a period during which it expanded vigorously in the Croatian-speaking districts, where the Benedictine and Franciscan monks adopted it as a weapon in their struggle against the influence of the Greek clergy; it thus acquired a new lease of life through the schism. In the thirteenth century its use was authorized by the Pope, and the Croatian monks carried it as far afield as Bohemia. The Catholic counter-reformation, with its dislike of the local and particular, caused it to recede rapidly; on the Dalmatian coast it was replaced by the Latin alphabet.

Religious Literature. Regional Dialects

The conquering mission of Cyril and Methodius was unsuccessful, and after their death the Slavs of Greater Moravia, represented by their Frankish clergy, remained under the aegis of Rome. But the brothers' exiled disciples found refuge in the kingdom of Bulgaria, which had become Christian in 864; and it was from this quarter that the new written language, after causing the extinction of the Turco-Tatar idiom of the proto-Bulgars, went forth to become the ecclesiastical language of all Slavs under the Greek rite. Introduced by Bulgarian clerks into the Russia of Kiev, it gave birth to Russian Slavonic, which remained the only literary language of the East Slavs until the eighteenth century.

The influence of Cyril and Methodius had begun by making its way into the regions which had been most accessible to Greco-Roman civilization. It was in Macedonia and Dioclea and along the Croatian coastline (Dalmatia) that the first literary works were composed – religious works almost exclusively, consisting mainly of translations and compilations from Latin (in the Slovenian and Croatian districts) and more especially from Greek (in Serbian and Bulgarian districts). In the tenth and eleventh centuries Old Slavonic began separating out – breaking down into regional idioms; ecclesiastical works appeared in Slovenian, Croatian, Serbian and Bulgarian versions.

But each region had its own dialect. Between Slovenian in the north and Macedono-Bulgarian in the south-east were the three major dialects of the Serbo-Croatian language, named after their respective interrogative pronouns for 'what?': the *kaj*-dialect round Zagreb, and the more widely spoken *ča*- and *što-(i)je*-dialects, the latter being preponderant in the sixteenth century. The boundaries of the second and third fluctuated considerably at different times. The *ča*-dialect and its variant forms were current over a wide area in Croatia, Dalmatia and Bosnia; medieval

Catholic Slavonic literature is in the *ča*-dialect, and so is some of the later scholarly literature. But population movement from the inland regions to the coast (westward migrations caused by the Turkish invasion) reduced the area covered by this dialect and extended the area of the *što*-dialect, a group of inland idioms from Serbia and Montenegro which provided the foundations of literary Ragusan and eventually, as we shall see, of modern literary Serbo-Croatian.

A manuscript in Latin characters, from Brizin (Freising), is the oldest known example of written Slovenian; it dates from the year 1000. A Glagolitic inscription in the Church of Saint Lucy, on the island of Krk, is the earliest Croatian literary document (1120). Croatian and Serbo-Bulgarian literature at this stage shows little originality, but is more plentiful than Slovenian literature. It consists of translations of the Gospels; prayers and sermons; apocalyptic writings, elements from which made their way into folksong; and a category which is specially interesting from the Slav and national viewpoints, namely an apocryphal literature (lives of the saints, and secular stories) which was banned by the Church but was better adapted to popular sensibility and was perhaps connected with the Bogomil heresy of a later period.

Under the first Bulgarian kingdom (created by Simeon, 893–927), Okhrid, the religious centre of the region, and Plovdiv, its political capital, were the focal points of literary production. Notable figures included the Exarch John, whose writings celebrate the valour of Tsar Simeon; the missionary monk Clement; Bishop Constantine, the author of the first treatise on Slavonic versification, and a champion of the national literary tradition; and the monk Khrabr, whose *Treatise on Letters* defends that tradition against aggressive Greek criticism. Resistance to the Latin and Greek clergy, especially the second, was the atmosphere surrounding the development of this literature, which took most of its material from Latin and Byzantine religious sources but transposed it into the Slav idiom.

Bulgaria and the Bogomils

This nascent culture and national literature were an all too frail and tender growth. When the Bulgar areas fell under Byzantine domination the Greek clergy became all-powerful. We may well wonder, however, whether all the Bulgars without exception deserved the strictures of Theophylactos, bishop of Okhrid, who described them as 'barbarians, slaves, filthy people, listening to the chanting in church as donkeys might listen to the notes of a viol'. The sources are not quite sufficient for us to judge how far Bulgarian society had progressed at the time. Bogomilism was in a sense a revolt of 'Circumcellions' against a Hellenized ruling class. The contempt of the educated, cultured clergy was directed indifferently at the whole of a rebellious majority, who were not in fact uniformly uncultivated. The survival of a Slav national tradition under Byzantine overlordship is testified by a few naive works, such as the *Legend of Thessalonica* and the *Life of St John of Rila*.

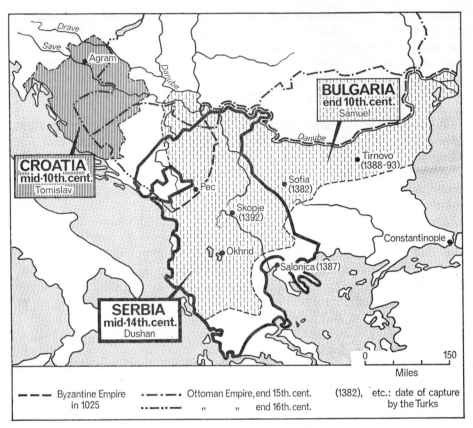

Map 7 Ephemeral Balkan States, 10th–15th Centuries

The Bulgars threw off the Byzantine yoke at the end of the eleventh century. The 'second Bulgar kingdom' (1185–1396) was confined to the eastern part of the country. The centre of intellectual life shifted from Okhrid to Tarnovo; the struggle with Byzantium stiffened the patriotism of a powerful clergy whose church had become autocephalous in 1235, though in the literary field it was still dependent on the Greeks. Bulgarian literature in this period consisted of translations and compilations in a learned idiom which the people did not understand.

As early as the tenth century, society in general and the Church in particular were shaken by a dualistic heresy, derived from Manichaeism, which under different names permeated the whole of southern Europe from east to west and had a long life despite persistent persecution. The Bogomils were the Bulgarian counterpart of the Cathars in southern France. Originating among the lower ranks of the clergy, the heresy quickly attracted popular support; it was a social protest embodied in a religious form, a reaction against the exploitation of the people by the nobility and higher clergy. Most of our information having come from its persecutors, our knowledge of it is far from adequate. Its literature perished at the stake with its supporters. The *Tract against the Bogomils* by the late tenth-century pamphleteer Cosmas describes them as a menace to society and as enemies of established religion: '. . . They decry the rich, abominate the Tsar, ridicule their superiors, forbid slaves to obey their masters. . . . They refuse to worship the Cross, which they call a weapon of Satan, or icons, which they call idols . . .'

Bogomilism spread from Bulgaria to Bosnia, where it took root firmly, almost succeeding in becoming the official religion, and lasting until the Turkish conquest. In the fourteenth century the last Bogomils were converted to Islam. Certain strange funerary monuments are commonly thought to have been erected by the Bogomils – the enormous standing stones, weighing ten tons or more, which can be seen in many parts of Bosnia and especially Herzegovina (as at Radimlje, near Stolac, for example). But these archaically decorated steles (plate 7) may belong to an earlier period (figure 21).

FIGURE 20 Illumination from a Bulgarian MS of the eleventh century.

Unobtrusive Nationality: the Slovenes

The Slovenes came in with the Avars in 568, and took over a larger area than the one they now occupy (map 21 b). Having shaken off Avar domination they set up a more or less independent state under the leadership

of their dukes, though the Slovenes of Carinthia were included for a time
in the empire of Greater Moravia. They were converted to Christianity in
the second half of the eighth century and received their ecclesiastical organization from the bishops of Salzburg and the patriarchs of Aquileia, thus
placing themselves permanently in western Christianity's sphere of influence. Meanwhile their ducal line began losing its hold and was supplanted
by German feudal lords; and after the Hungarians were defeated at
Augsburg in 955, Slovenia was subjected to a steady stream of German
colonization. From now on the Slovenes lived as people usually do in
mountainous regions. Each valley had its own somewhat enclosed existence; Slovenian customs and dialects survived intact; and a few local
liberties were retained under the administrative authority of the German-
dominated towns and the Holy Roman Empire, to which the country now
belonged.

Political Durability: Croatia
Dalmatia, populated in antiquity by Dalmatian settlers, was frequented by
Greek merchants, who founded a string of colonies there in the fourth century BC. It was subsequently conquered by the Romans (AD 6–9) and became a Roman province, and, until the fifth century, continued to enjoy
the brilliant civilization which it had developed, and to which the excavations of archaeologists on the sites of its cities have borne witness. It had
become Christian during the third century, and after escaping almost untouched by the Teutonic invasions – save for a short period under the
Ostrogoths – it came under Byzantine rule in the reign of Justinian and
was finally submerged by the Slav invasions of the sixth century, when it
was temporarily held by the Avars. The latter were displaced by the arrival
of the Croatians, a warlike tribe who gave their name to the greater part of
the region. The interior, the coast and the islands were completely Slavicised, the only exceptions being a handful of fortified towns: Krk (Veglia),
Rab (Arbe), Osor (Ossero), Zadar (Zara), Split (Spalato), Trogir (Trau),
Dubrovnik (Ragusa) and Kotor (Cattaro). These towns, whose mixed
population kept up the maritime connection with Byzantium, remained
under the emperor's authority and for some time continued to use Latin.

Thereafter the name Dalmatia was applied only to a narrow coastal
strip sprinkled with Byzantine towns (Split, Zadar, etc.) whose churches
came under the Patriarch of Constantinople. The rest of the country was
Croatia, which remained pagan until converted to Christianity under
Charlemagne, after which its religious allegiance was to Rome.

The Croats threw off the suzerainty of the Franks and put a royal line of
their own in power; under Tomislav (ninth century), the kingdom thus
created extended north as far as the country between the rivers Save and
Drave, and had administrative control of the Byzantine towns on the coast.
Under King Krešimir (1058–74) these towns were embodied in the kingdom of Croatia-Dalmatia, whose political and religious capital was Nin,
on the northern border of Dalmatia. The Hungarian conquest in the

eleventh century put an end to Croatian independence; from 1102 the throne was occupied by a Hungarian sovereign, though the Croats retained their army, royal seal and institutions (including a deliberative assembly of nobles). Croatia subsequently lost much of Dalmatia to the Venetians, who occupied it until the eighteenth century, and much of her southern territory to the Turks. She nevertheless succeeded in preserving the 'triple kingdom' – Croatia proper, *plus* Slavonia and what remained of her Dalmatian possessions – the reconstruction of which was the basis of the programme of the Croatian nationalists in the nineteenth century.

The king of Hungary governed the Croats through the intermediary of a *herceg*, but the administration of the coastal towns was entrusted to a '*ban* of Croatia and Dalmatia' or '*ban* of the maritime provinces'. The hinterland fell into the hands of a feudal class which grew up in the late thirteenth century on the ruins of the previous social structure of tribes and *župas*,

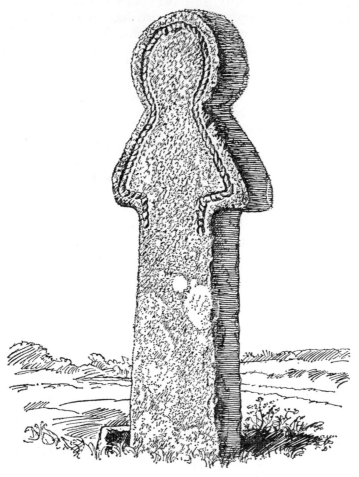

FIGURE 21 Funerary stele, possibly of a Bogomil, fifteenth century, at Bileca (Yugoslavia).

and which consumed its strength in savage vendettas. The leading families were the Kurjaković in Krbova, the Kačić in the region of the Neretva, and the Šubić – the most eminent being the last-named, who received the title of *ban* of Croatia and Dalmatia in 1293, imposed their authority on the coastal strip, and set up a branch of the house of Anjou to reign there. During the fourteenth century these Angevin rulers devoted their energies to trying to break the power of the feudal class.

Meanwhile the coastal towns, whose main interest was in close relations with foreign countries, and which were strong in defence (the fortress of Klin, above Split, and the town of Trogir, successfully resisted the Tatar invasion of 1242), were bent on maintaining, or, as the case might be, acquiring, autonomy. They took advantage of the favourable attitude of the king of Hungary, who was anxious to keep his outlets on the Adriatic; they also benefited from friction between Hungary and Venice, which weakened the kings' authority. In this manner the towns of Šibenik and Nin, between 1167 and 1205, obtained privileges resembling those of the ancient towns of Roman origin, such as Split, Zadar and Trogir. Life in these municipalities revolved entirely about seaborne trade; the atmosphere was quite different from that of the inland districts, whose agricultural existence was dominated by the local warlords. Municipal authority was held by a patrician class of Roman descent, speaking a language of their own, of which no written records have remained, and issuing official edicts in Latin or Italian. The lower classes – the shopkeepers, craftsmen and servants – were Slavs. These aristocratic communities, fairly free under the Hungarians but rather less so under the Venetians in the sixteenth century, were agitated by social upheavals in which Venetian intervention was aimed at curbing the proud and unruly patricians.

Croatia, as a seafaring power with a large number of ships on the Adriatic, had quickly come into conflict with Venice. In the ninth century she even imposed a tribute on the Venetians, payment being eventually refused in the year 1000. Thereafter Venice, in need of timber and sailors, and anxious to suppress piracy, engaged in a protracted struggle against the Dalmatian towns, which were inadequately supported by the king of Hungary. The contest swung to and fro for three centuries; Venetian pressure became heavier in the fourteenth, and, after a fifty-year interlude during which Venice (by the treaty of Zadar, 1358) renounced all her Dalmatian possessions, a naval expedition commanded by Admiral Loredan in 1420 took successively the fortified towns of Trogir, Split and Kotor and the islands of Brač, Hvar and Korčula. The Venetians' hold on the coastal towns and the Ottoman conquest a century later of the inland regions and the remainder of the shoreline, with the exception of Ragusa, opened a new chapter in the history of Croatia.

Croatia possessed a very ancient tradition of building in stone, a tradition represented in the eleventh century by numerous small churches, most of which have since vanished or nearly so. Combining simple construction with great freedom of plan, and topped with vaults and cupolas, they were

FIGURE 22 St Marina,
tempera on wood, central
panel of a Bulgarian
triptych, late fifteenth
century.

directly inspired by Byzantine example. But in the same century, as a
result of the country's adherence to the western rite, a surge of building
began: a profusion of Benedictine monasteries, and of larger churches
whose model was the three-nave basilica. The only one to have survived
intact is St Peter's, at Rab. Altars, pulpits, doorways and window-
embrasures were ornamented with reticulated work carved in low relief, a
type of decoration doubtless derived from Byzantium but mixed here with
Lombard influences. At the end of the eleventh century, the motifs of this
type of carving were combined with the new motifs of Romanesque.

   During the period of the free communes on the coast, that is to say from the eleventh to the fifteenth century, and especially during the thirteenth, the prosperity of the towns gave rise to a remarkable growth of religious architecture. All the cathedrals are Romanesque: such are St Triphon at Kotor (1166), reminiscent of the Apulian churches to which the Croatian nobles made pilgrimages; St Mary of Zadar, the tower of which reflects Lombard influence; and the cathedral of Trogir (Trau, the town with thirty-two churches, the 'Slav Bruges of the Adriatic'), whose decorated porch by the Yugoslav carver Radovan also derives from Italian models. The wooden doors of the cathedral of Split, by Andrej Buvina, portray scenes from daily life in naive style, but the spirit of Gothic architecture is noticeable in the tower.

Gothic was introduced into Croatia by the new religious orders, the Franciscans and Dominicans; it took the form of churches with a single nave which were convenient for preaching, and which had timber roofs instead of stone vaulting. An example is the fourteenth-century church of St Dominic at Trogir.

Book Two

THE BALKANS
IN TURKISH HANDS
RUSSIA:
A CONTINENTAL
EMPIRE

16th and 17th Centuries

4

The Serbs on
the Crest of the Wave

IN SOUTHERN and south-eastern Europe the Serbs and Bulgars, under the
domination, sometimes real, sometimes shadowy, of Byzantium, strove to
organize themselves into bodies politic on the Byzantine model. But the
Slavs of the western fringe, along the Adriatic, had their own way of life;
one manifestation of it was the little kingdom of Dioclea, governed from
Zeta, its capital; another was the emergence of Montenegro, whose record
down the centuries is one of perpetual resistance to outside interference.
Other, larger political entities, which proved ephemeral, depended for
their existence on Byzantine toleration or recognition. In the tenth century,
Simeon the Great set up a Bulgarian empire which covered the greater
part of the Balkans until it was destroyed by Byzantium; it was partially
built up again by Samojlo, with Macedonia as its basis. In the eleventh, it
was the state of Dioclea on the Adriatic coast which held out against
Byzantium. In the twelfth, Serbian history began; originating with the
local chieftains (*Knez*) of the Nemania family, and benefiting from the conflict between the Byzantines and Hungarians, the Serbian state in the
thirteenth century included Dioclea, the country behind Ragusa, and
Macedonia. Surviving invasion by the crusaders and the Mongols, and
warring with Hungary, Byzantium and the reconstituted power of Bulgaria,
the Serbia of the Nemania dynasty reached its zenith under Tsar Dushan
(1331–53), who styled himself, 'emperor of the Greeks and Serbs' and
ruled over Albania, Thessaly, Macedonia and Epirus.

A Hardworking Peasant People
The Turks brought progress to a standstill, and even in some cases caused
retrogression, in the regions they conquered in the fifteenth century; this
has created a false idea of those regions, an impression of deep-seated,
ineradicable backwardness. In reality, fourteenth-century Serbia was not
backward and uncouth. Less frequently ravaged than its neighbour
Bulgaria, and situated on lines of commercial communication leading to
the Mediterranean, the Adriatic ports, Germany and Hungary, Serbia
under Tsar Dushan made remarkable economic progress and entered a
phase of social development to which the Turkish conquest called a halt.

Rural activities flourished: pig-farming in the oak forests; cattle, sheep and goats (managed on the seasonal migratory system); lumbering (especially in the western districts, close to the coast); cereal cultivation (wheat, oats, millet); fishing; hunting; bee-keeping. Gold was extracted near Novipazar and Prizren; iron, which was commoner, in a number of places; lead, at Olovo and Kucevo; and silver at Rudnik. The mining and smelting of all these were carried out by Saxon miners who started entering the country in the thirteenth century. Transport – by pack-horses and mules on sketchy, ill-maintained tracks – was slow and inconvenient; communication was nevertheless maintained between the market towns of the interior, such as Péc and Prizren, and the seaports, outstanding among which was Cattaro (Kotor), whose leading merchants were admitted to the royal council and were sometimes employed as diplomats by the king. The merchant class, among whom partnerships were not uncommon, and who gave visiting foreign merchants a privileged reception as *gosti* (hosts), did not belong exclusively to the Greek and Dalmatian (especially Ragusan) bourgeoisie: the rapid growth of small towns and mining centres created the nucleus of a Serbian bourgeoisie, whose subsequent development was arrested by the unpromising economic conditions imposed by Turkish domination.

The Serbian population seems to have increased rapidly, to judge by the large number of village settlements dating from this period; it consisted mainly of farmers and stock-breeders, all of whom lived under the domination of feudal lords to whom the king had given estates as a reward for their services. The Vlach stock-breeders had their own special way of life and enjoyed greater liberty from compulsion. The ordinary peasants were less fortunate; a few were serfs, the rest owned small hereditary properties to which various obligations were attached, and were compelled to give a *corvée* of two days per week to their *seigneurs*. An even heavier imposition may have been the *corvée* devoted to public works, a task allotted by a royal administration whose resources consisted mainly of taxes on mining and trade, and which was intent on maintaining the country's security by keeping the forts and roads in good repair. Serbia's economic progress in the thirteenth and fourteenth centuries was of greater benefit to the king, the feudal grandees and the merchants of Ragusa than to the peasantry. Hence the sharp social contrasts which, at that period, were the price to be paid for the political and social organization of the state.

Serbia's achievement during the fourteenth century was, although short-lived, something original, something all her own. The constant aim of her ruling line, the Nemania family, was to set up a centrally administered state on the Byzantine model, based on a land-owning aristocracy and defending its existence alike against Hungarians and Byzantines before succumbing to the advancing Turks. The king governed Serbia proper (*Rassia, Rascie*) – the interior of the country, including Greek provinces wrested from Byzantium – and part of the Adriatic coast; the latter being divided into provinces of which one, Dioclea (the coast of Montenegro), was allocated to the heir to the throne, who also ranked as joint sovereign of the whole country. Unlike the Russian and Bulgarian sovereigns, the king of Serbia had no fixed capital but led a nomadic existence between various castles and monasteries which were his summer and winter residences up and down the kingdom. In 1346 King Stephen Dushan proclaimed himself 'emperor of the Serbs and Greeks' and made his court adopt Byzantine titles, functions and ceremonial dress. He governed through high-ranking officials, the Knez (*comes*) who represented his authority down to village level, and Diets (*Zbor*) whose members were representatives of the nobility and of the clergy, both Serbian and Greek. His decrees and charters were drawn up in Serbian, Greek and Latin. The Serbian used in these documents was the *što* dialect, the diplomatic language of the Balkans at that time.

His reign saw the establishment of a Code of Peace and Justice whose two hundred articles laid down the structure of feudal society, the privileges of the Church, the rights and duties of the nobles and their dependent peasants, and the scale of penalties for offences against the law. This 'code of Dushan' is a valuable source of information on Serbian society on the eve of the Ottoman invasion.

The king's authority was exercised not only through the lay administration but also through the Serbian Church, which was independent of Rome after 1219 and became the national church. Okhrid remained an autocephalous archbishopric; under Dushan its archbishop was even elevated to the rank of 'Patriarch of the Serbs and Greeks'. After Žiča, the residence of the archbishops was at Peć until the eighteenth century. The network of churches and monasteries, many of which were of royal foundation (examples are Studenica and St George of Rin or Nemania), covered the whole country; they were particularly numerous in the south, where the Serbian clergy were anxious to force out their Greek rivals. The monasteries, which, unlike the Bulgarian monasteries, were large, owned much land and by the fourteenth century had become powerful feudal manors, and remained so until overtaken by the ruinous consequences of Turkish invasion. Along the coast, the Serbian sovereigns in their age of greatness extended their friendly protection to the Roman Catholic churches of Cattaro and Ragusa.

Serbian Art

The kings and emperors of Serbia in the thirteenth and fourteenth centuries were prolific builders of churches; according to G. Millet, their architectural heritage is 'the richest of all those bequeathed to us by ancient Christian art in the East'. The explanation is that monastery and royal residence both served a dual purpose, at once political and religious. The founder of the Nemania dynasty became a monk, ruled under the name of Sava and instigated the building of the famous monasteries of Studenica and Chilandari (on Mount Athos). It was during his reign that work started on the building of the cathedral of Žiča, the Serbian Rheims. For a hundred years, Romanesque art, with local adaptations, became a national art.

Sixteen magnificent churches were built in Serbia between the thirteenth century and the end of the fourteenth, a notable instance being Serbia's national religious sanctuary, St Nahum, on Lake Okhrid, which has a Byzantine ground-plan and Serbian vaulting.

The interior walls of these churches were covered with frescoes, most of which have unfortunately disappeared; we have at any rate almost none which are as old as the twelfth century. The most important are those in the church of St Michael, near Ston, Sancta Sophia, at Okhrid, and the monastery of Nerezi, near Skoplje (1164); in the last-named, the faces have an individuality which is scarcely to be found elsewhere than in Italian frescoes of the thirteenth and fourteenth centuries. Surviving examples from a later period are those in the churches at Gracanica and Nagorica (1337), whose bright colours and supple drawing recall Sienese painting, and at Liubostinja, which date from Dushan's reign.

Serbia's Independence Obliterated; the Turkish Conquest
The frailty of the Serbian state was demonstrated by its breaking up under Turkish pressure on the Balkans after the death of Dushan. The political structures set up by the Balkan Slavs were, indeed, dependent on contingent circumstances: they were the handiwork of a single princeling or family, they lacked economic and social foundation, they were resisted by the feudal landowners; and their crowning weakness was their inability to hold out for long against attacks from neighbours more powerful than themselves. The centrifugal tendencies which they contained, and which had been temporarily suppressed, broke out afresh to restore the anarchy which was the peninsula's chronic condition. Vestiges of authority remained only in limited sectors. As soon as Dushan was dead, Trvtko, the *ban* (ruler) of Bosnia, assumed the sovereign title and founded a new, tolerably powerful kingdom, which, however, soon succumbed to the attacks of the Hungarians and the Turks.

The Ottoman conquest put the Balkans back into a state of political childhood and kept them there. Between 1371 (Turkish victory on the Marica) and 1526 (victory at Mohács), Turkish raids penetrated farther and farther to the north, disorganizing the country and, after each fresh victory, leaving it to disintegrate for a while beyond the Turkish advanced positions. The battle of Kossovo (1389) reduced Serbia to Turkish vassalage. Bulgaria and Macedonia were the next victims. In the following century, such Serbian districts as were still uncaptured were added to the list, the last autonomous 'despot' being removed in 1459; Bosnia fell in 1463, and Herzegovina in 1481. The Turks crossed the Danube, entered Hungary, sent raiding parties into Slovenia, and threatened Vienna.

The frontier was stabilized, however, and the lot of the Southern Slavs on both sides of the Danube was sealed for the next three centuries. The Slovenes and Croats placed themselves under Hapsburg protection.

Southern Hungary was peopled by Serbian refugees who joined forces with the Hungarians to fight the Turks. Venice possessed herself of Dalmatia. Only the proud and independent republic of Ragusa, in its craggy home, held firm against all comers.

When the Turks invaded the Balkans, Serbia was a state on its way towards modern forms of political organization. The customs governing the succession were unfavourable to that fragmentation of the central power which, in Russia, had strengthened feudal divisions. Trade between the coast and the interior reinforced the royal authority by making the town-dwelling middle classes an important element in the kingdom and limiting the power of the large landowners. Turkish pressure in the fourteenth century, and the all but complete conquest of the peninsula in the fifteenth, brought this forward trend to a dead stop, revived old social patterns, and froze the fate of the Slav peoples of the Balkans into immobility for more than three hundred years.

The abolition first of the imperial and later of the royal title, a quarter of a century after the death of Stephen Dushan in 1355, is merely a symbol of a long process of disintegration which went on for over a century. The anarchy caused by the Turks' forays into the country was manifested by attempts at local self-defence and by profound changes in the patterns of political and social life.

The immediate consequences of the invasion were burnt, deserted villages, rural indigence, decline of the manorial and ecclesiastical estates, and a withdrawal of the population to the mining communities and fortified towns, which were capable of self-defence or at least of maintaining a somewhat problematic survival. Later, there were peasant migrations from the great open plains to the shelter of the forests, to the powerful coastal towns, and over the frontier into Hungarian Pannonia. Self-governing communities were set up everywhere – groups of rich or noble families whose leading members became warlords, and which were allied to one another by ties of blood; this stage was followed by a grouping on a wider social scale – groups of villages, which soon fell under the domination of these new-made feudal lords; and these local combinations were quick to give birth to clans and tribes and to reconstitute a 'primitive democracy', in which ancient traditions were preserved and law was based on custom. This turn of affairs constituted neither the rise of a new system nor the revival of an old one; it was an alignment of society with the social patterns of the Vlachs, who, even in the great days of the now defunct central authority, had been less affected by it than anyone else.

5

From Moscow to Eurasia

MUSCOVY had her own destiny to work out in her own way. She threw off
the Mongol yoke, extended her dominion to the Pacific coast, and, to
administer these vast and almost uninhabited expanses, exercised an iron
tyranny and imposed serfdom on her peasants. Entrenched in Orthodoxy,
she turned her back on the comparatively liberal West (map 8).

I EXPANSION IN SIBERIA: THE RUSSIANS ON THE PACIFIC

The reign of Ivan IV (1553–84), in whom brutality and indeed cruelty
were combined with a remarkable sense of political realities, earned him
the epithet *Grozni* (but how are we to translate this: 'the Terrible', which
is the usual version, or, less damningly, 'the Redoubtable', as certain historians, anxious to rehabilitate him, would have us do?). The two achievements to be placed to his credit are Russia's expansion into Siberia, and
the consolidation of the centralized state structure.

Conquest in Siberia
The last check to Russia's eastward expansion was suddenly removed by
the capture of Kazan in 1552. The Stroganov clan moved forward from
Solvytchegodsk into the lonely forests about the River Kama, started new
saltmines there, and set their hearts on crossing the Urals. With the government's tacit approval they commissioned a mercenary Cossack general,
Ermak, to advance into the valley of the Ob; his victories caused the downfall of the Tatar kingdom of Kutchum. In 1582, western Siberia became a
Russian possession. Thereafter a gradual infiltration of peasants from the
central regions, relying for protection on the existing military posts,
progressively imposed the Russian presence on the whole of Siberia
(map 8).

In this vast and almost uninhabited continent, where the biggest obstacle to conquest was nature, rather than the scattered, numerically insignificant native tribes, the Russians made rapid progress. After the Time
of the Troubles (1596–1613), it took only some thirty years for Cossack
detachments, setting up one forward post after another, to advance more
than 2,500 miles from the region of Tomsk to the Pacific coast, where they

founded Okhotsk in 1649. Employing throughout Siberia the colonial policy which the rulers of Novgorod had applied to the non-Russian inhabitants of the Kama valley and the northern part of the Ural valley, the Tsar's agents maintained Russian dominance by means of a network of strongpoints (*ostrogi*), in which they held the hostages they had seized to ensure payment of the tribute in furs (*jassak*). These posts were the footholds marking the progress of the expeditions, at once military and mercantile in character, conducted up and down the country by these bold, unscrupulous pioneers who enriched themselves by barter and disguised pillage, and thus increased the numbers of the as yet embryonic trading middle class. These *promychlenniki* (business men, *entrepreneurs*), sprung from the lower class of peasants in European Russia, became employers as soon as they achieved merchant status; their representatives travelled Siberia, collecting furs on their behalf and even making contact with the merchants of China, and led their masters' caravans of goods to the great trading centres in the west, Nijni Novgorod and Moscow. The merchants also helped to enliven Siberia's new 'towns' during the long winter months.

Russian civilization had entered the Siberian continent in no uncertain

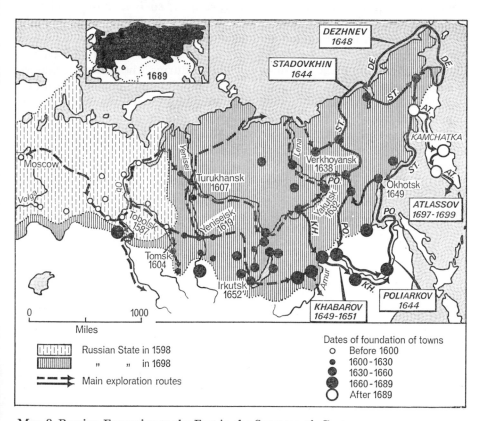

Map 8 Russian Expansion to the East in the Seventeenth Century

manner; but its lines of penetration were so many separate threads consisting of settlers and functionaries in small numbers, and isolated Cossack bands. Siberia was not absorbed; the indigenous peoples, though exploited and thrown on to the defensive, continued to live very much as they had before. What Russia had achieved was to reach the Pacific in a single thrust, and to pave the way for the more substantial occupation which, two centuries later, fashioned a new Russia in Siberia.

Russians and non-Russians

The peculiar character of the Russian colonial drive to the east is just this, that it penetrated regions which were almost uninhabited but not quite. The Russian peasant settled in at the expense of nomadic or semi-nomadic alien peoples who resented and resisted the newcomers; a climate of lasting enmity and insecurity was soon created.

Before reaching Siberia, where they were so few that they simply settled in alongside the local population, the Russians on their eastward way had encountered the Finno-Tatar peoples of the middle Volga (Chuvashes, Cheremis, Volga Tatars, etc.) and the approaches to the Ural valley (Voguls and Bashkirs). Hostilities were limited, the population being sparse and lightly armed. Nevertheless, a town such as Novgorod (the present-day Gorki), which long remained Muscovy's eastern outpost, could be alarmed even in the seventeenth century by Mordvinian raids on set-tlers' villages near its own walls. Farther away, south-west of the Urals, the Bashkirs represented a continuous threat during the early period of Russian settlement. But despite increasing colonization around the middle Volga and its left-bank tributaries (the Kama, etc.), hardly any of the non-Russian elements were assimilated. The Voguls are the only example of an indigenous people which disappeared almost without trace, doubtless be-cause they remained pagan at first and, after being won over to Orthodoxy, were submerged in the tide of Russian immigrants. It was quite otherwise with the Moslem peoples along the Volga and the Ural River; they kept up their cultural and religious links with the Turcoman states of central Asia and so retained their individuality. It was a case not so much of simple juxtaposition (as in Siberia) but rather of 'imbrication' – a patchwork of communities and their territories, a complicated jigsaw in which Russian and Tatar villages existed side by side; continuous trade between them provided a link; religion on the other hand was an invisible line of demarcation which was seldom if ever crossed.

But the non-Russians had their own social hierarchy; hence the Russian peasant, so heavily burdened with taxes and the *corvée*, and the Tatar peasant, exploited by his own overlord, had much in common. Whenever the two were not in direct competition for their daily bread, differences of race and religion became less obstructive and even left room for an obscure, ill-defined sense of solidarity which rose to the surface whenever rebellion occurred against state tyranny. The history of these regions is not simply that of the East Slavs conquering almost uninhabited tracts of country;

nor is it merely a chapter in the history of colonization, in which a race of colonists impose themselves on an oppressed and stifled native population. It is a curious story of furtive reconciliations and temporary alliances between communities normally hostile to each other, but equally subject to oppression and exploitation. In the series of popular uprisings of which Russia was the theatre from the late sixteenth century onwards, Russians and non-Russians were always active simultaneously, and sometimes unitedly or in concert. And when the mines and foundries established in the eighteenth century in the Ural region began draining the surrounding districts of workers, peasants threatened with this industrial conscription fled southward for refuge and freedom, or at least a breathing-space, among the Bashkirs.

Russian Siberia

When the Cossacks appeared on the Pacific shore and set up the station of Okhotsk in 1649, Siberia had already been brought under the authority of the Tsar by means of a network of military posts – a net whose meshes were doubtless very wide but which was adequate to overawe the native peoples and exact the tribute in furs (*jassak*), the natives being, after all, not very numerous (perhaps 250,000 souls in the whole of that immense region). This was colonial exploitation, but it was also colonial development. Settlers began coming in and the population began growing, at least in western Siberia, in the triangle between the Rivers Tobol and Tura, an area of approximately 30,900 square miles containing most of Siberia's agriculture and three-quarters of the Siberian peasants (numbering between 35,000 and 40,000). Farther east, on the Lena and the upper Yenisei, and in Transbaikalia, there were only minute communities here and there, surrounded by the solitudes of forest or steppe.

To speak of the conquest of Siberia is really to overstate the case. The Russians set up a loose but very extensive system of fortified posts, sited at river-crossings, which kept the natives under control and whose walls and watch-towers of timber enclosed a social microcosm, Russia in little. Tomsk in 1646 had just over 1,000 inhabitants, more than half of whom were employed by the state (Cossacks and functionaries). The remainder consisted of about a hundred craftsmen and shopkeepers in the *posad*; a hundred peasants on state plots, whose compulsory contributions in kind helped to feed the garrison; and a further hundred or so composed of new arrivals, whom the authorities were trying, with some difficulty, to settle in some suitable way.

This was a typical Siberian 'town'. But humanity was in short supply a good distance west of the Yenisei, and in these remoter regions the only signs of the Tsar's authority were occasional *zimovie* – small armed posts garrisoned by a few soldiers who endured a pitiless climate as best they could and terrorized the natives into paying the *jassak*. In such places, Russian power was represented only by a prison for accommodating the hostages held for this fiscal purpose.

Thus the 'conquest' of Siberia merely set down small groups of Slavs among the natives, whose way of life was hardly changed and who influenced the Russians not at all. The emptiness of the country – the very low population level, and the distances, which rendered contacts fleeting and superficial – explains this unalloyed transference of a style of life which was modified in a few particulars by natural conditions, but remained fundamentally Russian.

Can it be argued nevertheless that there is a Siberian sub-species of the Russian people? The way of life, and more especially the background, of the immigrants, many of whom were fugitive peasants or religious refugees (heterodox victims of Orthodox persecution), might lead one to conclude that there was a special Siberian mentality. But in fact Russia transported herself entire into Siberia; her organization, administration and social patterns were the same there as at home. Siberia was populated by such a piecemeal process, and society was composed of such small groups, that authority met with little opposition; minds could be moulded on the same lines there as elsewhere. The Siberian people was simply the advance-guard of the Russians in their movement towards the Pacific.

II THE CENTRALIZED RUSSIAN STATE

The process by which the sovereign acquired complete authority over all Russian territories reached its culmination under Ivan IV. And although the Time of Troubles (1598–1613) was marked by political anarchy, Polish invasion, armed risings by non-Russian elements of the population, and peasant revolts, so that at times the state was in danger of collapsing altogether, the final result demonstrated that the foundatinos of central authority had been well and truly laid and that the nation was now a strongly cohesive whole. In the seventeenth century, under the Romanovs, the Tsar once more enjoyed complete authority (map 9).

Authoritarian Reforms
Arbitrary power, with no real check upon it, had been established in the sixteenth century. The sovereign set up the Duma of the Boyars and thus consulted, at any rate nominally, the representatives of the great families; and at crucial junctures he appealed to opinion by convoking a representative assembly which was rather like the States-General in France: the *Zemsky Sobor*, consisting of the Duma *plus* deputies representing the clergy, the nobility, the *posads* and even, on occasion, some of the free peasant communities. But at that period the *Zemsky Sobor* was authority's tool rather than an obstacle to arbitrary government. It made it easier for the ruler to impose sacrifices on his subjects. In Moscow itself, Ivan appealed even more directly to the people at large by assembling them in the Red Square and requesting their support for his decisions.

In all likelihood, popular backing was as useful to him as his armed forces and the support of the Church in enabling him to subdue the unruly boyars (who had been in power effectively if not legally during the four-year regency, 1553–6), and to introduce changes in the administration of the country which strengthened the power of the throne and even altered the structure of Russian society.

There were two periods of reform, separated by the military victories of 1555–6. The first and more moderate period paid a certain measure of attention to the complaints of the people at exploitation by the Tsar's officials; the second, which was more revolutionary, encroached rudely on the various hierarchies of privilege, bringing them more closely to heel but at the same time delivering the peasants into their hands.

The first reforms improved the functioning of the state apparatus for the future, and gave Ivan the means with which to launch his offensive against the Tatars. The system of *kormlenie* (functionaries picking a living for themselves from the districts they administered) was suppressed in 1555. Central control over revenue was instituted, taxes being henceforward to be paid directly to the treasury. And the landowners' military obligations were fixed by regulation.

But the more decisive series of reforms was that initiated in 1565. With the support of the docile Zemsky Sobor, Ivan organized the *oprichnina*, a system which placed him in direct personal control of the central — the most populous and prosperous – regions of the country, and left the remaining regions (*zemshchina*) to be administered by the Duma of the boyars under his overriding authority. At the same time he decimated the ranks of the aristocratic boyars and reapportioned the lands awarded for past services. Many large landowners had their hereditary estates confiscated; boyars suspected of disaffection found themselves being removed to remote, comparatively unprofitable 'benefices'; and many of the small and medium landed gentry, suddenly promoted, became more faithful than ever and were wedded henceforth to the service of the state. These were the successive stages of a brutal, pitiless policy of reform to which history seems to afford no parallel, and which, though its life on the plane of practical administration was short, produced decisive effects on the social plane: it extinguished the boyars as a political force and, by sealing the alliance between the Tsar and the reconstituted nobility, created a supply of potential administrators. The boyars themselves felt obliged to fall into line and serve. Meanwhile the *namestniki*, maintained by the population and enjoying wide personal powers, were replaced by *voevodas* dispatched by the Tsar throughout the kingdom to represent his authority. They enforced respect for it by every means within their power.

Monarchical Compromise: A Brief Interlude

The Time of Troubles, during which state power in Russia was nearly obliterated, intensified the desire for freedom and the forces of regional autonomy. In the ensuing period of recovery, the *Zemsky Sobor* played a very important part between 1613 and 1648, sitting almost continually until 1621 and thereafter meeting less and less often until absolute power was eventually resumed by Alexis Mikhailovitch. As anarchy receded, a kind of moral unanimity in the governing aristocracy and the urban classes, both of whom induced the Tsar to sanction measures serving their own interests, coincided with a cautious attitude on the part of the sovereigns, whose prospects were for the time being uncertain, to produce this short and exceptional interlude of modified monarchy, with less than absolute power (plates 9 and 14).

The Code (*Ulozhenie*) of 1649 was its death certificate. This document, which included the provisions embodied in the *Sudebnik* of 1497 was not merely an attempt to codify the existing regulations governing Russian administration; it contained new provisions, relating to the royal power, and defining the duties of all classes, including the administrators, to the state. Retained as the foundation of Russian law until the nineteenth century, it confirmed the Tsar's authority over the whole of society; each class was considered separately, but all were united by a common bond of obligation and also, in the case of the privileged classes – the nobility and the merchant class – by appropriate rights. The Code abandoned the principle of a national representative assembly which, having voted, would issue a decision or make recommendations. The administration of the country's affairs was handed over once and for all to the bureaucracy: the *prikazes*, directed by boyars but obedient tools of the sovereign none the less.

Under the feudal system in the West, the sovereign repaid his political supporters with estates and privileges, and the fabric of society depended on protection and vassalage. Just when the elements of such a system had emerged in Russia, the royal will abruptly arrested their further development. The causes of the break were complicated and do not yield easily to scrutiny. Historians have adduced the personal qualities of the grand princes of Moscow, Byzantine traditions of government, ecclesiastical support, and Mongol domination; to these we may add the fact that, even in Russia, no local leader bent on autonomy had the necessary means to stand up to a sixteenth-century sovereign. Gunpowder had transformed the relations which had previously tended to develop between the boyars and the grand prince of Moscow. It was at a lower level, in the relations between landowner and peasant, that feudalism strengthened its hold and, strangely, retained it till the dawn of the twentieth century.

From Feudal Supporter to State Servant
In the seventeenth century, the distinction between absolute property (*votchina*) and conditional property (*pomiestie*, property awarded for services past and future) virtually disappeared. Whichever the nature of his tenure might be, permanent or precarious, the landowner stood in the same relationship to the sovereign as the peasants on his estate did to him. His obligation to serve and obey was absolute. Similarly, his own almost unlimited power over his peasants made him an owner of souls as well as of land.

Gone were the days when the boyars, as in the great Moscow rebellion of 1341, could drop out of a prince's service, retire with their wives and children to their estates and refuse to serve anyone. By the end of the fifteenth century a vow of service had been instituted, the terms of which compelled them to be in the service of a prince and forbade their leaving one prince for another. And in the sixteenth century the elimination of the autonomous principalities, and the rise of the centralized power of Muscovy, left them with only one prince to serve – the Grand Prince of Moscow, the Tsar; in addition to which, the Church, underwriting Moscow's policy of centralization and conquest, made the vow of fidelity more alarming by giving it a religious character; the wording of the oath associated traitors with Judas. The exchange of letters between Ivan the Terrible and Prince Kurbsky (1564–1679), who had fled to Lithuania, is a case in point: Ivan's retort, in violent, picturesque language, to his vassal's reproaches, is that he holds from the Almighty a power which even the highest in the land, the greatest churchman or noble in the kingdom, may not dispute; the Tsar's right to distribute rewards and punishments is absolute; Prince Kurbsky is henceforward, inescapably, a traitor, a man without honour.

The result of this state of affairs was the creation of a class of 'servitors'; Peter the Great, by drawing up the *chin* or Table of Ranks, merely gave official status to an accomplished fact.

Enforced Decline of the Trading Cities

Novgorod, like Pskov, lost its independence in the sixteenth century. It had submitted perforce to the Grand Prince in 1471 and had been conquered by Ivan III in 1478; a century later its recalcitrance had caused it to be ruinously damaged by Ivan IV, and it had sunk into gradual decline. The catastrophic conditions under which it was integrated into the Russian state – its aristocracy and bourgeoisie were decimated, the resulting gaps being filled by servants of the Tsar, and merchants from Moscow – were too great to be counterbalanced by the accompanying advantage, that of participating henceforward in the extensive national market.

True, Novgorod's links with Moscow were strengthened. In the sixteenth century, the trade route connecting the two cities via Vyshny-Volotchek, Torjok and Tver became an important artery. In the seventeenth, the Tikhvin district, with its craftsmen and the little mining and metalworking centres they operated, took part in Novgorod's trade with the interior. And despite the expulsion of the Hanseatic merchants in 1494, Novgorod had never stopped trading with the West. The city grew and its population rose, being estimated about 1550 at some thirty thousand inhabitants.

But this apparent prosperity was deceptive; in reality Novgorod was stagnating while the rest of the Russian economy was going ahead, the acceleration being particularly marked in the seventeenth century. The state, which had become the prime mover, was not anxious to hand out special advantages to a suspect city. Novgorod's last vestiges of independence disappeared at the close of the sixteenth century. Its guilds and corporations, which other Russian cities did not possess and which gave it its distinctive character, lost their privileges; and the destruction of the boyars of Novgorod as a political force was accompanied by the suppression of the local institutions, the *veche* and the whole traditional hierarchy of administration. The city, governed by *namestniki* and later by *voevodas*, was gradually drawn into the administrative system of the whole country. Local landowners, most of whom were Muscovite boyars transplanted for the purpose, assumed the preponderant role at the expense of the merchant class. The city's final ruin was consummated under Peter the Great, when the extension of the commercial axis running up from Moscow through Vyshny-Volotchek towards the Baltic bypassed Novgorod and reduced it to the status of a little provincial town, a living museum (plate 15).

III FROM FREEDOM TO SERFDOM

The East Slavs, like the Poles, never underwent the gradual process of emancipation which, in the European West, culminated in the freedom of the peasantry. On the contrary, the Russian peasant, who was a free man juridically speaking, and remained fairly free in practice until about the fourteenth century, lost the absolute freehold of the land he cultivated and thereafter became progressively more closely tied to it, until in the eighteenth century he became an article of property: the landowner owned the peasants too.

The only peasants to escape serfdom were those on government estates, and even these enjoyed fewer rights than peasants in the West. They had an oppressive amount of *corvées* to discharge and could not move from their villages without permission, and in many cases appeared to resemble the serfs so closely that they were thought of as such. But their position was in fact rather different. Most of them lived in Muscovy's southern and eastern borderlands, where more land was available because not much of it had been appropriated by the aristocracy.

In those parts of old Muscovy where the land had been farmed for centuries, the peasant could not avoid being oppressed twice over, by the aristocracy and by the state. The princes' 'servitors', on being granted fiefs (*pomestia*) to support them (all land being in the gift of the Tsar), placed such a heavy load of dues on the peasants that the latter became permanent debtors. The land was often ravaged by war; the harvest was frequently poor – and where agricultural methods are so backward a poor harvest is a calamity. Many peasants sought to escape to the tracts of free country in the east. This tendency was encouraged in the sixteenth century by Ivan the Terrible's conquests, which suddenly expanded the frontiers of his kingdom to the Caspian and Siberia.

This was a period of capital importance in the history of the peasants. Hitherto any peasant not encumbered with debt was allowed to move from the estate on St George's Day (26 November, by the Julian calendar), provided the harvest had been got in. But the land meant nothing to its owners unless it was occupied and profitably worked, and they had soon begun seeking for every possible device by which the labour force could be kept on the spot. In this they were at one with the princes of Moscow, whose drive for a well organized state, administered from the centre, made it desirable from the military and fiscal points of view to keep the peasant population immovably settled. The relations between the peasants and their lay or ecclesiastical master were not determined only by the latter's personal decisions; on top of these came royal ukases of wider import, embodying

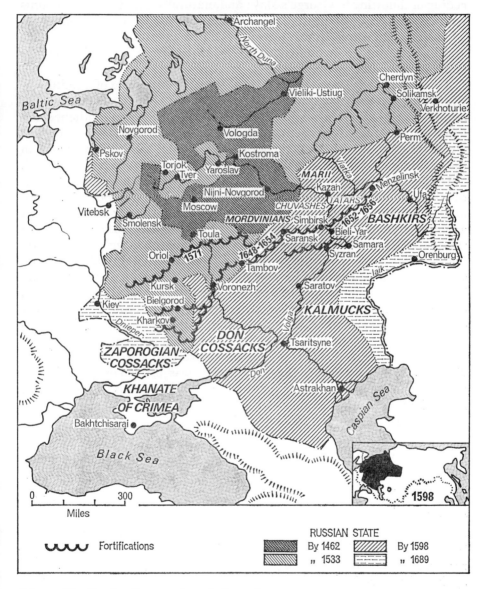

Map 9 The Russian State, 15th–17th Centuries

some new demand by the state, and emphasizing anew the depth of the peasants' servitude.

One of the first stages on the road to serfdom was reached in the Code of 1497, under which a debt-free peasant was no longer allowed to remove himself from the estate at any time of year he pleased, but only on St George's Day (peasants with undischarged debts were of course not free to go at all). In other words, he could leave the feudal domain only when the main agricultural work of the year had been completed, in the week preceding or following St George's Day; and, naturally, had to settle accounts with his lord before going, and in particular pay off any outstanding rent. Thus the ukase was far from enslaving the peasant and looked reasonable and logical enough: it limited the right of departure in the interests of cultivation, but did not abolish it.

The Code of 1550, which was part of Ivan IV's first series of administrative reforms, merely confirmed this arrangement. But the *opritchnina*, the administrative reorganization initiated in 1565, which strengthened the framework and augmented the personnel of the administration, and subjected the estates to stricter control by the Tsar, also laid its heavy hand on the peasants themselves by tying them more closely to their masters' land.

In the atmosphere of violence surrounding the politically motivated redistribution of land – a redistribution in which numerous boyars lost not only their estates but their lives – the peasants came in for a good deal of arbitrary treatment. Many peasants who had previously been farming on state property were transferred to these new landowners and consequently had heavier services to discharge, and found their rights all the more severely curtailed because the new owners were hard masters, men who had risen from practically nothing and were avid to use their authority. Still more distressing were the forced deportations of peasants from one part of the country to another, a method often employed for supplying manpower when a servant of the Tsar had been given an estate in an underpopulated area. Practically speaking, the peasant came to be regarded as a kind of tool; his existence, in the owner's eyes, was justified only by his connection with the soil; he became a thing, an object, for his landlord's use. And this attitude was tolerated, even encouraged, by the state.

Since these changes in landownership were often accompanied by violence, many estates were devastated and the tenant-farmers on them were ruined and even forced to flee; peasants thus impoverished were an easy prey to the landlord class, and their economic subordination became more complete. In the history of a country like Russia, we must never overlook the catastrophic eventualities which abruptly aggravated the peasants' lot from time to time. It was not only by a gradual, evenly-paced development that much of the peasant population was brought into serfdom: wars and internal dissension inflicted damaging crises on the economy and created new situations with bewildering suddenness. Ivan IV's punitive expedition against Novgorod in 1570, for example, and the massacres and devastation involved in it, turned the peasants of the surrounding country into debtors, fugitives and beggars who were willing to accept the feudal yoke in exchange for – as they hoped – a quiet life.

Ivan IV's measures were no doubt justified: the state was gravely handicapped by the danger of disintegration, the country's feudal disunity had to be overcome and the Tsar's authority imposed firmly throughout Russia's territories. Socially, however, it was another matter; the results for the peasants were unhappy.

Self-interest cannot be held entirely responsible. The state could survive only if the land was cultivated; it could not afford to see the land neglected and deserted; it shared with the landowners an interest in limiting the peasants' movements. State intervention was born of necessity; it arose when the troubles of the time had reduced the peasants to helpless distress, increasing their mobility and imperilling the state's economy. From 1570 onwards (perhaps earlier, but if so there is no documentary evidence to show it), the Tsar periodically declared that for a certain length of time (five years) no tenant-farmer would be allowed to leave his holding, even if he was not in debt. Later, the practice was increasingly adopted of renewing this close season as soon as it came to an end, so that the ban became continuous – an exception being the year 1601, when it was lifted by an ukase of Boris Godunov. In 1649 the Code of Alexis Mikhailovitch expressly attached the peasant to the land he worked; serfdom *de facto* became serfdom *de jure*.

The destiny of the peasants in Russian history has indeed proved curious. Serfs almost to a man in Muscovy itself, they were the source of continual emigration to the newly conquered regions beyond the middle Volga, in the direction of Siberia and the Pomorye (the White Sea littoral), where they constituted a free peasantry, released temporarily from the demands of the exchequer, and permanently from the grasp of the landowning nobility. Rural communities formed in this way by fugitives succeeded in living undisturbed for many years in the heart of the forests; in their lonely, almost inaccessible clearings defended by tracts of marshland into which the Tsar's employees were not anxious to venture, taxes and the *corvée* were a thing of the past. Most of the emigrants, however, settled in less isolated vicinities, accessible by tracks and rivers, and remained in contact with the administration as it followed up behind the advancing conquest. The forest solitudes of the Ural region, and western Siberia beyond them, were peopled by this irregular process.

Of course the estate owners demanded the return of their runaways, and a mass of laws was passed appearing to meet their wishes. But threats of punishment, however harsh, were impotent against the force of fact: men were needed to colonize the eastern territories, and the garrisons of the armed posts set up at intervals along the lines of penetration were obliged to provide for their support. The new settlers, shielded by the many hundreds of miles between themselves and their former masters, were allowed to take up plots of ground of which one *desiatin* (hectare) was cultivated for the state, to feed the officials and soldiers of the Tsar.

The landed aristocracy found these distant territories unappealing, preferring in almost all cases to be given estates in the south, moving gradually
into the Ukraine as it was recovered from the Tatars (map 9).

The land eastwards from the Volga, through the Ural region (where, in
the seventeenth century, the Stroganovs were the only noble family to
carve out gigantic domains for themselves), and on into Siberia, became a
vast national reserve; here a section of the peasantry rehabilitated themselves, surviving and developing in almost total immunity from serfdom,
and, by Peter the Great's time, constituted a special social category, as we
shall see. Geography, the local conditions by which this eastern colonization
was shaped, precluded serfdom, which until 1861 was the essential feature
of peasant society in the western regions, where settlement and cultivation
had been established so much longer and the rigorous imposition of state
authority depended precisely on preventing population movement.

Popular Revolts
Neither the subjection of the peasants nor the organization of a centralized
state, which consolidated its hold on the country after Ivan IV's reign, was
accomplished without resistance. The seventeenth century was marked by
disturbances whose scope and continuity are equalled by no other period.
The complexity of the causes behind this unrest accounts for the surprising
temporary alliances springing up between peasants, urban craftsmen and
landed proprietors, who joined forces briefly from political motives only to
be at once divided again by social ones. The resistance was ineffective – it
lacked the necessary resources, and the various insurrections took place too
far apart, without co-ordination. But the participation of military elements
– the boyars, and more especially the Cossacks of the southern borderlands
– rendered it formidable. And there was the additional support, indirect for
the most part, of the non-Russian population, which took advantage of the
circumstances to try to shake off Russian tutelage.

During the heyday of Vassily Shuisky (1606–10), 'the tsar of the boyars'
(a 'tsar' not without rivals), the whole Russian kingdom was affected by
revolts which originated in the countryside and got as far as the suburbs of
Tver, Pskov and Novgorod in the north, and those of the cities of the south-
west, to which many peasants had fled from the central districts. The only
one of these risings to threaten the central power (in 1606–7) found a leader
in the person of Ivan Bolotnikov, a former Don Cossack who had escaped
from a Turkish galley. He gathered serfs from the southern frontiers, advanced from one small town to another and accumulated a raggle-taggle
army which he launched against Moscow, and which had been joined
meanwhile by a few boyars with a view to diverting it to their own ends.
But the revolutionary tone of Bolotnikov's proclamations was not to their
liking and they soon abandoned him, with the result that the siege of
Moscow was a failure and the army was compelled to withdraw to Kaluga.
Cossack reinforcements enabled Bolotnikov to advance north to Tula,
where, however, besieged by Shuisky's troops, he surrendered and was

tortured. Despite ferocious repression, the movement continued in the middle Volga districts, where a force raised by the Mordvinian and Cheremis minorities, supported by some of the Russian serfs, marched on Nijni Novgorod, from which they were repulsed (1607–8).

A few years later (1616) the peasants of the same region rose again, simultaneously with the Tatars of Kazan. Though this flare-up was short-lived, it showed the precarious position of authority and the tensions of society along Muscovy's southern and eastern fringes, where conquest and colonization were recent and where Russian serfs co-existed with unruly non-Russians and free Cossacks.

In the early days of the reign of Alexis Mikhailovitch (1645–76), heavy taxation touched off a string of disturbances among the lower orders in the *posads* (1648); these outbreaks were specially serious in Moscow, where the Tsar sacrificed a few of his administrators to the demonstrators' anger. This disquieting situation caused the convocation of the *Zemsky Sobor* and the publication of the new legal Code (*Ulozhenie*) of 1649, one of whose prominent features was increased penalties for attacks on the person of the Tsar. Novgorod and Pskov revolted again in 1650, and the latter held out for three months against the Moscovite troops; executions and deportations struck once again at these merchant cities, whose former independence rendered them suspect, and which the central authority had no desire to treat tenderly. As elsewhere, the movement was complex: the landowners, whose peasants rose throughout the region, soon decided in favour of surrender, and took part in the ensuing repression; thus the social drive underlying the insurrection was overshadowed by the threat to property.

At the same period, Polish Ukraine, where religious and national causes were added to the social incentives to revolt, underwent similar disturbances, which broke out in 1648 and were directed against Poland by the Cossack hetman Bogdan Khmelnitski. The almost permanent state of war in those parts, where the Cossacks, sometimes uniting with the Tatars against the Poles, sometimes attacked by Poles and Tatars at once, finally went over to the Tsar in 1654 (thereby incorporating Ukraine in the Russian kingdom, but also triggering thirty years of Russo-Polish war, which ended in the partition of Ukraine in 1666) should not cause us to overlook the struggle of the Ukrainian peasants against their Polish masters; a struggle which provided the background, and occasionally the determinant, of military events.

The Moscow revolt of 1662 (at one moment during which the Tsar, at his residence in the Kolomenskoye suburb, engaged in a hypocritically pathetic dialogue with a crowd of demonstrators from the city, who were brutally dispersed) was merely a fleeting expression of discontent by the poorer classes, hard hit by the financial measures of Alexander Mikhailovitch – he had made a massive issue of copper coinage, which sent food prices rising steeply (plate 11).

A much more real threat to the recently developed unity of the state was the revolt of the Don Cossacks under the leadership of Stenka Razin (1669–71). Razin, who had been in command of an expedition pillaging the Persian towns on the Caspian in 1667–9, appeared before the walls of Astrakhan in the latter year, augmented his troops with volunteers from the serfs of the district, executed the Tsar's envoy at Tcherkassk (at the mouth of the Don), made his way up the Don valley, and seized Tsaritsyn and Astrakhan, on the lower Volga, in the summer of 1670.

This was more than a mere expedition of conquest. It was greeted by complicity and support in the towns, whose ramparts would otherwise have proved impregnable. Discontent and hope, divergent, confused, were polarized by it. Its target was not the Tsar; the insurgents believed him to be favourable towards the movement, but considered his wishes had been betrayed by the boyars. The revolt was anti-administrative and anti-aristocratic. It liberated anarchial instincts; it appealed to the urge for freedom prevalent in communities oppressed by the growth of centralization and the arbitrary tyranny of the Tasr's officials. It was supported by a mass of runaway peasants who had settled among the Cossacks and were afraid of being recaptured by their masters; and wherever it went it was greeted by a rising of the serfs. This widespread, spontaneous reaction was characteristic of all these large movements, the hard core of which – the precipitate, as it were – was the military activity of the Cossacks.

In the event, Razin's successes were short-lived. After capturing Saratov and Samara (the present-day Kuibyshev), he was halted before Simbirsk (now Ulianov), where an army rapidly raised by Alexis Mikhailovitch drove him back towards the south. Having withdrawn to Kagalnitsky in the lower Don valley, a town of which he himself was the founder, he was handed over by the Cossacks and executed in Moscow.

Nevertheless the rising had spread far beyond the districts traversed and controlled by the troops of Stepan Razin. It affected an enormous area, reaching the central regions in the proximity of Nijni Novgorod and inflaming the whole basin of the Donets and Don, where it touched off a rebellion among the non-Russian elements, the Kalmucks, Tatars, Mordvinians and Chuvashes. For several months there was merciless guerrilla warfare between peasant bands and the Tsar's troops. The destruction of estates by one side was met by the other with mass hangings of insurgents, some of whose names have been enshrined in revolutionary tradition, such as the peasant woman Aniosha, of Arzamas, where she was put to death. The recapture in November 1671 of Astrakhan, which had held out under one of Razin's lieutenants, marked the end of a movement which, to an even greater extent than that of Bolotnikov, has been kept alive in folksong and popular memory, and, like the great insurrections of Bulavin and Pougachev in the eighteenth century, marked one of the principal phases of the struggle of the peasants against the feudal regime.

6

Foundations of
Russia's Power

IN PRINCIPLE, all Russian territory belonged to the sovereign; in practice, most of it was controlled by a landowning aristocracy. The members of this class might be secular or monastic, and the estate might be held as a grant from the Tsar (*pomestie*) or as a freehold patrimony (*votchina*); but in all cases the relationship between the owner and the peasants working for his benefit was the same. The sixteenth and seventeenth centuries were a crucial period: juridically the peasant on a monastic or private estate had previously been free; he now lost that freedom and became for all practical purposes a serf; in particular, he lost his right to quit the estate at will. The owner, whose land, in the primitive agricultural conditions of the time, was rarely very productive, had every incentive to keep the peasant on the spot, and pressed the government to place legal restrictions on the right of departure. Arbitrary action by the landlords, combined with legislation in the second half of the sixteenth century, gradually subjected most of the peasants on the estates to a system of serfdom which was the most striking characteristic of the old regime in Russia.

I A MERCANTILE ECONOMY

Slow Progress in Agriculture
Another characteristic was economic backwardness, an inevitable result of which was increasingly harsh exploitation of human beings. It is true that cultivation on burnt clearings, involving a simple 'nomadism of the fields', had virtually ceased in the seventeenth century, except in a few isolated regions of northern Russia, where the population was insignificant in relation to the vastness of the forests. Nevertheless the prevailing agricultural technique was still one of small patches of cultivation surrounded by relatively extensive fallows, the former being shifted around every few years.

Under this system (*perelozhnaya sistema*), cultivation was shifted within a rather small area, which never altered; the ground was worked with a primitive type of plough which had no fore-wheels; and the fallows were not manured. Nevertheless in the more populous regions of the centre (round Moscow, Yaroslav, Tver, Vladimir, Kostroma and Nijni Novgorod) and the north-west (Novgorod and Pskov), where the fallows were smaller and were brought back into cultivation with increasing frequency, a system of crop-rotation (*parovaya-zernovaya sistema*) had already come into use, under which the fallows were manured and were cultivated every alternate year. Cultivation had reached a more advanced stage; the primitive plough had given way to one of normal type. This system had begun developing by the end of the sixteenth century. But yields were low on the whole, harvests were at the mercy of the slightest vagaries of the weather, and agricultural progress was slow and very localized.

Stock-raising played only a minor part in this agrarian economy, its principal function being to provide draught and pack animals, except in the western regions (along the Dnieper) and the south-western, where there was a trade in cattle on the hoof and in lard and undressed hides. The animals, according at least to foreign travellers, were thin and underfed. But our information about this side of agricultural activity is scanty.

Progress in agriculture was far from being continuous; it was halted and even reversed in periods of recession; war and conquest, and Ivan IV's high-handed intervention whenever he undertook the redistribution of the *pomestia*, caused a return from intensive to extensive cultivation in a number of districts.

Urban Growth

But of course agriculture was not the sole occupation of the Russian peasant. Russian crafts slowly surmounted the bad times caused by the Mongol invasion. And in the little fortified townships, as in the villages, the prosperity of the artisan class bore witness to the steady growth of a national market and to the importance of mutual trade in the general economy. An indication of this activity is the number of 'towns' whose Kreml was surrounded by a *posad* and by *slobodas* inhabited by craftsmen and merchants; there were between three and four hundred of these places in the sixteenth and seventeenth centuries. But the figure is putative – at that time any place was a town if the central administration said it was; judged by their population and activities many of these towns were only villages. The important point is, however, that most of them supported other occupations besides agriculture.

The rising tide of trade caused new centres, *riady*, to spring up in completely rural areas. These, which were situated at points intermediate between village and town, consisted of rows of shops and workshops on the main arteries of communication, and were future towns in embryo. After the decline in urban life following the Mongol invasion, economic recovery began at the end of the fourteenth century. In addition to the towns dating from the kingdom of Kiev, and others which had been created for strategic or political reasons in the eleventh and twelfth centuries, there were now these new communities, the *riady*, each with its shops, granaries and

Gostinni dvor (a bazaar for merchants from elsewhere). In the sixteenth century, most townships of any importance were surrounded by broad earthworks and deep moats which protected the artisan population living outside the Kreml; thus integrated into the whole, the *posad* ended by virtually becoming the town – a process observable in Yaroslav, Vladimir, Tver, Novgorod and Moscow. Frequent fires, destroying whole quarters at one sweep, disorganized town life; nevertheless timber continued to be used for all building purposes except, in some cases, fortifications. After the great fire of 1658, which demolished much of Yaroslav, stone towers were erected on the ramparts; with the exception of such Lithuanian towns as Vilno, almost the only places defended by stone walls were Novgorod, Pskov, Izborsk, Ladoga and Moscow; in the last named, the merchants' quarter (*Kitaigorod*) was surrounded by a fortified wall between 1534 and 1538, and the entire *posad* (*Beili Gorod*) between 1585 and 1591. New Kremls were built, however at Tula (between 1514 and 1521), Zaraisk (1531) and Kolomna (1525–31).

Moscow: Religion in the Life of a Great City
These towns and cities, dominated by throngs of onion-domes and glittering crosses, bore visible witness less to the power of the tsar than to that of religion. Every quarter had its own church, in many cases more than one; every street-intersection had its shrines and outdoor icons, with lamps and candles burning before them by night and day. There were shrines and icons too along the city wall or palissade. And from one church tower to another the chimes rang out – marking the time of day, striking up a noisy welcome on special occasions, such as the visit of some notable personage, and warning the population of fires and other calamities. And when night had fallen and the city was silent, the archers on guard at the gates of the Kreml used the names of saints as passwords.

The rhythm of the working year depended on the Church; all business ceased for the great religious feasts of Easter, Christmas, the Assumption and St Nicholas's Day, and on every Saturday from the moment of the first vesper bell. The Church was unsuccessful, however, in preventing the sale of liquor on these occasions, except for a few years (1652–8) under the Patriarch Nikon. Nor could it interfere with the fair-days, which were frequent (eleven a year at Zvenigorod, for instance) and which were always held on a saint's day.

The city's approaches were guarded by fortified monasteries a few miles away to the east and south: powerful bastions against possible Tatar aggression and the ever-present threat of a peasant insurrection. There were the Andronikov monastery, built of stone between 1410 and 1427, on the lofty band of the Yaouza, dominating the road from Vladimir; the monasteries of the Saviour (early fifteenth century, but rebuilt in 1446) and Simonov (founded in 1379) on the left bank of the Moskva – the second of which was destined to play a decisive role in the agrarian revolts of the seventeenth century; the Danilov monastery, an older foundation (1272),

erected after a victory over the Tatars and overlooking the roads from the
southern steppes; and finally the Novo-Dievitchy monastery (1524) in the
bend of the Moskva, an advanced post towards the roads from the south-
east. By the seventeenth century the Kremlin had lost its military significance; the inhabitants of the *posads* and *slobodas* depended for their
security on external fortifications.

The city of Moscow put on a big spurt of growth in the seventeenth century. The population, estimated at 41,500 by Herberstein (Charles v's
ambassador) *circa* 1550, had doubled by 1600; but 80,000 is a small figure
compared with the population of western European cities at the same
time. It was after the Time of Troubles that the Muscovite capital, benefiting from the presence of a court, the development of the administration,
the creation of a small militia of *streltsy*, and, above all, the swelling current
of trade, became a populous city; by the end of the seventeenth century it
had 200,000 inhabitants.

How the People Lived

It has often been asserted that Peter the Great's reign marks a watershed
in Russian history, a critical period during which the westernization of the
upper classes destroyed the fundamental unity of the Russian people, producing a chasm between the rulers and the ruled and an antagonism between two mentalities, two ways of life, with disastrous consequences for
the country at a later period. But, as we shall point out in Book Four, the
cleavage was more apparent than real.

Even in the centuries when the skills of civilization were in their infancy
and life had few material comforts to offer, there were big differences between the way of life of the poorer people in town and country, and that of
the landowners and merchants. The psychological unity of society was precarious, shattered from time to time by violent class hostilities. As for
western influences, they had been penetrating in considerable volume
from the end of the sixteenth century; no one waited for Peter the Great's
advent to go clean-shaven in the Polish manner – a fashion which came in
during the period following the Time of Troubles – and the terrible ukase
of 1634, which banned the use of tobacco under pain of death, proves that
people in Moscow had taken to smoking. Social differences were doubtless
little more striking than at the present day, for Russian society was already
highly diversified. Undoubtedly, however, the contrast between the richest
and the poorest was enormous.

The poorest, who were also the most numerous, lived in little log-built
isbas roofed with straw or dried mud, with crude heating arrangements (*po
chernomou*) and no chimneys; the smoke made its way out through the narrow windows, which, when shut, were covered with the stretched bladders
of fishes or cows or sometimes merely with oiled cloth, and admitted little
light. In winter the *isba* gave shelter to the small livestock and poultry.
Tables, with benches fixed along the walls, were the only furniture. Clothes
were of linen or coarse woollen cloth, and footgear was fashioned from

birchbark. Sheepskins were the poor man's only furs. The peasant's table-ware was made of wood or earthenware, his food consisted mainly of cereals and vegetables prepared without cooking, in some cases fermented, salted or dried; cabbage, cucumbers and beet were the main items. Berries and mushrooms were preserved for the winter. Meat and butter were rarely seen, except on feast days, but much fish was eaten. For drinks there was *kvas* (made from fermented barley) and beer. Dessert consisted of *kisel* (fruit jelly made with starch).

The richer peasants lived more comfortably: their *isbas* were roomier, and their furniture included chests containing clothes of English as well as Russian cloth, often richly ornamented. High leather boots were worn and were the first sign of having risen in the scale of prosperity (two centuries later they were still the first purchase of a peasant who had come to work in town, with his savings in his pocket). Alongside the wooden kitchen utensils appeared others made of copper (stewing pots), iron (saucepans) and pewter (dishes).

The lower classes in town lived like those in the country. But the exercise of a particular craft or trade sometimes caused modifications, in cases where the family dwelling incorporated the shop or workroom; the latter had better illumination. The more prosperous inhabitants of the *posad*, whether craftsmen or merchants, lived in larger houses – sometimes of two storeys, and having chimneys (whence the name *bielaia isba*, white *isba*); and the windows had panes of mica or even glass. The living room was decorated with carved chests reinforced with decorative ironwork and containing silk clothes, blankets, and fox and marten furs. Utensils were of metal (copper, iron and tin); sometimes even gold and silver, as in the Stroganov household at Solvytchegodsk, but this was uncommon. As a rule, one corner of the room was set aside for prayer and was hung with icons. The owner's working hours were spent outside the home, in a workshop or business establishment nearby.

The expansion of business and the crafts, in this period when the cities of Muscovy were growing at a quickened tempo, increased the numbers of a middle class which had become detached from the countryside, looked at life from a town-dweller's point of view and was regarded as a model by the peasant masses.

Novgorod, which had been the pacesetter in the arts, performed the same function in the social field with the *Domostroi*, a sixteenth-century manual for householders which gives an ideal picture of life as conducted in a well-to-do town family, and the social and religious observances with which such a family should comply. This treatise, which derives from Byzantine literature both in its didactic moralizing and in its form, was adapted and completed in Moscow by Sylvester, priest of the Church of the Assumption; and although it expresses an ideal of austerity, industry and piety which was not for everybody, and which no one could have realized in its entirety, it possesses an undeniable historical value. In his own composition, *Instruction to his Son*, which he appended to the treatise,

Sylvester describes a style of conduct which, in its prudent egoism, its reconciliation of morality with self-interest and the pursuit of a tranquil life,
would seem to be closer to reality.

The Upper Classes

In the houses of the *gosti*, and in those of the nobles (called 'palaces', but
they were really large timber-built houses), touches of western luxury,
indicating Polish or German influence, were visible in the details of furniture and decoration: carved tables; chairs (both upright and easy); pictures, even portraits. But the well-to-do classes differed from the people
not so much in the comfort of their lives as in the way they spent their time
and, despite violent opposition from the Church, in their greater freedom
to indulged in worldly pleasures. Except in Moscow and its environs, however, there was little change. Only the capital with its foreign residents, its
diplomatic contact with foreign governments, and the commercial intercourse by which the needs of the court and the wealthy Muscovites were
supplied, was open to the outside world; it thus became the theatre of open
conflict between the partisans of tradition and the continually increasing
number of those who succumed to the lure of an imported modernism.

But both parties to this conflict affected the badges of wealth which distinguished them from the common herd: silk blouses, ceremonial dress
stiff with gold and silver brocade, embroidery, heavy fur pelisses, knee-
boots of red leather; their women went in for elaborate hairdressing and
heavy make-up, and wore *kokochniki* embellished with pearls and precious
stones. Western clothes were rarely to be seen; so were clean-shaven faces;
to this extent the boyar resembled the moujik. The difference was not in
the design and cut of the clothes but in the quality of the materials. The
gulf between the outward appearance of the rich and the poor was doubtless greater in the seventeenth than in the succeeding century, when the
difference came from the nobility's adoption of western fashions.

The Position of Women

A shadow lay over half the population: women, weighed down by the
doctrine of original sin and by legislation enacted by men, possessed no
rights and were subordinated to the will of fathers and husbands. The
injunctions of the *Domostroi* provide a convincing reconstruction of the
atmosphere governing married life:

If the husband finds that order has been disturbed by his wife or servants, or
that the rules prescribed in this book are being disregarded [rules for household
management and control of the servants], he should speak the language of reason
to his wife and instruct her. If with docile heart she amends her conduct to con-
form with her husband's teaching, he should love and reward her.

If the wife or son or daughter do not pay attention to the words or instructions
of the father of the family, if they do not listen to them with respect and fear, if
they do not do what they are ordered by husband, father or mother, they should
be whipped in proportion to their offence.

On the other hand, however grave their offence, they should not be struck on the ear or face, or with a stick or any instrument of iron or wood. . . . You should administer punishment with a whip, and watch where you are striking; that is reasonable, and terrible, and beneficial to health. If some grave fault has been committed, such as to excite anger, some act of glaring and inexcusable disobedience, or of negligence, the culprit's shirt should be removed and his hands held, and he should be whipped, without excessive violence, in accordance with his fault, and when you have finished striking him you should speak a few kind words to him.

A wife, ranked with minors and servants, had to obey the head of the family. Nevertheless her position differed greatly according to whether the family lived in town or country, and was rich or poor. Women took part in agricultural work; besides, the continual migrations of peasants put large numbers of families on the roads, severing them from their original surroundings; both these factors gave women a certain freedom and authority, though just how far this went it is impossible to say.

Moreover, when some of the men were away, women participated in the village assembly on their behalf. Woman's position of inferiority, born of the discredit cast on her by religion and in many cases aggravated by the coarseness, brutality and desires of her husband, was compensated in some degree by the important, indeed indispensable, role she played in the economic life of the countryside.

Women in well-to-do town families led a more sheltered, restricted life, in a degree corresponding to the family's position in the social scale.

Economic Independence in Jeopardy; a Policy of Mercantile Self-Defence
Russia possessed maritime outlets neither to the west, on the Baltic, which was in the hands of the Swedes, nor to the south, where the Tatar tribes roamed the northern shores of the Black Sea; her Siberian expansion had therefore the effect of reinforcing her continental character. Nevertheless it was not with Asia that the main part of her commerce was conducted. The infrequent caravans connecting Russia with central Asia and, across almost uninhabited Siberia, with China, carried only a thin trickle of trade. Russia's face was turned towards the west. It was the White Sea port of Arkhangelsk, unfortunately closed by ice during the long winters, and the transit towns on the frontiers, Pskov and Novgorod – no longer quite their former selves – which received manufactured goods (arms, pig-iron, precious metals, fabrics and luxury commodities) from Scandinavia and western Europe, and exported the products of the Russian soil and forest: timber, pitch, potash, leather, suet, hemp, flax and furs. But the Russian merchants did not as yet venture beyond Arkhangelsk and the land frontier to any great extent; and Russia had no fleet; it was through German and Swedish merchants, and English and Dutch ships, that Russian traders made connection with the outside world.

The attempts made to acquire a Baltic outlet in the sixteenth century had come to nothing. Russia's subordinate position in this respect appeared

as a great advantage to her neighbours. Gustavus Adolphus told the
Swedish Diet in 1629; 'Great lakes, Ladoga and Peipus, and the country
round, thirty leagues of vast marshes, and impregnable forts, separate us
from these enemies of ours; Russia has no access to the sea and, thanks be
to God, will henceforward find it difficult to overcome the obstacles which
separate her from it.' On the other hand, English, German and Dutch
merchants were making their way into Russian territory; so far from being
limited to the external trade which they were permitted to carry on
directly, they also participated in the country's internal trade through
middlemen. The beginnings of foreign commercial exploitation were
already threatening the country, which had resumed regular relations with
the West only within the last century, but was able to parry western
initiative only by political means.

For her economy was still rudimentary. Her craft industries were not
strong enough to meet the needs of the army, the court and the great landowners at a time when the demand for both necessities and luxuries was
increasing with the development of the state. Imports were essential; but
their value exceeded that of the agricultural products which provided
Russia's exports, and the resulting cash payments were a drain on the currency. Her lack of currency, and the simplicity of her trading methods,
were the great weakness of a Russia which knew nothing of the financial
practices that were already commonplace in the West, and whose merchants were incapable of reacting effectively to foreign commercial
penetration without help from authority.

As in the West, the government sought to devise a trading policy and
technique which would protect the country's economic independence and
at the same time consolidate its own power. This was a new stage, the
second, in Russia's transition from medieval to modern times. The establishment of a treasury – regarded at that time as an instrument for the
sovereign power alone to manipulate – was the objective of Tsar Alexis
Mikhailovitch; it inspired all the other economic and financial measures
by which his reign was distinguished, and whose purpose was to prevent
too much of the country's prized and scanty currency from going abroad.
About 1640, to the south of Moscow, near Tula, the first ordnance factories
were set up under the direction of two Dutchmen, Vinius and Marselis –
the first, hesitant step towards limiting costly imports. In 1654–5 Alexis
accumulated silver ingots and coinage purchased abroad and had them
melted down or re-stamped with Russian markings, and followed this up
with a massive issue of copper money for foreign trade. These monetary
manœuvres, undertaken when Russia was at war with Poland, were undoubtedly something of a makeshift, and they caused a serious social crisis
which spread into the Ukraine.

An action more in conformity with the mercantilist spirit was the state's
direct intervention in economic activity. Half the state's income was derived from taxes on alcohol, and customs duties, which had risen; the
government now began trading on its own account, establishing a state

monopoly in 1662 in five export commodities: sables, potash, pitch, suet and hemp, and exercising a pre-emptive option on all imported goods.

A Plutocratic Class and Its Brief Political Power
This new role brought the administration into close contact with a small but extremely active class of the population, the big merchants or *gosti* ('hosts'). More precisely, the *gosti* were given official positions; they became advisers to the government, and carried out commercial operations on its behalf. They had much influence with the tsar, and used it at once to limit competition from foreign merchants and to acquire a near-monopoly of large-scale trading, both internal and external. The Commercial Decree of 13 January 1667 gave them what they wanted; it appointed them as sole middlemen for all internal wholesale trade and turned them into a privileged caste, lording it over the small merchants and shopkeepers, of whom there were multitudes in both town and country, and whose numbers were quite out of proportion to the quantity of goods changing hands. The Decree bears witness to a sharp reaction against the foreign merchants, who now became liable to heavier taxation; it completed the protectionist measures which were placed on a more systematic footing in the next century.

Nor was this the whole significance of the Decree. It gave official sanction to the prominence of a new social class, one which owed its existence to the accelerated tempo of trade, was already wealthy in movable capital, had become necessary to the government, and was capable of bringing political pressure to bear on it. But this momentary phase, in which a section of the wealthy bourgeoisie transcended its professional competence to play a larger role, turned out to be unique in Russian social history. At no time, including even the years preceding the First World War, did the Russian bourgeoisie acquire such influence again. During the reign of Alexis Mikhailovitch, Russia was close to becoming a bourgeois monarchy. The tardy pace of economic development, and the subsequent orientation of the state, whose power under Peter the Great and his successors was derived consistently from the landed aristocracy, curtailed the prospects of the Russian bourgeoisie and relegated them to the subject classes.

A Burgher Grandee: the 'Gost' Nikitin
The Russian commercial operators who worked on a big scale in this immense country, trading from the frontiers of Poland and Sweden to China (with which relations developed after the treaty of Nerchinsk, in 1689) were few in number, but rich and powerful. Such a man as Gabriel Romanovitch Nikitin, who at the time of his death (1689) was being tried for having too freely criticized the policy of Peter the Great, is a typical example of these colourful individuals whose ability and lack of scruple, in a favourable economic climate, carried them to the top of the social hierarchy. Of peasant extraction, Nikitin rose in the service of a wealthy trader and, in the sixteen-seventies, with the help of his brothers and nephews and

a large staff of employees, set up his own business organization and
launched out on a remarkable scale. He scoured the towns and markets
for supposedly imported 'German' and 'Persian' textiles – which had in
fact been produced by Russian craftsmen – and sent out his caravans to
Siberia year after year; long trains of wagons, drawn by teams of ten
horses, made their way towards the Ural River and Verkhoturie, and were
accompanied either by Nikitin in person or by his *prikazchiki* (factors).
Travelling from there onwards sometimes by water, sometimes on land,
for which purpose even skis were used, the caravan made for Irkutsk on its
way to China. In Siberia Nikitin collected considerable quantities of furs;
the commoner varieties were sold in China, the rest were sent to Russia
with the returning caravan. Perpetually on the move, Nikitin would
appear at the fair at St Macarius, or Ustiug, or Irbit, but also took care of
his warehouses in Moscow, where he had a private house which was built
of stone, and supported a nearby church at his own charges, with a priest
retained for his personal service.

His fortune was large by the standards of the time. He himself valued his
capital in 1697 at over 20,000 roubles (two thirds of which was in the form
of goods), a figure which is certain to have been misleadingly low. His
accounts show that in a mere two years (1697–8) he brought back more
than 36,000 roubles' worth of miscellaneous merchandise from Siberia.
The large profits on his trading activities (as when, for instance, a consign-
ment of furs bought for 720 roubles at Yakutsk was sold for 3,600 roubles
in Moscow) were increased by his business as a usurer. He lent considerable sums – hundreds of roubles at a time – to his fellow-merchants, and
smaller ones to a host of craftsmen and peasants. The Siberian administration also borrowed from him; the voivodas' relations with him were
complicated by loans and less orthodox 'considerations' which were interwoven with the pattern of his ceaseless bargaining, which, though profitable, contained a high element of risk. Admittedly, it is difficult to estimate
the purchasing power of the rouble; it varied greatly from one region to
another. Some eighty years earlier in 1623, a functionary of the Tsar reported that a certain Ivan Afanasiev, as a result of stealing two fox-skins
which must have been exceptionally fine, since they were worth 110
roubles, was able to buy more than twenty hectares of land in Siberia,
build an isba, buy five horses, ten head of cattle, twenty sheep and several
dozen poultry, and still have half the original sum left. The figures, though
very dubious, give a rough gauge of values.

Nikitin's arrest took place on his return from one of his Siberian journeys.
The ostensible charge was a loan at extortionate interest; the real motive
was political. Proud and over-confident, Nikitin had been too outspoken
and seemed to oppose the new régime. He is the typical example of the rich
Russian burghers of the seventeenth century whom Peter the Great broke
and subdued.

II INTELLECTUAL TRENDS – NATIONAL CULTURE

Attachment to the Past

From the close of the sixteenth century the grand princes of Moscow, the consolidators of Russian territory, invoked the traditional connection with the kingdom of Kiev. Overlooking the interim of feudal dispersion and anarchy, they not only maintained, less accurately than artfully, the power that had been handed down to them in unbroken succession; they extended the limits of that power beyond their own borders, proclaiming themselves the heirs to the imperial glories of Byzantium, now in Turkish hands. The *Tale of the Princes of Vladimir* (early sixteenth century), which establishes the direct descent of the Rurik dynasty from Augustus Caesar, tells of Vladimir Monomakh receiving the symbolic attributes of sovereignty from the last Byzantine emperor. And the abbot of the Eleazar monastery in Pskov promulgated the notion of 'Moscow, the third Rome', the previous two being Rome and Byzantium. But the religious aspect of these claims, which made Moscow the centre of the Orthodox faith, was merely window-dressing. Not so the revival of the traditional link with Kiev, which gave the grand princes of Moscow a pretext for claiming lands now forming part of the combined kingdom of Poland and Lithuania. History and legend are interwoven in the chronicles of the time, all of which are inspired by the thirst for continuity which is expressed in the *Book of Degrees*.

Religious Trends. Frustrated Heresies

The creation of a centralized state, uniting territories which had existed separately during the period of political fragmentation, and each of which had developed in its own way round its own principal city, brought with it an incipient unification of cultural elements, which from now on were shaped and co-ordinated by the overriding conception, and the existence, present and prospective, of Muscovite Russia. Regional originality gave way; uniformity in literary and artistic styles and themes gradually took its place. Above all, the extension of sovereign authority stimulated political awareness. The relationship of the tsar to the other holders (lay or ecclesiastical) of power and prestige in the kingdom; the nature of power; the role of the Church; the place of the various groups and classes within the state – as early as the end of the fifteenth century and more particularly in the sixteenth, reflection on all these crucial points was manifested in literary works which were deeply engaged with contemporary realities, and whose authors were not exclusively members of the clergy.

The Church, as a wealthy landowning body closely linked with the secular power, was in intimate and active contact with secular life, to the detriment of its own unity. There was no rigid isolation about the Orthodox clergy; they were militant in every sense of the term. And they were divided by bitter controversies, in which two main trends stand out. Joseph (of Volotsk) (1439–1515), abbot of the monastery of Volokolamsk, was the leading figure of the so-called Josephist school, which defended the Church's political powers and the wealth of the monasteries and, while remaining comparatively independent of the state, was prepared to foster the state's authority just in so far as the Church could count on state backing. In his *Instruction*, Joseph of Volotsk enjoined fear of God, detestation of heretics and absolute submission to the ecclesiastical hierarchy; he and his disciples, such as the Metropolitan Daniel (1552–9), were responsible for the 'cold and austere ritualism' (L. Behr-Siegel) against which a section of the Church was in revolt in the seventeenth century. At the same time, though their general tendency was to support the actions of the throne, they were a state within the state; they constituted that official Church, at once rigorous and adaptable, vigilantly aware of political realities, whose power was broken two centuries later by Peter the Great.

A very different position was assumed by the monastic clergy on the state's eastern borders, in those recently conquered regions where the monks, far from Moscow, lived under precarious and sometimes dangerous conditions. The monasteries beyond the Volga represented the real religious life of the time. The ascetic tendency, renunciation of this world's goods, an indulgent attitude to heretics, and some degree of mysticism, are expressed in the *Eight Thoughts*, and the *Letter to his Disciples on the Monastic Life*, of Nil Sorski (1433–1508), who represents the voice of isolated, rural monasticism: a religious element which was more or less cut off from ordinary life and had no great cultural influence, but which was better suited to the religious needs of the people. Despite its spiritual, unworldly quality, this element produced the practical energy of the *startsy* – wise, experienced monks, friendly, confidence-inspiring, who counselled those in perplexity and even emerged from seclusion to intervene in public affairs, sometimes at the risk of their lives.

Various heretical offshoots from orthodox doctrine were sternly opposed by the official Church. Their main breeding-ground was the Novgorod region, which had been incorporated in the Muscovite state in 1478, and whose economic and social decline precipitated a condition of crisis in which the flagrant wealth of the Church, and its connections with the central power, provoked the antagonism of two sects, the *strigolniki* and the 'Judaizers'. They adopted an extreme position, denying Christ's divinity and the mysteries (as the sacraments are called in the Eastern Church); driven at once by material anxieties and a craving for religious purity and simplicity, they withdrew their recognition from the ecclesiastical hierarchy and turned to the sovereign (regarding him not as hostile but as having been led astray by bad advisers) to protect the poor and humble against the landowners. In a recently integrated and still suspect part of the country, they represented a danger to the social and political order; they were condemned and punished in the early years of the sixteenth century. But the underlying causes of heresy remained untouched, producing sectarian trends whose development inside the official Church went on for the next two centuries.

National Culture

It was not only by foreigners – Greeks and South Slavs – that external influences were introduced into Muscovy. By the end of the fourteenth century the Russians already had numerous colonies of monks in Constantinople and on Mount Athos, who copied Greek manuscripts and formed a permanent link between Russia and the Byzantine empire. Literary culture was powered for the most part by religion and history, and its centres, dating back beyond the Mongol conquest to the glorious Kievan past, were no longer Novgorod and Pskov alone; the monasteries of Tver, Rostov, Vladimir, Suzdal and Moscow had joined in the work. In Moscow, with the support of a secular power which, in the second half of the fifteenth century, laid claim to the mantle of Byzantium after that city had fallen to the Turks, archives were accumulated, and libraries of ancient manuscripts were set up in which Greek and Roman antiquity were strongly represented. The grand prince's library was remarkably rich; but so were those of the monasteries of the Trinity and St Sergius, of the Solovki Islands, of St Cyril at Bieloozero, and of Volokolamsk. In addition to religious works they contained historical narratives in which it is often hard to disentangle the materials contributed by older chronicles, now no longer extant, from the imagination of the copyists, who quite consciously strove to glorify the Russian past.

The twin preoccupations of cultivated people in the sixteenth century, in whose eyes the practice of religion and the exercise of political functions were inseparably connected, were the problem of power and the validity or otherwise of doctrinal texts. Hence when Maxim the Greek, a monk from Mount Athos who came to Russia in 1528, attacked the overdue task of correcting some of the Russian devotional literature, he encountered strong opposition from the 'Josephists'; accused of discrediting the Russian saints, he was condemned by a council held in 1531 and died in sequestration at the monastery of the Trinity and St Sergius.

These preoccupations were of course confined to a minority, the highest circles in Church and state, who in many instances were the same people. They reflect a genuine spiritual life, and a lively political awareness, on the part of administrators both secular and ecclesiastical.

This is not to say, however, that those circles had a monopoly of education; sixteenth-century Russia was less barbarous that its western contemporaries believed. Monasteries had their schools, in most of which, admittedly, the young were taught to do little more than pick their way through the Gospels. Not many people received this elementary education; and only a certain proportion of the monks, and a few boyars, went on to anything more advanced. It has been calculated (but the figures are by no means certain) that in the region of Moscow at the beginning of the sixteenth century, 65% of the landowners could read and write, and from 25% to 30% of the inhabitants of the *posad*. The peasant was of course illiterate, and remained so unless he took holy orders. It is reasonable to assume that the proliferation of towns in the sixteenth century caused an increase in education; new administrative needs, greater commercial activity, and increasing contact with the West, made it imperative to have people who could write, do simple calculations, and speak foreign languages. The political unification of the Russian lands, and the conquest of new territories in the east, both of which made new demands on the administration, called for larger numbers of 'geometers' and 'calculators' (*arifmetiki*) and increased the Russian's practical knowledge of the ever more extensive area controlled by successive grand princes. Correspondingly, the rudiments of practical science can be seen in the chronological tables fixing the date of Easter for a century at a time, and in the medical treatises listing the symptoms of certain diseases and the specific virtues of plants.

Outside the ranks of the clergy there were not many educated people. The correspondence between Ivan the Terrible, 'a thinker and writer' as Pierre Pascal justly calls him, and his renegade vassal Prince Kurbsky, stands out as a rather unusual phenomenon – a set of remarkable letters exchanged between 1564 and 1579, which express the conflict between authority's centralizing trend and the forces of conservatism represented by the boyars. Nevertheless the sixteenth century produced considerable progress in this respect, for it was then that education and culture began eluding the Church's monopoly and acquiring a secular tinge. The extremely harsh struggle which, in Ivan the Terrible's reign, went on between the landlords on one hand and the peasants and the poorer townsfolk on the other, and the conflict between the old and the new boyar aristocracy, generated a literature of fierce political polemic which the art of printing, still in its infancy, was capable of diffusing only on a small scale.

Ivan Semenovitch Peresvietov (mid-sixteenth century) is the most remarkable representative of secularized political thought. He constructs a theory of absolute monarchy, which he compares with the political system of the Ottoman empire (interpreted very much in his own way) and that of the fallen empire of Byzantium, and allows the reader to infer certain allusions to the tsar and the boyars; and he does all this without invoking literary precedents or the authority of the fathers of the Church. He was the first of the 'publicists' who, under each tsar in turn, used the power of the pen to reinforce the royal authority. His tendency is thus in line with that of the 'Josephist' clergy and their leader, the Metropolitan Macarius (*c.* 1482–*c.* 1563), who held all the influential positions in the Church in the time of Ivan the Terrible.

The growth of the grand princes' power at the expense of the boyars, and their role in the defence of the Orthodox faith, are echoed in legends such as the *Tale of Peter and Febron of Murom* (Peter and Febron were the tutelary saints of the princes of Muscovy from the time of Ivan III). But opposition to that power, or at least resentment of their victorious undertakings, also acted as a source of literary creation; certain stories composed in Novgorod and Pskov, for example, express the pride and bitterness of an aristocracy who had been brought low but remained aware of the part played by their cities in the advancement of civilization.

It was at the instigation of Macarius, in about 1562, that his successor Athanasius put the finishing touches to the *Book of Degrees*, a genealogy of the Russian princes from Vladimir to Ivan IV, displaying the continuous development of the state from the tenth century to the sixteenth, and glorifying the close collaboration of the Church and the royal line in their common political task.

This militant clergy had its own manual of conduct and policy, which remains a valuable source of information on Russian society of that time: the *Stoglav* or 'Hundred Chapters', consisting of decisions taken at the Council of 1551, and defining the relationship between Church and state. This was the Russian Church's golden age, in which the religious ideal was identified with the national principle (*Danzas*). But it was also the period in which the expression of that principle ceased to be the exclusive privilege of an educated clergy.

Meanwhile the great, motley mass of the Russian people themselves lived unconscious of these ideological currents, on which their own future destiny depended. The mere fact of knowing the three Rs was not enough to elevate anyone to these lofty levels of discussion. It is true that the rich and the humble, though divided by conflicting interests on the material plane, were brought together in apparent community of feeling in church, where the faithful, standing, participated in those long ceremonious services whose hypnotically beautiful ritual made brilliant use of spectacle and music. But the people had a literaure and music of their own; professional reciters of *byliny*, gipsy singers and musicians, and dancers, mimes and puppet showmen, travelled from village to village bringing joy to the heart, and pleasure to the eye and ear, without the threat of eternal punishment. All these were under the darkest suspicion from the Church, which held profane music to be an art of the devil and did everything possible to suppress it. As early as the thirteenth century, Archbishop Kiril and the Archimandrite Serapion regarded the Tatar invasions as a visitation of divine wrath upon the Russians for their excessive love of music; and profane music was condemned by Article 92 of the *Stoglav*. A by-product of the need to combat its attractions was the magnificent development of church music which began in the sixteenth century.

Kiev's Contribution

The cossack-dominated Ukraine was united with Moscow in 1654, but this change produced smaller consequences than it might have done: war between the Poles and Russians ended in a partition of the Ukraine under the truce of Andrussovo (1667), confirmed by the 'perpetual peace' concluded in 1681. Poland renounced her claims to the left bank of the Dnieper and to the district of Kiev. Henceforward the intellectual capital of the East Slavs, with its ecclesiastical Academy in which Latin was the official language, and which had supplied Moscow with educated priests, no longer enjoyed the independence it had derived from its extra-territorial position. Simultaneously, the schism of the Old Believers had pushed the Orthodox

Church in Moscow into setting up a system of higher education of its own; this undertaking involved a clash between the partisans of Greek and those of Latin; and beyond the dispute about the learned languages lay a wider conflict, that between minds already receptive to western influences, and the majority, who feared those influences as a danger to Orthodoxy. The Academy founded in Moscow in 1687 used all three languages, Greek, Latin and Slavonic, but this show of harmony was merely a gesture. During its early years the Academy was not so much a training-school for theologians as an office from which a rigorous censorship was imposed on foreign books of Catholic, Lutheran or Calvinist inspiration.

Kiev retained its religious role in the newly enlarged state of Muscovy, which was still very short of schools and, in this respect, played second fiddle to the Poles, Serbs and Bulgars.

Time-lag in the Sciences

Russia's progress in the seventeenth century was real but slow, and she lagged grievously behind the West. The advance of knowledge was hampered by three factors: shortage of educated men; economic backwardness; and the Church's rooted aversion to any sort of novelty. Recent experiments and scientific discoveries remained unknown; in this sector, Russia was still living on the intellectual capital of medieval Europe. Her notions of natural history, medicine and pharmacology were still drawn from archaic compositions of Byzantine origin. History was represented by a manual of universal history, *The Chronographer*, written in the Balkans in the sixteenth century and subsequently adapted to Russian needs. On the credit side, decimal calculation was rendered possible by the adoption of Arabic numerals in the second half of the seventeenth century; and Mercator's *Geography* was translated in 1630.

But the principal tool of culture – the officially consecrated language of scholarship and the upper classes – was still Old Slavonic, slightly modified. Its rules were established by Smotricky's grammar (1619), reprinted in Moscow from 1648 onwards. Slavonic was a barrier to progress; the proper literary medium of human activity was not this artificial idiom but the language of the bureaucrats in the *prikazy*, self-educated men of culture such as Pososhkov, the language of priests who had remained close to the people, like Father Avvakum – the language of Moscow, which was to acquire its characteristic stamp about a century later.

Birth of the Theatre

After the death of Alexis Mikhailovitch, who beguiled his leisure with falconry and unfortunate attempts to grow southern crops on his estate at Ismailovo, court circles became more interested in enjoying themselves; in 1673 a new entertainment was born, the theatre, firmly confined to Biblical subjects by the Church, but enlivened by burlesque interludes in which the instinctive side of human nature was let loose.

III THE CHURCH IN THE SEVENTEENTH CENTURY

Power of the Church

To the humblest people as to the most powerful, the Church perennially offered its multiple vision of life: inspiring fear of authority and respect for the established order by its depiction of eternal punishment; admiration, by its splendid and moving ceremonies; and heartfelt devotion by representations of the Virgin's gentle, tender face. Painted icons, however, cost more than the common people could afford; the peasants set up iconostases in their homes by decorating one corner of a room with small religious prints which were disfigured by the smoke and flies and periodically replaced from the market or a pedlar's pack. Grouped round the Virgin were patron saints, to whom the protection of domestic animals and the harvest was entrusted. The efficacy attributed by popular superstition to these naive depictions, the liberties taken by their artists in the interpretation of the Gospels, and, worst of all, their imitation of western iconography, rendered them suspect in the eyes of the Church. But this type of art, which flourished without interference until the time of Peter the Great, frequently displayed qualities of poetic fantasy which had almost entirely disappeared from the authorized icons, which had degenerated into lifeless echoes of Byzantine prototypes; in the seventeenth century the Church had prescribed a repertory of stock patterns, from which artists were not permitted to deviate; the art of the icon was paralysed. With the spread of the printing-press, the peasants acquired more and more of these popular devotional pictures, which the retailers and pedlars bought at the five annual fairs of Kholui, in the Shuia-Vladimir district.

At no time was the Church possessed of greater privileges, or more closely involved in the lives of the people, than in the seventeenth century. It not only dominated the country's spiritual and intellectual life but, through the monasteries, played an important part in economic life as well. It has been estimated that in the seventeenth century the two branches of the clergy owned two thirds of Russian territory. The Church owned 118,000 buildings (83,000 of which were monastic property). It must of course be remembered that monasteries, as distinct from churches, were forts; like our western castles, they were essential to the framework of public authority; hence they were specially vulnerable to the vicissitudes of conflict, as well as to natural calamities. About two thousand monasteries were in existence in the seventeenth century; more than a thousand of them disappeared as a result of fires, epidemics and the disasters of war. During the eighteenth century the number remained steady at about a thousand. Many of them possessed only a little land. But the biggest owned vast estates, populated by serfs, and did a long-distance trade in wheat and salt, untaxed by the tsar. The monastery of Volokolamsk sold an average of 60,000 puds of wheat per year; that of Solovki, 130,000 puds of salt. The monasteries enjoyed this favourable treatment until the time of Peter the

Great, and though their property stopped increasing from the middle of the seventeenth century, and their privileges were reduced, they remained one of the key factors in agricultural and commercial life: in 1762, Russia's 921 monasteries owned more than 800,000 serfs, slightly over 100,000 of whom were attached to a single monastery, that of the Trinity of St Sergius at Zagorsk.

FIGURE 23 Church of the Saviour, in the Kremlin, after an eighteenth-century engraving.

In the villages, the priest was often the only person who could read and write; and because he was indispensable as an intermediary between the rural community and the local representatives of the central authority, he enjoyed great importance. Even if he lived like the peasants, crushed by the weight of a large family and wretchedly poor, and even if he was a drunkard into the bargain, he was feared and respected. Contempt of the villagers for their priest is a late phenomenon, occurring first in the eighteenth century. When education, struggling slowly ahead, had progressed far enough to produce a few peasants in each community who were able to read and write a little, the parish priest became a slightly less important figure, especially as these literate peasants (*gramatnye*) mostly belonged to heretical sects, on the fringe of the established church, such as the Old Believers. And the spiritual influence of the priests on the faithful was never as great as that of the monasteries. Moreover, in spite of the general conversion of the country to Christianity, many pagan features, and in some cases actual pagan worship, survived. Macarius, Archbishop of Novgorod, complained in 1533 that in his district the old idols were still worshipped and that secret sacrifices were offered in the forests to the *russalkas* and woodland deities. The *Stoglav* (1551) mentions the persistence of pagan customs.

The fifteenth, sixteenth and seventeenth centuries were the period when the Church covered the country with a denser network of churches and monasteries and brought the struggle against paganism to a victorious conclusion.

By the time the Church was rocked by the schism of the Old Believers witch-burning had almost become a thing of the past. The priests were active everywhere and churches were being built in considerable numbers, especially in the towns. At the beginning of the seventeenth century Moscow had 400 churches for a population of 17,000 households (say 60,000–70,000 inhabitants). It has been estimated that by the end of that century there were 20,000 churches in all Russia, an average of one church to every 20 or 25 households (say 100 people) in the oldest towns, one to every 40 or 50 households in the newer towns, and one to every 50 or 100 households in the countryside. The only places which more or less eluded clerical influence were the isolated villages in the almost uninhabited regions of the north and north-east, into which the priests found it as difficult to make their way as the tax-gatherers, and where some very curious varieties of heresy developed in the eighteenth century.

A Great Schism

There was no Reformation in Russia. But the country was split in the seventeenth century by a schism which was just as deep and momentous in its own way, and which removed from the established church, and therefore from full allegiance to the centralized secular authority, an enormous mass of believers whose numbers cannot be precisely estimated but who, until the Revolution of 1917, constituted a kind of latent resistance movement. The schism of the 'Old Believers', which has been penetratingly studied by Pierre Pascal, had its origin in purely religious factors going back to the Time of Troubles. At the accession of the Romanov dynasty, Russia's moral decadence, and the menace of 'western impiety' in the provinces bordering the combined Polish and Lithuanian kingdom, forced the Orthodox Church to set about its own regeneration in close concert with the programme of political reconstruction undertaken by the tsar.

This necessary movement of reform was divided into two trends. On the one hand stood the zealous champions of authority and regimentation: the proponents of a state religion, an official church, who felt no compunction in altering the well-loved customs of the faithful, and, in default of creating a Muscovite theocracy, were glad to compound with the government and society. The other party, concerned with moral perfection and lofty religious experience, were upholders of tradition; they had a purer conception of Christianity, a faith at once closer to the feelings of the masses and further from pragmatic realities; they were against any changes in the regular forms of worships, which for them were not merely an empty system of symbols but the expression of a truly Christian conception of life.

The two tendencies came into open conflict in 1653 with the clash between the archpriest Avvakum and the 'Friends of God' on the one hand – the champions of ascetic Christianity, as Pierre Pascal says – and, on the other, the new patriarch of Moscow, Nikon, who succeeded in getting

6

Avvakum exiled to Siberia in 1655. Nikon's resignation, Avvakum's return to Moscow (1664), and his final deportation in 1667 to Pustozersk where he was mutilated and buried alive in 1682, are the main episodes in a religious war which, after the Tsar had set the seal of his approval on the reform movements in 1664, was marked by the torture and execution of large numbers of those whose attachment to tradition caused them to be designated as the 'Old Believers'.

Meanwhile, by the labours of Kievan monks taking the Greek liturgy as their model, the service books of the Muscovite church were revised and its ritual modified. The substantial, important changes which reform introduced in Church organization were of less significance to the people than certain innovations which flew in the face of time-honoured customs. The ban on multiple prosterrations, and the new practice of crossing oneself with three fingers instead of two, elicited a stubborn passive resistance which the martyrdom of Avvakum merely served to strengthen.

The schism of the Old Believers (or Old Ritualists) was far from being just a monkish controversy. The religious struggle by which ecclesiastical circles were so distressingly agitated between 1653 and 1667 was not only a confrontation of two different Christian attitudes to life, the first realistic and politically-minded, visualizing religion in the framework of public affairs, and the second more idealistic and anarchial, tending to asceticism and even to a rejection of society. It was, rather, an aspect of the development of a modern state, in the special conditions of Russian political and social life. The crusading spirit which provided an intimate connection between government and Orthodoxy could continue to exist only if government became the junior partner. The growing supremacy of the secular power, with an army and a civil service to give it the necessary support, was incompatible with the creation of a Christian state of Muscovy such as was desired by the Friends of God. The Tsar took over Nikon's reforms for his own ends, seeking to curb both the Church and, through the Church, the people, who at that time were unusually full of unrest.

The reforms associated with Nikon's name, which caused such pain to all who lived in an atmosphere of daily piety, were in effect only one element among a number of measures taken about that time to deal with a situation which contained the threat of revolution. It is true that reform won the day during a breathing-space, the interim between the Moscow insurrection of 1662 and Stenka Razin's rebellion (1669–71), in neither of which can the influence of the Old Believers be discerned. But resistance to reform undoubtedly owed some of its strength to the disturbed condition of the country. It cannot be said that opposition to the centralizing policy of the government, or to the oppression of the peasants by the nobles, actually caused the schism (*raskol*); but it was the reason why the schism went so deep and spread so widely.

The raskol was political opposition in a disguised, unconscious form. It took root and spread not only in the middle Volga districts which were Avvakum's home country, but also in the frontier regions of the south and east, where the Old Believers were either given refuge from government persecution by the Cossacks, or were tolerated because they were the only available colonists. Avvakum counselled retreat to the 'desert' for religious reasons, a retreat extolled by him thus:

> As it is written by the son of Basil,
> Our venerable father Ephraim:
> Fly, my dear ones,
> Into the black woods;
> Take refuge, my dear ones,
> In the mountains and the caves;
> Hide, my dear ones,
> In the depths of the earth.
> Ah, if someone would but build me
> A cell in the heart of the woods,
> Where no man went
> And no bird flew;
> Where only thou, O Christ, wouldst dwell
> For the good of our souls;
> And where I would no longer see
> All the scandal of this world.

But in the forests of the Urals and Siberia, on the tundras of the Pomorye and the steppes of the south, the 'desert' also offered a means of escape from the exactions of the state and the landlords, from the necessity of getting a passport for any journey, from military recruiting, and from priestly pressure and 'exhortations' (Pierre Pascal). It meant a return to freedom, for the time being at least, freedom from the order imposed by authority both civil and ecclesiastic. The schism therefore swelled the flow of migration which was helping to extend Slav civilization in the direction of Asia.

The schism did not cut the Church in two, but it placed a significant fraction of Russia's population beyond the bounds of the official Church (it has been estimated that there were several million Old Believers at the beginning of the twentieth century); it caused new sects to proliferate, and the more remote the regions in which these flourished the greater was their deviation from orthodoxy. It was difficult to maintain an ecclesiastical hierarchy outside the Church, and many of the Old Believers accordingly dispensed with priests; hence the division of the schismatics into *popovtsy* and *bezpopovtsy* ('priestless'). Others fell into aberrant varieties of faith which arose spontaneously through isolation from the established religious centres. But these strange, picturesque sects had no effective significance.

What really was significant, for Russia's economic as well as her religious future, was the groups of Old Believers who remained within the Christian fold and settled firmly in the middle Volga districts and the new areas of colonization, and showed in the maintenance of their own way of life that solidarity which is found only among persecuted minorities. A high moral level prevailed in these closely knit communities, which in this respect were often superior to the Orthodox majority. Moreover, the necessity of defending the faith demanded a higher level of education. And everyone prospered all the more in his day-to-day activities through being able to count on community support. Regarded with suspicion, yet tolerated on the whole, the Old Believers were to play a prominent part in Russia's development and progress. It was they who in the eighteenth century constituted the well-to-do peasantry of the Volga lands, practising every kind of rural industry, and who, in the factories of the Ural region, became overseers renowned for their strictness and attention to duty. In the nineteenth century it was from the upper ranks of their peasantry that most of the textile manufacturers, bankers and business men were drawn. The greater part of the people had been permanently forced into a comparatively passive condition; the Old Believers – the Puritans of Orthodoxy – were an active principle, a dynamic progressive force.

The conflict which thus relegated a substantial minority to a position of fruitful obscurity produced different results on the national level. The whole reform movement, the endeavour to regenerate the Church and effect a widespread moral improvement, was carried on both by the Friends of God and by Nikon and his partisans in a spirit of hostility to western influences, and was the religious side of a general reaction against foreigners. The discriminatory measures adopted during Nikon's patriarchate affected foreigners living in Moscow and were welcomed by the Muscovite merchants — a case of religion coming to the aid of commerce. Men had to grow beards, which were officially proclaimed to be a mark of Russian nationality. The conservation of old traditions, representing a conscious reliance on the past – a temporary withdrawal, incompatible with economic progress – was a symbolic weapon against foreign competition and the growing participation of foreigners in the life of the capital. This narrow nationalism, echoed in the reign of Peter the Great by the writings of Pososhkov, who recommended closing Russia to the outside world, was a characteristic reaction by a country rendered vulnerable by its backwardness, a reaction which had already manifested itself in the mercantilism of Alexis Mikhailovitch.

Book Three

MODERN STATES
1700–1860

7

The Dawn of Capitalism
in Russia

RUSSIA was now equipped with all the attributes of power; and she had resumed her contact with the West. With Asia behind her like a bastion, she both learned all she could from Europe and intervened actively in European affairs yet remained, with her traditional customs and institutions, apart and alone. The earliest forms of capitalism were different in Russia from what they were elsewhere. Russia was a country of contrasts: a modern state yet retarded, lingering in the past; civilized, ignorant; authoritarian, anarchic; and obscurely agitated by demands for essential reforms.

I NOVEL ACHIEVEMENT AND OBJECTIVES

Creative Practicality: Peter the Great

Superficially westernized, but in everything else, including this excesses, thoroughly Russian in character and temperament, Peter the Great inaugurated a thoroughly novel period in Russian history. His reforms were not unique in themselves; many of them had been tried, or toyed with, or merely planned on paper, before his time. What was unprecedented was that he pushed them through, overcoming not only the natural obstacles but the human ones – the passivity of a people for the most part ignorant and superstitious, and the resistance of the upper classes, whose habits he disturbed and whose traditions he despised. He was in fact a highly untraditional person, this cleanshaven, pipe-smoking tsar who wore German clothes and insisted on imposing the most sophisticated refinements of the western courts on his reluctant entourage.

Yet it would be a mistake to imagine that his spectacular break with the past, this surface adhesion to foreign ways which were adopted perforce by those about him but hardly at all in the country at large, put him out of touch with the people. What makes him such a distinctive figure is precisely the way he chose to govern: his personal, day-to-day contact with his subjects. Alexis Mikhailovitch had harangued the people of Moscow in the Red Square; Peter mixed with them. He was less interested in men themselves than in what they did, their crafts or professions; but he was always ready to put his hand to the job himself, and this brought him close to them. He was good with his hands and prodigal of his energy; he learnt the rudiments of innumerable trades and would often intervene in the enterprises he himself had instigated, lending a hand, even taking charge if necessary. He would go to any amount of trouble and cared nothing for danger. He was a man of familiar manners, a tsar who imposed his remorseless will directly, with little regard for the underdog, and who was admired as well as feared.

He was the opposite of an intellectual; less cultivated than Ivan the Terrible or Alexis Mikhailovitch; a practical man, who got things done; terrifyingly dynamic, a bit muddled, but a force of nature – always in a hurry to see the job through and get on to the next one, incapable of long-range imaginative vision but full of plans, full of curiosity, pouring out quick and sometimes contradictory decisions, and implacably determined. He was a tsar of reform, and his administrative and economic achievements, most of which remained effective for over a century, laid the foundations of modern Russia.

But despite invading every sphere of action, this dictatorial tsar was none the less a servant of the state. His decisions rode roughshod over everyone and seemed arbitrary; but they were conceived in the public interest (which, it is true, was identified with that of the upper classes) and were not imposed without explanation. This was the new, original feature of Peter's rule: he sought to justify himself in the country's eyes; he appealed to his subjects' goodwill, patriotism and zeal for work. In so far as this self-justification was propaganda, intended to popularize the régime, it can be accounted for by the difficulties and resistances Peter had to overcome, of which there were plenty, and by his desire for a glorious name; he had plenty of that, too. Thus, for example, the appearance of the first Russian newspaper, the *Viedomosti* ('News'), in 1703, kept a small but influential public informed of the progress of the war and the activities of the bureaucracy. The same trend is apparent in the treatises and addresses of Feofan Prokopovitch (1681–1736), Archbishop of Novgorod, and of Shafirov, both of whom expounded the reasons for the Russo-Swedish war, and the writings of Saltykov, who was the spokesman for the interests of the nobility but also supplied theoretical arguments for the sovereign's mercantile policy. But behind these works of propaganda can be seen the growth of a larger conception, that of a state which was more important than its leaders, and exacted their dutiful service.

This political ideal, and the devotion aroused by Peter's character and zeal, permeated the bureaucracy, from the highest servants of the régime to the multitude of petty functionaries whom the state's increasing powers had made necessary. The military schools, and the various permanent councils created by Peter, contributed to the building up of a loyal and comparatively effective administration and a tradition of service from which his eighteenth-century successors were to benefit. The *pitomki*, his administrative protégés, were great administrators; some were Russianized foreigners, such as Osterman, who was in charge of foreign affairs, but there were also native-born Russians like Tatishtshev, whose functions were extremely varied and who was the very type of the cultivated noble with a passionate interest in Russian history. The state now possessed all the basic departments of administration, and although these were still dependent on foreign countries for some of their personnel, they were increasingly devoted to the national idea.

Peter, with his passion for reform, has often been taxed with steering Russia into paths which were not truly her own. He enlisted the services of foreigners, and enforced the imitation, at least by part of the governing class, of western styles, a trend especially visible in architecture and costume; and for this he has been accused of severing the government and the upper classes generally from the people. But the rift was only apparent, not real. The outlook of the boyars was perpetuated by the eighteenth-century nobles, and there was very little change in class relationships. 'Europeanization', in its external and visible aspects, was superficial; and its administrative applications in the army and government were not only highly beneficial but in many cases were simply earlier projects, of national origin, with a new look. The 'European' tendency neither destroyed tradition nor disrupted social unity. The Slavophils, who depreciated the achievements of the enlightened rulers of the Russian eighteenth century, have portrayed Peter the Great as the destroyer of an old and better order which is supposed to have been more in tune with the psychology of the Russian people. But this is illusory; there was no such golden age. The seventeenth-century boyar was no closer to the moujik than was the landowning noble of the next century. Both lived in a world the peasant could never enter; feudal privilege made it impossible for him to acquire land and the means of production. All that Peter the Great's measures did with regard to this situation was to harness the ancient social structure to the service of a modernized state.

No side of life escaped Peter's exuberant, all-embracing attention. As soon as the danger from Sweden had been liquidated by the victory at Poltava (1709), he embarked on a series of administrative measures which was interrupted only by his death (1725). The provincial governments were organized systematically for the first time; regulations were introduced for the management of the army and navy; a census of the peasants was attempted for the first time to facilitate regular collection of the poll tax; a hierarchy of grades and functions (the Table of Ranks, 1722) laid down the services the nobility were to render to the state in return for their privileges; and the government acquired power over the Church, which lost its patriarch and was ruled thereafter by a Holy Synod which took its directives from the tsar. All these measures were aimed at strengthening the state and subordinating the economic and spiritual power of the nobility and clergy, the power which held the people in perfect subjection. And they were only one part of a manifold, detailed, fruitful lifetime of activities whose scope also included industrial development, monetary

6*

policy (Russia now had a single currency for the first time), and public education (military schools were established, and a system of elementary education was initiated paralleling that already provided by the clergy). On the day he died, Peter the Great signed the decree for the creation of the Academy of Sciences.

Peter's outstanding achievement was that he brought into being the essential administrative mechanisms of a modern state and found people to run them. It is hardly surprising that his efforts in this direction remained incomplete. The prevailing ignorance made it difficult to recruit state servants. Outside the military schools, education was almost non-existent: in 1725, the total number of pupils in the diocesan schools of the clergy was only 3,000 (and half the available teachers were concentrated in the region of Kiev); the government-created schools under lay auspices had barely 2,000 pupils in 1722, and the number went down in the following years. The idea of universal, popular, national education was born during that period, but started coming into practice only at the end of the century. Consequently foreigners (including some from the Baltic cities, newly annexed after Russia's victories over Sweden) played an important part in the administration. But they had no influence on the shaping of policy; that was dictated by the government. Moreover, the situation was gradually altered under Peter the Great's successors; the reaction of 1740 against 'the reign of the Germans' demonstrated the vigour of a genuinely Russian bureaucracy which, in that cosmopolitan century, limited foreign collaboration to the minimum.

The Reign of Bluff: Catherine II

Catherine II, who was of foreign descent but rapidly became thoroughly Russian, ruled over a powerful empire to whose fundamental strength she herself contributed little. Her reputation was spread throughout Europe by the French *philosophes*, who were stuffed with illusions and lavished unbridled praise on her as 'the Semiramis of the north'. But what they said and what she did were two different things. Her success consisted of reaping where her predecessors had sown. A symbol of a long-standing debt, recognized by her, was the statue of Peter the Great which she ordered to be erected on the bank of the Neva, and which inspired Pushkin to write his *Bronze Horseman*:

> Erect beside the lonely waters,
> His mind full of great thoughts,
> He gazes into the distance . . .

When Catherine mounted the throne as a result of Peter II's assassination, Russia gave her all the assets which enabled her to become a glorious sovereign – an army which had recently camped in Berlin, and some of whose leaders were subsequently to distinguish themselves in fighting the Turks abroad and revolutionaries at home; an administration imbued with Peter the Great's devotion to Russian development and prestige; a powerful metallurgical industry, which had made new strides in Elizabeth's reign; a busy flow of trade, in both directions, with the western countries; and a strong diplomatic position.

Over the next quarter of a century, Catherine consolidated this inherited situation. Her statesmanship, unoriginal but adroit and opportunist, followed the directions imposed by the pressures of the dominant classes and dictated by her own alert awareness of her popularity. There were no sweeping decisions or profound creative changes; just a combination of liberal gestures and skilful accommodation. Her policy at home was compounded of adjustments, tactful manoeuvres and more than a dash of hypocrisy. Many of Peter's measures, taken in haste, had fallen by the wayside; under Catherine this teeming, fertile disorder was replaced by prudence, deliberation and bluff. It was typical of her to condemn the confiscation of ecclesiastical estates which had been started by her predecessor, and to go on confiscating them.

In 1767, with a view to establishing a new legal code, she assembled a commission which was reasonably representative of all ranks in society; but though she accepted the lists of grievances drawn up by this body she took notice of its deliberations only in so far as they coincided with her own opinions, which were far from liberal. The commission's work paved the way for the administrative measures of 1775, by which the provincial governments were reorganized, and those of 1785, which reaffirmed the privileges of the aristocracy (Charter to the Nobility) and gave statutes to the towns (Charter to the Towns). But the edifice of serfdom was left as firm as ever; and, though the spread of industry was increasing the number of serfs who, with or without permission, went off to work in factories, a tendency which weakened their owners' hold upon their lives, the new measures gave the owners greater statutory powers over their peasants. Catherine II's reign would appear to constitute a defensive reaction by an aristocratic society bent on preserving an unjustifiable system.

Catherine's educational policy, which resuscitated former plans for public education dispensed by the state, and which was inspired by the example of Austrian school organization, eventually produced only some three hundred popular schools for the people. The nobles had their own educational institutions, like the Smolny Institute for girls, founded in St Petersburg in 1764. In this field as in others, the empress's achievements were unoriginal, falling far short of the schemes for educational reform by which she appeared to be so greatly preoccupied. Her favourite, Potemkin, is remembered among other things for the villages he 'created' for her during her journey to the Crimea in 1787, his intention being to give the illusion of a Ukraine abundantly inhabited by prosperous peasants. Publicity sometimes fashions unmerited reputations; and Catherine's entourage was efficient. The glories of her reign were really due to the remarkable progress achieved by the country over a period of threequarters of a century.

II BROADER SOCIAL AND ECONOMIC FOUNDATIONS

Development of Trade and Transport
Russia's territorial immensity still consisted, in the eighteenth century, of isolated, loosely connected regions; but the trade routes running through them were becoming steadily busier, and the seas at which the routes terminated were free. Peter the Great's conquest of the Baltic coasts, and his creation of St Petersburg, turned the once glorious cities of Novgorod and Pskov into second-rate provincial trading towns. The heart of Muscovy was directly connected with the Gulf of Finland by water, after the construction of the Vyshnevolotsky Canal (1706–30) and the lateral canal skirting Lake Ladoga (map 15); used only in the south-to-north direction this artery had as its main function, until the end of the century, the transport of the slow-moving consignments of iron which were produced in the Urals and travelled by way of St Petersburg to the workshops of England. Farther east, two canal-systems linked the Volga with the Baltic, the Mariinsky (1798–1810) and the Tikhvin Canal (1802–12). Other canals were built during the same period, from the West Duna and Niemen to the North Duna, and in the Dnieper basin. Goods circulated more freely as a result; people and ideas did not. Roads would have been needed for that; they were cruelly lacking in eastern Europe, whereas the West at that time was developing a magnificent road network, subsequently extended by Napoleon's conquests.

The lack of roads, a Soviet author has written, has been the curse of Russia, exerting a negative influence not only on her trade but also on her culture. The majestic barges laden with charcoal (figure 24), corn or iron, which, except when held in check by the winter ice, floated down the rivers or were hauled up them by the *burlaki*, and which docked at the Neva quays, did not transport couriers and mail, or government orders, or books. On tracks which were dusty in summer, and unusable during the spring thaw, horses provided speedy transport only in winter, and even then not always safely.

Siberia was several months distant from Moscow by combined road and water transport; the newly created frontier town of Kiakhta, on the Mongolian border, was made the compulsory terminal for trade with China; but tea, which was becoming the Russians' customary drink in the eighteenth century, did not travel only by this route – it was easier to import it from England, via St Petersburg.

It was in the nineteenth century that tea-drinking became really widespread in Russia. Their first acquaintance with what is now one of their national drinks is said to have resulted from chance. In 1638 the khan of Mongolia presented a hundred pounds or so of tea to a Russian embassy, who apparently did not find this new drink much to their liking; but not wishing to offend the khan they took it back to Moscow. It was tried and relished there, and its use caught on at court and among some of the boyars.

The first commercial imports of tea were made by buying it from the Dutch and shipping via Arkhangelsk and later St Petersburg; the quantities were very small. Commercial relations with China, which were irregular at first, did not begin until later, after the treaty of Nerchinsk in 1689 and more especially the foundation of the frontier-post at Kiakhta in 1728, through which all trade between China and Russia had to be conducted (map 12).

FIGURE 24 Barge carrying charcoal to the forges of the Ural region.

Imports of tea were still under 500 tons at the end of the eighteenth century and the maritime route remained important (because it was easier and cheaper) at least until 1822, at which date the government banned it in order to encourage trade through Kiakhta, through which 8,000 tons of tea passed in 1862. In the latter year the ban was lifted. The opening of five Chinese ports to the Russians in 1858, that of the Suez Canal in 1869, and the development of Russia's commercial fleet towards 1880, took most of the profit out of the Siberian route, though tea imports along it were revived by the building of the Trans-Siberian railway: in 1896 Russia imported 50,000 tons of China tea in addition to what she got from Ceylon and Japan. Tea had become the everyday drink of all the peoples of the empire; its use was made easier by the fact that every home possessed the traditional samovar (kettle constructed on a tubular plan, providing a

MAIN EXPORTS FROM ST PETERSBURG, 1752	
GOODS	VALUE (in roubles)
1 Iron (bars, anchors)	729,886
2 Copper	61,284
3 Russian leather	616,382
4 Various textiles	314,105
5 *Calemande* (coarse bleached broadcloth)	150,800
6 Sailcloth	167,040
7 Hemp	137,640
8 Ropes and cables	52,954
9 Flax	133,858
10 Hemp oil and linseed oil	105,290
11 Suet	131,997
12 Beeswax	129,311
13 Furs (ermine, hare, grey quirrel)	68,652
14 Silk	81,996
15 Hogs' bristles	57,082
16 Caviar	28,642
17 Saltpetre	13,992
	4,208,145[1]

SOURCE: *Dictionnaire universel* (Larousse), vol. v (*Commerce de Russie*)

[1] Out of a total of 4,353,696 roubles

constant supply of boiling water). Attempts had even been made, from 1833 onwards, to grow tea, near Echemiadzin (Armenia).

In the south, where the treaty of Kuchuk-Kainardji and the conquest of the Crimea gave the empire the north coast of the Black Sea, the increasing population and importance of the Ukraine caused the rise, from about 1800, of the port of Odessa – the chief outlet for Russian grain, and the point from which Russian influence now began to spread throughout the Mediterranean, from Constantinople to Marseille. But Ukrainian wheat was handicapped by high transport costs; it came down from the steppes in endless trains of wagons drawn by teams of oxen. Topography thwarted

Main Imports through St Petersburg, 1752

GOODS	VALUE (in roubles)
1 Cloth (fine, medium and ordinary)	507,590
2 Cloth for the troops	230,182
3 Velvet, taffeta, silk, etc.	420,566
4 Gold and silver braid, Spanish lace	106,867
5 Fashion accessories	412,202
6 Worsteds	156,683
7 Short-nap worsteds, etc.	209,727
8 Cotton fabrics (plain and printed)	138,060
9 Cambrai linen, muslin, etc.	67,178
10 Handkerchiefs (silk, cotton)	78,390
11 Lump sugar, candy sugar, etc.	255,196
12 French wines (red and white)	174,977
13 French brandy and liqueurs	56,487
14 Burgundy, champagne	115,982
15 English beer and cider	21,301
16 Herrings, hake, etc.	39,389
17 Tea, coffee, chocolate	50,782
18 Raisins, almonds	33,823
19 Ginger, pepper, cinnamon	28,027
20 Indigo, cochineal, etc.	96,562
21 Dyestuffs	43,606
22 Alum	18,916
23 Furniture, etc.	112,654
24 Tin (crude and finished)	94,448
	3,470,595[1]

SOURCE: *Dictionnaire universel*, loc. cit.

[1] Out of a total of 3,979,352 roubles.

NOTE: This list indicates only the range of goods passing through St Petersburg. The figures, based on customs dues, are misleadingly low.

the enterprise of its rulers, and the energy of its people, with natural obstacles which were defeated only by the coming of the railways in the second half of the nineteenth century.

Inadequate communications and transport greatly hampered Russia's economic growth precisely at the period when her increasingly close relations with the industrial countries of western Europe had fostered the introduction of modern methods, the development of new needs, and the more regular production of an export surplus. Moreover, industrial expansion in Britain, France and the German-speaking countries exerted an adverse bias on trade between Russia and the rest of Europe. From this point of view, Russia was less backward in the eighteenth century than in the first half of the nineteenth. In the former, she exported pig-iron as well as agricultural produce and a considerable quantity of finished products, such as Russian leather and various textiles (see the table on p. 154). A century later, in the period 1856–60, textiles and leather accounted for only a minute proportion (1·9%) of the total value of the country's export and wheat (35·1%) had usurped the position of iron. In overseas markets, the agricultural character of the Russian economy became increasingly evident by comparison with the already powerfully industrialized West.

The Century of Iron. A Great Industrial Region
Yet things had once been the other way round. Surprisingly, a region of heavy industry had developed in the Urals as early as the reign of Peter the Great; there was nothing to equal it anywhere in the world at the time. Operations were on a small scale at first, the sole purpose being to provide

FIGURE 25   Rolling mill in the Ural region, eighteenth century.

cannon for the army shortly to be launched against Sweden (1699). But the age-old practice of using wood as fuel for smelting was hard on timber supplies; production in the West was therefore limited; and for a century Russia, with Sweden, was the chief exporter of iron billets. The prosperity of the industrial centres in the Urals during the eighteenth century was based on the foreign rather than the home market, which, despite frequent wars, was not large (figures 25 and 26).

This industry did not arise spontaneously but was set up at the tsar's command in the lonely eastern forests, to which it was necessary at first to transport both equipment and workers, the latter being forcibly recruited among the ironworkers round Moscow and near Lake Onega. The foundation of the works at Neviansk (1699–1700), which were handed over to an ironmaster from Tula, Nikita Demidov, compulsorily transferred to the Urals, was the first step in a long process which completely changed the face of an enormous area measuring some five hundred miles from north to south by three hundred from east to west (map 10).

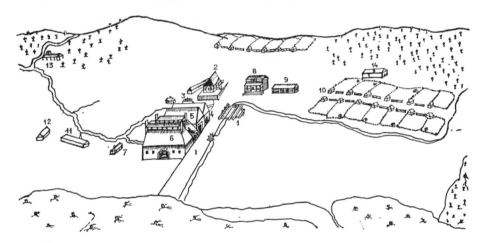

FIGURE 26 Works at Utkinsk in the Ural, belonging to Akinfi Demidov, in 1734
1 Dam. 2 Management and other offices. 3 Sawmill. 4 Ore intake, grading, crushing. 5 Blast furnaces (under construction in 1734). 6 Main forge (4 hammers). 7 Small forge. 8 Granary and timber store. 9 Main timber stocks. 10 Workers' houses and plots. 11 Ore stockpile. 12 Off-loading point for ore from mine. 13 Brickyard. 14 Workshop supplying bellows, tools, etc.

Demidov and the state between them started a whole network of establishments, of which there were about fifty by 1745 (thirty-five working iron, and nineteen copper). In the early days these works were sited on the rich banks of ore near the headwaters of the Tura and the Tagil, and there were always more of them in those districts than elsewhere; as the Urals became more populous and accessible, new establishments were built farther from the mines, from which the ore was sent to them by water. In 1735 the great landowners in that part of Russia, the Stroganov family, entered the industrial arena; and in the second half of the century industry spread to the south, where foundries – mostly copper – were set up by wealthy commoners and by nobles who were in favour with the government. By 1763 there were sixty-three establishments in the Urals (twelve of which worked both iron and copper); some of these were not single works but groups under single ownership, so the real figure must have been higher. Out of the total Russian production of 54,000 tons of iron in 1767, the Ural region provided 30,000 tons, two thirds of which was exported.

The transformation of the Urals by about a hundred small industrial centres, many of them scattered in outlying positions, must be reckoned not in terms of their number but of the busy life they engendered in the area. Industry created a special type of village: workers' settlements, consisting of rows of *isbas* on plots of ground which were granted to part of the labour force and had to be hacked out of the surrounding forest, in the immediate neighbourhood of the works and of the dam which supplied power. There was only one sizeable town, Ekaterinburg (the present day Sverdlovsk), named after the wife of Peter the Great; the site was chosen in 1721 by the director of the government factories in the region, V. N. Tatishtshev; construction was undertaken by his successor, de Hennin, in 1723. Industrial workers constituted the bulk of its population; and the government office for the administration of the Ural mines was set up there.

These villages were the focal points of the intense activity which now began spreading through the forests. The Ural establishments were not little workshops but up-to-date installations, whose output was high for the period. Those at Kushvinsky and Nizhni-Tagilsk produced over 3,000 tons of iron in 1766–7; even the smallest of them produced 300 tons or more.

PROMINENT IRONMASTERS IN THE URALS, 1777					
Ironmaster	Blast furnaces	Power hammers	Copper foundries	Foundry workers	Peasants enrolled for auxiliary services
Demidov family (24 works)	17	143	20	16,000	21,500
Yakovlev group (16 works)	11	92	5	7,900	13,000

They naturally required large quantities of wood. While relatively few workers were occupied in the establishment itself, running the blast furnaces, hammers and rolling-mills, thousands were busy outside to supply these few with raw materials: woodcutters, charcoal burners, and carters to transport charcoal and ore. The peasant population of the whole region was mobilized, working in *artels* on a job-contract basis, to keep the works going.

The Last Great Popular Revolt

As the foregoing details indicate, industry in the Urals was just as oppressive to the local peasantry, forcibly enlisted for these auxiliary services, as to the foundry workers themselves, who were hereditarily tied to the establishments. As industry spread southwards, it pushed the Bashkirs out of their agricultural and migratory areas, and they periodically rebelled in an attempt to throw back the tide of colonization. Apprehension lest the Bashkirs surround the foundry and massacre the Russians, and fear of the army and the tsar's police, kept the region fairly quiet. But the number of disturbances began rising in 1764; the workers went on strike or seized the foundries, and the enlisted peasants frequently deserted and fled to the Yaik, in Bashkir territory, where a feeling of class solidarity caused them to be tolerantly received by the tribesmen. The situation was such that when in 1773 the cossacks of the Yaik rose in revolt, what had begun as a local rebellion spread almost instantaneously to the whole of the southern Ural region, affecting a large number of foundries and sweeping beyond the Ural basin to the estates along the Volga.

Most of the central Ural establishments were frightened by the possibility of Bashkir attacks into organizing for self-defence; this limited the northward advance of Pugachev's forward detachments. Pugachev joined them after his defeat outside the walls of Orenburg and slipped away to the west, being deserted *en route* by the Bashkirs, who went home, and was accompanied thereafter only by a small body of Cossacks and workers. He appeared outside Kazan and moved down the Volga, causing a general uprising of the peasants. A miscellaneous army, undisciplined but large, collected round him, a human flood which pillaged Kazan, Saratov and Tsaritsyn, while reports of his victories or approach touched off disturbances in rural areas remote from the scene.

The real significance of Pugachev's revolt lies in the reaction of the peasantry against a feudal system of which they had become increasingly intolerant. Both serfs and compulsorily enlisted peasants responded to Pugachev's proclamations, which promised that industrial enlistment, and the poll-tax and other taxes and the *corvée*, would be abolished, and the farm-land, woodlands and pastures would be redistributed. But, as with earlier insurrections, the temporary success of *Pugachevshchina* ('Pugachevism') was due to the military backbone provided by the Cossacks and also to the weakness of the tsarist administration in these distant, outlying territories. When Catherine II was able to dispatch to the Volga the troops liberated from the Russo-Turkish war by the treaty of Kuchuk-Kainardji (12 July 1774), Pugachev's mob of peasant followers was quickly dispersed. Pugachev himself, fleeing across the steppe, was betrayed by his associates, handed over to the authorities and executed. Terrible reprisals brought unrest to a standstill during the summer of 1775.

Pugachevshchina was not the end of the armed struggle between serfs and landowners; there were further formidable risings, though none of them was such a danger to the government, in the closing years of the eighteenth century. But it was the last rebellion on a really big scale. Henceforward serfdom was doomed; it was a declining system undermined by new conditions of economic development and exposed to pressure from the awakening masses. During the first half of the nineteenth century there was always a peasant disturbance going on somewhere, and these continual and increasingly numerous outbursts, though sporadic, showed how impossible it was to preserve a feature of the social structure which enlightened opinion, and even some of the tsar's advisers, considered harmful to the national interest.

First Steps towards Industrial Capitalism

A transformation came over the Russian economy during the first half of the nineteenth century. The western market for the output of Russia's foundries ceased to exist when the introduction of coke-firing relieved Britain of the necessity of importing Russian pig-iron. Industry in the Ural region was not thereby forced into decline, but confined itself to the slowly developing home market. The growth of that market also conditioned the rise of the textile industries, which were gradually making the transition from cottage industry to factory organization (map 10).

Stimulated by the protective tariff of 1822, cotton weaving (which began supplanting linen at the end if the eighteenth century) became intensely productive in St Petersburg and even more so in the Ivanovo district, the speciality of which was cotton prints. Work was shared out among the weavers and executed in their homes, on handlooms; power looms, first seen in St Petersburg in 1808, were not in general use until the eighteen-forties. Even 1860, two thirds of the Ivanovo weavers still worked at home, and in all Russia there were only about 10,000 power looms (as against 80,000 or 90,000 handlooms), representing one fifth of the total production of cotton fabrics. The corner was turned in the eighteen-sixties, when mechanized production quickly gained the upper hand.

Technical advance was similarly slow in the printing side of the textile industry. The printing cylinder was first used 1817, in St Petersburg; fabric-printing by this method, which was established with the help of skilled workers whom the manufacturers recruited from Alsace, did not displace printing from blocks until about 1860.

As for linen, hemp and silk, traditional methods of production by hand remained unaltered. Woollen production, however, whose principal customer was the army and which was controlled by landowners with their

own serfs as labour force, had achieved a fairly high degree of concentration; yet at the middle of the century these large textile mills were still
almost entirely dependent on handlooms, which according to a rough
count made in 1859 numbered 4,916 as against 261 mechanical looms.

Industry, in this period of nascent capitalism, had not yet transformed
the habits of the peasants; it had to accommodate itself to their way of life,
which was governed by the soil. So its labour force was hybrid, at once
agricultural and industrial; some peasants divided their time about equally
between weaving at home and working in the fields, others were industrial
workers most of the time but periodically went back to their agricultural
tasks. Industry nevertheless changed the face of the suburbs in both capitals
and that of the entire countryside in the triangle between the Rivers Volga,
Oka and Moskva. Industrial villages or embryonic towns sprang up round
industrial undertakings which became powerful businesses in the second
half of the century. These new centres, being spread out over such a wide
area, escaped the notice of contemporary travellers, who hardly suspected
what important developments were going on and how much they would
affect Russia's future.

There was hardly any industrialization outside this clearly defined area.
But when certain territories in the south were brought under cultivation to
produce wheat and sugar beet, a thoroughly modern sugar industry was
created as a result. The manufacture of beet sugar, which began in the
early years of the nineteenth century and was carried out under very primitive conditions in central Russia, was introduced in the Ukraine in 1835.
The government refineries at Kiev, Poltava, Kharkov and Tchernigov
were large factories run on steam and using the latest methods. They were
capitalist enterprises, dominating the economy of their respective districts,
and were thus an exception to the general trend. The growth of industrial
population centres in Russia was usually connected with the accumulation
of wealth by artisans (many of whom went in for money-lending as a sideline and in some instances set up small businesses of their own), rather than
with the investment of capital (as in the sugar industry) by the commercial
middle class. Russia's backwardness, as compared with the expansive, progressive West, was caused by her weakness in the accumulation of capital.
Technically, however, she was progressive; puddling was adopted in the
metallurgy both of the central regions and of the Urals (where it accounted
for 45% of production as early as 1845). By 1860, this method was responsible for half of Russia's total production of iron. But it would be too much
to say that Russia had undergone an industrial revolution by that time.

Demography and Migration
The Russian population, almost all of which was still to be found in
European Russia, was growing fairly rapidly, the rate of increase being
0·8% per annum between the first and fifth censuses (1734–96) and 0·7%
between the fifth and ninth (1796–1851). The total has been estimated as
approximately 15 million in 1725, 36 million at the end of the century, and

nearly 70 million in 1851 (at which time the area of the Russian empire was some 6,641,000 square miles). In 1865, shortly after the abolition of serfdom, the population of Russia (excluding Poland and Finland) was in the neighbourhood of 75 million.

The population increase was naturally highest in the fertile 'black earth' country of the Ukraine and the middle Volga, which attracted a continual flow of settlers. But the bulk of the population was still concentrated in the north-western provinces (St Petersburg, Novgorod and Pskov); in Muscovy

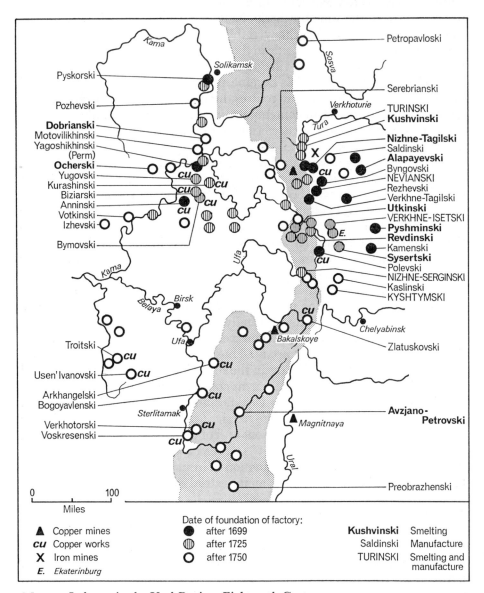

Map 10 Industry in the Ural Region, Eighteenth Century

the country's comparatively industrial central region (Moscow, Tver, Yaroslav Kostroma, Vladimir, Kaluga and Nijni Novgorod); the agricultural southern central regions (Tula Riazan, Orel, Tambov, Kursk and Voronezh); and the corresponding regions in the west (Smolensk, Vitebsk, Mohilev, Minsk, Grodno, Vilno and Kovno). In 1863 the population of these, respectively, was three, eight, ten and six million. The huge area of the Ukraine (the provinces of Tchernigov, Poltava, Kharkov, Kiev, Kherson, Ekaterinoslav, Tauris, Volhynia and Podolia, and the Don Cossack territory) had over twelve million inhabitants. Beyond these areas, to the north and east, the density was much lower; the population was still small and scattered; and Siberia remained almost deserted.

The population was the result of immigration and the birthrate. But it would be a mistake to reduce the dynamics of the situation to a mere overspill draining off of the excess population of the centre into the areas of colonization in the south and west. The birthrate was much higher in the recently colonized regions than in the western ones. Whole families migrated, settled down in their new homes and multiplied rapidly. What they created was not a new culture; on the contrary, the Russian peasantry retained the same characteristics for thousands of miles of territory; the little islands of population which they formed were the advanced posts of a single civilization.

Villages and Towns

These colonists were a people on the march, and what they wanted was land and liberty. They were fugitive state peasants, and serfs whom the most oppressive ukases were powerless to recall to the bondage of the estates; they passed beyond the territories where colonization was well established, creating huge new zones of Russian settlement in which, however heavy the obligations placed on them by the state, they at least had no other master to serve. Thus the ratio of serfs to total peasant population became smaller; from two thirds at the beginning of the eighteenth century it went down to 55% by the beginning of the nineteenth; by 1815 it had sunk to 46%, and was barely one third on the eve of the abolition of serfdom. On the other hand, almost all the peasants were serfs in the busiest, most populous places, the regions which counted for most in the life of the nation.

The overwhelming majority of Russians were villagers: in 1794, hardly more than two million of them could be considered urban dwellers, and the urban population grew slowly. In 1811 630 urban communities were recorded, most of them with less than five thousand inhabitants. Small towns contained 26% of the total urban population, nearly 20% of whom lived in the two capitals (St Petersburg 335,000, Moscow 270,000), and who numbered about three million in all. By 1863 this figure had doubled, but still represented only 10% of the total population.

Many of the towns were really only large villages; they were called towns only by virtue of their administrative functions and a governmental stroke of the pen. Others (in the neighbourhood of the capitals, and in the provinces of Ivanovo and Kostroma, where the first half of the nineteenth century had seen the growth of genuine, though small, industrial towns) really were towns but were not officially called so. Hence the statistical classification of towns, which the administration tended to distribute evenly over the whole country, does not yield a true picture. In certain parts of the country urban centres were numerous, in fact if not in name, and created their own particular kind of material and human environment.

Just because there were two capitals, containing one fifth of the urban population; and because in the vicinity of each of them there was this irregular constellation of small, semi-agricultural, semi-industrial towns, which were increasingly full of commercial activity and enterprise, the strictly limited areas in question exerted a highly formative effect on the national life.

Travellers' accounts all agree in saying that the Russian towns, being built of wood, had a dingy, ancient, neglected look, accentuated by contrast with the sparkling white roughcast walls and colourful onion-domes of the churches, and the russet brickwork of the monasteries. The number of towns went on going up during the eighteenth century, less by the administrative promotion of existing centres than by the creation of new ones in the lands bordering European Russia: the industrial Urals, where Ekaterinburg was built in 1723 and Orenburg in 1735, and the Ukraine, where the development of colonization and of commercial access to the Black Sea caused a number of new towns to appear, among them being Ekaterinoslav (1778–83) and the ports of Kherson (1778), Sebastopol (1784) and Odessa (1794–1800).

The Beginning of Deliberate Urban Development
Catherine II gloried in founding new cities, some of which, however, never got beyond the planning stage, while others, such as Ekaterinoslav, remained villages for many years after their foundation. Catherine must nevertheless be given credit for inaugurating what had been merely foreshadowed in a tentative way under Peter the Great: a deliberate policy of urban development. Peter's efforts were confined to building St Petersburg, which was still monopolizing the country's architectural activities long after his death. The ukase of 1714, making it illegal to build in stone anywhere except in the capital, was not repealed until 1728. And urban development in Moscow itself, despite the foundation there of a school of architecture in 1749, proceeded in a slow and disorderly fashion. Catherine II's formulation of a general policy of urban development was thus an entirely new departure.

The measures taken by her to safeguard her power in the remoter provinces, following the suppression of Pugachev's revolt, included appointing high officials to serve in numerous towns, which were thereby elevated to a position of importance in the organization of the state. But, even before that tragic insurrection, it had become clear that the chief administrative centres needed to be brought up to date on the lines of their western counterparts. During her journey on the Volga in 1767, Catherine herself had publicly expressed disgust with cities which were 'magnificently situated and ignobly built'. A general scheme of reorganization was entrusted in 1769 to a Commission for Masonry Building in St Petersburg and Moscow, which produced a series of projects for rebuilding the country's administrative centres. This step was taken in the context of a new social and economic situation, in which the nobles were no longer compelled to enter state service and in consequence were leaving the capital to resume a country existence on their estates and, in some cases, to undertake building activities in the provincial towns, whose society now included the high officials appointed by the government. The various skilled trades had been developing; so had business; the provinces could now provide all the appurtenances for intensive society life, with balls, assemblies and official ceremonies.

Urban layouts of this period all display the same features: a central section (*gorod*) comprising public buildings, covered markets, and dwelling-houses, two or three storeys high, for merchants and aristocratic officials; and suburbs (*predmiestie* or *forshtaty*) for professional people, craftsmen and peasants, whose masonry houses or wooden cottages had a ground floor only.

The *gorod* was disposed about two major axes, at whose intersection an open space, which might be either a rectangle or a trapezium, formed the centre of the town; near this was the fort (*kreml*), at the crossroads of the four main streets, which were metalled. The height of the houses, and their roof materials, were strictly governed by regulations; sanitary measures and fire-fighting precautions were also laid down. In practice, the architects were always very respectful of the existing buildings, especially churches, round which their plans were arranged. Yaroslav is an excellent example of this intelligent adaptation, with almost every street leading to a church and the whole forming a collection of admirable vistas.

Catherine II's town-planning policy was not destructive; and its actual achievements – which fell far short of the planners' intentions – in no way diminished the piquancy of traditional regional styles. In all towns possessing a rich heritage of religious buildings and works of art, these styles were cultivated in what amounted to professional schools of architects and artistic craftsmen, based on the monasteries and churches. Hence the fashionable architectural style of the time percolated rather slowly, with much leisurely delay, into the provinces from its fountainhead, the Academy of Arts and the Moscow School of Architecture. The provinces were still in the first stage of Russian classicism – that embodied in the early works of Bazhenov, Starov and Kazakov – when the two capitals were already witnessing the triumph of high classicism in the later works of these three Russians and those of the Italian, Quarenghi, and the Scot, Cameron.

Urban Life

The population of the small towns remained fairly stable. That of the larger towns and big cities fluctuated a good deal, going up in winter and down in summer; the bigger the city the greater the fluctuation. Moscow, towards the end of the eighteenth century, had a population of approximately 175,000 rising to 300,000 in winter. Winter was the season of industrial work, and also of society life. Summer was the season of farm work and the big fairs, the season when the nobles saw that the harvest was brought in on their estates and stored for the winter. In autumn the muddy tracks were travelled both by peasants walking to the city for work and by merchants' pack-trains and the local estate-owners' carriages, the latter laden with domestic utensils, poultry, hams and preserves.

As soon as they had settled down again in their town residences the nobles organized their social season. The richer ones had private theatres, where performances were given by choirs or acting troupes composed of serfs. Western dances (minuet, polonaise, quadrille and the German *grossvater*) were danced at balls. The retinue of servants included picturesque Russian subjects of non-Russian race, such as Kalmucks and Cherkesses (Circassians); and there was a vogue for dwarfs in Chinese costume. But things of this kind were the exception; as a rule the nobles, if they were not detained by state service (which had become voluntary in 1762) and were able to spend some time in town, merely continued their somewhat rustic existence in a different setting.

The brilliant, frivolous side of aristocratic life lent gaiety to the two capitals, especially St Petersburg. The middle classes, on the other hand, however rich some of them became, were always much less showy. And the city's true face was to be found rather in Moscow's central business quarter, which had grown up on lines reminiscent of an Oriental bazaar, and in the suburban fringes, where artisans' workshops stood huddled side by side with tumbledown wooden houses.

III AN AGE OF ACHIEVEMENT — THE EIGHTEENTH CENTURY

The combination of foreign influences and native dynamism made the eighteenth century of Russia what it was for the rest of Europe: a *grand siècle*, an age of triumphant achievement, analogous to the reign of Louis XIV in France in the preceding century. It was now that efforts by earlier Russian sovereigns to organize a modern state came to fruition. By the foundation of St Petersburg in 1703 Russia became more open to western influences by way of the Baltic, which was free to the shipping of all nations. Under Peter the Great the new capital was little more than a collection of workshops, but in the course of the century it grew and changed and eventually took over all the country's foreign trade, to the exclusion of Arkhangelsk; at the same time, with the island bastion of Kronstadt to protect it on the western side, it was Russia's greatest military port. The life of the court, the activities of the administration, the city's building development, and its trade and shipping, turned St Petersburg into a human hive; a field of every technical skill, a crucible teeming with foreign influences, a cosmopolitan city through which came immigrants making for the interior but where most of them stayed, attracted by the opportunities they found there. The great eighteenth-century rulers, not only the leading figures, Peter the Great and Catherine II, but also Anne and especially Elizabeth, with her appetite for display, fine living and the pleasures of the arts, strove to make St Petersburg a setting worthy of themselves and fit to sustain comparison with the great capitals of the West. The city's animation radiated beyond its boundaries, and the building fever produced the handsome summer residences of Tsarskoe Selo (1749–56), Peterhof (1747–52), Gatchina (1766–81) and Pavlovsk (1782–6).

These palaces were the work of foreign architects, mostly Italians, and, despite being executed by skilled Russian craftsmen, owed little to the national tradition. They are a visible reminder of a period when it seemed that the triumph of foreign influence was complete; when Russia's successive rulers, bent on modernizing the state, felt obliged to send for growing numbers of specialists from Holland, Germany, Britain, France and Italy. Peter the Great recruited a steady flow of architects, decorators, painters, metalworkers, shipwrights, sea-captains, doctors and so on. A foreign *décor* was transplanted to Russian soil; meanwhile military needs caused factories and workshops to be set up, in which foreigners occupied the leading positions.

All of which may seem to be no achievement at all, but to represent, rather, a 'new' Russia which merely aped the West, left its former capital to doze on the banks of the Moskva, and looked exclusively to the Baltic trade-routes for the seeds of progress and the forces shaping Russia's future civilization.

In reality, however, imitation of things foreign was strictly limited. In art, it was confined to the court, the aristocracy and a minute fraction of the urban population; the new artistic and, above all, architectural achievements, designed for highly specialized local purposes, simply emphasized the contrast between the indigenous and the imported: between Russia's traditional, popular arts, which continued to flourish and give their own character and flavour to life all over the country, and the alien art-forms, which were applied with hardly a detail altered and which stood for a class civilization, the reign of privilege.

In the economic sphere (with the exception of shipping and shipbuilding), the Russians owed no part of their essential knowledge to foreign experts. The latter were simply auxiliaries, extra technicians demanded by the protean task of national development; travelling from one workshop to another, they made their contribution mainly by training new workers and increasing the amount of skilled labour available. The reign of Peter the Great was marked by rapid progress in the metallurgical industries round Lake Ladoga and in the Urals. In both areas, the number of foreigners employed was lower in proportion as the degree of specialization was higher: in the ordnance shops of Petrovski (Ladoga) in 1721 there were hardly any foreigners, the Russians having been for long familiar with the manufacture of guns; foreigners constituted one third of the skilled hands working the blast-furnaces, trip-hammers, wire-drawing machines and rolling mills; and there was a large number of apprentices, all of whom were of course Russians.

It may also be noted that these foreigners, not all of whom were highly skilled and who mostly knew several trades, were employed on a wide variety of jobs, and learnt about as much as they taught during their stay in Russia. The context in which they were taken on was a combination of some trade already known to the Russians, and a novel technical process; their contributions were quickly absorbed into a body of technical practice whose development thereafter went on independently of foreign guidance. An example is the Saxon engineer de Hennin, director of the Ural mines and foundries from 1722 to 1724; he put his administrative ability at the service of the Russians but built his dams in accordance with the old, traditional Russian method, which was well adapted to local conditions of soil and climate.

All Russia's previous development had culminated in a situation which makes it permissible to speak of the eighteenth century as a *grand siècle*, not because Russia went to school under western teachers, but because the constructive and productive energies of the nation blossomed out in achievements of various kinds which constituted a Russia modern and original.

The great research and teaching institutions, the Academy of Sciences (1725), the University of Moscow (1755), and the Academy of Arts (1758), which had originally been staffed mainly by foreigners, especially Germans, were rapidly Russianized. The first timid reforms of spelling, under Peter the Great, were followed by the formation of a literary language, the foundations of which were laid by Lomonosov, the presiding genius of the age, in his grammar. The Vyshnevolotsky canal, and the creation of the port of St Petersburg (map 15), had provided easier communication between the Moscow region and the Baltic; the result was accelerated trade – a growing market which provided the finance to carry the administration and army, the twin pillars of the royal power. It was this which rendered possible the first appearance of Russian troops in Berlin (1760) and of a Russian fleet in the Mediterranean (1770). After centuries of a withdrawn, inward-looking, precarious existence, continually threatened by the Tatar hordes in the south and the effectively organized states which were Russia's western neighbours, the Russians had now crossed their own frontiers in force; no longer did the outside world know them only in the guise of ambassadors and delegations.

In this agricultural country, whose exports were almost exclusively the products of field and forest, manufacture was now flourishing; and where the mining and working of metals was concerned, Russian manufacture was modern. Under Catherine II the Urals became Europe's most highly industrialized region, the main supplier of pig-iron to industrial England. It is true that most of Russia's export manufacture consisted of half-finished articles. And though the production of linen fabrics and even cotton prints was developed in the Ivanovo district after 1750, this industry, like all other Russian manufacture of finished goods, was based wholly on the home market. The fact remains that the nuclei of an industrial civilization did make their appearance, though a little later than in some of the western countries, in eighteenth-century Russia.

Economic Thought

This aspect of Russian development is reflected in the attention paid, in certain educated circles, to the problem 'of riches and poverty' – to borrow the title of a book by Pososhkov (1724), a self-made, self-educated man, of peasant origin, who is sometimes regarded as the father of Russian mercantile doctrine. The question naturally arises whether there ever was such a doctrine in Russia, in the sense in which it existed in England or France; and, if so, whether it was merely borrowed from foreign sources; and whether it was derived from the facts of the situation, or simply applied to them.

Russian mercantilism consisted of recipes for filling the state coffers and, with this end in view, of promoting industrial activity and foreign trade. Sometimes Russian economic policy took the form of direct state intervention; this happened in the early part of Peter the Great's time, when in the absence of individual initiative, the government set up its own industrial establishments and compelled Demidov, the blacksmith from Tula, to become the ironmaster of the Urals. In other instances, the government confined itself to encouraging manufacturers by means of subsidies, privileges, tax-exemptions and protective tariffs. But in either event, Russian mercantilism was adapted to circumstances, and was the offspring of necessity. It was a practical expression of economic thought – thought which in the mind of Peter the Great, thirsty for immediate results and distracted by the pressure of events, was no doubt still somewhat confused, but which was clarified and rendered more methodical by the civil servants who during his reign were trained by their experience in the *Prikazy*, and whose successors continued to steer the administration long after Peter himself was dead.

There was nothing specifically Russian in the methods employed. The striking thing, even more than in the corresponding context in the West, was the attitude which accompanied their application. Russian mercantilism, which was associated with an elementary stage in the development of an industrial economy, and, as elsewhere, with a policy of economic warfare grossly exceeding the bounds of normal competition, was permeated with a narrow nationalism; Pososhkov, for example, inveighs violently against foreigners. The same tendency is visible in the restrictions which, from the seventeenth century onwards, were increasingly effective in loosening the grip acquired by Dutch and English traders on the Russian market. The Russian eighteenth century, though so glad to welcome foreign influences and foreign help, was coloured through and through by this struggle; even industry was affected – an example being the abrupt expulsion, in 1740, of the German technicians who had been attracted in large numbers during the reign of Anne by the patronage of her favourite, Bühren.

Development of a National Spirit

National feeling, which past struggles against Polish, German and Tatar invasions had crystallized around the cross of Orthodoxy, was further consolidated as a result of eighteenth-century administrative reform. In the years 1699–1705, Peter the Great had organized regular military recruitment, to which the traditional enrolment of volunteers became merely supplementary. The new system weighed heavily on the peasants; but it had the advantage of bringing men from different localities together and filling the country with ex-soldiers who had a formative experience in common, that of having served their country in uniform. The exploits of the army, which had appeared in Berlin, and of the fleet in the Mediterranean, made little impression on the population outside the two capitals and the other major cities, where each new feat of Russian arms was celebrated with feasting and a march-past. But national pride and solidarity were stimulated by resistance to Sweden at the beginning of the century and by the conquest of the Crimea at the end of it, when the Cross took revenge on the Crescent by destroying the Crimean mosques.

Interest in history became even stronger under Catherine II than under Peter. Both these sovereigns encouraged research into ancient documents, including the chronicles which had been preserved by generations of churchmen and which recorded the great deeds, real or legendary, of the Russian people. Between 1762 and 1796, 'the history of medieval Russia took shape and came to life', as André Mazon has written. The Academy sponsored the publication of the *Chronicles* of Nestor, Nikon and Novgorod. In 1768 the first *History of Russia* made its appearance, a posthumous work by a disciple of Peter the Great, V. N. Tatishchev (d. 1750), one of those enlightened administrators of whom there were still so few in the first half of the century. A copy of the *Lay of the Warriors of Igor* (the *Slovo* of Igor) was discovered in 1795 and presented to the Tsarina a few months before her death; its editor, Prince Musin-Pushkin, wrote in 1800: 'It shows us that our own ancient heroes, like those of other peoples, had bards to sing of their glory.' It seems, however, that this epic poem was written at a later period and must therefore be placed in a different category: one of those patriotic literary works serving as prelude to a national history which is in process of reconstruction or, where necessary, of invention.

The sovereigns themselves were not content merely to encourage this resurrection of the past. Peter the Great, who often likened himself to his predecessors, especially Alexis Mikhailovitch, had thoughts of causing an official chronicle of his reign to be compiled; he left a *Journal* of his military activities, a document supervised if not actually written by him, and published at the end of the eighteenth century. Catherine II, whose passion for history was inspired by political motives, was eager to compose 'a kind of manual of patriotic education' (A. Mazon) for schoolboys; helped by a team of archivists, she herself took part in collecting original documents for *Notes on the History of Russia* and in publishing the work, in which she displayed a powerful feeling for dynastic tradition and Russian greatness.

This growing nationalism, with its quest for the pristine sources, caused a revival of interest in the ancient art of Russia. Modernism in a western key, which had been so much the fashion under Peter the Great, had discredited the art of the icon; icons had their religious function to fulfil but had lost all aesthetic prestige. At the beginning of the nineteenth century they were allowed to re-enter the realm of the beautiful. The name of Rublev, whose works could no longer be identified with certainty, even his great *Trinity* being attributed to him only with hesitation as later as 1840, became the approved symbol of Russia's artistic past.

The Old and the New

This sense of greatness permeated the court and also the aristocracy, despite the fact that the latter, at any rate in outward appearance, was abandoning the national customs. It also permeated, and more powerfully, the urban middle class – a business class no longer consisting, as in the previous century, of a few *gosti* who had a monopoly of the country's foreign trade, but extending, in every town of any size, to include a small number of merchants and wealthy craftsmen who had local administrative duties. This class remained Russian and dressed in Russian style. A glaring contrast, indeed, separated the aristocracy, and the handful of merchants aping their ways, from the rest of the population. 'Town dress', western and principally German, which had been introduced into Russia by the ukases of 1700, was compulsory for all citizens – in theory; in practice, it was worn chiefly in St Petersburg, where the nobility clustered round the court and police control was effective. After Peter's death, everyone of moderate or less than moderate means reverted to national costume, and the comparatively few Russians affecting western dress stood out sharply from the broad mass of the people.

But although the use of western clothes had been limited to a fairly small area before Catherine's reign, the end of the century found them spreading even to the remotest provinces. The nobles, relieved of compulsory state service in 1762 and consequently more interested in making profits from agriculture, were living on their estates, increasing their incomes by exploiting their serfs more intensively, and devoting more money to personal expenses. Western fashions, brought back from London and

Paris by rich landowners or bought from tradesmen who imported them, became commoner; the less wealthy landowners had tailors and dress-makers among their serfs, who copied the genuine article.

In the nineteenth century the development of democratic ideas was re-flected in urban sartorial fashions. Formerly, the model for admiration and imitation was the officer or feudal grandee; now, it was the thinker, the liberty-loving romantic. More and more young men appeared in the great-coat, *siurtuk*, instead of the more modest frock-coat, *frak* (respectively the French *surtout* and *frac*). Loosely flowing silk cravats, and tartan waistcoats, recalled Lord Byron and the heroes of Sir Walter Scott's novels. But there was a difference between St Petersburg, the capital, which was more austere and conservative, and Moscow and the provinces, where greater freedom of dress was in vogue. In the towns and cities, certain details of national dress reflected the influence of foreign fashion, and, as fashion does, kept varying. But generally speaking the people, in both town and country, remained faithful to tradition, which was almost changeless in time but differed from one district or group of villages to another; each generation handed on to the next the patterns and the ways of making them which it had received from its predecessor, and which were best suited to the natural surroundings, practical needs and physical types of the wearers.

Though women and girls had different hair-styles respectively, their clothes were alike: a sleeveless coat (*sarafan*), a woollen skirt (*panieva*), a short pelisse (*polushubok*) or a quilted wrap (*telogreika*). Men, in the northern, eatern and central provinces, wore a shirt (*rubashka*), narrow trousers (*porty*) and a long coat (*kaftan*); in the southern and western provinces, broad trousers (*sharovary*) and an upper garment, the *svita*. At least, these were the typical clothes. But the peasants' lives were closely mingled with the aristocracy's; in particular, the women and girls in the nobles' enormous domestic staffs dressed differently from those who had stayed at home in the villages, exchanging the *sarafan* for a blouse and, if they were wet-nurses, wearing a bonnet. Though their costume was dic-tated by their employers, there can be no doubt that this enforced elegance produced a good effect on the general standard of peasant dress.

Traditional observances, such as the celebration of weddings and feast-days, made the peasants spend more money than most of them could afford; there was a glaring discrepancy between the wretched drabness of everyday life and the deceptively gay, colourful occasions when their vitality and capacity for enjoyment found an outlet. It would nevertheless appear that towards the end of the century the general standard of living, to judge by the standard of dressing, went up slightly. The brisk trade done by the serf craftsmen of the Ivanovo region, who sold their printed fabrics (cotton as well as linen, even at this early period) in the market place, would have been impossible without increased purchasing power among the peasant class generally.

Simultaneously with an improvement in the appearance of the isbas, whose exterior became gayer and more decorative, there was an upsurge of artistic taste in the making of articles of daily use.

The Popular Arts at Their Best

The latter part of the eighteenth century was the great period of the popular arts in Russia, when the traditional forms of various articles in daily use were brought to a pitch of delightful and often humorous perfection.

The centres of artistic popular craftsmanship lay along the oldest-established trade-routes radiating outwards from Moscow: to Arkangelsk through Zagorsk, Rostov, Vologda, and Kholmogory; to Siberia through Veliki Ustiug and along the northern road; and to Nijni Novgorod (Gorki) through Vladimir.

No village of any prominence was without its own speciality. Fedoskino, near Moscow, was 'the home of Russian lacquer-work'. In or near the triangle formed by the Volga and Oka there were three groups of villages in which these peasant arts were principally concentrated: between Moscow and Yaroslav, particularly in the Old Believers' communities, there was enamel-work round Rostov and in the neighbourhood of the monastery of the Trinity and St Sergius, and wood-carving at Bogorodsk, Kudrino and Khotkovo; between Moscow and Nijni Novgorod, in the area of Vladimir, Mstera specialized in icon-painting, metalwork and embroidery, and Kholui and Palekh in the first of these three; and to the north of Nijni Novgorod, in the Semenov region, painted wood and carved bone were produced at Khokhloma, the filigree at Kazakovo. Further north, near Kostroma, there was silver-working at Krasnoe and lace-making at Vologda; in the valley of the Sukhona, not far from Veliki Ustiug, there was niello-work; on the banks of the Semogsa, near Kholmogory, carved bone, and objects cut out of bark. On the northern route to Siberia, Dymkovo, in the Viatka region, made terracotta toys. To the south of Moscow, gold-working went on at Sinkovo, near Bronnicy; and there were pottery and lace-making in the region of Riazan. At Krestsy, east of Novgorod, there was embroidery.

Luxury in the peasant home at this period took the form of perfect craftsmanship in wood, both turned and carved. Intricate, lacy structures overhung porches and window-embrasures on the most prosperous *isbas* in the middle Volga region. Carved flowers, animals and geometric designs embellished dippers, salt cellars, dies for stamping spiced cakes, spinning-wheels, dishes, pots, boxes and canisters. Vessels and containers cut out of birchbark were covered with plant-form decoration. Children's toys were brightly-coloured *matrioshki* (puppets) and groups of very lifelike people and animals, carved in woods which are easy to work such as lime, aspen or birch. Also used in decorative miniature sculpture were boxwood, cypress (imported from the south) and walnut.

Wooden dishes, plates, cups and so on were painted in many cases, like the toys; the village of Khokhloma in particular had a reputation for skill in the use of gold, black and red pigments which were fixed by heating and

7

protected by polishing with linseed oil, to which age imparted a glowing patina. Goldsmiths found plenty of customers for their jewellery, in which filigree played a prominent part. But the most valuable pieces, executed in gold or more frequently in silver, were enriched with niello work – a peculiar type of engraving in which the hollows were filled in with a powdered alloy, the latter being fused under heat and polished; the design might be purely abstract and decorative or, alternatively, represent military victories, panoramas or architectural views. Russian niello craftsmanship originated during the sixteenth century in the workshops round the Palace of Armour and the monastery of the Trinity at St Sergius, and spread northwards. In the seventeenth century the artists of the Palace of Armour, which has been described as the 'academy' of Russian decorative craftsmanship, began popularizing new motifs in the carving of bone and ivory (walrus and mammoth tusks); these were adopted by craftsmen in the Kholmogory region, where such carving had been carried to a high level of accomplishment in the preceding centuries.

All these arts were popular in two senses: their motifs were drawn from the life of the people, and they were produced in the villages, where the peasants earned so little in agriculture that they had to add to their income by working for the town market. But the peasants themselves almost never bought niello work, or carvings executed in expensive materials; similarly, wealthy townspeople were the purchasers of the early lacquer-work which gradually, at the end of the eighteenth century, took over from icon-painting in the villages of the Vladimir region. Moreover, the trend of a certain amount of popular art was dictated to the craftsmen producing it, who were serfs, by their owners.

When, in the eighteenth century, lace began to figure so prominently in both men's and women's clothes (frills for the fronts and cuffs of shirts, lace caps, and trimmings for *corsages* and skirts), an increasing number of female serfs were put to lace-making; this applied both to the household serfs and to those on the estates. It was only in the making of straightforward, everyday articles – and also in the art of embroidery, which was indispensable for clothes for wedding-days and festivals – that the folk-crafts served the perennial needs of the people. It happened, however, that both luxury production and the genuinely popular crafts reached their greatest artistic perfection in the eighteenth century.

Noble and Official Art

In the process of modernization that Peter the Great did his best to force on his country, art had a function to fulfil; and, in so far as it was treated as a means to an end, a device for adding dignity and lustre to his reign, it turned its back on the Byzantine tradition in Russia's artistic past. Civil architecture took precedence over religious, and the portrait over the icon. Western influences became preponderant, almost to the exclusion of indigenous sources of inspiration. Nevertheless this art derived from abroad, developed by artists imported for the purpose, was soon absorbed into the national patrimony. It is quite untrue to maintain that this imitation of foreign art (really no more than a decorative addition), or even the appearance of new art-forms (such as sculpture, which was prohibited by the Orthodox Church), created a split between the classes and the masses. Both the new buildings and their interior decoration were executed by Russian workmen and artists. And in every country, official art in the grand style has always sought to impress the masses without much recourse to popular artistic tradition. A peasant from Auvergne, under Louis xiv, knew as little of the glories of Versailles as did a moujik from Suzdal of those of Peterhof. The introduction of the baroque and classical modes in Russia, and their integration into the country's architecture, did not constitute a break with the past but simply a new development, dictated by the tastes and desires of the oligarchy.

The sovereigns focused their architectural ambitions on St Petersburg, which was originally laid out by Peter the Great and developed in the reign of Elizabeth. The capital owed its architectural masterpieces to Bartholomeo Rastrelli (1700–70), the creator of Russian baroque, who designed the Winter Palace, erected 'to the glory of all the Russias', the Stroganov Palace, the Smolny Convent, and the nearby summer residences of Tsarskoye Selo and Peterhof. The polychromy of his exteriors, partnered by sumptuous interior decoration and much marquetry and carved wood, provided a luxury setting for the giddy extravagance of the court under Elizabeth, who had fifteen thousand dresses in her wardrobe and enjoyed showing them off in an endless round of festivities. Catherine ii's reign was less frivolous; baroque made way for classicism; the new style was propagated by the Academy of Arts, which dominated artistic life in Russia until about the middle of the nineteenth century. St Petersburg was enriched with a considerable number of buildings, the style of which became successively more severe from the reign of Catherine ii to that of Nicholas i, and which gave the city the majestic physiognomy which it has kept to the present day.

It was likewise to foreign architects that St Petersburg owed the construction, under Catherine ii, of the Academy of Arts, by the French architect J. B. Vallin de la Mothe (1729–90), and the Marble Palace, by the Italian Antonio Rinaldi (1709–90). Another Italian, Giacomo Quarenghi (1744–1817), whose abundant output was continued under Alexander i, built the Theatre of the Hermitage, the English Palace at Peterhof, the Alexander Palace at Tsarskoye Selo, the Smolny Institute, and, in Moscow, the Sheremetev Hospital. The interiors of the apartments at Tsarskoye Selo were entrusted to the Scottish architect, Cameron, who was deeply versed in antiquity and decorated them in Pompeian style.

But Russia now had architects of her own in Ivan Starov (1743–1808) and Vassily Bazhenov (1737–99). The first-named built the Taurid Palace, with its Roman cupola; the second, who drew up a project for rebuilding the Moscow Kremlin which was too expensive to carry out, trained pupils, including Matvey Kazakov (1738–1841), who built the Senate Palace in classical style alongside the old onion-dome churches. But Moscow, remote from the seat of government, was more traditional, slower to welcome the new baroque style and its classical successor; the chief field of architectural activity in Moscow was the building of private houses in a peculiar style, where the most affluent members of the nobility led a life of luxury.

The first half of the nineteenth century, during which the activity of French architects in Russia came to an end, brought nothing new in architecture – only a heightened taste for the grandiose and pompous, visible in such imposing buildings as the Cathedral of Our Lady in Kazan, by the Russian Andrey Voronikhin (1759–1814), and the Cathedral of St Isaac, by the Frenchman Ricard de Montferrand (1786–1858) (plate 13). Secular architecture, proceeding on a more modest scale, produced more elegant results, like the Marine Exchange buildings by Thomas de Thomon (1756–1813) and the reconstruction of the Admiralty building to plans by Adrian Zakharov (1761–1811). It was St Petersburg which provided the right conditions for the extraordinary fertility of Russian classicism, which influenced the development of architectural design all over the country. Russian classicism has been accused of being alien to Russia. Critics have repeatedly echoed Custine's assertion that the architecture of St Petersburg is an anomaly, a false trail (*contresens*). No doubt it does impose itself on the landscape instead of accommodating itself to it. But it is not a disfigurement. The horizontal lines of 'Greco-Roman' temples harmonize perfectly with the misty climate. And with their uniformity, their severe exteriors and their sometimes immoderate size, these classical, monumental buildings, both religious and secular, are in keeping with the character of Nicholas I's reign.

In the palaces built for the landed nobility from Peter the Great's time onwards, family tradition was perpetuated by the portraits covering the walls. This was a new side to Russian art, a necessary, useful one in which, moreover, Russian painters excelled from the start and continued to do so throughout the eighteenth century. The leading figures in that period were Andrey Matveyev (1701–39), Ivan Nikitin (1690–1741), Alexis Antropov (1716–95), Ivan Argunov (1727–97) and Fedor Bokatov (1736–1808). In the reigns of Catherine II and Alexander I, most of the portraitists were Ukrainians; outstanding among them were Dmitri Levitski (1735–1832), who after a time unfortunately allowed his talent to be diverted into official academicism, and Vladimir Borovikovsky (1757–1825).

Landscape painting was almost unknown in Russia before the end of the eighteenth century. Fedor Alexeev (1753–1824), a pupil of Canaletto, lived at the court of King Stanislas Augustus and left a complete visual documentation of Warsaw (figure 28); he also painted, rather inexpressively, the Neva Quays and the various quarters of St Petersburg. The first real landscape painter in the history of Russian art, Silver Shchedrin (1791–1830), who died at an early age in Italy, found almost all his subjects outside Russia.

The rise of Russian painting, and its acquisition of European stature, date from the nineteenth century. A feeling of power, resulting from the war of 1812 – faith in the uniqueness of Orthodox Russia and her superiority over the West – influenced artistic trends and encouraged two painters who lived mainly in Rome but had a considerable reputation in both Russia and Europe, Karl Bryulov (1799–1852), a historical painter ('The Last Days of Pompeii', 1834), and Alexander Ivanov (1806–58), who attempted in his monumental 'Appearance of the Messiah before the People' to express an ideal at once religious and national.

The art of the portrait continued to be represented by numerous painters such as Orest Kiprensky (1783–1836), who was already living in Rome when Bryulov and Ivanov arrived there; Vassily Tropinin (1776–1856); Varnek (1782–1842); and Zarianko (1818–70). Meanwhile the spectacle of a colourful, divided society, agitated by social problems, gave birth to descriptive painting, which in some instances confined itself to observation and, in others, pointed a moral. The first of these tendencies is represented by such painters as A. Orloski (1777–1832), a Pole by birth, 'the perfect illustrator of Russian life between 1800 and 1830' (L. Réau), and A. Venetsianov (1780–1847), who portrayed peasant life and customs; an example of the second tendency is Fedotov (1815–52), whose *genre* paintings (with highly explicit titles, such as 'Presentation of the Future Bride in a Merchant's House', and 'Morning Scene – A Newly Promoted Civil Servant') are of great value to the social historian for the light they throw on mid-century life.

IV RUSSIAN SOCIETY ON THE EVE OF THE GREAT REFORMS

Russian society at this period, that is to say on the brink of capitalistic development, was still rigidly divided into its various 'estates'; but it was less uniform and more fluid than might appear. The churchmen, the nobles, the middle classes and artisans, the free peasants and the serfs, differed from one another both in juridical status and in material prosperity. There was a big gap between the village priest and the bishop in a provincial capital, between the poor nobleman and the rich landowner with tens of thousands of serfs, between the poverty-stricken peasant and the landlord whose agricultural profits were supplemented by money lending and local trade. New avenues to wealth were available in the nineteenth century. In the space of one or two generations it was possible to go right up the ladder: from serfdom to freedom (by purchase), from peasant status to admission to one of the merchant guilds, and from aristocratic privileges (which could be granted to individual members of the middle classes) to the acquisition of noble rank. But in practice these opportunities for betterment affected only a small percentage of the population.

The Church in State Harness

The Church under Peter the Great was considerably involved in an activity for which Pierre Pascal has borrowed the term 'Caesaropapism'. The secular priests virtually acted as civil servants, closely directed by the Holy Synod and expected to explain the tsar's decisions to the faithful, most of whom were illiterate, and to assist the local authorities. But the lowliest clerics occupied a socially inferior position and did not always have much control over the population. The village priests, who were married and usually produced large families, handed on the job from father to son and endeavoured to find places for their numerous other children in the various branches of the Church's organization. It thus came about that whereas in isolated regions the priests and their assistants were few, in the central regions they were many, sometimes excessively so; a village of two hundred households (say eight hundred inhabitants) might have five priests and fifty deacons, beadles and sacristans. It is only fair to add that in every field of activity the number of minor employees or domestic retainers was very large – a characteristic feature of life in economically backward countries – and that the Church simply followed the accepted pattern.

Religious life, and also intellectual culture and religious authority, were concentrated in the monasteries, from which the higher ranks of the secular priests were drawn. The monasteries had a hard time of it under Peter the Great. Monks and lay brothers were regarded as idlers; they were also suspected of being, all too frequently, opposed to the tsar's programme; their numbers accordingly went down, shrinking from 25,000 at the beginning of the eighteenth century to a mere 14,000 in 1730. But the decline did not last long. Monasticism recovered under Elizabeth; in 1760, all the restrictions imposed on monastic life were removed; anyone could enter a monastery. By 1762, Russia had over a thousand monasteries, a quarter of which were for women. But the Church was unable to retain the property it had accumulated in the course of the century. By an ukase of 1764, Catherine II secularized all monastic property, imposed an annual tax, and set up a classification of authorized monasteries in order of importance.

At the top of the list came the two Lavras of Pechersky, at Kiev, and the monastery of the Trinity and St Sergius; later, two further monasteries were elevated to the same rank (map 17). On the next level came six monasteries known as *katedralnie*, those at Tchernigov, Kostroma, Vladimir, Novgorod-Severski, St Petersburg (this later became a Lavra) and Moscow (the Chudov monastery). The final group consisted of all the remaining monasteries, divided into three categories according to how many monks they had: thirty-three, seventeen or twelve. In practice, the number of monasteries greatly exceeded that shown by this official register (318 tax-paying monasteries and 67 convents), since authorization without taxation was granted to other monasteries, which were not added to the register. In about 1900 there were nearly a thousand altogether (540 monasteries, 370 convents) with a total of some 43,000 monks, lay brothers and novices (7,464 monks, 7,566 lay brothers). This is a small figure for a population of

130 million. But the importance of the monasteries cannot be judged by their number: they were places of pilgrimage, whose saintly monks attracted crowds of the faithful in search of comfort and advice; they were also centres of study and mystical life; their influence was wide.

The secular clergy did not rise to similar heights. But they did not really deserve the sweeping accusations of ignorance which have been made against them. Educational progress, what there was of it, was mainly their handiwork. It was from among the 'priests' sons' that the most active, exigent elements were recruited, those who were most aware of the obstacles placed in the way of progress by Russia's political and social system. The *raznochinets* ('men without rank') were a category of individuals for whom there was no definition in law, and who had escaped from their class background by virtue of their education; they were drawn from all sections of the population – peasants, *meshchanie* (who were part of the lower middle class), impoverished nobles, and, most of all, the clergy. As we shall see, the irony of history made the Church one of the main sources of the Revolution.

The Nobles and the Nation

The administrators and military commanders required by the state were drawn from the nobility, who combined the habit of authority with some degree of secular education, which they were alone in possessing. The reforms of Peter the Great obliged them to become educated along western lines, at schools in which technical and military instruction took precedence over general education and which were intended as copies of similar institutions in the West. The fashion for German or French clothes and hairstyles was symbolic of the attraction exercised by the more advanced countries of central and western Europe. Russian ruling circles encouraged such imitation, because it seemed that without it Russia would never succeed in sloughing off her backwardness.

The nobility's western ways were consequently not just a superficial garnish. Although their basic mentality and daily habits were derived from centuries of tradition, their 'opinions' – the ideas they formed of society and the world – were derived less from the realities of Russian life than from an education which had left tradition behind and, from the very nature of elementary technical instruction, led them into the realm of generalities and abstract ideas and fostered a Utopian rationalism in the style of the European eighteenth century. It was the nobility who, as the only educated class (outside the Church, that is), gave birth to the intelligentsia; the latter went into opposition, and in 1825 were to unleash the Decembrist rebellion.

The very attachment of the nobles to the state was what impelled the more thoughtful individuals among them to borrow their ideas for reform from foreign countries. Moreover their education and way of life were such as to inspire them with delusions of easy success. Western nobles, because of their estates, had powerful local roots. Their Russian counterparts had not; the tsar had given them scattered demesnes which divided their attention, and on which they did not reside for long at a time; service in the army or administration ruled their lives and took them indifferently to any part of the empire. Their children were brought up by women and surrounded by serfs, with the result that they acquired the habit of giving orders and developed exaggerated ideas of their own authority. After a few years of this conditioning they were removed very young from their families and given a military-type education, in many cases far from the estates where they had spent their childhood, so that they became estranged from the social realities of country life and developed yet further their sense, and enjoyment, of command. On succeeding to the family estates they tried to impose something like military discipline on their peasants; and in state service, which took first place over the profitable management of their properties as the aim and object of their lives, they were motivated by a powerful feeling of duty towards Russia. Devoid of any real ties with the land, trained from youth to devote their careers to the state, and accustomed from early childhood to exercise arbitrary authority over humble peasants, they were almost without exception imbued with the same ideal of enlightened despotism as the government. Consequently their political attitude, in cases where it diverged from perfect conformity, never got further than the abstract, Utopian stage and was easily reconciled with a lively sense of their material interests and a stubborn defence of their rights;

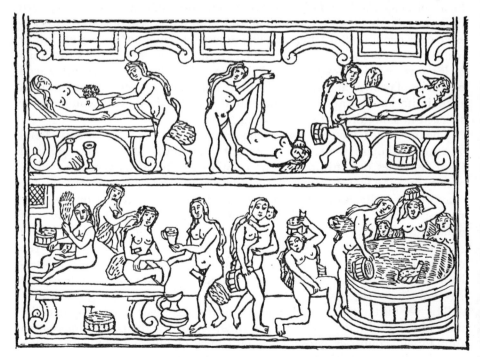

FIGURE 27 A steam-bath establishment in Russia (eighteenth century, after an old engraving).

a liberal aristocrat was no less intent than anyone else on getting the utmost out of his serfs.

The nobles reached the apogee of their power under Catherine II. They had absolute powers over their serfs and greater freedom from obligation to the state, which, by the ukase of 1762, no longer exacted compulsory service in return for their privileges.

In 1785 the nobles received a charter confirming the privileges which they were to retain intact until 1861. This charter later provided the basis of article 15 of volume 9 of the Code of Laws (*Svod zakonov*), which defined the nobility as follows: 'The title of nobleman originates in the abilities and virtues of men who in the past wielded authority and distinguished themselves by their services; such services, having become merits in themselves, have acquired for the descendants of those men the right to call themselves nobly born.' This very general definition led to claims for noble rank being founded in many instances on some *de facto* situation rather than on pedigree; and in fact the majority of noble titles had been created by civil servants following the establishment of the *Chin* (Table of Ranks) under Peter the Great.

The nobles did not make any very striking change in their way of life as a result of being liberated from compulsory state service. A certain number of them did indeed spend more time on their estates and show more interest in the management of the land; the members of the St Petersburg Free Economic Society – which was founded in 1765 and whose published *Works* are a valuable source for the history of Russian agriculture – represent a new race of enlightened landowners, eager for progress and closer to the realities of peasant life.

But tradition, education and the prospects of a career all tended to keep the majority of the nobles in state service, as before. The court and city of St Petersburg accounted for a good many, who had their principal residences on the banks of the Neva. Officers and administrators went on being recruited from the nobility, who now had more chance than before of being allowed to carry out their functions in the neighbourhood of their estates.

As might be expected, the better-educated type of landowner, living on his estates or at least visiting them frequently, became commoner after 1815, when the return of peace brought back large numbers of Russian officers from the battlefields of Europe. The nobleman nevertheless remained at once a state official and a landed proprietor. In the management of his land he applied to his peasants the discipline and authority which he had used elsewhere, and which were second nature to him. A patriarchal bureaucracy, whose attitudes were those of the military and the police, held the countryside firmly in its grasp.

Even if a nobleman had big estates – which, however, were always a collection of isolated bits and pieces – his mentality was that of a small holder. His thinking was small, his methods a mixture of automatism and rule-of-thumb. This was inevitable. The Russian agricultural system,

7*

characterized by the *mir* (undoubtedly a restrictive, reactionary influence) and the excessive division of landownership, in which the landlord's plots and those of the peasants were mixed up together in a complicated jig-saw, was an obstacle to efficient operation and the introduction of new agricultural methods; in short, to progress.

Noblemen Wealthy and Needy

In these circumstances, the rich, magnificent noble, living in broad, open style, spending freely and conspicuously, was a type not often to be met with. A more familiar figure was the needy nobleman struggling to make ends meet, not over-endowed with foresight, spoiled by the system of serf-dom – which gave him labour and raw materials for nothing – and unable to distinguish between selling-price and profit. Lack of ready cash forced him into making quick sales; he tended to conceal the unrewarding state of his farming operations behind a smokescreen of sidelines, such as dis-tilling spirits and levying profitable tithes on the craftsmen and petty manufacturers on his estates, but was none the less obliged to mortgage the latter, so that the abolition of serfdom in 1861 found him burdened with debts for which his own peasants were the surety.

The structure of aristocratic society had thus been greatly altered since the reign of Peter the Great. Despite having kept their essential privileges, the nobles had been unable to dam the rising tide of officials. As the de-velopment of the state proceeded, its functionaries naturally became more numerous: the old nobility (whose own titles had in many cases originated with the exercise of a function) found themselves drowned in a wave of individuals recently promoted to aristocratic rank, who were noblemen in the sight of the law but not regarded as such by society. In the nineteenth century there were only a hundred or so left of the families, some with titles and others without, whose noble rank dated from the origins of the Russian state. The great honorific distinctions (the first three classes of the Order of St Vladimir and all classes of the Order of St Gregory) automatically conferred hereditary noble rank, among whose recipients were middle-class men who had made fortunes. Thus the numbers of the aristocracy were rapidly swelled, and the ownership of land was by no means always the essential characteristic of noble status. Economic differences within the aristocratic class became more pronounced.

There were plenty of nobles who did not live in palaces or maintain an expensive style. Most of them could not afford such exceptional places as the celebrated residences in the Moscow suburbs, like Arkhangelskoye (originally the property of Prince Galitsin, acquired in 1810 by the Yusopov family); Ostankino (now Pushkinskoye); and Kuskovo, a mini-ature Muscovite Versailles belonging to the Sheremetev family, who also owned the castles of Voronovo, Ostafievo and Viazomy. Of comparable splendour were the palaces in the capital, where the families most prominent in imperial court circles lived for part of the year.

The houses described by Turgenev in his novel, *A Nest of Gentlefolk*, are all built on much the same lines. The mansion has only one upper storey. On one side it faces an enormous courtyard; on the other, a terrace beyond which lies a park in the French style. There are two wings, and a central façade with columns. But the reception rooms, arranged in either a straight line or a circle (as at Arkhangelskoye), are not necessarily as luxurious as those at Ostankino, with its profusion of tapestries, its French, Flemish and Italian pictures, and its family portraits painted by serf-artists. Nor do the service quarters and stables take up as much room; the great landowners all had large staffs of servants, but not all of them owned 140,000 serfs, as did Prince Sheremetev, or were able to support a theatre, choirs and troupes of ballet dancers.

This luxurious life, though unattainable by the rank and file of the nobility, was a model for imitation in matters of detail. Paris and London fashions found their way eventually into remote corners of the provinces through being adopted by the rich city-dwelling nobles, who had direct contact with foreign countries.

The Troubled Conscience of the Nobles
The aristocratic class, being of such varied composition, did not react unanimously to events and adopt a uniform attitude to the way in which the country was ruled, and the problems with which it was confronted. The aristocracy constituted Russia's most cultured, progressive, enlightened and, since Catherine II's reign, independent class, the members of which were tempted to develop political views just in so far as they recognized – despite their own privileged position – that serfdom was an institution which no longer made sense, that autocracy was inconsistent with the new conditions of economic life, and that patriotism itself supplied the motive for far-reaching reforms.

Much heart-searching about the Russian political and social structure went on among a minority of nobles whose knowledge of French, their second language since childhood, enabled them to read the *philosophes*. The more sensitive among them found the poverty and servitude of peasant life a distressing spectacle. A typical example of these young noblemen, who had the courage to denounce autocracy and serfdom, is A.N.Radishchev (1749–1802), the publication of whose *Journey from St Petersburg to Moscow* (1790) was followed by Siberian exile and early death.

The influence (curbed as far as possible by strict censorship) of the United States and the French Revolution, and the Napoleonic wars, which took the Russians into Paris and brought large numbers of aristocratic army officers into direct contact with the French, caused a few of them to harbour thoughts of a change of régime. They discussed projects for reform in masonic lodges and secret societies, and used the death of Alexander I as the occasion for instigating the so-called Decembrist or Dekabrist revolt (14 December 1825), which was quickly put down by the new Tsar, Nicholas I. This revolutionary movement, whose aim was to overthrow tsarism and institute democracy but whose only means were secret meetings and a military plot, lacked support among the people and even among the nobility.

Although some of the nobles were liberals, especially in the army, the majority of the class remained attached to the old order of things in Russia, and consistently supported the conservative policy of the government. The Slavophils drew their supporters largely from the nobility; and however many nobles acquired a cosmopolitan tinge, travelling or even living in Europe, very few of them wanted to see Russia following the same paths as the western countries. The nobles who went travelling and were in evidence in the capitals of Europe were a minute fraction of their class; most of the others could not afford foreign travel and remained chained to their native soil, shut in by their traditional environment, imbued with a conservative vision of society, living not very prosperously on the income from their diminishing estates, and exerting little influence on the conduct of the state. The part once played by the nobility had in fact been taken over by highly placed officials and by the leading families, who preserved their importance by adapting themselves to the rise of capitalism and taking part in commerce and industry.

'Dekabrism' was the army's first and last revolt against tsarism. Ideas of liberty and equality continued to spread among the nobles. But from now on, through the combined influence of German philosophy and the revolutions of 1830 and 1848 in France, those Russian nobles who were given to thinking about their country's future (and these were all indigent nobles) joined the small band of intellectuals who were concentrated in the universities – mostly at the University of Moscow – and who, finding no place for themselves in Russian society, felt like foreigners in their own country. These proletarians of the intellect have been described as 'internal *émigrés*'. Feeling to the full the oppressive weight of Nicholas I's régime, and disillusioned about the chances of a successful military *putsch*, they resorted to extreme doctrines of revolutionary but, as yet, idealistic socialism, with a bias in favour of uniquely Russian features of social organization. They regarded the village community, which ensured something like equality between the peasants, as socialism's necessary foundation; the artisans were to act as a counterpoise, preventing economic development from becoming lopsided; the rise of the middle classes, resulting inexorably from technical progress and the spread of industrialization, was felt to be suspect. The revolutionary writers, including Herzen himself (except towards the end of his life), were faithful to the idea of an essentially Russian socialism which was to be set up at a single stroke as soon as the country had struck off the fetters of serfdom and tsarism. The image of the Russian people, four out of every five of whom were peasants, was constantly before these writers' eyes; and in the prevailing ignorance and poverty their hopes were strengthened when they saw industrial serfs amassing money and rising to a higher status, and educated serfs who became actors, artists or craftsmen for the delectation of high officials and the aristocracy. But their hopes were unreal. In the controversy over serfdom which began in 1855, the nobles, almost to a man, stubbornly defended their privileges.

From 'gosti' to 'bourgeois'

The *gosti* and merchants of the time of Alexis Mikhailovitch were succeeded in the eighteenth century by a larger class, the 'bourgeois' (if such they can be called), who, under Peter the Great's policy of classification, continued more intensively by Catherine II, were divided into three 'guilds' according to the amount of their declared capital. These 'merchant' guilds also included metallurgical industrialists, though the richest of these, such as the Demidov family, escaped guild registration by acquiring noble status. Since the textile industries in the eighteenth century were in the hands of nobles (as was the case with woollen cloth) or of serfs and hence, indirectly, of nobles (as was the case with linen and subsequently cotton as well), the Russian middle class remained essentially commercial, not industrial, and numerically weak, until the second third of the nineteenth century; especially as the members of the third guild were too rustic in their outlook and way of life to have typical middle-class characteristics.

But the development of the port of St Petersburg, Moscow and the provincial cities of the central region, which were near the industrial towns, brought about concentrations of these middle-class elements (represented elsewhere only by very small groups, which included non-Russians, especially Tatars). These middle-class people, whose names were registered under the first two guilds, made a big difference to life in the cities concerned, both by their commercial activities and by the responsibilities they undertook in urban administration.

MERCHANT GUILDS IN RUSSIA

Year	Total population	First Guild	Second Guild	Third Guild
1830	56,000,000	1,510	3,928	68,279
1857	72,000,000	1,440	5,005	137,198

SOURCES: State Archives, Leningrad, folio 869, op. 1–165.1.2, and A. KEPPEN, Ninth Census 1857.

Origin of the Industrial Middle Class

During the second half of the eighteenth century and the first thirty years of the nineteenth, the growth of the textile industry enabled a number of peasants to make money and rise into the merchant category. Most of them were not free men; curiously, the great estates were the environment in which the industrial middle class came to birth. At Ivanovo, on the estates

of the Sheremetev family, where it was customary for the peasants to supplement their meagre agricultural earnings by manufacturing printed
linen fabrics, petty capitalists appeared from 1750 onwards, authorized by
their landlord to set up workshops, engage local craftsmen and, by a tacit
delegation of authority, exercise privileges over the free men and serfs in
their employ. The industry gradually changed over to cotton. Serfs
who had made good, such as the Gratchovs, and later the Garelins,
Baburins, Kuvayevs, Burylins and others, bought their freedom – at a very
high price – and had themselves registered in the merchant guilds, the
ranks of the middle class thus being augmented by some very able people.
Emancipation by this means was particularly common in the eighteen-
twenties, during which period the production of cotton prints was rising

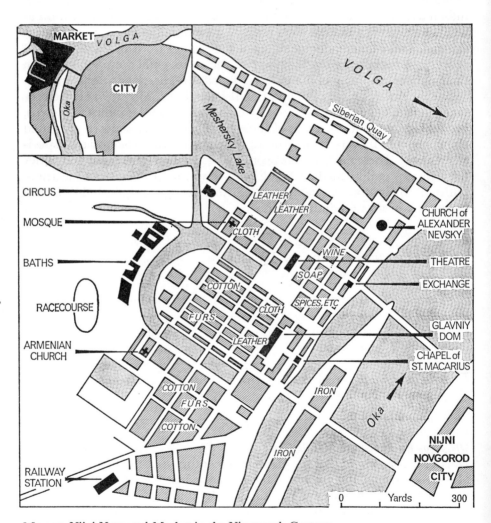

Map 11 Nijni Norgorod Market in the Nineteenth Century

rapidly as a result of their being protected in the home market by the tariff bill of 1822.

Ivanovo is only one example among many. In an enormous area comprising the provinces of Moscow, Vladimir (where Ivanov lies), Kostroma and Tver, small-scale industry gave rise to industrial villages dominated by families who had only recently put serfdom behind them, and who were eventually to rise to the highest stratum of the middle class; such were the Konovalovs near Kineshma, the Krasilshchikovs at Rodniki, the Gorbunovs near Nerekhta, and the very successful Morozovs, who branched out from Zuievo in the province of Vladimir to found numerous businesses both in that province and in the other three. These wealthy ex-serfs were accompanied in their rise by men who had always been free, peasants employed by the treasury, or small merchants who had taken advantage of the favourable commercial climate to set up workshops or business houses; families in this category included the Baranovs at Alexandrov, the Khludovs at Egorevsk, the Maliutins at Ramenskoye, and the Prokhorovs in Moscow.

Many of these industrialists were Old Believers, who brought their habitual qualities of perseverance and industry to their new occupations. Another factor contributing to their social elevation was their loyalty to one another; communities of the sect were scattered up and down the upper Volga, affording not only assistance and safe stopping-places for a fellow-sectarian's caravans but, if necessary, financial backing in his business. Regarded with suspicion by the government, these heretics nevertheless had protectors in high places, including the entourage of the tsar; but through distrust, and doubtless also from conviction, they avoided getting involved in public life; they played no part as yet in municipal administration; they concentrated on their work. Belonging to the first, or less frequently the second, merchant guild, they already constituted the élite of the middle class, and their names figured prominently in the large firms controlling the textile industry before the outbreak of the First World War. The sons of the pioneer industrialists among the Old Believers inherited sound businesses which became powerful factories after 1861.

The smallness of their numbers, and the speed with which they made money, are explained by the special conditions prevailing in Russia in the period of nascent capitalism. The market was expanding but was still fragmentary, cut up into separate areas by poor communications, and the isolation of certain border-areas caused considerable price-differences, which the industrialists took care to profit by. These advantageous circumstances were most favourable to the most active entrepreneurs – who were also those protected by the landlord-serf relationship; by the time they were emancipated they had achieved a virtual monopoly with which it was hard for anyone to compete. The number of these rising 'merchants' was small, moreover, in relation to the economic setting in which they operated; and the majority of them were mere shopkeepers, who could hardly yet be called middle-class. In 1845, the three guilds had a total membership of some 130,000; of these, about 5,000 were registered in the second guild, and less than 1,800 in the first (both merchants and industrialists). The middle class, as represented by the first two guilds, may have numbered, with their families, about 30,000 people, in a total population of approximately 65,000,000.

Paternalism and the Working Class

'The working class' is a term which, at least in its customary western acceptation, has almost no place in a description of Russian life at this period. About 1860 the existence of some 15,000 industrial undertakings was recorded, most of which, however, were craft workshops and employed only a few hands; the total labour force in these undertakings was between 500,000 and 600,000, of whom 300,000 were in the textile industry. The overall figure is small for a total population of 74,000,000. Moreover, the majority of these workers remained peasants; their links with the countryside were hardly loosened, their industrial jobs being only part-time or temporary occupations which they went to in the winter, returning to their native villages for summer and the harvest. Many of them at this period, the textile workers for example, worked in their own villages for a local firm, usually in local workshops, which were listed in the census as industrial undertakings; in this way they were able to combine industrial and agricultural work, dividing their time between the two. Whether free men or serfs, they were wage-earners, and could move from one place to another with approval of the *mir*; if they were serfs they had also to obtain the agreement of the landlord's steward (unless, of course, they were escaped serfs).

But manufacture was already tending to have a full-time, permanent work force. The metallurgical industry had done this from the first; its skilled workers were attached to their place of work by force of law; in the Ural foundries owned by the state, the workers were regarded in the same light as soldiers and subject to military regulations; and in the private factories they were really industrial serfs, even if they had originally been free and in theory were so still.

Mobility of labour was greater in the textile industry, where the workers were treated by the manager as free men, even in cases where they were serfs and therefore dependent on a landlord. But even here serfdom of a kind, backed by substantial if not legal compulsion, made its appearance in the establishments of the Old Believers, who took in fugitive serfs, concealed them so as not to have to restore them to their owners, and imposed on them a discipline which extended not only to their hours of work but to their private lives as well. It is true that under this arrangement the runaways escaped from legal serfdom and, by means of forged documents and the communities' help, were admitted to the registers of the *meshchanstvo*. But they bought their social promotion at the price of aligning themselves with a way of life almost entirely organized by the sect.

The powerful industrialist Efim Gouchkov, who managed the capital resources of the Community of the Theodosians in Moscow, and ran woollen, cotton and silk weaving mills employing close on eight hundred men in the eighteen-forties, ruled his workers with tyrannical authority, making them marry or separate as he chose and even, quite illegally, acting as their judge in criminal offences. This patriarchal conduct was typical; Orthodox owners went in for it too, but did not carry it quite so far.

Wages in the proper sense there were none; payment was complicated, variable and irregular, and its exact nature is not simple to discover. The worker was paid by the day or at piece-rates, either in cash or household provisions (which were often supplied by the establishment's own shop). Wage payments were almost always incomplete and were made at variable intervals; the largest were those made at Christmas and Easter; advances were given in the form of presents, which, except where the owner had forbidden it, sometimes consisted of vodka. But as a rule, wages were paid not directly, to the worker, but to the *artel*, the co-operative to which he belonged, and which might be external to the factory (as in tree-felling, charcoal-burning and other auxiliaries of the metallurgical industries) or internal (as in the textile industry, where the work in the fabric-printing shop was undertaken by an *artel*). In broad terms, the worker drew his pay from different sources, the main ones being the factory office and the leader of the artel (*artelshchik*). The type and method of payment, and a system of fines the exaction of which was ensured by simply deducting them from wages before the pay-out made the worker's position insecure and his future uncertain.

The workers were too few to constitute an influential force; their links with the soil prevented the growth of class-consciousness; their ignorance isolated them from the opposition, which was still confined to the intellectuals, and also from the currents of socialist thought with which, at that time, the élite of the western working class were preoccupied. The workers' movement in Russia accordingly manifested itself only in local and often individual conflicts, which involved small numbers and were fought out on purely professional, non-political issues.

Peasant Life: Subjection and Hope
During the century and a half preceding the abolition of serfdom, the majority of the Russian people – the peasants – were held in contempt. Yet they looked forward in hope. From the reign of Peter the Great to that of Catherine II, legislation reinforced the landowner's authority over his serfs, extended serfdom to the Ukraine, and, by creating the industrial serf category, appeared to treat serfdom as a permanent institution by adapting it to the country's economic development. But at the same time peasant resistance – marked by incessant disputes over tithe payments and the *corvée*, and by the disturbances and great revolts of the eighteenth century – showed that relations between serfs and landowners were founded on deep hostility, on the peasants' rejection of a system which new developments in the economic field were eventually to invalidate.

In the nineteenth century, a market economy rapidly developed and squeezed natural economy almost out of the picture. Urban growth, however slow, and the multiplication of industrial villages and small towns in the central regions, created new masses of consumers; this was a challenge to agriculture, which was simultaneously stimulated by cereal exportation through the Black Sea ports. But attempts to raise output were blocked by the passivity and ill-will of the agricultural serfs. The system was thereafter already doomed in the minds of the landowners; they foresaw its abolition, and sought only to retain as many of their advantages as possible, and to liquidate it in whatever way would be most profitable to themselves. The peasant disturbances, some of them extensive, which were common under Nicholas I, and the lesson of defeat in the Crimea in 1855, led the government to eliminate this obstacle to progress and to force the still-hesitant nobles to set their peasants free.

Serfdom had already been potentially undermined by the new structures which Russia's rudimentary capitalism had introduced into the economy. The increasing employment of regular wage-earners in factories – not only state peasants, who were free, but also serfs who had their owners' permission to work elsewhere than on the estate – was a sign that the compulsory tie between the worker and the land, which was the essence of serfdom, had become weaker.

Travel was still restricted; any peasant wanting to make a short stay outside the village needed the landlord's consent; even free peasants had to get a written permit. Peasant mobility was nevertheless increasing, stimulated by the demand for labour in the newly-developed southern regions. Agricultural day-labourers were becoming more numerous; the wage-earning agricultural class was growing.

In the central regions, where village life revolved round the *mir*, the community of interest essential to that institution was tending to break down in the years preceding 1861. Many of the periodical distributions no longer took place; the only ones that did were partial distributions, intended to adjust the size of the holdings under cultivation to the needs of families whose sizes had changed with time. The peasants were coming to regard the strips they cultivated as their own property. The growth of a market economy, and the impoverishment of families who had bred too plentifully and were weighed down by usury, enabled a minority of peasants to get rich and farm out their land to other peasants, who worked for them; a parallel to the situation in the Ivanovo district, where serfs ran their own textile mills and had other serfs working under them.

The methods and implements of Russian agriculture were hardly calculated to raise the standard of living among the peasants. Plots were tiny; they were also dispersed, one man's property being in several places; money for development was lacking; all these factors inhibited agricultural progress. Cultivation depended on a primitive plough with two shares, the *sokha*; a less common, more advanced type, with two wheels and a coulter, used in the south, where the soil was heavier, was the *plug*, 'the implement of the rich peasant' (Confino), which required a team of several oxen. The kinds of soil available for cultivation, and the scanty development of stock-breeding, favoured the *sokha*, which could if necessary be drawn by a single horse. The three-year rotation (winter wheat, barley, oats, peas, flax or hemp, and fallow) was the commonest system; but older methods of temporary cultivation on soil cleared by burning were still used, especially in the north and in the newly deforested areas in the south. The land was poorly worked, poorly manured and quickly exhausted.

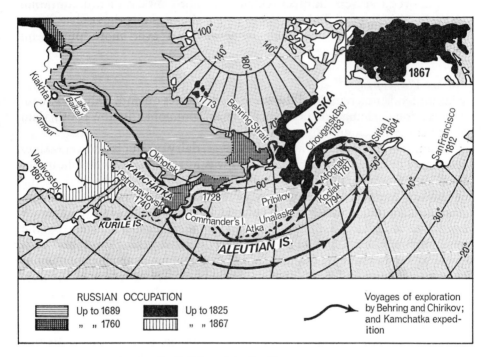

RUSSIAN OCCUPATION		Voyages of exploration by Behring and Chirikov; and Kamchatka expedition
Up to 1689	Up to 1825	
„ „ 1760	„ „ 1867	

Map 12 The Russians on Both Sides of the Pacific

Yet the taxes levied on the peasants were high and were being steadily raised for the majority of the serfs, whose masters were hard up and determined to improve their incomes. Tithes (*obrok*) and *corvées* (*barshchina*), which were increasingly combined in a mixed system which was more profitable for the landlord, were demanded ever more rigorously. The peasant disturbances, so common under Nicholas, were touched off by bitter arguments about the landlord's rights.

This sombre picture should not cause us to overlook sockal inequalities between one region and another and also one section and another of a single class, especially where the peasants were able to add to their income by craft manufacture. Siberia, still almost uninhabited, was a comparatively advantageous place to live in; so were the middle Volga regions, where the peasants were sometimes highly prosperous. Decorated *isbas*, with their carved and painted porches and window-embrasures, and richly embellished clothes for feast-days, were a visible pointer to the fact that some peasants at least were in easy circumstances and that, although the majority were still needy, the standard of living was slowly rising.

There was no real class-consciousness among the peasants. The Russian peasant class – spread out over an enormous area, varying considerably in its structure, and divided internally by conflicts of interest between its own strata – suffered under an outworn system whose abolition was imposed from above, and from motives which were not political or humanitarian but economic; a partial liberation to which the peasants themselves, however, had contributed by their tenacious and ever more purposeful resistance.

Peasant Ways of Life

Peasant foodstuffs remained the same for centuries on end. Salt pork, with an occasional change to beef (which was commoner in the south than elsewhere), was eaten only in winter.

In summer, the peasants ate poultry, eggs, dairy products and vegetables (cabbages and cucumbers); the potato was introduced into Russia under Peter the Great but was not generally cultivated until the end of the eighteenth century. Wild fruits and berries, and honey rather than sugar (the consumption of which began rising in the second half of the eighteenth century), completed a diet which was supplied almost entirely by the family's own labours. Vodka added gaiety on non-working days; and banquets to celebrate feast-days or family ceremonies, introducing various culinary refinements (meat or vegetables in pastry [*pirogi*], pancakes, rolls), were attended by a multitude of guests and cost the Russian peasant as much as would normally have supported him for several weeks.

Ordinary meals consisted of thick soup, gruel (a saying attributed to the peasants was '*Shchi da kasha, pishcha nasha*' [Cabbage soup and *kasha* are our food]) and fried potatoes; the fruits most often eaten were the sweet cucumber (*oguriets*) and the apple. Fish was a staple article of diet everywhere. In some regions the peasants held on to ancient taboos of obscure origin. Bear, hare, venison and swan were hardly ever eaten in the St Petersburg region. In some villages of the Ural region, cabbage was not eaten on St John the Baptist's day. And the diets adhered to by some religious sects (such as the *molokanes*, milk-drinkers) add a note of variety to a somewhat monotonous gastronomic scene.

Hunting, though no longer the means of procuring food and clothing, was still an important activity to the peasant in the forests of the north, the Urals and Siberia. During the winter months, from September to March, it might take the hunter, who almost always went alone, a hundred miles or more from his home. Warmly dressed and wearing a sheepskin cap, with boots of leather or bast reinforced with in-soles of hemp, and carrying a knapsack with two compartments, one for game he could eat and the other for the kinds he took home with him (fox, squirrel, otter, mink and so on), he was armed with an axe, a knife and a flintlock; in the remote northern areas and in Siberia, the latter was home-made. He moved on very broad skis and fixed strips of reindeer-skin on the bottom of them for uphill travelling, since in order to keep his hands free he used no ski-sticks. A few cooking utensils completed his outfit. The gun was not always included; powder and bullets being expensive, firearms were not widely used; traps, snares and nets were the hunter's stand-by.

Fishing was even more important than hunting, since it contributed directly to the peasant's larder; it was essential to life, especially in the northern regions with their numerous lakes, and had as a rule the advantage of not taking a man away from his village; it also demanded less skill and was a sociable occupation. It was most highly developed in the country round Novgorod, where the equipment and methods were perfected which were to be found all over Russia in the nineteenth century. Net-fishers got together in *artels* (*vataga*) of about ten men each, which divided up the local fishing-grounds between them. Net-fishing was a group activity and fostered a group spirit for which there was no place in the lonely life of the hunter.

The place where the rhythm of life was most closely geared to fishing was the Caspian region, where it was the principal means of support of the Yaik Cossacks. Below Yaitski Gorodok on the Ural River, up which the various species of sturgeon made their way in spring, the Cossacks obtained permits from the administration and, in groups of from three to five, fished during three periods: in January, when they speared the fish under the ice; the second in May, using nets; and the last and least important in October, again with nets. A further expedition was made in winter, on the tributaries and in the lakes, using nets under the ice; the purpose of this was to make provision for the winter. The catch in January and May was bought up by merchants who came to the region from all over Russia and for whom it was prepared and frozen for transport: there was a busy trade in sturgeon and beluga – some of which weighed three or four tons and yielded well over a hundred pounds of caviar – and the Cossack communities were correspondingly prosperous. Fishing, and the ancillary occupation of salt-gathering in the neighbourhood of the Ural River, provided the people's entire livelihood.

V INTELLECTUAL TRENDS — LITERATURE AND THE ARTS

The University's New Role

The policy of Nicholas I (1825–55), inspired by narrow-minded nationalism and based on the defence of autocracy and Orthodoxy, was applied to a changing society; the contrast between the two brings out all the more clearly the new intellectual currents which were flowing, and the reforming trend which drew hope from the fact that serfdom was visibly falling to pieces. The desire to control people's minds, to avoid a resurgence of Decembrism and keep the country on the beaten track of tradition, impelled the government to undertake an educational programme; primary education was left as rudimentary as before, but the stimulus given to secondary and higher education, within a framework of administrative and police supervision, produced a higher general level of intellectual life.

The number of secondary schools was increased. University entrance was restricted (by the University Statute of 1835 and later discriminatory measures) but the attempt to confine it solely to members of the aristocracy was unsuccessful. The faculties of law, language and literature were hampered by official supervision, the aim of which was to produce docile conformists who respected religion; but scientific studies were, in the nature of things, largely exempt from interference. In the eighteen-forties the University of Moscow displayed a vigorous development which was limited only by the small number of students it was allowed to enrol.

Freedom of thought was confined to small circles of students and professors, mostly aristocrats, who met more or less secretly. Opposition to the régime, after the failure of the Decembrist rising, passed from military into civilian hands. The University of Moscow became the focal point of an ardent political life, concentrated in student societies led by such men as Stankevitch and Herzen; the noblemen and commoners (though there were not many of the latter) for whom these gatherings provided a meeting-ground were the best element of that 'intellectual proletariat' which was the type and essence of the intelligentsia.

The intelligentsia were not, in the proper sense of the term, a class. Highly educated but also relatively poor, they were characterized above all by their sense of alienation from Russian society; they were, as someone remarked, the '*émigrés* of the interior'. Some of them still accepted their links with their own 'estate' (i.e. class), others, the *raznochintsy*, were voluntary *déclassés*; all were distressed by the political and social situation, opposed autocracy and Orthodoxy, and were regarded as a suspect element. Some compromised themselves with the authorities and became martyrs for their ideals. Gradually assuming a more and more radical position, they provided, from 1860 onwards, the hard core of the revolutionary movement.

Russia's Future Debated

From the beginning of the eighteenth century, enlightened opinion was divided by the reforms of Peter the Great and the road followed by the tsarist state. To a section of the conservative nobility, who idealized old Russia and its values, westernization and modernization were a denial of all they held dear. When the economic development of Europe posed the problem of Russia's material backwardness more acutely than hitherto, and made serfdom look outworn and deleterious, voices were heard among the nobility proposing its abolition but at the same time condemning the civilization of the West, which appeared to be in the later stages of decline, and defending Russia as an original civilization with a contribution to make to the future of humanity. Russia, though deflected from her true path by Peter the Great and his successors, was nevertheless still superior to the West by virtue of her national religion and her peasant institutions; the rural community was cited in this context as the great symbolic example of spontaneous unity between state and people. At once conservative and liberal, these 'Slavophils' were regarded with suspicion by the government and ridiculed by their opponents (Soloviev accused them of a religious nationalism which Russianized the Holy Ghost); and their vague Utopian theorizing was a fairly typical example of the mixture of romanticism, nationalism and mystical credulity which filled the heads of the European aristocracy at this time. The merit of such men as the brothers Kireyevsky, A. S. Khomiakov, the brothers Aksakov, and Samarin, in the 'forties and 'fifties, was that they extolled folklore, rediscovered the art of the icon, and insisted on the important place occupied in Russia's historic past by the Russian people (or rather, by an idealized version of it). In previous Russian historical studies, only the state had been glorified.

The same social background and university training produced another group of intellectuals, headed by Belinsky (1811–48) and Herzen (1812–70), who refused to reject the legacy of Peter the Great, holding, on the contrary, that the way to eliminate Russia's backwardness was to borrow the finest achievements of the West. Most of these 'Occidentalists', who envisaged Russia's future as similar to that of the western nations, were liberal reformers who adopted a line of moderate opposition to the policy of Nicholas 1; B.N.Chicherin, K.D.Kavelin, V.P.Botkin and P.V.Annenkov, among others, represented the outlook of the wealthy bourgeoisie – a small class which had little influence and no programme. The most revolutionary of the Occidentalists held considerable appeal for the intelligentsia, winning a certain amount of support among the students both for their social programme and for their somewhat surprising traditional leanings.

The movement split in half about 1845. One trend was represented by the circle of Utopian socialists who met for discussions under M.V. Butashevitch-Petrashevsky, a disciple of Fourier; the other, by Herzen, who was exiled in 1847 and disappointed by the failure of the European revolutions of 1848, and who, as the son of a big landowner, retained a romantic fondness for the peculiarities of Russian life. Herzen imagined Russia making the transition to Socialism without passing through an intermediate phase of capitalism, the rural community being in his view a symbol of the innate socialism of the Russian peasant. Smuggled copies of his periodical *Kolokol* ('The Bell'), published abroad from 1857 to 1867, exerted a profound influence on the revolutionary movement in Russia.

Reformist thought, even in its extreme forms, was at this stage conducted almost exclusively in terms of a Russia whose life was based on agriculture and the handicrafts, a Russia whose revolution was to be carried through by peasants. The reformers had little time for the bourgeoisie; and the development of a modern industrial system, in which the West was showing the way, was still regarded with suspicion. The revolutionary writers were preoccupied by the social conditions of peasant life and the controversies arising from the proposed abolition of serfdom.

Russian Literary Greatness

This is the period of the first great names in Russian literature: Griboyedov (1795–1829), Pushkin (1799–1837), Lermontov (1814–40), Gogol (1808–52) and Turgenev (1818–83). They described the injustices of a divided society, or appealed to the human thirst for freedom, and thus helped to inspire the opposition movement without directly participating in it. Griboyedov's most important work, *The Misfortune of Being Clever*, an attack on social inequality, was banned by the censorship. Pushkin, whose versatile genius matured so early, and who showed his mastery in poetry (*Eugen Onegin*), drama (*Boris Godunov*), the novel (*The Captain's Daughter*) and history (*The History of Pugachev's Rebellion*), was exiled for his fiery, revolutionary verse and led the life of a political suspect. Lermontov, a lyric poet in love with freedom, also incurred exile for his writings (*A Hero of our Time*, *The Demon*). The tsarist government was not unaware of the danger inherent in a literature whose libertarian romanticism or social realism drew attention to the régime and unmasked its vices. Irony was one of the devices by which the censorship could be evaded, an example being Gogol's novel, *Dead Souls*; contrary to what the author intended, his recantation in old age merely increased the influence of a work which, according to Herzen, had shocked all Russia. As for Turgenev, his volume of short pieces, *A Sportsman's Sketches* (1852), written in Paris, described peasant life so revealingly that Alexander II declared the book had influenced him greatly in his decision to abolish serfdom.

The whole period leading up to the great reforms of the eighteen-sixties was characterized by intense literary activity. Many periodicals were founded; publishing, after the death of Nicholas I, was relatively free from interference. The régime's attackers and defenders, though constantly engaged in polemics, often found themselves on common ground in their tendency to idealize Old Russia.

Before the Reforms

Annals of the Fatherland, founded in 1818 but suppressed until 1830, became in 1839 the centre of attraction for the most eminent representatives of Russian letters. The critic Belinsky was one of its leading figures, and its articles covered every aspect of national, literary, economic and artistic life. Its influence was eclipsed by that of other periodicals during the eighteen-fifties, but became important once more after 1868. The *Moscow News*, which appeared from 1850 to 1855, and *The Russian Messenger*, founded in 1856 and edited by M. N. Katkov (1818–87), were the standard-bearers of conservatism and authoritarian monarchy; *The Contemporary*, founded in

1836 by Pushkin and edited from 1847 onwards by Nekrassov (1821–77), was the voice of the younger generation and of revolutionary democracy.

National Music
In the eighteenth century the Russian aristocracy had been entertained by foreign operas. In the nineteenth, the compositions of M. Glinka (1809–57) marked the birth of Russian opera, in which western influences were combined with the utilization of folk melodies, a taste for which was becoming widespread among cultivated people. Glinka's operas, with their subjects drawn from the nation's past (*Ivan Susanin*, also known as *A Life for the Tsar*) or the great storehouse of popular legend (*Ruslan and Ludmila*), were not received without reservations; yet they and his symphonic works (such as *Kamarinskaya*) were to determine the course of Russian musical development throughout the second half of the nineteenth century. The Moscow Grand Theatre, built in 1780, destroyed by fire in 1803 and rebuilt in 1825, entered upon a glorious career.

VI THE TURN OF THE CENTURY

A conviction of Russia's greatness sustained the government and state during the reign of Nicholas I. Memories of the war of liberation in 1812 and the westward sweep of the tsarist armies which had camped in Paris in 1815, combined with recognition of the tsar as the policeman of Europe, whose power was sufficient to preserve apparent tranquillity in Russia while other countries were undergoing the revolutions of 1848, contributed to a national pride whose latent presence can be felt even in the most violent criticisms of the régime.

Official illusions were abruptly dispelled by the Crimean disaster. The state apparatus was seen to be unequal to its tasks; nor was the country equipped to sustain a lengthy war. The Russian social structure was exposed not merely as unjust but as a source of weakness. The need for reform, admitted henceforward by those in authority, created a comparatively liberal climate in the early years of the reign of Alexander II (1855–81), and prospects for the future were the subject of much excited debate. Over the course of a decade, while Russia was moving towards the partial liquidation of an obsolete system, the various shades of political thought became more sharply defined, ranging from revolutionary radicalism to the most narrow-minded conservatism; and, in the process, the arguments for opposition or active resistance were developed – arguments which, in the absence of organized parties, were adopted as weapons by the representatives of enlightened opinion. The period of the reforms was characterized by a sudden (and temporary) burst of freedom, freedom to think and feel and speak. Earlier economic developments, and the growth of towns, and the rise of new social strata, began to exert their influence: a steadily increasing minority was becoming aware of the questions at issue.

8
From Greatness to Decline –
The Polish State

POLAND's political institutions were potentially a model for the admiration of Europe. But she was too far ahead of her time; and divisions within her borders made her vulnerable, so that she was unable to resist the military power of her neighbours. Yet even after her political disappearance her spirit was kept alive by her record of civilization, her long struggle for existence, and her attempts at the eleventh hour to adapt herself to a world bent on destroying her.

I FROM THE 'GOLDEN CENTURY' TO THE PARTITIONS

Liberal Aristocratic Monarchism

Sixteenth-century Poland achieved a remarkable political stability, in which the power of the throne was sufficient as yet to control the nobility, whose privileges were considerable. The 'lands' or 'countries' of which the kingdom was composed were allowed a high degree of autonomy; administered by their own Diets and the palatines and castellans who, with the bishops, were also members of the king's council, they were dominated in practice by assemblies of their nobles, who were remarkable both for particularism and for their readiness to fall in with the manoeuvres of foreign powers. In the sixteenth century the Royal Council was transformed into a Senate, and Casimir Jagellon assembled the delegates to the local Diets as a Chamber of Nuncios. The Senate and Chamber constituted the national Diet, on which the statute *Nihil Novi* conferred powers unknown elsewhere: 'Nothing new [said the statute] shall be enacted by ourselves or our successors, regarding personal rights or public liberty, without the common consent of the senators and the deputies of the country.' But the principle of unanimity, which meant that any dissentients in the country at large either stood out against the régime or kept their views to themselves, had not yet laid the curse of sterility on the Diet's deliberations. Poland was in advance of her contemporaries – too far advanced, as it turned out – and had achieved an aristocratic parliamentary monarchy under which a precarious balance of forces safeguarded the essential liberties of the privileged classes. Elsewhere in Europe at this period, intolerance was the rule.

The institutions of the grand duchy of Lithuania had been undergoing a rapid development along similar lines from the end of the fourteenth century. A series of decisions taken by the grand dukes (who were also the kings of Poland) between 1387 and 1492 had followed the Polish model in defining the legal rights of the various classes of society, the analogy being particularly close in the case of nobility; Lithuania's political system, with its enlarged grand ducal Council and its provincial Diets, was very like Poland's. The resemblance was made absolute in the sixteenth century, in the reign of Sigismund Augustus. The grand duchy adopted all the Polish 'liberties', the local Diets, the Chamber of Nuncios, and the national Diet, which met for the first time in 1566. In addition, Sigismund Augustus used the Tatar menace, which was a standing danger to the southern areas of the grand duchy, to persuade the Lithuanian rulers to accept closer union with Poland.

The Union of Lublin (1569) made a single 'republic' of the kingdom of Poland and the grand duchy of Lithuania; each partner to the agreement retained its own laws, administration and army, but the two were governed by a single Diet under a single sovereign, who was elected by mutual consent. This unification, the last act in a long history of collaboration, took place after the grand duchy had been deprived of one third of its territory, including the Russian town of Smolensk, by Muscovite expansion (1514). Even so, the new state covered an area of more than 332,000 square miles.

Religious Toleration in Poland
Poland had been powerfully agitated by the Hussite movement. The doctrines of the Reformation flowed copiously into the country: Lutheranism in the northern areas and Great Poland, Calvinism in Little Poland and Lithuania. They made such headway that, by the time Sigismund Augustus came to the throne, a substantial fraction of the nobility, previously Catholic or, in Lithuania, Orthodox, had been converted. The Chamber of Nuncios had a Protestant majority; the great Sapieha and Czartoryski families went over to the Reformation. But Poland underwent no such horrors as were caused by the Wars of Religion in France. After a brief attempt at resistance, marked by a massacre of Lutherans at Danzig in 1526, the Catholic rulers were obliged to recognize the reformed religion, deny the help of the secular arm to the Catholic tribunals, and support a condition of mutual toleration which, while exceptional for the period, did not extend beyond the aristocracy. Poland gained the reputation of being a refugee for heretics; yet the passionate controversies in which the sects engaged, and in which numerous scholars from other countries came and took part, never ended in recourse to arms.

When the Jagellon dynasty became extinct, a Diet (1573) was convoked in Warsaw to decide under what conditions the new king should be elected. On the Protestants' initiative, and in an atmosphere of horror created by the news of the Massacre of St Bartholomew, the assembly succeeded (against opposition from the bishops) in passing the pact known as the Confederation of Warsaw, which guaranteed freedom of conscience and equal political rights to the adherents of the various confessions. This was in fact toleration at the top and nowhere else; it did not include commoners, and it did nothing to reduce the rights of the secular and ecclesiastical grandees on their estates, and of the king over his cities. However, it did make for religious peace – with the curious result that, by non-violent means, the Counter-Reformation was able to reconvert the country to Catholicism.

The 'Golden Century'

The Renaissance, Reformation and Counter-Reformation made the sixteenth century a capital period in the history of the civilization of Poland; a golden century. Literature in the Polish tongue made a brilliant start; the main trends of Europe's intellectual life, both political and religious, met and mingled; the liveliest arguments were conducted in a spirit of toleration which was far from typical of the age; the University of Cracow blazed with vitality; literature, the arts and the sciences overflowed with creative activity. And in this ebullient century the state, under the last representatives of the Jagellons, Sigismund the old (1506–48) and Sigismund Augustus (1458–72), still wielded power with a sufficiently firm hand to preserve the country's unity (map 13).

A cultivated society came into being among the aristocracy and the rich burghers of the towns, a society which was no longer satisfied with building castles, town halls and patrician houses, but welcomed artists, writers and scholars into its patronage and took an active part in the life of the mind. The court was no longer just a collection of customers; it became preponderant by the directions it imparted to culture and the *milieu* which it created about itself. Sigismund I's wife, Bona Sforza, an Italian princess, and her son, Sigismund Augustus, who collected a very fine library and the Wawel collection of so-called Gobelin tapestries, were true humanists.

The investigations of Nicholas Copernicus were the pride of the school of astronomy at Cracow at this period. Copernicus, the son of a rich middle-class family of Torun (a centre of the Polish export trade in wheat *via* the Baltic), was born in 1473 and educated at the University of Cracow, where he studied under two well-known astronomers and mathematicians, Wojciech of Brudzevo and Jan of Glogów. He next went to Italy, as the custom was, and studied for a further eight years, learning law and medicine at Bologna and Padua, followed by a period at Ferrara, where he was awarded a doctor's degree in canon law. But he had been making astronomical observations since 1497; he returned to Poland, and after executing several ecclesiastical commissions on behalf of his uncle, the bishop of

Warmie, he devoted himself to scientific work from 1512 to his death in 1543. His was a universal mind; in a little-known work, *De moneta cudenda ratio* (1517–26), he formulated the law later to be rediscovered by Gresham; and in his famous treatise, *De revolutionibus orbium coelestium*, published at the time of his death, he rejected the Ptolemaic system and opened the way for a new explanation of the movements of the heavenly bodies.

Polish university life was intensely active at this time and made a notable contribution to the European Renaissance. Scholarship was not devoted to classical antiquity to the exclusion of all else: the birth of Polish literature had given rise to philological research, and Jan Maczinski published a Polish-Latin dictionary; contact with the Turks and the Tatars created an interest in oriental languages. Above all, the problems of government and society, which had become acute and underlay much of what passed for religious conflict, were discussed in learned treatises which reflected hostility to the régime and expressed desires for reform. In his *Monumenta pro reipublicae ordinatione*, Jan Ostroróg put forward his theory of a sovereign national state, with a disestablished church, equality of all before the law, and universal military service. These proposals were developed more forcefully by Andrzej Frycz Modrzewski (1503–72) in his *De republica emendanda* (1551). In this work, which was translated into Polish and several other languages, the powers of the Church and the influence of Rome were subjected to sharper criticism; and though aristocratic privilege as such was not condemned, the middle class and peasants were more explicitly defended against its encroachments.

The Polish régime, which has been described as an 'aristocratic democracy', was unable to bridge the contradiction between the sovereign power of the state and the 'golden freedom' enjoyed by the happy few; the example of the western monarchies, with their growing centralization, their armies, and their reliance on a corps of 'officers' who discharged governmental as well as military duties, excited the approval of these scholarly jurists, who were concerned for the greatness of Poland and whose patriotism was alarmed both by internal dissension and by the dangers threatening the country's eastern borders. Similar preoccupations inspired Polish historians and geographers, who had been caught up by that great wave of curiosity about the world which was characteristic of the Renaissance. It was Poland which introduced the countries of eastern to those of western Europe. The rector of the University of Cracow, Maciej of Miechów, wrote a *Tractatus de duabus Sarmatis, Asiana et Europiana* (1517), a geographical and ethnographic description which went through eleven editions in the sixteenth century and was translated into Polish, Italian, Dutch and German. Meanwhile Bernard Wapowski was making his maps, which were published in 1526, of the Baltic coastal territories, Poland and Sarmatia (which meant, at that time, the countries stretching east from the Vistula to the Don and Volga basins).

Historians eager to present a picture of a strong Poland, governed by an unbroken dynastic line, devoted themselves to the critical scrutiny of the nation's origins and its present-day conditions; abandoning the old chronicle form, they composed the first great descriptions of the country: the History of Poland (*Djiejów Polski XXI ksiang*) in twelve volumes by Jan Dlugosz, the *Polish Chronicle* by Maciej of Miechów (the first history of Poland to be printed, 1519), and the two works of the bishop of Warmie, Martin Kromer, *De originibus et rebus gestis Polonorum* (1555) and *Polonia* (1570), which became better known abroad than at home.

As for the artistic field, the late fifteenth century had bequeathed to the Polish Renaissance a Gothic architecture of truly Polish character and inspiration which remained an active stylistic force for a further hundred years. Cracow provided a link between the realism of the medieval painters and miniaturists who created their works for a Gothic setting and were inspired by the local landscape and peasant life, and the new school, inspired by Italian influence, whose works were commissioned by the sovereigns from Sigismund onwards.

The medieval style, which was religious, reached its peak in the sculpture of Wit Stwosz (figure 46): the altar-screen of Our Lady of Cracow, the *Codex picturalis of Behem* (1503), a colourful record of the life of the craftsmen of Cracow, and King Casimir's tomb (1492). Thereafter the Jagellons, whose lead was followed by the court and the wealthiest section of the bourgeoisie, were responsible for the spread of an Italian style which was closer to their desire for regal magnificence. This phase was marked by the arrival in Cracow of Florentine architects and painters, and the building of the castle of Wawel (1508–16) and the memorial chapel of the Jagellons (1517–33), to which the Italian sculptors Berecci, Padovano and Canavesi contributed the tombs of Sigismund the Old and Sigismund Augustus between 1522 and 1572. But the massive, sober buildings, like fortified castles, which continued to be erected in the provinces, showed that the medieval tradition was still alive, and the Italian style itself acquired certain special characteristics through being influenced in matters of detail by regional and local peculiarities. Some of the many churches and town halls (such as that of Sandomierz), which were put up in that period of urban prosperity, display a mixed architectural ancestry, a manner which has been described as 'Polonized Renaissance'. Baroque came in later, at the end of the sixteenth century, and was slow to develop (plate 18).

Literature and Language: Polish and Latin
Latin was still the language of the administration and also of science. Copernicus and Modrzewski wrote their works in Latin; so did Klemens Janicki, who received financial patronage from Pope Paul III for his *Elegies*. But the Protestant sects used Polish in their services; the Catholic Church was obliged to use it both in theological controversy and in propaganda among the common people; thus the origin of Polish literature coincides with the Reformation.

Prose and verse are equally represented in Polish sixteenth-century literature. Most major literary effort at that time was militant; it was

involved in the clash between Catholics and Protestants and in the con-
comitant struggle between two views of the state, one section of opinion
being relatively tolerant towards foreign influence, including Rome's,
while the other was more strictly national and more sensitive to popular
feeling. The Calvinist reformer Mikolaj Rej (1505–69), who knew no Latin
and declared that he wrote 'in order that the peoples of other lands shall
know that the Poles are not geese, and that they have a language of their
own', is honoured as 'the father of Polish literature'; his copious output in
verse and prose consists of treatises, pamphlets and satires in which the
clergy and the *szlachta* are sharply criticized and Polish life is picturesquely
portrayed. *The Polish Courtier*, by Lukasz Gornicki (1527–1613), depicts a
humanist of the court. Jan Kochanowski (1530–84), one of the great Polish
poets, lived in Italy and France and finally at the court of Sigismund
Augustus before retiring to his estate at Czarnola. In his poems he sings of
his love for Poland, invoking its history and traditions and urging his compatriots to live in amity with one another. In a different key, an appeal for
unity and concord is also made by the Jesuit Pietr Skarga (1536–1612) in
his polemical writings against heresy.

Rocks and Shoals

Poland's greatness was maintained, at least in appearance, until about the
middle of the seventeenth century. The victorious campaigns of Stephen
Bathory (1575–87) in Livonia, and the still greater successes of Sigismund
III Vasa (1587–1632), who took advantage of the Time of Troubles to
quarter his troops in Moscow (1610) and recovered Smolensk by the truce
of Deulino (1618) – the provisions of which were confirmed by the 'perpetual' peace concluded in 1634 in the reign of Ladislas IV (1632–48) –
temporarily secured the eastern frontier; but the rising power of Muscovy
was still a danger to these territories, which were populated by Orthodox
Russians. Turkish raids in the Ukraine (1620), and the attempts of the
Swedes to establish themselves on the mouths of the Vistula, kept the Poles
on the alert; the position was precarious. They did manage, however, to
avoid taking part in the Thirty Years War, despite solicitations from
France and Austria.

Poland Recaptured by Catholicism
After the death in 1573 of the last member of the Jagellon dynasty, the
Diet managed to fend off the candidates put forward by the Hapsburgs.
The system of election, and the resistance of the Protestants and moderate
Catholics, saved Poland from the fate of Bohemia. However, religious
toleration was gradually working more and more to the benefit of the
Catholic Church, the side favoured by Stephen Bathory and more par-
ticularly by Sigismund III Vasa, who began excluding Protestants from
official appointments. Within fifty years the Counter-Reformation had
won. The Society of Jesus, which had been at work in Poland since 1565,

was represented by such outstanding men as Pietr Skarga, a brilliant
orator who secured the conversions of prominent noblemen, both Calvinist
and Orthodox. The intellectual superiority of the Jesuits, whose Academy
at Vilno was raised to university status while Stephen Bathory was on the
throne, is not by itself sufficient to account for the gradual return of most
of the great families to the Catholic faith. Career prospects, the court connection, and the attraction of a religion of greater social lustre more
universally recognized, and which linked its adherents with Rome, the
centre of the arts, were not without effect on Poland's cosmopolitan
aristocracy.

Catholicism gained a firmer hold through the schools which the Jesuits
set up all over the country, especially in the Ruthenian provinces, where
Orthodoxy was strong. The high quality of their teaching brought them
large numbers of pupils. Fierce competition caused the University of

Map 13 Poland in the 'Golden Century'

Cracow to decline; the transfer of the capital to Warsaw, at the end of the sixteenth century, had already dealt it a fatal blow.

The victory of Catholicism restored the country's religious unity, with the exception of the Ruthenian provinces. A residual minority of Calvinists and Lutherans was allowed to survive and to keep up its own schools and places of worship. But freedom of thought, the pioneering independence and modernity of which the University of Cracow had been the centre, was effectively stifled.

The most radical element in the sectarianism dividing religious life in sixteenth-century Poland, the element most strongly attached to a critical rational approach, was that represented by the Polish Brethren, whose doctrine was antitrinitarian and who were commonly known as the Arians. For the most part they were middle-class men, not aristocrats; they were against luxury, state authority, intolerance and war; and eventually, through the rigorous scrutiny of the recognized truths of religion, they took their stand on freedom of conscience, which implied the separation of church and state. They were persecuted by the Counter-Reformation, and their headquarters at Rakow, near Sandomir, were destroyed in 1638; in 1658 they were driven out of Poland, settling in Ruthenia, Hungary and Holland; their ideas, which exercised much appeal in western Europe, were later to inspire the philosophers of the Enlightenment.

Disaster Begins

Poland, greater than ever – prosperous, and to all appearances strong – was suddenly invaded and suffered grievous territorial losses under John Casimir (1648–68). The deluge had begun. The Ukrainian Cossacks rose against their masters, the Swedes attacked, and the Polish state narrowly escaped annihilation. Its internal weakness was shown up.

The Polish-Lithuanian territories west of the Dnieper had been gradually populated by free peasant settlers; on these the magnates (i.e. the ruling caste; nobles with hereditary official positions) were eager to impose serfdom, which was on its way to becoming the normal condition of the Polish peasantry. The territories in question were designated as feudal lands by Bathory and Sigismund III, divided into gigantic fiefs and handed over to the aristocracy, the intention being at once to integrate them more closely into the composite, varied fabric of the Polish economy and to supply the great families with a supplementary source of wealth. But though the population of that part of the Ukraine, who were not only Cossacks but Orthodox, were in principle Polish subjects, they constituted a military buffer between the Poles and the nearby Turks and Russians, and were therefore in a position to defend their independence and to exact payment for their services. After fighting the Muscovites at the side of the Poles, they spent many years resisting the policy of colonization and enslavement adopted by the kings of Poland, but were eventually overwhelmed by the Polish army. In 1638 a minority of the Cossacks, numbering 6,000, were registered as a standing mercenary force; the rest were

8

pushed down to peasant level. This was only a precarious conquest by the Catholic Polish landowners of an Orthodox and for the most part Little Russian peasantry, who could always find refuge and assistance across the border.

In the tract of country bounded on the east by the lower bend of the Dnieper – the no man's land separating the state of Muscovy from the khanate of the Crimea – the most powerful branch of the Cossacks had developed, that of the Zaporozhe ('beyond the rapids' of the Dnieper). These Zaporozhe Cossacks, whose numbers were increased by refugees from western Ukraine, were incessantly engaged in fighting the Muslims. In addition to being champions of Orthodoxy they had developed a comparatively democratic form of social organization which made them an inflammatory example to all Ukrainians who had been reduced to serfdom under the Poles. In 1648 they welcomed the Cossack leader Bogdan Khmelnitsky, who created a rising throughout the Ukraine, wiped out the Polish nobles there and defeated the king of Poland's army; finding himself unable to secure the sweeping, decisive guarantees he wanted, he treated with the tsar of Moscow and was offered control of the Ukraine.

Muscovy's reacquisition of the Ukraine caused a protracted war, which was interrupted by the truce of Andrussof in 1667 and ended by the 'perpetual' peace of 1681, under which the Ukraine was partitioned between the two countries. Poland lost a long strip of territory on the middle and upper Dnieper round Smolensk and Tchernigov.

Meanwhile the army of Charles x of Sweden had swept into Poland. Cracow fell in 1656; Danzig and Leopol were the only towns to repel the invaders; some of the castles and isolated monasteries held out, as at Czestochowa, where the monks had put their house in order for defence. All classes of the nation were on fire with the spirit of resistance. The king, who had had to flee to Silesia, resumed the attack, but although he succeeded in expelling the foreign troops from Polish soil he was obliged to cede Livonia to Sweden by the treaty of Oliva (1660); he had already renounced his claim to sovereignty over Prussia.

The 'deluge' marked the beginning of Poland's decline. By 1660, when war with Muscovy was still in progress, the rural population had diminished and agriculture was in a state of collapse; towns had been damaged and looted and in some cases destroyed, with the result that their trade never recovered in the interim before partition; and social unrest was aggravated by poverty.

But these were temporary handicaps. A graver source of weakness was disunity among the nobles who ruled the country without being willing to yield any of their privileges; thus they opposed any reform which might tend to strengthen the power of the throne. John Casimir had a plan for suppressing the *liberum veto* and creating permanent taxes, but was unable to carry it through. It was in this unhappy period that the problem of Poland's political system became endemic. It was no longer merely a matter for academic controversy; the Polish state – a constitutional oddity among the semi-absolute monarchies of Europe – was henceforward gambling with its own existence.

In contemporary eyes, however, the dangers looming over Poland's future were less obvious. The indefatigable Polish army, the rampart of the Christian world against the Turks, was still famous despite its reverses. The splendour of this military tradition was maintained for a while longer, notably by John Sobieski, who reigned from 1674 to 1696 and, in response to an appeal from the emperor Leopold, delivered Vienna from the besieging Turks in 1683. The death of this outstanding military leader, who was obsessed by the crusading spirit but enough of a realist to foresee the dark times lying ahead for his country, brought Poland's epoch of greatness to a close.

Stagnation of the Nobility

Science and letters in seventeenth-century Poland declined along with the universities and aristocratic culture. The course of events, and the guidance imposed on intellectual life by the Counter-Reformation, did nothing to encourage their development. The fostering of the best minds in the country was hampered by an increasingly aristocratic régime, by which in practice if not in principle the middle class was excluded from reaching high office in the Church, which held a virtual monopoly of control even in the economic field. Essentially, Polish society consisted of an enormous mass of peasantry dominated by swarms of nobles; the bourgeoisie was a comparatively small class. They had been an important factor in the country's culture in the past, especially during the period of urban prosperity at the beginning of the seventeenth century, but had sunk back into insignificance in the sixteen-fifties. The sole guardians of intelligence were the *szlachta*, who became more ignorant with every passing year; the great families, among whom a Maecenas cropped up here and there; and the clergy, absorbed in their task of reconquest.

Thus this period can show few writers of outstanding merit, and even these tended to produce memoirs, historical epics or accounts of contemporary events. French influence, moreover, was prevalent at the court, where the leading figure was Marie-Louise de Gonzague, the wife of Ladislas IV and subsequently of John Casimir. The most notable of the writers, Andrzej Morsztyn (1613–93), belonged to the French party and translated *Le Cid*, by Pierre Corneille, which was acted at court in 1661; he also published a volume of poems, *The Lute*, in a rarefied baroque style. The tradition of criticizing the régime was kept up by Marshal Stanislaw Herakliusz Lubomirski, in his *De vanitate consiliorum*. But the two most prolific writers of the time were the poet Waclaw Potocki (1625–96), who was a member of the Polish Brethren but left the movement during the persecution of 1658, and whose most interesting poem describes the campaign of 1621 against the Turks; and Jan Chrysostom Pasek, whose anecdotal memoirs reflect the great national events of the day and contain violent attacks on Queen Marie-Louise and the French party.

II DEATH OF A STATE, SURVIVAL OF A NATION

During the period of the Saxon kings (1697–1763), Poland, in the words of Lelewel, was 'sunk in a state of stupor . . . as if paralysed'. Her kings were foreigners, who for the most part ruled her without leaving their own country; she was abandoned to the intrigues of the *szlachta* and the great families; in the grinding hostilities between the Russians and the Swedes her territory was used as a transit zone, pillaged by the troops of both sides and falling progressively under the domination of Russia, whose possessions had been suddenly enlarged under Peter the Great; in short, she had lost her independence only to watch the internal causes of her decay becoming more pronounced than before.

Facts and Conditions

The period of the Saxon kings began in 1697 with the nomination of the Elector of Saxony, Frederick Augustus, to the Polish throne; and the new king's alliance with the Russians against the Swedes, in 1700, placed Poland at the centre of a war in which she played a semi-neutral role throughout. The Saxon, Russian and Swedish armies used her as their battlefield. Charles XII passed through the country after his victory at Narva, beat the Saxons near Cracow and set up another king, Stanislas Leszczinski (1704), who was soon compelled to flee. Russian troops advanced into the eastern provinces, rallying the supporters of the king of Saxony, and entered Warsaw after defeating Charles XII at Poltava (1709). The new king, Augustus II, was acknowledged by the Tsar but suspected of authoritarianism by the Polish nobility, and appealed to the Russians for military help to deal with the Confederation of Nobles, who had gathered in force at Tarnograd. The Confederation made the same appeal and the Tsar became the arbiter of Poland's destiny. There was a plan among some of the nobles to obtain augmented powers for the Diet, but this was defeated; and though the Saxon troops left Poland the Polish army was reduced in size and was thereafter too small to defend the country.

Hopes for independence were now transferred to the exiled king, Stanislas Leszczinski. His supporters in Poland, who were grouped round the great Potocki family, intrigued against the Saxon court and succeeded, on the death of Augustus II in 1733, in getting their candidate elected – the rival families of the Potocki and the Czartoryski having reached a reconciliation in order to avoid compromising the national cause. But the Russian army intervened, entered Warsaw and forcibly secured the election of Augustus III (1733–63). Stanislas Leszczinski, taking ship at Danzig, once more left Poland, and his remaining partisans were compelled to submit to the Diet of Pacification (1736). Augustus III ceded the duchy of Courland, where the empress Anne of Russia set up her favourite, Bühren.

After this, Poland ceased to count as a political power. She remained neutral during the War of the Austrian Succession, despite the empress Elizabeth's urgent requests to the Diet of 1744; during the Seven Year's War Polish territory was freely crossed by Russian troops on their way to conquer Berlin, and was even invaded by the Prussians, who got as far as Poznan. The end of the war (1763), the death of Augustus III, whose son was too young to be placed on the throne, and the coronation in 1764 of a member of the Czartoryski family, Stanislas Augustus Poniatowski, marked the inception of a new phase, in which Poland's political decline became more marked but proceeded in a new atmosphere of national recovery.

Poverty of the People

The peasants, silent and oppressed, found their position deteriorating in the period of reconstruction which followed the 'deluge'. The rehabilitation of agriculture which was set on foot by the great landowners involved breaking down large areas of cultivation into much smaller ones, and also forced many smallholders into employment on the landlord's personal holding, which was worked by a combination of agricultural serfs, wage-earning labourers and peasants liable to the *corvée*. The amount of the *corvée* demanded kept on going up, reaching six days a week in some instances. The free peasant became nearly extinct; most of the peasants fell into the iron grip of serfdom.

This general fall to a proletarian level was not absolutely universal; there was a certain amount of variety. The necessity for inviting German settlers to help in colonizing the western districts augmented the proportion of peasants who were free of the *corvée* and paid their dues in grain and money. In a few localities, German village rights also applied to the adjacent Polish village; an example was the rural estate of the municipality of Poznan, where the *corvée* was abolished from 1728 to 1747. In some cases the tenant-vassals in the royal villages benefited from special terms, particularly in Lithuania, where the *corvée* produced such a low output that it was abolished between 1680 and 1712, a measure affecting some 100,000 peasants. But these were very minor variations. The oppression and poverty weighing on the bulk of the peasant population were so heavy that they even made a dead letter of the legislation by which the peasant was tied to the estate; the colonization of the eastern provinces, for example, was made possible by the stream of fugitives who had avoided recapture.

The townsfolk suffered even more severely from the ravages of war, and the middle class, which had been numerically weak in the first place, became of still smaller account. Invasions and epidemics reduced many towns to the level of insignificant hamlets. The growth of Russia's external trade, a development noticeable even before Peter the Great's reign but specially prominent in the eighteenth century, faced the Polish towns with a new source of competition and was a further obstacle to their recovery. The impoverished peasants bought fewer manufactured articles than

before, and the needs of the aristocracy were increasingly satisfied by imported foreign merchandise. The commercial middle class found its economic position being eroded by the nobility; nobles were settling in the
towns, where residential 'islands' belonging to them, or to religious communities, obtained a dominant economic position and precluded the
development of any independent business activity or craft manufacture.
Whenever there was a clash of interest between the wealthiest commercial
element – the patricians of the trading classes – and their poorer competitors, the nobles who held local powers from the king supported the
popular side, in order to weaken the bourgeoisie and whittle away their
privileges.

Some 2,000 towns had acquired municipal charters; among them were
400 royal towns, and eight cities with a population of over 10,000 (Danzig,
50,000; Warsaw, 40,000; Lwow, 30,000; Wilno, 24,000; Cracow, 20,000;
Torun, 13,000; Lublin and Poznan, 10,000 each); the remainder were
secular or ecclesiastical properties .In the larger towns, fire and war had
not destroyed the town hall, market buildings and fine old houses, which
remained as monuments to former prosperity. But commercial activity had
dwindled sharply; exports of wheat and timber had diminished by one
third.

Religious Differences

The presence, within frontiers extending unnaturally far to the east, of
large religious minorities, so that loyalties were divided between Catholicism and Orthodoxy and, still more acutely, between Poland and Russia,
increased Poland's external difficulties in the eighteenth century: the
situation gave the Russians an excuse for intervening in her internal affairs.
Yet religious diversity would not have become a disruptive factor in the
Polish state without the proselytizing policy of the Catholics after the
Counter-Reformation.

The Protestants – Lutherans in the northern provinces, Calvinists in
Lithuania – were now reduced to about two hundred thousand, belonging to
the bourgeoisie and nobility and, in practice, long since deprived of the
rights expressly acknowledged by the settlement of 1573. Gradually excluded
from the provincial diets and the senate, from judicial office and finally (in
1718) from the Chamber of Nuncios, they were forbidden to hold public
office of any kind in 1733. A military career was the only one now open to
them. Not allowed to build churches after 1717, and subjected not to
general persecution but to a steady bombardment of petty restrictions,
they began to turn a hopeful eye on Prussia; this happened particularly in
the north, in Torun and Danzig, where they still had the right to hold
municipal office and commerce was still partly in their hands. Violence
was rare, however; in 1724 the burgomaster and nine burghers of Torun
were executed for sacrilege, but this was an isolated case. Lack of fanaticism is a fairly constant feature of the Polish mentality, and there was
a longstanding tradition of genuine tolerance; thus Catholic pressure,

encouraged from abroad, was to some extent curbed. Local autonomy, and the peculiarities of regional and individual liberties, created a variety of situations, in which the personal inclinations of bishops and office-holding landowners were the decisive factor. In Lithuania, the Radziwill family protected both Calvinists and Orthodox. The Protestant question nevertheless remained a source of division; all the more so when the Protestants' numbers began tending to rise, the need for repopulation having led kings and magnates to introduce colonists of German origin, even in Warsaw, where heretics had previously been banned.

A more serious problem was that presented by the Orthodox minority and the Ruthenian Uniates. The Polish provinces bordering on Russia had a population of half a million, who were Orthodox. These were Byelorussians for the most part, with concentrations of considerable size in the Ukraine; all they had was a bishopric at Mohilów (under the Patriarch of Kiev), a school at Vilno, and approximately fifty monasteries, for which they had difficulty in finding enough monks; they were essentially a peasant element, poor, illiterate and totally without influence in the state, but constituting a target for Russian irredentism.

Catholicism, moreover, was disunited. Alongside six million Catholic Poles (nearly all of whom were in the kingdom, i.e. Poland proper) were four million Ruthenians, who worshipped according to the Greek rite, in the grand duchy of Lithuania.

Polish colonization in these parts of Lithuania – Red Russia, Volhynia, Podolia and the Ukraine – was indeed successful in establishing islands of Catholics and even in winning over the Ruthenian bourgeoisie and nobility, who spoke Polish, and some of whom adopted the Catholic rite; but the overwhelming majority of the people remained faithful to the eastern form of Christianity. Under the Union of Brzesc (Brest) (1595) they were formally attached to Rome; but this move, which was purely the work of the higher clergy, had no effect on the loyalties of the peasantry and lower clergy, both of whom 'did not so much support as endure it' (Jobert). Orthodox pilgrimages to Kiev continued to attract crowds of Ruthenian peasants from Poland. And the struggle between Orthodoxy and Catholicism for the control of bishoprics went on for over a century after the Union and was still in progress at the beginning of the eighteenth century: the dioceses of Lwów and Luck came over to the Polish side only in 1700 and 1701 respectively. The Ruthenian Uniate Church was dominated by the excellent educated Order of the Basilians, whose members came from aristocratic families, had no influence on the lower clergy, and held a complete monopoly of ecclesiastical dignities.

Meanwhile the policy of successive Polish kings was inimical to the Greek rite; they regarded the Union as a step towards complete assimilation. Thus the Ruthenian Uniates did not enjoy the freedom and equality which had been accorded to them in principle; their Metropolitan, whose see was at Vilno, and who had the archbishop of Polock and six bishops under him, was not given a seat in the Senate, nor were the few noble families who had remained faithful to the Greek rite. In their distrust of the sovereign's intentions, the higher clergy and Ruthenian nobility sought the support of the Vatican, which considered the Union imprudent, and opposed it.

But the common people had nothing to do with such conflicts; speaking various Ukrainian dialects, and living on estates many of which were owned by Polish magnates, they constituted a mass of dissentients to whom the Greek rite was a means of expressing their hostility to the Poles and their solidarity with the Orthodox population on the other side of the border.

The Catholic Church, with its six million faithful who adhered to the Roman rite, dominated the situation. Farming seventeen per cent of the land under cultivation, and possessing considerable sources of revenue as well as owning houses, businesses and manufacturing concerns, it covered the country with its religious establishments and, in its aristocratic structure, reflected the inequalities of Polish secular society. From the sixteenth century onwards, even members of the upper middle class could not attain the rank of bishop or abbot. Commoners in the Church provided the indigent, ignorant ranks of the lower clergy. The most profitable cures of souls, and all the higher dignities, were monopolized by the nobility. The king's right to nominate bishops and the heads of thirteen of the big monasteries underlined the aristocratic character of the superior clergy, as did the fact that a number of bishoprics were owned and controlled by great families such as the Czartoryski, Potocki, Zaluski and Szembek. Thus there were representatives of the Polish nobility who by virtue of their family position drew considerable revenue from ecclesiastical estates; and this income was a measure of their standing and influence in the country. Financially speaking, the bishop of Cracow's income of 1,200,000 florins put him third on the list of European prelates, just below the archbishop of Toledo and the bishop of Strasburg. Material wealth, moral influence and political power went together: the seventeen Catholic bishops had seats in the Senate, with the magnates.

Interplay of Patriotism and Self-Interest

The Polish aristocracy were not exempted from the difficulties of the time by the dominant and exclusive position they had attained. But power, and most of the available land, and opportunities for culture and progress, were all in their hands. They were a numerous class, representing ten per cent of a population which had reached something like twelve millions; and a uniform class as regards their pretentions, if not their means. Half of them were almost as poor as the peasants; a blue-blooded proletariat, restless and unruly, more or less attached to the great families, whose wealth contrasted more strongly with the poverty of the peasants than in any other country. The resources of Prince Charles Radziwill were on a par with the king's. The property of the Lubomirski and Potocki families was to be reckoned in terms of dozens of towns and hundreds of villages. The magnates had not only their private properties but their *starostie*, state properties allocated to them by the king as a reward for their services. In the Ukraine, veritable *latifundiae* were set up in this way for some of the great families, the Lithuanian Radziwills and Sapiehas, the Polish Lubomirskis, Potockis and others. Both extremes and all possible intermediate levels were represented, from the half-starved nobleman, proud of his privileges but driving his own cart, to the great lord, the furnishing of whose town and country residences was on an oriental scale of luxury. In such a wide and varied class – half of whom, Stanislas Augustus used to say, could not read – the minority possessing both wealth and refinement was small indeed.

The condition of Poland in the first half of the eighteenth century has been described as 'Saxon lethargy'; an apt label for an exhausted country, where it seemed that all development was at an end and that society had lost the capacity for change and growth. Yet latent forces of progress were present; otherwise there could not have been the final burst of activity which held such importance for the future, and which demonstrated the vitality of the Polish nation under partition. Unfavourable accounts from western travellers, whose own countries were much more advanced, underline a contrast which both surprised and shocked them (but which applied, of course, to all the countries of eastern Europe, especially Russia).

After the 'golden century' the gap between Poland and the West had in fact become greater, and Poland's future looked extremely unpromising. Nevertheless, as early as the reign of Augustus III (1733–63), that is to say in the Saxon period, there were signs of recovery by comparison with the preceding period; signs of progress, even, however unobtrusive.

The Polish magnates, their country's only capitalists at that time, showed in the face of economic difficulty that they were by no means passive owners of the means of production. They made a real effort to preserve and increase their wealth. Agriculture moved slowly forward; fallows were reduced, within the framework of an old-established three-year system of cultivation, in which spring and winter wheat and forage crops were beginning to play a bigger part. Craftsmen in certain luxury trades were brought in from abroad. Abandoned mines were brought back into production. Several kinds of manufacture appeared on the estates of the great landowners. In Lithuania, Princess Anne Radziwill instituted the production of woollen cloth, pottery and tapestries. The clergy played a part in this economic recovery; Andrew Stanislas Zaluski, bishop of Cracow, developed iron production on his episcopal estates.

After the Swedish wars the ruined towns started coming back to life; especially Warsaw, where the population was rapidly increasing and the first Italian cafés and French dress-shops were appearing. A superficial observer might have thought Polish society ultra-conservative, stuck in the rut of its obsolete institutions; at the same time, however, steady progress towards economic recovery brought with it a social fluidity whose effects were already perceptible by the time of Augustus III's death. The excess of births over deaths came at the right time to meet new needs. Impoverished

8*

nobles were attracted to the city, where they found administrative posts and came into touch with the resurgent bourgeoisie. During this period were laid the social foundations on which future reformers of the state were to build.

Meanwhile, however, the *liberum veto* – 'the eye of liberty' – was operating in such a way as to make the Diet increasingly powerless to get anything done. The proportion of Diets dissolved after reaching a stalemate was 50 per cent in the years 1700–20, between 50 per cent and 60 per cent in 1720–40, and 100 per cent in 1740–60. The 'sickness of the Diet' was not exclusively caused by aristocratic self-interest and an anarchical conception of freedom; it was deliberately cultivated by foreign agents, Prussian, French and Russian. Whereas the magnates were too powerful not to align their political outlook with the interests of the country, the impecunious *szlachta* were open to corruption.

FIGURE 28 A wherry on the Vistula, Warsaw, eighteenth century. After a picture by B. Belotto, known as Canaletto, entitled *A View of Warsaw*.

This was the epoch, nevertheless, in which the more enlightened minds became aware of the political problem confronting the country. The Russian protectorate, foreign pressures, and the impossibility of implementing even the smallest reforms which might have arrested the decline of the state presented the Polish nobility with a dilemma: they must modify the régime or perish. But the fear of imminent catastrophe was for a long time overshadowed by anxiety to safeguard private interests and also by the feeling that the existing structure, with its peculiar local and regional autonomies and the individual rights it conferred on the privileged few, created a society which, if less firmly knit together, was also more liberal than any of the western monarchies and imposed fewer restrictions on the people. Hence the very moderate attitude adopted by the advocates of reform, such as Stanislas Dunin-Karwicki, the Abbé Konarski (in his earliest writings), Jan Stanislas Jablonowski, and the exiled king Stanislas Leszczsinski. In their pages the 'republican' nature of the state is taken for granted; so is the individual's right to be as free and independent as he likes; and an attempt is made to reconcile the power of the Diet with a more effective, more highly centralized government. The social order is left almost uncriticized.

Of greater significance for the future was the development of education at the hands of the clergy, who were numerous (about fifty thousand towards the middle of the century, half of these being regular, i.e. belonging to an order). They set up schools and seminaries all over the country.

The inferior education supplied by schools run on traditional lines, with Latin and rhetoric as almost the only subjects, had caused a decline in intellectual standards which the clergy strove to resist. The progress achieved was due less to the Jesuits, who ran the University of Vilno and some forty secondary schools and had a virtual monopoly of the teaching profession, than to the Piarists, in whose establishments, created as a result of the educational reforms of the Abbé Stanislas Konarski, a whole generation of patriotic nobles received the training which enabled them to form the backbone of the national movement at the end of the century.

In 1740, in Warsaw, Konarski started a *Collegium nobilium* (College of Nobles) whose curriculum found room for modern philosophy (Descartes, in particular), constitutional law, history and foreign languages. All the Piarist schools were reformed on these lines. The pupils' exercises, stripped of the 'baroque' eloquence against which Konarski had rebelled, bore on subjects of wide scope and general concern: the problems of aristocratic privilege, serfdom, the *liberum veto*, industrial development. Academic discussions of this sort were common to the Age of Enlightenment in general; applied to the special case of Poland, they had the merit of developing civic consciousness, and a sense of responsibility towards the nation, among a nobility which tended to be a law unto itself and to be much too fond of its privileges.

Finally, in a remarkable work on *The Effective Means of Deliberation*, published in four volumes between 1761 and 1763, Konarski attacked the principle of the *liberum veto* – the principle of unanimity which was at the root of his country's misfortunes – and argued in favour of decision by majority vote.

Apart from political writings, the literature of the first half of the century is very poor. Two of the few names worth mentioning are those of the first Polish women of letters, Elzbieta Druzbacka and Franciszka Urszula Radziwillówna; the second (1705–53) put on performances of plays by Molière at her castle of Nieświez. Foundations were laid for the renaissance of Polish science by the bibliographical labours of Bishop Andrzej Zaluski

(1702–24), who, with his brother, Josef, gathered an enormous library, one of the largest in Europe, containing 300,000 volumes and 100,000 manuscripts.

Poland as 'the Paradise of the Jews' ?

Poland had a million Jews (nearly a tenth of the population), constituting a 'Jewish nation' which was represented in the Diet. Speaking Yiddish more than Polish, organized autonomously, with their own schools, police and justice, and living in urban sections which were in no sense ghettos, the Polish Jews enjoyed greater tolerance than those of other countries. It may be doubted, however, whether Poland was exactly a paradise for them. They were despised, subjected to continual annoyances, and exploited by the nobles, who made use of them for their own ends. Access to the royal cities was often made hard for them by the city council; and in Warsaw they were banned altogether, at least in theory. But they played an important part in the feudal economy as tax-farmers and go-betweens, and small-scale commerce was largely in their hands. They resisted the Church's attempts at converting them under Augustus III, and constituted a human wedge of near-foreigners, separate, as yet, from the rest of the nation.

The Partitions

As early as 1764, at the opening session of the Diet, members of the Czartoryski family had raised the question of the *liberum veto*, and the voivode Andrzej Zamoyski, in a speech which became the point of departure for the reforming policy adopted by the king and one section of the magnates, demonstrated the link between the majority principle and republican government. Russia and Prussia ensured the failure of the project for reform, and two years later, alarmed by measures of the Diet which aimed at strengthening the king's hand and reorganizing the administration, encouraged those of the aristocracy who were against reform to combine in the Confederation of Radom; they also compelled an extraordinary Diet (1767–8), whose deliberations took place under the pressure of a Russian army of occupation, solemnly to uphold the principles of the king's election, the *liberum veto* and aristocratic privilege, all of which were raised to the dignity of 'cardinal laws'. Resistance from a handful of nobles, who formed the Confederation of Bar (1768), started a civil war which went on for two years and was complicated by peasant riots in the south-east of the country. Frederick II having profited by the opportunity to occupy part of Great Poland, Catherine II had started negotiating with Prussia and Austria with a view to carving up Polish territory for the first time; her Manifesto of July 1772 justified armed intervention by alleging the need to 'quell the Polish disorder' and to ensure 'the just satisfaction of her legal rights' (map 19, p. 339).

East of the upper Vistula, Poland lost the whole region of Léopol (Lwów), later known as Galicia, West Prussia with the exception of Torun and Danzig, and a wide belt of territory east of the Duna and in the region of Mohilev. The most agonizing amputations were those profiting Prussia and Austria. Catherine II got her hands on Russian territories, whose population was Orthodox and which were of slighter economic significance; but from now on she controlled Poland's internal politics through her ambassador, and instigated a certain number of limited reforms which further diminished the king's power, to the advantage of the magnates and impotent diets.

However, the partition of 1772 at least put an end to the civil war and abruptly opened the eyes of the Polish ruling class to the magnitude of the threat looming over the very existence of the state. The patriotic magnates, in the new Permanent Council which had been imposed on the king and shared executive power with him, and also in the Diets which, until 1786, did a modest but useful job, supported Stanislas Augustus in his efforts to foster the growth of a national spirit and to improve the country's institutions without incurring the Russian government's displeasure. This admirable work of recovery could not be carried out completely: the 'proconsul', the ambassador Stackelberg, put obstacles in its way; and its effects were curtailed by the selfishness and shortsightedness of many of the nobles, and the inertia of the masses, who had never been given a part to play in political life and whose only interest was the struggle for a living. Yet the work was lasting; it created a psychological climate in which an increasing proportion of opinion was trained into patriotic habits of thought, and progress was made towards national unity.

A Crowned philosophe – Stanislas Augustus

The reign of Stanislas Augustus (1764–95) is one of the paradoxes of Polish history. He had been elected on 7 September 1764 with the support of the 'Family' (i.e. of the Czartoryski) and under the protection of the Russian armies. After this, Russia's intervention in Polish affairs became more and more direct and pressing, opposing every serious attempt to improve the country's political machinery and, in particular, to abolish the *liberum veto*. Poland's political weaknesses made her more vulnerable to Russia's ambitions. What Catherine II dreamed of was a Poland closely linked, through Stanislas Augustus, her former lover, with Russia. Political interest was reinforced with the idea of Slav solidarity, which was not without supporters on the Polish side too. But competition from the ambitions of Poland's western neighbours forced Russia to limit and adapt her plans, and led to the country's dismemberment. In the partitions of 1772, 1792 and 1795, the Polish state disappeared.

Yet these years of calamity were also those of a last burst of vigour, a period when national consciousness flared up and the people learned the basic lessons of patriotism. The thirty years which began with the speech of Andrzej Zamoyski to the Diet of 1764, and ended with the national insurrection led by Thaddeus Kosciuszko in 1794, were the most tragic and discouraging which Poland had so far experienced, but also the richest in promise for her future.

After a long eclipse, the throne was once more occupied by a Polish sovereign. A '*philosophe* with a crown', the sensitive and cultivated Stanislas Augustus had travelled widely in the Europe of the Enlightenment, frequenting the *salon* of Madame Geoffrin in Paris, discovering a political ideal in England, and the example of a hard-working commercial nation in Holland. He had made himself learn all he could; thus prepared, he looked with an educator's eyes on his chosen task, that of 'restoring the political state of the Fatherland, and of developing the genius of the nation'.

His most fruitful achievement was to found a Commission of National Education in 1773. But all his measures, whether carried out or only planned, were inspired by the same preoccupation with national unity, the same desire to extend the country's administrative and professional structures beyond the narrow, exclusive bounds of the aristocracy and to draw all classes closer together by improving the conditions of the peasantry and enlarging the rights of the middle class.

Himself a member of the Czartoryski family, he had nothing of the revolutionary in his make-up; he was by nature an enlightened moderate. Even so, until catastrophe finally swept him aside, he was forced time after time to give way; compromise, concession and withdrawal were typical of his lifework, a work pursued tenaciously but doomed in advance to almost certain failure, a task carried out under the tragic conditions of a foreign protectorate and continuously-endangered frontiers. He has been called '*l'homme du sursis*' (Fabre), 'a specialist in postponement'. He was certainly a specialist in conciliation, which he would go to great lengths to secure. He was gifted neither with a strong will nor with much love of action; the resources he was given to govern with were not great; and Poland was under the shadow of foreign domination. Such were the circumstances in which he undertook to defend her national interests.

Before the partitions, Jean-Jacques Rousseau told the Poles: 'You cannot stop them from devouring you; make sure at least that you prove indigestible!' The Polish state's last twenty years of life created the preconditions for the survival of a nation about to lose its frontiers.

This final burst of national vitality was not solely the achievement of the 'patriotic party' which supported the king's endeavours and which, with representatives of the great Czartoryski, Potocki and Malachowski families among its members, had the power and personal influence to enlist the co-operation of the educated nobility; it was also the result of economic development and the advance of education, two factors which had been gradually transforming Polish society. The magnates and other rich nobles were exploiting the natural resources on their estates more energetically. and building factories; from 1764 onwards, they could engage in business and the industrial professions without loss of dignity; and this middle-class slant on the part of the aristocracy was undermining their traditional attitude, based on personal privilege and the exploitation of the peasants.

Simultaneously, the hitherto insignificant middle class was strengthened by the economic recovery of the towns and by the new little centres of industry springing up on the feudal estates themselves, especially in Great Poland. Although the partition of 1772 reduced the size of the national market and cut off some of its outlets. Poland continued on the whole to take part in the contemporary increase in the volume of trade. Cracow, despite being a frontier town, became a 'greater Cracow' which, with its suburb, Kazimierz, attained a population of thirty thousand and developed its trade with neighbouring Silesia.

There were more jobs available in road and river transport; there was also an increase in the number of shopkeepers; both factors, particularly the first, had the effect of freeing a certain number of peasants from the soil, some of whom managed by this means to enter commerce. Social mobility became greater and feudal ties were further weakened.

A sense of national unity was still confined to a minority, but pressure of circumstance was driving the lesson home and their number was growing. The same effect was produced by Piarist education, both in the College of Nobles, which the new king visited directly after his accession, and in the public schools run by the Order. The urgency of the need to develop education in the national interest was increasingly recognized.

In 1765 Stanislas Augustus founded a Cadet School to educate the penurious sons of the *szlachta* for a career in the army or the civil service; this school, maintained largely by the king and Prince Adam Czartoryski, produced several leaders of the national uprising, including Kosciuszko. All the teaching orders had royal backing and encouragement, including the Jesuits, who during the reign of the last Saxon king founded new schools (at Vilno, Ostróg, Warsaw and Lublin), and who gradually shed the trammels of scholasticism, turned towards the sciences, and supported the movement for political and social reform. There was a wave of activity among all the best-educated people in the country, a wave which reached its height during the years of anarchy between 1768 and 1772 and which resulted, directly after the partition, in the establishment of the Commission of National Education, 'the crowning achievement of the reign' (Jobert).

The Commission of National Education

The suppression of the Jesuit order by the Pope (1773), a decision which aroused the indignation of the court and Diet, resulted in the drawing-up of a comprehensive plan for education. Under the law of 14 October 1773 there was set up in Warsaw a 'commission responsible for providing education for young noblemen, under the protection of His Majesty the King'; the commission was given authority to supervise 'all academies, secondary schools, academic colonies and public schools, and everything connected with the studies and instruction of young noblemen'. This was the initial programme.

But in the next twenty years the commission made a gradual transition from this aristocratic point of view to a wider conception, under which education was to be made available to all classes without discrimination. Led by remarkable minds – Prince Michael Poniatowski, the king's brother, who became its chairman in 1786, Ignaz Potocki, one of Konarski's old pupils, and the chancellor Chreptowics, the author of the plan – the commission battled against severe financial difficulties and the rivalries of different confessions and social interests, and was spied upon meanwhile by the Russian embassy, which had planted its agents among the patriotic magnates; a programme of educational development was patiently and effectively carried out, with Jesuits and the secular priests of various denominations collaborating with each other and with a large number of laymen, of both aristocratic and middle-class origins. The new spirit in education, with official recommendation and encouragement, was especially effective in disseminating the principles of progress and creating a climate in which reform could flourish.

Cracow, the Home of Patriotism

A young canon named Kollontaj (1750–1812), the son of a poor family in Volhynia, was entrusted by Michael Poniatowski with the task of reforming the University of Cracow, founded under the Jagellons and now in a very depressed condition. In 1780 the University was promoted to the position of Principal Crown School, whose best students became teachers in secondary schools; it was provided with scientific collections and apparatus, which it had not had before; the curriculum was overhauled new teachers were recruited among the middle class in Cracow; thus reorganized and rejuvenated, without recourse either to the monastic orders or to foreign countries, the University regained its intellectual standing, started a course in Polish law in 1788, and became an important training-ground for Poland's future citizens.

The University of Vilno, which was also raised to the rank of a Principal School and was staffed by priests and foreigners, played a similar part, though on a more modest scale, in Lithuania.

Upsurge of National Literature. Committed Writers

From the very beginning of his reign Stanislas Augustus invited writers and artists to his Thursday dinner-parties, and the court became a centre of brilliant intellectual life. Naturally enough, members of his familiar circle tended to possess a courtier's attitude; not all of them were sensitive to their country's misfortunes. One of them, Ignaz Krasicki (1735–1801), bishop of Warmie, who slipped into Prussia at the time of the first partition and was a master-hand at taking evasive action ('*virtuose de l'échappatoire*' as Fabre calls him), wrote comic poems which show both talent and realism in their caricature of manners and morals at court and among the monks.

Stanislas Trembecki (1735–1812), who was a disciple of the Encyclopaedists, was more attached to the king and followed him to Russia during his travels in exile. Trembecki, whose poetry reflects his vivid interest in

Slav brotherhood and friendship with Russia, was motivated by what he had learnt from history – distrust of the Germans, and the conception of a community of the Slavs which required to be defended against German aggression. But he was also a courtier; at the time of his death his patron was the leading member of the Potocki family, to whose wife he had dedicated a poem and on whose lands he was living.

The National Theatre, founded in 1765 by the king, performed the plays of its director, Wojcech Boguslawski (1757–1829), in which mountain-dwellers and other peasants of the country round Cracow were featured in national costume for the first time. Some of the other plays presented were by the secretary of the Education Commission, Franciszek Zablocki.

A more important part than that of the court was played in Polish national history at this period by the Pulawy family's residence, south-east of Warsaw, where Prince Adam Kazimierz Czartoryski and his highly cultivated wife Isabelle were surrounded by young intellectuals and foreign scholars, whom they engaged as secretaries, tutors and theatrical pro-ducers. The surrounding atmosphere was romantic and the prevailing spirit patriotic. One of the poets there, who had been discovered by Prince Adam among the novices of the suppressed order of the Jesuits, Franciszek Dionizy Kniaznin (1750–1801), was later to go out of his mind at news of the defeat at Maciejovice.

Prince Adam has been given the credit for sheltering and fostering the last generation of Polish writers before the destruction of the country's independence. However that may be, Pulawy was certainly the cradle of much verse which overflowed with love of Poland, if not with poetic merit; an outpouring which had no practical consequences and produced little or no effect on the selfishness of the nobility, but which did prepare the way for the great romantic movement which, in the nineteenth century, was to give added strength to Polish national feeling.

All these writers expressed themselves exclusively in Polish, as did another poet in the prince's circle, Franciszek Karpinski (1741–1825), whose themes were religious and patriotic. Meanwhile research into Poland's past was kept up, for example by the bishop and historian Adam Naruszewicz (1733–96) in his *History of the Polish People* (to 1386). The Polish press and theatre originated during the period of transition preced-ing the second partition, of which an even more noteworthy feature was a remarkable political literature of a new character, evidence of the country's social development.

The Polish political writers of this final phase of the century were no longer mere theorists; they were personally involved in political conflict and in the tragic events precipitated from 1788 onwards.

The Epoch of the Reforms; Patriotism Resurgent
Literary activity, educational endeavour and artistic development, though impressive, could not disguise the weakness of the state. Reform was obstructed as much by group interests as by the ill-will of the Russian

government. Poland had neither substantial financial resources nor adequate military strength. Faced with the impossibility of imposing the requisite sacrifices on the well-to-do classes, the government was obliged in 1776 to reduce by a half the credits with which it had intended to organize an army of 30,000 men.

The year 1788 saw the inception of the famous 'Four Years' Diet, which attempted to establish the state on a sound footing. Its antagonism to Russia caused it to negotiate with Prussia, which was pretending to favour the reform programme; it also abolished the Permanent Council and voted the creation of an army of 100,000 men. But the tax designed to finance this undertaking fell heavily on the landed proprietors, and, despite the special commissions sent out to collect it, yielded less than half the sum hoped for; by a law passed in 1790 the target for the army was reduced to 65,000 men, yet even this projected figure had not been attained when, in 1792, Poland had to face a Russian army of 100,000. The whole preceding period of 'convalescence', from 1776 to 1788, had in effect been a period of unrelieved political stagnation, without any sign of the state's recovery; the Diet's measures had been ineffective medicine, tardily administered.

Now, however, the Diet – dominated by the 'patriotic' party, which included all the leading families, and responsive to the mood of the towns, which were thrusting their demands on its notice – proceeded to impose on the nobility a reconstruction of the state which matched the way Polish society had developed; it granted citizens' rights to the middle classes, gave greater power to the king, and hinted at the eventual liberation of the peasants. This programme, over which loomed the black prospect of foreign intervention, was carried out in a fever of patriotism stimulated by the events of the French Revolution, and was as it were the visible confirmation of the obscure travail which, during the period of convalescence, had produced the country's economic recovery – characterized by the abolition of internal customs dues, increased road-building, and improvement of the postal service and monetary system.

A new Poland was coming to birth amid the weakness and anarchy of the state organism. The middle classes, in one town after another, were organizing their strength, formulating their demands, and joining up with the patriotic party. Politically, it was conceded for the first time that plebeians as well as patricians had a place in the scheme of things.

When the Diet of 1788 met for the first time, its programme had been mapped in advance by Stanislas Staszic (1755–1826) in his *Remarks on the Life of J. Zamoyski* (1787) and Kollontaj in his *Letters* to Malachowski (1788). Zamoyski was a former chancellor of Poland; the Abbé Staszic was a miller's son who studied in France and became Zamoyski's tutor. According to Staszic, Poland should seek salvation in a hereditary monarchy wielded by a strong foreign dynasty. A permanent Diet, including representatives of the middle class, would limit the authority of the monarchy, whose power would be secured by a strong army and by taxes levied on all classes without exception. The peasants would receive protection and education and would no longer be tied to the land.

Much the same moderate programme, more extensively developed and conceived in a more republican spirit, was put forward by Kollontaj, whose view was that the hereditary monarchy should hold only moral authority, the real power being exercised by a central Diet which would periodically account for itself to the provincial diets. The strength of the Diet would be based on a reorganized army and on national unity, which would be fostered by public education with the emphasis on citizenship, and by the use of a single common language, Polish. The government's financial resources would depend on the maintenance of the rights of property-owners, whether nobles or bourgeois; the peasants, though they were to have personal liberty, would not acquire the freehold of the land they farmed. The authority of the government would derive from a 'new alliance' between the aristocratic and bourgeois classes, the latter being thus redeemed from their 'vile indifference'.

Both writers advanced the doctrine of a conservative state wedded to the protection of public liberties and the interests of the propertied classes, a doctrine borrowed from contemporary European economists and physiocrats (proponents of Quesnay's maxim, '*Laissez faire, laissez passer*'). These plans, which had great appeal for the patriotic party, were taken up briefly realized by the Four Years' Diet. They made their appearance during a phase of novel and unusual excitement, brought about by events in France. They attracted the younger generation of nobles, more ardent than their elders and possibly less anxious to cling to their privileges, and in any case more alive to the dangers threatening Poland, and determined to put their country's interests first. Half the deputies in the Diet of 1788 were unusually young: new men, who set the tone in debate and gave indispensable support to the patriotic party.

Poland was still politically divided at the moment of her downfall; had, in fact, never ceased being so. It was never possible to secure unanimity among the magnates and the turbulent *szlachta*. Two parties faced one another: the pro-Russian *hetmans*, who were feudal lords obstinately clinging to their rights, and the patriots, who had adopted Kollontaj's programme and who looked to the West where external affairs were concerned. A royalist group, including Stanislas Augustus himself, wavered between these two positions, gradually dissociating itself from the Russian protectorate and rallying the patriotic party to the consolidation of the royal power.

During its first two years the Diet had only a small majority in favour of reform and a change of foreign policy. In March 1790, Poland and Prussia signed a defensive alliance. In November the Diet was due for dissolution, but decided to continue in being and to admit the newly elected deputies, thus doubling its numbers. It also demanded that the provincial Diets pronounce for or against the election of a hereditary monarch who, when Stanislas Augustus died, was to be chosen from the house of Saxony. That the great families should thus step down in favour of foreign royalty was a pointer to the tragic situation in Poland. But at least the acquiescence of the provincial diets, and the doubling of the number of deputies in the central Diet, gave the patriotic party a large majority, and moreover showed that aristocratic opinion had moved forward considerably.

The first big measure voted by the Diet, on 18 April 1791, was concerned with the towns and therefore with the middle classes. The latter had strengthened their social position in the big cities, particularly Warsaw, which had a population of 100,000. The 'Perpetual Offering', the property tax voted on 26 March 1789, proved so difficult to collect that middle-class financial support for the state was indispensable. As early as October 1789, 'the magistrature' (municipal council) of Warsaw called a congress of the royal towns, whose three hundred delegates set up a union and sent the king a demand for participation in the Diet and government – the first concerted action of the bourgeoisie, a 'black procession' of whose representatives caused them to be denounced by the hetman Branicki as revolutionary agitators. At first the Diet did little, merely conferring nobility on a few manufacturers and lawyers; but after a more favourable climate had arisen as a result of doubling the number of deputies, the statute of 18 April 1791 gave a uniform charter to the towns, ridding them of aristocratic immunities and privileges and placing urban administration in the hands of the middle classes. The latter also acquired guarantees of individual liberty and greater ease of promotion to the aristocracy; there was no longer any bar to their acquiring real property, and they were given a share in the work of the Diet through being admitted to membership of the Commissions dealing with urban affairs.

Several members of the Diet at that time were making the chamber ring with their impassioned speeches. There was Kollontaj, who, in 1790, published his book on *The Political Rights of the Polish Nation*, and who gathered a few of the most advanced patriots into a propagandist group, 'The Forge' (*Kuznica*). There was Stanislas Staszic, who inveighed against the selfishness of the feudal landlords and the machinations by which national division was perpetuated. And there was Julian Ursyn Niemcewicz (1757–1841), Adam Czartoryski's aide-de-camp and a former pupil of the Corps of Cadets, who wrote satires against noble circles and their hostility to reform.

The central problem was still that of reforming the constitution. The solution was found in a *rapprochement* between the patriotic party and the king, and the secretly prepared *coup d'état* of 3 May 1791. The patriotic party took advantage of the absence from Warsaw of many of their opponents; manifestations of popular feeling, intended as a means of bringing pressure to bear on the Diet, occurred in the towns; and the king secured approval for a draft Constitution of which he and Kollontaj were the joint authors, and which had already been approved in secret.

The 'Governmental Law' of 3 May 1791, modelled on the constitutional practices of Great Britain, the United States and France, was also to some extent an echo of the traditions of freedom and independence which had come down from Poland's Golden Age, and which were modified to suit modern conditions and the need to provide broader social foundations for the edifice of the state. It was a compromise measure; it spoke of 'civic liberties' yet excluded the peasantry from acquiring them, and showed a desire at once to curtail the disorderly power of the magnates and to safeguard the country against the dangers of social revolution. A hereditary monarchy was constitutionally established, the elector of Saxony, Frederick Augustus, being designated as the first of the new line. The king was to govern with the help of ministers, who were responsible to a Diet elected by majority vote; five of these ministers, together with the king, the Marshal of the Diet and the primate chosen to represent the clergy (who was also president of the Commission of National Education), constituted the Guard of the Laws, the supreme administrative body, with control over the Commissions (Ministries).

The Diet was still an assembly of aristocratic representatives; the urban delegates, under the law of 18 April 1791, though sitting as 'plenipotentiary envoys', were there only in a consultative capacity and as members of ministerial Commissions.

Abandoning the title 'Republic' and abolishing the union between Poland and the grand duchy of Lithuania, the Constitution declared the existence of a single centralized 'State', in which 'the national will' was supposed to hold sovereign sway but which in fact kept the aristocracy on top, though in a more liberal atmosphere. The state and the nation coincided only in the military sector, all 'citizens' (not just the nobles) becoming the 'defenders of the national integrity and liberties'.

The Constitution's progressive character was apparent nevertheless in its recognition of changes in the structure of Polish society. The rights of the nobility were safeguarded no longer in the name of traditional privilege but by virtue of wealth, in the form of property. If a nobleman possessed even a few square yards of land, he also possessed political rights; but not otherwise. The landless nobles, who had been mere hangers-on of the magnates, were now eliminated from public affairs. For the middle classes there was a *cursus honorum* of which the most successful could avail themselves, and which gave them an excellent chance of acquiring noble status and the privileges which went with it.

In effect, Poland had anticipated the system by which, in nineteenth-century Russia, the best elements were skimmed off from the commercial and industrial classes and added to the aristocratic ruling class. The most radical of the Polish patriots, the left wing of the Forge, led by F.S. Jezierski, expressed fears on this score; they would have preferred the straightforward abolition of aristocratic privilege, following the example recently set by France.

As for the peasants, the Diet was not indifferent to their lot; yet the Constitution had confined itself to 'taking the agrciultural class under the protection of the law and the national government' and appealing to 'the natural and well-understood interest' of the nobles in the hope of prevailing on the latter to conclude free contracts with their peasants. The only sign of genuine reform was a single, limited measure: the peasants on former royal estates which had been acquired by noblemen were granted personal liberty and, in cases where they were farming a piece of land themselves, were made tenants of it in perpetuity. Nevertheless, the mere rumour of the timid measures discussed in the Diet was enough in several regions to set off disturbances among the peasants, who were sure that the abolition of serfdom was at hand.

The essential result of the Diet's labours, was, in fact, to administer a severe shock to the social order. To borrow the terms of the Polish historian Lesńodorski, 'the process of integrating and unifying the country . . . the broadening and modernization of the apparatus of the state' was inevitably only provisional. But the new institutions created at that time did reflect

Social Structure of Poland, c. 1791

SOCIAL GROUPS (%)		DISTRIBUTION (%)	
Peasants	75	Noblemen's properties	42
		State properties	9
		Church properties	10
		Royal properties	2
		Settlers	2
		Itinerant journeymen	10
			75
Urban citizens	6		
Jews	10		
Nobles	8		
Clergy	1		
	100		

SOURCE: Lesńodorski

NOTE: Distribution as given here is based on a total population figure of 8,545,000. According to recent research the figure was in fact over 10,000,000.

contemporary economic and social tendencies and the long-term trend which had taken hold of society; 'they mobilized the most active groups in an attempt to defend the country and rescue and regenerate its civilization.'

The effect on Poland's neighbours, however, was to provoke intervention and thus to hasten the end; the last act of the drama of her obliteration as a European state was now imminent.

Insurrection of a People

The Constitution of 3 May 1791 had been voted through, despite an official note from the Russian ambassador, Stackelberg, threatening punitive measures. The enthusiasm with which the Constitution was received in Warsaw and all the other Polish cities and towns, and which was a sign of nascent national unity, could not obscure for any length of time the hostility of the conservative magnates; invoking the spectre of a 'Jacobin' revolution, they dispatched Felix Potocki and the hetmans Branicki and Rzewuski to St Petersburg, where they asked Catherine II to give them funds and the support of her army. On 14 May 1792, with the help of their landless supporters of noble rank, they formed the Confederation of Targowica, which issued a manifesto calling on Poland to rise in defence of her faith and liberties, threatened by the 'crime' of 3 May. The Russians invaded Poland, occupied Warsaw, and forced the Polish army, in which, under the command of the patriotic Prince Joseph Poniatowski, General Thaddeus Kosciuszko was already covering himself with glory, to fall back behind the River Bug; meanwhile King Stanislas, out of opportunism and a concealed desire to restrict the extent of the defeat, had himself joined the Confederation. Prussia, for whom the defensive treaty of 1790 had no practical meaning whatsoever, and who was alarmed by the threat presented to her expansionism by the Polish *risorgimento*, took advantage of the situation to thrust her troops into Great Poland, and occupy Danzig, in January 1793.

The Russian and Prussian governments, after consultation, proceeded to the second partition of Poland, on grounds of the imperative need to destroy 'the influence of the horrible tendencies of the abominable Parisian sect and of the spirit of the French demagogues, who have extended their dominion to the Republic and are menacing the peace of Europe'. An obliging Diet, assembled for the purpose at Gordon, where the Confederates, who had no serious support in the country, had set up their headquarters, had no choice, under the threat of reprisals by the Russian troops, but to sign the treaty of partition in July 1793 and accept its conditions without protest in September. Poland was reduced to its central provinces and their three and a half million inhabitants.

The national insurrection broke out at this juncture, and Thaddeus Kosciuszko took command of it. The appeal to the country which, despite the instances of Joseph Poniatowski, King Stanislas had been too politic, too shy of the prospect of action, to venture upon, was made by a group of patriots with differing social backgrounds and in many cases with conflicting opinions, who were nevertheless united in their enthusiastic passion to defend Poland to the end and, if they could not gain the victory, at least to save their own and the national honour. Magnates of the patriotic party, officers and soldiers of the Polish army (whom the Russians dismissed as fast as they installed their own garrisons throughout the country), intellectuals, students and middle-class townsmen, were among the initiators of a broad movement which rapidly spread so far as to attract recruits even among the peasants, the majority of whom remained passive and unresponsive.

This desperate, romantic convulsion was incapable of saving the state, precisely because there was no state machinery to give it the means of fighting successfully. Another obstacle was the territorial insignificance of a Poland mutilated beyond hope of survival; and another, the presence of Russian troops in this shrunken territory, surrounded by powerful neighbours. But this final exertion, in which all classes took part, was to remain a symbol of national unity; it marked, in the words of Fabre, 'the end of a state, the birth of a people'. The rising provoked by the second partition was no mere simple plot on the part of a few enthusiastic extremists, it was a spontaneous outburst of patriotism which for the first time brought the poorer townsfolk and the most advanced peasants into partnership with the nobility and middle class.

The insurrection began in Cracow, where a cavalry raid forced the Russians to evacuate the city. In his famous vow, taken publicly in the Rynek Square, Kosciuszko called the nation to arms against the Russians and Prussians; and, gathering an army which included local peasants armed with scythes, routed a Russian column at Raclawice (4 April 1794). While a revolutionary committee was being formed in liberated Cracow, the Russians were pushed out of Warsaw by an attack from the Polish garrison, helped by the people, who had broken into the Arsenal (17 April). Vilno was liberated on 23 April. By the end of the month the Russian troops had been pushed back to the new frontier.

These successes were fated not to last. In an admirable effort to unite the country, Kosciuszko did everything he could to stand up for the king, who was being virtually held prisoner in his castle in Warsaw; to attract the peasants to his cause by means of the manifesto of Polaniec, which promised them personal liberty and a reduction of the *corvée*, with release from serfdom for any who took up arms; and to maintain his hold on the nobles, who were disturbed by the democratic complexion which the insurrection was assuming. The Supreme National Council which he instituted on 21 May in Warsaw, and in which, under Count Ignaz Potocki and Kollontaj, nobles and commoners sat together (including the shoemaker Kilinski, the hero of the rising in Warsaw), succeeded in raising 150,000 men in eight months, and was able to throw a force of between 70,000 and 80,000 troops into battle. This was far short of the general uprising which had been hoped for, but which was precluded by abstentions among the *szlachta* and by passivity among the peasants; and which would have been rendered impossible in any case by the lack of money and equipment. The sombre future looming over the revolt, which was entirely unsupported from out-side, was another reason why a morally unanimous people was relatively unwilling to commit itself to the ultimate sacrifice.

As early as 15 June, the Prussians broke the movement by taking Cracow. In August the Russians recaptured Vilno; on 10 October they overwhelmed Kosciuszko at Maciejowice and took him prisoner. General Suvorov appeared before Warsaw, and after taking its suburb of Praga, whose population were massacred, forced the city to surrender on 4 November. The king, placed under residential surveillance at Grodno, and persistently hoping that Catherine II would keep a Polish state in existence under a Russian prince, was reluctant to abdicate; when he finally did so, on 25 November 1795, Poland was no more. The third partition, in which Austria shared, amounted to complete liquidation. Austria, following an agreement concluded with Russia on 3 January 1795, acquired new terri-tory between the Bug and the Pilica, which included Cracow; Prussia obtained Mazovia, which included Warsaw. Russia took the rest of Volhynia and Lithuania (map 19, p. 339).

Survival of a Nation

'Finis Poloniae'! The obliteration of the state did not mean the extinction of Poland. The defeat of the insurgents, and the complete partition of the country by three foreign powers, caused an emigration which was the chief factor determining the character of the national movement until the middle of the nineteenth century. While those patriots who were unable to flee were, like Kollontaj, interned by the Austrians, or, like Kosciuszko, Count Ignaz Potocki and Kilinski, imprisoned by the Russians in the Peter and Paul Fortress, the officers who fled to Italy enlisted in the Polish Legions. Founded on 29 January 1797 under the command of General Dombrowski, the Legions subsequently gave practical effect to the spirit of the insurrec-tion's leaders, by fighting side by side with the French army for the liberation of Poland.

During the immense upheaval in Europe, caused by the later activities of the French Revolution and the rise of the Empire, Poland's future seemed in fact to be once more at issue. The Polish patriots imprisoned by the Russians were released by Paul I in 1796; some of them joined the emigration, which was carried out under the moral leadership of Kosciuszko; and the Polish Legions, amounting to over 15,000 men by 1801, took part in all the French army's Italian campaigns. The Treaty of Lunéville in that year, and the disbandment of the Polish Legions, caused hopes to ebb; but they sprang up afresh in 1806, when Napoleon formed a new Legion to fight the Prussians, raised a revolt in Prussian Poland, and eventually created a duchy of Warsaw which, in 1809, after the defeat of the Austrians, included Galicia. This resurrection of the Polish state as a satellite of French policy was not destined to survive Napoleon's downfall.

Meanwhile the permanence of Poland as a nation had already been asserted, even before the creation of the duchy of Warsaw: abroad, the signs
were the Polish army, and the courage displayed by the *emigrés* in the
battles in which they were gradually fighting their way back to their own
country; at home, in the conquered territories, there was an intellectual
and scientific life which went on in default of political activity, and which
the conquerors could not easily extinguish. In this respect Russian Poland
benefited from specially favourable treatment. Whereas Prussia and
Austria put in colonists of their own on state lands, and German functionaries in the administration forbade the use of the Polish language, and
the 'Principal School' of Cracow was turned into a Teutonic university,
Alexander I's liberal policy allowed the eastern territories to retain virtual
autonomy, under the general control of Russian governors.

The Polish nobility remained in charge of local affairs. The policy
adopted in no way contradicted the existing traditions of colonization and
absorption, and is further to be explained by the emperor's personal sympathy with Poland, by the community of attitude between the Russian and
Polish aristocracy, by Russia's desire to have the Polish people on her side,
and by the sentiment of Slav solidarity. Alexander invited Prince Adam
George Czartoryski to become a member of his private committee (or
unofficial committee, as it was sometimes called); the Prince also became
Minister for Foreign Affairs and subsequently rector of the Principal
School of Vilno, which had been converted into an Imperial University.
Vilno, a centre from which Polish influence radiated all over the territories
annexed by Russia (and beyond them, to the Kiev region), welcomed
scholars who had fled from Cracow, among them the brothers Sniadecki –
Jan, rector of the university in 1807, well known for his astronomical research, and Jedrzej, a chemist and biologist who devoted much energy to
securing Polish staff for the university and establishing the use of the Polish
language in science. Conditions in Prussian Poland were less favourable;
nevertheless, the creation in 1800 of the Society of the Friends of the
Sciences (the later Academy of Sciences) provided a rallying-point for men
of talent who, under the leadership of Stanislas Staszic between 1808 and
1826, worked together to build up the economy and educational system of
the temporary grand duchy.

A member of the Society, a Polonized Swede, Samuel Bogumil Linde,
published a *Dictionary of the Polish Language*, of which the first volume appeared in 1807, and which contained all the words in use from the
sixteenth to the eighteenth century.

The pro-Russian trend was strengthened by the return of a large number
of *emigrés* to Russian Poland after 1801. But the emergence of a miniature
Poland, created as a mercenary tool by Napoleon, placed the patriots in a
dilemma whose drawbacks became apparent after the rupture of relations
between France and Russia.

As long as the entente between the sovereigns lasted, the duchy of
Warsaw, under the nominal authority of Frederick Augustus of Saxony,

organized its administration and army on the French model and, as a cog in the Napoleonic machine, devoted its energies to the service of France in the hope that the fortunes of war would eventually supply an opportunity for the total restoration of the Polish state. When hostilities broke out between France and Austria in 1809 and the fighting spread to Polish soil, Prince Joseph Poniatowski was enabled to make a liberator's entry into Lublin, Lwów and Cracow (18 July) and, after Napoleon's victory, to enlarge the duchy considerably; with a population of 4,000,000 (a homogeneously Polish population, moreover), and a modern, experienced army, ducal Poland effectively embodied the national energies which remained undiminished through the ensuing ten years of dependence. Many of those who had striven to save their country during the glorious period of the Four Years' Diet now saw their efforts renewed in the activities of the younger generation, who entered the civil service or became volunteers in the Polish army.

But the military, bellicose side of the national movement once more gained the upper hand, smothering the democratic tendencies which had emerged during the insurrection, and whose representatives had been dubbed 'the Polish Jacobins'. The ducal government espoused the prudent policy which Kosciuszko himself had defended. The peasants were liberated anew but given no land, and the *corvée* was retained; the landlords, being hard up, worked their labour force as hard as they could, and the peasants were no better off than before. The agrarian problem was therefore still a source of national weakness, a potential cause of disunity.

Though it lived under French protection and had cast in its lot with the fortunes of Napoleon, the ducal government shared the ever-present fears and uncertainties hanging over the future of Napoleonic Europe. A pro-Russian faction – representing, at bottom, Prince Adam George Czartoryski – pinned its hopes on the good intentions of Alexander, to whom Poland was simply a pawn in the struggle with France, as it was to Napoleon in his dealings with Russia. The campaign of 1812, in which Polish troops fought in the ranks of the Grande Armée, and Napoleon's defeat, placed Poland's fate in the hands of the Tsar. What he would have preferred was the restoration, under Russian protection, of the Poland of before 1772; but he was obliged to negotiate with the Allies a new partition of Poland, sanctioned in 1815 by the Congress of Vienna, which was favourable to Poland's future at least to the extent that, on the country's Russian flank, the duchy of Warsaw and its capital were left intact, under the new guise of a kingdom. Prussia gained possession of Poznan and the surrounding region; Austria, of Galicia; and Cracow became a free city, which it remained until 1846.

9

Dependent and
Subject Nations

INVADED from the north by the Germans and from the south by the
Ottoman Turks, the Slav peoples of central and southern Europe lost the
independence they had spent so many years defending. They constituted
thereafter two dissimilar worlds; the one benefiting from a high degree of
European culture, despite national oppression, while the other fell back
into the rut of obsolete traditions and dragged out a sleepy existence on
the margin of Asia.

I DECLINE OF BOHEMIA

A Czech Sovereign: George of Podebrady
A Hussite defeat rather than a Catholic victory, the battle of Lipany (1434),
though it enabled Sigismund to place himself on the throne of Bohemia,
did not immediately weaken the Utraquists' power. But the fulcrum of
events was transferred from the religious field to the political. Independently of the intransigent Taborites, a small number of Czech nobles organized the management of affairs in eastern Bohemia in such a way as to
withstand the pressure of the Catholic party. One of them, George of
Podebrady, the Utraquists' bright particular star, first captured Prague
and became administrator of the land of Bohemia, in 1452, and then, after
the death of Wenceslas IV in 1458, its king.

Tolerant, yet vigilant for unity, compelling recognition of his authority
in Moravia and Lusatia as well as Bohemia; a moderate Utraquist, yet an
ardent defender of the Compacta; an adroit politician, yet generous and
very 'European' in attitude, George of Podebrady, who spoke German
extremely badly, was the only genuinely Czech sovereign Bohemia had
ever known. Supported by the urban middle classes and the lower nobility, he set himself to build up the power of a monarchical state, in which
Czech had become the language of public affairs and even of diplomacy.

Temporary Religious Peace
The Bohemian Brethren were disciples of Peter Chelčický, a peasant
thinker of the first half of the fifteenth century. About 1450 the Brethren
formed a Union, a society which dissociated itself completely from the

Church of Rome. Recruiting their followers mostly from the artisan and peasant classes, the Union of Bohemian Brethren, whose ideal was to return to a simple life in accordance with the precepts of scripture, were in line with the Taborite tradition; standing a little aside from the quasi-official Utraquist church, which was part of the Roman Church and adopted an over-conciliatory attitude towards it, the Brethren represented a reaction on the part of the common people, an indigenous Czech manifestation arising out of the defeat at Lipany and foreshadowing the Reformation.

However, after the death of George of Podebrady (1471), the new king, Vladislas (1471–1516) (a member of the Jagellon line, and son-in-law of the king of Poland), conducted an uncompromising campaign of Catholic restoration, and the Utraquists were hard put to it to maintain their position; in Prague the struggle culminated in a riot in 1483. In 1485 a treaty of toleration was signed (from which the Bohemian Brethren were excluded); the treaty was renewed in 1512 and religious peace was secured for the time being.

The Nobles in Power

The end of the fifteenth century marked a new period in the history of the Czech people, who came under Hapsburg domination in 1526 and suffered the crushing defeat of the Battle of the White Mountain a century later. The origin of the events leading to Bohemia's loss of independence, and also to her return to Catholicism after the episode of the Reformation, must be traced to a fundamental dislocation of her economy.

There was a shift in the position of the major axes of commerce; during the sixteenth century they increasingly by-passed central Europe, whose trade and political influence declined while the West grew richer. The great discoveries overseas, and the influx of precious metals from the American continent, reduced the importance of the Bohemian silver mines; the time was not far distant when Bohemia, like her neighbour, Saxony, would be in effect little more than a training centre for miners who went out to exploit the mineral resources of other countries. The trade boom in the maritime countries which had the ocean at their doors naturally benefited the continental regions too; at the same time, however, the proximity of the Turks, who by their victory at Mohács, in 1526, removed the last obstacle on their way to Vienna, meant that the position of Bohemia, screened only by the Austrian marches and what remained of Hungary, was no longer secure.

Danger from the Turks caused the leading place in Bohemia's affairs to pass to her military leaders, in other words the aristocracy. The absence of King Vladislas, who had acquired the throne of Hungary in 1490 and had left Prague, gave the ambitious nobles an easier field in which to work, and in 1500 they obtained a constitution which virtually placed the powers of both legislature and executive in their hands. Preponderant in the Diet, in which they even tried to exclude the towns from representation (a right formally established in 1517 by the so-called 'treaty of St Wenceslas'), they accentuated the divisions weakening their country by turning it into an oligarchic republic.

Aristocratic pressure was also evident in the economic and social field. Having been compelled to keep the peace, and finding themselves obliged, during a period of high prices, to increase their incomes in order to maintain the style proper to their rank, the nobles were paying more attention to their estates and doing their best to make every penny they could. The peasants, whose freedom of movement had already been restricted, found their bondage officially sanctioned in 1487 by a decision of the Diet, and confirmed by the Constitution of 1500.

The landowners were tending to let out less of their land to rent, preferring to farm it themselves on a large scale by means of serf labour and the *corvée*. They had other resources besides agriculture proper: fish-farming, for which ponds were artificially constructed, was universal; and a number of nobles became brewers, started mines and forges, distilleries or glassworks, or set their peasants to weaving. A certain amount of economic activity was gradually taken away from the middle classes, whose difficulties, however, were not much in evidence until the second half of the sixteenth century, and did not preclude their living in considerable luxury.

While the peasants were sinking deeper into hardship, the urban middle class had to struggle against the determination and energy with which the nobles attempted to snatch away their commercial privileges. Stern clashes of interest were involved in the settlement of political issues: in 1517 the towns won the right to representation in the Diet only at the cost of surrendering their monopoly in the brewing of beer! And when, under the Habsburgs, Bohemia was forced into the centralized imperial structure, the pressure of the royal authority was added to that of aristocratic privilege, and the towns felt the squeeze from both sides at once. The glories of the urban past were past indeed.

The Reformation in Bohemia

In Bohemia, the seed of the Lutheran Reformation fell on fertile ground. Having originated in Germany – where Luther defended the good name of the Hussites – it had no flavour of Czech nationalism and could therefore draw Czechs and Germans together, though its strongest appeal was to the poorer classes of Czechs and its most zealous followers were recruited among the Bohemian Brethren and the urban middle class. A new-style Utraquism, which favoured the Reformation and received majority backing in Bohemia, now arose in opposition to the conservative Utraquists, who were faithful to the Compacta and willing to compromise with Rome. Prague was split between the two tendencies and an agitated period ensued, to be ended when Ferdinand of Habsburg mounted the throne of Bohemia in 1526. Elected by the Diet with the support of the higher aristocracy, the new king firmly set about the realization of the great project that had been cherished by the Roman Curia since the Hussite period: the subjection of heretical Bohemia to Rome. But this religious unification was only one aspect of a policy whose general theme was monarchism and centralization: the higher aristocracy were brought to heel, the privileges of the Estates were reduced, and, to the great satisfaction of the towns, the restoration of peace in the kingdom enabled commerce to get on its feet again.

German and Catholic Pressure
But centralization had this disadvantage, that the administration set up by Ferdinand was run by German functionaries, with German as the official language. Czech now lost, for three centuries, the leading place it had occupied not only in Bohemia, where it was the national language, but at the Hungarian and Polish courts. Moreover, while firm government was good for the economy, the result was to intensify, rather than diminish, the social inequalities which provided such excellent soil for the growth of heresy. Nor did improved economic conditions compensate the nobility and urban middle class for the piecemeal removal of their privileges, in which they foresaw the eventual destruction of all their liberties. Despite the headway made by the king, whose policy was to frighten off his subjects' consciences when he could and buy them off when he had to, opposition began accumulating; a complex, composite growth, whose tangible effects were an increase of strength on the part both of the Union of Bohemian Brethren (who were gradually being won over to Lutheranism) and of the Utraquists. In addition, plans were being discussed for religious independence in the form of a Czech national church.

The conflict was going on in a fairly peaceful way when events in Germany forced Bohemia to take sides. Charles v demanded troops to help him fight the League of Smalkalde, and without consulting the Estates Ferdinand gave orders for levying a force. Prague and the royal towns rose in revolt, carrying with them part of the nobility. But this was only a passing gleam of independence; the defeat of the German Protestants at Mühlberg (1547) caused the Czech nobles to give in, whereupon the king rounded savagely on the towns and put them under strict surveillance. He took advantage of the occasion to impose a stronger censorship, to persecute the Bohemian Brethren and neo-Utraquists, and – notwithstanding the Peace of Augsburg, which appeared to establish toleration by defining the respective spheres of influence of the central European Catholics and Protestants – to set about reintroducing Catholicism all over Bohemia with the help of the Jesuits, who had started working in Prague in 1556 and later in Moravia, where they founded schools at Brno (1572) and Olmouc (1566).

Most of the nobility now came down on the Catholic side. The younger nobles, who were pupils of the Jesuits or were completing their education in the universities of Italy, constituted an intolerant rising generation with a strong background of Latin culture. The royal towns were given Catholic administrations. A minority which wielded power under two intransigent kings, Maximilian II and Rudolph II, strove to extirpate heresy by banning the Bohemian Brethren and purging the administration of neo-Utraquists, among whom strong Lutheran and Calvinistic influences were in evidence. This was a difficult undertaking, because it had the effect of drawing together the urban nobility and middle class, whose interests were normally divergent but who now combined against the Catholic nobles. Through their representatives in the Diet of 1575, these two urban elements essayed a move towards religious pacification by presenting the king with a proposal for a 'Czech confession' to which they appended a draft ecclesiastical settlement based on the Confession of Augsburg and inspired by the Hussite tradition. Maximilian's oral promises, given in exchange for the Diet's sanction of the taxes he wanted from Bohemia, were not kept. But the tactical position of the Utraquists and Bohemiam Brethren was too secure to be overridden without violence; toleration, however unwilling, and the persistent efforts of a Catholic minority whose power was growing, marked the closing years of the sixteenth century.

Brilliant Cultural Achievements

The cultural heights attained by the Bohemians were in no small measure due to the Hussite contribution. Printing was introduced from Germany, and the first Bohemian printed book was produced at Plzen in 1468; the many which followed had earned a select place for Bohemia among the countries of Europe by the end of the fifteenth century. Through the printed word, Bohemia played a considerable part in the Renaissance. Not, however, in all sides of it: the most important works appearing in Bohemia – mostly in Latin, though Czech was also used – were either religious or technical in character.

The specifically Czech aspect of Bohemian literature at this period is represented principally by the Bohemian Brethren, who had much influence among the middle-class town-dwellers. Chelčický had despised literature and the arts, but since then the movement's exclusive austerity had softened a good deal. Jan Blohuslav (1523–71), even more markedly than Brother Lucas, his successor as leader of the Brethren, was a true humanist; in addition to founding a school and a printing-shop at Ivančice he produced notable literary work in several fields, from the religious and musical (*Anthology of Anthems, Treatise on Music*) to the linguistic (*Czech Grammar, 1571*), and also translated the New Testament. The labours of the scholarly group associated with Blohuslav resulted in the famous Bible of Kralice, which was later to exert a powerful influence on Slovakian Protestantism.

In such undertakings, all the vitality of the Czech mind was called forth by religious preoccupations; by comparison, literary compositions produced by imitating ancient models were mere barren exercises. It was in the technical field that Czechs and Germans, writing in Latin, made the greatest contributions to man's knowledge of the world; the high level of development attained by Bohemia is reflected in books on the natural sciences, medicine and political economy. The two most famous are about fish-farming, one of the country's essential activities, and mines, the respective authors being Jan Skal Dubravsky (Dubravia) and the Saxon physician Bauer (Agricola). Agricola's treatise on mines, *De re metallica* (1556), written at Jachymov, one of the most important Bohemian mining centres, gives a complete picture of the mining and metallurgical techniques of the time. The sixteenth century also saw the appearance of the first maps of Bohemia (1518) and Moravia (1569). Prague in the sixteenth century was an international centre where Bohemia's scholars and technologists, both Czech and German, extended a welcome to colleagues from abroad: Tycho Brahe and Kepler spent some time there in the reign of Rudolph II.

The new age also stamped its character on architecture. Gothic died out in the late sixteenth century. The aristocracy, as elsewhere, vacated their fortified strongholds and went to live in the plains. Their palaces were built by Italian architects. But the most characteristic legacy of the Renaissance to Bohemian architecture is to be found in the blocks or rows of houses built by the urban patricians, which make such a graceful harmony of the central squares of towns or quarters of towns, as for example at Telc.

The National Catastrophe
The religious conflict dividing Bohemia appeared to have been resolved in 1609, when, under pressure from the Estates, King Rudolph II signed the 'Letter of Majesty' by which freedom of conscience and of worship was granted to non-Catholics. But the accession of Ferdinand of Styria was followed by the triumph of the Counter-Reformation and of centralization, and the rebellion of the Estates in 1618 initiated the Thirty Years War. On 8 November 1620 the Czech troops were crushed by the imperial army. Over Bohemia fell what was known as the 'time of the night' (*doba temna*).

Subjected to an extraordinary régime, the country suffered from both political and religious persecution: executions of rebels, confiscations of property (which was either distributed to the Catholic Church and the military leaders, or sold off cheaply) and violent persecution of non-Catholics, marked the period 1620–7, at the end of which the granting of a new Constitution made the Bohemian crown hereditary in the Habsburg family, removed the remaining powers of the Estates and put the German language on an equal footing with Czech.

The White Mountain was a national catastrophe. Religious persecution and the decree of 1627, which faced the nobles with a choice between Catholicism and exile, caused the departure of some thirty thousand middle-class families and a substantial fraction of the nobility. One of the exiles was Jan Amos Komensky (Comenius), bishop of the Union of Bohemian Brethren (1592–1670), who took refuge in Poland in 1628;

9

settling in the town of Leszno under the protection of Count Rafaël Leszcynski, he wrote works which laid the foundations of new pedagogical methods and of democratic education. Compelled to flee during the war between Sweden and Poland (1656), he ended his days in Amsterdam.

The economic and social consequences of the Bohemian national disaster were considerable, and were aggravated by the misfortunes of the Thirty Years War, by which the country was ravaged until 1648. The redistribution of confiscated lands, and speculation, which was encouraged by the depreciation of the currency, helped the Catholic aristocracy to amass large estates. These conditions enabled the *condottiere* Albrecht von Wallenstein, who had played a leading part in the opening phase of the war and, at the time of his assassination in 1634, was casting an ambitious eye on the Bohemian throne, to form the powerful duchy of Friedland. The minor Czech aristocracy and the towns, whose political influence was already weak, were badly off under the new régime and were further affected by the wretched conditions engendered by war, famine and epidemics. When peace returned, Bohemia had lost half its population (perhaps about a million people); Moravia had lost 500,000. Copious German immigration, officially encouraged, did something to repair these losses, especially near the country's borders. Thus war and Hapsburg policy had not only decimated the middle ranks of the Czech nation, but had thereby fostered Germanization. As for the peasants, their lives were made still harder than before by increased *corvées* and tithes, and by the contempt attaching henceforward to anyone who spoke Czech, the language of rebellion and heresy.

From 1630, however, the war, which had brought the imperial and Swedish troops alternately into the country, had interrupted the Counter-Reformation, which vigorously resumed its activities under Jesuit leadership after the Treaty of Westphalia. But even in 1651, a census showed that barely a fifth of the population of Bohemia had gone over to Catholicism. By 1657, there was not officially a single non-Catholic commune left. A shadowy conversion; the substance took a century to achieve.

The period extending from the Treaty of Westphalia to the accession of Joseph II (1780) was the logical consequence of the Czech defeat in 1620. Bohemia's independence, which was at least nominally maintained within the imperial setting, did not actually disappear until all the affairs of the Bohemian crown were placed under an imperial chancellery in 1749. The main characteristic of the period was re-Catholicization, which was energetically supported by the government. The proximity of Protestant Saxony and Silesia, from which came books of a heretical tinge and clandestine preachers, and the resistance of the people, who constituted a kind of 'Church in the desert' and secretly celebrated communion in both kinds, handicapped the Catholic missionary orders, whose final victory was delayed until half way through the eighteenth century.

The Slovaks and the Czechs

The Hussite movement had a lasting influence on the religious development of Slovakia, where Lutheranism had put down strong roots and was
nourished by the scriptures, which were smuggled in from Bohemia, and
the propaganda of the United Brethren. In the kingdom of Hungary the
Hapsburgs had trouble in keeping the Catholic nobility in order; hence the
accommodations which gave Hungary, unlike Bohemia, something like
religious freedom. Lutheranism retained firm footholds there, despite
anything the Jesuits could do.

But Slovakia never achieved any real national life; it was part of the
Hungarian kingdom, lacked any political institutions which might have
given it some measure of autonomy, and was dominated by an aristocracy
which went back to Catholicism after the Thirty Years War and was
acquiring an increasingly Magyar character. Almost all the Slovaks were
peasants and mountain-dwellers, and kept their own customs and dialects;
but their relations with Bohemia persisted and were facilitated by the
Counter-Reformation, which used the Czech language as an instrument of
propaganda, and by the accession of the Hapsburgs to the Hungarian
throne in 1687. Slovakian art-craftsmen were drawn to Prague; and the
minds of educated Slovaks were orientated towards Bohemia rather than
their own capital. Bratislava (Pressburg) occupied a marginal position not
only on the map but in their minds.

The Age of Baroque

There now arose in Bohemia and Moravia something which contrasted
sharply with the sufferings of the Czech people, namely that elegant,
luxurious architectural *décor* to which Prague and the whole country owe
their distinctive baroque charm. We could regard this as foreign art, of
Italian inspiration, brought in by the Counter-Reformation and the
Jesuits. Or we could diagnose it as a compensation-mechanism – the sensibility of the Czechs seeking refuge in unreal creations whose mobility,
fantasy, oppositions and complications expressed a flight into ideal realms,
a return to the distant glories of the national past, and an obscure protest
against the wretchedness of popular life. Baroque lends itself to the most
diverse interpretations.

The detailed execution was collective; the general conception was imposed from outside and above, by Italian artists commissioned in the first
place by King Matthew, then by the great *condottiere* Wallenstein, and, after
the Treaty of Westphalia, by Czech and German feudal aristocrats;
though it certainly was an alien importation, it harmonized with the local
landscape and natural conditions and drew its decorative inspiration from
the country's oldest religious traditions. As V.L.Tapié remarks in his delicate evocation of Moravian and Bohemian baroque (*Baroque et Classicisme*
[1957]), the statues and painted altar-tables of the Wallenstein Palace in
Prague, which was built between 1625 and 1929, transform the whole
into 'an immense hymn to St Wenceslas'. And the painter Karel Skieta

(1610–74) recreates the life of the saint in an authentically Czech landscape, in which scenes of peasant life are going on.

Between 1680 and 1740, Bohemia was covered with palaces and churches whose magnificence corresponds to the wealth of those who built them. It was then that Prague acquired the appearance it has had ever since on both sides of the Charles iv bridge (plate 16), 'the royal road of baroque statuary' (V.L.Tapié). The sculptures on the bridge, where tradition says there was only a single crucifix in 1648, are a solemn testimony to the victory of the Counter-Reformation; erected between 1704 and 1714, they are the work of several Czech and Slovakian artists, including the Brokovs, father and son. The art of the baroque imposed itself on the Czech landscape, and dominated the country's architecture, painting, music and popular art in the eighteenth century. Baroque supplied the setting for the religious festivals and ceremonies in which the people, more or less re-converted to Catholicism by persuasion or compulsion, celebrated the cult of the Virgin and the Saints – including an otherwise unknown Saint Nepomucene, who was canonized in 1719 and whose day was substituted by the Jesuits for the national festival commemorating Jan Hus.

Though the peasants' standard of living gradually rose during the eighteenth century, there was still much hardship. Some degree of solace was available in the type of religion offered to them by Counter-Reformation Catholicism: the Marian cult and that of the saints, and the ceremonies connected with both (solemn, sumptuous festivals, and processions for which the peasants put on their finest clothes, and pilgrimages to the numerous localities reputedly associated with miracles), shaped the religious calendar and provided simple souls with an alluring world of forms, colours and sounds which was more novel, more captivating even, than any secular merrymaking.

All the same, spontaneous protest against injustice and compulsion found an outlet in the people's fondness for the puppet-theatre; a very ancient institution, in which Kasparek, the Czech equivalent of Punch or Guignol, thumbed his nose at feudal grandees, monks and the military. This theatrical medium, which the authorities distrusted and occasionally banned, was also used for popular adaptations of the serious drama, such as *Doctor Faustus*. It was an unusual art-form, which was taken up and cultivated in the nineteenth century as part of the national renaissance.

Folk pottery, which had produced some really fine work in the sixteenth and seventeenth centuries, with much regional variation (the oldest known Czech pottery, dated 1584, comes from Hostomice), declined and became rather ordinary (plate 20).

Popular amusements included dance and song. There were dances of ancient origin for whirling couples, with sung accompaniment in Eastern style, for which various tunes might be used for a single type of dance; and men's dances, with much leaping, in Slovakia and eastern Moravia; both of these retained their archaic character into the contemporary period.

There were also the so-called figured dances, popular in Bohemia and western Moravia, in which only one tune was used for a given type of dance, the musical style being that of the western song with instrumental accompaniment; these proved amenable in due course to the influence of ballroom dancing and modern songs. All these dances were based on the activities of daily life and were often accompanied on the bagpipe, the typical popular musical instrument, which joined forces with the violin and clarinet to make up the village band. Some dances reflected social and political feelings in a very real way; there were 'Hussite dances' and a 'dance of the *corvée*'. The characteristic setting of Czech peasant life, that mixture of traditional features and surprising novelties which is so admirably described in the famous novel by Božena Nemcova, *Babička* ('The Grandmother', 1854), reached its most typical form in the eighteenth century, when it masked considerable poverty and, under the externals of fervent piety, a somewhat temperate attachment to Catholicism. The conditions under which the Catholic Church achieved its victory were such that it was incapable of erasing the people's memories of the Hussite movement.

Economic and Social Inequalities
The restoration of Catholicism was accompanied by an economic oppression so severe that the lot of the Czech peasant, compared with the wealth of the upper classes, was tragic. He was very heavily taxed, liable to corporal or capital punishment, subjected on the feudal estates to a continual *corvée* which frequently obliged him to till his own ground by night, and unable to better himself without the landlord's permission, even in cases where he was sufficiently well-off to give his children a good start in life. Bohemian society was split into two worlds, and the barrier between them was one of education as well as class. The Czech landlords largely adopted German ways; both they and the German landlords spent most of their time at the Viennese court. Peasant emigration and frequent risings were the result, though the peasants did benefit slightly from the empire's economic progress in the eighteenth century.

The magnificent style in which the nobles lived required great wealth. The economic hardships of the Czech people under foreign domination must not be allowed to obscure the general trend towards rapid enrichment, mainly benefiting the landed aristocracy and the Church. The population was rising fast (Bohemia had 3,000,000 inhabitants by 1791). The customs union between Bohemia and Austria was a stimulus to commerce. On the big estates, where potatoes, clover and beet had been introduced, marketable surpluses increased the landlords' incomes. One result of this general forward surge, from which all classes profited, though in very uneven proportions, was the reconstitution of the Czech middle class and intelligentsia; though their numbers were small at first, they were subsequently able, given more promising political conditions, to take the lead in the Czech national renaissance movement.

II THE SOUTH SLAVS: THE SLEEPY BALKANS

Partition by Ottoman Conquest

The Turkish conquest stabilized the social structures of the Slav peoples included within the frontiers of the Ottoman empire. The Turks interfered hardly at all with the lives of their Christian subjects, demanding only that they pay their taxes and supply recruits for the Turkish army. Holding down the country with fortresses which in many cases were the nuclei of future towns, they ruled by means of a feudal administration consisting of pashas and beys living on enormous estates, and an army of cavalry (spahis) and infantry (janissaries) which was originally composed of Christians who had adopted Turkish ways, but in which Turks also began serving in the second half of the sixteenth century.

Conversion to Islam, which to a Christian represented a means of rising in the social scale, skimmed off the best elements among the subject peoples. The administration and army, in fact, were run by these 'Turkicized' Europeans, many of whom were Slavs. Even the Sultan's immediate circle – his grand vizir, the highest officer of the state, and the vizirs composing his 'Divan' – consisted of foreigners. Between 1453 and 1623 there were twnety-one grand vizirs, of whom eleven were Yugoslavs, five Albanians and only three true Osmanli Turks.

Bosnia was where Islamization went furthest, doubtless because persecution of the Bogomils had swayed the people in favour of the invaders, who were more tolerant in religious matters. Towards 1600 Bosnia was three-quarters Muslim, and a long process of Christian reconquest, which was never fully successful, was required to reduce this proportion. There were also many renegades from Christianity in Macedonia, which was nearer the Turkish capital and in which the Turks themselves, outside the towns, constituted a substantial fraction of the population. Thus a minority of the Slavs had adopted the victors' culture and had supplied it not only with officials and soldiers but also writers and poets, such as Suzi Celebri, of Prizren, and Sudi, who came from near Sarajevo.

On the other hand, the Turkish invasion across the Danube, by which Vienna was threatened in the sixteenth century, caused migrations which intensified the preponderance of Slav settlement on the plain of Hungary. In addition to the northward flight of Serbian peasants and petty landowners, an exodus soon checked by the victorious advance of the Turks, there was voluntary resettlement of Vlach herdsmen along the road to Buda, and of peasants from Bosnia between the Save and Drave. Syrmia, Banat, Batschka and Slavonia were thus colonized by Serbs, and the ethnographic limit of the South Slav peoples was permanently fixed. The Slav character of the coastal zone, moreover, was accentuated by the fact that the Turks shifted the Bosnian Vlachs into the Dalmatian hinterland, where they became farmers and beekeepers.

The population along the fluctuating frontiers organized their own militia bands to resist the advancing Turks, and were supported on occasion by the imperial forces. The Turks, when their first impetus had spent itself, fell back a little; the Turkish and Austro-Hungarian frontier was defined under the Treaty of Karlovci (1699); and a 'march' was established, consisting of some three hundred and seventy-five miles of territory, from the Velebit to the Carpathians, inhabited by those of the Serbs and Croats who were still subjects of the Hapsburg empire. The peasants in these 'military confines' were also soldiers; they were provided with little freehold estates and made responsible for guarding the frontier. There was a high degree of ethnic homogeneity, the inhabitants' lively patriotism was made all the keener by the struggle against the Turks, and they enjoyed greater freedom than their brothers under Ottoman domination, south of the Danube; with the consequence that the 'military confines' were to become one of the leading areas in the national revival movements of the eighteenth and nineteenth centuries.

Dubrovnik, a Gateway to the West

Dubrovnik (Ragusa) was the only large town on the east coast of the Adriatic to escape Turkish rule, which it bought off with an annual indemnity. Through its patrician traders and its fleet it connected the Balkan territories with Italy and Spain, from both of which there was a continuous influx of western influences. As the intermediary between the Ottoman empire, which constituted a vast unified market, with customs duties to be paid only at the frontiers, and the Western countries, which in the sixteenth century were looking for outlets for their textiles, Ragusa was well represented in the ports of the Balkan peninsula, where her merchants' colonies enjoyed fiscal privileges and from which they sent home the wheat and animal products on which Ragusa depended. Ragusa, with two hundred ships, totalling 25,000 tons, and thousands of sailors, had a very considerable carrying trade; and there was a Ragusan consul in every large port in the western Mediterranean. The city's government was aristocratic, but economic power was shared by the nobles and middle class; in the sixteenth century Ragusa experienced great prosperity, but this was later much reduced by the displacement of the trade routes following the great discoveries, and by competition from the French, English and Dutch fleets in the Mediterranean, and from Muslim, Armenian and Jewish merchants in the Balkan towns. Although ruined by the earthquake of 6 April 1667, which killed between 3,000 and 4,000 people (over half the population), Ragusa regained her commercial vigour in the eighteenth century, and contrived to flourish by remaining neutral in the conflict between France and England. In the Napoleonic era the Ragusan republic was occupied by the French and lost its independence in 1808.

Dubrovnik, whose Latin population had been rapidly submerged by immigration from the interior, was a Slav town by the fifteenth century. From then until the eighteenth century it was the only centre of high culture in the countries of south-east Europe. The educated inhabitants spoke Italian, which was also the official language and remained so until the nineteenth century. But Dubrovnik's literature was Slavic, owing to patriotic spirit and a sense of Slav community.

The republic's independence, and its relations with Italy at the time of the Renaissance, led to the development of a humanist literature and, in the comedies of Marin Držić, of a theatre of manners depicting Ragusan life. But the power of the Ottoman empire, and the necessity of nursing the republic's commercial connections, also made it desirable to cultivate friendly relations with the Sultan, whose fame inspired the poet Mavro Vetranović (1482–1576). In the seventeenth century, when Turkey had entered on decline and Catholicism was energetically advancing, stamping its imprint both on baroque architecture and on literature, Ragusa's greatest poet, Ivan Gundulić, wrote his epic, *Osman*, in which he celebrated the Poles' great victory over the Turks at Chocim (1621) as a victory for Catholicism, and wove a connection between Slav popular tradition and western Christian civilization.

The Slavs in the Holy Roman Empire

Three nuclei of Slav population had survived in the rich Pannonian basin north of the Danube, which the Mongols had invaded in the tenth century: Banat, Batschka and Baranja (map 14). These were added to in the fifteenth century by a wave of fugitives from the Ottoman conquest, and again, in the sixteenth, when the Turks got as far north as the gates of Vienna, by peasants from the poorer, southern districts. In Batschka, eighty per cent of the population at that time were Serbs. At the beginning of the eighteenth century the frontier – the Ottoman front line, as it were, on the Hungarian sector – was fixed before Belgrade; meanwhile, however, Austrian troops had made a brief penetration into Serbian territory, with the result that, after their final withdrawal north of the Danube, the 'great emigration of 1690' further intensified the Serbian character of southern Pannonia. Despite considerable Hungarian and German colonization, the Serbs in this area (which at a later period, in 1848, became autonomous for a few years, when it was known as the Voivodina) presented a fairly homogeneous mass which played a leading role in the development of Serbian nationalism. Because they were obliged to defend their Orthodox faith against a Catholic régime, they were never lulled by the contemptuous tolerance displayed by the Turks towards their brothers across the Danube; moreover, their land being more fertile, they benefited from the general development of the Hapsburg empire.

Slav Unity and the Reformation

The Reformation produced profound repercussions in Croatia and Slovenia; it stimulated the opposition of the leading classes to imperial rule, and that of the peasants to the landowners; and it encouraged the written use of the popular dialects, thereby making the various sections of the Slav population more aware of their regional individuality.

Slovenia became, for a time, the platform of Protestant heresy. In

Croatia the Reformation swept the board in the coastal areas, the military confines and the country between the Mur and the Drave, but met strong resistance, based on Zagreb, from the Croatian nobles, who supported their Catholic sovereigns on account of the Turkish danger.

The Reformation, whose history in Slovenia is linked with the name of Primoz Trubar, was responsible for the creation of literary Slovenian, used in catechisms and translations of sacred history. But the Slovenian partisans of the Reformation were far from confining their activities to Slovenia; their zeal for conversion took them into Croatian and Serbian districts and even into Muslim Herzegovina. The fact that Reformation supporters in these different Slav environments were working for a single objective, though by various means, endowed their common undertaking, essentially religious though it was, with a pan-Slav character. And while the multiplicity of scripts (Glagolitic, Cyrillic and Latin) and languages (various dialectal forms of Slovenian, Croatian and Serbian) emphasized what a multiplicity of different nationalities was involved, it also emphasized their common features, the closeness with which their cultures were related.

The Counter-Reformation, unleashed by the arrival of the Jesuits in Graz in 1573 and carried on under the violent leadership of the sovereigns

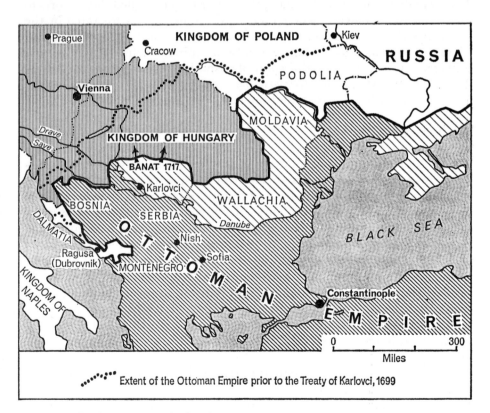

Map 14 The Ottoman Empire in 1699

9*

and the Church, rapidly demolished heresy, which was defeated by the beginning of the seventeenth century. The reconquest was even accompanied by pressure on the Orthodox Croatians, who were urged to go over to the Uniates. But the Reformation's linguistic legacy remained; the vernacular was accepted by the Church, and the Jesuits, by employing the *stŏ*-dialect of Croatian (the most widely used, and the most similar to Serbian) for their written propaganda, were in effect supporting one of the current ideas of the time, that of an 'Illyrian' linguistic unity.

As early as the sixteenth century, indeed, the idea of an ethnic and linguistic community of the south Slav peoples had been increasingly voiced by a number of writers and other cultivated people, mostly churchmen.

In the seventeenth century one of these was a Croat who spent much of his life in Russia, Križanić, who urged the union of Catholicism and Orthodoxy and also propounded the idea that Russia had a mission to fulfil among the southern Slav peoples. But the most important advocacy came from the Franciscans. Their propaganda was more effective among the country people than that of the Jesuits, and it was they who were chiefly responsible for restoring Catholicism in such Slav-speaking territories as had not fallen into Turkish hands; thereafter they extended their efforts to the whole of the Balkans, where their establishments were tolerated by the Turks; and by encouraging resistance to the highly unpopular Greek clergy, they helped to crystallize a national spirit which at that time was still compatible with a nebulous pan-Slavism. It was a Franciscan, Andrew Kačić Miošić, who, in his *Discourses for the Slav People* (1756), extolled the joint past of the Serbs, Croats and Bulgars.

The Slavs in the Ottoman Empire

Apart from religious works of no originality, almost nothing of a literary kind was produced in the countries under Turkish rule. But national feeling was kept alive by a rich and colourful folk-poetry, orally transmitted, whose themes were everyday life and distant or legendary memories of the past and of resistance to the Turks. In Serbia this grew into the great treasury of the *pesme*, ballads and lyrics which were accompanied on the *guzla* (a sort of guitar; figure 39, p. 373), and which caused Mieckiewicz to declare that the Serbian people was destined to be the bard and musician of the whole Slav race. These songs immortalized the *haiduks*, those heroes of the Balkan *maquis*, half brigands, half patriots, in the Turkish-occupied areas, and the *uskoks*, who set out from Croatia or the Dalmatian coast to raid the Turks and who, after spending some time as privateers in the emperor's interest, were given official status and transferred to the Confines (map 14).

In their struggle to preserve their national identity, moreover, the Serbs had to fight on two fronts. At the beginning of the sixteenth century the Greek Church, through the archbishopric of Okhrid, had tried to take over the Serbian Church, which had remained autonomous in northern Serbia and in Bosnia, Herzegovina and Montenegro. This was resisted by those of the Serbs who had gone over to the Turkish way of life but were still mindful of their family loyalties, and who now made use of their high positions in the sultan's personal service to favour the Serbian Church. The latter extended its influence southward; in 1557 the grand vizier Mehmed Sokolovitch re-established the former patriarchate of Peć, to which he appointed his brother, the monk Macarius; for the next two centuries the patriarchate of Peć (abolished as a result of Greek pressure in 1767) was the religious focus of the Serbs' national life.

The cultural life of the Bulgars, like that of the Serbs, was severely restricted. They were nearer the hub of things and had the Turks right on top of them; Turkish domination was particularly oppressive in the western Bulgarian-speaking areas. At popular level, an obscure national consciousness was expressed by veneration of St John of Rila and admiration for demotic heroes, the leaders of armed bands on the mountains at the time of the Turkish invasion. But Turkish was the language of administration; Greek, of education and refinement; the Bulgarian dialects were merely what the peasants spoke, and were despised accordingly.

The literary works produced when the Ottoman empire was at the height of its power, in the sixteenth century, owe such interest as they possess to the anti-Turkish feeling expressed in them; examples are the writings of the monk Pomen, who was also an icon painter, and those of the priest Peïo and of Matthew 'the Grammarian'. After this the failure of the insurrection at Tarnovo (1595), which had been fomented by the Ragusans, initiated a peculiarly tragic period, the dark night of Bulgarian history. There was armed resistance on the mountains and passive resistance elsewhere. In these areas close to Constantinople the Turks appear to have pursued what was for them a quite exceptional policy of compulsory conversion to Islam (which may perhaps account for the Muslim Bulgars, the Pomaks). The higher clergy, as foreigners (Greeks), were hated by the people, who nevertheless continued in the seventeenth and eighteenth centuries to find a focal point for their national feelings in the worship of the popular saints – George, Nicholas, and John of Rila.

The rich, corrupt Greek clergy looked down on the Bulgarian lower clergy and had little contact with the people. It was the Bosnian and Croatian missionaries of the Franciscan Order who took most interest in the latter and who, in the seventeen century, operating like commandos in advance of the great Catholic offensive, carried the faith to the Bulgars. A Bulgarian Catholic, Philip Stanislavov, bishop of Nicopolis, wrote what appears to be the first work in the Bulgarian vernacular, *Abagar*.

In the late seventeenth century, when the Austrians were penetrating deeply into Serbia, the Bulgarians rebelled (1688). When the rebellion failed they began looking to Russia as their possible future liberator. Seven hundred years earlier, religious life in Russia had been initiated by the Bulgarian monasteries, and it had been nourished by them ever since; now they in their turn, during the eighteenth century, received from Russia not only books in Russian Slavonic (itself originally an offshoot from Bulgarian) but also a new spiritual impetus. The treaty of Kutchuk-Kainardji (1744) placed them under Russian protection. Pioneered by the monk Païssi, a cultural renewal took place; but from this time forward Russia became the Bulgars' intellectual and spiritual guardian.

Book Four

NATIONALISM AND THE SLAV PEOPLES
1861–1917

10

Russia at the Crossroads - Accelerated Development

THE SUPPRESSION of serfdom, in the period of the reforms, was a turning-point in Russia's history. Even more important, however, was the rapid, long-delayed growth of her industry. Among this fertile peasant people, which had colonized Siberia, there now arose an army of proletarian workers and a middle class which, as yet, was passive. The bustle and diversification of Russian society produced many signs of high civilization; Russian literature and music became world-famous.

I DEMOGRAPHY AND THE ONWARD DRIVE OF COLONIZATION

Acquisition and Settlement of New Territories
Considerable changes in the nature of Russian society became evident in the years following 1861. New fields were open to officials, soldiers, colonists and business people. Central Asia was conquered or placed under protection (the khanates of Khiva and Bokhara). The building of railways to the Black Sea (between 1870 and 1880) and the Urals encouraged migration, travel and transport. The Ukraine, whose dusty tracks were no longer clogged by long lines of ox-drawn carts taking the year's grain crop down to Odessa, became Russia's foremost industrial region soon after 1885, when the Donets coal basin was connected by rail to the mines of Krivoy Rog. The Trans-Siberian line, which was built between 1892 and 1902 and extended the European rail system across the continent of Asia, brought Vladivostok within a week's travel of Moscow and, even more significantly, connected European Russia with western Siberia, which underwent a rapid increase in population and became the empire's new granary, second in importance only to the Ukraine. Communication with the Far East became easier. Thus, for example, the wholesale merchant Alexei Fedorovitch Vtorov, who had settled in Irkutsk in 1866, no longer had to lose months in organizing and dispatching his strings of heavily-laden carts from Siberia to Moscow and back; and he himself was able to live in Moscow. The extension of the state towards the south-east was in itself less

important than the fact that the country had now acquired means of transport which made it possible to bring into production rich, fertile tracts of territory, previously almost untouched.

The population of the Ukraine, after the introduction of industry, was no longer augmented only by the seasonal influx of agricultural workers from the north. The factories attracted a large permanent accretion of workers, mostly from outside the Ukraine; this additional population, in which the Russian element predominated, increased the size of the towns.

POPULATION OF THE PRINCIPAL TOWNS OF THE UKRAINE (in thousands)

TOWN	1863	1897	1914
Nikolayev	64·6	92	103·5
Ekaterinoslav	19·9	112·8	211·8
Kharkov	52	174	244·7
Kiev	68·4	247·7	520·5
Odessa	119	403·8	499·5

Between 1863 and 1914 the population density was more than doubled in the southern provinces; in that of Ekaterinoslav the increase was particularly great, from 7·8 to 23·9 per square mile. The rapid economic development of the Ukraine caused a mingled tide, a mixture of various East Slav peoples, to flow into the inland towns and also accentuated the cosmopolitan character of the Black Sea ports, whereas the country districts retained their local dialects and remained thoroughly Ukrainian.

In Siberia, the process by which the population was increased was of a different character. Agricultural colonization by Russians, Ukrainians and Byelorussians caused the Siberian population to double between 1860 and 1897 (from 3,500,000 to 7,000,000, both figures including 870,000 native inhabitants). Deportees, despite totalling 300,000 at the end of the nineteenth century, became a relatively unimportant category, numerically speaking; so did the Cossacks, of whom there were a few hundred thousand in Siberia and whose considerable privileges made the prospects for newcomers appear all the more uncertain. At first it was the population of western Siberia which was increased by immigration; with the building of the Trans-Siberian railway the influx extended further, to the foothills of the Altai, the Semirechye and central Siberia, and even to the Far East, which was also accessible by sea. The rate of settlement became higher after the revolution of 1905. The number of immigrants rose from 100,000 in 1900 to nearly 600,000 in 1907, and was more than 700,000 in 1909. The number of immigrants settling in Siberia between 1903 and 1913 – after discounting those who changed their minds and came back – was 4,400,000 (three quarters of whom settled in western Siberia). Except on the southern fringes of the area affected, where the wave of colonization – partly official, partly spontaneous – encroached on the Kirghiz-Kazak territory and pushed the native population, settlement was effected in empty country, entailing neither territorial partition nor cultural influence, and simply transplanting Russian life to Asiatic soil.

The same transplantation took place in central Asia, where however the groups of colonists were much smaller and there was an indifferent or hostile indigenous population to reckon with. These already inhabited regions were regarded mainly as a centre of cotton production and an imperial Russian bastion against British India; agricultural settlement occurred only on an insignificant scale. As late as 1892, in the region of Tashkent, there were only some two or three thousand families pursuing the ordinary round of Russian peasant life in the little villages they had created. These private citizens were outnumbered by the administrators: members of the army and the customs and postal services, and, with the extension of the Russian rail network into the area between 1881 and 1899, railway staff. The new population centres arose in the vicinity of the old-established towns; the two co-existed but did not influence each other. At Tashkent,

Russian Cities with more than 100,000 Inhabitants in 1914

St Petersburg	2,118,500	Ivanovo-Voznesensk	147,400
Moscow	1,762,700	Samara	143,800
Riga	558,000	Tula	139,700
Kiev	520,500	Omsk	134,800
Odessa	499,500	Kishinev	128,200
Tiflis	307,300	Minsk	116,700
Kharkov	244,700	Tomsk	114,700
Saratov	235,700	Nijni Novgorod	111,200
Baku	232,200	Yaroslav	111,200
Ekaterinoslav	211,800	Vitebsk	108,200
Vilno	203,800	Nikolayev	103,500
Kazan	194,200	Ekaterinodar	102,200
Rostov-on-Don	172,300	Tsaritsyn	100,800
Astrakhan	151,500	Orenburg	100,100

across the wide canal on which the fertility of the region depended, the jumbled mass of Uzbek dwellings, built of rammed earth, confronted the large, luxuorious villas and gardens composing the residential quarter of the Russian functionaries. Russian penetration in the protectorates was of the same character: New Bokhara, for example, founded in 1888 near the old city, had acquired by 1914 a mainly Russian population of about ten thousand postal and railway officials, bank employees and skilled manual workers, a social microcosm representing the farthest advance of Slav civilization in the south-east.

Russian colonization had previously been slight and sketchy on the southern Ukrainian steppes and in the Volga territories and Siberia; but the gaps were now being filled in, and the Slavs were firmly established in every part of the state where conditions were at all practicable. Land hitherto unused was cleared by the incoming Russian peasants, and the numerically weak non-Russian communities, undermined by infiltration, found themselves being either pushed back into smaller areas or diluted by successive waves of invaders. By the beginning of the twentieth century the Tatars, the Chuvashes, the Mordvinians on the Volga, the Mariis, the Udmurts on the Kama and the Bashkirs of the Ural region had become mere islets in a sea of Slavs, whose outermost waves in Siberia had reached, but not submerged, certain scattered tribes protected by distance, nature and their own insignificance: the Tunguz on the Yenisei, the Yakutsk on the Lena, the Buriat-Mongols round Lake Baikal and the Chuckshis on the Anadyr were unable, despite their tiny numbers, to preserve their cultural identity on the fringe of the imported Russian way of life.

It was in European Russia that peasant settlement was carried out most intensively, as can be seen from statistics compiled by the Soviet historian Yatsunsky. Whole regions were brought under cultivation. In the Ekaterinoslav, Kherson and Tauris provinces, the area cultivated increased from 4,855,620 acres in 1796 to 15,627,000 in 1860, 22,733,700 in 1881, and 30,915,357 in 1921. In the Don basin the figures for 1860, 1881 and 1912 respectively were 3,528,665, 10,358,658 and 18,302,096 acres. The rise was even steeper in the provinces of Samara, Orenburg, Ufa and Astrakhan: 2,928,000, 4,164,000, 18,861,000, 22,892,000. Though less spectacular than this victorious advance of the Russian peasant into new agricultural areas, the increase of cultivation in the 'black earth' country was a further pointer to the strength and persistence of demographic pressure.

The fecundity of the Russian people, necessitating the occupation of the most fertile and accessible areas in this vast expanse of Euro-Asiatic territories, caused the Slav element to predominate even in places where there was a relatively high concentration of Finno-Turkish inhabitants. The Russian state which this process produced was one in which the various non-Slav groups, though preserving their individuality, were now merely the majority or a significant minority in territories which had once been their own but in which they could not longer pretend to any degree of real independence. A map of the ethnographical composition of imperial

Russia in 1914 is like a partial forecast of the solution adopted by the Soviet government to the problem of these subordinate nationalities.

The Cossack Hosts

There had been a continual flow, as the centuries wore on, of colonists, runaway serfs and outlaws into the country on Muscovy's southern border, where Slav territory abutted on that of the Turkic peoples af the steppes; a frontier zone known as the 'wild field' (*dikoye polie*) over which no governmet had been able to establish control for any length of time. The newcomers formed armed bands which, as they became more organized, developed into the 'Cossack Hosts'. In the thirteenth century the term 'cossack' seems to have been applied to the Polovtsian mercenaries employed as frontier guards by the Genoese trading cities of the Crimea; it reappears in the fifteenth with wider, vaguer meaning which includes not only the Turkic mercenaries whom the Russian princes used as a buffer against raids by the peoples of the steppe, but also that floating population of the frontier zone which must originally have been of mixed Turkic and Slavic composition but was soon Russianized by the arrival of runaway peasants, to whom these disputed areas held the promise of freedom and a new start in life.

The Cossacks of necessity built up their communities on military lines; and though their living came mainly from agriculture they also went in for a mixture of alternate trade and pillage. Tactically, they commanded the caravan routes which, partly overland and partly by river, somewhat precariously connected the Black Sea and the central Russian principalities, across the Tatar-dominated steppes between; they sold their co-operation to the highest bidder, but from the fourteenth century onwards they were gradually drawn into the Russian orbit by community of religion, self-interest, and the pressure increasingly applied by the Muscovite rulers. The Don Cossacks rapidly became a defensive barrier against the Tatars, and received Russian support in return. The territory of the Ukrainian Cossacks was divided by the frontier between Muscovy and the Polish-Lithuanian kingdom, a fact to which they owed an independence of long duration. The southernmost part of that territory, in the bend of the Don, was the home of the curious Zaporozhe Cossack community, a kind of military republic which played a very active role in the conflicts between Poland, Russia and the Ottoman Empire. Impatient of outside control, but gradually converted to the Russian cause by its successive leaders, this community did not finally disappear until the reign of Catherine II: it was crushed and dispersed in 1775, by which time the Russians had installed themselves permanently on the Black Sea coast under the Treaty of Kutchuk-Kainardji (1764) and the intensive colonization of the southern steppes was turning the warlike organization of the Cossacks into a useless anachronism. Similar reasons led during the eighteenth century to the extinction of the other Cossack communities in the Ukraine, which was joined to the Russian state under Alexis Mikhailovitch.

The Zaporozhe *Sietch* has nevertheless survived in traditional memory as the perfect example of a Cossack society, and has been the chief source of the Cossack myth: a conception partly legendary and partly real, in which the Cossacks are pictured as living in a free democratic community, showing superlative courage as defenders of Orthodoxy against the Crescent, and staunchly championing the Russian people against the nomads of the steppe.

In reality, however, the Zaporozhe *Sietch* followed the same path of development as the other Cossack societies, whose structure was democratic in appearance only; their military hierarchy masked acute inequalities of personal wealth. Decisions were reached in open discussion, everyone had his say, but the liberty and equality fostered by this oral, public procedure were unreal. And anti-Turkish feeling, strengthened by constant guerrilla warfare and by strict adherence to Orthodoxy – which, in the seventeenth century, was to make the Cossacks into pillars of the 'Old Believers' heresy – did not preclude accommodations and even temporary alliances with the Ottoman Empire.

Some branches of the Cossacks lived on until the Revolution of 1917. They took service under the state and, as the Russian Empire developed, constituted the forward elements of expansion to the south and east and guarded the Caucasian and Asian frontiers. The Cossacks of the Ukraine and the Don provided the detachments which the Stroganovs sent eastwards from the Ural and which, under Ermak, conquered western Siberia. Russian power was extended to the Pacific shore by Cossacks. Dezhnev, the discoverer of the Behring Straits, was a Cossack.

The Russian government, strengthening its grip from the seventeenth century onwards in the lands along its southern borders, across the Don, in the valleys of the Kuban, the Terek and the Yaik, transformed these unruly mercenaries into faithful soldiers of the tsar. On the pattern of the existing communities (which were refashioned, amalgamated, or transferred from their old areas), it created new ones along the Asian frontier by a combined process, which went on until the end of the nineteenth century, of importing real Cossacks and 'cossackizing' the local peasantry. In 1914 there were eleven Cossack *voiskos* (armies, divided into *stanitsas*): those of the Don, the Kuban, the Terek, the Ural, Siberia, Astrakhan, Orenburg, Transbaikalia, Semiretchensk, the Amur and the Usuri, in addition to three city-based Cossack regiments.

Although in the late eighteenth century the Cossacks were still taking part in the great agrarian revolts which rocked the imperial throne and inflamed vast areas of southern Russia – and a highly important part at that, since they provided the unorganized peasants with such leaders as Bolotnikov, Stenka Razin, Bulavin and Pugachev – they subsequently aligned themselves completely with the country's political structure and became the foremost defenders of the existing order. As the most reliable troops the army possessed, they became shock-troops and took part in the most important battles; but these proud horsemen in their black sheepskin caps (*papakha*) were feared as well as admired by the civilian population on account of their absolute fidelity to the tsar in times of unrest, when they drove back the crowds of peasants or workers with their *nagaikas*.

The traditional image of the Cossack has inspired both novelists (such as Gogol, with his legendary *Taras Bulba*, 1837) and painters (Repin, *The Zaporozhe Cossacks' Letter to the Sultan*, 1891, inspired by a forged document of the eighteenth century and referring to the Turco-Polish war of 1677–8).

The Cossack societies were an exceptional, privileged element in the Russian social scene, and their influence was large in relation to their numbers. The largest *voisko*, however, that the Don, with a territory of some 23,200 square miles, which included the Donets region as well as the middle and lower Don, comprised 1,750,000 people in all – approximately 43 per cent of the total population of the area. Capable of providing 200,000 men for military service, it had been given the freehold of 7,413,000 acres of farming land, owned enormous herds of horses and cattle and flocks of sheep, held exclusive fishing rights on the Don and in the bight of the Sea of Azov, and was exempted from taxes on its wine trade and tolls on the transit of other goods.

In such circumstances, this 'Cossack' population was concerned only to a slight extent with military activities. With its fertility, its mineral wealth (the Donets coalfield) and its outlets on the Sea of Azov, the region took part in the country's general economic development; it had technical institutes as well as numerous schools, and produced engineers, doctors, architects, teachers and scholars. Even so, the past was remembered and traditions were preserved; there was a consciousness of privilege, a peculiar psychology which made this a special society with a powerful common bond of feeling, though the social structure was identical with that of the Russian people everywhere.

The other Cossack *voiskos* were less imposing in size, but, like the Don, constituted a distinctive, unusual element in the peasant population of the frontier areas. Ethnically speaking, moreover, they were a transitional element, since both in the northern Caucasus and in Siberia the Cossacks had acquired an admixture of non-Russian blood, Tatar, Chechen and Buriat. Their clothes were modified by native tradition; even their language, in some cases, was contaminated by the local dialects. Some Cossack units consisted wholly of non-Russians; the *voisko* of the Terek included several contingents whose standards displayed the Crescent. Service life and conditions, and obedience to the tsar, ensured unity. All the Cossack armies were given plenty of land to use and move about in, and possessed considerable privileges.

The Cossack stock-breeders of the Kuban, the largest group after the Don Cossacks, concluded profitable leases with oil companies and also had salt-marshes to exploit. The Ural Cossacks had a monopoly of sturgeon-fishing in the Ural River and its tributaries. The Cossacks of Transbaikalia had a monopoly of the sale of timber to the Siberian goldmines. They were a wealthy peasantry and supported the existing order; in 1917 they sided with the counter-revolutionaries in the civil war.

II THE EFFECTS OF THE GREAT REFORMS

Peasant Emancipation: Dependence in a New Form
The Slav colonial drive within the boundaries of the Russian empire was bound up with the new conditions of peasant life in the second half of the nineteenth century. The population was rising rapidly, by about a million a year: the total, which according to the census of 1897 was 127,000,000, had reached 175,000,000 by 1914. There was too little land under cultivation to induce the peasant to stay where he was, and in order to try his luck outside his village he had no need to emigrate to a foreign country; he took a job in one of the new factories or went to till virgin soil in Siberia.

The abolition of serfdom had not really made the peasants any better off. The Emancipation Act (the 'Statute for peasants liberated from serfdom') affected an enormous number of people – over 20,000,000, which was half the total number of peasants. Both psychologically and legally, these had undergone a sudden change of status; their rights as citizens were recognized; they had become equal with the state peasants and recovered their human dignity, though memories of serfdom continued to overshadow their attitude to life for many years (plate 21).

But the freedom conferred by the Act was only relative; it was complete only in the case of those who possessed nothing; the household serfs became proletarians in the fullest sense of the term and joined the rank and file of the agricultural labourers and industrial workers. Those who had been farming on their owners' property were now given a smallholding (*nadiel*) of their own, but the size of these freehold plots varied from one district to another, and was often less than the plots they had been allowed to farm before becoming their own masters. The transfer depended either on a unilateral decision by the landlord, or on an amicable arrangement between him and the rural community (except in Byelorussia and the Ukraine, where landownership was vested not in the community but in the family). The second procedure was the commoner; the *mir* was thus the intermediary, responsible for negotiating the agreement on the peasant's behalf and seeing that it was carried out. But with the abolition of the peasant's personal dependence on the landlord the entire feudal administrative structure had been abolished too; peasant self-government, effected through the *mir*, was the result. The village assembly (*selski skhod*) and its elected mayor (*starosta*) continued to discharge the traditional economic functions of the commune (periodical reallocation of land, management of communal property, etc.); in addition, they now transmitted government orders, assessed the individual's share of the tax payable by the commune (and collected it), exercised police powers, and, pending final transfer of freeholds from landlord to peasantry, ensured fulfilment of the landlord's customary rights to tithes and *corvée*. This state of 'temporary dependence' lasted until the deeds of purchase were signed; if the landlord refused to sign, it could last indefinitely.

The purchases in question arose from the fact that land was not distributed free of charge (whether directly to the peasant or through the *mir* as agent for the transaction); and payment was waived only if the peasant was prepared to content himself with one quarter of his allocation – the 'beggar's share', as it was called. The act of purchase conferred promotion from the category of 'dependent' peasant to that of 'peasant proprietor'. The purchase-price, advanced by the government and repayable in forty-nine annual instalments, was remitted to the original owner in the form of bills guaranteed by the state. In practice, the state advanced only four-fifths of the price in cases where no obligation to purchase had been imposed by the owner; the remaining one fifth was a supplementary payment which the commune could discharge in goods or labour. All in all, the former serf was less than wholly free. In one form or another, substantial traces or serfdom persisted long after publication of the Act. The process of land-transfer dragged on into the 'eighties. In relation to the state the peasants even found themselves in a worse position than before, with their annual redemption-instalments to pay in addition to the usual taxes; sometimes the burden was too much for them, and on several occasions the government was obliged to declare a permanent moratorium on arrears; redemption was finally abolished in 1906. The rural community, which had become an organ of the state rather than the representative of the peasants' interests, resorted on occasion to all the usual legal sanctions applicable to debtors: it confined the offender to his village by refusing him a passport, withheld his wages, distrained on his furniture or even confiscated his land. The effect of the Act of 1861 was to intensify the tyranny of the mir.

The old arrangements survived in various ways. The nobles' and peasants' properties were not separate units but were intricately entangled, and in many cases the plots retained by the former landlord were simply the snippets (*otrezki*, division of ground) lopped off the fields which were being looked after by the peasants at the time of the new dispensation, when the boundaries of their freeholds were worked out. The peasant went on cultivating these *otrezki* and paid rent either in cash or by working on some other patch of ground owned by the landlord. Piece-meal cultivation perpetuated dependence, at the same time as it prevented agricultural progress.

But although it was essentially a conservative compromise, the Act did in the long run constitute a turning-point in the social history of Russia. The freeing of millions of serfs made migration easier and accelerated the influx of peasants into the towns, despite the check on movement so jealously maintained by the *mir*. The labour market was reinforced by a flood of new recruits and this was a benefit to industry. A large number of peasants, moreover (perhaps as many as half a million), left their villages by accepting the 'beggar's share' and immediately selling it. The application of the Act took place in an atmosphere of dissatisfaction and hard bargaining which brought increased social tension and made the villagers still more foot-loose than before.

In effect, the social promotion of the peasants was little more than illusory. The combination of low agricultural output and a high birthrate would have sufficed in itself to cause continual emigration from the central regions to untouched land farther east. But the Act had made village life even worse by accentuating economic differences; the new division of property occasioned much buying and selling, in which the haves rose still further above the have-nots. While the majority of peasants lived wretchedly on inadequate holdings and had to hire themselves out part-time to make ends meet, there was a minority who made money, bought up more land from needy nobles and, developing into the *kulak* class, were an object of envy to the village poor. The word *kulak* means a clenched fist, grasping money; the *kulaks* were 'the tight-fisted ones', in fact.

In reality this development, which antedated the Act and to some extent received a fillip from it, would have gone ahead much faster if reform had been more radical. On the whole, the Act had the curious effect of putting a brake on it. Angrily, the under-privileged peasant saw that the aristocracy's estates were still in existence and that the *kulaks* were amassing possessions, and he became resigned to the prospect of yet further reductions of his property; he was painfully aware of the formidable precedent set by the current expropriation, devised and executed from above, by the state. At the same time, however, the retention of the *mir* kept property-transactions within certain bounds and hindered the formation of a large rural middle class. The social advantages of capitalism were less in evidence in the countryside than the drawbacks of a social order which, for most people, meant the continuation of economic servitude.

Harder Times for the Peasants

The new economic conditions of the final twenty years of the nineteenth century, combined with the tardy repercussions of the Act, played as large a part as the liberation of the serfs in determining marked changes in the conditions of peasant life. As an exporter of cereals on a large scale Russia suffered from falling wheat-prices in the international market. To balance the country's trade and pay for capital equipment, the government's economic policy tended to increase the amount exported (which rose to one fifth of the harvest in European Russia throughout the eighteen nineties), though of course the financial return did not increase in proportion.

The peasantry – burdened with crushing taxes, and compelled to sell more of their produce, leaving less to live on – found their standard of living, broadly speaking, deteriorating.

The situation, naturally, was not the same everywhere. In the central regions, where grain crops were not the main source of income, craft earnings and part-time industrial wages kept some of the peasants on a fairly even keel. In the southern and south-eastern regions, which were becoming Russia's granary and one of the granaries of Europe, and where the area under wheat had increased by 14 per cent, the capitalistic nature of agriculture – a characteristic also found in Lithuania and certain parts of Byelorussia – favoured the development of a rustic middle class. Population-increase combined with a market economy made social inequalities sharper – to a different degree, however, in different regions, since the system of the *mir* remained an obstacle at once to agricultural improvement and (though less markedly) to the rapid enrichment of a minority.

WHEAT EXPORTS FROM RUSSIA		
YEAR	WEIGHT	VALUE
1876–80	287,000,000 puds	291,000,000 roubles
1896–1900	444,000,000 ,,	323,000,000 ,,

There were real advances in agricultural technique on the big estates and the property of the richest peasants; progress elsewhere was insignificant. Output was still low; an estimated average of 39 puds per desiatin (slightly over 535 lb. per acre) on peasant land, and 47 puds (660 lb. per acre) on the big estates. Harvests varied enormously from one year to another; even if the great famines, like that of 1891, are overlooked, there were few years when the yield could be called really satisfactory. High productivity was impossible when cultivation was split up into such small units. In European Russia, according to Lenin (*The Development of Capitalism in Russia*), one fifth of the families farmed more than half the land redeemed under the Emancipation Act or leased out by the big landowners, and the same families owned a large proportion of the cattle and modern agricultural equipment; 50 per cent of families could be classified as poor. Repayment of grants for land-purchase became more and more difficult, and the government was obliged on several occasions to waive the accumulated arrears.

In the latter part of the century there was a perceptible increase in the number of unfit men examined by army medical boards, from which it must be inferred that the standard of health among the peasants was not high. Certainly the government, in 1901, considered it advisable to appoint a commission to investigate the causes of poverty in the central regions, where the condition of all peasants wholly dependent on agriculture was particularly wretched. The investigators reported that the majority of the peasants were undernourished and rarely ate meat. It is true that opinion at the time had become more sensitive to the lot of the individual and that the inquiry was merely discovering something which had been going on for very many years. Undeniably, however, there had been some increase in poverty among the majority, precisely during the period when greater opportunities of betterment had been made available. Even in Siberia, where the peasants, whether Cossacks or not, had more land and lived much more comfortably, the influx of immigrants, after the completion of the Trans-Siberian railway, increased the proportion of agricultural proletarians.

The Nobles and the Wind of Change

The effects of the Act on the circumstances of the nobility were no less important. Insolvent nobles, who had mortgaged most of their serfs to the state, had to pay their debts out of the money they got by selling their land to the peasants; all they were left with was the difference, in the form of rapidly depreciating bonds. But impoverished though they were, they were able, once quit of debt to the government, to raise considerable sums and invest them in profitable improvements on their estates. What was more, the Charters which laid down the detailed application of the Emancipation Act in relation to property and various existing rights resulted in a rigorous interpretation of those rights, mainly to the nobility's advantage. The opportunity was seized of annulling many burdens previously borne by the estates (free use of woodland and pasture, the right to gather firewood, etc.). The minute patchwork of cultivated holdings, and the fact that sundry uncultivated but useful features, such as paths, fords and brooks, were still in the nobleman's hands, gave him openings for putting the squeeze on the peasants in the vicinity and supplementing his income. Last but not least, the nobility were suddenly and brutally confronted by the economic realities of farming. However irritating the vestiges of the feudal system may have been to the peasantry they represented no more than a sideline to the nobleman, now that he no longer had serf labour with which to prop up his affairs. Long before 1861, a few landowners (including some who owned serfs on the *obrok* system) had been aware of the need for rational management; the same awareness was now forced on all the rest. The spirit of the up-to-date agricultural proprietor began to spread. Its effects were limited; still, the Act had undoubtedly given the nobility a salutary shock.

The healthy influence exerted by the Act on the mentality of the nobles was restricted by the financial difficulties from which their class suffered in the late nineteenth century. The richest and most enterprising nobles reacted to the fall in wheat prices by turning to other, more profitable crops and also to stock-farming (including dairy products for urban consumption); and the introduction of agricultural machinery enabled them to cut down their costs. But most of the aristocracy were too short of funds to adapt themselves to new conditions; the consequence was a general tendency for them to get rid of much of their land. By 1902 the nobility had sold a quarter of the land they had owned in 1882 (the purchasers being rich peasants and members of the urban middle class), and were personally farming only a third (as against 40 per cent) of what they still owned; the other two thirds were let. As at an earlier period, there was an increasingly sharp contrast between the few nobles who tried to keep pace with progress, and the majority, who found their financial position declining.

Development of the Middle Classes

Alexander II's liberal reforms – the creation of the *zemstvos* and the reorganization of the judicial system, in 1864 – were influential beyond the confines of the peasant class. These measures, which were intended to improve local administration and promote respect for the law by securing active participation from well-to-do people generally, brought all classes together, breaking down their isolation from the state; part of the result was therefore to confer new responsibilities on the peasants, outside the orbit of the rural community (the *mir*) though without releasing them from its authority.

In practice, these newly-created bodies were run by landowners – nobles, and members of the urban and rural middle class; the former were slow to lose their leading position in society, the latter played an increasing part from the eighteen-eighties onwards. Presided over by nobles, the district *zemstvos* elected provincial *zemstvos* which performed similar functions over a much wider area, and whose deliberations were steered by the marshal of the nobility.

However undemocratically their members may have been recruited, the *zemstvos* played an enormous part in the changes taking place in various sides of country life. They increased the number of elementary schools, organized the beginnings of a public health service, and allocated funds for road-building. They became one of the nodes round which social life revolved; they promoted the activities of professional men (doctors, teachers, engineers and so on) who either practised in the village or were in direct touch with it; they contributed to the diffusion of knowledge among the ignorant peasant masses; they created openings for social advancement, and, in short, introduced even into the remotest backwaters of the country (at least in the thirty-three provinces to which the reform of 1864 applied) the spirit of the towns, the spirit of progress.

The judicial reforms of 1864 were inspired by similar principles. The judicial system was detached from the administration; judges were appointed permanently, their independence being thereby safeguarded; proceedings were conducted orally and in public, to the benefit of the accused. But reform was by no means limited to these innovations. The old courts, which had been controlled by the administration and were differently constituted for different social strata, were abolished in favour of a new system which was the same for everyone and which included justices of the peace, district courts, assizes and higher courts; this system was to some extent controlled by those to whom it applied – the public – since the justices of the peace were elected by the *zemstvos* (or by the urban *dumas*, in the towns)

and the district courts functioned with the aid of juries. The census qualifications demanded for jury service were much less exclusive than those for
election to the *zemstvos* (for which only one twentieth of those registered in
the census as landowners were eligible); the lower middle class, in both
town and country, was thus able to take part. The same class was also
enabled to supply judges, who had to possess a certificate of secondary
education and a certain income (not large) from land or buildings.

These reforms were of capital importance; they improved relations between classes, made society less rigid and more amenable to change, caused
new posts to be created, and increased the numbers of officials and of
members of the liberal professions. The speeding-up of economic development in the closing years of the century, and the increased demand for
public servants on the part of a state whose activities were growing, augmented yet further the middle strata of society – the strata which from this
time onwards supplied the intelligentsia and the basis of opposition to the
régime. The image of Russian society appeared to be moving gradually
closer to that of the societies of western Europe.

III A DELAYED 'INDUSTRIAL REVOLUTION'

On the Road to Capitalism. Uneven Development
Conditions unfavourable to industrial development – the most obvious of
which was lack of capital – were tackled by the state for reasons at once
economic and national. The whole policy of Finance Ministers Reitern
(1862–78), Bunge (1878–87), Vishnegradsky (1887–92) and Witte (1892–
1903 – nicknamed 'the father of Russian industry'), consisted of laying
firm financial foundations and, in the absence of Russian capital, creating
an atmosphere of confidence to attract investment from abroad, which
flowed in briskly during the 'honeymoon' period of the Franco-Russian
alliance (1893–5).

About the middle of the nineteenth century, Russia was described as
being still no more than 'a huge village'. Certainly its cities and small industrial towns presented the appearance of being lost in the vast spaces of
the countryside; the busy life of a few urban concentrations and even of
whole districts or regions (St Petersburg, Moscow, the Ural valley, the
central provinces) was powerless to offset the impression of unchanging
immobility received by the hasty traveller. The impression was a false one
created by distances over which all human activity was spread out. It is,
however, true that the great changes, both quantitative and qualitative,
which were taking place in the country's economic and social structure,
and which in the West constituted 'the industrial revolution' (a customary
and convenient label whose aptness is now contested, but which has been
taken over by the East), hardly began to make their appearance in Russia
before the eighteen-eighties. Russia's industrial revolution was a late phenomenon, brought into being on a permanent, traditional, rural back-

ground which gave it special social characteristics. It had been preceded by technical progress whose course can be traced from the early years of the century; it was helped on its way by the reforms of Alexander II, particularly the abolition of serfdom, whose full effects (liberation of the labour market, and the increased importance of the peasants as consumers) were not felt until after 1880; and it was accelerated by the state, which built factories in order to supply the country with railways.

Technologically, Russia's industrial revolution was only partial. It had comparatively little effect on the ancient metallurgical industries of the Ural, which were still using wood for fuel at the end of the century;

GEOGRAPHICAL DISTRIBUTION OF RUSSIAN INDUSTRY IN 1887

REGION	NUMBER OF ENTERPRISES	NUMBER OF WORKERS	% OF TOTAL NUMBER OF WORKERS
Whole Russian empire	27,247	789,322	
Russian Poland	2,288	105,494	
Russia (*minus* Poland)	18,959	683,824	100
including the 'industrial centre' (provinces of Moscow, Tver, Kostroma, Vladimir, Nijni-Novgorod, Riazan, Tula, Kaluga)	4,440	373,055	54·6
North-west (St Petersburg, Narva, Riga)	997	72,947	10·7
South (Ukraine)	3,809 (initially)	64,939	9·5
West (region of Minsk and Smolensk)	2,213	50,299	7·4
Ural	1,523	26,814	3·9
'Black earth' region of the centre (link between centre and south)	1,345	31,638	4·6
Volga cities (from Simbirsk to Astrakhan)	1,969	30,836	4·5

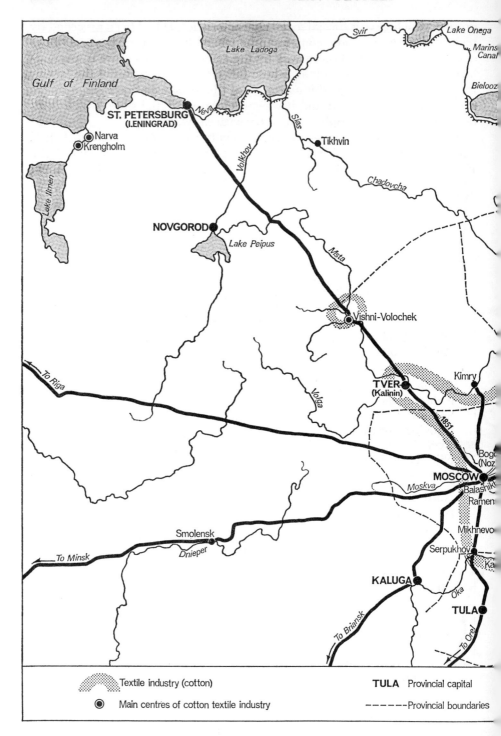

Map 15 The Cotton Industry in Nineteenth-Century Russia

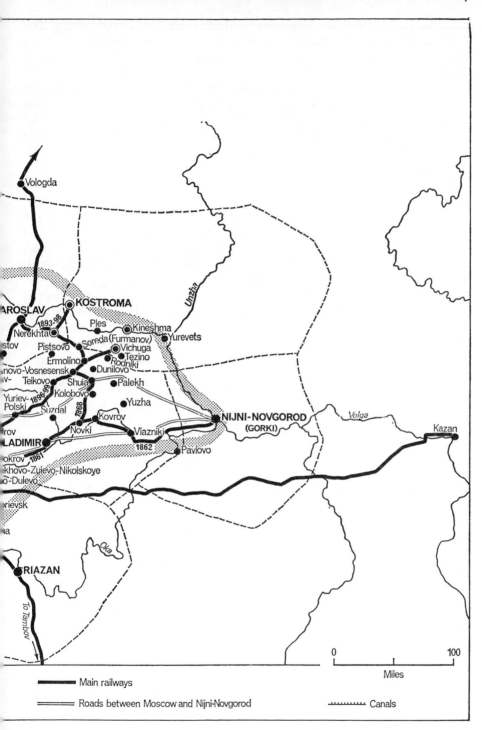

Vologda

YAROSLAV · KOSTROMA

1893-98
Nerekhta
stov
Pistsovo
Ermolino
novo-Vosnesensk
ov-
Teikovo
Yuriev-
Polski
Suzdal
rov
Novki
LADIMIR
okrov 1861
khovo-Zuievo-Nikolskoye
o-Dulevo
rievsk
ia

Ples
Soreda (Furmanov)
Rodniki
Dunilovo
Shuia
Kolobovo

Kineshma
Vichuga
Tezino

Yurevets

Palekh

Yuzha

Kovrov
Viazniki

NIJNI-NOVGOROD
(GORKI)

1862
Pavlovo

Unzha

Volga

Kazan

Oka

RIAZAN

To Tambov

0   100

Miles

▬▬▬ Main railways

═══ Roads between Moscow and Nijni-Novgorod

⌢⌢⌢ Canals

according to the scientist Mendeleyev, that region was sound asleep (*Spit Ural*, 'the Ural sleeps'). However, Martin furnaces were gradually replacing puddling furnaces, and the use of the Bessemer converter was becoming more widespread. In the Ukraine, on the other hand, which woke suddenly into industrial life after 1880, the new factories, almost all of which were set up by foreign firms to supply the railway companies with rails, used mineral fuel and were equipped with all the latest 'American-style' devices. In the textile industry, progress was slower and above all much less even. The mechanization of cotton weaving, which ousted domestic weaving by hand and brought the workers together in the mill, was almost complete by 1880; between 1866 and 1879, the number of weavers working at home for the wholesale warehouses had dropped from 66,200 to 50,000, whereas the number of machine-loom operators had risen from 94,600 to 162,700. Nearly all cotton fabrics were now produced in factories. Linen and woollen goods, on the other hand, continued to be produced on a craft basis outside the big concerns with state contracts; and for family needs both spinning and weaving were carried out at home (map 15).

The coming of the machine resulted in concentrations of industrial labour; this happened even in the new, underpopulated regions, once their isolation had been broken down by the railways. Mechanization also caused migration of workers and their families in the case of certain skilled trades: for example, steam navigation reduced the number of boatbuilding yards on the Volga. Between 1860 and 1870, 12,500 miles of railways were laid. By 1880, the shores both of the Baltic and of the Black Sea had been linked with the central regions; after 1890, the Urals and Siberia became the goal. The rail network altered the country's industrial anatomy and opened up new fields of enterprise. The Moscow-St Petersburg line was opened in 1855; 1857 saw the inauguration of the spinning-mills of Krengholm, at the mouth of the Narva, which were destined to employ more than 12,000 people and to become one of the largest centres of the cotton industry in Russia before 1914.

Similarly, the linking of Moscow with the Black Sea ports by way of the Ukraine, and of the Donets coalfields by a lateral line to the iron of Krivoi Rog, caused the creation of a new industrial region in the provinces of Ekaterinoslav (the present-day Dniepropetrovsk), Kharkov and Kiev; by 1890 the Ukraine had outstripped the Urals in the produuction of cast-iron. In so far as Russia had an industrial revolution, the Ukraine is a typical or perhaps, rather, unique example: new undertakings sprang up rapidly, the existing towns expanded and new ones were built, workers came flooding in and settled round the factories. The economic complex was characterized by a vigour unrivalled elsewhere in the country. In 1900 the Ukraine had seventeen factories (mostly in or near Ekaterinoslav) with twenty-nine blast furnaces between them, and was producing more than half the pig-iron in Russia and a little less than half of the wrought iron; it also produced coal; and its northern provinces supplied nearly all the country's refined sugar (map 16).

1a. (*Top*) Novgorod in the 14th century. Reconstruction based on archaelogical excavation.

1b. (*Bottom*) Inscription on birchbark, 11th or 12th century, found at Novgorod. It is about a woman who was dismissed by her husband and is complaining of having been deprived of property inherited from her own family.

2. (*Top*) Typical Romanesque carving, cathedral of Strelzno, 12th century.

3. (*Bottom*) Early evidence of a monetary system: coinage of Boleslas the Valiant (12th–13th century). Warsaw Museum.

4. (*Top*) Church of St John Kaneo (late 13th century), above Lake Okhrid.
5. (*Bottom*) The bridge of Arslanagić at Trebinje (Bosnia), built by order of Mehemed Pasha Sokolović in the 16th century.
6. (*Right*) 13th-century Romanesque porch, cathedral of St Laurence, Trogir.

YUGOSLAVIA

7. Gravestone, thought to be of Bogomils, 13th–14th centuries at Brotnjice, Cavtat.

BULGARIA

8. Three saints, 11th–13th centuries. Tempera on canvas on poplar wood. National Gallery, Sofia. Exhibition 'Treasures from the Museums of Bulgaria'.

9. One of the typically Muscovite tsars who were Peter the Great's predecessors: Michael I, the first Romanov, who came to the throne in 1613. This portrait by the icon-painter Ivan Maximov was commissioned by a boyar. Collection Dominique Aronson, Paris.

10. Church of the
Assumption, Vladimir, 12th
century, showing Byzantine
influence.

12. Domed churches
named after St Basil,
overlooking the Red Square,
Moscow. Built between 1554
and 1560.

11. The remarkable
church of the Ascension
(1532) at the village of
Kolomenskoye; a
masterpiece of
authentically Russian
art.

13. The cathedral of
St Isaac, Leningrad
(1819–58).

14. An imposing setting for a tsar's receptions : the court of Alexis Mikhailovitch in 1662.

15. Novgorod after its decline from a busy city to a virtual museum. Its two parts (the 'Sancta Sophia's side', named after the cathedral, and the 'merchants' side', recalling former commercial prosperity) are separated by the Volkhov. 18th-century engraving after Lespinasse.

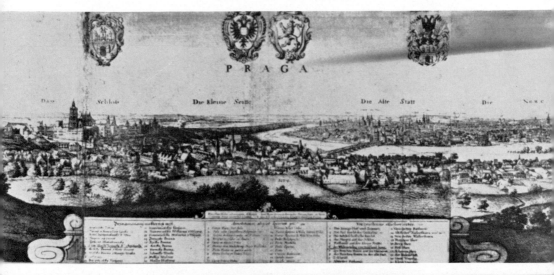

16. (*Top*) Prague in 1642. Old engraving with trilingual legend (Czech, Latin, German).
17. (*Bottom*) The emperor Sigismund with the kings of Bohemia and Hungary, by the Master of 1424. Musée du Louvre.

18. Statue of a female figure, in the baroque chapel of the school church of St John of Legnica, which contains the tombs of the last Piasts of Silesia.

POLAND

19. Castles and churches.
   a. (*Top left*) Castle of Baranów, late 16th century, Polish Renaissance period.
   b. (*Middle left*) 17th-century house at Kazimierz (*voivodia* of Lublin), with ornate façade.
   c. (*Bottom left*) Wilanów Palace, near Warsaw (1680–1733).
   d. (*Top right*) 17th-century wooden church at Haczow (*voivodia* of Rzeszow).
   e. (*Bottom right*) Church of the Visitandines, Warsaw (1755–61).

20. Jug decorated with a fish
and a crayfish, a much-used
motif (1792).

21. Official propaganda : printed cotton kerchief, produced and distributed in large
numbers to commemorate the abolition of serfdom, 19 February 1861.
Collection Dominique Aronson, Paris.

RUSSIA

22a. (*Top left*) Leningrad, 'the Venice of the north'. The Griboyedov (formerly
Ekaterinsky) Canal. Background: the Church of the Blessed Saviour (1883–7).
  b. (*Top right*) Square of the Winter Palace, Leningrad.
  c. (*Bottom left*) The Orthodox church, Tunis, in the style of Suzdal, built 1956.
  d. (*Bottom right*) Modern Kiev: a new school in Sverdlov Street.

RUSSIA

23. Tolstoy and Gorky, a photograph taken in 1900 by Countess Tolstoy. Tolstoy Museum, Institut d'Etudes Slaves, Paris.

POLAND

24. Small rural house with polychromed decoration, about 1950, at Zalipie (*voivodia* of Cracow).

CZECHOSLOVAKIA

25. Spartacus Day: the spirit of the famous Sokols can be seen in the harmony and control of these fine gymnastic performers.

MODERN YUGOSLAVIA

26. Strip-cultivation, a survival from an earlier age.

SOVIET UNION – The modern city

27a. (*Top*) Group of buildings in Moscow.

b. (*Middle*) The new town of Darnitsa, a suburb of Kiev (capital of the Ukraine):
living accommodation for railway rolling stock repair workers.

c. (*Bottom*) Gagarin Avenue in the town of Thorez (formerly Chistiakovo), inhabited
by miners of the Donbas (Ukraine).

The social consequences of the industrial revolution were nevertheless limited. In principle, the Emancipation Act of 1861 had had the effect of creating a free labour market; in practice, the effect did not reach significant proportions until after 1880. Where this side of economic life was concerned, the new mthods of production affected only a small fraction of the population. In other countries, the soaring growth of industry had caused powerful industrial concentrations and large-scale migration of workers; this phenomenon was hardly visible in Russia. Population movement was still controlled by the requirements of agriculture; urban expansion proceeded at a moderate pace; and the fertility of the Russian people was such that, in relation to the enormous and increasing mass of the peasantry, the number of permanent immigrants to the industrial centres was minimal.

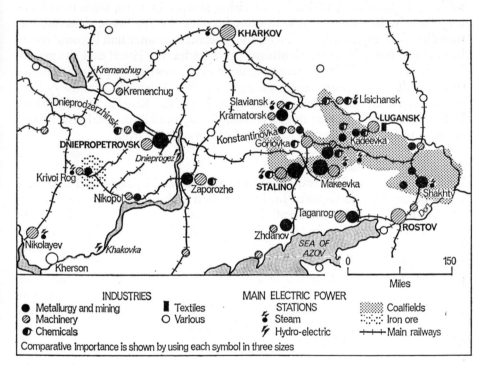

Map 16 Industry in the Ukraine, Nineteenth and Twentieth Centuries

But industrial development did modify the structure of society by creating a proletariat, and to this extent it can justly be called an industrial revolution. Dementiev (1850–1915), a doctor employed by a *zemstvo*, wrote a study, *What the Factory Gives to the People and What It Takes Away from Them* (1893), in which he showed that a high proportion of villagers (80 per cent by 1890, in the region of Moscow) had in fact become detached from the life of the soil; though appearances were all the other way, since most villagers were still registered as inhabitants of their native communes and therefore counted officially as peasants. The number of temporary workers was tending to diminish rapidly, and though they kept their peasant outlook their jobs made them town-dwellers – not yet wholly absorbed into town life, but already detached from their peasant background.

After the long drawn-out crisis of 1900–6 and the rather slow recovery from it, which was complete by 1909 or 1910, Russia once more experienced, in the three years preceding the war, a remarkable period of industrial progress, comparable to that of the 'nineties. But whereas the industrial revolution in the late nineteenth century, though supported by a gradually extending consumers' market protected by high tariff walls, had owed its rapid advance to foreign investment and to orders placed by government departments, it was the ordinary home market which now became the mainstay of industrial prosperity. Railway-building, and also military expenditure, which began rising steeply in 1910, were contributory factors. But there was a sudden increase in the home demand for metallurgical and textile products; the peasant customer had become more important, the prices of agricultural produce having risen; and the growing towns were building in masonry instead of wood and equipping themselves with the appurtenances of modern life. A length of railway-line could have been the symbol for the expansion of the Russian metallurgical industries in the 'nineties; the corresponding symbol in the early twentieth century would be a sheet of mild steel or corrugated iron.

Monopolistic Tendencies

The closing years of the tsarist régime were marked by the rapid development of capitalism. General business activity, the proliferation of credit transactions, and the accelerated movement of capital, reached an unprecedented pitch. Foreign capital was still playing an essential part, since in 1914 it represented a third of all private investment and held a commanding position in the key industries. But there was a new feature; the growing proportion of capital of Russian origin, in itself an indication of the increased strength of the home market. Russia's position on the eve of the 1914–18 war was peculiar, in that the growth of her industries was no longer keeping pace with demand; it had ceased to correspond to the effective level of purchasing power; though the potential needs of the bulk of the population were of course considerable, the actual standard of living was, in the main, still low. It is possible that the monopolies which came into being during the crisis period exerted a restrictive influence; Soviet historians hold them responsible for the under-production which was starving Russia of coal, metals and oil at the beginning of the First World War. It is true that Russia's considerable dependence on foreign capital and control militated against the alignment of her industries with her national needs. The report of the meeting of the Council of Ministers on 23 January 1914 placed the blame for high prices and the coal-shortage on the policy of the Prodameta, a sales-cartel which had been in control of industrial undertakings in southern Russian since 1902.

The interests of the nation and those of capitalism were interwoven, sometimes identical but often in conflict with each other, and the clash between them was rendered more acute by the monopoly tendency. The Prodameta cartel, which had extended its range between 1902 and 1909 to include a number of metallurgical products, was in competition with the Krovlia cartel, in which several of the leading iron and steel manufacturers in the Ural region had been associated since 1905.

The Prodameta, which, in 1908, marketed 90 per cent of metallurgical products in the south and 45 per cent of such products in the empire as a whole, and had gained the agreement of the two largest joint-stock companies in the Ukraine to the formation of a trust, found itself up against violent opposition which was a mixture of competitive jealousy and patriotic feeling, and which received wide publicity in the press. This hostility came from various right-wing circles. The landed proprietors were worried by the accelerated industrialization of the country and the development – and the demands – of the industrial working class; in addition, they were genuinely anxious about the increased economic pressure under which the national economy was labouring, and which offered foreign bankers the necessary opening for setting up this trust in southern Russia. The industrialists in the Baltic regions were also hostile, alarmed at the prospect of having to pay monopoly prices. And there was hostility from the industrialists of the Ural region, which was awakening from slumber at last and clashing in the Russian market with the triumphant advance of the Ukraine. The birth of a trust was an object of dread, and was described in the *New Times* of 8 April 1899 as an even greater evil than revolution; the theme of the trust as a political power was developed by the conservative right; that of the trust as a leviathan devouring the market, by competitive industrialists. The Muscovite middle class invoked the cause of patriotism; they were in favour of industrial development but feared foreign financial domination.

Dissension between firms belonging to the Prodameta, and the more or less subterranean opposition which was active even in the corridors of the Duma and in government circles, caused the project to fall through; a victory hailed with resounding acclamation by a section of the press. But the affair had stirred public opinion: it had exposed the chaotic nature of an industrial development which led to unbridled competition, diverted a large part of the profits abroad, and placed the government in a dilemma, caught between economic arguments and the wider interests of the nation.

The tendency to industrial concentration nevertheless continued until the outbreak of war; it took the form of arguments between firms and, though more rarely, of mergers. In 1913, the five most powerful mining and metallurgical companies in the Urals were responsible for half the iron ore extracted in that region and a quarter of the coal, and half the production of coke. Industry in the south captured most of the market in European Russia from industry in the Urals. The latter had been eaten into less deeply by monopolistic tendencies and had remained largely in the hands of family firms – it was, in a word, more Russian. Its chief customers were in eastern Russia, central Asia, and Siberia.

The oil industry was the one in which the concentration of ownership, and also the influence of foreign capital, were most marked. The cartel formed in 1905 by the Nobel and Mazout companies controlled, by 1910, 80 per cent of sales of petroleum and petroleum products; in 1913 it was still controlling 77 per cent, and was doing 40 per cent of the carrying trade with its own fleet of tankers. But new agreements were made in 1910: Royal Dutch Shell set up a Russian branch, absorbed various provincial companies, and was responsible for 20 per cent of oil production in 1914. In 1912 the Russian General Oil Company was started; it was run from London, with British and Russian capital, and had between 20 per cent and 30 per cent of production in its hands by 1914. In the struggle for markets between the three organizations, RGO became a serious threat to the monopoly of the Nobel group by 1913. The oil industry was even more dependent on foreign banks than the metallurgical industries of the Ukraine, and was sometimes described as 'semi-colonial' in consequence.

RUSSIAN AND FOREIGN COMPANIES

Year	Total number of companies	Capital in millions of roubles	Joint-stock companies, industrial and commercial, Russian and foreign	Capital in millions of roubles	Number of foreign companies	Capital in millions of roubles
1881	635	839·4	372	349·1	5	6·3
1900	1,369	2,402	1,009	1,558·9	125	281·4
1914	2,235	4,720	1,835	3,425·6	176	498·4

The remaining sectors of industry were not subject to the same forms of monopolistic organization; they were based on capital of which a substantial proportion, often a majority share or even the whole, was Russian; and some of them (textiles, for example) remained independent of the major banking houses, which were financially linked with western capitalism. Broadly speaking, however, the years 1910–13 were a period in which banking strode rapidly ahead, acquired control over the main industries and remained – despite the increasingly large part played by Russian capital – dependent on foreign finance-houses.

The chronic shortage of capital which obliged the government to have recourse to endless borrowing from abroad, and to grant considerable economic privileges to companies and banks which in fact, if not always in appearance, were controlled from abroad, placed Russia in a position of economic dependence to which, in the years just preceding the war, no end could be foreseen. Some of her resources were completely outside her control: Russia mined nine tenths of the world's platinum, for instance, but its marketing and price depended on Great Britain. Indeed, Russia's external trade as a whole was in the hands of foreign middlemen, chief among whom were the Germans.

Some people have described the Russia of this period as an 'economic colony'. Though exaggerated, this description is not altogether without truth. For although the nation had a dynamic though small middle class, the requisite economic and banking structures, and a growing army of technicians, it lacked the necessary financial power. However, there was a growing awareness of Russia's dependence on foreigners, a dependence whose effects extended even into political life; and a growing reaction, on a national scale, against it. The war, by eliminating German influence and tightening up controls, started the process of disengagement. And the Revolution, in its task of effecting a state take-over, was supported by a wave of popular patriotic feeling.

Revival of the Manual Crafts

Russia remained, as ever, a land of contrasts. The development of large-scale industry was not accompanied by the extinction of the *kustary* (rural craftsmen) or even by the total disappearance of cottage industry attached to factory production. By the end of the century nearly all textile workers, it is true, were proletarians who had quitted the family workroom for a job in the factory. But there was still a large range of crafts which were not in competition with modern industrial methods, or not very much so, and which were very much alive: the woodworkers, such as the coopers, cart-wrights (one of whose products was the *telega*), boat-builders, sledge-builders and makers of various household equipment; the metalworkers, with their pots and pans, samovars, fish-hooks; and the leatherworkers, such as the cobblers who made knee-boots.

As in the past, there were whole villages devoted to a single speciality. Sergievsk, north of Moscow, made toys; Boldino, in the province of Nijni Novgorod, sledges. The province of Moscow at the end of the century had 180,000 factory workers and 190,000 *kustary*. In the neighbouring provinces, where industrialization had not progressed so far, the ratio of the second to the first was even higher: in the province of Kostroma there were 35,000 factory workers, in that of Tver, 23,000; each of these provinces had 140,000 craftsmen. The individual craftsman still represented at once the most picturesque and the most widespread form of manufacturing activity. The government looked upon him with a favourable eye, and populist thinkers regarded him as supplying one of the stable, prosperous components in the structure of peasant society.

In this new Russia, which was uprooting the peasant from the soil and creating cities that were an inhuman environment for the workers inhabiting them, the craftsman was the inheritor and guardian of tradition, the last relic of a golden age; but he was also, through the highest and most refined varieties of his handiwork, a man in a special position, the privileged representative of the common people of Russia, of their creativeness and their desire to adorn their daily lives, as well as providing a by no means negligible contribution to the luxurious homes of the rich.

Nevertheless, the standard of the more artistic crafts had deteriorated since the eighteenth century. In the latter part of the nineteenth there was an attempt to pump fresh life into them by means of government aid, the patronage of industrialists and society ladies, and collaboration in matters of decorative design from well-known painters of the day. One of the centres of this movement was Abramtsevo, north of Moscow, where the manufacturer Mamontov gathered writers and painters and set up studios for cabinet-making and wood-carving in 1882, with pottery added later. Popular art received most help, however, not from ventures of this kind, but from a market which now included the rich peasants and the nationally-orientated middle class, and from another material factor: improved facilities for transport and display, which made it possible to show the craftsman's finest creations to the public in every part of the country.

IV THE CHANGING SOCIAL STRUCTURE

A Two-way Process: Decadence and Enrichment among the Nobility
The Emancipation Act of 1861 accentuated a process which had already caused striking changes in aristocratic society. The number of titles conferred, after a period during which it was greatly reduced, rose to a higher rate than before. Between 1858 and 1897, the number of nobles (including their families) in the fifty provinces of European Russia increased from 609,673 to 885,745, a jump of about 45 per cent. Even if we confine ourselves to the Slav nations within the empire's borders, another 135,000 must be added to account for the Polish nobility. But statistics also record a rapid increase in the non-Slav nobility: Caucasian (171,000), Asiatic (nearly 12,000) and Siberian (16,000); and though there was much variation according to nationality and the type and rank of title awarded, the position of these newcomers from the social and administrative point of view placed them more or less on a level with the Russian nobility.

Because official responsibility and a noble title were always, in the nature of the administrative system, connected, and because the growth of the state organism automatically necessitated a larger number of officials, the old nobility found themselves swamped by a flood of these new arrivals, who were nobles according to the law though not quite accepted as such in society. According to Prince Dolgoruki's *Book of Genealogies*, there remained in the nineteenth century barely a hundred families (with or without titles) whose ennoblement dated from the origins of the Russian state. In the twentieth century the number went down much further.

The state favoured the ennoblement of commoners who had succeeded in business. Access to noble status was also provided by honorific distinctions: elevation to the hereditary nobility accompanied the three first class of the Order of St Vladimir and all classes of the Order of St Gregory. In the twentieth century, anyone who served the state for thirty-five years in a civil department, or twenty-five in the army, had a chance of being rewarded with the Order of St Vladimir and therefore with hereditary noble rank.

Less than ever did the nobility form a homogeneous whole; some nobles were rich and others poor, some influential, others obscure, lingering in backwaters and regarded as insignificant by commoners who were at home in the main stream of life, such as business men and industrialists. Even now, however, on the brink of their disappearance, the nobles retained much of their former power. True, their resources had been reduced by the implementation of the Act of 1861, and they were continually selling off land to wealthy peasants and increasingly, as time went on, to middle-class town-dwellers. The Revolution of 1905 caused further grants of land to be made to the peasants, and by 1912 the total area in aristocratic ownership had dwindled by nearly half.

But the nobility, like others, profited from the general economic trend of the time. Many nobles started industrial enterprises on their estates, or invested capital in the railway companies and new industries. Part of Russian industry was still owned by this class: mining and metallurgy in the Ural region, some textile manufacture (notably woollens), and a cluster of activities connected with profitable estate-management, such as boatbuilding and the manufacture of pitch, potash, etc. Others (and these too were many) rationalized their farming methods to some extent and obtained higher yields. The richest nobles came off best: while the minor and middle nobility were going rapidly downhill, the great families with plenty of money, such as the Yusupovs, adapted themselves to capitalism and tapped new sources of wealth. Out of some one hundred and fifty thousand names, a small number stand out prominently: Sheremetev, Stroganov, Demidov, Yusupov, Kochubey, Galitzyn, Saltykov, Vorontsov, Dashkov, Chuvalov, Tolstoy, Bariatinski, and a few more, to which must be added the names of certain recently ennobled middle-class families. Changed conditions for the Russian nobility had not cut off their resources, far from it, indeed; and though the class as a whole was growing poorer it included a number of wealthy capitalists whose political influence was great and whose social position imposing. But the nobles were acquiring a middle-class character themselves. Industrial profits supported the standing of the great families and protected their landed possessions.

There was an enormous gap between these powerful, influential nobles and the needy minor aristocrats whose grounds were no roomier than those of their neighbours – a rich peasant, say, and a merchant from the nearest town. Equally wide was the gap between the great nobleman and the government official whose many years of loyal service had been rewarded by elevation to the hereditary nobility. An example of this species was Lenin's father, Ilia Nikolayevitch Ulianov, director of the rural schools in Simbirsk province, who was promoted to be a counsellor of state on the active list and, in virtue of this, acquired hereditary noble rank at the age of forty-five; but who, in circles beyond his professional environment, never enjoyed the recognition and influence of an authentic nobleman.

Nobles who had no official appointment and salary, and whose private means were limited, did not suffer as severe a setback in 1914 as might be imagined. Selling their farm produce, even in years when prices were high, and playing the stock-market, were not in all cases their main sources of income. Land values had risen considerably, particularly on the outskirts of towns, and in the vicinity of railways under construction, and in regions where agricultural development was proceeding rapidly. If selling slices of land reduced the size of a nobleman's estate, it also lined his purse and enabled him to buy more industrial shares. Any nobleman whose land was favourably situated did well out of the country's general economic advance. It is easy to talk of the decline of the nobility; but in fact the Revolution of 1917 did not shake a tree whose fruit was already over-ripe and shrivelled.

The Church's Apparent Power
In Russia, a Christian state where the powers temporal and spiritual were intimately connected, the Church enjoyed not only an authority recognized and indeed upheld by the state, but privileges which were reinforced by the policy of Alexander III and that of the procurator-general of the Holy Synod, Pobedonostsev, from 1881 to 1905. It will be readily understood what a special position the Church acquired as the prop of autocratic government, at whose disposition it placed a clergy who explained the laws to the peasant, preached submissiveness, and rendered the people's sufferings in this world supportable by promising the blessings of divine justice in the next.

But the Church's position, partly because of this compromise with a régime whose authority was by no means unanimously accepted, was not as strong as it looked. The number of monasteries was increased under Alexander III; yet they and the churches together provided a singularly tenuous network in relation to so vast a country. There were 85,000,000 Orthodox worshippers (according to the census of 1897), spread out, moreover, through an immense area; in 1905 there were 48,000 churches (and, it is true, about 19,000 chapels as well), mostly in the towns, and slightly over 100,000 priests. The regular clergy (monks and nuns) hardly exceeded a total of 40,000 in their 724 religious houses (about 500 of which were monasteries and the rest nunneries); and the monks and lay brothers (whose numbers were about equal) totalled only some 15,000 as against 30,000 novices and male and female domestics (map 17).

The monasteries, some of which were famous places of pilgrimage, sustained the people's faith but had no continuous, direct contact with the

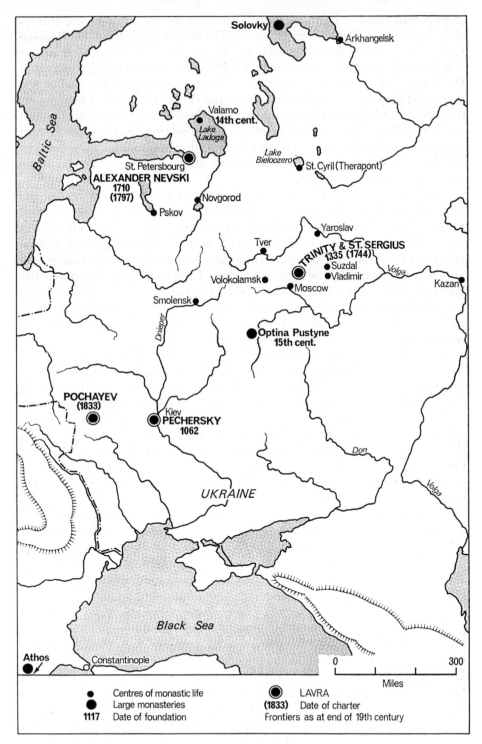

Map 17 Russian Monasteries in the Nineteenth Century

population. Besides, many of them had been founded in remote, thinly-populated parts of the country, along the routes carved out by Russian expansion in earlier days. The secular clergy on the other hand were rather few in numbers and, in the country, fairly poor and often despised (though their material circumstances had been improved towards the end of the century); they made the people observe the rites of the Church but had no deep religious influence. In the towns the priests were better educated and more worldly, a different kind of person from their brothers in the country; they belonged to the upper classes; their authority was a social as well as religious force and they elicited fear and distrust, as well as veneration, among the common people.

But it was especially in the country that the population really eluded the Church's grasp, despite appearances to the contrary. Everywhere beyond the outskirts of the towns the Russian peasantry had retained all the old superstitions and many of the pagan customs, thinly disguised with a veneer of Christianity; wherever there was contact between Russian and non-Russian peasants, the former borrowed the spells and charms of the latter; in Siberia, the Russians consulted the local shamans. Some highly unorthodox sects, whose numerical strength is difficult to estimate, were still active in the most isolated regions. The clergy's hold over the people was much more superficial than it seemed to be.

In addition, the rent which the schism of the Old Believers had made in the fabric of Orthodoxy was still making itself felt. The Old Believers' heresy possessed an austerity and moral elevation which placed it on a high level – it is in no way to be compared to the various freakish sects with which Russia abounded – and its authority over its adherents was undeniable. But it regarded the official Church with a distrust born of persecutions too recent to have faded from memory. It is true that the lines of demarcation in Russian society in the early twentieth century were economic rather than religious. The Old Believers, whether they were prosperous craftsmen of the Volga region or business men or industrialists of the provinces of Moscow and Ivanovo, were hardly to be distinguished from their Orthodox competitors. The fact remains that this important minority was not part and parcel of Orthodoxy, and that Orthodoxy was, among other things, a pillar of the established political order. However loyal the Old Believers might be, and, in the twentieth century, however close to the official Church, they were a separate element.

The Orthodox Church did not possess that monolithic unity which its position as the approved religion of the state appeared to give it.

Despite its integration with the state, the financial help the Church received from that quarter was not very large. Out of a normal budget which had risen by 1898 to the sum of 1,356,576,000 roubles, the amount allocated to the Holy Synod and the Orthodox Church was only a little over 20,000,000 roubles (half of which was for the secular clergy and the missions). The Church's educational establishments received a further 7,414,600 roubles.

The Church maintained a large number of parish schools, and more of these were set up under Alexander III; but in this field it met with severe competition from the state schools, to whose annual budget the Ministry of Education gave 26,921,000 roubles. The Church possessed considerable resources, however, and was also able during the nineteenth century to recover the land confiscated from it in the eighteenth by Catherine II. Its main sources of income were collections and donations, and profits from manufacture, business and agriculture. The sale of candles (manufactured by the Church) to pilgrims and others brought in an enormous amount of money, after travel to Russia's holy places had been made easier by the abolition of serfdom and the growth of the railways. It should however be noted that ecclesiastical wealth was concentrated, all too evidently, in a few highly prosperous monasteries and churches, while the rest scratched along as best they could. This glaring contrast between riches and poverty in the Church itself did nothing to strengthen its moral position.

Ecclesiastical society thus exhibited the same social inequalities as Russian society in general. The country clergy did indeed receive land from the commune (and the priest was more liberally provided than others), and a stipend, which they drew not without difficulty. But the priest's modest resources had to provide for his family and assistants; an extensive brood. His economic position would have pushed him down into the proletariat were it not that his profession was still a more or less exclusive caste, with hereditary succession from father to son or son-in-law. But the fact that the clergy had so many children was a contributory factor in the formation of the intelligentsia, that stratum of *déclassés* which was so prolific a source of revolutionaries.

Rise of the Industrial Middle Class

Russia's industrial revolution, or what there was of it, shook up a society in which opportunities for advancement were limited. It enriched a minority among the peasants, swelled the ranks of the industrial and commercial middle class, and brought to birth an industrial proletariat. Quantitatively speaking, its results were restricted by the economic backwardness which Russia never succeeded in throwing off under tsarism. But it did initiate social changes and a popular upsurge which account for the fact that, shortly before the First World War, aristocratic, autocratic Russia entered belatedly on the path of constitutional government in the Western manner.

The accelerated tempo of trade had increased the number of merchants registered in the three guilds to a total of 280,000, according to the census of 1897; a very small figure, as yet, for a total population of 128,000,000. But another 343,000 should be added, to include the category of 'honourable citizens' who had received a title placing them just below noble status, and who represented the richest section of the industrial and commercial middle class. This section had not grown much in numbers, since it had arisen almost exclusively in the period of embryonic capitalism, and the dynasties into which it had developed had entrenched themselves in monopoly positions.

The great manufacturers in the cotton industry, the Morozovs, Prokhorovs, Konovalovs and so on, had developed their fortunes and their power unimpeded: no new competitors had arisen on the same scale as themselves. They, with a few wholesalers (the *Skupshchiki*), composed the élite of bourgeois society. By now, the men of these families were graduates of universities and technical schools; they knew foreign languages (German for business, French for culture); they travelled in Europe, not for amusement, like the nobles, but to visit the factories of England, Alsace and Switzerland – they were interested in progress; they were very different from the merchant type depicted in such sombre colours by Ostrovsky, whose descriptions refer to an earlier period, before the liberal reforms of Alexander II. They did not stand aloof from the world; they sat on town councils, presided over stock-exchange committees, and entered fashionable society; some of them, such as the Shchukins and Tretyakovs, were patrons of the arts. The new conditions of social life and economic development after 1861 triumphed over the old, worn-out system of education and caused a rift between the generations. The founder of the M.J. Riabushinsky cotton spinning mills was an Old Believer, austere and unbending, who would not let his children learn music and broke a violin over the head of his son Paul; the latter, after becoming chairman of the business, led a society life, was a devotee of the arts and used to invite the actors from the Mali Teatr to his house.

These *grands bourgeois*, whose public activities, prior to 1905, were confined to the municipal field, were not opponents of the régime. Traditionally loyal, and confident of authority's support in the event of riots or strikes, they had no feeling that they constituted a political force. They knew their fortunes were secure, and their only ambition was to penetrate further into the aristocratic structure of the state and rise by means of titles. They bought estates (a very unusual thing to do, before 1861) not only for factory-building but also in order to live in aristocratic style. They played little part in the events culminating in the revolution of 1905, but the new constitutional régime brought them closer to government circles. They supported the liberal KD party (Constitutional Democrats) but were active in the wings rather than on stage; in the lobbies rather than in the Duma. During the years preceding the First World War they constituted a pressure group whose unity was effectively maintained by fear of revolutionary movements.

The remaining strata of the bourgeoisie – the middle and lower-middle classes – increased considerably in numbers. They belonged either to the lower guilds, especially the *mestchantsvo* (which had grown to a total of 14,000,000 members by 1897) or to the category of non-aristocratic functionaries; they were essentially town-dwellers, and their position in urban life became more prominent after the 1905 revolution. They gained the upper hand in many municipalities after 1910, when the qualifications for suffrage, based on the value of an individual's urban property, were lowered and the number of voters went up. The thrusting, newly-important middle classes were a source of strength to liberal opinion. In this respect, tsarist Russia appeared to be following in western footsteps.

The Self-made Man

The cotton industry was the cradle of a rich bourgeoisie whose names dominated Russian business activity in the second half of the nineteenth century and the early years of the twentieth. Most of them were of serf origin, such as the Garelin, Kuvayev, Gandurin and Burylin families at Ivanovo, the Konovalovs at Vichuga, the Razorenovs at Kineshma and the Gorbunovs at Nerekhta.

In the province of Moscow the best-known family, the one playing the biggest part in the conclaves of late nineteenth-century industrialists, were the Morozovs. The first Morozov, Savva, who died in 1860 at the age of ninety, had run a cotton weaving mill at Zuievo (province of Vladimir) in the early part of the century. The Morozovs are a typical example of those prolific middle-class families who benefited from favourable conditions to become numerous throughout central Russia, creating new businesses which were always ruled by a member of the family and which employed altogether some 50,000 workers; the factories at Orekhovo-Zuievo alone (where in 1885, the first big strike marked the beginning of the workers' movement in Russia) had a staff of 8,000.

There powerful manufacturers, who exercised a paternalistic authority even in the day-to-day running of their factories, played a major part in municipal affairs. With the exception of the provincial capitals, industrial towns tended to be more or less synonymous with local industrial enterprise. It has been said that 'a cotton-print royal family' reigned at Ivanovo, where one town councillor in three was an industrialist; there was a Gandurin and a Burylin, and the mayor himself, one of the Derbenevs, was a weaver and exporter of cotton – a local potentate with a ferocious appetite for work, who was merciless in his treatment of his workers, went about shabbily and untidily dressed and hardly allowed himself time to eat stew out of a wooden bowl; though when he had guests they were received with ostentatious luxury and the tableware was of gold and silver.

These former serfs, who had gained their freedom in the eighteen-twenties and were so quick to rise in the social scale, were by no means the only Russian industrialists. A good many had sprung from the free peasantry or the urban artisans; they began making money in the first half of the century and transformed themselves into wealthy middle-class citizens. Such were the Baranovs at Alexandrov (province of Vladimir), the Khludovs at Egorevsk (province of Riazan), the Maliutins at Ramenskoye (province of Moscow), the Riabushinskys in Moscow itself and later at Vyshni Volotchek, and the Prokhorovs, also in Moscow. The fourth-generation descendants of the founder set up the so-called Three Mountains Company in 1874, but the family's continued ascent carried it into the ranks of the hereditary nobility in 1912.

After 1861 it was unusual for anyone to make the great breakthrough by the same means. But there was a wave of *entrepreneurs* who founded their fortunes not on a combination of craft-manufacture and business (as did those just described) but on business alone – business with the state, in the form of contracts and sub-contracts for government supplies or the distillation of liquor (for which the state held the monopoly and drew royalties). Having accumulated an abundance of capital, a man of this type would emerge suddenly as a large-scale industrialist. Examples of this transition from commerce to industry are the Balin family at Yuzha (near Viazniki, in the province of Vladimir), whose mills had 130,000 spinning-machines, and a work-force of over 5,000, in 1914; and the Riabushinsky family at Vyshni Volotchek, who extended their activities beyond the industrial sector and founded banks in Kharkov and Moscow.

The Middle Class on the Threshold of Politics

The professional bodies created in the reign of Nicholas I under the title of Councils of Manufacturers, later known as Councils of Commerce, were conceived as consultative organs, performing an intermediary function between the bureaucracy and the commercial middle class; and they might have caused the latter to take stock of themselves and become aware of their collective importance. Nothing of the sort resulted, however, because the bureaucracy, with its arbitrary habits of behaviour and its distrust of all initiative, created an atmosphere unfavourable to any real collaboration with professional groups. Once again, the chief obstacle to progress was the régime itself.

The new Council of Commerce and Manufactures, set up in 1872, was expressly provided with the right to make recommendations and to present practical plans to the Minister of Finance; but it never fulfilled the purpose intended for it, and businessmen lost interest. It was only in the financial committees (the number of which was increasing: there were seventeen in 1906, eighty-seven in 1911) that the richest section of the bourgeoisie acquired the habit of meeting for discussions on economic problems of general significance. In the last years of the century the representatives of the commercial and industrial middle class, while not attacking the régime, took a sharper, more exigent tone when commenting on questions of immediate concern to themselves, such as the customs and excise system. But the reception accorded to their wishes by the administration showed how little importance was attached to the requests of businessmen acting collectively. The Russian bureaucracy was undoubtedly susceptible to pressure from individuals, or to group pressure exerted by devious means; but manœuvres of this kind were concerned only with immediate ends. Publicly, the administration affected indifference to corporate desires. Not until after 1905 did circumstances force it to change its attitude.

Growth of a Proletariat

Large-scale industry engendered a new element, the proletariat, which displayed signs of class-consciousness towards the end of the nineteenth

NUMBER OF WORKERS IN THE FIFTY PROVINCES OF
EUROPEAN RUSSIA IN THE LATER TSARIST PERIOD

Year	Mining and smelting	Subsequent manufacture and processing	Railways	Total
1879	235,000	763,000	191,000	1,189,000
1890	340,000	840,000	252,000	1,432,000
1900–3	477,000	1,262,000	469,000	2,208,000

SOURCE: Lenin, *The Development of Capitalism in Russia*

century, and, in the social history of tsarist Russia, played a much larger part than its small numbers might lead one to infer.

The size of the industrial working class is really almost impossible to estimate: even up to the Revolution, there were still a great many nomadic or seasonal workers who were strongly attached to the soil, and whose rustic attitude to life remained the same even in the factories. At the turn of the century, the figure may have been over a million and a half; by 1914 Russia had 3,000,000 industrial workers (in a total population of 175,000,000).

This estimate, however, accounts only for factory-workers properly so called, as recorded by the Inspectorate of Factories and the Inspectorate of Mines. In studying the proletariat we must include regular staff of various kinds: railwaymen (over 80,000 in 1913), navigation and waterways employees (500,000), posts and telegraphs (80,000); and various others such as building workers (2,500,000, of whom however two thirds were casual labourers and still primarily peasants), the most subordinate grades in commercial employment, agricultural workers (4,500,000), domestic staff, and manual workers who worked in their own homes. The economist Rashin, in his study of the origins and development of the working class in Russia (1958), gives the following table of the wage-earning population in 1913, whose total numbers he puts at 17,815,000:

Industrial workers
Factory-workers   3,100,000
Wage-earners not on a factory payroll, working at home
   or in a craftsman's shop   3,000,000
Building workers   1,500,000
                                                                       ——————
                                                                       7,600,000

Transport workers	
Railways	815,000
Water transport	500,000
	1,315,000
Agricultural workers	4,500,000
Miscellaneous (general labourers, occasional day-labourers, and hotel trade employees, domestic servants)	4,065,000

In this mass, the greater part of which was still not yet detached from the peasantry, and whose diversity bears witness to the degree of economic progress achieved by Russia before the First World War, but also to the strength of traditional social attachments (as indicated by the number of servants), the factory-workers nevertheless represent the keynote, the most specific ingredient, the genuine proletarians (at least if we leave aside those semi-civil-servants, the railway and water transport workers).

Most proletarians came from the villages, where they either possessed no land at all or lived wretchedly on inadequate plots; the central regions were the principal reservoir of industrial labour. Very many peasants prac-tised a craft as an extra source of livelihood, and began to lose their con-nections with village life when they obtained a passport from their rural community and went off to find work elsewhere. Those who entered indus-try chose the nearest factory, moving as short a distance as possible from their province and even their home district; this was especially true of the central regions, where the factories were mostly situated in villages or little country towns. Thus there grew up in the provinces of Ivanovo and Kostroma, for example, a local proletariat, who had practically shed their links with the soil but not with the preoccupations of peasant life and its periodical diversions; particularly as the worker was a social outcast in the village or small town where he had come to live.

At their places of work and in their residential quarters, these proletar-ians constituted a considerable section of society; in some small places, indeed, they were almost in the majority. In a big city like Ivanovo-Voznesensk, the 'Russian Manchester', whose inhabitants numbered 100,000 in 1905, the workers represented over a quarter of the population but were still newcomers, more than half of them having been there for less than five years and more than a quarter for less than one. Much the same was the case in all the old industrial areas (except the biggest cities and the surrounding country) and also in recently industrialized areas such as the Ukraine, where the workers had come from far and wide and soon dis-carded their ties with life on the land. In the province of Moscow in 1855, 55 per cent of workers were the children of workers; the proportion was as high as 77 per cent in the textile industry. The number of workers who went back to their villages to help with the harvest was particularly low (3 per cent) in the spinning mills.

There were some peasants who, instead of being absorbed into industry, went off while they were still young men to find town jobs and save up for a *troika*, an embroidered shirt, a pair of varnished knee-boots and an accordion, with an eye to subsequent conquests among the girls of the village. But the general tendency was for the worker's connection with the soil to be broken for good; the number of full-time workers, forming an integral part of the life of the cities and industrial villages, was continually growing. Russia, like other countries, had acquired her labouring masses.

They were not uniformly distributed: the true proletariat, dependent solely on industrial employment, originated mainly in St Petersburg, on the Baltic coast, whose hinterland was an inadequate reservoir of labour, and the Ukraine, whose prosperous agriculture kept most of the local population busy. The Putilov factory at St Petersburg was employing nearly 11,000 workers in 1907; the total number of workers in the city was some 25,000. In the Ukraine, the factories of the New Russia Company at Yuzovka employed 14,000 workers; those of the Briansk Company, not far from Ekaterinoslav, 5,200; those of the Dnieper Company at Kamenskoye, near Alexandrovsk, 6,500; those of the Donets Foundry Company and the Russo-Belgian Company near Bakhmut, 7,000. It would be easy to multiply examples, all showing the same state of affairs: the Russian workers were few but always densely concentrated; still close to country life in spirit and outlook, but bound to their employers by the traditional policy of protective authoritarianism which, in the late nineteenth century, resembled the situation obtaining in western factories fifty years earlier.

Urban Outcasts

The workers were like a foreign body in the organism of city life, taking no part in municipal affairs. The factory-owners' authority over them was complete; in addition, they were subjected to a system of police surveillance which became even more thorough after the emergence of institutions ostensibly favourable to them, such as the Inspectorate of Labour, which was founded in 1880 and extended to the whole country in 1899, and which functioned less as an impartial referee than as a tool of the employers and the state. As for the *starosty* of the factories, who after 1903 were elected by the workers (subject, however, to the owners' approval), they were never really representatives of the employees. Not until 1906 did the workers win the right to organize trade unions, whose existence was always precarious and which were constantly being suspended 'for reasons of public security'.

In the circumstances, the workers did not start becoming class-conscious until the 'eighties, when in the absence of union organization they were compelled to press their demands by isolated acts of resistance, each local strike subsequently becoming – as did that of the 8,000 workers of the Morozov factory at Orekhovo-Zuievo in 1885 – an example and encouragement to a workers' movement which took shape in the late 'nineties and, of necessity, assumed a political complexion.

The influence of the revolutionary leaders, writing from abroad, was still very slight; but the men who organized strikes and demonstrations were almost always former deportees, members of secret societies who had been in prison and acquired an active knowledge of revolution; a few of them had read Marx and Plekhanov. The first Marxist groups among the workers were formed after 1890; from then onwards, led by Lenin (who settled in St Petersburg in 1893 and left it for exile in 1896) and by the Union of Struggle for the Liberation of the Working Class, the workers' movement, prevented from turning to trade unionism, took extreme forms and resorted to mass action in support of its claims. All the St Petersburg workers came out on strike in 1896, during the festivities for Nicholas II's coronation; in the following year the government reduced the working day to eleven and a half hours.

Conditions for the Russian workers were extremely harsh. Wages were low and were frequently reduced by stoppages and fines, which were justified in the employer's eyes by poor work, poor care of machines, and Monday absenteeism; the worker, on the other hand, would have argued that if his workmanship was clumsy and his output low the cause was fatigue brought on by under-nourishment, and that his weekly abuse of vodka was merely an artificial attempt to top up his energy.

The existence of a working-class élite, few and far between and without much influence as yet, did nothing to disguise the moral degradation of the workers as a whole. The situation in this respect was not always as bad as in the eighteen-eighties, the period described in the Reminiscences of A.A. Shapovalov; in the railway repair-shops at St Petersburg at that time any excuse was good enough for a drinking-bout or a murderous brawl, the apprentices were quick to learn coarse, drunken ways, scrounging, thieving and lying were accepted as normal behaviour, and the dead weight of servility inherited from the past was evident in the hypocriticial humility of the workers towards the boss. During the final decade of the century the atmosphere in the shops was improved, though only slightly, by organized action on behalf of workers' demands and by the influence of the skilled tradesmen (mechanics, locksmiths and so on) who were the aristocracy of the industrial working class.

To pay wages irregularly was common practice in the older establishments. The worker was issued with an official certificate whose terms placed him completely at the disposition of the employer. He was protected in principle by social legislation introduced gradually between 1882 and 1905, regulating such matters as the length of the working day, the employment of women and children, accidents, and medical care; but in practice these provisions tended to go by default. The great textile undertakings of the Muscovite manufacturers, and the factories set up in the Ukraine by foreign companies, took a paternalist line which secured certain advantages to the worker. Cases of sickness or injury were admitted to the factory's hospital; on the other hand, few workers' sons went to the school which was provided by the firm but which was so small that it could take only foremen's children. The co-operative shops installed by the management came in for rather more criticism than they deserved; but the prices charged were often high in relation to the quality of the stock. The effect on the worker – underpaid, and housed in hutments belonging to the factory, regardless of whether he was a bachelor or married – was to make him feel despised and a captive.

V PROGRESS IN EDUCATION AND THE SCIENCES

Universities and Schools
Notable cultural advances were achieved after the reforms of Alexander II. The increase in the number of intellectuals, which was proceeding faster than can be ascribed to population-growth alone, was not prevented by the state's distrust of unruly, politically recalcitrant students in seminary and university alike; a distrust which took the form of discriminatory measures and police surveillance. It was in fact mainly after the Revolution of 1905 that the higher educational establishments were inundated by the younger generation; but student numbers had already started rising perceptibly by the end of the century, when the country's economic progress demanded a steadily increasing supply of technically qualified men, whom it was no longer convenient to recruit solely from abroad. As early as 1900, the number of students in the then existing universities had risen from 3,659 (the total in 1855) to 16,357.

DISTRIBUTION OF UNIVERSITY STUDENTS IN RUSSIA			
Moscow	4,562	Kharkov	1,506
St Petersburg	3,613	Odessa	954
Kiev	2,602	Kazan	906
Dorpat (now Tartu)	1,647	Tomsk	557

However, this was a small figure in a population of 130,000,000. It rose more steeply after 1900, the total mounting from 21,506 in 1904 to 38,440 in 1909. Thereafter it receded slightly, falling to 34,538 in 1912. But this figure must be taken in conjunction with that of the pupils of the higher schools (military, technical, scientific and archaeological institutes, schools of languages, etc.), which contained some 40,000 students in 1912–3.

According to the census of 1897, 22 per cent of the population could read and write, the proportion being 30 per cent of the men and 13 per cent of the women. But it is interesting to note that the percentage was much higher for the 10–40 years age-group, a fact which indicates a substantial advance in adult education.

PERCENTAGES OF RUSSIANS ABLE TO READ AND WRITE		
Age Group	Men	Women
10 – 19 years	45·5%	21·8%
20 – 29 years	44·9%	19·5%
30 – 39 years	39·5%	16·7%
SOURCE: Johnson, *Educational Heritage*		

These are average figures; they refer to Russian territory as a whole and do not reflect the considerable differences obtaining between one region and another; in Central Asia and the Caucasus, for example, little more than 5 per cent of the inhabitants had received any schooling. There was also a difference between the towns, where nearly half the total population, including one third of the women, had been to school, and the country, where only a quarter of the peasants, and one tenth of their womenfolk, were more or less able to read and write.

The network of elementary schools had been extended. Apart from establishments run by various ministries and by other, semi-official institutions – the two accounting between them for a mere fifty thousand students or thereabouts – the majority of pupils in 1898 were attending schools administered either by the Ministry of Education (37,000 schools with 2,650,000 pupils) or the Holy Synod (40,000 schools with 1,476,000 pupils).

In the early years of the twentieth century these figures increased rapidly (at least where public education was concerned), more rapidly than the population, but still fell far short of the country's needs.

SCHOOL ATTENDANCE IN RUSSIA IN 1911		
Educational Authority	Number of Schools	Number of Pupils
Ministry of Education	60,000	4,200,000
Holy Synod	38,000	1,800,000
Other institutions	2,700	200,000

Four years later, the Ministry of Education was responsible for 80,000 schools with 6,000,000 pupils (2,000,000 of whom were girls); mostly, however, in the towns.

Education in the rural areas had made little progress, despite the efforts of the *zemstvos*.

Secondary schools were attracting an increasing number of pupils but the total intake was still small. In 1912–3 they had less than 700,000 pupils (and this includes the seminaries). By the outbreak of the First World War the total number of school and university pupils had risen to about 9,000,000 in a total population of 175,000,000.

Russian Contributions to Science

Scientifically, Russia lagged behind other countries and was largely dependent on them. She nevertheless produced a few scientists and technologists who went abroad to find a more congenial atmosphere and better working conditions; such were the biologist Mechnikov (1845–1916), a Nobel prize-winner in 1908, and the physicist Yablochkov (1847–94), who invented a spark-plug. Inside Russia, the physiologist Pavlov (1849–1936) won fame by his work on digestion, founded a whole new school of thought in psychophysiology, and won a Nobel prize in 1904. But such successes were few; general education was still too undeveloped, and serious obstacles made it difficult for the universities' most brilliant pupils to enter research. Pavlov's life is a case in point: one of the eleven children of a priest, he was educated at the seminary at Riazan and the University of St Petersburg, where he took his medical degree in 1883; led a poverty-stricken existence for a number of years; was obliged to accept the chair of pharmacology at the University of Tomsk; and was able only in 1895 to embark on his research at the University of St Petersburg, where he taught for thirty years.

Prominence of Women

At every level of Russian society, women occupied an important position and to some extent an independent one. This was due to a combination of factors: distance – the geographical scale of Russian life; and the fact that, in the rural areas, the men often had to be away for long periods at a time; and the scarcity of women in the recently colonized regions. The role of women in both town and village was often a leading one; at the very least they worked in close partnership with their men; there was no room in life for the submissively feminine attitude implied by certain literary sources which are few in number though great in fame; penned at early periods (the *Domostroi* is an example), they are not above suspicion of partiality and moreover refer only to special cases.

Admittedly, the gloomy realism of Ostrovsky's plays about life in the merchant class depicts the abasement of women under the will of the tyrannical head of the family. But that was only one part of the truth, one which moreover applied specially to the first half of the nineteenth century. Among the 'merchants' (which means registered members of the merchant guilds) the industrialists, who were more advanced, constituted an élite, a special environment in which a wife often had a special position to fill: her husband's factory, with its multitude of workers, clerks and so on, gave her the chance and indeed the duty of entering a field of activity to which there was no parallel in commercial circles, at any rate on the same scale and with as much responsibility. It was the achievement of industrialists' wives not only to do the conventional thing by building churches in the villages near the factory, but also workers' housing, communal baths, schools, libraries and theatres. Sometimes their opportunities were even wider: it was not unknown, if the husband died while the children were minors, for the widow to take over the chairmanship of the firm.

Even in the background position assigned to them by the Church, wives, or rather mothers, exerted a significant influence in some cases on prominent figures in literary and religious life.

Women played an active part in literary movements, and still more in artistic ones. The list of contributors to *Mir Iskusstva* contains such names as Polenova, Yakuchikova, Ostrumova, Goncharova and Princess Tenisheva.

Women made a big contribution to the revolutionary movement; large numbers of them undertook the humbler tasks, a few participated directly in terrorist activities. The Land and Freedom party, founded in 1876, included Vera Figner and Sophia Perovskaya among its members; in 1879 the latter with her own hands placed a bomb on the railway line along which the Tsar was to travel. In 1878 another woman revolutionary, Vera Zasulich, shot down the chief of police, Trepov, with a revolver.

Woman's role in society had been suddenly enlarged by the application of the reforms of 1860; the *zemstvos* created and managed a number of institutions which offered them an immediate outlet for their energies.

Nor did the educational system debar them from culture. The proportion of women who had received schooling of some sort was, of course, smaller than that of the men: here again we can turn to the census of 1897, which tells us that 13 per cent of the female population of Russia had learnt to read and write, as against 32·2 per cent of the males. The proportion was higher: 26·8 per cent and 34·2 per cent respectively, in the Vistula territories (the former Polish kingdom); and lower in Siberia: 5·1 per cent and 19·2 per cent.

But a distinction must be drawn between the country districts, where ignorance was the general rule, and the towns, where a third of the female population had been to a school of some kind. A further distinction is that between classes: nearly 70 per cent of women in aristocratic and administrative circles could read and write.

On the other hand it is to be noted that at secondary level the ratio of men to women was much higher: 528,232 women had received a secondary education, as against 717,134 men (72,441 of whom had received it in military academies). And the universities (representing higher education and higher technical education) had trained no less than 7,000 women (as compared, admittedly, with a much larger number of men, namely almost

132,000). All these figures are small, but they point not so much to any inferiority in the position of women as to a low level of education among the population as a whole.

Although admission to the universities was denied to women under the University Act of 1863, a certain number of institutions were open to them, including the medical schools; towards 1865 there were some 200 women medical students in the capital. Secondary education being already available to girls (St Petersburg's four high schools for girls had approximately a thousand pupils in 1862), a press campaign to broaden their opportunities was mounted in the liberal atmosphere of the Great Reforms; conducted by the *Sovremennik* (*The Contemporary*) and by the magazine *Nedelia* (*The Week*), a feminist organ, the campaign failed to get women admitted to the universities but did win for them (or at least for those who had gained diplomas as secondary teachers) the right to attend the extension lectures given voluntarily in the evenings and on Sundays by professors of St Petersburg University. In 1876 this right was extended to all universitity cities; by about 1880, women could take four-year courses whose intellectual level was in no way inferior to that of the regular courses.

Meanwhile women were being admitted to certain professions: they were becoming medical assistants, telegraph operators and, from 1871, accountants. They were excluded from service in government departments until 1914. But the first women doctors had made their appearance during the Russo-Turkish war of 1887–8; their numbers increased rapidly, and special institutes were set up for training them.

VI THE ARTS AND THE NATION

Half a Century of Great Literature

A great literature had been born in Russia in the years preceding the emancipation of the serfs. This literature reflected a society agitated by violent ideological conflicts and by the reforms of the 'sixties; it was caught in the crossfire of criticism from the Slavophils on the one hand and the Westernizers on the other, and subsequently from the conservatives and the liberal intelligentsia; it was under constant scrutiny from the standpoint of the existing political and social order, and was plagued for years by a vigilant and touchy censorship; it was nevertheless sufficiently free to expand and blossom magnificently. But along with this free creativeness, it was always – though not all of it was 'engaged' in the narrow sense – strongly influenced by the moral and social problems posed by Russia's backwardness.

Turgenev (1818–83) is much more than the delightful writer who gave us *A Sportsman's Sketches*, a portrayal of the peasantry; he also wrote, for example, *Fathers and Sons* (1861), a novel which shows the clash between two generations and in which a new type, the 'nihilist', makes his first appearance, a character the author perhaps based on Bakunin. Turgenev's contemporary Goncharov (1812–91) delineated in *Oblomov* a landowner afflicted with chronic indecision, one of those provincial noblemen who 'began by forgetting how to pull on their stockings, and ended by forgetting how to live'. Ten years later, when the aristocracy's very existence was in question, this vice of *oblomovshchina* had come to be regarded as an ingrained characteristic; generalizing inaccurately, the public attributed it to the nobility at large, whereas a good many nobles were in fact struggling hard against poverty and the stagnation of provincial life.

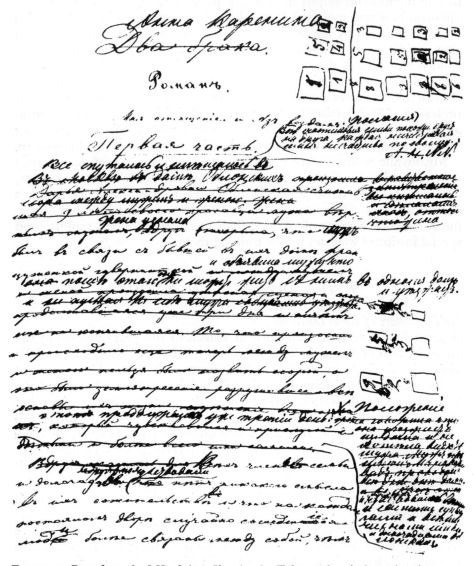

FIGURE 29 Page from the MS of *Anna Karenina*, by Tolstoy; the ninth version, in which the initial plan, involving Anna's divorce and her remarriage to Vronsky (whence the deleted title, *Dva braka* [Two marriages]), was abandone .

Dostoevsky (1821–81), who underwent four years of imprisonment with hard labour, followed by five years of exile, in Siberia, from which he returned in 1859, contemplated human suffering, both physical and moral, with sympathy and keen sensibility. His prison experiences provided the material for *The House of the Dead* (1861). His novels (*The Insulted and the Injured*, 1861; *Crime and Punishment*, 1866; *The Idiot*, 1868; *The Possessed*, 1871; *The Brothers Karamazov*, 1879), show him to be a profound psychologist who is attracted by the lower depths of society and by the troubled, questing soul and the unbalanced mind. Deeply concerned with the Christian conception of life, the search for God, the necessity of defending the rights of the spirit, and the problem of moral freedom, he became in later life an adherent of the 'Slav idea', which in his case meant a naive, unrealistic Pan-Slavism and a religious nationalism which led him, in his reaction against materialism and the radical intelligentsia, into political conformism.

A very different temperament is evident in the works of Tolstoy (1828–1910), whose appetite for life frequently overrides his moral and religious tendencies. He was full of fads and fantasies (*'lubies'*), as Legras remarks; excited, for a while, by his educational experiments in his school at Yasnaya Polyana; 'an anarchistic prophet, excommunicated by the Church but tolerated by the government, surrounded by hangers-on and famous throughout the world; punctuating his long life with works of uneven value, some of which bear the stamp of genius; abandoning his family and dying shortly afterwards, alone, at a small country railway-station', Tolstoy, with his 'unquiet spirit and lack of balance', is the personification of nineteenth-century Russia (Legras). The whole of Russia becomes a living presence for the reader of Tolstoy's masterpieces *War and Peace* (1864–9), in which the campaign of 1812 provides the setting for a panoramic picture of Russian life, and *Anna Karenina* (1873–7), which unfolds the destinies of two noble families (figure 29). Abandoning the novel, he turned to the novella and the stage-play; in *The Power of Darkness* (1886), his intentions as a moral and religious propagandist are entangled in a lurid plot reminiscent of the old-fashioned spine-chilling melodrama.

A better exponent of the theatre was Ostrovsky (1823–86), whose characters are authentic Russians in their everyday environment, in most cases that of the Muscovite merchant class. From *The Storm* in 1859 to *Wolves and Sheep* in 1875, his plays allow us to follow the development of social life, in which the narrow, tradition-bound mentality of the mid-century bourgeoisie is overlaid by the broader and more unprincipled attitudes of the new-style business man.

The leading reviews, such as *The Contemporary*, and subsequently *Annals of the Fatherland*, published contributions in prose and verse from authors who were of noble origin for the most part, and to whom Alexander II's relatively liberal attitude permitted a certain freedom of expression, though they had to be careful not to go too far.

N.A.Nekrassov (1821–77), who edited *The Contemporary* from 1846 to 1866, and *Annals of the Fatherland* from the latter year until his death, was a poet whose tenderness and compassion were excited by suffering. His 'generous poetry' belongs to the democratic and liberal trend of the eighteen-seventies, a trend of which the title of his volume, *Who In Russia Lives At Ease?*, is a characteristic example. His lyricism reached a considerable public, not so much by its quality as poetry as by the nature of the sentiments expressed.

Grisha's Hymn to Russia

You are poor,
You are rich,
You are impotent
And omnipotent,
O Mother Russia!
A free heart which finds its salvation
Even in slavery,
The people's heart
Is gold, pure gold.
The strength of the people
Its mighty strength,
Lies in possessing
A pure conscience
And living justice!
Strength and injustice
Cannot abide together,
And by injustice
No sacrifice
Has ever been called forth . . .
Russia does not stir,
She is as one dead.
But if the spark
Hidden within her
Bursts into sudden flame,
Then all rise at once
With no one to wake them,
All advance
Though none entreat them;
Grain by grain
The wheat is heaped up, mountain-high!
An army arises
In ranks beyond number,
Bearing within itself
Invincible power!
You are poor,
You are rich,
You are oppressed
Yet omnipotent,
O Mother Russia!

N.A.Nekrassov
(from *Who In Russia Lives at Ease?*)

M.E.Saltykov (1826–89), writing under the pseudonym Shchedrin, contributed to *The Contemporary* and succeeded Nekrassov as editor of *Annals of the Fatherland*. He represents 'the literature of accusation'; his aggressive criticism is camouflaged by enigmatic wording and humorous allusion; his copious output (*The History of a Town, Letters from the Provinces, Sketch of a Province*, etc.) describes the follies and foibles of the upper classes, both nobles and bourgeois. This humorist, who simultaneously carried on a brilliant career as a provincial administrator, wielded considerable political influence in educated circles for something like forty years.

The same period was marked by the development of a type of literature which, though more conformist in tone, is none the less of interest by virtue of the picture of popular life which it offers to the historian. P.I.Melnikov (1818–83), a civil servant in Nijni Novgorod who wrote about the Old Believers as well as persecuting them, left two works, *In the Forests* (1868–74) and *In The Mountains* (1875–82), whose vigorous character-drawing conveys the life and outlook of the religious minorities along the middle Volga, a region which owed is activity and animation largely to them. N.S.Leskov (1831–95), in his novel *Church People* (1872), takes the reader into ecclesiastical circles, described with sympathy and, indeed, a certain partiality.

The great period of poetic romanticism, the period of Pushkin and Lermontov, was over. But the lyrical tradition continued to be represented by aristocratic poets of high quality, though the audience to which they appealed was smaller: F.I.Tyuchev (1803–73), the quiet tones of whose verse are full of melancholy, vibrating with the sadness of the close of day and the evening of life; Alexis Tolstoy (1817–75), the novelist's cousin, who was not only a 'pleasing lyrical poet' (Legras) but also wrote a novel (*Prince Serebriany*, 1862) and a dramatic trilogy set in the time of Ivan the Terrible (*The Death of Ivan the Terrible*, 1868; *Tsar Fedor Ivanovitch*, 1868; and *Tsar Boris*, 1870); and A.A.Fet (1820–92), who, in his poetry, dealt with the intimate atmosphere of the family circle, and, in his life, had the distinction of being one of the landowners who actively looked after their estates and not only maintained their material position but improved it.

The most characteristic representatives of Russian literature towards the end of the old régime are, however, Chekhov and Gorki.

A.P.Chekhov (1860–1904) belonged to the new generation which the reforms of Alexander II had enabled to rise from the ranks of the underprivileged to a higher social position. Chekhov, who had become medical officer to a *zemstvo*, published humorous stories; in the eighteen-nineties he applied himself to writing for the stage, providing the Moscow Art Theatre, founded in 1898 by a businessman, A. Alexeyev (Stanislavsky), with part of its repertory. His most interesting plays are not his farces, such as *The Bear* (1888), but his dramas, whose characters are comic on the outside but are inwardly profoundly sad; indifferent to active life, and pathologically self-concerned, they remain immured in their personal problems. Helped by Stanislavsky's remarkable production, Chekhov's 'comedies'

(*Ivanov*, 1887; *The Seagull*, 1896; *Uncle Vanya*, 1897; *Three Sisters*, 1900; *The Cherry Orchard*, 1903) attracted a large urban public who adored the theatre and discovered in these moral and emotional problems (which were essentially a refuge from the real problems of life) innumerable features of the middle class and its fears – some members of the middle class, that is to say those who could not adapt themselves to new economic conditions and were in danger of going under.

M. Gorki (1868–1936), whose real name was M. Peshkov, was the orphaned son of a working-class family who earned his living in all manner of jobs and fed his mind with revolutionary writings; and it was with him that literary art in Russia took a leap forward into the Revolution. He became famous as a writer in the 'nineties. His literary achievement is inseparable from his political activity. He took part in revolutionary agitation among students and workers (and was arrested in 1901), early became a contributor to the newspapers *Novoye Slovo* (1899) and *Zhizn* (1899–1901), fought in the 1905 Revolution and was compelled to flee abroad in the following year, settling in Capri after a short stay in the United States and remaining outside Russia until 1913, when an amnesty enabled him to return; in his stories and novels (*Foma Gordeyev*, 1899; *The Three*, 1900; *The Mother*, 1906), his plays (*The Lower Middle Class*, 1901; *The Lower Depths*, 1902; both of which were performed at the Art Theatre), his reminiscences (*My Childhood, Earning My Bread*, 1913–1916), he portrayed a society torn by the class struggle and the conflict between the generations, and bestowed a new dignity on the lowest grades, the most completely disinherited, in the social hierarchy, introducing the 'fourth estate' into literature (*The Lower Depths*) and insisting on the importance of the industrial proletariat (*Foma Gordeyev*). The romanticism of his early style was gradually replaced by a socialistic realism which was strongly influenced by contemporary social and political events; at the time of Stolypin's reforms, his interest was aroused by the village scene and the struggles of the peasants (*Among the People*, 1909). But his broad fresco, of which his autobiography forms a part, is based above all on the lower strata of the city population: the outcast and destitute, the proletarian workers, and the reactionary lower middle class. During the years preceding the First World War, Gorki, who had met Lenin on 27 November 1905 and had not lost touch with him, and who was on the staff of *Pravda*, was thoroughly involved in revolutionary activity (plate 23).

Realistic Painting and Abstract Art
In 1863, a group of pupils of the St Petersburg Academy of the Fine Arts broke away from that institution and formed an 'Artel of Free Painters'. Financially supported by a Muscovite merchant and art-patron, Tretyakov, the Artel changed into a 'Society for Itinerant Exhibitions' in 1870, and dominated artistic life in Russia until the end of the century.

The reaction was not only against the Academy but also against St

Petersburg: the intention was to blow away the aristocratic atmosphere in which artistic creation was carried on and bring art to the people, the whole people; exhibitions were to be held from one end of the empire to the other, so as to educate the people's taste. This new school, born of a new society, adopted Chernyshevsky's ideas about the relation of art to reality; the work of art was now to depict real life, pass judgement on society, convey a definite moral attitude, and stimulate reform and progress; and, since it was an instrument for the education and emancipation of the masses, it must be within the understanding of the simple moujik. It was the ambition of painters, as of writers, in these ebullient years of reform and enthusiasm, to go to the people. It was not, however, among the ignorant peasants that they succeeded in attracting a public, but those sections of the middle class, both upper and lower, which were then on the increase in Russia.

The movement was at once a reaction against academicism and in favour of national and patriotic ideals, and seems to have been a delayed offshoot from the nationalism of the earliest years of the century. The two trends of utilitarian realism and a return to the past can sometimes be seen in one and the same painter.

Repin (1844–1930), the most popular of the Itinerant Painters, evoked episodes famous in history and legend, such as 'Ivan the Terrible before the Body of his Son' and 'The Zaporozhe Cossacks Making a Mocking Reply to a Grandiloquent Decree of Sultan Mahomet VI'; but he also treated the newly-sensitive public to such scenes as 'Boat-hauliers on the Volga' (1870), 'Arrest of a Propagandist', and 'They were Not Expecting Him' (the return of a militant revolutionary from exile).

Surikov habitually took his subject-matter from history: 'The Conquest of Siberia', 'Suvorov crossing the Alps'. In his famous painting of 'The Boyarina Morozova', on the other hand, the commemoration of an episode in the persecution of the Old Believers seems to be merely incidental; the subject has been used mainly as an opportunity for catching the picturesque qualities of the people in Moscow in the seventeenth century.

I. N. Kramskoy (1837–87) and Nicolai Gay (1831–94) attempted to create a typically Russian Christ. Victor Vasnetsov (1856–1933) illustrated old Russian legends and *byliny*. Vereshchagin expressed his pacifism in 'The Apotheosis of War', Perov his anti-clericalism in 'Easter Procession in the Village'. These are a few of the most illustrious names among the Itinerants. But there were other, less-known painters who, coming a little later, won comparable success and exerted an equally deep influence by their treatment of social injustice and human wretchedness; such were Miasoedov ('The Zemstvo at Luncheon'), Prianishnikov ('The Bazaar'), Yaroshenko ('The Prisoner'), and Jacobi ('Marching Covicts: a Halt').

Realism continued to dominate most Russian painting; but its revolutionary purpose, which in any case was theoretical rather than something actually made visible on the canvas, gradually dwindled away. The Itinerants became reconciled to the Academy and the Moscow School of

Painting and Architecture. They exercised a powerful influence on the Union of Russian Artists, founded in Moscow in 1903. In their turn, they and their work acquired something of an official character. Their pictures had in fact been as little appreciated by the masses, who remained unaware of them, as had the efforts of numerous young intellectuals at that time to mingle with the people and educate them. The middle-class rich went on buying pictures on the conventional Russian school, which were easy for them to understand and admire; but the most highly cultivated, or the most perceptive, of the wealthy merchants, such as the Mamontovs, the Shchukins and the Morozovs, became interested in western painting and thus fostered the emergence of a new type of art inspired by Impressionism and Symbolism, an art of the *avant-garde*, based on St Petersburg and led by the magazine *Mir Iskusstva* (*The World of Art*, 1906): an individualistic, futuristic art which, having deliberately cut itself off from the people, was rejected by social-democratic circles and condemned by Plekhanov; later, too, by Lenin, who wrote in connection with it, 'Ought we to offer superfine biscuits to a tiny minority, when the industrial and peasant masses are short of black bread?'

However, these novel experiments, which brought artistic circles in St Petersburg into close touch with those in Paris, Munich and Rome, were continued in the years preceding the First World War by a small but highly active group of painters, in whose work it is a delicate matter to discriminate between foreign influences and spontaneous creativity.

These artists included M. Larionov (born 1881), leader of the 'Knave of Diamonds' group, and Natalya Goncharova (1881–1962), whose early works, exhibited in 1909 and 1910, prefigured Futurism. But both of them were in Paris by 1914 and thereafter worked for Diaghilev, for whose ballets they designed sets and costumes. In the field of painting, however, their influence was less than that of K. Malevitch (1878–1935), whose experiments ultimately produced, in 1913, a curious picture consisting of a black square on a white ground. This was the original nucleus of Suprematism, a doctrine launched by him in a manifesto dated 1915; later, in 1927, he defended it in a further essay in which art was defined as 'an element additional to life': 'Art must not continue serving the state or religion; it can no longer be employed to illustrate the history of manners and morals; it refuses to have anything to do with the object, it believes it can exist in and for itself, dispensing henceforth with life, its allegedly eternal source.'

Among the associates of this advanced movement were two great artists, both of whom were born in Russia and, after spending many years abroad, came back to work there from 1914 to 1921: Kandinsky and Chagall. The condemnation of abstract art, the impossibility of winning recognition for it by means of a Constructivist solution, and the triumph of socialist realism (which had a tradition behind it and possessed the further advantage of social utility), forced them out of Russia; Chagall went to Paris, Kandinsky to Weimar and then Paris. Kandinsky (1866–1944), whose reputation has steadily increased, is regarded as the father of abstract painting.

Russian Music Conquers the World

A friend of Pushkin, Dargomyzhsky (1813–69), composed an opera, *Russalka*, whose music leaned further in the direction of realism than Glinka's. Still more important was his treatment of the Don Juan theme, *The Stone Guest*, which Paul Dukas described as 'the corner-stone of Russian national opera'.

But Russian music first emerged in its true glory in the work of the 'mighty five': Balakirev (1837–1910), Cesar Cui (1835–1918), Borodin (1832–87), Mussorgsky (1839–81) and Rimsky-Korsakov (1844–1918), all of whom came unusually late to music after abandoning other careers. Balakirev, who had published a collection of folksongs in 1866, was the leader and driving-force of the group, the masterly compositions of whose members constituted a truly original, truly Russian music – emancipated from serfdom, as it were, by the study of folk-melody.

The talent of Cui was limited and he never succeeded in liberating his music from western models. But Borodin, in his symphonies, his tone-picture *On the Steppes of Central Asia* and his unfinished opera *Prince Igor* (in which 'heroic echoes from Russia's legendary age can be heard singing'), combined Russian, Caucasian and Asiatic themes. Even more markedly, Mussorgsky, in *Boris Godunov* and *Khovantschina*, spoke a 'new language' inspired by folk traditions and Russian liturgical music, and by means of his admirable choruses gave the common people the leading share in the dramatic action. At the time of his death he was planning to compose a *Pugachevschina* which would have evoked that terrible popular insurrection of which the memory hung like a shadow over the whole of the nineteenth century. Rimsky-Korsakov, whose output was copious and very varied (but less original than Mussorgsky's), also made use of oriental themes (in his symphonic poem *Antar*, for example) and took his subjects from Russian history and national customs (*The Girl of Pskov, Russian Easter, Christmas Night*). It was from him that the publisher Bielayev acquired the idea of running a series of symphony concerts in St Petersburg and thus of creating a wider audience for the new school of thought in Russian music. Rimsky-Korsakov was a liberal and the authorities eyed him with suspicion; his opera *Le Coq d'Or* was banned from public performance.

The tendencies of Tchaikovsky (1840–93) were in the main more classical, but he too had recourse to popular sources. He was a composer of big successes; his symphonies and operas (*Romeo and Juliet, Eugene Onegin*), though perhaps too facile in their fluency, have a moving sensibility and melancholy and are of immensely wide appeal. His *Swan Lake* is still the great bravura piece of classical ballet.

All these composers, also Glazunov (1865–1936) in his opera *Stenka Razin*, rallied to the historical national tradition to which Pushkin, in both prose and verse, had given so brilliant a form. Their works are more or less consciously steeped in Russian nationalism and show a profound feeling for popular values. In particular their operas, sumptuously staging the most dramatic events of the Russian past, were welcomed by an ever larger public which by this time consisted of the urban middle classes. But the main mass of the people left these costly spectacles almost unsampled. Secular music, whose original themes were their own unwitting contribution to the new movement, remained a closed book to them. They were not opera-goers; the church and the Orthodox rites offered them the splendours of a religious music whose authentically Russian character had been firmly established since the seventeenth century.

Both St Petersburg and Moscow had a conservatoire and in the early twentieth century these two cities were musical centres represented by composers such as Taneiev, Gretchaninov, Skriabin, Rachmaninov and many others. World renown for Russian music came through the work of Diaghilev (died 1929), who organized concerts of Russian symphonic music in Paris from 1907 onwards and presented the ballets of Stravinsky (born 1889), *The Firebird, Petrushka* and *Le Sacre du Printemps* (*The Rites of Spring*). These ballets were a revelation to the French public; the first performance of *Le Sacre*, 29 May 1913, provoked a new '*bataille d'Hernani*'. It can be argued that Stravinsky, whose musical genius defies categories and transcends frontiers, has ceased to be Russian. None the less, his first large-scale works, exploding the musical conventions of the day, contributed by their originality to the expansion of the nation's music.

11

Russia as a
Bourgeois National State

ASIATIC conquest had swollen the Russian empire to colossal size; a Colossus under suspicion of possessing feet of clay. Notwithstanding the rise of a wealthy bourgeoisie, the state was still an autocracy managed by a bureaucratic noble caste. The social order placed a heavy weight of oppression on the people, among whom the premonitory rumbles of revolution were to be heard, and on the non-Russian subject nationalities, which were in danger of assimilation. The explosion of 1905 resulted in a superficial change, the erection of a constitutional screen behind which tsarism struggled in vain to prolong the existence of the old social and political forms.

I THE CAPITALS AT THE TURN OF THE CENTURY

Slav Russia at this period had virtually only two great cities, St Petersburg and Moscow. The first was the frontier-capital, born of the will of Peter the Great, with only a century and a half of life behind it; the second, the ancient metropolis in the heart of the country, was the centre of Russian tradition, saturated in history and viewing the modernism of St Petersburg with distrust and disapproval (maps 22 and 23, pp. 392 and 412).

The very sites on which the two cities were built formed a contrast. St Petersburg, the Venice of the north – or, rather, the Slav Amsterdam – reared its magnificent palaces and mansions along the banks of its canals and the grim, spacious River Neva which connected the city's energies with the Baltic and the West. Moscow, an inland centre, with a layout resembling that of Paris, was dominated by its citidel, the Kremlin within whose confined space the city's finest monuments were concentrated, and whose streets, extending like spokes from a hub, and punctuated at intervals by monasteries which had been defensive strongpoints in times gone by, provided a connection with Russia's continental sectors and orientated the life of Moscow towards Asia and the southern steppes.

Geographical position dictated the nature of the economy in both cases. The cities' interests were diametrically opposed, suggesting a difference in psychology. St Petersburg was more of a consumer than Moscow. Its industries fed on imported raw materials. It was much involved in international trade, and struggled to escape from the shackles of economic nationalism. Its merchants and bankers had the open minds and broad views of businessmen more European than Russian in spirit. Moscow, the home of textile industries requiring state protection, was the commercial centre of the inland provinces, the focal point for a nationally-minded middle class who rubbed shoulders with Tatar traders in embroidered skull-caps. The Urals and Asia came gliding into Moscow with the heavy barges which tied up at its quays. St Petersburg, where the court and westernized high society set the tone, exhibited greater urbanity and elegance; Moscow, whose links with rustic existence were always strong, was more conservative, more attached to traditional styles of dress and a typically Russian way of life.

But Moscow, like the rest of the country, depended on St Petersburg as the door through which news from the West arrived – not only the authorized foreign press but also clandestine literature and revolutionary directives. The two capitals had one point in common: the proletarian masses in both were equally wretched, identical in outlook, unanimous in their demands, and constituted an exceptional element in a mainly rural country.

St Petersburg (whose population was 1,265,000 in 1897, and 2,000,000 in 1912) lacked the advantage of possessing an immediate hinterland; but it had its port, and was the seat of the court and the government; it continued to be the capital. It was the chief centre for the redistribution of finished manufactured articles imported from abroad, and, in 1900, was the outlet of 75 per cent (by weight) of all Russian exports. It was the base for Russia's naval forces. And it was an industrial city, with shipyards, foundries, powder factories and weaving mills (which put on a sudden spurt of development after 1870). In and around the centre the canals were lined by countless palaces, while the working population (150,000 in 1900) swarmed in the poverty-stricken suburban slums; the Putilov factory alone, which towards 1870 was providing half the rails made in Russia and had since turned to the manufacture of machinery and armaments, employed 12,000, and was the dominating factor in the city's industrial life (plate 22a and b).

St Petersburg was the home of a solidly-established commercial middle class; 85 per cent of the population were *mieshchanies* and peasants who, for the most part, had dropped their connections with village life.

St Petersburg was of a much more urban, cosmopolitan character than Moscow. The high proportion of nobles living there (137,825 in 1910, representing about 7·2 per cent of the population) is accounted for by the presence of the court and government. Accordingly, as in Moscow, there was a large number of servants and their families (192,000 in 1900, representing about 13·2 per cent of the population). But to an even greater degree than in Moscow, the contrast between rich and poor was visible in the overcrowding of the workers' quarters, where anything from ten to

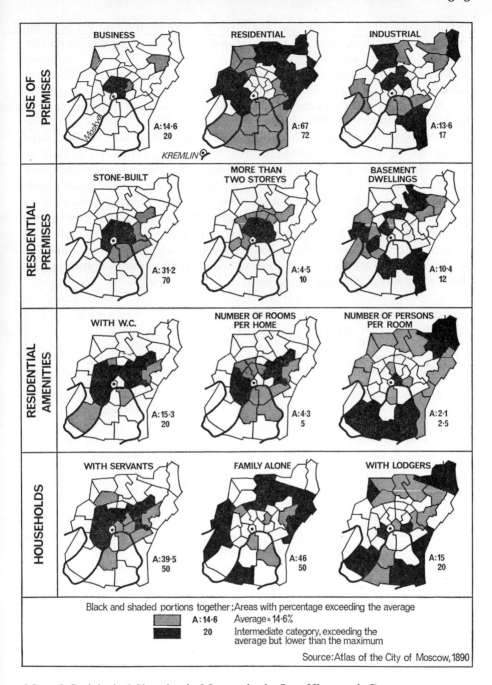

Map 18 Sociological Situation in Moscow in the Late Nineteenth Century

twenty people slept in one room, though rents were high (from 7·5 per cent to 10 per cent of wages in the case of family apartments, and from 12 per cent to 33 per cent for bachelor lodgings).

Moscow had become a great city, with 753,469 inhabitants in 1881 and over 1,000,000 according to the census of 1897 (a figure which was to rise to 1,600,000 by 1912). It extended over an enormous area, 45 per cent of its houses consisting of ground floor only and another 25 per cent having only one upper storey. Half these houses were of timber; only in the centre of the city, in the network of boulevards, were 95 per cent of them built of stone. Moscow was over-populated; a quarter of the inhabitants lived four or more to a room; a third were grouped in 'associated households', with shared kitchens. Many of the houses were unhealthy; half of them had no privies. Though Moscow was a commercial and industrial city many country landowners also had residences there and there was a high proportion of servants among the population, amounting (if servants' children are included) to 10 per cent, 15 per cent or even 20 per cent of the total in the central districts (map 18, p. 303).

POPULATION OF ST PETERSBURG IN 1910

Total population	1,881,300—labouring population, 25%
Peasants (families included)	1,310,429—born in the city, 65% estab- —lished in it for many years.
Mieschanies, shopkeepers, artisans, lower middle class (families included)	—50% born in the city, 40% 295,000—established there for many —years.

Moscow's central situation, and the proximity of the Ivanovo industrial zone and the market of Nijni Novgorod, combined with its distributive and intermediary function on the routes to the south and to Asia, gave the city an active, bustling atmosphere comparable to that of St Petersburg. Economically speaking, it recovered its capital status and was equal in importance to the great Baltic port. The writer A. N. Tikhonov has evoked in the following terms the swarming Muscovite population, the contrasts between rich and poor in the various quarters, the picturesque qualities and social variety of Moscow life, and the open agitation and secret resistance of the city's revolutionary groups:

The Moscow of wily, resourceful manufacturers, the kings of cotton, alcohol and iron; the city of self-made Maecenases who hastily crammed their sham-Gothic castles and decadent 'cottages' with fashionable collections of French pictures, negro monstrosities, Sèvres porcelain, anything and everything which was in vogue in Paris, and who regarded themselves as Russian Medicis. Their grandfathers, in many cases at least, were serfs who wore *tille* instead of shoes, and who as they ate their horse-radish soup never dreamed that one day their grandsons would drive about Moscow in gigs, sit in the Duma, run banks, edit newspapers, eat oysters, and organize Attic nights in a suburban villa, *The Black Swan*, with naked actresses.

This was also the Moscow of the big merchants in long, skirted coats, who, after spending the week in their dark shops in the Zamoskvoretche quarter [beyond the Moskva, on the right bank] or the Riady [in the centre of the city], selling ironmongery, medicines and leather, took their families to the bathhouse for a steam bath on Saturday and spent Sunday touring the churches to find the one where the deacon sang the deepest bass . . .

. . . But it was also the Moscow of secret revolutionaries, the members of local or foreign committees. You never saw them, yet their activities were in evidence everywhere: at a meeting of some artistic and literary circle an unknown orator would deliver a Bolshevist speech; a pamphlet would appear in a factory; the police would unearth a secret printing-press; and sometimes, out in the suburbs, a revolver-shot would ring out, its target a policeman or informer.

Again, it was the Moscow of the working-class quarters of the Presna, on the outskirts, in the Zamoskvoretche, which I must admit to knowing only by hearsay, and with which indeed it was difficult for a stranger to become acquainted more directly. The workers maintained a sombre silence, immured in their stone-built cubes – the factories and workshops – and surrounded by police spies and *agents provocateurs* trained in the school of Zubatov [a former revolutionary who had joined the police]; yet there was not a man in Moscow who could not feel this sombre silence behind his back.

In December 1905 the silence was broken by salvoes from the barricades. That Moscow, however, I shall describe later.

Alexander   Serebrov   (A.N.Tikhonov),
Times and Men. Reminiscences 1898–1905
(from Aslanov's translation, pp. 105–110).

II FROM AUTOCRACY TO THE CONSTITUTION

Revolutionary Agitation

The reforms of the eighteen-sixties, by creating a new political climate, enabled broad currents of ideas to develop, ideas whose origins can be traced back to the closing years of Nicholas I's reign. The perspectives envisaged were still those of intellectuals, but they were being sketched now by a greater number of groups and were winning wider attention.

Slavophilism on the Defensive

Slavophilism, the pioneers of which had been Ivan Kireyevsky (1806–56) and Khomiakov (1804–60), had become the magic carpet of a section of opinion at once conservative yet anxious for progress; a combination which was widespread among those of the landowners whose estates were neither very large nor very small. It was characteristic of the Slavophil movement, which was as it were tinged with religion at the edges, to see the past through distorting spectacles and to idealize Russian civilization; the result of the schematic comparisons drawn by the Slavophils between Russia and the West was to create a sense of irreducible opposition and of national superiority. But the Slavophils were not against economic progress provided the traditional framework of Russian life was left untouched. They wanted 'western machines, not western ideas'. They were caught between contradictory factors – on the one hand their own interests, which they had not as yet formulated clearly, and which presupposed their adapting themselves to capitalism, now penetrating Russia; on the other, their adherence to class relationships which they regarded as instruments of social stability and human happiness. This contradiction they veiled in cloudy verbiage. Slavophilism had in any case dwindled, after the reforms of the 'sixties, into a mere reflex of national pride – a state of mind which also emerged as part of the powerful current of populism then sweeping all before it among the younger generation.

In the course of the 'sixties the intelligentsia underwent a certain change in character. The word itself made its first appearance during that decade, and was used in retrospect as a label for intellectuals in general, and, in particular, for the enemies of absolutism. Economic development, and the real progress made in education under Nicholas I, added a large number of functionaries to the ranks of the intelligentsia and stimulated the recruiting of the latter from a miscellaneous or, to use Herzen's word for it, 'chaotic' environment: a confused stratum of students who were priests or sons of priests, plus cadets from the military academies, young officers, ruined nobles, merchants of the third guild, and those odd-men-out the *raznochintsy*, a rootless and somewhat indefinite category composed of urban plebeians who did not fit into the old division into 'estates', or indeed any other social classification. This new intelligentsia was radical, excessive, extreme; disappointed by Alexander II's reforms, which were a mere compromise, leaving the social and political order inviolate, but which did give them freedom to express their views, they demanded changes of a more sweeping kind. Fascinated by science, believing in progress, and rejecting religion, the intelligentsia subordinated all human activities to social utility. Disinterested, austere, anxious for the people's welfare on principle rather than from affection, and uncompromising in thought and action, the intelligentsia constituted the yeast in the dough of Russian society.

Populism and Marxism

Populism (*narodnichestvo*) was a revolutionary trend with socialist tendencies, all of whose very varied forms were inspired by strong feelings against the prevailing social order, and hostility towards capitalism.

The image of Russia cherished by the Populists was that of a peasant country without a proletariat; a country in whose privileged classes the bourgeoisie were only an infinitesimal fraction and in which, therefore, there could be no social basis for capitalism. In their eyes, revolution in Russia was bound to be a peasant revolution, providing a direct transition to socialism, favourable conditions for which were already present in the shape of the rural community and such forms of co-operative production as the artel. The Populists feared capitalism because it reduced the peasant masses to proletarians, destroyed small-scale industry and the artisan class, and depressed the life of the people. Its drawbacks, they felt, could be avoided by utilizing and expanding the existing, time-honoured structures. Populists of every shade had moreover an aristocratic idea of revolution; they were confident that the intelligentsia could prepare the way, supply leadership and ensure final triumph. It was the intelligentsia's function to rouse the masses, who were already ripe for insurrection (according to Bakunin, 1814–76), or to educate them into revolutionary consciousness (according to Lavrov, 1923–1900); the Russian people was 'instinctively communistic'. Both these thinkers believed insurrection would spontaneously generate a federation of free communes; whereas according to Tkachev (1844–85), the first step must be the capture of the state apparatus by a revolutionary organization.

These doctrinaire theorists, some of whom had been able for a while to write openly in the press (an example being Lavrov's *Historical Letters*), fled abroad after 1870. Their writings were smuggled into Russia and exerted an influence on small action-groups who could not gain much of a hearing and who, in the capitals and a few other large cities, soon passed from open propaganda to secret terrorism.

The Populism of the 'seventies sought to collaborate with the peasants, unrest and disturbances among whom were kept smouldering by the difficulties encountered in administering the Emancipation Act. Land distribution set nobles and peasants at loggerheads, and the hardships resulting from the Russo-Turkish war of 1877–8 caused a crescendo of discontent in the countryside. But the passive peasant multitude, struggling to defend its immediate interests, was almost completely indifferent to the revolutionary propaganda of the Populists, who 'went to the people' in order to educate and convince them, and also to get to know them better. These intellectuals – mainly students – full of faith and illusions, who travelled from village to village, and, in the southern regions along the Don and the Volga, strove to arouse memories of Stenka Razin and Pugachev, were totally unsuccessful. Hounded by the police, they were soon filling the gaols and penal settlements.

The foundation in 1876 of the secret society *Zemlia i Volia* (Land and Freedom), one of whose organizers was Plekhanov, was a turning-point. Renewed attempts had been made to carry out a continuous propaganda programme among the peasants, the disseminators being revolutionaries functioning in this capacity wherever they themselves worked and lived. But these attempts had failed; the movement now went over to violence and adopted terrorism as its weapon. A short-lived group, the *Chernyi Perediel* (Black Partition), remained faithful to a policy of agitation; but a new secret society, the *Narodnaia Volia* (People's Will), struck at the state in the person of its leader and organized the assassination of Alexander II on 1 March 1881.

The growth of the Russian revolutionary movement, though governed by conditions peculiar to the country, did not take place in hermetic isolation. The foundation in 1864 of the First International, which was joined in 1870 by a Russian *émigré* section, and the insurrection of the Paris Commune in 1871, caused profound reverberations in Russian revolutionary circles. But whereas in the West the 'seventies saw the emergence of the first workers' organizations, the Russian revolutionaries of the same period were unorganized, divided by passionate theoretical disputes, hampered by constant police pressure, and devoid of any real support among the peasants; meanwhile they found it hard to gain a hearing from an industrial proletariat which was insignificant in size, and whose associations with country life were still strong. Breathing a rarefied, unrealistic atmosphere, thirsting for action, and attaching too much importance to individual acts of heroism, they were an advance-guard whose efforts were doomed from the first; but though in the immediate view they achieved little or nothing they blazed the trail for militant working-class action on a large scale at the end of the century, in a changed economic and social context.

Russia's industrial development induced among the Populists of the 'eighties a rigidity, a political hardening of the arteries, which estranged them from revolutionary activity. Their ideal, which they never abandoned, was a socialism of peasants and craftsmen; large-scale industry, supported by state capitalism and foreign banks, they regarded as essentially artificial. Their pessimism concerning its future was voiced in the speeches of Vorontsov. They pointed to the low purchasing power of the home market, and emphasized the sacrifices imposed on the peasants by industrialization. They attributed little significance to the industrial proletariat, which they felt was incapable of providing the motive power of revolution. Their critical attitude took precedence over any active programme, and their theoretical views had ceased to present any danger to the government. In the leading reviews, such as *Annals of the Fatherland* and *Russian Wealth*, the public could watch their transition from the denial of an industrial workers' movement to the denial of any political movement of the masses whatever.

After acquiring this peaceful character, Populism no longer supplied the revolutionary movement with any active supporters; but some of its arguments were taken over by the great current of revolutionary socialism which exerted such a profound effect on political life in Russia at the beginning of the twentieth century. Even in the 'nineties, the heirs of Populism had been unable to go on denying the importance of the proletariat: for in addition to peasant disturbances there were now factory strikes, which took place in urban surroundings and produced far more spectacular effects. But those revolutionary socialists who recruited their adherents from the rural intelligentsia continued the Populist tradition, and regarded the peasant masses as the foundation of their endeavours; in their eyes, the proletariat was at the most an auxiliary force. The rural community and its institutions still seemed to them to offer a stepping-stone towards socialism. As they were now operating among a peasantry which, though still ignorant, was politically less passive than before, they revived the procedures of militant Populism, which were propaganda, agitation and terrorism.

Meanwhile the progress of industrialization was enlarging the proletariat, whose strength lay less in its overall numbers than in its being concentrated round the big enterprises in the two capitals and in the factory-towns near Moscow and in the Ukraine. Wretched living conditions for the workers were responsible for the first great strikes, which arose spontaneously, not as a result of political agitation, in the textile mills of St Petersburg and Krengholm (1870), and later (1875) in the metallurgical plants recently set up in the Ukraine. But only a few of the workers at this period were reached by socialist propaganda. The International's influence was weak: the 'Workers' Unions' founded in both south (Odessa, 1875) and north (St Petersburg, 1878) had no more than a few hundred members and were soon broken up by the police.

It was during the 'eighties that Marxism came into Russia and the first study-circles were formed in which *Das Kapital* (already known in extracts in the 'seventies) was discussed by a tiny minority of intellectuals. The influence of these small Marxist groups was negligible until Lenin, in 1893, began co-ordinating them and converting Marxism into an instrument of political working-class struggle.

Initially, however, it was against Populism that Marxism battled its way forward. Plekhanov, who in Geneva in 1883 had founded a group called 'Emancipation of Labour', became the educator of the Russian Marxists through his translations and his own fundamental work, *The Development of the Monistic Conception of History*. He restored the status of capitalism and placed the proletariat in the foreground of social struggle. His severe criticism of the conservative moujik, and of the peasantry as a formless mass and a class divided against itself, was the practical reaction of a fighter. The reinstatement of the peasant among the forces of revolution came later, with Lenin.

An extensive polemical literature was begotten by Marxist opposition to the Populist trend. This was a theoretical warfare, a surface conflict, waged partly in public, since the government tolerated a 'legal Marxism' which looked forward to the development of capitalism with state support and which, to this end, strove to reconcile the interests of the workers with those of the middle class. The phase through which Russia was passing at the time was such as to place a premium on any doctrine stressing the importance of economic factors in moulding history, and of industrialization as a source of progress. Hence the fact that so many books and articles published by economists and university teachers in the eighteen-eighties appear to be impregnated with Marxist influence. The tendency had been anticipated by the lectures on Russian history delivered by Kliuchevsky (1841–1911), a professor at Moscow University, who had attempted to analyse the past in terms of a complicated nexus of causes, among which a prominent place was given to the economy and to social change. He was claimed as a precursor by the legal Marxists, one of whom, the economist Tugan-Baranovsky (1865–1919), brought out in 1898 a book on *The Russian Factory, Past and Present*. Another was I. V. Yanzhul (1845–1914), an inspector of factories who became a professor of the University of Moscow and was elected a member of the Academy in 1895; the emphasis in his writings is on the mechanics of the economy, visualized in the setting of a kind of state socialism. All the literature of this nature, whether descriptive or doctrinaire, is in line with the surge of industrial development in a Russia faced with new problems which were the fruit of capitalism, and which Populism tended to ignore.

The legal Marxists and their near relations the 'Economists' (whose programme included illegal work but not necessarily revolution – they were revisionists) came in for sharp criticism from Lenin, who founded a Union for the Liberation of the Working Class at St Petersburg in 1895, and, during his exile in Siberia (1897–1900), wrote some of his most important works. One of them in particular is of classic quality, rising above the polemical level and constituting a historical study of great value: *The Development of Capitalism in Russia* (1898) is a remarkable analysis of conditions among the peasants and workers at the close of the century.

While the Marxists were busy staking out their theoretical positions, both against Populism and against the conformism, the watered-down interpretations of Marxism, which were favoured by the legal Marxists and 'Economists', a broader political opposition was developing, a movement which had many active adherents but remained fundamentally conventional, even respectful, in its attitude to established authority. The 'nineties were a decisive decade. The terrible famine of 1891 spotlighted the negligence and indifference of the tsarist administration; the wave of strikes in 1894–6 was characterized by a premonitory tinge of political motivation. Both of these developments occurred when the attitude of the régime was hardening: the ukase of 1890 had restricted the comparatively democratic conditions of popular representation in the *zemstvos*; and that of 1892 reduced the number of municipal electors. This reactionary policy was out of step with social progress, and the atmosphere created by the Franco-Russian alliance made it all the more irritating to the non-aristocrats, the middle classes, now more numerous than ever before. In theatres and concert-halls the *Marseillaise* was received with enthusiastic applause, as a symbol of liberal aspirations, by the bourgeoisie who constituted the bulk of the audience.

Opposition to the régime was reinforced by the economic crisis of 1900, which crystallized the revolutionary movement into its definitive groupings and also stimulated the formation of political parties, whose existence was recognized by the constitutional state born of the 1905 revolution.

Out of the liberal movement, whose hopes were centred on creating a general assembly of *zemstvo* delegates as a kind of rudimentary parliament, there came the party of the Constitutional Democrats (KD). The Constitutional Democrats were mostly middle-class people; their programme was based on the principles of liberty and equality, and on the notion of a Russia destined to travel the same road of political development as the western countries. Without connections among the peasants and workers, and hostile not to tsarism but to autocrasy, the KD party, represented by gifted intellectuals such as the historian Miliukov (1859–1943), occupied the forefront of the political scene. It offered the immediate hope of practical reforms in a state which stood condemned by its own anachronisms. The KDs distrusted the politically unawakened popular masses and shunned the idea of revolutionary adventure; the body of opinion for which they spoke, though as yet amorphous, became increasingly extensive in the early years of the twentieth century.

Under this cloak of reformism the revolutionary opposition secretly continued its work. Its main currents were revolutionary socialism and Marxism; the later was split into two by the schism between Bolsheviks and Mensheviks in 1903.

The revolutionary socialists drew their support from the intelligentsia in town and country, especially the latter; most of them were functionaries with a modest position in the salary scale, schoolmasters, agronomists, hospital workers, clerks and so on. More and more groups of them sprang up in the most heavily industrialized areas, organized themselves into a union in the north, and were in touch with a Union of Russian Revolutionary Socialists abroad. The year 1902 saw the creation of a Socialist Revolutionary Party, the volume of whose activity in the propaganda field is indicated by the estimated total of over a million leaflets, newspapers and pamphlets distributed by it in Russia from 1901 to 1903. Its programme was based on two aspects of Russian life at the time: peasant society, with its very low cultural level, and the imperial policy of Russianizing the non-Russian subject peoples.

This party took the view that the path to socialism was inseparable from national conditions; its political programme was one of federalism. The success achieved among the non-Slav peoples of Russia by the SRs (Socialist Revolutionaries) arose precisely from their drawing a distinction between the uniformity of social conditions throughout the empire, and the diversity of the national interests of the peoples struggling against the oppression of tsarism. The SRs were concerned less with the industrial proletariat than with the peasantry, whose traditions they regarded as indicating a ready-made inclination towards socialism; in this respect the SRs were the heirs of Populism. In addition, they attributed much importance to terrorism in the task of preparing the ground for revolution. Most of the assassinations between 1901 and 1904 were their work. They lived in the present, basing their actions on the short view and devoting themselves to immediate and visible aims; they were agitators, instigators of violence, precursors and servants of the Revolution.

Their opponents, the two Marxist fractions, appeared to be throwing away their energies in sterile theoretical discussion and controversy. It was nevertheless in the period 1900–5 that Lenin, in his articles in *Iskra* (*The Spark*) and in his famous book *What Is To Be Done?* (1902), defined the principles of Marxism-Leninism.

The basis of this political philosophy was the organization of a party composed of a limited number of professional militant revolutionaries, at once the advance-guard of the working class and the cadre on which its future prospects depended. The working class was the instrument and weapon of revolution, the only class capable of enlisting the peasant masses in the struggle for better immediate conditions and ultimate political control. The Marxists, who were accused by the Socialist Revolutionaries of wanting to 'boil the moujik in the stew-pot of the factory', kept their eyes on the future; they deliberately aligned their activities with the general tendency of industrial development. To their contemporaries they seemed far less extremist in their approach than the Socialist Revolutionaries; yet until the events of 1905 their direct influence on the people was very much slighter.

After its London Congress of 1903 the party was divided into two factions, each with a different conception of what the party ought to be: the 'Bolsheviks' or majority faction, headed by Lenin, believed it should be a highly organized group of picked members, and to that extent detached from the rest of society, whereas the 'Mensheviks', the minority, wanted membership kept open to anyone who believed in the party's aims. The split was fundamental, the Bolsheviks giving priority to efficiency and the demands of action, the Mensheviks holding democratic principles and a certain degree of freedom to be essential; though the two were united in their determination to work for the overthrow of tsarism and to carry out a socialist revolution under the dictatorship of the proletariat. The harshly-contested struggle which ensued between the two sections of the social democratic movement resulted in the founding, in 1912, of a Bolshevik Party, which had been taking shape gradually within the movement itself. In his book *One Step Forward, Two Steps Back* (1904) Lenin had refuted the Mensheviks' arguments and drawn a clear picture of what the party of the working class was required to be: a fighting party, restricted in numbers, highly centralized and intensely disciplined, adapted to the practical conditions of agitation and struggle, absolutely united in its aims, and distrustful of intellectuals, who were regarded as unreliable revolutionary elements.

These controversies, which suddenly acquired acute significance as a result of the events of 1905, were confined to the narrow circles of militant revolutionaries and left the masses practically unaffected. Russia presented every appearance of strength, with the régime firmly entrenched and the police and bureaucracy all-powerful. This was the Russia of the Universal Exhibition of 1900, a Russia whose official self-portrait was reassuring to

French financial circles and conducive to French loans; a Russia whose response to modern economic conditions was an enlightened despotism, unwilling to concede much liberty to its subjects, and careful to reinforce the aristocracy by conferring titles on wealthy members of the middle class; a Russian which had thawed out, and in which, over the last fifty years, there had been sufficient social mobility to admit a growing minority to a position of opulence if not of political power. In spite of strikes and peasant disturbances, the prospects for revolution in Russia seemed remote; the country's only outstanding problem appeared to be that of the political liberties desired not only by the liberals, but even by a section of the aristocracy.

The economic crisis at the beginning of the century, and military defeats in the Far East, suddenly brought to the fore a Russia which had hitherto remained submerged and concealed, and also exposed the inefficiency and weakness inherent in the régime.

The Great Turning-Point: 1905

An economic crisis, caused by over-production, broke out in 1899 and was made worse by bad harvests, by which the purchasing power of the peasants was reduced. Crisis conditions dragged on for several years, damaging heavy industry in particular; some firms went bankrupt, others were forced into amalgamation. Manufacturers reacted to the emergency by forming 'syndicates'. This had the effect both of strengthening the influence of foreign capital and of connecting industrial groups more closely with government circles, which were rocked by the pull of conflicting interests in consequence; the wielders of power came under stronger pressure from business circles than hitherto.

The crisis hit the industrial workers in various ways. Hundreds of thousands of them found themselves unemployed. Working conditions deteriorated; more women and children, at low rates, were taken on in the factories – in 1903 they represented 27 per cent of the total labour force. Firms took to paying a higher proportion of the individual's wage in the form of foodstuffs. Meanwhile the concentration of the industrial working class was becoming more acute: in 1904, factories employing an average of 1,300 were accounting for 850,000 workers, or half the total number of workers. The accumulation of a poverty-stricken proletariat was particularly striking in the suburbs of St Petersburg, in the vicinity of the Putilov factories, and in the Khitrovo quarter in Moscow, near the Yaouza, a district whose doss-houses and hazardous streets were Gorki's model when he came to describe the lower depths. A certain number of unemployed workers made their way back to the countryside; but the majority remained in an uprooted, helpless condition, even in the provincial towns and cities. The growth of class-consciousness and the increase in the number of militant revolutionaries were both connected with this phenomenon of concentration, whose dangerous implications for the social order were heightened by poverty.

Where the countryside was concerned, the crisis had supervened at a time when social and economic inequalities were becoming sharper. The amount of property held by the aristocracy was still being reduced by sales of land to rich peasants and middle-class town-dwellers. Despite this, in European Russia in 1904 some thirty thousand landed proprietors still owned an average of five thousand acres apiece, amounting in all to a quarter of the total area of the country. And among the peasantry, who numbered twelve million families, a prosperous minority (one fifth of the whole) farmed half of the total acreage in peasant ownership; the remaining four fifths lived on little family holdings of a dozen acres or so; 2,800,000 peasants in this category, indeed, depended on holdings of seven acres.

Population growth and inheritance were whittling down the size of family holdings and increasing the number of landless agricultural labourers. Some peasants did make purchases of land, but they were very much in the minority; and in any case they merely bought tiny strips to round off their existing property, or else were too poor to become more than part-owners, part tenant-farmers; some of them also worked part-time as farm labourers. Three quarters of the land sold went to the rich peasants and middle-class townsmen. Agricultural rents were rising to such an extent that there was hardly any margin of profit for the peasant farmer. Productivity was still low; the only places where it was improving was on the big estates, worked by wage-labour.

Land-hunger had thus become more urgent than ever. There was a swollen army of land-workers who were in fact largely superfluous. As early as the census of 1897 it had been shown that there were over 4,000,000 day-labourers, and that 1,600,000 of them found only occasional employment. All of them sought work in the towns, where jobs had become scarce because of the crisis, or in the Ukraine, the Volga region, the Caucasus or Siberia, where, however, deforestation proceeded slowly and not much surplus manpower could be absorbed: the total area cleared advanced only from 82,200,000 desiatinas in 1900 to 87,600,000 desiatinas in 1905.

This was a period of social tension; of demonstrations, strikes and peasant disturbances, interconnected by the workers' continual migrations.

Agitation in the towns and cities now became an organized movement, political in character, and all the stronger for there being no trades unions. The workers demanded political liberties as well as higher wages and the eight-hour day, and sometimes combined their agitation with that of the students protesting against university regulations, as in Moscow, Kkarkov and Kiev in 1901. Strikes originating in purely industrial grievances took place in such a climate of social tension that they turned almost at once into something else, with wider objectives. That at Rostov-on-Don, in November 1903, gradually brought out the whole labouring population of the city and some of the railwaymen as well; it gave rise to mass meetings, dispersed by the army and police, and can be regarded as the first major expression of class-consciousness among the Russian workers.

Disturbances such as this aggravated the country's difficult industrial plight, and the government took them seriously. In an attempt to divide the workers it adopted a device suggested by Zubatov, the chief of the Moscow police, and created 'independent' associations of workers; it also made certain nominal concessions.

Workers' demonstrations nevertheless increased in 1903 particularly in St Petersburg and in the south. It is true that they affected only a small proportion of the working class:

Numbers of Workers Striking, 1900–3

1900	29,000
1901	32,000
1902	37,000
1903	87,000

But such strikes as did take place were so spectacular as to constitute a precedent, an example for imitation; contemplated in retrospect, they take on the appearance of a rehearsal for 1905. In July 1903 there was a strike involving simultaneously the workers in Baku, the railwaymen and other workers in Odessa and in the industrial towns of the Ukraine, and the miners of the Don Basin. In the development of this strike, which was at once general and regional in character, we can discern the influence of revolutionary committees acting on a mass which was torn between conflicting approaches and appeals and mainly intent on immediate gains of a professional order, but which was already, in a minority of its members, responsive to the call for action against autocracy and in favour of freedom of the press and freedom of association.

There was also unrest in the countryside, especially in the Ukraine and the Volga region, where the harvest had been poor. And there were sporadic, less threatening disturbances in central Russia. A problem which now became specially pertinent was that of the *mir*, the institution by means of which the rulers of the state had hoped to keep the peasants quiet and ensure a modicum at least of social justice. A special commission, created in 1902 and headed by Witte, observed that what the *mir* was really doing was to keep the peasants in a state of chronic indigence and to prevent any sort of agricultural progress; the commission recommended breaking the hold of the *mir*, empowering the peasant to withdraw from it at will and, by means of bank loans, making it easier for him to acquire property of his own – the hope being that a rural middle class would rapidly spring up and act as a pillar of the social order. The government rejected these proposals, which were shelved until 1906. The existence of the *mir* was confirmed by the ukase of 8 June 1904; certain measures were taken to relieve the peasants' wants, however, notably the suppression of the 'circular guarantee' (collective responsibility for the payment of taxes).

No picture of revolutionary agitation in this period would be complete without mention of the individual acts of aggression, carried out by the Socialist Revolutionaries, which accounted for the lives of two Ministers of the Interior (Sipyagin in 1902 and Pleve in 1904), one Minister of Education, and two provincial governors, those of Kharkov and Ufa. The higher administration lived in continual fear. Pleve, who was obliged to take a train once a week, always at the same time, from St Petersburg to Peterhof, where he attended the meetings of the Imperial Council, used to say, 'Every Tuesday, when I have reached home safe and sound, I tell myself that I have one more week to live.'

Such an atmosphere prompted the government at once to the severest repression and to an understanding with the moderate elements in the liberal opposition, which was developing openly, in the foreground of the political landscape. This section of opinion, which had originated in the administrative climate of the *zemstvo*, had already formulated its programme in the 'nineties in an appeal to the government, demanding 'a representative government on the basis of universal suffrage, freedom of worship, an independent judiciary, and the inviolability of the human person and human rights.'

In 1900, delegates from the provincial *zemstvos* began holding combined meetings behind closed doors; they constituted a semi-secret opposition which resulted in the formation of the KD (Constitutional Democratic) Party in 1905, and which passed resolutions demanding political reforms; meanwhile *Osvobozhdenie* (*Liberation*), a periodical edited in Paris by Struve, defined their position by declaring that 'Russia's cultural and political liberation cannot be exclusively or principally the work of one class, one party, or one doctrine'. But, as early as 1903, Minister of the Interior Pleve and Finance Minister Witte, negotiating with the representatives of the liberals, ensured their continued loyalty and, by letting them go on holding their meetings, put a damper on their political aspirations. This compromise was a makeshift depending on the ostensible power of the state.

The disastrous issue of the Russo-Japanese war was to wring from the government the concessions it had previously refused.

No signs of impending storm, however, heralded the sudden though transient collapse which occurred in 1905. The peasant multitudes had for the most part remained unaffected by the revolutionary movement, however violently they were stirred by it in certain well-defined areas. Unrest among the industrial workers, despite its political implications, constituted no danger to a régime equipped with a powerful army and a still more powerful police. The liberal opposition could do nothing, though its aristocratic and bourgeois supporters carried much weight both socially and economically and had the ear of the government; to the authorities the liberals were simply a tactical reserve, a screen to be set up against the revolutionary opposition as occasion might demand.

In a matter of months the situation was transformed. The government's nerve was shaken by military defeats in Manchuria and by social agitation, which sprang up with renewed vigour and was marked by 'Bloody Sunday', 9 January 1905 (Russian calendar; 22 January according to the European calendar). Semi-official recognition was accorded to the Assembly of the *zemstvo* delegates, and after much faltering and fumbling the government was obliged to sanction the formation of a Legislative Assembly, the Duma, a decision promulgated by the Tsar's Manifesto of 17 October 1905. This was a triumph for the liberal constitutionalists, who had organized as a party (KD) only a few weeks before, in September.

Meanwhile, however, revolutionary action was developing throughout the country on such a scale as to make 1905 a prefiguration of 1917. What had previously spent itself in sporadic local movements now expanded into a general rebellion whose success, though short-lived, showed up the weaknesses of the apparently all-powerful autocracy. There were anti-Russian disturbances among the non-Russian population in Finland, Poland and Transcaucasia; in some cases, as at Baku, the non-Russians fought each other; the government had to use force to clear the road by which the visiting Shah of Persia returned to his own dominions. There were peasant revolts which, for the first time, showed a tendency towards co-ordination, a tendency engineered by militant revolutionaries who had come out from the towns to foster it and which, initially at least, excited the favour of the *kulaks*, who hoped for a chance of buying up noblemen's properties. There were outbreaks of mutiny in the forces, including the celebrated episode of the cruiser *Potemkin*. And there was working-class militancy, which, in the big cities, used general strikes as an opportunity for uniting the various revolutionary parties in the struggle against tsarism, and was transformed by the zeal of the Bolshevik fraction into an armed rebellion.

The Tsar's October manifesto had had the effect of rallying part of the opposition to his side and forcing a cleavage between the liberals of the middle classes, satisfied by political reforms which placed Russia on the path of constitutional development, and the revolutionaries, who persevered in the fight against tsarism and made use of the 'days of liberty' which followed the issue of the manifesto to prepare for a general insurrection.

October and November 1905 were characterized by the creation of *soviets* among the sailors stationed at Kronstadt and Sebastopol, the workers in St Petersburg and Moscow, and the railwaymen of the Trans-Siberian line. The Revolution of 1917 caused a revival of interest in features which, at the time of their appearance, seemed to be merely by-products of civil war, without much rhyme or reason, and to which only the revolutionary parties attributed any significance for the future.

Some of the troops who had been fighting in Manchuria, for instance, were disarmed by the soviet of the Trans-Siberian railway workers, transported west under its orders, and had their weapons restored to them at the end of the journey, after which they demobilized themselves of their own accord and hurried back to their villages in order not to miss the hopefully anticipated redistribution of land. The episode foreshadowed the disintegration of the tsarist armies in 1917. Again, there was the St Petersburg soviet which included the dazzling figure of Trotsky, but which was dominated by its Menshevik fraction and concentrated on building up a revolutionary government instead of organizing armed rebellion; and the Moscow soviet, in which the Bolsheviks were in the majority and which called strikes and formed combat sections in an attempt to instigate a nation-wide revolt. Both of these were tragic experiments, foredoomed to failure, but in them can be seen the conflicting tactical policies of the Revolution which, twelve years later, was to sweep forward to victory.

Meanwhile, however, the most important instrument in the maintenance of order, the army, had remained comparatively unaffected by revolutionary agitation; after putting down the Kronstadt and Sebastopol mutinies it broke up the St Petersburg soviet and crushed that of Moscow.

The agitators resumed their work all over the country, both in industrial centres and in the rural areas; but the counter-revolution, with the majority on its side, was equally widespread. Backed by the government, the 'Black Hundreds' harried socialists and, on suspicion, intellectuals, and diverted the passions of the populace on to the Jews by means of a wave of pogroms. By the early months of 1906 the government once more had the situation well under control. The insurrection (of which Lenin was to say that 'without the dress rehearsal in 1905 our victory in 1917 would have been impossible') appeared to have been a flash in the pan. However, Russia had become a constitutional monarchy complete with a Duma, a public tribunal in which, for the first time, the government's actions could be discussed and criticized and political demands could be voiced. Progress by peaceful means appeared possible.

The 1905 collapse was followed by a recovery on the part of autocracy; the KD Party's hopes of a liberal régime were blighted. Progress towards parliamentary government was abruptly forestalled by the authorities, who were at once lulled into over-confidence by the ostensible affection of the masses for the Tsar and the Orthodox faith, and frightened lest the exercise of political liberties prove too much for the edifice of imperial power.

This first Duma was 'a parliament in leading-strings' ('*parlement en tutelle*' – Chasles); the landed proprietors, who were favoured by the electoral system, held a substantial majority in it, and the preponderant influence in its debates was that of the liberal intelligentsia. It nevertheless represented all classes and nationalities in the empire. It was the Duma of hope – and of disappointment. The Tsar's refusal to set up a ministry answerable to the Duma, and his conception of the latter as a merely consultative assembly, led to a clash of interests terminated by the dissolution of the Duma on 7 July 1906. The Second Duma fared no better, and the Electoral Statute of 3 June 1907, which was virtually a *coup d'état*, predetermined the nature of the third, the 'Black Duma' or 'Duma of the landlords', which was sufficiently subservient to stay put and was in fact the only one which lasted its full term (1907–12), during which it deferred all attempts at reform and left the realities of power to the government.

This return to autocracy, a 'liquidation of liberty' not wholly to be explained by the blindness of the not particularly intelligent Tsar, took place against a background of political and social unrest. Although their movement had been practically shattered early in 1906, the revolutionaries were once more at grips with the forces of the imperial régime, whose successes had rendered them more intransigent. The mutinies, peasant disturbances and political assassinations which followed the dissolution of the First Duma continued through 1907 and beyond, though more sporadically as time went on. But, by the time the Duma turned itself as it were into a House of Lords without a House of Commons to balance it, police tyranny had largely subjugated 'terror'.

Meanwhile it looked as if tsarism had time on its side. The Duma did nothing but what was wanted of it; in a total voting strength of 442 the government had a majority of 30. Nature herself added a bonus, in the form of the exceptional harvests of 1908 and 1909. Industrial recovery, from 1910 onwards, refuted the charge of governmental incapacity. Pressure of opinion was compelling autocracy to behave more circumspectly than usual. And the fundamental liberties granted in 1905, and never revoked, were tolerated under a totally arbitrary régime which, by its very inconsistencies, enabled the opposition to build itself up again. The press was free to adopt a tone which would have been out of the question a few years earlier. The electoral campaign of 1912 was fought in a relatively liberal atmosphere; it crystallized opinion to such an extent as to determine not only the positions of the parties from then until 1917 but also the government's resolve, henceforward irrevocable, to keep the powers of the Duma permanently curtailed.

The electoral system, combined with pressure from the administration and police during the elections, enabled the government to contrive that the resulting assembly would represent yet another step towards reaction; the right wing was strong, the opposition parties had been weakened.

However, the real meaning of the elections of 1912 was that they deepened the gulf between Russia as it actually was and the Russian régime as a legal fiction, and that under cover of this fiction the revolutionary parties had gained in strength: a fact apparent less in the results, which were distorted by the electoral system, than in the hurly-burly of the elections themselves.

The rural proletariat was almost unrepresented in the Fourth Duma. But the precautions taken by the government to ensure that only docile representatives were elected show how apprehensive it was. Elections took place in three stages, and the peasants in the villages were divided into groups, confined under surveillance, severely lectured, and isolated from contact with opposition supporters; the delegates elected to take part in the next stages were sometimes expelled from the district or put in prison. Later, on arrival at the towns (often from a great distance) for the tertiary elections, they were given board and lodging and carefully segregated.

The results consequently gave very little idea of the real state of rural opinion. Interest in politics, though weak and inoffensive in large tracts of the country, had been aroused and maintained in all areas where the propagandists of revolution had been at work; but the most obvious feature of the situation was the peasantry's inertia, a factor which from the revolutionary viewpoint justified Lenin's opinion that the industrial working class, however small and undeveloped, was politically the most alive, and the only one capable of 'leading the people along the highroad'.

But the desire for progress, and a longing to lay the foundations of a more equitable social order, were not wholly absent from the minds of the privileged classes, including even some of the most conservative; particularly those who, as faithful Christians, attributed a practical value to the laws of God. In the 'eighties the mystical philosophy of V. Solovyev (1853–1900) had appealed to the intellectuals of the liberal right wing, who were joined after the troubled period of 1900–6 by a few repentant apostates from Marxism. This minor cultural renaissance was brought about by the rising tide of social peril and fears of a 'Red flood'. It was a curious phenomenon; very limited in its appeal, but interesting in that it embodied a revived Slavophilism which had come to terms with modern economic conditions and, as a retort to the growth of atheistic materialism, proposed to 'place socialism on idealistic and ethical foundations'. The volume of essays entitled *Vekhi* (1909) (*Navigation-marks*), whose contributors included Berdiaev (1874–1948), Bulgakov (1871–1944) and Struve (1870–1944), condemned the revolutionary intelligentsia and reaffirmed the primacy of spiritual life as the great creative power, the one source of progress. But this hopeful attempt at reconciling tradition and actuality bore a religious and theoretical character; hence the current of thought which it represented was marginal to the practical problems of Russian life, and was influential only in a very small way.

New Social Forces

A Rural 'Third Estate' ?

The revolution of 1905 had dispelled once and for all the illusions of the imperial bureaucracy concerning both the *mir* as a bulwark of social stability, and the fondness of the peasants for the system of collective ownership. It showed that the needier peasants had only one idea in their heads, to acquire property of their own – a change which could be effected only by a further nation-wide redistribution of land and the seizure of the aristocratic estates, on which some of the peasants in question were already settled on a tenant-farming or crop-sharing basis. The power of the *mir* had in any case been progressively undermined for years past by irregular personal arrangements which allowed surplus peasants to leave the village, and which led to transfers of title and an uneven division of land. Even the practice of periodically reallocating the land held by the community had fallen into abeyance in many cases; by 1905 there were an estimated three-and-a-half million peasants who could regard themselves as permanent landowners, their holdings not having been subjected to redivision for fifty years or more. The importance of the *mir* as an institution was further lessened by the fact that the colonized territories had never adopted the system. It was almost unknown in Siberia, which was fast becoming more populous and was turning into one of the empire's granaries.

After the epidemic of peasant revolts between 1900 and 1906, and, more important still, the arrival in the Duma of peasant deputies demanding the compulsory purchase of such estates as the aristocracy still possessed, the government could no longer consider the *mir* as the cornerstone of the social edifice. The peasants, perversely, had voted the wrong way. The drawbacks of the rural community had begun to outweigh its advantages: it was held to be a cause of rebellion because it perpetuated poverty; but it obstructed the growth of a village bourgeoisie, which would have been a factor of stability and order. Hence, after crushing the insurgent peasants and rejecting the proposals, modest though they were, of the Agrarian Commission of the First Duma, and finally dissolving the latter, the

FIGURE 30 Russian popular picture (*lubki*), *The Bear Working*. (The moujik succeeds in making saplings into hoops but the bear is clumsy and fails).

government revived the earlier projects of Witte and embarked on the series of reforms to which Minister Stolypin attached his name.

The Council of State which examined the text submitted by Stolypin included some of the most opulent Russian landowners; twenty of them owned well over 20,000 acres apiece, not counting forest and woodland. Acutely aware that the very principle of property had been temporarily in jeopardy, the Council made no secret of the fact that its purpose was to combat revolution. Thus the motive for abolishing the *mir* was primarily political. Already in 1904 Witte had written: 'Egalitarian government destroys the idea of the strength and inviolability of the rights of property, and offers the most favourable soil for the propagation of socialist conceptions.' The Council of State echoed him by declaring in 1906: 'Failure to distribute land in the provinces must be brought to an end, since it is becoming a threat to the ultimate retention of our own property.' At the same time the economic and social advantages expected from the abolition of the *mir* were also invoked: a newly prosperous peasantry would arise and would cultivate its land more efficiently through being able to pay higher wages; living standards would rise; the home market would expand and provide increased outlets for industrial goods.

The ukase of 4 November 1906, supplemented in 1911 by the laws of 14 June 1910 and 29 March 1911, had the same end in view. Any community land which had not been redistributed since 1861; or since 1886, under the law of 1910) was declared the individual property of its holders. In the case of land not redistributed since 1893 the law reaffirmed the necessity of a two-thirds majority vote (altered to a simple majority in 1911) as the condition for abolishing a *mir*, but it also authorized any peasant to quit the community at will while retaining full proprietary rights in the land farmed by him. He was given the same freedom with regard to land which had been more recently redistributed, except that the amount retained by him was to be determined by the size and needs of his family.

Application of the ukase of 1906 was slow, so much so that in 1913 only 1,500,000 peasants had been satisfied out of a total of nearly 4,000,000 who had demanded proprietary rights in community land. If the 3,500,000 peasants who were made landowners by decree in 1906 be included, 5,000,000 landowners in all were created by the so-called Stolypin reforms. Since the main effect of the programme was simply to confer legal sanction on situations already existing, this result may look meagre. Nevertheless the increasing numbers of peasants applying for undistributed community land (651,000 in 1910, 1,226,000 in 1912) shows that the dissolution of the *mir* was being accelerated and that Russia was ridding herself of an institution which, in the conditions of the time, was becoming an obstacle to agricultural progress.

Meanwhile, however, the social problem remained intact. The acreage available for cultivation was not enlarged simply by releasing it from the shackles of the *mir*; and increased facilities for transfers of title, and for purchase with help from the Agricultural Land Bank, were chiefly of benefit to the richest villagers. True, the property of the aristocracy – that perennial provocation to the poor – continued to shrink rapidly, falling to 50,000,000 desiatinas in 1910 (a reduction of one third from 1877). But this was a drop in the ocean. The population, which had risen to 160,000,000 by 1910, was growing so fast that the agricultural central regions were permanently over-populated, and the empty spaces of Siberia never succeeded in absorbing the surplus. Agricultural improvement was still proceeding at a crawl; yields were low; agricultural education, which had been set on foot in the late nineteenth century, affected only a few hundred thousand farmers. The development of a rural 'third estate' was accompanied by increasing disparities in living standards. Hostility between the poor peasant and the kulak became more and more intense and dominated social relationships in the village.

By the outbreak of the First World War the general condition of agriculture had undoubtedly improved and the standard of life had risen. But over-population, and land-grabbing by the well-to-do, rendered the social climate oppressive. It is true that, omitting crown lands and apanages, the comparative figures for 1913 are just over 420,000,000 acres owned by peasants as against 178,000,000 acres by the nobility and middle classes. By the peasantry were a vast mass – over 130,000,000 human beings of whom a certain number had no land at all or lived meagrely on inadequate strips, and gazed enviously at the estates of the rich peasants and of some 2,000,000 non-peasant proprietors.

The Middle Classes on the Make

The revolution of 1905, which turned Russia into a constitutional monarchy, might have been expected to create more scope for the middle classes in the political sphere. But no such result was forthcoming. When, in late 1905, the revolution was assuming a more violent character in both capitals, fears of social cataclysm caused big business to align itself with the aristocracy. These two elements joined hands in the 'Union of 17 October', declared their approval of the Tsar's political concessions and gave him their full support.

The revolution of 1905 did not transform the bourgeoisie into a class with a political role of its own to play, even after divergences of interest had destroyed its temporary alliance with the nobility. In spirit it was always the government's obedient servant, and any criticisms or demands it presented were couched in the most prudent terms. Its spokesmen were careful to confine any problem under discussion to the specific interests of industry and commerce, avoiding all topics outside these professional boundaries.

Between 1906 and 1914 the middle classes had the opportunity of making their wishes known both in electoral campaigns and through their representatives in successive Dumas; yet no coherent political platform emerged. Certainly the middle strata of society were by this time no longer unanimous in their support of the régime. The wealthy upper middle class, the best educated and most enlightened section of the bourgeoisie, retained their usual loyal attitude but wanted a more liberal spirit at government level, and fairer representation of the various strata of society in the Duma. This section came under attack from the right-wing press, which denounced the progressive industrialists and accused them of collusion with the KD party; the latter, though drawing its membership mainly from the intelligentsia, was more or less openly supported by the upper-middles. These were accused of criticizing the government on principle, at every opportunity, and hence of being hostile to the country's governmental system *en bloc*. In reality, however, the middle classes' opposition was expressed sporadically, diffusely, and was particularly active in municipal and professional life in the big cities; in St Petersburg and Moscow it emerged in the form of two newspapers, respectively *Slovo* (*The Word*) and *Utro Rossii* (*Russia's Awakening*). The latter, which was owned by the Riabushinsky family, set itself up as the champion of the bourgeoisie, the empire's third estate, buoyantly in the ascendant, superior in both importance and effectiveness to the decadent nobility and fossilized bureaucracy. But the voice of *Russia's Awakening* fell almost entirely on deaf ears. In 1914 the bourgeoisie still was without the active role in the state's affairs which its economic importance might lead one to infer; nor was it playing any effective part in the industrial alliances which had taken shape by that time and which were continually bringing pressure to bear on the government. Russia was still an aristocratic and military state, in which the nobility – who had acquired a strong bourgeois tinge themselves – were, as ever, the leading element.

III NATIONALISM OR FEDERALISM?

The Problem of the Nation and Its Nationalities
Russia during the final epoch of the old régime was still something like a 'prison of peoples'. Ethnically, her empire was a complex structure, three quarters Slav and preponderantly Great Russian, which the policy of Russianizing the alien indigenous nationalities had saddled with the redoubtable task of maintaining national unity; though this policy had been moderated after 1905.

Russia's non-Slav peoples were not only impressively numerous (between 150 and 200 ethnic groups and languages or dialects); they also differed enormously in size, cultural attainments and historical connections with the empire. The western and southern fringes were occupied by peoples who were conscious of a lengthy national past and had enjoyed independence prior to absorption by conquest. Finland, which no longer figured much in official statistics, had its own institutions and was a precarious acquisition. The 8,000,000 Poles who had lost most of their political liberties after the insurrection of 1863 resented the oppressive weight of Russian autocracy. The Armenians (1,200,000) and Georgians (1,350,000), now were linked with the empire through their reigning obligarchies, were subject nations but possessed their own ancient culture. The case of the Estonian, Lettish and even Lithuanian peasantry was different. The Greater Lithuania of earlier days had included only a minority of the Lithuanians, nor had either of the other two ever set up a state of their own; but a modern literary renaissance had now made them conscious of their existence as distinct nationalities.

No comparison can be drawn between these large and important groups, whose cultural level was high, and the swarm of small minorities (in some cases reduced to a few thousand people who had kept their dialect and customs) inhabiting the Caucasus – a region described by Marc Bloch as 'a museum of ethnographical relics'. Clearly, such minorities as these, possessing neither the numbers nor the cohesion which are the foundation of a state, could hardly aspire to a national existence of their own. A common feature on both fronts, however, was that Russian colonization had been largely or wholly lacking. The peoples concerned had retained their original characteristics.

The same was true of the central Asian nationalities, which had been recently incorporated into the empire and were of considerable size (1,700,000 Uzbeks, 4,300,000 Kirghiz and Kazaks); despite remaining almost unaffected by Russian penetration they were regarded as 'colonial' peoples, on the same footing as the very much less numerous Siberian native nationalities. These were thinly scattered in vast areas, and their geographical position on the flanks of the living-space settled by the Russians cushioned them against the thrust of colonization, though not against colonial exploitation.

The Turko-Finnish populations in the Volga and Ural regions, on the other hand, forming an irregular checker-board pattern with the Russian element, constituted enclaves which were proof against assimilation. The largest of these populations were the Tatars, totalling three and a half million inhabitants in eleven provinces, though they were nowhere in the majority; even in Kazan province, the centre of their culture, they were only 30 per cent of the total population. Mohammedanism not only protected these peoples against assimilation but provided a cultural link between them; and the Volga Tatars, to some extent through their aristocracy but mainly through their merchant class, both of which were powerful, exercised an influence which was strongly felt by the neighbouring Bashkirs (1,500,000) and extended into central Asia. In the late nineteenth century they took the lead in a Pan-Turk movement, the prelude to which was an intellectual and religious revival associated with the names of Nasyri (1825–1902), 'the Turkic Lomonosov', and the teacher Gaspraly (1831–1914).

Despite the danger from the Russification policy of the 'eighties, which by means of conversions to Orthodoxy, compulsory use of the Russian language, and administrative assimilation, tended to weaken national characteristics, the non-Slav peoples were closely involved in the general activity of the country. Caucasian nobles were received at court, Polish engineers fostered progress in Siberia, Tatar merchants imported cotton goods from Ivanovo into Asia, the oilfields of Baku were partly manned by labour from Azerbaijan; social contacts and economic connections were far advanced and appeared to herald final integration. But national susceptibilities, offended by the deprivations imposed by tsarist policy, were fuel to an endemic, latent hostility directed less at the Russians than at the régime.

There were as many nationality problems as there were peoples within the empire. Until 1905, it was the western non-Russians who caused tsarism's greatest difficulties: the Finns, already almost separated from the empire, the Poles, struggling against invasion by the Russian language as well as Russian functionaries, and the Balts, whose national feelings were aroused against the Germans of the towns and cities even more than against the imperial administration. After 1905 the non-Russian peoples had their own representatives in successive Dumas; the problem of the subject nationalities became more urgent and provided a spring-board for opposition to the government, and the political parties were forced to define their attitudes towards it.

The Conservatives persisted in holding narrowly nationalistic views, in some cases even with a specifically Great Russian bias, at the expense of the Ukrianian and Byelorussian interests; the liberals, on the other hand, were hard put to it to reconcile their devotion to national unity with their sympathy towards the oppressed peoples. The Social Democrats, through their spokesman Lenin, emphasized the right of self-determination but gave priority to the class struggle, rejecting any idea of separatism not associated with the victory of socialism, since the latter would maintain the solidarity of peoples. These left-wing theoretical discussions were carried out in a tense atmosphere of political and syndical conflicts, reverberations from which were carried over into the Congress of the Second International.

A Special Case: the Jews

It was at this period that the Marxist definition of a nation, destined to figure so prominently some years later, was first formulated: the nation is inconceivable without a territory. Now the Jews, who were regarded as constituting a distinct nationality, numbered nearly 5,000,000 in the Russian Empire, 1,500,000 of them being in Poland and the rest officially allotted (with individual exceptions) to the provinces of the west (former Polish territories now assimilated into the imperial system: the provinces of Grodno, Kovno, Minsk, Mohilev, Vitebsk and Vilno); the south-west (Podolia, Volhynia, Tchernigov, Poltava); and the south (Bessarabia, Crimea, Kherson-Odessa, Ekaterinoslav), where they constituted from 5 to 18 per cent of the population (in some towns and villages the proportion was considerably higher). The diaspora never prevented them from remaining distinct in religion, customs, social organization and to a certain extent language. Yet they were in a curious position: they were admitted to be a separate nationality (despised, persecuted and rejected not only by the administration but even by the Russian people) without being recognized as a nation; so they were not entitled to claim independence.

Anti-Jewish feeling was frequently in evidence at that time as a trait of the Russian mentality. Even left-wing intellectuals displayed it; the Zionist leader Yabotinsky put his co-religionists on guard against them.

The national aspects of the Jewish problem, however, did not come up until the end of the nineteenth century, and then only in discussions in the working-class parties, which were faced by the conflict between the ideal of internationalism and the recognition of national aspirations. The special position of the Jews had brought about the founding of the *Bund*, a Jewish working men's organization whose programme, inspired by Martov (1873–1923), was based on the recognition of a cultural autonomy devoid of territorial links. The hostility of the Russian Social Democrats, who held that a nation could not be said to exist apart from a territory, caused a temporary severance of the Bund from the rest of the movement in 1903, but after the revolution of 1905 the activities of the Jewish socialists were included once more in the mainstream of the Social Democrats' anti-tsarist propaganda; solidarity in the struggle against the régime took priority over nationalism.

Every possible theoretical position, from integration to separatism and from non-territorial cultural autonomy to a federal union of nationalities, was canvassed between 1905 and 1914. The Finns and the Poles were in a category apart; there was talk of imminent war, in which event they would obviously cease sooner or later to be bound both to the Russians and to the non-Slav peoples of the empire. Independence for the latter, indeed, would not only have shattered the state but made any sort of political grouping impossible, a fact which leaps to the mind if one thinks of the distribution of Slav and non-Slav peoples in that vast expanse, from the middle Volga to the Pacific shore, which the Russians had colonized. No Russian, whatever his ideals, could be expected to countenance such a collapse. A highly characteristic example of the nationalistic sentiments prevailing among intellectuals, even liberal intellectuals, is to be seen in the controversy waged in 1911 in *Russian Thought (Russkaya Mysl)*, between Struve, the ex-Marxist, and Yabotinsky: the first maintained that the Great Russians, Ukrainians and Byelorussians, representing 65 per cent of the empire's population, constituted a single nation and that Russia was therefore a national state (*Nationalstaat*), within which the Poles and Finns possessed cultures of their own; the second writer argued that Russia was not a national state but an association of nationalities (*Nationalitätenstaat*) on which a Russian culture had been imposed by 43 per cent of the whole, the Great Russian minority.

The Ukrainian Nation

The adjective 'Ruthenian' goes back to the period succeeding the fall of Kiev, that is, to the dismemberment of the 'Rus' by Mongol invasion. The lands on the right bank of the Dnieper, which escaped Mongol occupation and later became part of the Polish-Lithuanian kingdom, were known for a time as Little Russia; their inhabitants were called *Rusini* (Ruthenians). But in the usage of Byzantine diplomacy, and, more important, among the ecclesiastics of the Patriarchate of Constantinople, the term 'Little Russia' was adopted to denote the southern regions of the 'Rus' as distinct from the central, Muscovite regions, known as 'Great Russia'; and these names were subsequently taken up by the tsarist government and used in official edicts and other documents.

The word Ukraine ('border country') is first attested in the late eleventh century, at which time it denoted the country on the right bank of the Dnieper, a territory disputed between the 'Rus' and the invading nomads. Thereafter the term occurs with increasing frequency in the Chronicles; in the eighteenth century it had come to denote the inhabitants of Little Russia, known as 'Ukrainians'. Progressively, as the linguistic and cultural unity of the population on both sides of the Dnieper (a population divided only by the unstable Polish-Russian frontier) suggested the distinct idea of a nation, the epithet 'Ukrainian' tended to cover this population as a whole. After the partition of Poland, 'Ukrainian' largely displaced 'Ruthenian' in popular speech, both in the former Polish territories regained by Russia and in those transferred to Austrian control. And 'Ukrainian' continued to be applied as a label of nationality to the inhabitants of eastern Galicia, who were Polish subjects between the world wars; while the term 'Subcarpathian Ruthenia' was retained for the most easterly part of Czechoslovakia, which was inhabited by Ukrainians.

The rearrangement of frontiers after the Second World War made it possible to include the whole Ukrainian people in a federal Ukraine.

The various Slavic languages in use among the East Slavs had acquired their respective individualities by the eleventh century, broadly speaking; Ukrainian dialects were a permanent feature thereafter. A consciousness of Ukrainian nationality, on the other hand, did not arise until later. It was the outcome of a lengthy past, and was connected with the history of the Cossack communities in southern Russia; it sprang fully into life only in the late eighteenth century, gaining firmness and consistency in the second half of the nineteenth. Its taproot was the development of Ukrainian as a literary medium.

Written Ukrainian prior to the late eighteenth century had been a mixture, its ingredients being Slavic or Old Russian, Polish, Lithuanian, and the Ukrainian vernacular of the people. The man who created the foundations of Ukrainian as a literary language was Ivan Kotlarevski (1769–1838). His poem *The Aeneid* (1798), whose subject is the dispersion of the Cossacks after the suppression of the Zaporozhe Sietch by Catherine II, and his other writings (comedies of manners and descriptions of Ukrainian villages), convey his affection for the Ukrainian people and his desire to give them an instrument of literary expression. Nowhere does Kotlarevski show any disposition to rebel against Russia or the prevailing social order.

He was an official of the Ministry of Education and an officer on the military reserve, and volunteered in the struggle against Napoleon in 1812.

The eighteen-forties saw the growth of a Ukrainian intelligentsia whose tendencies were democratic, protesting against the condition of society but not opposed to the Russians or the Russian state. The dream of this new class was a federation of the Slav peoples, on a political basis of democracy. A Brotherhood of Saints Cyril and Methodius was secretly created, but quickly detected by the police and harshly suppressed. Among its members was Taras Shevchenko (1814–61), who came of a serf family and whose writings, unlike those of Kotlarevski and others, convey a protest at once national and social. His poems, collected under the title *Kobzar*, caused him to be exiled to Orenburg from 1847 to 1857. His vocabulary is free of the Russianisms still to be found in Kotlarevski; his output marks the beginning of a truly Ukrainian literary language.

From this time on there was an increase of national spirit among the intellectuals as a reaction against the government's endeavours to impose Russification (a leading instance occurred in 1876, when it was declared illegal to publish books, or even to perform plays, in Ukrainian). But the movement's main goal was simply to safeguard the civilized values for which the Ukraine was noted, and to give the Ukrainian people as high a level of cultural life as possible. All that even the most advanced patriots wanted was autonomy in a federal setting.

Despite Russification, the Ukraine continued to produce talented writers, such as the poet, novelist and historian Panko Kulish (1819–97), and Marko Vovchok (1834–1907). The latter name was the pseudonym of a woman who had loved Shevchenko; she was a novelist, and described the life of the Ukrainian peasants in her *Tales* (translated into Russian by Turgenev); she translated Jules Verne into Russian (she was a Russian herself and wrote in both languages). These authors belonged to the period of the great reforms, the abolition of serfdom. Vovchok was part of the literary movement, based on democracy and Populism, which was represented by a large number of contemporary Russian authors; Kulish, on the other hand, belonged to a liberal right wing which was more anti-Russian, more strongly tinged with Ukrainian nationalism.

The realistic novels of Ivan Nechni-Levychki (1838–1918) deal with peasant life both before and after the abolition of serfdom, and also depict the Ukrainian intelligentsia. Those of Panas Myrni (Rudchenko) (1849–1940) are more radical in tendency; they had to be published in Geneva. The Ukrainian past, as revealed in folklore, occupied the historian and sociologist Myshaïlo Drahomanov (1845–95), whose role was political as well as literary but who worked mainly outside the Ukraine. Two other outstanding writers of the late nineteenth century were the novelist Myshaïlo Kotsiubinski (1864–1913), a friend of Gorki, and Larissa Kossach (1871–1913), who wrote poems and verse-plays under the pseudonym

Lessia Ukrainka; her social ideas placed her in the vanguard of the feminist movement.

Another Centre of Ukrainian Nationalism

When the government's Russifying measures had gone so far as to extinguish hope inside the Ukraine, Austrian Galicia became the home of the national movement with the foundation in 1873, at Lvov, of the Shevchenko Society, whose purpose was to 'foster the development of Ukrainian literature'. A leading part was played by Franko (1856–1916), a disciple of the Ukrainian Professor Drahomanov (who had been excluded from his chair at Kiev University in 1876 and had become a kind of travelling salesman in Europe on behalf of Ukrainian nationalism). In 1890 Franko founded a Ukrainian Radical Party. A man of peasant origin who had graduated at the University of Lvov, he represented the democratic and revolutionary tendency among the Galician intelligentsia. But his broad Ukrainian nationalism isolated him not at all from Russian and Polish culture, and the esteem he enjoyed in Russia won him a degree as doctor *honoris causa* at the University of Kharkov.

The Travelling Theatre and Its Contribution

The development of a national outlook was helped by the use of Ukrainian on the stage; the vernacular of the people had got into the theatre by way of the entr'actes in religious plays as early as the seventeenth century, and was subsequently encouraged when some of the great landowners organized acting troupes of serfs. Kharkov, Kiev and Odessa had their own theatres by the early nineteenth century. From 1882, a travelling company run by Michael Kropyvnitchky (1840–1918) toured all over European Russia, performing plays mainly in Ukrainian. A group of playwrights, who also produced and even acted, organized tours in the Ukraine; the leading figures were the poet and Shakespeare translator Myshaïlo Starytsky (1840–1904) and the realistic playwright Marko Kropyvnitchky (1840–1918).

The cultural unity of the Ukrainians was expressed within the span of a single century by a literary output which straddled frontiers, and which concerned not only the Ukraine and Galicia but Bukovina (annexed by Austria in 1775), where Czernowitz (Cernivci) played a part similar to that of Lvov in Galicia. The poet Yuri Fedkovitch (1834–88), who used the racy language of the huzules of Carpathia, also wrote stories describing the wretched condition of the peasants in Bukovina. In the newspaper *Bukovyna*, which he edited, he expressed at once his opposition to the idea of a 'Bukovinian nation' and his lively sense of the unity of the Ukrainian people. The life of the peasants, treated in the same spirit, also appears in the books of the novelist Ol'ha Kobulanska (1863–1942). This writer was an active member of the feminist movement stemming from the Society of Ruthenian Women.

Austria, which regarded the Ukrainian national movement favourably in so far as it was anti-Russian, permitted a chair of Ukrainian history, which was entrusted to the historian Krushevski, to be instituted in 1894 at the University of Lvov. In Galicia before the First World War a National Democratic Party was organized, whose dual programme, maximum and minimum, provided either for the creation of an independent Ukraine including all the Ukrainians on both sides of the frontier, or, alternatively, an Austrian Ukrainian province within the Austro-Hungarian empire, consisting of eastern Galicia and Bukovina. Meanwhile readers were not lacking in Galicia for the pamphlets put out by Ukrainian patriots in the Russian empire, the membership of whose secret organizations was drawn from the urban lower middle classes, and whose programmes were more violent and revolutionary.

By this time the national problem had been complicated by new factors. During the final third of the nineteenth century the Ukraine had been developing at a heightened tempo. The biggest change was industrialization, which created new towns and inflated those already existing, attracted labour and specialists from the central regions, and brought an influx of Russian-speakers to mingle with the Ukrainian population; at the same time the cosmopolitan character of the seaports was becoming more pronounced. The Ukraine's geographical position, astride the routes to the Black Sea, and the overriding influence of economic interests, unifying peoples who had been existing symbiotically for centuries, rendered Ukrainian separatism quite unthinkable from the government's point of view. As for the Ukrainians, their national movement concentrated mainly on cultural objectives, as before. Its political programme was a united Ukraine under federal auspices, which, it was hoped, would include all the Ukrainian areas.

IV BEFORE THE STORM – A SUMMARY OF RUSSIAN PROGRESS

At the outbreak of the First World War, Russia was to all appearances a firm pillar of the Franco-Russian alliance. Her army's initial victories – won by the courage and numerical strength of her soldiers rather than by good equipment or the abilities of the high command – forced the Germans and Austrians to retreat in considerable depth and confirmed the impression that the government was firmly in control. The liberal opposition was ineffective, revolutionary agitation carried no punch; neither seemed capable of giving serious trouble.

The revolution of 1905 had in fact contained the seeds of advance; in retrospect, it appeared to have set the régime on the path of orderly progress towards institutions of a more modern, democratic kind, which the forces of reaction had managed to cripple in the immediate outcome but would be unable to inhibit indefinitely. The time-honoured anachronisms of Russian life were withering. The aristocarcy, many of whom had entered industry and commerce, had been reinforced by the wealthiest section of the middle class, now solidly supporting the régime. In all sectors of the country's activities, economic expansion and the needs of the state were stimulating the growth of the middle class as a whole and thus contributing to social stability: the small landowners who had sprung up after the Stolypin reforms, the businessmen in the towns, the engineers and technicians and civil servants, were a highly diverse multitude but a pacific one, whose modest demands for improvements of one kind or another were almost exclusively occupational or professional. Pressure groups such as these were capable of gradually modifying the political climate, making the administration work more efficiently and pushing the government towards wider, more radical reforms.

The Duma, though muzzled by the government, did at least enable the dissentients to make their voices heard. The freedoms won by the revolution of 1905 – freedom of association, professional combination and the

FIGURE 31
Mould for
spiced bread
(Russia),
nineteenth
century.

press – were still recognized in principle; in practice their operation was severely restricted, though not entirely blotted out, by the utterly arbitrary behaviour of the authorities. A reformism which threatened no harm to the government worked inside the narrow limits allowed to a tolerated opposition; it looked capable of ensuring a course of political development which, without violence, would gradually force the autocracy into the requisite concessions. Russia would tread the western path.

Such was the reassuring façade of an empire which was to show, under stress of war, how rickety it really was. The gigantic masses of the peasantry had never been totally passive or totally resigned to their lot, and the emergence of a new class, the well-to-do villagers, had as yet hardly begun; its main effect was to make inequality worse. Because there was an agricultural proletariat, whose size was increasing with that of the population, the forefront of the people's minds was occupied by land distribution. And in the towns there was a helot class: the industrial workers, present in ever larger concentrations and dominating the slums, got almost nothing either out of industrial prosperity or even the liberties proclaimed in 1905. They had no real rights, were distrusted by the governing classes, lived wretchedly, and had largely lost their connections with village life; they were ready to listen to revolutionary propaganda, and their demands were forced into a political form through being denied free expression in trade unionism.

The strength neither of agitation in the countryside, nor of the industrial workers' movement, can be estimated simply from the comparatively small number of those who declared their discontent visibly: the demonstrators and strikers. The deep-seated contradictions of a society which was adapting itself to modern life and its novel conditions, but making this transition too slowly, had excited the people to a resentment at once more general and more obscure. 'Underground Russia' did not consist only of the secret activities of a revolutionary minority; it was present also in a potential form, the future exigence and violence which were being worked up by the people's natural, and frustrated, sense of justice. The idea of a new distribution of land governed the minds of more than half the peasants; and in the shadow of the factories there simmered an obscure anger which the revolutionary agitators had difficulty in keeping in check.

This psychological element, which contemporaries hardly noticed or else underestimated, must be borne in mind if we are to understand the speed and scope of the collapse in 1917, which the effects of war do not in themselves sufficiently explain.

The actions of individual leaders played some part in the shaping of events. But the opposition politicians who figured most prominently on the political stage, though of consequence to the authorities, were out of touch with the masses and were swept away at the same time as the liberal republic, that short-lived experiment which was no sooner initiated than it became obsolescent and a failure. It was at the popular level, among the workers and peasants, half secretly and half publicly (revolutionary literature being tolerated as long as it confined itself to theoretical problems),

12

that the revolutionary cadres, who were to grasp control of the country's destiny, were being forged into shape. There were not many of them but they were already schooled for their task, well versed in revolutionary principles and tactical doctrine; they not only distributed pamphlets and newspapers printed in Russia and abroad, they explained them; and though their conflicting trends reflected the divergent tendencies of international socialism, they were all bent on destroying the régime. They were that vanguard of the Revolution whose duties and function had been defined by Lenin.

It may be reasonably doubted whether the agitators' influence was really very great. Even in the towns it was confined to a small circle here and there. And it was the work of the Socialist Revolutionaries rather than the Social Democrats, though it was the latter who imposed their leadership on the Revolution. But the danger the agitators represented to the régime even at this stage, however insignificant it appeared to the public, can be gauged from the anxieties they aroused among the tsar's police and indeed the police forces of Europe, anxieties reflected in archives once secret but since thrown open. One figure stands out above all: Lenin, whose extraordinary intelligence and tenacity during the twenty years before the war enabled him to work out the doctrine and tactics of revolution, in a form suited to the special case of Russia. What seemed at the time to be tedious Byzantine disputes on articles of theory was in fact an indispensable process, the forging of an effective instrument of civil war. The care with which deviationist opinions were mercilessly crushed, the ideological struggle against Populism, the Socialist Revolutionaries, Economism, Menshevism, and the 'liquidation' school of thought (terrorism, which, like other romantic methods, Lenin rejected) – all these, in the light of events from 1917 onwards, bear witness to Lenin's insight and realism.

Economic progress, mainly in industry but also, though to a far smaller extent, in agriculture, was beginning to catch up with Russian backwardness. But neither the bourgeoisie, nor the *kulaks* whom the state regarded as the potential foundation of a solid and stable régime, constituted a high proportion of the population. Economic development had not had time to cause a big expansion of the middle ranks of society, those which act as dampers on social conflict. Thus the KD party lacked a basis of support in the country at large. It was His Imperial Majesty's licensed opposition, carrying no real weight in the Duma (which was dominated by the wealthy nobility); it was suspended in a vacuum. The country's representative institutions were like a badly slipping clutch. Russia as a legal fiction was a different thing from the Russia of reality.

Meanwhile, the great mass of the people, the peasants and even the industrial workers, were indifferent to the long-term programmes of the parties devoted to gradualism, and, in almost all cases, maintained a cautious attitude towards revolutionary propaganda; fear and religious tradition guaranteed greater influence to the priest than to the political agitator. But they had urgent practical problems to cope with, matters of property, wages and conditions, and could easily understand the simple, immediate goals indicated by the revolutionary parties; consequently they became in effect an immense standing reserve of revolutionary power. Despite all obstacles, the social basis of the revolutionary parties had broadened; the campaigns of political 'animation' initiated by the militants of 1905 had penetrated deeper and deeper into the factories and villages.

Agitation was least effective in the countryside, where the gradual increase in productivity and a rise in agricultural prices had created slightly better conditions for most of the population; the same causes presumably account for the reduction in numbers of the 'agrarian movements' (6,000 in 1910, 4,500 in 1911, 647 in 1913). In the towns, especially the capital, it was different. Politically motivated strikes were frequent, and there was enough solidarity to ensure that, if one factory came out, others would follow; a situation which engendered a novel development, the employers' retort in the form of a lock-out.

While among the inert masses of the peasantry the persistent notion of a new share-out of land became stronger than ever, the urban proletariat, whose numbers increased with the surge of industrial development from 1910 to 1914, were becoming more class-conscious. Despite the freedom officially granted to labour organizations in 1905, trade unions were barely tolerated and were often harassed by the police; so there was no chance of their acting as a moderating influence. As already indicated, the workers lived beyond the fringe of society; though intimately involved in urban activity they were outcasts in terms of municipal affairs; they were excluded from the chances of betterment offered by a developing society, with a wider range of income and opportunity. Of necessity, their demands acquired a political stamp. The politically active working-class groups, though few in number, were organized by militants of remarkable ability. Lenin's role in secret activities must not be underestimated. His doggedness, doctrinal adaptability and sense of practical realities converted a muddle of agitation into the methodical preparation of that advanced striking-force of the working class, to which the events of 1917 were to throw open the strait gate of Revolution.

12

Vitality Undaunted:
Poland 1815-1914

POLAND as a state never completely vanished after partition. The 'kingdom of the Congress', provided with a constitutional charter, had a government and an army (commanded, however, by the Tsar's brother Constantine) and could hope, even within the Russian imperial framework, to recover its eastern provinces in Lithuania and Ruthenia, annexed by the Russians and absorbed into the Russian administrative system. The preservation of the throne made it possible to keep nationhood alive and to educate the younger generation, who, whether at home or in exile, continually voiced their resolute desire for national independence. The kingdom of the Congress gave birth to the two romantic risings, in November 1830 and January 1863, which brought about its decline and dissolution but which also demonstrated the strength of Polish patriotism.

I THE POLISH PEOPLE: PROLIFIC, UNANIMOUS, DIVIDED

Throughout the nineteenth century, a high birthrate maintained a secure foundation for the nationality of the Poles. The population of the kingdom of the Congress went up by 77 per cent between 1816 and 1850, and by 100 per cent between 1850 and 1900, rising from 4,800,000 inhabitants in 1850 to nearly 10,000,000. In Galicia and Prussian Poland the increase was less marked. In the Poznan region and Polish Pomerania the corresponding figures were 65 per cent between 1816 and 1850 (the total in the latter year reaching 1,300,000), and 35 per cent between 1850 and 1900 (when the total was 1,900,000). In Galicia, half of whose inhabitants were not Poles but Ruthenians (Ukrainians), the figures were 22 per cent (population in 1850: 4,600,000) and 60 per cent (population in 1900: 7,300,000). At the dawn of the twentieth century the Polish element in the population of the three territories amounted to some 15,000,000, a mass whose very size was a complete safeguard against assimilation.

The fortunes of this divided people, however, varied greatly from one territory to another. Prussian Poland, where the towns became strongly

Teutonic but the country districts remained Polish, was dominated by an agricultural policy which encouraged good husbandry on the part of the big landowners and the more prosperous peasants. Under the law of 1823 the richest Polish peasants acquired perpetual ownership of their land against periodical payment; the remainder joined the ranks of the day-labourers or were absorbed into town life. It was at least possible, in the prevailing conditions of agricultural progress, for a small part of the peasantry to become wealthy, establish themselves strongly on the land, keep their national traditions and resist German colonization, which did not become dangerous until the second half of the century.

But the pressure of Prussian assimilation was already beginning to show in the German functionaries who spoke Polish badly or not at all, in unsuccessful attempts to introduce bilingual education, and in the creation of numerous German Protestant schools, which soon outnumbered the Catholic schools in a region where the Catholics formed two thirds of the population.

FIGURE 32
Polish peasant
costumes,
nineteenth
century.

In Galicia, the emperor had created a Diet which had no powers, and almost all the seats in which were given to the big Polish landowners and the representatives of the clergy. Serfdom was still in force; the unrest it caused took the form of frequent disturbances and the indifference of the peasants to political issues. Half the population were in any case Ruthenians (Ukrainians), most of whom worked on estates owned by Poles. The government concerned itself little with these areas, in which agriculture trundled monotonously on, and which served as outlets for the industrial products of Austria and Bohemia. It deliberately weakened the Polish nobles by intervening in their clashes with the peasants. But its actions made virtually no difference to the main mass of the people, who kept their traditions and language intact. The free city of Cracow, thanks to its university, had become once more a centre of Polish science.

The Kingdom of the Congress

The Polish kingdom had inherited a difficult economic predicament, produced by the partitions, the territorial reshuffles between 1806 and 1815, and the course laid down for a ducal state whose chief purpose, in Napoleon's eyes, was to maintain a body of troops. The manufacturers of the eighteenth century had died out; they had contributed, however, to the creation of a labour force whose skills and attitudes were still available in the nineteenth.

Russian Poland had now been made part of the imperial economy, and its industrial history developed similarly to Russia's – but with this difference, that capital accumulation was almost nil and that Poland's nascent industries were even more closely geared to ordinary day-to-day consumption. A capital market to foster investment was forthcoming neither from the peasants nor even from the big landowners. The vast majority of the former lived on small plots and produced very little for sale; the latter, benefiting from an abundance of cheap labour and from the automatic and continuous rise in land-values, had little incentive to modernize their methods and raise output. Consequently industrialization, in spite of state encouragement in the eighteen-twenties, remained almost static in the first half of the century. Its main signs of life were the development of Lodz as a textile centre, and, for a short time only, of mining and metallurgy at Kielce, which was overshadowed by the factories set up in 1834 at Huta Bankowa, based on the Dombrowa coal basin.

Old-fashioned craft production went on as before, with a sprinkling of big establishments which, as in Russia, were very much in the minority. The large linen mill started by Girard in the eighteen-thirties, which was responsible for the birth of the town of Żyrardów and was a concentrated capitalistic enterprise with bank credits and modern equipment, controlled a large number of home weavers but did not, at least in its early years, wipe out village craftsmanship, the most widespread form of industrial production. One of the first establishments to manufacture machinery, Evans's factory in Warsaw, which was supplied with ore by peasants discharging their *corvée*, also put work out to the small local foundries.

The Polish economy as a whole, in its new start in the period 1820–30, ran on the lines indicated here. However, the basic ingredient required for faster progress was already present, in the form of the capital supplied to Girard by wealthy Poles with which to start his mills. The textile establishments at Lodz, like their counterparts in Russia, brought themselves abreast with the times by undercover purchases of English machines, whose export at that time was illegal.

A protectionist régime, access to the Russian market, and resumed exports of agricultural products via Danzig, all encouraged this nascent industrial growth, which was also helped by the creation of a Bank of Poland; in this respect the kingdom was even ahead of Russia, which had no banking institutions on a national scale. But, as in Russia, the economy was handicapped by the continued economic servitude of the peasants and

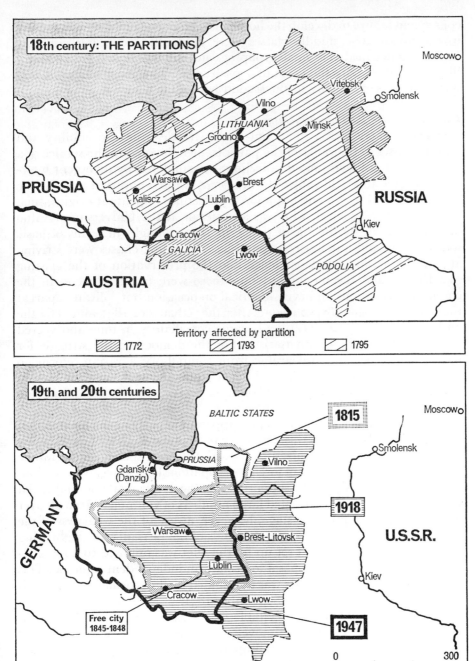

Map 19 Poland, from the Eighteenth to the Twentieth Century

consequent failure to develop the home market. Social mobility was greater in the towns. The middle classes were gradually increasing, and the workers, concentrated in small groupings and still half linked with country life, were as yet only the germ of a proletariat. The great economic and social changes came only in the second half of the century.

Romanticism and the Patriotic Upsurge

Meanwhile there was a small but steady trickle from the nobility and middle classes to the ranks of the patriots, men devoted to the service of a people which, though united in feeling, was sundered by divergent interests. The peasants, still subject to the *corvée*, wanted agrarian reform; the nobles withheld it. No one but a few intellectuals of peasant origins, such as the historian Lelewel, who was a professor at the University of Vilno until driven out by the tsarist police in 1823, thought in terms of basic social reform and a democratic republic. The ruling classes were striving at once for national independence and the preservation of the existing social order and the monarchy; thus there were two tendencies in the country, harmonious and even identical on occasion but splitting apart at the slightest danger of revolution. After the setbacks of 1831 and 1863 the nationalism of the conservatives became conciliatory in tone and veered towards collaboration with tsarism. For the democrats, the struggle for independence became inseparable from compulsory agrarian reform, to be imposed on the landlords, and hence from a struggle against tsarism which was in the interest of the common people alike in Poland and in Russia.

The two tendencies became clearly apparent as early as the insurrection of November 1830, which was a military plot similar to that of the Russian Decembrists and was organized by a patriotic secret society in the insane hope of ridding the country of foreign occupation. Based largely on wishful thinking, the uprising was supported by the craftsmen and industrial workers of Warsaw and attracted large numbers of volunteers from all over the country. From an early stage, however, aware of the weakness of the Polish army and alarmed by the demands of the peasants, the right wing in the national government set up by the Diet was opposed to a mass revolt and the democrats' proposal to declare an independent republic. This unpromising political wrangle was terminated by the Russian army, which finished crushing the revolt in September 1831.

The consequences of this inevitable defeat were, on the whole, advantageous to the Polish national movement. Fearful repression, employing the death-penalty, confiscation of property and deportation to the Caucasus or Siberia, caused a general exodus of patriots and cured them of any temptation to make their peace with Russia. The conservatives rallied round Prince Adam George Czartoryski in Paris, while Lelewel pursued his democratic republican objectives in Brussels. But the two groups were coming closer together and the aristocracy had begun shedding its hostility to agrarian reform, which it now recognized as essential to the realization of national unity – a goal which had become all the more urgent in that the kingdom had been deprived of its constitution and given an Organic Statute (26 February 1832), suppressing the Diet and army. The country had been allowed to keep its language and administration but was reduced to the level of a favoured province, dependent on the Imperial Senate and increasingly threatened by assimilation.

Beyond the boundaries of the kingdom, in the annexed provinces, where administrative assimilation was total, the passivity of the Uniate sect had enabled their superior clergy to swing them over *en masse* to the Orthodox Church in 1839, the only exception being the diocese of Chelm; a Russifying 'drive to the west' which advanced the religious frontier to coincide with the linguistic. The result was that the Polish clergy entered more deeply into the national movement, which acquired a religious as well as a political character and began to stir the peasant masses.

The notion of a general uprising in Poland, and of the rebirth of Polish liberty under cover of a European war, was promoted by the *émigrés*; they did their utmost to interest the governments of the West in the fate of their country, and in 1833 they initiated conspiracies inside the kingdom which were quickly suppressed. However, Poland had found herself a national anthem in the shape of the *Song of the Legions* composed in 1797 by Josef Wybicki (1747–1822); and hopes of liberation were fed by an ardently patriotic literature which spread its wings without impediment in foreign countries and aroused the sympathy of liberal intellectuals for 'heroic Poland'. The 'Great Emigration' which followed the defeat of 1831 is associated with such famous names as Adam Mickiewicz (1798–1855), Juliusz Slowacki (1809–1849) and Zygmunt Krasinsky (1812–1850).

The feature common to all such writers, who were so varied and indeed diametrically opposed in some cases, was the inspiration they drew from their country's misfortunes. Whether they were militantly political, like Adam Mickiewicz, or remained aloof from action, like Slowacki, the work of all of them was shaped by the events of 1830–1, the severity of Nicholas I's régime, and the need to safeguard Poland's nationhood. The most effective of them was Mickiewicz, who became more or less the spiritual leader of the struggle for liberation. He had been one of Lelewel's students at Vilno and was forced to leave Lithuania in 1817, when the semi-secret societies formed at the University excited Russian repression on grounds of 'unreasonable patriotism'. From Russia he travelled to Germany and France; during his stay in each country he wrote poems and romantic plays which soon ranked as the bible of Polish patriotism both at home and abroad. It was while in Paris that he wrote *The Books of the Polish Nation and Pilgrims* (1833), a passionate, poetic appeal to the Polish people, who were regaining their national soul by travelling the diverse roads which led to freedom.

Slowacki was less popular and won recognition as a great poet of the emigration only a short time before his early death. Like Mickwiewicz, he represents a specifically Polish romanticism; a typical example of his poetry is *Kordian* (1834), exalting a hero who has fallen a sacrifice to the struggle for freedom. Written in a Europe compelled to remain static by its conservative monarchies, works such as these were full of enthusiasm for the future and of incitements to revolt. Another work composed in exile was *Observations on the History of Poland and Her People*, by Joachim Lelewel, 'the father of modern Polish historiography', who demonstrated the importance of the masses in the development of states, and the significance of the agrarian problem.

Meanwhile Frédéric Chopin (1810–49), who had emigrated after the events of 1831, was finding in folklore, popular legends and Polish history the inspiration for his *Mazurkas, Polonaises* and *Ballades* – compositions which at once reaffirmed his own connection with Poland and, through their successful reception, contributed to the wave of sympathy aroused by the country's tribulations.

In this climate of turmoil and hope, the revolutionary events of 1848 produced a few repercussions in Prussian Poland and also in Galicia, where unrest among the peasants had been going on since 1845. Cracow, after the rebellion there in 1846, was stripped of its charter as a free city, and peace was quickly enforced in Galicia, where the peasants had risen against the Polish landowners; the latter veered thereafter towards political docility. The *corvée* was abolished, but opposition between the Ruthenian and Polish elements continued and the government exploited it to weaken the national movement.

The entire artistic life, not only the literary activities, of the Polish territories in the nineteenth century was impregnated with patriotism. Romanticsm in the plastic arts was inseparably associated with the national struggle, which had been weakened but not extinguished by the set-backs of 1830 and 1863. Not only Matejko but other, earlier painters, such as Piotr Machalowski (1800–55), had evoked memories of the glorious past and the splendours of the Napoleonic phase, both of which had been responsible for so many disappointed hopes. In the art of the portrait, represented in the early part of the century by Antoni Brodowski (1784–1894), international fame was won by Henryk Rodakowski (1823–94). But Poland though disemembered, was still alive to the major European trends; with the result that, for example, the realism of the landscapes and *genre* paintings of Wojcech Gerson (1831–1901) provided yet another outlet through which Poland could remind the world of her existence.

The accession of Alexander II, and the comparatively liberal atmosphere of the eighteen-sixties, roused fresh hope in the Polish patriots. The amnesty declared by Alexander enabled the exiled Poles in Siberia to come back, and although in his speech of May 1856 he enjoined the Poles not to indulge in daydreams he put an end to the state of war which had dominated life in the kingdom since 1833; he made a few concessions, one of which was to authorize, in 1857, the foundation of a Society of Agriculture. By the following year this body had acquired 2,500 members and represented the élite of Polish society, notably the small landed nobility, who were against land-reform and loyal to the Russian government but demanded the revival of the Polish state, and supported conservative claims for the return of the eastern territories annexed by Russia. Parallel to this there was renewed activity among the secret organizations of the democrats, which began building up again during the eighteen-sixties and were very active. They organized demonstrations to mark the anniversary of the insurrection of 1830–1; considerable sections of the population took part in these, especially the students, of whom there were many in Warsaw, and bloody clashes with the police resulted. The democrats, divided into two factions, 'Reds' and 'Whites', were no longer the mere advanced fraction, isolated from the national movement, which they had been thirty years before; the desire for independence expressed by them was now general, and while it was particularly keen in the towns, both large and small, it was also attracting the passive sympathy of the peasants.

The Insurrection of 1863
A call to rebellion was launched on 22 January 1863. Despite the presence of the tsarist police, preparations had been going on for three years in the army and administration, among the students, and in the factories. The call met with a powerful response in the kingdom and, after a few months, in Lithuania.

The insurrection was triggered by the Reds and taken up by the Whites. It was essentially a town-dwellers' revolt, with the petty nobility standing outside it; the main participants were the military, and the students, craftsmen, workers and priests. There was no effective support to be had from the peasants, who were keen to join in or adopted a wait-and-see attitude according to the amount of influence wielded by the leaders in different places. The revolt had insufficient resources and received no help from abroad, and had no prospect of defeating the powerful Russian army. Fighting was still going on as late as April 1864 but was sporadic and unco-ordinated, and had become confined to the southern districts. The Russian government began a merciless campaign of repression in the summer of 1863, and before long had deprived the Poles of the few liberties previously left to them.

The kingdom of the Congress disappeared; it was turned into an administrative unit of twelve provinces and called the Vistula Territory. The institutions the Russians had allowed to survive under the Statute of 1832 were abolished. The weight of the Russian police and bureaucracy became increasingly oppressive in Poland at a time when liberal reforms were being granted in Russia itself. The outlines emerged of a deliberate policy which looked like a death-sentence for Poland, destroying her hopes and progressively transforming her into a mere province of the empire: administration in the towns was centralized, a campaign was openly waged against the Catholic Church because it had taken part in the struggle, Warsaw University was Russianized, so were the Polish secondary schools, and there were concessions to the Polish peasants in the direction of land-reform – the purpose being to set them against their landlords and, if possible, turn them into loyal subjects of the Emperor.

II THREE CONFLUENT DESTINIES

The Polish Diaspora

The year 1863 marked a new milestone in the history of the Polish nation. The failure of the rising caused a diaspora of the country's intellectual forces to various quarters of the world, but especially to the enormous Russian empire. Numerous Poles were deported to Siberia, others took service in the Russian army or administration. All three categories contributed brilliantly to the economic and cultural development of Russia, which was short of trained men and derived much practical benefit from these newcomers. Scientific activities were transplanted from the lands of the Vistula to the universities of the empire and also to Siberia, where the names of Benedykt Dybowski, Aleksander Czekanowski and Jan Czerski (all political deportees), and Bronislaw Grabczewski, are associated with massive achievements in geographical, geological and archaeological investigation. The Poles also took root in other countries, where Polish naturalists, geographers, geophysicists and explorers took part in African, Oceanic and Antarctic discovery and study. It was thus the destiny of the Polish intelligentsia, in the absence of a state to keep them together, to be thoroughly involved in international life, without thereby losing their vital links with their mutilated and downtrodden country.

The Training-Ground: Galicia

Polish cultural life was kept going more strongly in Galicia than in the lands of the Vistula, where the Polish University of Warsaw, after a brief existence from 1862 to 1869, had been replaced by a Russian university. After being subjected to a powerful course of Germanization in the first half of the nineteenth century, Galicia from 1867 onwards enjoyed a substantial degree of autonomy within the political framework of the Austro-Hungarian Empire. It was administered by a Diet, had a Polish governor and elected its own representatives to the Imperial Council. Polish had replaced German as the language of administration and justice.

The University of Cracow was allowed to become Polish in 1870, that of Lwow in 1877; and the Cracow Academy of Sciences, founded in 1872, became a busy centre of Polish science, attracting numerous students from the other annexed territories. In particular there grew up under its aegis a School of History under Michael Bobrzinski, who pondered on the annihilation of the Polish state (which he attributed to the errors of the Polish people) with a certain pessimism and a somewhat conservative conception of the past which distinguished the historical thought of Cracow from that of Warsaw.

The cosmopolitan novelist Henryk Sienkiewicz, whose *Quo Vadis ?* won him a Nobel Prize, made only a short stay in Cracow; but the painter Jan Matejko (1838–93) worked there for many years, and his pictures constitute a magnificent fresco of Poland's glorious but tragic past. Another resident was the poet Stanislaw Wyspianski (1869–1907), whose plays, charged with symbolism, are based on episodes of the struggle of the Poles to defend their spiritual identity (*The Woman of Warsaw*, 1898). The University of Lwow was also not without its radius of influence, but it was a Polish island surrounded by Ruthenian territory in which the Austrian government was opposing the Russians by encouraging Ukrainian nationalism; the University had to compound with the Ukrainian interest, and was the scene of powerful political agitation after the end of the century.

Galicia has been privileged to play a special part in Poland's national history. As a peasant region whose agriculture was backward on the whole, and whose industry (which in any case was in Austrian hands) was represented only by a few coal-mines and oil-wells in the eastern districts, it was economically the Cinderella of the three territories. Many of its peasants went abroad to work or emigrated permanently. The national movement was complicated there by the existence of two nationalities, Polish and Ruthenian, the one in the west, the other in the east, but both dominated by an administration of Polish functionaries and big landowners, and united in a popular opposition more acutely aware of the social problem than of the political. However, the comparatively liberal rule of the Austrians made Galicia a refuge for Polish patriots who had been driven out of Russia and Prussia, and a training-ground for the struggles of the future.

Resistance to Germanization

In Prussian Poland, the vitality of the Poles persisted in asserting itself despite the highly unfavourable conditions created by the policy of the Prussian government. Here again was an essentially agricultural country, but one which shared in the general progress of German agriculture, and was moreover helped by high prices for rye in the late nineteenth century and by transit trade along the routes leading to the Baltic ports. The agricultural proletariat, working for Polish or German landowners, formed a large part of the population, but two other elements – the prosperous section of the peasantry, and an urban middle class in competition with the German minority – were developing. Unlike what happened in the two other territories, the denationalizing process imposed on the Poles of Prussia took the form of systematic German colonization, a drive which was intensified in the eighteen-seventies and thereafter. This was an internal concern of the kingdom of Prussia, and the Reich took care not to intervene; the problem of relations between Prussians and Poles was defined by the policy of Bismarck, who in his violent speeches denounced 'the Polish danger' and made the extinction of Polish nationality the condition of Prussia's existence.

In 1874 German was made the exclusive language of education, except in districts where only Polish was understood; the same was done for administration in 1876 and for justice in 1877. In 1886 a Commission of Colonization was set up, whose function was to make Eastern Pomerania and the country round Poznan more German by buying agricultural properties and dividing them among German settlers.

The year 1894 saw the foundation of a league to assist the German population in the eastern provinces. A succession of laws was passed in an attempt to take the land away from the Poles and install Germans in the districts along the Russian frontier: the colonization law of 10 August 1886, the law of 10 August 1904, forbidding building, the expropriation law of 1908, a particularly rigorous measure which, however, was hardly put into practice until 1913 – these enactments mark the stages of a harsh struggle between the Poles and Prussians, from which the latter, contrary to expectation, failed to emerge victorious.

The dynamism of the Poles was attested by the resistance with which, in all sorts of ways, they met the devices of denationalization. The Polish peasantry had a high birthrate and were increasing relatively to the Prussians, and though they lost over 741,500 acres of land between 1861 and 1885 they more than recovered their losses by their purchases in the ensuing years. And out of 1,112,000 acres bought by the Colonization Commission and transferred to German settlers, only a quarter had been in Polish ownership; the remaining three quarters were sold by Prussian landowners. Agricultural progress on Polish estates, the organization of co-operatives and credit societies, and the founding of a Land Bank in 1888, demonstrated the strength of the economic positions held by the Polish peasants.

Simultaneously there was a growing passive resistance to measures of assimilation, a resistance in which the Church, through its country clergy, played an important part. After 1900 the Poles were systematically excluded from all administrative functions, a wholly Prussian bureaucracy was installed, place-names were Germanized, and the police became busier and stricter than ever. And it was precisely in these circumstances that the Poles retorted with prolonged strikes by their schoolboys, backed by their families (that of 1906–7 was the longest); with patriotic demonstrations; and with continual protests by the Polish deputies in the Reichstag. All these were signs pointing to the failure of a denationalization policy which, on the admission of the Colonization Commission itself, the Poles had countered with a heightened consciousness of their nationality.

Attempted Russification

The Vistula territories, the former kingdom of Poland, which contained the essential part of the nation in a homogeneous whole, remained, as ever, the basis of the Polish economy.

The agrarian reform of 3 March 1864 produced the same liberating effects as that of 1861 in Russia, and displayed the same deficiencies. For political reasons the peasants, though apparently better off, received less land than they had lost in the period preceding the reform, and a form of *corvée* was retained as compensation for the survival of common rights (use of common land). So the peasant problem was incompletely resolved; but the reform did accentuate social differentiation in the village and facilitate the recruiting of new hands for industry. Russian Poland became a great industrial region. The cotton spinning and weaving mills of Lodz, the woollen mills of Sosnoviec and Czenstochova, and the linen mills of Zyrardów, were employing a total of nearly 100,000 in 1902. The Dombrowa coal-mines and the metallurgical industries, small, large and medium-scale, of the Dombrowa-Sosnoviec area, and of Warsaw, were booming.

It is true that most of the industrial establishments were owned by foreign firms; but the busy economic life to which they bore witness was none the less real for that. On the social plane, the corresponding phenomena were an industrial proletariat, and a bourgeoisie strengthened by the addition of numerous nobles who had been dispossessed after the insurrections and had become engineers, lawyers and doctors. This diversified society was of course subjected to a policy of progressive Russian assimilation, whose first outlines began to appear after 1863 and were accentuated in the eighteen-eighties under the direction of Gurko, the governor of Poland, and Apoukhtin, the chief inspector of schools; the policy's main target was the use of the Polish language, banned from teaching in 1885 and from the catechism in 1892. Other factors making for assimilation were the dispersion of Polish military recruits all over the empire, and of Polish students, whose numbers were not great, in Russian educational establishments; the development of a Russian bureaucracy; and the partial introduction of Russian law in the territories of the Vistula. Yet assimilation was a failure, here as elsewhere. Polish was taught in secret; patriotic memories were kept alive in the family circle, including memories of the late struggles for liberty; in 1886 a National League was secretly formed, and the most active sections of the middle classes in Warsaw joined it; the Polish Socialist Party was founded in 1892, the National Democratic Party in 1897; and Social Democratic groups began appearing in working class circles. These were the forms taken by a resistance which, after 1905, found more favourable conditions for development in the relatively liberal climate of the new Russian constitution.

III HOPES OF LIBERATION

The national struggle continued to produce reverberations abroad; at home it involved all classes of the people, without, however, preventing the Poles from taking a very active part in the economic and political life of the whole of Russia. Poland's entire industrial economy was orientated towards the Empire, to which 70 per cent of Polish textile output was sold in 1903, as against 30 per cent on the home market. Polish technicians scattered throughout the empire collaborated in Russia's industrialization, including the construction of the Trans-Siberian railway. The powerful material interests linking the Poles and Russians explain the attitude of conciliation adopted by much of the Polish bourgeoisie, those who favoured the objective of the National Democratic Party: the restoration of autonomy to a Poland which would remain a loyal member of the Russian empire. But the emptiness of the moderates' hopes, after the encouraging events of 1905, was revealed when the liberal mood of 1905–7 was replaced by universal reaction in the years from then to the First World War.

FIGURE 33 Contemporary Polish popular art from the *voivodia* of Cracow: *Christ in Torment.*

Peaceful struggle by legal means now appeared to be a lost cause. The romantic tradition of armed insurrection against the Russians therefore regained its attractions for the Polish Socialist Party under the leadership of Pilsudski, who had been a refugee in Austrian Galicia since 1900; meanwhile the Social Democratic groups, which were in communication with their Russian counterparts, worked for the overthrow of tsarism. The first of these activist minorities conceived the struggle in a political sense, the second in a social one. But what they were struggling against was a vast empire which, on its western periphery, was broadening the economic foundations of the Polish nation, and they could achieve nothing without a European war to help them. War was the means by which favourable conditions were suddenly created for the resurrection of the Polish state.

Political life in the Polish territories before the First World War became intensely active. The population was increasing by between 2 and 3 per cent per annum; the towns and cities, the source of every new political impulse, were getting bigger, and in this atmosphere a strongly youthful character came over the struggle for independence, a new element in which was a proletariat which though small (a few hundred thousand) was very active. The liberation movement was no longer the concern only of an aristocratic and middle-class élite but of all the Poles, on both sides of the frontiers dividing them. In the literary and aritstic fields the struggle was supported by a positivism which brought the peasants and workers into the main stream. The evocation of the past, with its extravagant glories and miseries, was succeeded by a more realistic depiction of present-day life and its difficulties, life in villages and factories: the writings of Stefan Zeromski (1864–1925) express a socialist ideology, those of Wladyslaw Reymont (1868–1925) give a picture of the peasant classes and the conflicts within them in the early twentieth century (*The Peasants*, 1904 and 1906–9). The novels of Boleslaw Prus (1847–1912), and the paintings of Aleksander Gierymski, present the labour and hardships of the common people.

13

The National Renaissance in Bohemia-Slovakia

THE CZECHS, who had undergone much German penetration but had also benefited from industrial development promoted by Viennese bankers, had an enlightened middle class and a growing proletariat, to whom the national history of the Czech people was a source of strength – of the will to resist, and of hope for eventual liberation.

The Slovaks, like the Czechs, looked towards Prague, and opposed the Hungarians by holding fast to their own culture.

I PRECONDITIONS OF REVIVAL

The Czech State: Fiction and Reality

Theoretically, the lands of the Crown of Bohemia had kept their independence after the Battle of the White Mountain; it was as kings or queens of Bohemia that the Hapsburgs ruled the country. But this was only the outward show of independence as far as Czech nationality was concerned. From this juncture onwards the crucial issue was Teuton *versus* Slav, especially on the linguistic plane. Educational progress under Maria-Theresa (1740–80) and Joseph II (1780–90) was accompanied by a campaign in favour of German, which was proclaimed the national language.

In the country districts, education was conducted in Czech; in the towns, Czech was used in the lower forms and German in the upper. But the higher educational establishments in Prague and Brno, where future teachers were taught, used German only. In the University German was gradually displacing Latin. Czech, spoken mainly by the peasants, was regarded as a plebeian vernacular and, because it awoke memories of Hus, as the tool of heresy. The Czech nobles and burghers had become almost completely German in their ways, and the functionaries, who were supposed to be familiar with Czech, knew it imperfectly.

However, the drive in favour of German, which had no justification on grounds of local nationality and was primarily an instrument of political unification, met with opposition, and this was indirectly assisted by Joseph II's reforms. An edict of toleration and the mitigation of the censorship enabled the dissentients to survive and organize themselves, and also allowed the ideas of the French Encyclopaedists and the English rationalists to penetrate freely. And thus there grew up a small intellectual élite, led by Gelasius Dobner (1719–90), 'the founder of Czech historiography', and the Slav scholar Joseph Dobrovský, and the work of these two men caused a genuine national renaissance on the literary and historical plane.

FIGURE 34 Peasant art of the Huzules, a Slav people of the Western Carpathians (Czechoslovakia): brightly painted dish.

The conditions in which this renaissance occurred were particularly difficult. Europe's permanent state of war in the late eighteenth and early nineteenth century had kept Bohemia in a state of siege, an extraordinary situation in which the Emperor Franz II had been able to pack the administration with German or Germanicized soldiers and noblemen. After 1806 the expression 'hereditary state' fell into disuse and was increasingly replaced by 'Empire of Austria' or 'Imperial Austrian State'; the Czechs got into the habit of referring to 'the emperor' instead of 'the king of Bohemia'. The fiction of an independent state nevertheless survived, and was useful later in the struggle for independence.

Meanwhile, the resistance of the Bohemian States General to Viennese centralism was much divided, and the Germanicized nobility showed little appetite for defending projected constitutions which would have pruned their privileges and given rights to the townsfolk and rustics. Few indeed were those who championed the cause of nationality, demanded an effective share in running the country's affairs, and, adopting the extreme position which this entailed, proposed the abolition of absolute rule, the exercise of civil rights, government by the people, and parity of the two languages, Czech and German. On its most radical side the opposition was, in fact, anti-German, and struggled, though with little success, against further enroachment by German influence. A chair of Czech language and literature was created in the University of Prague (which remained German); this was the only concession obtained by the States General. Ineffective in Metternich's time, the opposition grew in vigour and determination with the approach of the events of 1848, which were to shake the whole of central Europe.

Economic and Social Conditions

Bohemia shared in the economic revolution of the nineteenth century. In the countryside, where production was raised by improvements in farming methods, the standard of life rose rather slowly. By the middle of the century the population amounted to an impressive total of consumers, increasing from 4,000,000 in 1837 to 5,000,000 in 1869 (these figures are for Bohemia itself). The road network was being extended, and, still more important, Vienna was linked by rail during the eighteen-forties with Prague, Olmouc and Brno, the three most important cities. Apart from Russia, Bohemia was the only Slav country which was becoming industrialized at this period; Bohemia's first sugar refineries were appearing, and textile mills were multiplying round Prague. This accelerated economic growth brought an increase in social differentiation, with the accent on betterment; both of the country's ethnic groups benefited, the Czech bourgeoisie in particular becoming more numerous. Another consequence was the founding of more schools (Prague had already acquired its own polytechnic, in 1806). Some of these were technical, others non-classical without being specifically technical; many were bilingual; and conditions of enrolment favoured the Czechs. The main feature of the new phase was that the rural population was growing fast and was quicker than before to move into the towns, to which it was attracted by the growth of industry. This increase in the urban population consisted mainly of Czechs; the cities and towns were being slowly Slavicised, and even on the fringes of Bohemia, where the Germans were in the majority, the Czech element was eroding the German 'islands', in which it came into competition with local labour, causing considerable tension between the two nationalities.

II RECOVERING THE SLAV HERITAGE

Role of the Intellectuals and Scholars

During the first half of the nineteenth century the Czech renaissance experienced a 'heroic age' (Denis) which was also a distinct literary period. The renaissance was based on the impulse to return to the sources of national history, the appetite for folklore, the study of characteristics of popular life; a tendency which had emerged all over Europe towards the end of the eighteenth century.

The movement originated with a group of German and Czech scholars whose language and culture were German; university professors, priests, cultivated noblemen, all making a scientific study of the Bohemian past without any nationalistic ulterior motives.

But almost at once this renewal of acquaintance with historical traditions, and the revival of the language, effectively roused a dormant patriotism to the defence of the subject people's national values against foreign political domination; from which it was only a step to the defence of that people's rights as well. All the glories of Bohemia's past were brought back to life by the labours of the 'Awakeners', as they were called, and were used in support of Czech political and social demands. Other influences were there too: romanticism, seeking to make contact with the timeless soul of the people through the study of customs and language; and the spirit of the Encyclopaedists of the eighteenth century, the enemies of oppression and intolerance in any form. But the source of the movement's strength was in the struggles of ancient days, in which the Czech people had become conscious of its individuality. The Awakeners rallied to the standard of the Hussite tradition, and the first modern Czech poem, by Jaroslav Puchmajer (1769–1820), is entitled *Ode to Jan Žižka*.

The Czech renaissance soon turned into a campaign of resistance to German culture, and since its leaders, who were men of popular origin, were democrats by temperament, it also became a movement of social protest: it drew attention to the antagonism between the people, the main mass of which was essentially peasant in character, and an urban minority whose unpopular functionaries and businessmen represented German civilization. The Czechs resented their inferior position all the more in that, though their own language was the one they normally used, they had no chance of rising in society without learning German.

Consequently the scholarly achievements which laid the foundations of Slav and Czech philology and restored the eminence and dignity of the language, possessed a decisive importance. Joseph Dobrovský (1753–1829), at once a priest, a freemason and a disciple of the Encyclopaedists, converted Czech into an instrument of literary potentialities through his philological studies and his grammar, which was based on peasant speech. He himself, however, wrote in Latin and German. Joseph Jungmann (1776–1846), likewise of humble origin, a teacher, poet and journalist of a later generation, wrote in Czech and aspired to give his fellow-countrymen an interest in their own literature (*History of Czech Literature*, 1825). But both of these men saw things from a Slav rather than a Czech viewpoint and attracted only a limited following. The effect created among a wider public was due to another of the Awakeners, Kramerius (1759–1808), who was a real propagandist. He founded a printing firm in Prague (the Czech Exposition) from which a mass of works in Czech flowed into Bohemia, Moravia and even Slovakia.

The great names in Czech nationalism begin emerging after 1820. It is possible that the historian František Palacký (1798–1876) was the man who, as Ernest Denis puts it, at once dominated and epitomized the Czech renaissance. By birth a Moravian, he took the lead in the national movement in 1823 and in 1830 published his monumental *History of Bohemia* (from the earliest times to 1526), originally written in German, a work which made his name known far beyond the Czech homeland.

As the editor of various periodicals successively, he was the virtual organizer of Bohemia's literary and artistic life. His intention was that the future government of the Czech people should be based on the nobles and the rich (he has been compared with Guizot); he therefore sought support from those of his compatriots who were the most Germanized and, with few exceptions, the least affected by nationalist aspirations. His positive achievement was that he provided the Czechs with a conception of their own history, which he over-simplified by seeing it as the age-old conflict between the two nationalities, Czech and German, in Bohemia. Historically, this was an arbitrary interpretation; in the light of the contemporary situation, however, it appeared accurate, and it was supported by documents and the reasoning of a talented author; it was to prove a redoubtable weapon in the great conflict of nationalities in nineteenth-century Europe. Palacký was also the organizer of the Bohemian Museum which had been created a short time before, in 1820, and whose *Bulletin* became a Czech scientific and literary review. In 1831 a Czech publishing house (Matice Česka) was established in connection with the Museum.

A feature of the same period was the career of Havliček (1821–56), a journalist with a remarkable gift of popularization who commented on the Irish rising and other international events which caused a great stir in Czech circles.

The time had not yet come for an open confrontation between Czechs and Germans. Scholars and writers ardently explored the Slav past and everything to do with it, producing an idealized picture in which truth was mixed up with legend. Šafařik (1795–1861), a Slovak, published his *Slav Antiquities*. The language was being built up and its expressive powers extended; the physiologist Jan Evangelista Purkyne (1781–1869), and two naturalists at the University of Prague, the brothers Presl, developed it into a medium for scientific exposition. Gradually, in a romantic, patriotic atmosphere which generated a good deal of mediocre writing but also the poems (*Mai*) of Mácha (1810–36), there grew up an intellectual life whose political implications soon became suspect in the eyes of the government.

This development, the point of departure of the national movement and also its weapon, was still confined to a middle-class minority which was steeped in German culture. But the whole of Czech history had suddenly become a matter of first-class topical interest; and the vitality of the Czechs as a nation gave urgency to the question of their status in the imperial setting, a question which now actively engaged the minds of all classes in the community. Feeling was strongest among the poorer people in the towns and countryside, struggling as they were against Hapsburg absolutism, the tyranny of German officials, and exploitation by the great landowners.

The Polish rising of 1830 caused much excitement in Bohemia, and the decline of Metternich's system after 1840 opened the way for Czech propaganda to penetrate the countryside, while in the towns the movement was gaining strength from the use of Czech in the theatre (the first Czech opera, by František Skrup [1801–62], was put on in Prague in 1828). The Czech national anthem was composed in 1834.

The momentum of political life increased in the years leading up to 1848. But the Bohemian States General, dominated by nobles whose main attachment was to their privileges, were timorous in their claims; the immediate wishes of the educated patriots were more accurately reflected in secret pamphlets from abroad, which demanded a bigger share for the Slavs in the government of the empire and equality of the Czech and German languages. The two tendencies into which the movement was later to be divided were already apparent: the moderate conservatism, liberal in a mild way, led by Palacký and supported by middle-class intellectuals, such as the philologist Šafařik and the historian Tomek (1818–1905), Palacký's son-in-law Rieger (1857–1907), and Havlíček (1821–56), who in 1848 became editor of the newspaper *Národny Noviny*; and the radical wing supported by the urban artisans and the students, under the leadership of a group of writers which included Amanuel Arnold (1801–69), Joseph Vàclav Frič (1829–90) and Karel Sladkovsky (1823–80).

Prague as the Mecca of the Slavs under the Empire
Two things stand out from the failure of the European revolution of 1848, in which Bohemia was deeply involved: the strength of the national movement, and the illusions entertained by the liberals. In Prague, the revolution began with an illegal gathering on 11 March whose programme demanded political liberties for Bohemia as a whole, special rights for the Czechs, and social reforms, including suppression of the *corvée*. But the fate of the revolution in Bohemia depended on the situation in Vienna and, even more, on events then taking place in Germany, where one of the ideas

Map 20 Czechoslovakia, Historical Development in the Twentieth Century

in circulation among the revolutionaries was that of a Greater Germany, a resurrection of the Holy Roman Empire which would include Austria and her possessions. This objective was viewed favourably by some of the Germans in Bohemia.

The Czech patriots' retort was to insist on the territorial integrity of the existing empire, and to demand rights for the Slav peoples under its rule. This was the stand taken by Palacký and the liberals, who hopefully intended to shape Bohemia's future in a federal state embodying equal rights for Czechs and Germans. But in the eyes of the masses the political problem was secondary; the radicals' primary objective was to abolish feudalism and improve the workers' conditions; to this extent the Czech national movement was linked with the social revolutionary movement by which Europe (with the exception of Russia) was then being agitated.

Just one of all the radicals' demands for reform was satisfied: in September 1848, by a decision of the Parliament of Vienna, the peasants became owners of the land they cultivated, and the *corvée* was remitted against a monetary payment. Meanwhile the rioting crowds were put down in Prague during June and in Vienna during September, and heavy persecution fell on the Czech patriots, particularly the radicals. The latter were dispersed and were gradually forced into silence or exile. Their resistance crumbled: in 1856 Havlíček died of sufferings undergone in prison; in 1860 Frič was obliged to take refuge in France, where he made the Czech cause popular with a public which had previously been aware only of the Polish problem.

During the early months of the revolution there was held in Prague a Congress at which, for the first time, representatives from all over the Slav world came together; and a manifesto was issued proclaiming the right of every Slav people to determine its future. This ostensible unanimity, which appeared to override Palacký's conciliatory tendencies, was in fact barely sufficient to disguise the deep dissensions both between and within the Slav peoples – hostility between the Poles and the Russians, and the conflict of liberals and radicals. Though the Congress's programme, appealing to the Slav peoples to claim independence, was somewhat academic, its objective was, after all, nothing less than the destruction or diminution of three empires, the Russian, Austrian and Ottoman. The Czech politicians, drawn from a bourgeoisie which was no doubt pusillanimous but also prudent and sensible, remained, like Palacký, faithful to an 'Austro-Slavism' whose only fruits were a series of humiliating setbacks to the Czech cause. When the government in Vienna called a Constituent Assembly to settle the Empire's political constitution, the Czech delegates, led by Palacký, toed the line as before; and in the war against Hungary, in which the Slavs sided with Austria, the Slovakian militia units which were the first troops to clash with the Hungarian forces were commanded by Czech officers.

Yet victory for Vienna was followed by no concessions to the Czechs. As soon as the Austrians, with Russian help, had crushed the Hungarians, a constitution was granted which strengthened the Teutonic hold on

Bohemia, but remained in other respects a dead letter: from 1852 the empire was ruled by a succession of decrees from Bach, the Minister of the Interior, whose systematic oppression of the minorities continued until 1860.

Nevertheless the events of 1848 had promoted the Czechs to the front rank in the Slav liberation movement; from then onwards it was Prague to which the other Slavs under the monarchy came to learn, from the Czech example, the lessons of organized resistance. The country with the most advanced economic development and the most diversified society became a model for the Slovenes, Serbs and Croats of the empire. It was in Bohemia that Heinrich Fügner and Dr Miroslav Tyrs, in 1862, started organizing gymnastic clubs, the *Sokols* (Falcons), whose red shirts were a deliberate echo of Garibaldi. This youth movement spread to the other Slav countries under Austrian rule and provided the struggle for freedom with enthusiastic recruits. Serbian and Bulgarian contingents took part in the first great Congress of Sokols, held in Prague in 1912.

From a People to a Nation: Slovakia in Transition
Slovakia, with no independence on which to look back, no experience of life as an organized state, was an integral part of the kingdom of Hungary; at the beginning of the nineteenth century it was still only potentially a nation. However, despite being isolated, mountainous and almost entirely agricultural, the country had shared in the acceleration of economic life which mared the eighteenth century. Artisan families developed and prospered, their wares being carried by pedlars beyond the Slovakian borders into Moravia and Bohemia, to which Slovakia was intimately linked by community of culture and similarities of language. Contact between Bohemia-Moravia and Slovakia was naturally strong round Bratislava, a region where communications were good and the towns numerous; notable among the latter was Bratislava itself, the centre of the region's intellectual life, with Protestant schools staffed by graduates of German universities who were to train some of the most prominent leaders of the Slav renaissance, including Šafařik and J. Kollre, who were Slovaks, and the Moravian Palacký (map 20).

Prior to their emergence as a nation the Slovaks spoke their local dialects. The official language of the Hungarian kingdom was Latin. The educated Slovaks, of whom there were few, regarded Prague as the centre of their scheme of things; and when in the early nineteenth century Antonin Bernolak, himself of Slovakian birth, composed the first grammar and dictionary of his native tongue he chose the western dialect of Slovakia, that with the closest resemblance to Czech, as his literary medium. His efforts were received with indifference. The Slovakian people had been subjected by the Hungarians to a policy of deliberate persecution, culminating in the decree of 1847 by which Magyar became the country's only official language; this caused the Slovakian patriots to pick on the dialect of central Slovakia, which was less similar to Czech, as their weapon of resistance.

This linguistic separatism did not extinguish the community of culture between the Czechs and Slovaks, but it inevitably encouraged the enthusiasm then developing for the study of things Slovakian, the country's history, popular traditions and folksongs. This was the period of that towering personality, the patriot Ludovit Štur (1815–56), a Protestant who defended the language and its use in education; and of such literary pioneers as the poets Samo Chalúpka (1812–83) and Janko Kral (1822–76).

Czech Culture

The failure of the 1848 revolution, the persecution which followed it, and the establishment in 1867 of an Austro-Hungarian monarchy under which the Slavs were denied the position they wanted, were powerless to break the national movement; it had progressed too far. The Czech nation no longer had to demonstrate its existence. The high quality of its civilization was attested by a growing profusion of art and literature. Nearly all of the latter was inspired by patriotic feeling and affection for the people; subject-matter was provided by Czech history, the peasants' beliefs and customs, and the Bohemian landscape. Examples are Vitězslav Halek (1835–74), who wrote epics, travel books and lyrics; Jan Neruda (1834–91), a poet who became the intellectual guide of Czech youth (*Cosmic Songs*, 1878) and edited the newspaper *Narodny Listy* (*National Pages*), and whose *Good Friday Songs*, published posthumously, voice the sufferings of his country; and Alois Jirašek (1851–1930), whose historical novels evoke the Hussite wars and the nation's resistance to foreign domination.

Halek and Neruda belonged to the 'May generation' (so called after the title of the Almanach published in 1858, and of a poem by Neruda). During the 'seventies a cosmopolitan Czech literature began emerging from the swaddling bands of German influence; a literary tendency which looked to the west, especially France, and whose pioneer was Jaroslav Vrchlicky (1853–1912), a poet and prolific translator who enlarged the Bohemian literary horizon and, like Julius Zeyer (1841–1901), worked for the periodical *Lumir*. Simultaneously an attitude of direct involvement in the nation's life and struggle was exemplified by Svatopluk Cech (1846–1908), an epic poet whose patriotic verse was enthusiastically received and who also expressed 'the anger of the proletariat, bowed under the burden of omnipotent capital' (Denis), in his *Songs of a Slave* (1895). Towards the end of the century, realism and naturalism came to the fore in the books of Joseph Svatopluk Machar (1869–1942) and Petr Bezruč (1867–1958). The writings of Franz Kafka (1883–1924) are full of a morbid sensibility and express a more personal reaction to a complex and oppressive material world; they have exerted considerable literary influence, notably in France (figure 35).

Czech literature is deeply tinged with democratic feeling, social struggle, positivism and, in some cases, anti-clericalism. It mirrors the dramatic predicament – the aspirations, the fight for life – of the Czech people; and except when evoking the glories of the past, it becomes shrouded in melancholy. All Czech writers seem to be more or less committed to something or other, *engagés*. Some of them alternate between anarchism and constructive socialism, for example Kostak Neumann (1875–1947). On the eve of the Great War, literary life in Bohemia, though overshadowed and eroded by fears for the national future, was equipped with every form of expression and thought and linked with the literary life of the Western countries.

In all the arts the Czechs had a noteworthy contribution to make. Joseph Mánes (1820–74), Bohemia's great classical painter, portrayed the working life of the people and, like his successor Mikolas Aleš (1852–1912), evoked the Hussite period, which also provided subject-matter for Jaroslav Cermak (1830–78). Adolph Kosarek (1830–59) painted landscapes; Venceslas Brožik (1851–1901), scenes from everyday life. But where the Czechs particularly triumphed was in music; several of their composers became world-famous.

The Czech school of composers begins with Bedřich Smetana (1824–84), a political exile, who evoked a happy, boisterous Bohemia in *The Bartered Bride* (1866) and the country's historical and legendary past in his other operas (*Dalibor* and *Libuse*) and his cycle of symphonic poems, *My Country*. Nostalgia for his distant homeland inspired the *New World Symphony* of Anton Dvořák (1841–1904); in his *Dances* and operas (*Russalka*) he drew on folk-tradition. Ždenek Fibich (1850–1910), at the turn of the century and after, worked in the tradition of Smetana, as did Leos Janaček (1854–1928), a representative example of the type of composer nurtured in the social environment of a village shcoolmaster; a man of the people. Meanwhile a younger generation of composers was emerging who were to make their names after the First World War: Joseph Bohuslav Foerster (1859–1951), Vítézslav Novák (1870–1949), Joseph Suk (1874–1935), and Otokar Ostrčil (1879–1935).

The past springs to life in Czech music, whose heritage of anthems, hymns and folksong goes back as far as the Hussite epoch and the counter-reformation and, with Church support, was kept alive in the villages by

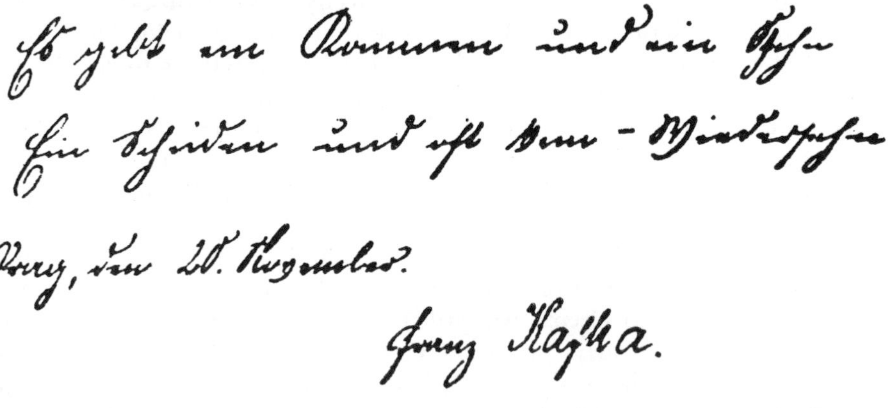
Es gibt ein Kommen und ein Gehn
Ein Scheiden und oft kein – Wiedersehn

Prag, den 20. November.

Franz Kafka.

FIGURE 35 First known MS of Franz Kafka, dated 1898, in Hugo Bergmann's album.

schoolmasters who were also precentors. Before Bohemia set up its official musical institutions (a goal that Smetana had much at heart), it was in this milieu, half-lay, half-ecclesiastical and essentially popular, that the vocation and talents of future musicians were discovered and encouraged.

From the time of the national renaissance the entire population was alive to national ideals. The intellectual young, who were enthusiastic and ardently patriotic, devoted themselves passionately to the furthering of popular culture; choirs and amateur dramatic societies were formed everywhere, with the object of encouraging a taste for Czech music and theatre. Their influence was greatest in the towns; in the country it was gymnastic clubs on the lines of the Sokols which mainly contributed to the cult of patriotism. The National Theatre, 'the temple of the Czech renaissance', founded in 1868 and rebuilt by Žitek (1832–1909), almost the only great Bohemian architect before Jan Kotera (1871–1923), and decorated by Julius Mařak (1832–99), Vojtech Hynais (1854–1925) and František Ženišek (1849–1916), demonstrated the wealth and variety of artistic talent at Bohemia's disposal. Only sculpture remained under the influence of Viennese romanticism. Myslbek (1848–1922) was the pioneer in whose work it began to throw off its chains and produce original creations based on Bohemia's past (the Wenceslas monument).

Most of the sculptors' work, however, was executed for municipalities, societies and institutions anxious to keep alive the memory of Bohemia's famous men. During the late nineteenth and early twentieth century, the public squares in Prague were provided with busts and statues of the 'Awakeners' of the Czech nation.

III PREMONITIONS OF THE FUTURE

The Germans in Recession

This brilliant picture had its dark patches. For all their enthusiasm, the patriots were somewhat sceptical of the chances for Czech political liberty in any near future. The power of the monarchy was one obstacle; another was the preponderance of the Germans in the economic field. The leaders of the liberation movement refused at first to have anything to do with the Parliament of Vienna but took their seats in it from 1879 onwards; behind the immediate political hurly-burly, however, the motto they adopted was that appearing on the title-page of the first volume of the *Great Czech Encyclopaedia*, inaugurated in that year: 'Our salvation lies in persevering toil.'

During this period the Czechs benefited both from favourable demographic conditions and from the recent development of the market. The ratio of Germans to Czechs was still falling, especially in the towns. In 1900 there were nearly 4,000,000 Czech-speaking inhabitants in the province of Bohemia as against 2,400,000 German-speakers. But in the big towns like Plzen and Brno the balance was altering in the Czechs' favour, and by 1910 Prague had only 35,000 Germans as against 538,000 Czechs.

The effect of this demographic pressure became manifest in the gradual capture of important positions on the economic front. The first phase of the industrial revolution, up to 1870, which was characterized by the growth of the textile industries, had benefited the German bourgeoisie almost exclusively. After 1870 an expanding market had caused the establishment or extension of a great variety of industries, particularly the manufacture of beverages and foodstuffs (breweries, sugar refineries, flour mills, etc.), started in many cases by Czechs who had recently risen to middle-class status and were closely in touch with the agricultural world, which was entirely Czech.

The Prague Exhibition of 1891 showed that Czech production was not confined to peasant crafts but included the most modern types of industrial manufacture.

The rise of the Czech bourgeoisie strengthened the foundations of the national movement. In the years following the Austro-Hungarian Compromise, the police measures taken by the government in Vienna – measures whose accumulation between 1867 and 1873 was recorded in *The Lamentations of the Crown of Bohemia* – provoked the Czechs into holding secret meetings in the open countryside; the years 1868–71 were the period of the so-called 'Tabors'. After 1867 the relatively conservative side of Czech patriotism began losing its influence; Austro-Slavism was discredited. Palacký died in 1876. The radical Young Czech Party, which appeared in the Bohemian Diet in 1874 and the Parliament of Vienna in 1879, triumphed in the 1891 elections. The two problems confronting Bohemia, namely German expansion and Austro-Hungarian federalism, merged into an ever keener struggle between Czechs and Germans.

The 'eighties brought a change: the political struggle was no longer carried on exclusively by the middle classes. Most middle-class people had gradually come over to the idea of an independent Bohemia, which presupposed the destruction of Austria–Hungary. The Czech deputies in the Parliament of Vienna were still known as the Young Czechs, but this had become merely a token designation: new middle-class parties were taking shape and one of these, the Czech National Party, was to give birth in 1899 to the Realist Party, whose numbers were small but which, through its leader Masaryk, was to play a vital part in the creation of Czechoslovakia during the First World War. Meanwhile, however, industrial development was striding ahead and the proletariat was growing in proportion. The May Day demonstrations in 1890, the disturbances of 1893–6 in Prague, and more particularly the strike of 60,000 miners in 1900, showed how strong the proletariat was. A Social Democratic Party had been founded in 1888. In the countryside, the progress of education had kept pace with that of agriculture, so that even before the First World War there was no illiteracy in Bohemia, an exceptional state of affairs for the Slav countries. An Agrarian Party had been started. Universal suffrage was established by the electoral reform of 1907 and enabled the people's representatives to participate legally in politics.

The recognition of Bohemia's political life by the Rescript of 12 September 1871 did nothing to improve the prospects for Czech national independence. Nor did the Language Decree of 19 April 1880 meet the needs of the Czechs, who were in the majority and whose intellectual level was high. Of greater importance was the inauguration in Prague, in 1882, of a Czech University which opened with 1,000 students and had risen to 3,000 (twice as many as the German University) by 1900. From 1890 onwards the issue dominating all electoral contests was the 'Punctations', a government plan for splitting Bohemia into two administrative zones, one Czech, the other German; but this geographical share-out of national rights was violently opposed by the Young Czechs, and the project was a help to them in winning the election. In an atmosphere of mounting tension caused by the spread of Pangermanism, a concession on the government's part in 1897 – a decree that all legal proceedings be conducted in the language of the plaintiff – was greeted with a storm of indignation from the Germans of Bohemia and aroused violent reactions in Germany itself.

Czech nationalism was now no longer simply an internal political question of the empire; the German nationalism it faced was supported from outside; Pangermanism, by indirect pressure on the government in Vienna, was striving to prevent any concessions to Czech demands, and to strengthen the resistance of the Germans living in Bohemia. When, in 1907, the weight of the working-class vote was thrown into politics, social issues became more prominent than before; but this, in so far as it was a matter of Czech peasants and workers urging their demands on German landlords and employers, did nothing to soothe the conflict of nationalities.

Independence and Revolution
The Bohemian and Slovakian proletariat was profoundly stirred by what happened in Russia from 1905 to 1907. The path of socialism, even more effectively than that of nationalism, would lead to the destruction of despotic empires and the economic system enforced by them. But this prospect, uncertain enough in itself, was rendered yet more remote by the partial failure of the first Russian revolution.

In the years before 1914 the most urgent problem was still that of the rights of the Czech people. These rights were discussed and argued in the Bohemian Diet (which the Germans boycotted after 1908) and in newspapers, books, club and society meetings and the political parties. Fighting in the Balkans had made the international atmosphere oppressively electric, and it appeared increasingly certain that Bohemia's future would depend on the outcome of a war whose imminence everyone could feel, and in which the existence of the Austro-Hungarian Empire would be at stake. Bohemia's two ethnic groups had arrived at deadlock, and the Czechs rallied to independence as the only possible solution. The prospect of a sovereign Czech state was a perspective in which the ideals of most of the

Czech patriots were fittingly represented by the sociologist T.G.Masaryk (1850–1937), whose whole political career from 1899 onwards had been committed to the struggle for independence. The Austro-Hungarian Empire having collapsed, the new state was founded in 1919; it included Slovakia, which was culturally so close to Bohemia and had shared Bohemia's struggles. For defence against German imperialism, Czechoslovakia relied on help from the bourgeois democracies of the West.

Individuality of Slovakia

After the suppression of the Hungarian rebellion Slovakia was subjected for a time to a limited amount of Germanization, but the comparatively liberal policy of the Viennese government largely prevented the treatment from taking effect. In 1863 a patriotic association was founded, the *Matice slovenska* (The Hive), with headquarters in the small town of Turčanski Svaty Martín, which had been selected as the token capital of a putative independent Slovakia. But from 1867 the Slovaks were exposed to an intensive process of Magyarization which was facilitated by the economic advances going on at the time. The mountains ensured that most of the country remained as isolated as ever, but the small towns on the plain were now connected with the outside world by the railway, which got as far as Košice in 1873. The middle classes were doing well out of stock-raising and animal products, and were tending to go Magyar. In the eyes of the Hungarian government the Slovakian language simply did not exist; the Slovaks were Hungarian subjects who spoke a Slovakian dialect. The use of Hungarian was compulsory in almost everything except primary education, and was supported by a campaign of denationalization to which every possible encouragement was given. The *Matice slovenska* was dissolved in 1875.

The Slovakian people's language and rights were defended by a handful of middle-class intellectuals, by the minor Catholic clergy, who stubbornly held their own against the Hungarian bishops, and, above all, by the Protestant pastors and their flock, many of whom were being sent money by relations who had emigrated to the United States. The Slovakian patriots turned for moral support to Prague, whose links with Slovakia were strengthened by the Czech University founded in 1882, which attracted Slovakian scholars and students. With Hungarian and Austrian culture looming over them, the Slovakians developed an independent intellectual and artistic life during the 'sixties; the country began to have its own writers, painters and scholars. In verse, one of the most prominent figures was the father of Slovakian poetry, a singer of the country and its people, Pavel Orszvagh Hviedoslav (1849–1921), and Martin Kukučin (1860–1928) was correspondingly eminent in prose.

14

The Balkans
Halfway to Liberation

DURING the nineteenth century the political life of the South Slav peoples underwent a transformation. All of them experienced a national renaissance; some achieved independence, the rest drew hope from the certainty of independence to come. All over Europe the subject peoples were carried away by a great tide of national feeling, the South Slavs no less than anyone else. Early in the century, the traditional resistance of the Serbian peasants of the Šumadija to Turkish overlordship suddenly expanded; after a protracted insurrection, the Sultan conceded the autonomy of a miniature Serbia which was recognized as a principality in 1830, became independent *de jure* in 1878 and a kingdom in 1882. Fifty years after the insurrection a slight enlargement of the new state was rendered possible by the Russo-Turkish war of 1877–8. But the biggest change resulting from this war was the partial liberation of the Bulgars: Bulgaria became an autonomous principality, and the Bulgarian people were brought together in a single territory when eastern Rumelia was added in 1885; the independence of their country was recognized in 1908.

Meanwhile the incipient break-up of the Ottoman Empire, and the rise of two new Slav states, were turning the Balkans into a cockpit for the diplomatic rivalries of Europe. The Russian Empire, which had supported the Serbs and Bulgars in turn, clashed with the Austro-Hungarian, whose economic interests and ethnic composition produced an aggressive Austro-Slavism driving down towards the Mediterranean. In 1878 Austria occupied Bosnia and Herzegovina (which she annexed in 1908) and the *sanjak* of Novi Pazar, the key-position between Bosnia and Macedonia (this, however, she subsequently handed back to the Turks). Finally the two Balkan Wars of 1912–3, in which the Turks were thrown out of nearly all of the Balkan peninsula but which left the victors fighting each other over the division of Macedonia, confirmed Serbia's dominant position and confined Bulgaria within the narrow limits of her ethnic frontiers.

I THE NORTHERN SECTOR: VIENNA AND BUDAPEST

Illyrianism: Decline and Fall of a Dream
Among Croatian intellectuals, Illyrianism was the form assumed by the thirst for independent nationhood. The seeds of the doctrine had been sown

by an ephemeral creation of Napoleon's, an Illyria comprising Dalmatia and part of Croatia: after Napoleon's fall the importance of Zagreb and the force of Croatian nationalism perpetuated the Illyrian concept as an ideal for the Yugoslav peoples, an ideal based on a shared language.

Ljudevit (Louis) Gaj (1809–72), who was a follower of Šafařik and deeply imbued with Panslavism, laid the foundations of Illyrianism where the linguistic side was concerned. In 1835 he started a Croatian newspaper, with a supplement entitled *The Morning Star: Croatian, Slavonic, Dalmatian*. After much wavering between the various forms of Croatian the one he chose was the *što*-dialect, which was closest to the Serbian spoken north of the Danube. He gave it a Latin alphabet, the result being a literary medium available to Serbs and Croats alike, which could be written with either Latin or Cyrillic characters. Meanwhile the Croatian national awakening went on; reading-rooms were being opened, theatrical performances were being given in Croatian; another development, outside the literary realm, was the forming of an economic association by middle-class Croats who were anxious to foster industrial growth and their own banking accounts.

Gaj was never able to rally the South Slavs as a whole to the banner of Illyrianism; he encountered much hostility in Slovenia, whose dialects differed greatly from Croatian, and in Dalmatia, where the intellectual élite spoke Italian. The language of officialdom varied from region to region – it might be Latin, Hungarian, Italian or German; and the aristocracy were foreigners by extraction (German or Italian) and Magyars by culture. In this situation Illyrianism, as a programme for effecting Croatia's national resurgence, restored the traditions of the people, their language and costume and customs, to their true worth; and incidentally brought regional differences into prominence. And though it had originated in the linguistic and literary field, Illyrianism as an attempt to unify the South Slav peoples soon gave rise to territorial claims and the aggressive Croatian self-aggrandisement which ultimately caused its downfall. But the lifework of Gaj, by bringing the Serbs and Croats closer together, also paved the way for the eventual unity of Yugoslavia.

Croatian Literature

The impetus of the defunct Illyrian movement survived in the South Slav peoples' efforts towards an *entente* which, after the Austro-Hungarian Compromise of 1867, became the goal of Bishop Josip Juraj Strossmayer, the founder of the Yugoslav Academy of Zagreb. Croatia, whose officially recognized autonomy meant little or nothing, went its own way; as a relatively advanced country, whose aristocracy supported the Hungarian government but whose urban lower middle class were nationalists, it provided suitable conditions for the growth of a literature reflecting the problems of the day: such problems as relations with the empire, Slav solidarity, Croatian nationalism, social antagonism, the drift to the towns, and the creation of a modern attitude to life.

13

After the wave of romanticism represented by Mirko Bogović (1816–93), Luka Botić (1830–63) and Janko Jurković (1827–89), realism made its appearance with August Šenoa (1838–81), who, in addition to editing a review, *The Crown*, was a poet, critic and descriptive writer who portrayed Croatian society, depicted the class-conflicts of the sixteenth century, and dominated the literature of his time. An equally ardent patriotism, though more sentimental in tone, is expressed in the historical novels of Josip Eugen Tomić (1843–1916).

Realism, under Russian and French influence, swept the board in the eighties. Evgenij Kumičić (1850–1904), however, remained faithful to the patriotic romantic tradition.

The opposite is true of Ante Kovačić (1854–99), Josip Kozarac (1858–1906) and Vjenceslav Novák (1859–1905), whose works picture the transformation of society by modern economic conditions, analysing the psychology of the *déracinés*, the newcomers to urban life, and exposing the poverty and wretchedness of the workers. Critical and revolutionary thought also found a voice in poetry; but the only figure to stand out from a host of mediocre poets is Silvije Strahimire Kranjčević (1865–1908), a pessimistic observer of an imperfect society.

Violent political upheavals after 1895 had forced young people to complete their education at foreign universities, from which they returned in the early days of the twentieth century with their minds enriched by a knowledge of European literature and, if they had spent their time in Prague, by the teaching of Masaryk.

A fever of modernism brought out a rash of magazines devoted to literary research and criticism, a noted example being the *Sovremenik*, which was edited by Branimir Livadić (1871–1949) and took the place of the *Vijenac* in 1903. The dominating note in a medley of tendencies was pessimism, an impulse to fall back on art and leave political and social preoccupations to others. Patriotism nevertheless still functioned as a source of literary inspiration, even for the poet Antun Gustav Matoš (1873–1914), who wrote in exile and became one of the masters of the younger generation, and more particularly in the case of Valdimir Nazor (1876–1949), who dominated the literary scene with his abundant output and vigorous national feeling. The works of the best of the younger prose-writers, Dinko Simunović (1873–1933), show much affection for the Dalmatian peasants, whose way of life was threatened by urban proliferation. The social changes going on in Croatia, which benefited from progress in the empire generally despite failing to achieve any genuine independence, can be inferred from the period's writing. But this literary harvest, though varied and full of individuality and flavour, had largely ceased to play any part in political life.

Birth of a Nation: the Slovenes

The Reformation had caused a vernacular literature to spring up among the Slovenes; the restoration of Catholicism in the seventeenth and eighteenth centuries had tended to discourage it. But religion could make headway only by appealing to regional patriotism; hence the consciousness of possessing an indigenous culture owed much to Church propaganda and the writings of Bishop Thomas Hren (who lived in the first half of the seventeenth century).

Towards the end of the eighteenth century some of the Slovenian intelligentsia began emancipating themselves from clerical influence. Literary circles arose, among them that of the baron and art-patron Zigo Cojz, one of whose members was the poet Valentin Vodnik (1758–1819). A Slovenian newspaper was published at Ljubljana from 1797 to 1800. During the Napoleonic period the Slovenes had their own schools and, surrounded as they were by Teutonic culture, were (as Vodnik expressed it) 'no longer content with little'. But, as elsewhere, the romantic movement was the decisive factor in the national awakening.

The Slovenian intellectuals, confronted by Pan-Slav ambitions and Croatian Illyrianism, were obliged to justify the existence of their own language, still in process of being built up as a literary medium. This was the point at issue in the controversy between Kopitar and the great Slovenian poet France Prešren (1800–49). Slovenian literature developed rapidly under the guidance of Prešren (whose *Garland of Sonnets* was published in 1846) and his friend Matija Cop (1797–1838), who wrote the first history of that literature; *The News* was founded by Janez Bleiweis in 1847; the poetry of Simon Jenko (1835–59) made its appearance; and the true founders of Slovenian prose, Josip Jurčić (1844–81), Josip Stritar (1873–1923) and Janez Trdina (1830–1905), wrote their novels.

The guiding preoccupations of these and other writers were Slovenian national aims and the description of Slovenian life, whose traditions were threatened by the steady advance of the Teutons; indeed, its very existence was in danger. The former living-space of the Slovenes had been much reduced by the Austrians' gradual drive to the south. The Slovenian population was a bloc of a mere million and a half, concentrated for the most part in Carniola, round Ljubljana; there were also Slovenian minorities tucked in between the islands of German colonization in Styria and Carinthia. The towns were dominated by the Austrian middle class; their architecture, their officials' uniforms and their way of life were all Teutonic. However, the authorities did not suppress the activities of the Slovenian intelligentsia, who wrote works in the regional tongue and distributed them in the country, gradually achieving publicity for their claim that, within the empire, the Slovenes had a right to a cultural life of their own.

During the second half of the nineteenth century, the literary movement was closely connected with political activity inspired by regional feeling. There were two trends, associated respectively with a liberal minority and a conservative and clerical majority; the first was more dynamic and got more done, the second was moderate and, being under Church direction, had to keep its peace with the Vatican as well as Vienna, and played down the animosity of the broad mass of the Slovenian people towards German landlords in the country and German capitalists in the towns. Both trends, and even the competition between them, contributed to the growth of national consciousness.

The Slovenes' defence of their culture and way of life was characterized by migration in opposite directions: many members of the rural proletariat emigrated (there were 25,000 Slovenes in Cleveland in 1910), others moved into the towns of Slovenia itself. After 1870 the younger generation, being more patriotic and also better educated than its predecessors, strengthened the ranks of the Slovenian urban middle class, previously represented almost entirely by intellectuals. Although legislation fostered the teaching of German at the expense of Slovenian, the population as a whole benefited from the high quality of the educational system; of all the South Slav peoples the Slovenes had the lowest illiteracy rate (3 per cent of the under-twenties in 1910).

The press, whose main interests were two, namely political and literary, was divided, like the public it served, into two groups, liberal and conservative. And there was plenty of it – no less than a hundred and twenty-two papers in 1914.

The Slovene's moderate demands were voiced in the *tabors*, popular assemblies which were the vestigial survival of an ancient tradition, bringing the people of town and country together and giving the national movement a more or less democratic flavour. Patriotic propaganda permeated the athletic clubs which played such an active part in the political life of the Slavs under Austro-Hungarian rule. As a counterblast to the *Sokols* (Falcons), founded in 1863, the clergy started the *Orli* (Eagles) in 1903.

But although the national movement was acquiring a broader social base it never won the concessions it sought from the empire. The prevailing literary atmosphere before the First World War was one of dejection and pessimism; meanwhile the political climate was hardening, and among the members of the Slovenian Renascence Association there were proponents of total independence who no longer drew the line at acts of violence.

The Voivodina and the Rise of Serbia

Among the Serbs of Hungary, whose material and cultural level was higher than that of the Serbs under the Ottoman yoke, a precocious national renaissance, connected both with the Enlightenment and with 'Josephism' paved the way for the emancipation which the Serbs of the Šumadija were to wrest from the Turks during the first third of the nineteenth century. With the intention of offsetting Russian influence, which from the time of Peter the Great had become preponderant in both literature and art among the Serbs of southern Hungary, Joseph II's policy of enlightened despotism encouraged the printing of Serbian books and the establishment of Serbian schools. The first Serbian secondary school was founded in 1791, the year after his death, and the first Serbian newspaper appeared in Vienna in the same year. Behind all this lay a secret hope that the Hungarian Serbs, who were Orthodox, might be swung over to the Uniates and hence in effect to Rome. Joseph II's attitude brought him the support of educated people and also of the lower middle class, both of whom were attracted by his policy of economic development and his opposition to the Turks, which enabled him to figure as the defender of Balkan Christendom.

The Serbs of Hungary, whose demands were resisted by the government in Vienna as well as by the Hungarians, failed to get permission to govern their own territory. However, they enjoyed civic rights and freedom of worship; they already had writers who glorified Serbia's past and extolled her future liberation (*The History of Serbia*, by Jovan Rajić); and they were full of baroque influence, expressed in the luxuriance of their churches. It was they who supplied the cultural weapons in the struggle against the Turks in the early years of the nineteenth century.

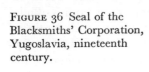

FIGURE 36 Seal of the Blacksmiths' Corporation, Yugoslavia, nineteenth century.

During the first half of that century, intellectual life continued to burgeon in the region which was briefly promoted (1848–58) to autonomous existence as the Voivodina. The year 1826 saw the founding of the *Matica srpska* (a literary society and publishing house combined) and of newspapers whose patriotic aims were reflected in their titles (*The Serbian People's Page*, *The Serbian People's Journal*). There were talented writers and painters. People of advanced taste abandoned the baroque, a western importation which had been all the fashion in Joseph II's time, and steered architecture and painting towards a simplicity which was closer to the spirit of the folk. Within the limits imposed on these developments by the clergy, who were wedded to tradition, and the Imperial Court, which was distrustful, the Voivodina continued to be indispensable as a cultural nucleus for the divided Serbian nation.

II THE ISTANBUL SECTOR

Serbia's Progress towards Independence
The long war of liberation which forced the Ottomans to countenance a miniature autonomous Serbia, on whose throne the Karageorgevitch

dynasty was succeeded by the Obrenovitch, was accompanied by a creative effort on the institutional side, to which the Serbs of Hungary made a decisive contribution. Since 1808 there had been a training school for civil servants in Belgrade, whose teachers were Serbians from the Banat. Karageorge's children's tutor was Dositej Obradović (1739–1811), who was born in the Temesvar district, wrote books in the language of the people, and was 'the founder of modern Serbian'. The Serbia of 1835, with 700,000 inhabitants, had 60 schools containing 2,500 pupils. In 1859 there were 352, of which 15 were girls' schools. A secondary school was opened in Belgrade in 1855.

Some of the forms assumed by the national fervour which gripped the country after liberation were religious. Churches and monasteries were being repaired or rebuilt even while the fighting was still going on. But it was during the reign of Miloš Obrenovič, in the midst of internal struggles between the liberal spirit of the intelligentsia from the Voivodina and the Turkish-style despotism of the sovereign, that the foundations of Serbia's cultural development were laid: schools and hospitals were built, an Orthodox seminary, a printing house and a theatre were set up, an official gazette started coming out, and the National Library and National Museum were founded. It was during this epoch that Vuk Karadžič (1787–1864), a patriot and self-educated man, collected folk epics, legends and songs, compiled a Serbian dictionary (1818), worked out a new spelling, and, 'breaking with the artificial idiom of Church Slavonic', wrote in a language which most of the South Slavs could understand. The adoption of the *što*-dialect as a written language by Serbs and Croats simultaneously, and its recognition as their common language in 1850, became, despite political divergences, the determining element in the history of the South Slavs on both sides of the Austro-Hungarian frontier.

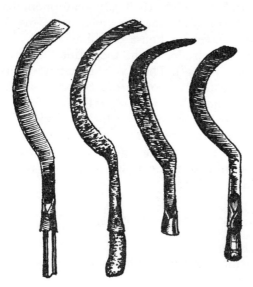

FIGURE 37 Sickles used in Yugoslavia, nineteenth century.

Autonomous Serbia was a blend of opposites: a country which had kept its popular traditions and way of life (figures 36, 37 and 38) but whose political leaders after 1830, educated in German, Austrian or French universities, were striving to organize it as a modern state. The most active of these leaders, such as Ilya Garašanin, the 'man of the reforms', were ex-pupils of the Faculty of Law in Paris (and were known as 'the Parisians').

In the villages, where each thatched, plastered, lime-washed house stood in its own plot of ground, a family might number anything from thirty to sixty people, working in common under the absolute authority of its senior members, who met in a council, the *skupe*, and administered the affairs of the whole under the leadership of a *staresina*. The *skupe* also constituted the municipal council in large communes, whose leader was a *knet* (mayor). The sense of local independence was extremely strong, and in the process by which the country's constitutional arrangements were hammered out during the nineteenth century, the demands of the various parties were often really just those of large clans with wide regional influence.

This closely-knit familial structure was compatible with a high degree of liberty: marriage was free, depending solely on mutual consent, and there was no control over the bequeathing of movable property. There was also much freedom in religion, and an admixture of picturesque pagan customs; on Midsummer Eve, for instance, if there was a drought, a girl wearing nothing but flowers, grass and leaves was escorted through the village by the peasants while other girls and women, walking with her, invoked the sun and moon and begged for rain. It was during this post-liberation period that the country's inheritance of folk-song (*pesme*), hitherto a matter of purely oral tradition, was recorded in writing – changing somewhat in the process – and became fuel for both literary and political romanticism.

Serbian Literature and the Patriotic Movement

Devotion to the past and to Serbia characterized the writing of the Serbs in the nineteenth century: a literature reflecting the life and vicissitudes of a people which history had torn asunder, and of which only one portion had won its fight for freedom. Petar Petrovič Njegos (1813–51) depicted

FIGURE 38
Plough in use in Yugoslavia during the second half of the nineteenth century.

Montenegrin life and the great deeds of the Karageorgevitch family in his poems; he was at the same time the political and religious leader of the Montenegrins, who were independent in fact if not on paper and were defending their freedom against the Turks at the point of the sword. Another romantic poet, his contemporary, Branko Radićevič (1824–53), was the first writer to employ the new language and spelling. The plays of Jovan Stenja Popvić (1806–56) portrayed the customs and behaviour of the Serbian middle class.

Literature kept time with its guiding force, the varying pulse of national feeling. The initial romantic upsurge favoured poetry; the leading figures during this phase were Jura Jakšić (1832–78), Laza Kostić (1841–1910) and, in particular, Jovan Jovanović Zmaj (1839–1904), whose patriotic aspirations took on a religious complexion and were recited like prayers:

Lord, tell us that Thy anger is appeased and that Thou hast pardoned our transgressions.
Lord, put an end to the torments of the sons of Lazarus, the martyr of Kossovo.
Lord, restore unto us the place that is ours in the midst of the nations, and deliver us from the Turks and the Shvabé [Germans].

After the disappointments of the 'fifties, romanticism as a source of poetic inspiration dried up; the lyricism of Radićevič did, however, find a latter-day resurrection in the work of Vojislav Ilić (1862–94). Realistic prose with a progressive social bias, a *genre* initiated by Svetozar Marković (1846–75), who lived and wrote abroad but became the guide of the younger generation of writers, was the new instrument of the national renaissance.

This was the period when less of the writing produced came from outside the free Principality of Serbia than had been the case hitherto. The new state had its own writers, various both in temperament and political orientation, but almost unanimous in their determination to convey the reality of Serbian life both past and present. The exiled Josa Ignatović (1814–88) wrote novels about peasant poverty; so did Milovan Glisič (1847–1908), a disciple of Marković. The novels of Svetolik Ranković (1863–99) deliberately seek the gloomy side of life and turn a critical eye on the idealized heroes of Serbian national history and the Orthodox monks. Laza Lazarević (1851–90) wrote nostalgic evocations of the past; Janko Vesselinović (1862–1905), of an idyllic rustic present. Stevan Stremač (1855–1906) accepted society as he found it and portrayed it amusingly.

The early twentieth century was a new chapter in the story of Serbia's progress as a nation. After the *coup d'état* of 1903 she concluded political alliances with the West, and intellectuals both young and old who had studied in France came to the fore in consequence. Writers, as hitherto, were preoccupied by two things: hope for the complete liberation of the Slavs, and the problems of contemporary society. The poet Aleksa Šantić (1868–1924) was distressed by the sufferings of those (and they were many)

who were compelled to emigrate to find a living; so was the novelist Ivo
Cippico (1807–1923); a more important member of the same category was
Peter Kočič (1877–1916), whose sharp anti-Austrian feeling suffuses his
description of the Bosnian peasants. At the same time, however, western
influence, combined with the uncertainty and oppressive disenchantment
of the contemporary scene, generated poetic individualism in the case of
Jovan Dučić (1874–1943) and even pessimism in that of Vladislas Petković
Diš (1880–1917) and Milan Rakić (1876–1938); the last-named was the
most important of the trio. Nor was the best prose-writer of the period,
Bora Stanković (1876–1917), exempt from this reaction; his novels and
plays reflect the anxieties of an intellectual who has difficulty in adjusting
to modern life and new conditions.

The Bulgarian Renaissance
National feeling among the Bulgars had been stifled by two kinds of domination: political, from the Turks, and religious, from the Greek clergy,

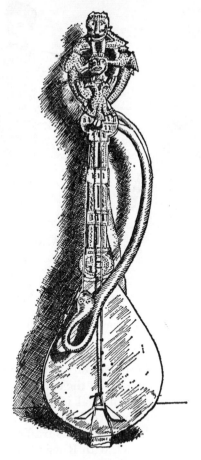

Figure 39 Njegoš's guzla, made in 1801.

who would have nothing to do with anything written in Bulgarian. In Bulgaria as in other countries, the awakening began with a historical and literary revival.

A monk on Mount Athos, Païssi, who was born near Somokov in 1722, was anxious to 'serve the Bulgar race' and wrote a *Slavo-Bulgarian History of the Peoples, Tsars and Saints of Bulgaria and of Everything which has Happened There*. The work appeared in 1762 and, though not printed till 1844, circulated in manuscript all over the country; and because it recalled Bulgaria's glorious past and the achievements of her tsars and clergy it became 'as it were the Gospel of the Bulgarian revival' (Bernard); a struggle which extended from the second half of the eighteenth century to 1878, when the Ottoman yoke was thrown off. Païssi, with his cry of 'Bulgar! know thy own race and thy language!', had condemned the Greek tyranny even more powerfully than the Turkish; it was in a religious context that the 'first murmur of the Bulgarian awakening' made itself heard.

FIGURE 40 Bulgarian costumes. *Left*, from the region of Stara Zagora. – *Right*, from the Haskovo region.

But the linguistic problem, the necessity of putting Bulgarian on its feet, was what first engrossed the patriots in the early nineteenth century. Some of these pioneers were men of unusual intellect in ecclesiastical circles, thoroughly versed in Greek culture but up in arms against militant Hellenism; others were middle-class traders trafficking over the Black Sea with Odessa and in constant touch with Russia, whose influence gradually became preponderant in Bulgaria. At the same time, the need to create schools in which the vernacular would be taught, and which therefore had to be independent of the monastic education system, gave the movement a secular tone; in spite of which its basic objective was still, in most people's eyes, the establishment of a national church.

The year 1835 saw the foundation of a school at Gabrovo which became a centre of cultural development based firmly on the Bulgarian language. The school was endowed by a wealthy merchant who was devoted to literature, Vasil Aprilov (1789–1847). The director was a Hellenist, Neophytes of Rila (1793–1881). Branches were set up in a number of towns. The awakening had now definitely begun. Much patient work by Neophytes and his assistant, Naïden Gerov (1823–1900), resulted in the grammars and dictionaries which bear their names and eventually in the formation of a literary language derived from the dialects of eastern Bulgaria. Meanwhile the memory of Bulgaria's one-time independence, an awareness of the specific and authentic quality of her culture, and the Bulgars' antagonism to Hellenism and the domination of the Turks, were begetting a polemical literature, from the famous pamphlet by Neophytes Bozneli (1785–1848), *Our Mother, Bulgaria* (first published just before the outbreak of the 1876 insurrection), to the patriotic poetry of Petko Staveïkov (1827–1897).

But it was mainly abroad that the Bulgarian people's destinies were being hammered out. The first magazine written in Bulgarian was published at Smyrna in 1844; the first newspaper, at Leipzig in 1846. And it

FIGURE 41 Bulgar costumes. *Left*, from the Harmanli region. – *Right*, from the Ikhtiman region.

was at Zagreb that the Miladinov brothers compiled their collection of Bulgaro-Macedonian folk-songs (1861). Another refuge was Rumania, where the poet and journalist George Rakovski (1821–67), 'the Bulgarian Garibaldi', guided the activities of *émigré* circles, in which capacity he was succeeded by Ljuben Karavelov (1835–79); and it was in the same country that the great poet Christo Botev (1848–76) wrote in praise of the nation's heroes. All these men were revolutionaries and romantics with socialist leanings, who regarded both literature and journalism as weapons to be used in political struggle and who, in some cases, became actively involved in that struggle themselves. Christo Botev, for example, returned to Bulgaria and fell in battle against the Turks in 1876.

By the inauguration of the Bulgarian Exarchate in 1870 the Bulgars secured the Orthodox Church in their own country and Macedonia from direct administration by the Greek Patriarchate; the final step, liberation from Ottoman rule, was eventually achieved during the period 1878–85. But the relative strength of Bulgarian and Turkish influence in the country's life had been undergoing a change since the eighteenth century as a result of the increasing prosperity of Bulgarian commerce and craft manufacture. There was less of a contrast than before between the countryside, with its little villages tucked away here and there, and the large towns, few in number and of ancient origin (Sofia, with a population of 100,000, Plovdiv, Kustendil and Varna), which contained a high percentage of Turks. Bulgarian peasants had been settling in the towns; simultaneously the villages and small towns, in which the Bulgars predominated, had been growing.

The process was slower in Macedonia: when Greece and Serbia became independent a large number of Turks moved out into the Macedonian towns, which did not acquire a Slav character until the middle part of the century.

Bulgaria before liberation was still living in the Middle Ages. The peasants cultivated the Turkish landowners' estates. Their condition had been deteriorating since the beginning of the nineteenth century: tithes and taxes had been raised, and fines were imposed after every rising; many peasants fell into debt and lost their land. The result was that a few Turkish families owned vast properties cultivated partly by tenant-farmers on a crop-sharing basis, but largely, and increasingly, by day-labourers or serfs whom the landowner could order about as he pleased.

The Orient began on the plains of Bulgaria. Transport consisted of ox-wagons constructed exclusively of wood; the driver protected his beasts in winter by rugging them up in woollen blankets, and kept them cool in summer by watering them from a wooden jug on the end of a pole. The roads were improved under the rule of Midhat Pasha (who was dismissed in disgrace in 1867), and brigandage was decreasing; but it was still possible to meet horsemen armed with revolvers and carbines, with bandoliers slung crosswise and knives in their belts. At wide intervals would be found a *khan* (an inn and staging-post combined) with a shed or stable for the horses, mules and donkeys and, for the human guests, a large room lit by unglazed windows; along one wall ran a low wide bench or divan; a flat-topped chest was the bar-counter; stew, or gruel seasoned with red pepper, was accompanied by *raki* and wine from a firkin and cask in a corner of the room.

The towns, dominated by their minarets and churches, were of Turkish appearance. The houses were built of timber and rammed earth and the streets were muddy or dusty according to season. Craft industry was very active and was organized in guilds, each with its own quarter, laid out as a bazaar: dyers, tinsmiths, turners, weavers (who made the national woollen cloth known as *shaiak*), and the busiest trades of all: the blacksmiths, tanners and furriers.

When Bulgaria became independent (1878–85) nearly all the Turks left the towns, which became wholly Bulgarian but whose population was correspondingly depleted; a deficiency offset by the new communities which developed along the railways built towards the end of the century.

Bulgaria had approximately 3,000,000 inhabitants in 1885, a fifth of whom were town-dwellers; this semi-urban character, resulting from the large number of small towns with a population of anything from 5,000 to 20,000, has persisted to the present day. In 1926 the proportion of town-dwellers was still 20 per cent and the country was still essentially agri-cultural; there were three cities with more than 50,000 inhabitants (Sofia had 213,000), two between 30,000 and 50,000, and approxi-mately fifty towns between 5,000 and 30,000, the total population being 5,483,000.

The national reawakening, prior to independence, had produced an effect only on people's minds; independence itself was followed by social changes and some degree of modernization. The departure of the Turkish landlords, who were expropriated and compensated, enabled the govern-ment to divide their estates among those already working on them. But the peasants had to purchase their new holdings by annual instalments and remained badly off in consequence.

Industry made little headway after independence; Bulgaria was still a country of small businesses. During the years preceding the First World War two factors, both fostered by the authoritarian monarchy, seemed likely to make her the future 'Japan of Eastern Europe': state investment (which was encouraged by a remarkable climate of commercial growth) and the provision of sources of credit. But the first-fruits were not imposing: in 1910 the country possessed some two hundred industrial establishments (tobacco factories, sugar refineries, flour mills and breweries) employing little more than 20,000 people. On the other hand, the liberal institutions which had been founded ensured some degree of freedom of thought, and political life was very active; the protagonists were the agrarian parties and a social-democratic movement whose influence spilled out some way be-yond the borders of the kingdom, making itself felt especially in Macedonia.

Bulgaria was no longer subject to direct pressure from Russia, to whom she owed her independence; she had a powerful army; and the appearance she presented was that of a solidly established nation, homogeneous and well-knit – but also an expansionist one, with territorial designs on Macedonia.

The changing times left their mark on culture: the heroic age was succeeded by the age of organization, and the literature of national struggle came to an end with independence. What influenced writers now was the unfolding life of the new state, which gradually obliterated the vestiges of Turkish rule, brought modern institutions into being and, in its march towards capitalism, found itself grappling with social problems not previously encountered. Memories of lost battles and reverberations from contemporary politics mingle in the poems and novels of Ivan Vazov (1850–1921); and a cult of the people, a *mystique* of the peasantry, an outlook peculiar to Bulgaria, that land of peasant smallholders, pervades the works of M.Georgiev (1854–1916), T.Vlaikov (1865–1943) and A.Strachimirov (1872–1937).

On the threshold of the twentieth century, the younger generation – among whom were those 'aristocrats of high art' (Bernard) who collected round the literary magazine *Thought* (founded in 1892) – rejected lyrical romanticism and utilitarian realism and, as in the rest of Europe, devoted themselves to the quest for formal perfection from a standpoint at once more universal and more individualistic. On the other hand, devotion to the nation's past, nostalgia for Bulgaria's former greatness and even a patriotic desire for conquest are not lacking in the compositions of the poets of the time, such as P.Stvaikov (1866–1912), 'obsessed by the insurrection of 1876' (Bernard), P.Yavorov (1878–1914), who took part in the Macedonian risings, and P.Todorov (1879–1916), who drew his inspiration from the peasants' legends.

An Ally of Serbia: Bosnia

Bosnia and Herzegovina had been divided in the past between the Serbian and Croatian kingdoms, and lay moreover on the route of southbound travellers to Constantinople; the resulting interplay of influences had left its mark on religion. At the time of the Austrian occupation in 1878, the population consisted of 500,000 Orthodox, 450,000 Muslims and 200,000 Roman Catholics. The drowsy calm of life under the Turks was soon dissipated when the Austro-Hungarian Empire drew the territory into its economic orbit: railways were built, German officials, technicians and workers came in, and life in the towns was transformed. But in the countryside things jogged along as before, in the timeless fashion depicted by Ivo Andrić in *The Bridge on the Drina*.

There was a sense of Slav solidarity throughout the region, which was ethnically Serbian and whose emotional ties were stronger with Serbia than with Croatia. The insurrection of 1875, a prelude to the Russo-Turkish war of 1887–8, had united Catholics and Orthodox against the

Ottoman Empire. After 1878 there was a pro-Serbian and anti-Austrian freedom movement supported by the Orthodox majority and the Muslim Serbs; the Catholics, except for a few intellectuals, were pro-Austrian and maintained a prudent reserve. The Austrian government's refusal to recognize that the Bosnians were more Serbian than anything else, and native efforts to defeat 'Serbianism' and work up local patriotic feeling, were powerless against a movement led by the new intelligentsia of the towns, who were in league with Belgrade. When the First Balkan War broke out in 1912, Bosnia and Herzegovina – which had been held back in a state of quasi-colonial exploitation in spite of the Constitution granted to them in 1909 – became a rendezvous for terrorists bent on victory for the Slav nationalisms they respectively supported, and on union with Serbia.

III FROM PAN-SLAVISM TO 'BALKANIZATION'

Nationalism's Motley Victory
The nineteenth-century political awakening of the Balkan Slav peoples which had been initiated by Illyrianism, and which – at any rate among the intellectuals, the minority – had kept some sort of feeling for Slav unity, developed utimately into a cultural separatism which the possession of a common language, Serbo-Croat, did little to disguise.

The Slovenes, menaced by the German presence, acquired an acute cultural self-awareness. The Croats, in their political resistance to the Hungarians, and also as a reaction against the subtler pressure exerted economically by the Germans, lived in hopes of restoring their country to its position as a fully independent state; but memories of the former 'triune' kingdom caused them to take a nationalistic, aggressive attitude towards Bosnia and weakened their resolve to ally themselves closely with the Serbs – who, however, achieved a higher degree of progress in the period preceding the First World War. Moreover, the struggle for freedom divided the Croatian nationalists into two camps, one opting for conciliation with the Austro-Hungarian Empire, in which it was hoped Croatia would be given a statute like Hungary's, the other committed to intransigence and more alive to Slav solidarity, with which the continued existence of the empire was incompatible.

Independent Serbia consolidated her position in the Balkans, extended her frontiers, and moved forward from the Turkish-style despotism of Miloš Obrenovitch's time to a comparatively liberal régime after the change of dynasty in 1903, which was hailed with approval in western Europe. To the substantial Serbian minorities still under Austrian or Hungarian rule the country represented the hope of freedom. But Serbia's Mediterranean imperialism drew her eyes to the south, beyond Macedonia, thus putting her hopelessly at loggerheads with Bulgaria. And the Bulgars, though they had successfully attained their essential national ends, were unlucky in the outcome of the wars they engaged in and persistently

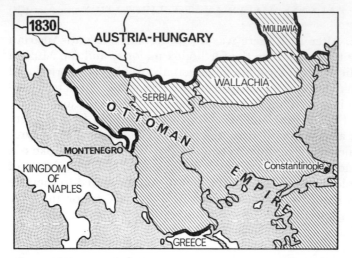

Map 21 Yugoslavia
and Bulgaria : Poli-
tical Development,
1830–1947

AUSTRIA HUNGARY TRANSYLVANIA RUMANIA CROATIA BOSNIA YUGOSLAVIA SERBIA BULGARIA DALMATIA MONTENEGRO ALBANIA Istanbul ITALY 1923 TURKEY GREECE 1919-1939

Austria-Hungary in 1913

Budapest HUNGARY 1942 Zagreb RUMANIA Bucharest CROATIA Belgrade SERBIA Sarajevo MONTENEGRO Sofia BULGARIA ITALY ALBANIA Istanbul GREECE TURKEY

AUSTRIA Budapest 1947 SLOVENIA HUNGARY Ljubljana Zagreb RUMANIA CROATIA Bucharest BOSNIA Sarajevo Belgrade SERBIA YUGOSLAVIA MONTENEGRO Sofia BULGARIA Titograd Skopje MACEDONIA ITALY Tirana ALBANIA Istanbul GREECE TURKEY 0 250 Miles

claimed those parts of Macedonia from which they were excluded as *terra irredenta*.

The ideal of unity through Pan-Slavism having been abandoned, a less ambitious idea, federalism, was obstructed by nationalistic small-mindedness on all sides. The nineteenth-century intellectuals had dreamed of a 'Yugoslav' nation covering the Balkans and the foothills of the Alps. More modest and realistic, yet not really in touch with facts and in any case as few in numbers as their predecessors, the leaders of the revolutionary parties now laboured to encourage a sense of solidarity between folk and folk and to reconcile the persistence of national characteristics with a proposed International of the peoples. But nationalism, as vigorous and uncompromising as ever, was still the ruling passion of the South Slavs (maps 21a and 21b).

Experiment in Macedonia

Geographically, Macedonia is an elevated plain dominated by mountains from 6,000 to 9,500 feet high, sloping down to the Aegean and intersected by four rivers, the Vardar, Mesta, Struma and Bystritsa (Aliakmon). Ethnically speaking it is a crossroads, the Macedonians proper being hemmed in by the Greeks of Salonica, the Bulgars of the Pirin mountains, the Serbs to the north and Albanians to the west. The Macedonians are differentiated from their neighbours by characteristics both ethnic and linguistic (though the language is in fact fairly close to Bulgarian); and their national consciousness was stimulated during the nineteenth century by friction with Greek influence and Turkish dominion.

In its earliest days the Macedonian patriotic movement was hardly distinguishable from the Bulgarian, just as the Macedonian dialects were closer to Bulgarian than to Serbian. But, because her geographical position kept her in contact with Serbia and Greece, Macedonia was decidedly more amenable to progress. The Greek Church played a dominant part in Macedonian education. The result was that until the emergence of an autonomous Bulgaria in 1878, Macedonia was one of the busiest centres of the Bulgarian patriotic movement: as early as 1814 books in Bulgarian were published at Tetovo and Doiran, in 1838 a Bulgarian printing business was set up in Salonica by an inhabitant of Doiran, and in 1810 a Bulgarian school was founded in Veles, twenty-five years before the first Bulgarian school was started (by a Macedonian, moreover) in eastern Bulgaria. Between 1800 and 1870, 178 Bulgarian schools were created in Macedonia.

At this stage the movement was Bulgaro-Macedonian and the reawakening was purely an intellectual affair, inspired by the Bulgarian Church's opposition to the Phanariot Patriarchate of Constantinople, an opposition which had increased after the founding of the Bulgarian Exarchate in 1870. In this sense, the movement represented an internal Orthodox quarrel, parallelled and stimulated by rivalry between Greek and Macedonian merchants. Concurrently, however, the dynamics of the region's economy directed Macedonia's energies northwards. Her crops (tobacco, cotton and opium) were exported in the annual caravan which gathered at Prilep and made its way to Austria, and her commercial relations with Serbia were fairly extensive. Consequently some of the Macedonian schools, whose pupils were merchants' children, were staffed by Serbian teachers using textbooks printed in Kragujevac or Belgrade. The Greek element nevertheless still constituted the major ingredient in Macedonia's cultural life; the first Macedonian patriots (such as Dmitre Miladinov, who taught Bulgarian in a school at Okhrid) came from the part of Macedonia where Hellenism was strongest.

The creation in 1870 of the Bulgarian Exarchate, which was independent of the authority of the Phanariot Patriarchate of Constantinople, brought the Macedonians and Bulgarians even closer to each other than before; from this time forward the Macedonians' resistance was directed exclusively against Turkish rule and was carried on under the aegis of the Bulgarian Church. But the final third of the century, during which Bulgarian as a written language was being worked up, was also marked by an emergent Macedonian nationalism, a regional reaction to the opposing claims of Bulgaria and Serbia, both of which denied the existence of a Macedonian nation. This 'Macedonization' of Bulgaro-Macedonian Slav nationalism was based on support from the Macedonian shopkeepers and petty merchants, whose commercial success was making them an important element in the towns and bringing them into competition with the Bulgar merchants. The prime movers in the movement's conversion were a very small minority, an intelligentsia whose members were themselves the product of Greek education but who, by researching into folklore and publishing the material they collected, strove to define the pecularities of Macedonian as a literary language and show that it was distinct from Bulgarian.

As presented in the work of Parteni Zografski (1818–75), a pupil of Miladinov, and Kuzman Šapkarev (1834–1904), Macedonian was still merely a 'Bulgaro-Macedonian compromise', the aim being the adoption of a common language with Bulgaria without sacrificing the special characteristics of Macedonian. Georgi Pulevski (1838–94), who composed dictionaries and a Macedonian grammar, went further in the direction of Macedonian as an independent language capable of serving as the foundation-stone of Macedonian national consciousness. But these were isolated endeavours, with no immediate practical bearing. The main problem being the struggle against the Turks and the liberation of Macedonia, the Macedonian movement was slow to make autonomy its objective. It turned first towards free Serbia; hence the demonstrations of pro-Serbian feeling which occurred in Macedonia between 1878 and 1880. Next, after the founding of the Bulgarian state, the Macedonian insurgent movement sought support from Bulgaria. The 'Internal Macedonian-Andrinopolitan Revolutionary Organization' (IMRO), which was set up in 1893, started by being mainly Bulgarian in complexion, the aim of the

Macedonian patriots being an independent Macedonia which would subsequently be incorporated into Bulgaria. Gradually, however, the movement became genuinely Macedonian and, under the influence of Delčev
(1872–1903) and his circle of socialist colleagues, hostile to annexation by
the authoritarian, monarchical régime in Bulgaria. And although it was at
Sofia that the Union of Macedonian Revolutionary Social Democrats was
formed in 1894, the Union's programme was the establishment of an
independent republic of Macedonia.

Round the turn of the century Macedonia became the theatre of continuous active resistance to the Turks, marked by the risings of 1894, 1897,
1900 and 1902, and culminating in the great rebellion 'of Saint Elias' (so-
called after the saint's day on which it began) in 1903: a 'Macedonian epic'
in which Macedonia's national awareness was brought finally to birth.
Hitherto the Macedonian people had thought mainly of resisting the Turks
and had formed no precise picture of what they wanted their political
future to be. The movement's socialist leaders dreamed of a Macedonian
state which, within the framework of an international union, would be on
a brotherly footing with its neighbours and whose right to exist as a nation
would therefore never again be questioned from either side, the Serbian or
the Bulgarian. The organization received secret backing from the Bulgarian
government which, as before, was determined on annexation. The failure
of the great rising in 1903 split the revolutionary organization in half; in
their disappointment some of the leaders of the insurrection fell in with the
Bulgarian position, but the rest stuck to the programme of independence
and, in the congress they held in 1908, announced their support for a
federal union of Balkan peoples in which Macedonia would be given her
rightful place. At Skoplje two years later a social democratic group was
organized, with backing from Belgrade.

But the Macedonians were caught between two fires – Bulgaria, who regarded Macedonia as part of her national inheritance, and Serbia, whose
arguments were economic and political – and in the resulting welter they
had a hard task to disentangle and maintain their rights to a separate existence. The outcome of the Second Balkan War, in 1913, enabled a victorious Serbia to grab most of Macedonia and subject it to a process of
Serbianization which the Macedonians resisted and which, in effect,
made them still more conscious of their nationality than before.

Book Five

THE SLAVS
DRAW CLOSER
TOGETHER

1917–60

THE TERRITORIAL adjustments effected after the war brought considerable changes in the western frontiers of the former Russian empire, which was now the Union of Socialist Soviet Republics. Finland regained her independence. A resurrected Poland rejected the Curzon Line, and expanded eastwards to regain territories which had once formed part of the Polish state but whose population consisted mainly of Byelorussians and Ukrainians. Three new states, Estonia, Latvia and Lithuania were set up in the Baltic lands; these contained very small Russian minorities except in the region of Estonia's frontier with the Soviets, a broad tract of country along the River Narova (Narva) and the shore of Lake Peipus; here, time-honoured economic and social structures were preserved which were disappearing in the Soviet Union, behind a frontier sealed with barbed wire and tall watch-towers. This frontier symbolizes a juxtaposition which has been dividing the world ever since the October Revolution, though the lines of division have shifted from time to time. Between the Revolution and the Second World War the Slav peoples were grouped in two types of organization: Poland, Czechoslovakia, Yugoslavia and Bulgaria, after surmounting the social upheavals of the immediate post-war period, joined the great family of capitalist states; the Soviet Union, once it had abandoned the dream of world revolution, lived in an atmosphere of siege, working out its own destiny and gradually obtaining the rest of the world's recognition of the first socialist state.

The frontiers of the new state of Czechoslovakia took in a small segment of the Ukraine (Subcarpathian Ukraine) and also, of necessity, included a strong German minority, thereby perpetuating the national problem. In Yugoslavia the problem was still more acute, not so much because of the country's small German, Hungarian and Italian minorities as because the government's policy of centralism thwarted the centrifugal or even, in certain cases, national aspirations of the various peoples in the kingdom. Only Bulgaria was blessed with unequivocal ethnic homogeneity; but she regarded her frontiers as an injustice and claimed possession of Macedonia, which had been embodied in the kingdom of the Serbs, Croats and Slovenes.

The new states, flushed with the dynamism of victory, could not but succumb to the charms of a policy of assimilation – precisely, however, at a juncture when the machinery of education and communication had been so extended as to make all ethnic groups more vividly aware of their national peculiarities and more determined to assert them. Internally, the history of these states between the World Wars consists of conflict between a dominant nationality (Polish, Czech, Serbian) and oppressed or frustrated nationalities; a conflict superimposed on social problems and interacting with them.

The Second World War was to bring about a solution more in conformity with the nature of the interests involved, by the simultaneous introduction of a federal system and a democratic régime.

All the Slav peoples went over to socialism, which conferred unity without assimilation. But the national problem had already ceased to exist for Poland and Czechoslovakia, whose German minorities had been almost entirely removed. Behind the new Polish frontier on the Oder, a Polish population was replacing the former German inhabitants; and the eastern territories were ceded to the Soviet Union and embodied in the Byelorussian and Ukrainian republics. In the Czechoslovakian republic, the Slovaks were allowed to keep their own language. Yugoslavia became a federation whose five republics were free to develop their indigenous culture. Provision was thus made for Macedonia, the youngest of the European nationalities.

A bloc of socialist countries was formed under the aegis of the Soviet Union. Yugoslavia broke away from this grouping and followed a path of her own, working out a system of decentralized socialistic self-management and seeking approval of it among the capitalist powers, with which she has maintained close relations. Poland occupies a special position in the bloc: she is a semi-socialized country, linked with the West by her history, her predilections and her active religious life (based on the genuine faith of the great majority of her citizens); a country of nuances, of agreements-to-differ, Poland is in simultaneous communication with East and West. Czechoslovakia and Bulgaria have advanced further on the road to socialism and are the most reliable members of an economic bloc which functions on lines peculiar to itself, and whose internal frontiers now permit greater freedom of movement than at first.

The liberalization which followed the anti-Stalinist reaction in the popular democracies marked the emancipation of the countries concerned from Russian leading-strings. The concrete realities resulting from ten years of enforced partnership, the logic of self-interest on either side no less than the similarity or identity of political systems, are what now keeps those countries attached to their eastern neighbour. But they have become more independent and are developing their relations with the West, at the same time as their importance in the Soviet bloc as a whole, though in different degrees in individual cases, is increasing. The Czechs have a low birthrate and perhaps a less promising future than the Poles, with their exceptional vitality. The Balkan peoples have as yet made comparatively little progress towards industrialization; and industry is an index of power. But despite differences in the speed of advance the Slav peoples seem to be moving unanimously towards a common goal. Paradoxically, however, may not their community of development be betrayed by the very potency of their national characteristics – a potency which has been singularly enhanced by the revolutions of which they have been the theatre?

15

The Soviet Union - a Great Example

THE OCTOBER Revolution marked the beginning of a new age in Russia: the country quickly transformed itself into a Union of Soviet Socialist Republics and set about defining the principles of a new state and a new social structure.

To what extent is Russia, in actual fact, a socialist state and a socialist society? That both was and is her goal and, after many vicissitudes, she is halfway towards achieving it. The period of 'war communism' changed the existence of the Soviet Union from a question-mark into an established fact. Next, the period of the NEP (New Economic Policy) produced material recovery, but only by temporarily placing fundamental principles in abeyance. Finally, the period of the Five Year Plans initiated a phase of substantial development in every department of the country's life; but progress was tragically interrupted by the Second World War and paralysed for a time by Stalinism. Such are the three stages of Soviet history from 1917 to 1950, a short but closely-packed history which inevitably compels us to inquire in what degree Russia has succceded in transforming society, creating an original civilization, and – a revolutionary ideal in the fullest sense – fashioning a new kind of human being, 'Communist man'.

I A NEW IDEAL

Changing the Mentality of the Peasant

Essentially, the Soviet régime is characterized by state appropriation of the means of production. Nationalization of industry and collectivization on the land have not merely created new patterns of outward behaviour but are tending to produce an inward, psychological change as well. Social thinking is beginning to replace individual.

The country districts have been less affected by the change than the towns. Of course memories of the rural community, the *mir*, are still to some extent present in people's minds; but peasant habits of mutual help, and the dim sense of community and comradeship in the face of natural difficulties and disasters, count for little against rustic individualism and that keen sense of property which has long created a climate of hostility and resistance towards the *kolkhozes*, and which has forced the authorities into one compromise after another.

It was the workers who had carried the Revolution forward to victory, but it was the peasants – to whom it handed over the land – who made the victory final and permanent. 'War communism', the rough and ready method without which it would have been impossible to feed the Red Army and the towns, had consisted of widespread requisitioning rather than collectivization. The NEP period was characterized by a rejection of the forms of collectivism born of the Revolution, and the preservation and even revival of the old rural communities, with their combination of periodical redistribution and individual enterprise; the effect was to reinforce the proprietary spirit of a peasantry whose ignorance, narrow realism and adherence to tradition rendered them virtually incapable of visualizing an agrarian socialism, integrated with the general economic development of the country. Thus the government, at grips with immense tasks and forced to select its priorities, at first merely encouraged co-operation in various forms and attempted to introduce socialism at village level, both from the outside, through price-fixing and market pressures, and from the inside, by propaganda and education. But social inequality was not only persistent but increasing, and though it ensured support for the government from such peasants as had little or no land, it was holding up the march towards socialism. The incompatibility of state-controlled industry with a vague, indefinite system of private property was glaringly underlined when the successes of the NEP were followed by new difficulties in 1927–8. The policy of progressive collectivization based on voluntary co-operation was replaced, at Stalin's orders, by compulsory collectivization. This was a second revolution in itself, one that cut deeper and was more traumatic because it concerned the vast majority of the population and abruptly introduced alien methods and an alien spirit into the rural environment.

The *kolkhoz* was in fact much more than a mere collective agricultural business undertaking which left room for small individual holdings as well. It was, and is, a production co-operative, with an overall plan which covers every activity of the group and includes the distribution of tasks and a special system of remuneration and sales. It presupposes a higher standard of education and stronger sense of intiative; but it also implies a continual check on results, with sanctions as required, and in effect mobilizes the peasant in the service of the state. The system was installed in an atmosphere of class-struggle which was partly spontaneous and partly cultivated, and whose vaguely, ambiguously labelled outlet was the 'war on the *kulaks*'. Hence no impartial judgement can be formed of its effectiveness, economically speaking, in the short period after its inception and before the Second World War. But the social objective, which was more important, was attained: 93 per cent of family holdings in the USSR had been collectivized by 1937, and 96 per cent by 1940; and very nearly the entire acreage of cultivable land was being worked by collective farms.

Compulsion by itself is not enough to account for the success of the undertaking. The new organization had much to offer the peasants in the village; but they were not always alive to its advantages. Eliminating the rich peasants also meant eliminating certain indisputable economic and social values. Hostility on the part of a capable minority with local influence, and the incompetence of *kolkhoz* personnel – sometimes chosen less for ability and skill than for their loyalty to the Revolution – caused

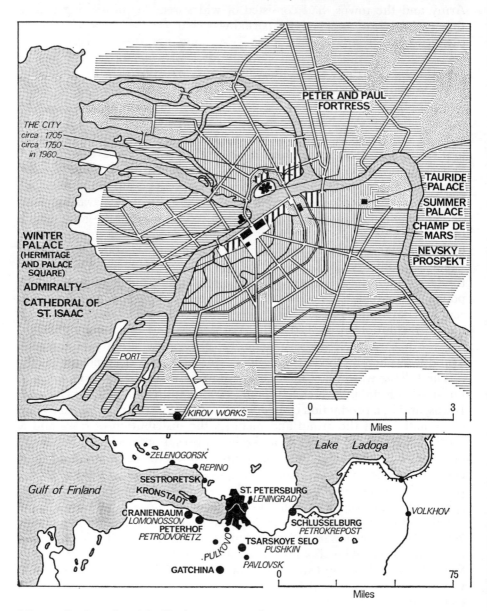

Map 22 Leningrad and Its Environs, 1705–1960

USSR: GENERAL STATISTICAL PICTURE			
Area	8,600,000 sq. miles		
Population		1959 census	1963 estimate
		209,000,000	224,800,000
Ethnic distribution	Russians	114,000,000	
	Ukrainians	37,000,000	
	Byelorussians	8,400,000	
Regional distribution	RSFSR	117,500,000	124,000,000
	Uk.SSR	42,000,000	44,300,000
	Byel. SSR	8,000,000	8,400,000
Percentage of population in towns	RSFSR	52%	57%
	Uk. SSR	46%	50%
	Byel. SSR	31%	36%
Principal cities in the three republics:	Moscow (present boundaries)	6,039,000	6,354,000
	Leningrad	3,321,000	3,552,000
	Kiev	1,104,000	1,248,000
	Gorki	942,000	1,042,000
	Kharkov	934,000	1,006,000
	Novosibirsk	886,000	99,0000
	Kuibyshev	806,000	901,000
	Sverdlovsk	779,000	869,000
	Donetsk (formerly Stalino)	699,000	774,000
	Cheliabinsk	689,000	767,000,
	Dniepropetrovsk	660,000	738,000
	Odessa	629,000	709,000
	Minsk	509,000	644,000

temporary confusion and retrogression. But as the organization of the *kolkhozes* has progressed new social elements have emerged, and time has brought greater experience; education both in school and through the job itself has benefited those who were children when the system was started and soldiers in the Second World War; these men have cast off the dead weight of tradition and constitute a new peasantry, psychologically integrated with their society.

Admittedly, the peasants took advantage of relaxed controls during the Second World War to enlarge their private holdings by encroaching on collective land. The *kolkhoz* system has nevertheless become an accepted part of Russian life. The spread of education, the mechanization of agriculture, the presence of numerous technicians and administrators, and the link which education has established between villager and townsman, are new features infusing the countryside with the spirit of the towns, where people's minds are quicker to adapt themselves to progress and move with the times. Broadly speaking, the régime has converted the countryside as well as the towns to the idea of public service, based on the universal adoption of salary or wages as the only means of livelihood and on the Communist citizen's sense of duty towards the state.

The *kolkhozes*, whose numbers are at present going down though the number of agricultural units run by them is going up, are an example of applied socialism which includes only a part – though the greater part – of the personnel engaged in agriculture. The state farms (*sovkhozes*) which were first started in the early days of the Revolution, were doubled in number between 1953 and 1962, and are a symptom of a tendency by no means confined to industry and commerce, the tendency to 'functionarization': a state of affairs in which personnel at all levels are full-time state servants.

'Communist Man': Myth or Reality?

Whether or no the Soviets have created a new man they have certainly created a new society. The way in which the various sides of a given individual's life are linked together by the interplay of institutions during his education, whatever his ultimate profession, dilutes or even precludes any feeling of belonging to a particular social class. Intellectual and manual worker stand side by side, and the exercise of authority implies neither contempt nor condescension.

At the apex of the functional hierarchy, the administrators and technocrats are powerful in that they are answerable only to the government, which controls them; but they do not own the means of production, or inherit the private fortunes without which the existence of family dynasties is impossible. Enrichment is limited and conditional; it does not in itself confer power. Of course the desire to rise in station includes a desire for a more comfortable life and more money; but increasingly, in a society where everything is conceived in collective terms, such a desire expresses the individual's duty – which has now become a need, an instinct – to take his place, at the highest level he can reach, in a professional order in which the exercise of authority and the sense of social utility tend to count for more than material advantage.

The narrow ideal represented to a Soviet citizen by the acquisition of a television set, a washing machine and, with luck, a car, is no different from the ideal of the average American citizen. But in the USSR there is no exceptionally privileged social minority whose example orientates the secret desires of the majority towards the kind of success which is measured exclusively in terms of money and luxury. The severity of the penalties inflicted from time to time on isolated profiteers – who are antisocial precisely because of their isolation – helps to keep the country tuned up to a morality which could in time become second nature.

This attitude is a definite, deliberate feature of the régime and holds good from one end of the territory to the other. All nationalities within the Union are controlled, though not always unresistingly, by this common trend. The tardy endeavours of tsarism to assimilate the non-Russian populations had had very little effect by the time the Revolution broke out; the revolutionary régime subsequently imposed one ideal, one rule of life, on everybody. The official use of national minority languages, not merely authorized but, for practical reasons, made compulsory, and the encouragement given to the expression of the peculiar genius of each people, has not hindered but actually promoted the moral integration which is being pushed through, and which is banding together the very varied ethnic elements composing the Soviet population. Integration is being achieved partly through economic development, which ignores the barriers between one social group and another, and also through education, which creates identical modes of thought – the same conception of life, the same social ideal. In this respect the more backward minorities, in which the educational system finds its most mallaeble material, seem to show a lower resistance to assimilation than the more advanced peoples; it may be, however, that this difference is really related to climatic factors. But in any case, socialist ways of thought are taking root all over the country. No longer, as in earlier periods, is there a mere juxtaposition of different peoples, connected but never in any real sense united by the exchanges of all kinds, both cultural and economic, taking place between them. The distinguishing mark of the current moral integration is that it respects and even fosters the peculiar characteristics of the peoples. The *décor* of their everyday lives, their languages and their artistic self-expression are not only kept alive but held in honour.

It is true that the smallest and most widely scattered nationalities, as in Siberia, for example, will perhaps be unable much longer to hold out against a Russification which, while not imposed, for practical purposes imposes itself on anybody aspiring to rise in the hierarchy and play more than a local role. But the large non-Slav nationalities in the Caucasus (Armenians, Georgians, Azerbaijanis, etc.) and central Asia (Uzbeks, etc.), despite expressing their national characteristics more freely than they were able to do in the past, do not for this reason conceive political, social and economic life in any way differently from the Slav Russians to the west of them. The vast Euro-Asiatic continent thus appears to have become the crucible in which a new civilization is being created.

Federalism and the Peoples: Byelorussia and the Ukraine
The time has now arrived when an objective judgement can be passed on the federal system in Soviet Russia. That system is the living embodiment

of the socialist dream of fraternal peoples united in the common possession of a democratic régime, the only form of government compatible with a supranational authority.

To confine the present discussion to the Slav peoples, the problem of reconciling a central, Russian-dominated, Moscow-based authority with the autonomy of the Byelorussians and Ukrainians was less acute in the case of the former, whose national consciousness was more recent and who had long been divided and confused by political domination from various sources; it was more difficult in the case of the Ukrainians, who had been opposing the tsarist policy of assimilation for a hundred years and, through their intelligentsia, had retained a lively sense of independence. The fact that many Ukrainians emigrated, and were hostile to the Soviet régime for national and religious even more than for social reasons, meant that, abroad, the image was perpetuated of a people living under the heel of an intolerable dictatorship.

The Soviet authorities have in fact entertained for many years a certain distrust, not unjustified by experience, towards the Ukraine, which despite being a federated republic is subject to close central control. The Ukraine, after all, was the region where the fiercest clashes had taken place between the Bolshevik forces and the White armies. And with German support it had seceded from Russia.

Traditional nationalism – which, at least in its final years, had demanded full independence, and which had been represented by social classes eliminated during the Revolution – was succeeded by a popular nationalism which has been allowed to play an increasingly large part in the multinational Soviet state. The Second World War, and the resistance to occupation which it developed, showed how strong were the common bonds of patriotism uniting the Russians and Ukrainians. The thorough mingling of the two in an industrialized Ukraine which has become a centre of attraction, and in which the entire Ukrainian people now lives, is helping to dissipate a hostility that belongs to the past. Nationalism's principal weapon, the language, previously feared and grudgingly accepted, is now recognized as the essential medium of expression for the genius of the Ukrainian people. The educational curriculum ensures that the Ukrainians are bilingual; most primary education is given in Ukrainian (in some schools the teaching is in Russian, Polish, Moldavian and Hungarian); Russian is learnt from the second to the eighth year of the course and is allotted the same number of hours in the timetable as Ukrainian. The recent proliferation of scientific works published in Ukrainian testifies to the vitality of Ukrainian culture.

In the main, Ukrainian culture was benefited by the Revolution of 1917. The poems of P.H.Tychyna (b. 1891), which are devoted to the life of the workers and the peasants, and of V.N.Sosiura (b.1898), which are full of revolutionary enthusiasm, and the novels of A.V.Holovko (b.1897), which describe the part played by the Communists in village affairs, prefigure the period of 'socialist realism' represented by the plays of Alexander

Kornezhchuk (b.1904), the novels of Natan Rybak (b.1913) and the poems of Rylsky (b.1895). The new writers to emerge since 1945 include Alech Honchar (b.1918), Yuri Yanovshki (b.1902) and Oleksa Dovzhenko (b.1916), who is even better known as a film-maker. The themes of this literature of reconciliation and Slav brotherhood are the Ukrainian people's heroic struggle for independence, the events of war, both civil and international, and the tasks of socialist construction.

In 1922 the Revolution caused the appearance of a new state whose historical antecedents were somewhat indefinite, but which enabled the Byelorussian-speaking population in the region of Minsk to constitute a distinct nation.

The Byelorussians, who had their own dialects and folklore, had been part of the grand duchy of Lithuania; they had even for a short time supplied the grand duchy with its administrative language (strongly contaminated, however, with Polish and Ukrainian). Religiously, they were split between Orthodoxy and Uniatism, and were pulled towards Russia and Poland respectively; and they had suffered much from their position as a frontier-march between these two powerful states, whose contending influences dominated the native aristocracy. Until the twentieth century the bulk of the people consisted of illiterate peasants. Byelorussian culture could nevertheless trace its roots back to the sixteenth, in the scholarly and religious works of Georgi Skorina and his successors such as Vasili Tiapinski (1540–1603) and Simeon Budny, all of whom represented Orthodoxy and anti-Polish feeling.

The awakening of Byelorussian national life began in the nineteenth century, when the distinctive character of the country was brought out by the study of dialects, research into folk-traditions, and the first literary creations in Byelorussian, which was acquiring a linguistic individuality of its own. This growing, initially linguistic, awareness was accompanied during the second half of the nineteenth century by the activities of an intelligentsia which, under the influence of the Russian revolutionary writers, was conducting a political and social struggle against tsarism. A desire for national autonomy began crystallizing in 1905. By this time the Byelorussians had their own poets, such as Janko Kupala (1882–1942), Jakub Kolas (1828–1956), Alois Pashkievich ('Tiotka') (1876–1916), and Maxim Bogdanovich (1891–1917).

The October Revolution, though followed by a bitter struggle between nationalist and revolutionary factions which went on into the nineteen-thirties, marked the beginning of the country's economic rehabilitation and the development of a specifically Byelorussian culture in line with Soviet realism. Kupala and Kolas were still writing, accompanied by a constellation of poets, novelists and playwrights including Kusma Cherny, Janka Mavr, Kondrat Kapriva (b.1896), and Petro Glebka, whose works, 'national in form and socialist in content', reflect the tragic history of Byelorussia, ravaged by two world wars and asserting its increasing importance among the Slav peoples of the Soviet Union.

14

II SOCIAL AND POLITICAL REALISM

Socialist Culture

Attitudes of mind change slowly; there is always a time-lag. Decisions can be taken, economic and social structures can be modified or overthrown, but the planners must armour themselves in patience if they propose to subdue the powerful forces of preference and habit. Soviet Russia has been in existence for less than half a century; in 1917 the theoretical principles of a new form of organized society had been enunciated but their practical application was bound to require several decades. On the other hand, the enthusiasm of the militants was a very real force, surrounding every decision with a messianic aura such as could call forth civic devotion and the spirit of self-sacrifice among the revolutionary élite. The Soviet Union has not been built up by compulsion alone; it is not merely the work of a new enlightened despotism. Its foundations were laid in a climate of hope and enthusiasm, of violence and heroism; in its early days its praises were sung by a group of poets in whose eyes the Revolution was the realization of a new gospel, the first act of a total transformation; from this time forward the world was illuminated by the 'star of blood and fire', as Bakunin had called it, which was rising over Moscow.

The Bolsheviks in power set themselves to found a Communist society, a task which implied rejecting the past *in toto* and building a new social edifice on Marxist principles. Every side of life was involved, because, on the basis of a new economic system and a society from which classes were eventually to disappear, a Communist culture, reflecting the political régime, was to be developed (figure42).

But the first years after the Revolution were marked by a terrible civil war and a fierce concentration of willpower on the most urgent problems; there was not much room for artistic preoccupations. Only poetry, the literary medium best accommodated to periods of poverty and rapid historical development, was free to celebrate the extraordinary events unfolding in Russia: Blok (1880–1932), author of *The Twelve*, Bielyi (1880–1934), Essenin (1895–1925), author of *Inonia*, and Volonin (1877–1932) were the most courageous of the poets who wove an aura of romanticism round the harsh realities of the Revolution.

But the government meanwhile had not lost sight of the necessity for a proletarian art, expressing the needs and duties of the working class and delineating the tasks and achievements of the new régime, an art whose realism and straightforward style would make it accessible to everyone. From inside the Communist Party, Lunacharsky and Bukharin mounted a full-scale campaign to organize publishing and art, with the intention of discovering new talent and giving it the material means of putting its work before the world.

The objective was nothing less than the complete transformation of culture: artists and writers whose tendencies or social origin rendered them

 НЕГРАМОТНЫЙ тот-же СЛЕПОЙ
ВСЮДУ ЕГО ЖДУТ НЕУДАЧИ И НЕСЧАСТЬЯ·

FIGURE 42 Russian poster, an example of the campaign against illiteracy: 'The illiterate person is like a blind man; failure and misfortune threaten him on every side.' Artist: A.Rudakov.

suspect were subjected to censorship or condemned to silence; newcomers who were judged less by their real abilities than by their promise and their political opinions, were given preferential treatment. To describe this literary upheaval simply in terms of propaganda and expediency would nevertheless be a mistake. Most of the young writers who responded to the call were full of revolutionary faith and an eager desire to share in the great enterprise; their works, though mediocre in many cases, take us into a world on the move, a world of infinite prospects, which did in fact offer writers a certain freedom of expression and an opportunity for investigating new aspects of experience. Hence the period of proletarian literature determined by the renunciation, or apparent renunciation, of 'bourgeois' culture was by no means a mere conformist interlude.

Realism and Truth: Literature, Painting and Music

Literature

The first years after the Revolution were a period of acute controversy between different schools, a battle of tendencies concerning the definition of ideal proletarian art. The authorities abstained from adopting any position in a field which, at this experimental stage, was of interest to hardly anyone except a tiny minority of intellectuals; though they did react against the claim of the extremist literary groups to reject the bourgeois past altogether; Lunacharsky, as Commissar for Culture (Narkom) in the Russian Republic (RSFSR), declared, 'To demand the instant appearance of proletarian culture is to believe in miracles.'

The Communist Party, mindful that the nation's cultural heritage could not be scornfully cast aside, allowed free competition between contemporary literary trends. The result was an outpouring which displayed the most various tendencies; many of these works were noteworthy and many more were not, but all were determined by the pressure of events and the perspectives revealed by revolution. To describe revolutionary reality in both its aspects, warlike and peaceful, the lives of heroes and those of the worker and the peasant, using for this purpose a 'socially-orientated naturalism' whose tone was often violent, was regarded as the main function of both poetry and prose. But while some writers, through conviction, conformism or mere lack of talent, were hostile to the analysis of individual feelings and indulged in frigid and tedious political disquisitions, there were others, such as Fadeev (*Defeat*) and Libedinsky (*Birth of a Hero*), who wanted to depict man, 'living man, with his sorrows and joys', and went back to the tradition of the Russian psychological novel.

The writers most strongly in favour of the new régime, the Communists and fellow-travellers, made it their business to equip the advance of the Revolution with the necessary literary weapons, and sought not only subject-matter, but new forms, appropriate to the circumstances. Folklore and the idiom of the people hung like millstones round the neck of both poetry and prose. In the delusive intention of spreading a gospel, rather than writing comprehensibly, the writer went in heavily for slang and dialect; the literary language was at once enriched and contaminated by the urge to be genuine and write like a real man of the people. This short-lived phase produced shoals of unreadable works which descended quickly into oblivion.

On the credit side, the excessive use of the language of the streets, the fields, the political meeting and the barrack-room – in short, of the people – revealed a profound national feeling whose content was cultural, not political, and which also underlay the encouragement given by the state to the literature of the different peoples of the Union.

Literary creation, in these years when the outcome of the Revolution was still at stake, and when circumstances forced those in power to offset terror with flexibility, wavered between conformity and revolt, or rather the affirmation of freedom. The young writers known as the Serapion Brothers, a group formed in Petrograd in 1921 and led by Evgeni Zamiatin (1884–1937), represented this latter position, an independence of mind which nurtured the development of some of the best writers of the period: Ivanov (1895–1963), Tikhonov (b.1896), Fedin (b.1892), and others. They cared for good writing and respected truth; they portrayed Soviet society as they saw it, a society still relatively unchanged by revolution, abounding with injustices and abuses; in many cases their criticism took the form of satire or the humorous story. The well-known works of Zoshchenko (1893–1958), Kataev (b.1897), Ilf (1897–1937) and Petrov (1907–42), author of *The Twelve Chairs*, were born of this state of mind; so were those of some other writers who had supported the Revolution from an earlier stage, such as the poet Mayakovsky (1893–1930) (among whose poems *The Bedbug* is one of the best-known).

Soon, however, a single general characteristic began to dominate Soviet literature, when, by approximately 1925, the régime could be seen to be internally secure and to have achieved recognition abroad. The tragic years during which the new social structures had been in course of erection, at the cost of many lives and much suffering, were still vivid in memory; writers consequently felt an impulse, if not to draw up a balance-sheet, at least to state the problem presented by the conflict between the individual and a collectivist society.

Doubt – which is in itself a form of liberty – makes its appearance in the novels (*Envy*, for example) of Yuri Olesha (1889–1960) and the symbolist poetry of Pasternak (1890–1960), the most notable of the Soviet poets, who incurred criticism from critical quarters precisely for his 'bourgeois individualism'. Similarly, in the raw realism of Babel (1894–1941) (*Red Cavalry*), and the novels of Fedin (*The Brothers*), Leonov (b.1899) (*The Badgers*), and Pilniak (1894–1937) (*The Volga Flows Into The Caspian Sea*), psychological analysis and a resolve to be true to the facts of human experience reveal the sufferings of the individual in his struggle to come to terms with a new world. Almost without exception, however, the writers of this period extol human solidarity and the socialist system, within which the realization of happiness is assumed to be implicit.

But the time was now approaching when the first Five Year Plan was to mobilize every sector of the country's activities for socialist construction, subordinating everything to immediate effectiveness and revolutionary utility. In June 1925 the Central Committee of the Communist Party had passed a resolution defining the duties of the Party in the struggle to promote the ideology of the Revolution, and declaring that literature must be 'nationalist in form, socialist in content'. This resolution now acquired its full significance, and creative writers felt the inexorable pressure of the 'social imperative'. The *mystique* of the Five Year Plan and the class war – the appalling struggle to annihilate the *kulaks* – took hold of most of the new writers and inspired the monotonous sameness of their books; a trend which bore fruit later, however, in the 'thirties, with the emergence in fiction of those heroes of socialist construction who personified the new society and its hopes.

The First Five Year Plan was accompanied by a period of literary stagnation lasting more than three years, which the Central Committee, in 1932, and the first Congress of Soviet Writers, in 1934, tried to end. Presumably creative freedom and social duty are always virtually incompatible. Despite the efforts of Gorki (1868–1936), who had returned from abroad in 1928, and continual resistance from non-Communist authors – the fellow-travellers, soon to be enrolled in the Union of Soviet Writers – Soviet literature became Party literature. Yet the effort to create a new culture, and at the same time to describe people who had been born and bred under the new conditions of Soviet life, conferred dignity and stature on the works of the best writers. The heroes of everyday existence created by those writers, characters portrayed as devoting their toil, their lives and their very thoughts to the cause of communism, doubtless possessed few counterparts in real life; but they were not just figments of the literary imagination. Korchagin, in *When the Steel was Tempered*, by N.A.Ostrovsky (1904–36), and Davydov, in *Virgin Soil Upturned*, by Sholokhov (b.1905), are 'Communist men' of a type which did in fact evolve in the staggering collective task proceeding in field and factory. Facile imitation of the type by numbers of mediocre writers, in all the republics of the Soviet Union, has undoubtedly obscured the fact that such 'model' characters really existed and that the uniform, monolithic character of Soviet literature corresponded to the substantial unity of a society from which classes were beginning to disappear, and where individualism was gradually yielding ground to a collective conception of life.

It is of course true that the novel which describes man at grips with nature and his daily work, and whose purpose is didactic, draws a veil over much of reality. Written to inspire new undertakings and encourage effort, and committing its author to the collective action of the society in which he lives, it glorifies lofty thoughts and feelings; it portrays obstacles only in order to show how easily they are overcome by the application of the human will; it breathes optimism, it commemorates success; and though it does not exactly betray the truth it frequently skirts round it.

On the other hand, the insistence on 'realism' as the writer's duty obliges him to reflect society as it is; so that a man's victories in his profession, in a life orientated towards the socialist ideal, cannot be imagined as having been gained without a struggle. The writer has to keep before his mind's eye the nature and prospects of Soviet society and describe the contradictions thrown up in the course of its development. Realism in subject-matter and situation drives the writer to seek greater accuracy and vividness in his picture of individuals and working groups, and the resistances and setbacks they encounter.

In this atmosphere of incessant, grinding struggle it would be unreasonable to expect the 'new man' to be at all a common phenomenon. The fearful war years, from 1940 to 1944 – which turned the most flourishing regions of European Russia into a wilderness strewn with corpses – forced the Russians into immediate tasks which devoured all their energies. The fight for the country's existence, and the struggle to keep the régime running, brought lassitude as well as victory; and as many of the younger adults as survived, never having known the enthusiasm and exaltation of the revolutionary period, now thought only of enjoying a fuller life in which to forget the ordeals of the last two decades. Stalin's harsh authority, in the aberrations of his old age, had rendered the forced march towards a better future intolerable and had temporarily masked the change occurring in the Russian outlook, a swing back towards traditional attitudes, manifested at present in a 'thaw' which poses considerable problems of interpretation.

Possibly the new man can evolve only in peace-time, not war. Soviet writing in the years immediately following the war continued the tradition of the war books; it described battles, obscure heroes, the crushing burdens and endless sufferings of the soldiers, 'a man's destiny'. But meanwhile the tasks of reconstruction were setting anew the problems solved in an earlier generation by the pioneers of the civil war. Once more the thread was there to be picked up, the way through the labyrinth; having escaped with their lives, people were anxious to resume the pursuit of happiness in a socialist society; the Communist Voropaev, in *Happiness*, by the novelist P. Pavlenko (1889–1951), is a case in point. In this atmosphere of resurgence and renewal, there have been books which acquire natural settings such as the forest and the fields, even the factory, a poetic character enabling the individual to reconcile the harsh dictates of duty with the demands of sensibility and emotion (Leonov, *The Russian Forest*, 1953). And the versatility of an Ilya Ehrenburg (b.1891), the background of whose writing includes experience in republican Spain and in France (the fall of Paris), is now free to manifest itself in his *Memoirs*, a fresco of literary and social history in the Soviet Union over the past fifty years.

The traumatic experience of war, exposing weaknesses, divergences and dissent and forcing the authorities to preserve unity by resorting to compromise, has partially loosened the iron rule of conformism. Post-war realism, with its more detailed portrayal of society, is admittedly a continuation of the realism of the 'thirties but shows a livelier concern for psychological truth. Its protagonists are no longer chosen exclusively from the shock-workers of the 'noble' industries – steelworks and so on – the engineers and 'cadres', chock-full of authority and initiative, depicted in the novels of Kochetov, Granin, Gorbatov, Rybakov, Sobko and others, but the humblest workers such as miners, drivers, ship's carpenters and bargemen. This invasion of the literary field by the people *en masse* has exposed, with a new raw clarity, the gap separating the average Soviet citizen from the rare socialist hero and the ideal Soviet man.

Painting

Soviet painting is similarly dominated by a realism devoted to events in social and political life, and to the heroes of history and the Revolution – and by 'heroes' is meant not only the obvious, famous figures but also the humblest: the militant rank and file and, in general, all those whose lives are dedicated to the construction of socialism. This painting, which reflects 'all that is best and most progressive' and expresses the goals of communism in concrete form, is didactic and is meant to have a social value; it must therefore be comprehensible to the people, demanding no effort of intellectual adjustment and eliciting an instant response from mind and heart.

It is representational (figurative), and presents immediately recognizable themes in a hackneyed though highly competent style. Work in the factory or on the land, sport, and everyday life, provide most of its subject-matter. Demands from officialdom have also produced a large number of portraits of the leaders of the Revolution, a *genre* which has a long tradition behind it; its most prominent exponent during the 'thirties was A. Gerasimov.

The effect of the Second World War was to send painters in search of historical subjects in which the country's heroic past sprang to life, arousing opportune emotions of national pride. More recently, however, the great actors on the stage of history, ancient or modern, have been increasingly replaced by the people – workers, peasants, soldiers – going about their everyday affairs.

This change in subject-matter has been accompanied by no corresponding change in style: literal representation is the rule. Abstract art is too bewildering for the masses; the general public, flocking into the museums and gallaries, wants to see things it understands. Such a price was bound to be exacted by a general attempt to educate public taste. This apparent backwardness is in fact continuity, the consistent application of a policy of popular education and culture which Lenin had outlined as early as 1919, in a conversation with Clara Zetkin: 'Soviet art must be the property of the people. What matters is the benefits which art can bring, not to a few hundred or even a few thousand individuals, but to the hundreds of millions who constitute the Soviet population. Art belongs to the people.'

It is nevertheless noticeable that the younger painters, while remaining faithful to the canonical repertory of subjects, are tending to abandon academic conceptions of form and explore the visible world in their own way. Their originality is tolerated in the somewhat more liberal atmosphere corresponding to the increasing sophistication of the public, or at least a section of it; taste and appetite in the visual arts are changing; new demands have arisen.

Music

The Revolution in no way interrupted the glorious course of Russian musical history. It provided new inspiration; at the same time, by impos- ing 'heroic and constructive' themes, it presented composers with a diffi- cult problem: that of 'remaining comprehensible to the big public without sinking to the public's level and sacrificing their artistic means of expres- sion on the altar of simplicity' (Hofman). Two names have dominated music in Russia since 1918, Sergei Prokofiev (1891–1953) and Dmitri Shostakovitch (b.1906).

FIGURE 43 Russian popular music: examples of *byliny*.

Sergei Prokofiev, already a celebrated and controversial figure inside Russia as an *avant-garde* composer before the First World War, with the *Scythian Suites* (1916) to his credit, made his career abroad from 1918 to 1933, revisiting Russia only for a triumphantly successful tour in 1928. After his final return home his output remained as copious as ever. Con- certos, symphonies, sonatas (including the famous *Ninth*, 1947), ballet- music (*The Buffoon*, 1921, *Romeo and Juliet*, 1936), operas (*The Love of Three Oranges*, 1921, *The Flaming Angel*, 1927), music for plays and films (*Alexander Nevsky*, 1939), symphonic Tales (*Peter and the Wolf*, 1936), oratorios (*Guard- ing the Peace*, 1950) – from 1934 this gigantic and varied harvest has been a vital element in Russian life and has made its own contribution to the national ideal and the building of socialism.

The music of Dmitri Shostakovitch evinces a spiritual dedication to the

14*

Russian fatherland, to social struggle and the Herculean undertakings of peacetime life. It consists mainly of symphonies (of which the *Thirteenth* is based on Yevtushenko's *Babi Yar*), oratorios, such as *The Song of the Forests*, and concertos. His opera *Katerina Ismailova*, based on folk-tunes and caricaturing Russian pre-war society, was banned by Stalin after its *première* in Leningrad in 1934, but was rehabilitated in the 'thaw'. His involvement in political life is greater than Prokofiev's; but, like Prokofiev, he has found an extra stimulus to creation in his sense of patriotic duty, an urge not always easy to reconcile with the free expression of personality; and, again like Prokofiev, he was accused in 1948 of a 'formalistic and anti-popular orientation'.

The best work of these composers has not always been elicited by official commissions, such as Prokofiev's *Canatata* (1937) for the twentieth anniversary of the October Revolution, composed to a libretto selected from the writings of Marx, Lenin and Stalin, and Shostakovitch's *Poem to Stalin* (1938). But these composers are of importance not only because of the aesthetic value of their music but because of their popularity, the enthusiasm they have excited among the masses as well as the advanced minority. Prokofiev's final musical utterance, recalling the calamitous sufferings of war, the labours of reconstruction and the rediscovery of the joys of peace, illustrates the trend to be found in a number of Soviet composers, a desire not only to awaken emotion but to elevate the mind.

Tradition and Revolution in Writing and the Film

During the immediate post-Revolutionary phase the traditional heroes of history went through a lean time: the vulgarized, over-schematic version of Marxism which was then in vogue made it seem as if their achievements were mere meaningless ripples on a stream, incidents in the impersonal flow of social-historical processes. According to Pokrovsky, the leader of Soviet historiography in the 'twenties, Peter the Great was a debauchee who had been a mere tool for the interests of the merchant class. But it was not long before the heroes were reinstated; their prestige was even heightened in so far as they had assisted progress, steering history on a course which, it was proclaimed, had culminated in the October Revolution. They were no longer visualized exclusively as the representatives of the ruling classes, exploiting the poor, and resisting the movements of popular liberation of which the peasant revolts were the historical milestones. On the contrary, they had demonstrated a desire for progress and even an anxiety for the common good which was now considered to have been a positive progressive factor. Excuses were found for their most violent or arbitrary actions, which indeed provided an indirect excuse for the harshness of the very régime which now pronounced judgement upon them; and they were included by implication in Lenin's eulogistic summing-up of Peter the Great, who, he said, had 'used barbarous means to drag Russia out of barbarism'.

These rehabilitated heroes were subsequently joined by other figures, previously obscure or reviled as agitators, brigands or robber chiefs; men like Bolotnikov, Stenka Razin and Pugachev, whose following of insurgent Cossacks and peasant mobs had threatened to topple the throne of the tsars. Individuals of the humblest social origins thus took their place beside sovereigns, and the most illustrious representatives of the aristocracy, in that vast historical panorama in which, from the time of the First Five Year Plan, nationalism was reconciled with socialism.

The task of disseminating this view of the past was undertaken by both history and literature. But the paramount influence in this connection was not that of the big, substantial works, like Alexis Tolstoy's *Peter the Great* (the three sections of which appeared in 1929–30, 1933–4 and 1944–5 respectively); a more important part was that played by the innumerable pamphlets and booklets which were issued for young people and the general public; the advance of literacy had made the country's history accessible through the printed word both at school and in later life. The defenders of Muscovy against the Germans, Poles and Turks, the great generals and admirals of the eighteenth and nineteenth centuries, and the sovereigns to whom Russia's greatness was partly due, were portrayed in short biographies which appeared in great profusion after 1940, when the Soviet Union found itself once more engaged in a ruthless struggle for existence.

From the first, tense, tumultuous years after the Revolution all the way down to the post-Stalin epoch, there can be seen an unbroken line leading to a total vision of Russia's historical past, a vision fostered by literature but presented even more effectively by the cinema. The film industry had been delivered from financial difficulties by nationalization and, like literature, had become an instrument of propaganda; but the change-over had involved no stifling of talent. Indeed, the daring experiments of the revolutionary creative period in the 'twenties led to the 'Soviet explosion', as Georges Sadoul has called it, which gave the world Eisenstein's admirable film *The Battle-Cruiser Potemkin* (1926), a masterpiece of tehnical innovation based on one of the most dramatic episodes of the 1905 revolution, and the epic excitement of Pudovkin's *Storm Over Asia* (1928). Film-making, like writing, took its subject-matter from political and social reality, past or present, in conformity with the prescriptions of social realism; it commemorated great historic feats of arms, and struggles for independence and freedom; the exploits of national and revolutionary leaders and heroes, and famous sovereigns, were the chosen material of cinematic geniuses such as Eisenstein (*Alexander Nevsky*, 1938, and the unfinished *Ivan the Terrible*, 1945), Pudovkin (*Suvorov*, 1941, *Admiral Nakhimov*, 1945), and lesser figures like Petrov (*Peter the Great*, 1937) and Donskoy (the *Trilogy of Gorki*, 1938–40).

Film-making also parallelled writing in that it created heroic characters as models for the rising generation: Vassiliev's Chapaev (1934), a partisan-leader of the civil war, became an image imprinted on the public mind, and Maxim (in a trilogy which appeared in 1925–14) symbolizes the life of a Soviet worker during the First World War and the Revolution. The Soviet film-makers have been described as 'engineers of souls'. It is undoubtedly true that, to an even greater extent than writing, the cinema, both in movie-houses and through mobile projection units, became a democratic, popular instrument of national culture under the First Five Year Plan, at first only in the towns and later also in the country. Nor was it grown-ups alone who benefited: children's films, which in the early days were practically a Soviet speciality, supplemented the ample output of children's books (animal stories and traditional legends). The cinema penetrated every corner of the republics comprising the Union. Those in the west and in the Caucasus were not slow to produce their own gifted directors, such as the Ukrainians Dovzhenko and Savchenko (the second of whom created *Bogdan Khelmnitsky*, 1941, commemorating one of the great popular insurrections of the Russian seventeenth century), the Byelorussians Dzigan, Spiess and others, and the Georgian Chyaourely (*The Fall of Berlin*, 1944).

The Second World War supplied a new crop of subjects calculated to stimulate national pride. Ermler's *The Turning-Point* (1945) showed the Russian generals reaching the decision to defend Stalingrad; the events of the defence itself were depicted by Petrov in *The Battle of Stalingrad* (1949); and Savchenko told the story of the battle for the Crimea in *The Third Blow* (1949). But despite the large number of war-films begotten by the tragic experiences undergone by the Soviet Union, the main body of Russian film-making continued to concentrate on those aspects of the national glories which were concerned less with the sword than with the ploughshare: peace, freedom and progress were the themes, and they included psychological observation of the inner crises suffered by the individual in his task of adapting himself to new conditions, imposed by Soviet life. Nor were the big creative achievements of the régime neglected. In addition, specialized documentaries were made, both for technicians and for a wider public which had developed an appetite for scientific popularization.

III PAST AND FUTURE

Have the Russians been de-Christianized?
Organizing a society on Marxist principles inevitably involves the propagation of atheism. During the militant period of socialist construction, the Orthodox Church, compromised by its profound connections with tsarism and, in the main, hostile towards the new régime, suffered grievous blows. The clergy were decimated and scattered; churches, monasteries and seminaries were closed; proselytizing was forbidden; might was right, and the Church was powerless to resist. At the same time the Russian people's faith – which, whether real or apparent, had many centuries of tradition behind it – was subjected to a heavy bombardment of question and discussion.

But the concentration of the nation's energies in the Second World War was perforce accompanied by a certain relaxation in the direction of tolerance; and the régime had become strong enough meanwhile to allow the two competing ideologies to coexist, provided the country's economic and social foundations were not thereby threatened. To what extent has the Russian people recovered, or never lost, its Christianity? Only an objective investigation – no easy matter! – would supply the answer. We must content ourselves with indefinite estimates based on superficial observations.

N.Struve considers it possible to assert that, of 160,000,000 Orthodox subjects of the USSR (Orthodox, that is to say, at least in the sense that their home background is Orthodox), two thirds have been baptized (though it must be noted that baptism was compulsory in the enemy-occupied zones during the Second World War); he also maintains that the majority of Soviet children receive baptism at the present time. Basing his conclusions on the numerous attendance of the faithful in the twenty thousand churches which were open in 1960, he estimates that the Soviet Union contains at least 40,000,000 practising Orthodox believers, amounting to about 25 per cent of those whose family background is Orthodox, and over 33 per cent of those who have received baptism.

The fact remains that the majority of practising believers are women, old people, 'pensioners, housewives and the infirm'. And just how are we to interpret the persistent fondness for celebrating feast-days which have lost their religious meaning but continue to give the peasants a pretext for merry-making? In the old days, the Orthodox Church had studded the calendar with such a succession of festival days, on which no work was done, that 'Old Russia' laboured under the stigma of crippling the nation's economic life. The Soviet government has had to struggle against customs to which the peasants remain attached.

Large crowds make their way to the old places of pilgrimage, in particular to the monastery of the Trinity and St Sergius at Zagorsk. But the main upholders of the religous tradition are the generation now drawing to an end, those born during the first quarter of the century. The young, generally speaking, seem indifferent; no metaphysical self-questionings appear to trouble their minds. Only time will tell whether this is a transitory phenomenon or whether it represents a permanent psychological transformation.

But the Church has gained in unity what it has lost in numbers. It would be hard to say which of two facts is the more surprising: that sects are disappearing; or that some of them have survived and that a few are even recognized by the State. Such is the case with the various communities of the Old Believers, who are especially numerous in the western region (Byelorussia and the Ukraine) but can hardly number more than one or two million adherents. Other Christians outside the ranks of Orthodoxy in Soviet Russia include tiny groups of Mennonites, Baptists, Evangelicals, Adventists, etc. But in any case these fractional residues, whether surviving spontaneously or by a deliberate act of will, are on a par with the alleged emergence of new sects under the Soviet régime: however interesting they may be as instances of psychological individualism they remain mere minor phenomena, of no consequence whatever amid the broad current of religious indifference on which the Soviet people is at present moving forward.

Rural Craftsmen

The nineteen-thirties saw the revival of an aesthetic tradition, namely the elevation of Russian rustic craftsmanship to the level of fine art. The craft-associations (*artels*) were resuscitated; some of them, notably those producing garments and table-linen, were organized on a systematic workshop basis. The training of skilled craftsmen was put on a regular footing, not without difficulty. The old techniques have been kept up, but subject-matter has been enriched with themes suggesting the progress of socialist construction. The lacquered boxes (painted *papier mâché*) from Palekh, a village which is at once a museum and an art-school, illustrate, as ever, the tradition of fairy-tale and legend; movement and colour, tenderly nursed,

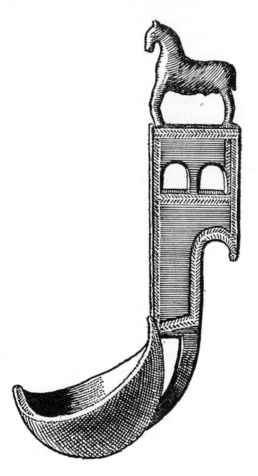

FIGURE 44 Popular craftsmanship in Russia in the twentieth century: wooden dipper with carved handle.

result in a romanticism full of charm. But work in the same medium from Mstera, and even more so from Fedoskino, also uses contemporary literary themes and subjects from pictures by contemporary Soviet painters, such as scenes from present-day life or recent wars of liberation; the tone and conception are more academic and in some cases reflect the realism officially prescribed by the Party.

All the old centres of craftsmanship have resumed activity; their geographical distribution is the same; the nature of their output is determined, as before, by climate, natural resources and tradition. Wood-carving is to be found everywhere, especially in the western parts of the Ukraine, round Zagorsk (toys, and dolls resembling the 'old woman who lived in a shoe'), Bogorodsk, and Gorki (utensils with red and gold decoration on a black ground). Walrus and mammoth tusks are carved in the north. Kostroma makes a speciality of silver filigree. Niello (engraved enamelled metal) is being produced once more at Veliki Ustiug.

This revival of the crafts has been typified by the same reorientation as was already visible, though less markedly, at the beginning of the twentieth century. With a few exceptions, such as wooden toys, this is luxury craftsmanship, with high production-costs and a small total output, intended for a minority market and above all for tourists and the export trade. It represents a marginal item in the general economy. But what it is achieving, with government backing, is the perpetuation of a cluster of popular arts which were in danger of being swept away beyond recall. This regard for traditional folkways and for the deep-seated national characteristics they express is perfectly compatible, according to Soviet conceptions of the new society, with industrial modernity. In embroidery, the old motifs, though simplified, are still plainly recognizable (and also in luxury linen goods, now almost entirely industrialized). Once, those motifs conveyed a whole world of beliefs – a lozenge with criscrosses at the corners, for example, meant a house for a young married couple. They have now been complemented by the addition of new forms, which vary from region to region. In the villages of the Krestsy district, near Novgorod, table linen is embroidered in white, pierced, geometrical designs. Mstera goes in for floral ornamentation and also produces multicoloured 'Vladimir lace'. The Kaluga region is noted for needlework on a coloured background, representing stylized animals and vegetation. In every region there are women who embroider, and every region has its individual type and style of work.

The New Image of the Towns

Since the Revolution the general physionomy of the country has changed. The ravages of the civil war and two world wars have confronted the State, twice, with the problem of reconstruction, a problem aggravated by demographic pressure and still more by industrial development. There is a steady flow of country people, attracted by the prospect of work, to the cities and towns. Under the old régime, the urban percentage of the population grew slowly; between 1922 and 1963 it has jumped from 15 per cent to 52 per cent. Existing towns have expanded, new ones have sprung up, stimulated by the provision of capital equipment, and hamlets have grown into important centres; Russia, a 'great village' in the nineteenth century, has become a country of big cities. At the same time the distances between them are so great that they do not present the image of that dense occupation of the ground which is so familiar to us in the West (map 23).

There has been little change in the villages, where the *isbas* (a word falling into disuse) have been replaced by *domiki* (cottages, small houses). But in the towns the transformation has been considerable. Organizational and administrative growth has made it necessary to put up large numbers of public buildings, an opportunity which might have called forth a new,

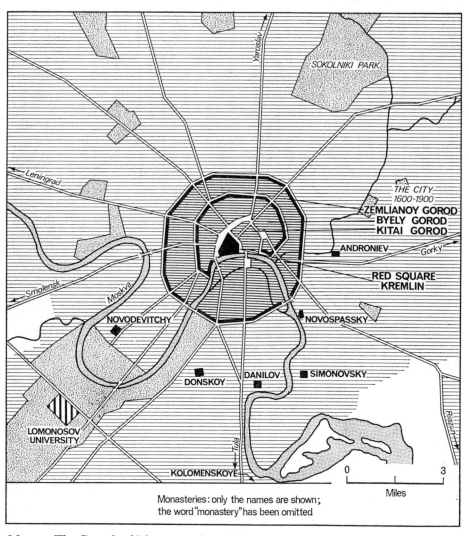

Monasteries: only the names are shown;
the word "monastery" has been omitted

Map 23 The Growth of Moscow, 17th–20th Centuries

officially-inspired venture in the art of architecture. Exploration in this field has been limited; cheapness and speed of construction were paramount. Originality is the exception.

The interlude of anarchy and civil war was the period of hope and innovation in the arts, a period whose vibrations lived on until about 1935.

'Constructivism', whose cosmopolitan character foredoomed it to early condemnation, made a short-lived break with tradition, striving to adapt style to function and create an expressive plastic elegance. But the régime was quick to fashion a new academicism, after the foundation of the Academy of Architecture in 1934. What was responsible for their resurgence of the past was the dead weight of the peasant masses, whose raw, barely urbanized mentality exerted a reactionary effect through the technicians recruited from their own ranks; a conservatism all too visible in the cornices, balustraded balconies and pedimented doorways adorning the façades of so many of the administrative buildings and apartment blocks erected in the 'thirties. Another factor was megalomania, the craze for sheer massive size which prompted Stalin to order the erection of some fifteen gigantic buildings on sites scattered about in Moscow; symbolizing power by their height, and attachment to tradition by their academicism, they soon came under criticism on the score not of poor style but of inconvenience. The new Lomonosov University, on the Hill of Birds, overlooking the western bend of the Moskva, is the most typical example of these outsize palaces, of which no more were built after the Second World War. The Moscow underground railway, in itself so rationally conceived for quick transportation of large numbers of passengers, reflects, in the sumptuous style and very uneven quality of its decor, the same attitude to life.

After 1945 the need to rebuild the country's ruined cities as fast as possible, and to create new residential areas in them for the ever-increasing urban population, caused these architectural histrionics to be abandoned; exteriors became simple without any sacrifice of comfort inside. Originality is to be seen not in the appearance of the buildings viewed individually (individual character is precisely what they lack), but in the creation of extensive functional *ensembles*: whole urban districts which have completely transformed the townscape. Everywhere, from Siberia, with its new city of Novosibirsk, to Moscow, urban life is undergoing a similar change. The capital, for example, has thrust out westwards beyond the new University and produced a twin for itself, a city of 100,000 inhabitants. Building policy today is firmly orientated towards giving the population full facilities for their domestic, occupational and social needs. In this field, the Soviet Union is following the same path as the West (plate 27).

Widening Power and Influence
In the space of fifty years a new super-power has come into being. Its influence on the world no longer radiates only through its writers and painters and musicians – and even, after so short a lapse of time, its scientists – but

through the infectious contact of its social and political ideal and its economic strength. The period is far distant (and yet so close – a mere thirty years) in which the Soviet Union, surrounded by a *cordon sanitaire*, was still struggling for existence in harsh circumstances and, despite an internal dictatorship which lent a specious appearance of power, could not treat with the capitalist states on a footing of genuine equality. The Second World War, after raising frequent false hopes that the régime would fall, was the triumphantly-surmounted test of success and durability.

Having become one of the two giants whose influence divides the world and even extends into space, the Soviet Union, now industrialized, exports machinery, capital equipment and technicians. Simultaneously it is putting its own house in order; a task covering the whole of the Union's immense territory, performed in the face of considerable natural obstacles, and imposing a crushing load of endeavour. The policy of trade with the capitalist states and aid to the underdeveloped countries is continually increasing Russia's contacts in all parts of the world and, in effect, stamps her recent history with the hallmark of success. Typically, the new dam put into service at Bratsk, on the Angara, the keystone of future development in eastern Siberia, was parallelled in 1964 by the work begun on the dam at Assuan in Egypt, an undertaking rendered possible by Soviet capital and engineers.

This rapid rise, however, would be devoid of new significance and perhaps short-lived in its importance, but for one thing: Russia is a socialist country, and the principles of socialism have therefore become an inevitable ingredient in any discussion of human life and the future of the peoples of mankind. All writing on social and political subjects is coloured today by the Marxist frame of reference – Marxism rebutted or debated or accepted, as the case may be, but there. By putting socialism into practice the Soviet Union has turned it into a concrete reality. Socialism has become an exemplar. It is an option for young states, and disturbs the conformism of the old.

Threats to Socialism
The Russian educational system being genuinely democratic, there is equality of opportunity. But equality has to be adjusted to the country's requirements. There are immeasurable resources to be exploited, a huge country to be equipped, a rapidly growing population to be harnessed to the nation's tasks; more and more people are therefore needed for the better-paid jobs, those in management and supervision. But the appeal of such jobs is less than it used to be, and the general drive towards comfort and success – a drive determined by the self-interest, preferences and prejudices of the individual – is perpetually creating obstacles to the development and maintenance of a harmonious socialist society.

This difficulty hardly arises at the higher levels of industrial employment, open only to a select minority; but it makes a great deal of difference at the middle levels, where the prestige of an intellectual career, divorced

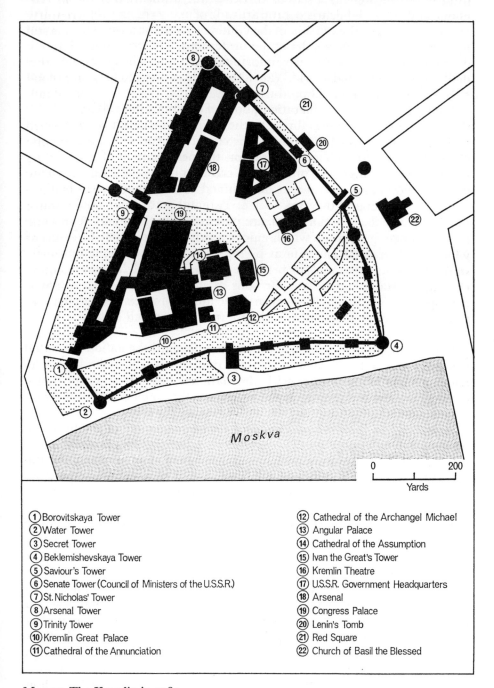

Map 24 The Kremlin in 1960

① Borovitskaya Tower
② Water Tower
③ Secret Tower
④ Beklemishevskaya Tower
⑤ Saviour's Tower
⑥ Senate Tower (Council of Ministers of the U.S.S.R.)
⑦ St. Nicholas' Tower
⑧ Arsenal Tower
⑨ Trinity Tower
⑩ Kremlin Great Palace
⑪ Cathedral of the Annunciation

⑫ Cathedral of the Archangel Michael
⑬ Angular Palace
⑭ Cathedral of the Assumption
⑮ Ivan the Great's Tower
⑯ Kremlin Theatre
⑰ U.S.S.R. Government Headquarters
⑱ Arsenal
⑲ Congress Palace
⑳ Lenin's Tomb
㉑ Red Square
㉒ Church of Basil the Blessed

from industry, presents a serious threat to recruitment. Khrushchev denounced the disdainful, aristocratic attitude of many young people towards manual work, and the worship of the Golden Calf in the form of the leather briefcase – that visible amulet of the professions. The present glut of budding intellectuals is particularly unfortunate at a time when the generation depleted by the Second World War (a 'bulge' in reverse, so to speak) ought to be just entering into full productivity.

But these objective considerations, born of economic imperatives, are not the chief danger. A graver threat to the future of socialism is the sense of social superiority which the professions confer. Of course the régime precludes the rise of new 'classes' based on the perpetuation of privilege by inheritance. But it cannot prevent the creation of mobile 'castes', dependent on individual success and determined to maintain a firm hold on whatever advantages they may seize. Parental status and family background, particularly in the towns, are paramount in the minds of a section of the younger generation which enjoys a privileged position *de facto*, and which constitutes, at any rate at present, the majority among university students. Between 30 and 40 per cent of the pupils of Moscow's higher education establishments are the sons of industrial or *kolkhoz* workers, a proportion which shows at once how much progress has been made towards building a socialist society, and how much remains to be made.

Soviet legislation is doing what it can to safeguard the nation's essential priorities and induce a new mentality, one which will make it easy to allocate tasks in conformity with the national interest, and which will develop the sense of the dignity of work, whether intellectual or manual. An attempt is being made, in fact, both to satisfy the economic needs of the moment and to lay the foundations of that ideal society of the future in which a university degree will be not merely a passport to a profession but, rather, a token of culture which will be regarded as compatible with employment of any and every kind. This distant prospect presupposes an era of development of which, at most, the dawn can just be said to be beginning.

At present, educational reforms in the spirit of Article 121 of the 1936 Constitution are tending to close the gap between intellectual and manual work by bringing them together as early as possible in the educational process, and by providing for contact, over a lengthy period, between the life of the pupil and that of the workaday world. This was the goal aimed at by the law of 12 December 1958. Schoolboys of ten years of age and upwards take part in a great variety of manual jobs, and university students are obliged to devote a small portion of their time to productive work; these provisions are intended not so much to contribute to the economy or merely to broaden the experience of the young, thus making them more valuable as future citizens, as to develop a new outlook to the whole vocational question, a new psychological climate.

Efforts such as these express faith in the possibilities of human beings, faith in progress. But the power of ingrained feelings and prejudices remains formidable. It can be seen in other fields besides education. The establishment not merely of peaceful relations, but of active harmony, between peoples formerly hostile to one another is by now an accomplished fact. The national individuality of the various peoples composing the Union is today of interest only on the cultural plane. All these peoples, Slav and non-Slav alike, are effectively united by socialism. The illustrious personages who founded the fame, and adorn the history, of the countries of central Asia are honoured and commemorated on the same level as the heroes of Great Russia. The ministries of the federated Republics are no longer exclusively in the hands of Slavs. All dangers of secession having been removed, the common task – whose setting is a whole continent rather than the administrative boundaries of its constituent Republics – confers genuine equality on all Soviet citizens, regardless of nationality. In cosmopolitan Moscow, the Tatar in his fur cap, dangling his tea-kettle as he strolls down a hotel corridor, enjoys the same rights as any Russian or Ukrainian. As regards the Jews, however, who were treated under tsarism as a separate nation, a nationality without a territory, there seems to be a residue from the past, an anti-Semitic tendency which though not widespread is still definitely there, a latent survival, an ancient bogey grotesquely out-of-date in the contemporary context.

Future Prospects

That the régime does in fact work is no longer seriously open to doubt. The pace of the country's evolution is increasing. Progress in the sciences, the advanced state of research, and the emergence of a numerous élite of technicians, tell their own story. The Soviet Union has abandoned isolation in favour of participation. It has become as powerful a centre of attraction as the United States, though for different reasons, and is making its influence felt everywhere through the perspectives of social choice which it offers. The Revolution was an experiment worked out in flesh and blood, one which questioned the very principles of human life, the foundations of society and the various possibilities of human relations; and with all its tragic errors, its successes, its failures, it remains an example for young nations to ponder and for revolutionaries to put into practice. In the countries of the peoples' democracies the new régime has been installed only with decisive support from Soviet Russia; and elsewhere, the sudden and spontaneous extension of Russian ideological influence is the most salient feature of a power and effectiveness which are largely due to the penetrative quality of socialism (map 24).

But what does all this mean in terms of human nature – of man, and in particular of Communist man? Are the policy of peaceful coexistence, and the liberalization of the régime, signs that the movement has stabilized itself and, as it were, cast anchor? Will socialism's accumulated prosperity, the rise in the standard of living and the development of collective well-being, have the paradoxical effect of inhibiting and eventually halting the gradual, indispensable transformation of men's mental habits? Communism has encountered resistance caused by passivity, by nostalgia for the old days of profit-making, by inadequate material incentives; human nature (perfectible maybe, but to what extent?) has visibly demonstrated these reactions at every level of the productive process, reactions which authority seeks to counter or anticipate by a continual alternation between freedom and compulsion. The strength or weakness of socialism's foundations resides, when all is said, in men's 'virtue', and in the degree to which they can actively embrace a system of values which, as yet, they have only passively accepted.

16

From Independence to Consolidation: Poland and Czechoslovakia

POLAND and Czechoslovakia sprang up as newly-constituted free countries after the Allied victory in 1918, though in both cases the strong national foundation required by the new edifice had been built during the previous hundred years. Both, as time went on, were menaced by the rebirth of Pangermanism, and were therefore compelled to seek outside support through alliances of doubtful value. Both were again crushed, both rose again and passed this time into the camp of the peoples' democracies, where the new régime struggles with the difficult problem of reconciling freedom with the practice of socialism.

I POLAND

Precarious Unity

The First World War restored independent statehood to the Polish people. After the defeat of Germany and Austria-Hungary, and a year of war between the troops of Pilsudski and the Bolshevik government (terminated by the Treaty of Riga, 18 March 1921), Poland regained her eighteenth-century frontiers; a return to the past which spelt grave difficulties for the future. Refusing the Allies' demand for an eastern frontier, the Curzon line, which would have corresponded roughly with the Poles' ethnic boundary, the Pilsudski government included within the new state the eastern territories, the *Kresy* or 'confines' which had indeed formed part of Poland before the partitions but were inhabited mainly by Lithuanians, Byelorussians and Ukrainians: 5,000,000 people, who, with the 1,000,000 Germans in the territories regained in the west, constituted more than a quarter of the total population of Poland.

This mixed bag of peoples and territories was provided with a unified political framework copied from those of the Western countries. Poland became a parliamentary democracy under a president designated by two assemblies, the Diet and the Senate, both elected by direct universal suffrage. The tasks of administering and co-ordinating the three territories, developing the economy, organizing the army, and establishing a budget, demanded a terrific effort from the government, which succeeded in carrying them out with the help of western capital – French, American and German. Unable to regain possession of Danzig, the Poles created the modern Baltic port of Gdynia.

Finance and the economy were put highest on the list of priorities, and the Polish government, which represented the propertied classes, gradually developed under Pilsudski's guidance into a semi-fascist régime. Pilsudski had ostensibly retired from political life in May 1923, but in 1926 he engineered a *coup d'état* with the support of the army and thereafter strengthened the power of the executive by remote control, working through intermediaries and reorganizing the military command until he was virtually able to rule the country himself. From 1930 to his death in 1935 there was open dictatorship, prolonged until the outbreak of the Second World War by the so-called 'régime of the colonels'.

The history of this second Polish republic was a succession of economic crises and social upheavals. Poland was the forward position of the western powers in their opposition to Bolshevism. She was, moreover, bound to them by defensive alliances and financial aid; dependent on them, indeed, for industrial investment. And she was in danger from a resurgent Germany insistently demanding the return of the 'Polish corridor'. It was not long before Poland found herself in a helpless condition against which no increase of governmental severity was of any avail.

Economic development had strengthened the left-wing opposition by creating a larger proletariat. But the biggest problem of all was still the condition of the peasants and the inequality of land distribution.

In the early days of the new state the socialistic appearance of the government had raised fresh hopes in the countryside. But the great estates were still intact and their owners as powerful as ever, and the expected agrarian reform never really got moving. A start was provided by the agrarian law of July 1920, under which the largest landowners were to be expropriated by forced purchase and their estates distributed among the peasants. Over 2,224,000 acres were reallocated in this way between 1920 and 1925, at which date a second agrarian law was passed to provide easier terms for the small owner and imposed an annual minimum redemption of 49,500 acres for the next ten years. But only half the programme, which in any case was rendered farcical by the rapidly rising birthrate, was ever carried out. Reform was successfully blocked by the stubbornness of the estate owners.

A graver threat to the unity and future of the state was that presented by the minorities.

The rise of Nazism, though temporarily accompanied by an unreal *rapprochement*, turned the German minority into a militant agency on behalf of German territorial claims; meanwhile the proletariat in the east and south turned hopeful eyes in the direction of Moscow, and the anti-Semitic policy of the government had produced poverty and discontent in

National Minorities in Poland	
Poles	20,000,000 (65·5%)
Jews	2,300,000 (7·5% if considered *en bloc*, but in practice merged respectively in the other minorities, especially the Poles)
Ukrainians	5,400,000 (17·8%)
Germans	1,250,000 (4·1%)
Byelorussians	1,000,000 (3·4%)
Miscellaneous (Lithuanians, Russians, Czechs, Tatars, etc.)	550,000 (1·7%)

large numbers of second-class citizens. After an initial partition imposed by Germany and the Soviet Union, Poland collapsed swiftly in 1940 and entered the horrors of the occupation period.

Resurrection among the Ruins
Perhaps no country in history has faced as grim a position as Poland at the end of the Second World War. Hitler's deliberate policy, pursued for four years, of exterminating the Polish people; the comings and goings of armies engaged in active fighting; attack from the air and systematic destruction on the ground – all these had affected practically the whole country except the southern regions. Forty per cent of urban investment had been wiped out. Warsaw, with 1,200,000 citizens in 1939, had lost just under 80 per cent of them; 240,000 were still alive among the ruins on 1 March 1945. Many small towns, such as Nowogrod and Rozan, had been totally destroyed.

The population had suffered enormous losses. Yet the figure of 600,000 dead in battle was nothing beside the 5,400,000 (one-fifth of the total population) who had died in the concentration camps, labour camps and prisons, or who had been executed in mass reprisals. Industry and agriculture had been ruined in a proportion varying from 30 to 50 per cent.

In this devastation a new Poland was set up, on new demographic foundations. The Poland of 1939 had consisted of 147,063 square miles, with 35,000,000 inhabitants. The Poland of 1946 found its frontier pushed back in the east but was allowed to advance to the Oder in the west, where the territory thus annexed to Poland contained only 6,000,000 people in place of its former 9,000,000 (a reduction caused both by war-time losses and by a mass emigration of the Germans, an emigration which moreover continued after the war and subtracted a further 1,400,000 inhabitants from

Poland between 1946 and 1950). The result was a population of 24,000,000 in an area of 120,362 square miles. This numerical loss was offset by a gain in ethnic homogeneity:

Poles	88% (21,000,000)
Germans	10%
Others	2%

Moreover, this new homogeneity was accompanied by a new fecundity, the highest in Europe. The average annual rise in the birthrate between the wars had stood at the remarkable figure of 14·3 per cent; between 1950 and 1956 it was 19 per cent. One consequence is that 40 per cent of the present population of Poland (25,000,000 in 1950, rising to 28,500,000 in 1957, with a density of 35·5 per square mile) are under-twenties.

Vitality of this order, though creating problems of subsistence, housing and education which complicated the task of national recovery, also produced an atmosphere favourable to activity and initiative; it facilitated the rapid settlement of the western regions, whose unquestionably Polish character it was necessary to establish for all time; and it supplied the nation with an increase in manpower whose effects would be felt in the near future.

Faced with gigantic problems of material restoration and also of national unity, the Polish government, supported by the political parties of the people, has set about a programme of socialist construction which from 1956 onwards has been noteworthy for its liberal and accommodating spirit. The Polish Constitution enacted on 22 July 1952 provides for a people's democracy in which the legislative power is vested in a Diet (executive responsibility being entrusted to a Council of State elected by the Diet) and a planned economy; external trade is a state monopoly, and the principal means of production are in public or national ownership. Collectivization, however, has not gone very far; this is particularly true of the countryside. Agrarian reform was set in motion as early as 1944 and has expropriated all owners of more than 124 acres, with the result that by 1950 nearly half of the rural population were cultivating properties of from 12 to 35 acres. But, within limits, the peasant classes have maintained a differentiated structure; the struggle against those sections of the population who previously exploited the peasants and workers, a struggle expressly built into the Constitution under Article 3, mostly takes the form of measures setting a limit to individual enrichment and encouraging production under co-operative arrangements.

Nor is the socialized sector co-extensive with the whole of industry: the industrial crafts and small private industrial concerns still have a considerable place in the scheme of things; they are treated as complementary, not superfluous. Socialized industry also takes the form of production co-operatives.

Finally, there is one field in which the new régime in Poland shows its originality: the relationship between Church and state, a peculiarly sensitive problem in a Catholic country under a Marxist government. The agreement of 14 April 1950 between the government and the episcopate left the Church with something resembling autonomy, and a guarantee of freedom in education. After violent arguments about the interpretation of this *modus vivendi*, the new attitude adopted by the government in the autumn of 1956 included a new agreement with the Church and established a state of equilibrium.

Meanwhile Poland has been rebuilding and developing her economy. The Oder districts are being repopulated and their economy revitalized; the ports (Szcecin, Gdynia and Gdansk, of which the last-named is now a Polish possession) have been equipped with the necessary installations – an important matter now that Poland has acquired an extensive coastline; progress in industrialization has been marked by such milestones as the creation of new metallurgical centres like Nowa Huta and, more recently (1952), Nowe Tychy, near Katowice; and the organization of scientific and cultural life has been stimulated by the Academy of Sciences (founded in 1952), which encourages research of every kind. These have been the principal tasks, carried through by the dynamism of the people and their leaders, in a country which after coming close to extinction has once more become an important state.

A Socialist City: Nowa Huta
Prior to the First World War, the ancient university city of Cracow had become 'a town of the retired' (in British terms, something of a Cheltenham). In the restored Polish state after that war, Cracow showed signs of new life: an industrial fringe grew up round it. Now, under the contemporary régime, the Lenin metallurgical complex has been added, and the new city of Nowa Huta has been increasing and multiplying on the left bank of the Vistula since 1950.

POLAND IN 1961: STATISTICAL PICTURE		
Area		121,000 sq. miles
Total population		30,700,000 (as against 28,500,000 in 1957)
Rural population (1950)		45·75%
Urban population (1950)		54·25%
Principal cities (1961)	Warsaw	1,162,000 (as against 1,200,000 in 1939)
	Lodz	721,000
	Cracow	488,000

That site was chosen for Nowa Huta precisely in order to revive Cracow. Nowa Huta consists of two parts: a complete steel-working complex with a production equal to that of all Poland in 1937 (2,200,000 tons in 1963); and an urban complex connected directly with Cracow. It is contemporary Poland's greatest achievement. It took some 30,000 workers about ten years' continuous work to build the city and factory. The permanent population, amounting to 100,000 or thereabouts, is accommodated in an extensive residential area whose buildings are disposed along arteries radiating like the ribs of a fan from a central open space on the bank of the Vistula. In ten years nearly 50,000 living-units have been built, a dozen schools, the hospital over two hundred shops, several cinemas, a library and a theatre, covering in all nearly four square miles and including a number of gardens and large stretches of greensward.

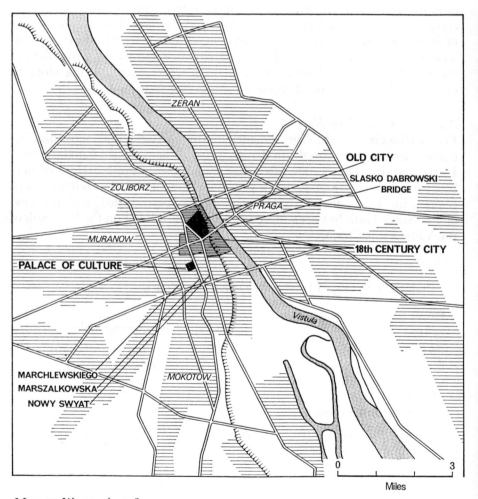

Map 25 Warsaw in 1960

The inhabitants of Nowa Huta consist largely of peasants from the surrounding districts and even from the voivodina of Katowice, that is to say from the coal basin of Upper Silesia, whose proximity was the *raison d'être* of the new community. But there is also a leavening of citizens from Cracow; that ancient university centre continues to contribute its quota of trained people and, in the heart of the new industrial region, has acquired a new importance. Nowa Huta, busy, dynamic and youthful (nearly a quarter of its population are under six years of age, and a third are between twenty and thirty), certainly personifies the contemporary social and economic revolution; but it turns to its neighbour for the necessary lessons which can be drawn from the culture and taste of so many previous generations. Cracow did not suffer, at any rate as far as its buildings were concerned, from the fearful destruction of the Second World War; intact, saturated with history, it has now been surrounded by a dense industrial ring and has practically become fused with Nowa Huta in a single conurbation and, in accordance with the decentralizing ordinances emanating from Warsaw, has begun to play the part of a great provincial capital.

The New Warsaw

In its reconstruction of the old quarters of Warsaw (Stare Miasto) the Polish government has displayed its loyalty to the past – the source from which Poland, in her many tragic crises, has always drawn courage and faith in the future. And the government is actively creating the future in the very way in which it is laying out the reconstructed capital, whose outlying parts are being developed into a huge, airy complex of new towns. Warsaw has become the typical specimen of those modern conurbations, not so much cities in the old sense as urban nebulae, whose economic and social activities have been decentralized and in which the original nucleus is mainly given over to administrative purposes (map 25).

Democratic Education

A feature common to all the left-wing democracies is that many more schools are being built and that culture has been democratized. In Poland, achievements in this field are all the more remarkable in that the war had destroyed the educational system in general and its buildings in particular; it had also killed off most of the staff and destroyed libraries (76 per cent of libraries were wiped out in Warsaw, 68 per cent in Poznan, 30 per cent in Lublin, and 14 per cent in Cracow).

Over and above the labours of reconstruction, progress by comparison with pre-war achievements has been considerable. Illiteracy is a thing of the past. The ratio of non-specialized secondary schools to the total population has greatly increased. The educational system is now better able to educate the masses; and the intake of the higher educational establishments is correspondingly larger.

The emphasis laid on professional and technical training is a sign of the times, a consequence of industrialization. Poland has no lack of natural resources, and the acquisition of the western territories has made an important addition to them (map 26).

HIGHER EDUCATION IN POLAND						
YEAR	NUMBER OF HIGH SCHOOLS	NUMBER OF STUDENTS (per 10,000 pop.)	SOCIAL ORIGIN OF STUDENTS %			
			Peasant	Worker	Intellectual	Miscellaneous
1937–8	27	14	8	9	58	25
1957–8	76[1]	45	21	32	42	5

[1] Including 8 universities

Variety in the Arts and Literature

Polish literature since 1918, though rich and varied, has moved continually round a central crux, namely the great problems confronting a state which has been successively re-established, destroyed and reconstituted, and which has never ceased tending its wounds and meditating on its own existence. Writers nurtured under the old order have been succeeded by generation after new generation, starting with those who were deeply involved in the artistic and literary pioneering of the experimental 'twenties; young people strongly influenced by the proletarian revolutionary writers of the Soviet Union, and drawing their subject-matter from the experiences of a society which, after the ordeals of the war, was seeking the path of justice and happiness but failing to find it.

These writers included not a few women, who had been roused by social injustice of one sort or another; for example Zofia Nalkowska (1885–1954) and Maria Dombrowska (1897–1962). The men included such writers as Bruno Jasienski (1901–42) and Wladyslaw Broniewski (1897–1962), who evoked the popular risings of the past, Julian Przybos (b.1901), a poet of industrial life, and Julian Tuwim (1894–1953), who described the working class. Social themes were the keynote; Polish writing in the years before the Second World War was increasingly dominated by opposition to the régime. The anti-fascism and anti-militarism of Antoni Slonimski (b.1895) make him a typical representative of the prevailing mood of dissent.

The Second World War and the German occupation brought a great change; an individualist such as Jaroslaw Iwaszkiewicz (b.1894), for example, became an *engagé*. Literary creation never ceased during those diffi-

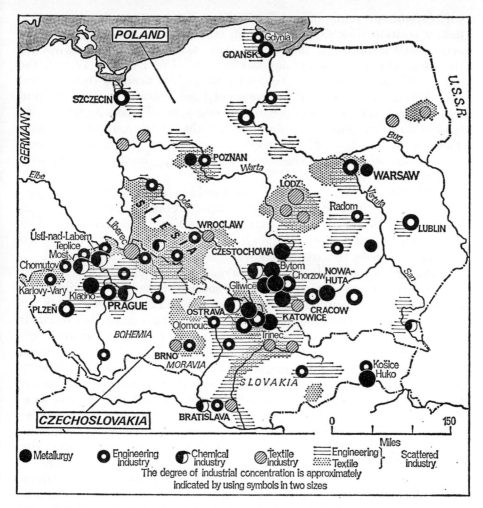

Map 26 Industry in Poland and Czechoslovakia, Twentieth Century

cult times; it was kept up by writers who had emigrated to the Soviet Union or the West (where the poets Tuwim and Slonimski continued writing, and Ksawery Pruszynski [1887–1950] produced his brilliant reporting). It sprang up vigorously in Poland itself as soon as the war ended, stimulus to freedom of expression from 1945 to 1949 being provided by the conflict of tendencies and by controversy about the new régime; the latter trend is typified by Jerzy Andrzejewski (b.1909) in his novel *Ashes and Diamonds*.

In 1949 the government demanded that the writers take their line from socialist realism; it was alarmed to see how small a part they were playing in the building of a new society. The resulting works were very uneven in quality. But thought remained free; criticism was never stifled. There was an immediate reaction against 'schematicism', a literary resistance whose fruits became apparent about 1954. Polish writing today has retained its variety without relinquishing its involvement in society's constructive task, a position which sets a premium on certain themes and places the accent on the future of the people. The memoirs of Lucian Rudnicki (b.1882), which started coming out in 1948 (*Old and New Things*), the stories of Tadeusz Borowski (1922–51), Kazimierz Brandys (b.1916) and Igor Neverly (b.1903), and the poems of Józef Putrament (b.1910), and many others, reflect an outlook which manages to reconcile truth with faith in socialism. But life abroad provides the strongest inspiration; thus Tadeusz Breza (b.1905), formerly a novelist of Polish life, is now preoccupied with his impressions of Italian life, with the Vatican as a background.

The Polish cinema is equally vigorous and has invaded the field of international competition in the work of Alexander Ford, Wanda Iakubovska, Jerzy Kawalerowicz (*Midnight Train*), and the New Wave directors such as Andrej Munk and Andrej Wajda. Of all the people's democracies, Poland has made the most remarkable contributions to the art of the film.

Although the nationalist bias of the Polish government between the wars had kept the country's eastern frontiers more or less closed, the influence of the Bolshevik revolution had made its way into Poland and affected not only the working-class masses but also the intellectuals and artists and their movements. The pictorial innovations of the young Polish 'formists' between 1918 and 1920 progressed in parallel with those of the Russian *avant-garde* painters of the same period. The main interest of their work (which was an amalgam of cubist and impressionist elements) consisted of their desire to create a national style inspired by folk-art. All too soon, however, Polish painters – many of whom frequented the studios of Paris – hitched their wagon to 'post-impressionist colourism' (Zygmunt Waliszewski, 1887–1936), a tendency which had no connection with social developments and moved steadily towards a new academicism.

The Second World War did nothing to shatter traditional conventions (figure 45), but it did give the arts a new general direction in which to steer; it weighed heavily on the painters' minds (and the sculptors'), and prompted them to use themes in which the depiction of events was at the same time a protest against the destruction of human values (Felician Kowarski, 1898–1948). The leading characteristic of Polish post-war painting, on the other hand, has been the variety of its tendencies, and an irresistible urge to branch out experimentally on lines which are foreign to social realism and are strongly influenced by the West. Meanwhile the building of socialism was creating a completely new atmosphere round the arts. Such a painter as Wladislaw Strzeminski (1893–1952), whose abstract, mathematical 'unism' was intended to contribute towards the beauty of the cities of the future, stands out in original isolation from the largest group of post-impressionist colourists, such as Pronaszko (1885–1958), Cybis (b.1897), Eibisch (b.1896), and various others.

In 1949 and 1950 the government embarked on an attempt to divert painting towards realism, and to give priority to figurative work which fulfilled a political and educative function by taking its subject-matter from popular life. Twenty years later than the Soviet Union, Poland underwent a phase of compulsion in the arts which failed, like its Russian predeccessor, and which was abandoned in 1954. While most of the modernists went on painting but did not exhibit, and others reconciled colourism with the new directives, officially-sponsored exhibitions offered the public works composed in accordance with the prescribed programme but evincing, however discreetly, a tendency to slip through the net. The sudden thaw of 1954, marked by the so-called Arsenal Exhibition – an expressionist display put on for the International Festival of Youth – was a typically Polish phenomenon.

Freedom of expression having been restored, talent of every species is

FIGURE 45 Polish popular art of the twentieth century: silhouettes in cut paper. The two cocks, a time-hallowed motif.

emerging. From figurative painting (Kazimierz Mikulski, b.1918; Jerzy Nowosielski, b.1923) to geometrical or expressionist abstraction (the former represented by Henryk Staszewski, b.1894, Marek Wlodarski, b.1903, and Tadeusz Kantor, b.1915, and the latter by Tadeusz Brzozowski, b.1918, and Adam Marczynski, b.1908), and from conventional neo-colourism to the combination of simplified colours and forms (Waclaw Taranczewski, b.1903, Jan Lebensztein, b.1930), a very wide range of *genres* is moving actively ahead.

More than any other of the visual arts, Polish painting is displaying the peculiar qualities of a highly individualistic people, thoroughly receptive to influences from abroad and very youthful in spirit, prone to gusts of enthusiasm and usually recalcitrant towards authority.

II CZECHOSLOVAKIA

The Masaryk Republic

Western-Style Parliamentary Democracy

In both Bohemia and Slovakia, the Austro-Hungarian collapse left control in the hands of a Committee of National Liberation which proclaimed the independence of the Czechoslovakian territories in October 1918. The new state, whose frontiers were defined by the peace treaty, organized itself under French protection. A middle-class liberal republic whose social structure brought it closer than any other Slav country to the western states, and associated with the latter by political and trade agreements, Czechoslovakia figured on the international level as a bastion against both German imperialism and the Bolshevik revolution. Its frontiers extended beyond Slovakia to Subcarpathian Russia, inhabited by Ukrainians; and since strategic necessities dictated the inclusion of the whole Bohemian quadrilateral within the country's borders, the population lacked homogeneity. A strong German minority, widely scattered in the towns of the interior and densely concentrated along the northern frontier, imposed on the new state a problem which the development of Germany towards fascism was soon to render insoluble. Czechoslovakia's 54,050 square miles supported 10,000,000 Czechs and Slovaks, 3,250,000 Germans, 700,000 Hungarians, and 1,000,000 Ukrainians and Poles (map 20, p. 355).

Czechoslovakia withstood without much difficulty the revolutionary wave which swept over Europe between 1918 and 1920, and which touched Slovakia in June 1919. This highly industrialized country, most of whose enterprises were run from Vienna, was also a country of modern agriculture, one third of whose forests and cultivated land consisted of big estates owned by a partly Germanized aristocracy. And it was governed by a Czech bourgeoisie which corresponded to the national feelings of the majority, and was thereby enabled to limit the amount of concessions wrung from it on the social plane.

The transfer of the headquarters of limited companies from Vienna to Prague, and the 'Czechization' of industrial financial capital, were not followed by nationalization measures. Out of 4,000,000 residents of big estates which were placed under sequestration and later partially restored to their owners, less than 2,000,000 moved into the ranks of the prosperous peasants, who supported the régime; agrarian reform made little headway. The failure of the general strike of December 1920 damped the popular hopes excited by the Russian revolution, which by that time had been successfully contained. Czechoslovakia between the wars, under the presidency of T.G.Masaryk, was the very type of a political democracy in which the basic freedoms (freedom of assembly, the right to strike, and freedom of the press) are accompanied by a residue of social legislation inherited from a less liberal past – from the Austro-Hungarian monarchy.

Like Poland, independent Czechoslovakia found herself suddenly thrust into the world, and compelled to take part in international material and

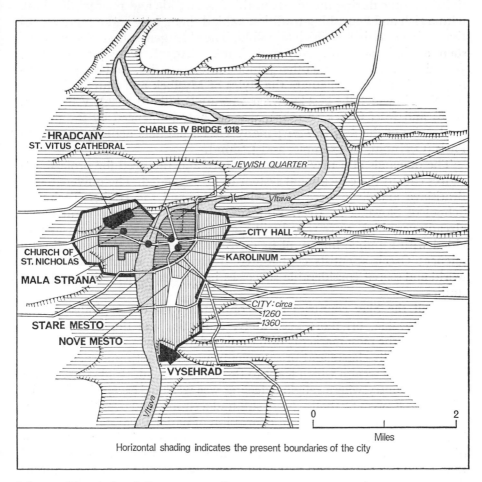

Map 27 Historical and Contemporary Prague

cultural competition. But by its own considerable exertions the nation rapidly lifted itself out of provincialism (map 27).

After a crisis of adaptation which resulted in further power for the bourgeois financiers, the Czechoslovak economy experienced high prosperity from 1924 to 1929. The Skoda steel factories of Plzen, the armaments factories at Brno, and the Bata shoe factories at Zlin (now Gottwaldov), sent their exports all over the world; Czech industry, highly diversified, and distributed throughout Bohemia, stamped its image on the landscape. Mountainous Slovakia, with the exception of its western fringe, remained agricultural and pastoral. A fever of building transformed the cities; the old quarters of Prague, with their outcrops of Baroque, were kept intact, but the rest of the capital put forth a quick growth of modern suburbs and soon had a population of 1,000,000. The country's urban, industrial character became more marked. The architects were trying to create a national modern style, influenced at first by cubism and dominated by a 'constructivist' attitude during the nineteen-thirties. Artistic and musical life, both with a rich and flourishing tradition behind them, now had a more receptive national setting in which to unfold. The older generation of composers, such as L.Janaček (d.1928) and J.Suk (d.1935), were joined by O. Jeremias, E.F.Burian and other junior contemporaries. And though sculpture continued to perpetuate the styles of Myslbek and Stursa (d.1925), painting, in which the best known names are E.Filla (d.1953), V.Spála (d. 1946) and Josef Čapek (d.1945), was strongly influenced by the diverse tendencies of the *école de Paris*; many Czech painters actually moved to Paris (O.Kubin, for example, and J.Sima).

The demands of a new national culture and the need for professional cadres caused the educational system to be expanded. The universities of Bratislava and Brno were founded in 1919, and the Higher Technical School of Slovakia in 1937. Educational standards in the rural areas, already very high, were raised still higher, and every commune was provided with a public library of its own. Publishing forged ahead. So did science; Czech scientists contributed freely to the scientific life of the world and scored considerable successes in physics, Orientalism and Slav studies.

Of all the Slav countries then connected with the capitalist world, Czechoslovakia, or, more accurately, Bohemia, was the one in which society was the most markedly differentiated, the standard of living highest and the middle classes and prosperous peasantry most numerous, despite inequalities of wealth which leapt to the eye in the industrial cities. It was also the country where religious feeling was weakest, except in Slovakia, where the Roman Catholic clergy still had a strong hold over the peasants. In Poland, Catholicism was an expression of national resistance, whereas in Bohemia it was compromised by its Hapsburg associations; but the indifference of a large proportion of the population (it has been estimated that 1,500,000 people had detached themselves totally from the Church) doubtless sprang from other, deeper causes, and merely showed up more obviously under a secular, middle-class government which had no desire to go on maintaining the Church in the station in life to which it was accustomed.

Literature, in this practical, pragmatic society with a keen eye for profits, but threatened from abroad, could hardly hope to avoid a precocious involvement in social and political issues. The struggle for independence was followed by resistance to the rise of fascism and the threat of enslavement. The most popular book in modern Czech literature, *The Adventures of the Good Soldier Schwejk*, by J.Hašek, had its roots in the Hapsburg past. But the first great prose artist of the period, K.Čapek (1890–1938), quickly made the transition from travel books to fiction and theatre (*War with the Newts*, 1934) of an anti-fascist tendency. The novelist V.Vančura (1891–1942) was at work on the third book of a patriotic cycle, *The Historical Images of the Czech People*, at the time of his assassination by the Gestapo. Social criticism provides the substance of the novels of M.Majerova and I.Olbracht, and the struggles and destiny of the Jews those of Hostovsky (b.1898). The poets S.K.Neumann (1875–1947) and J.Hora (1891–1945) were succeeded by a new generation, E.Halas (1905–49) and V.Nezval (1900–58), an outstanding figure whose imagination, formal virtuosity and rich intellectuality invite comparison with Eluard, Aragon, Neruda or Nazim Hikmet.

Through its middle classes the Czech people has been highly receptive to western influence; and through its workers, to the influence of Soviet Russia. While a docile middle-of-the-road Czech socialism was busy keeping in step with the government, the revolutionary left was sharply in opposition, organizing strike movements in the 'thirties, finding models for its own activities in Soviet experience, and endeavouring to reconcile the social struggle against the Czech bourgeoisie with the national struggle against the threat of Nazism. Though primarily political, this was also cultural action on behalf of a Communist ideal; supporters included the philosopher, historian and teacher Zd.Nejedly (1878–1962), the militant poet S.K.Neumann, the novelists Maria Majerova (b.1882) and I. Olbracht (1882–1952). Criticism of capitalist society and study of the relationship between culture and revolution received considerable impetus from an organization of left-wing progressives, *Levá Fronta* ('Left Front'), inaugurated in 1930, and J.Fučik's editorship of the new Marxist review *Tvorba* (*Creation*). Propaganda and the political education of the people were carried on not only by the press but also by theatrical performances by the Union of Czechoslovak Working-class Amateur Artists; these productions were put on all over the country. The Communist Party, which had been started in 1921, remained legally in existence until 1938.

Independence in Peril
The unity of Czechoslovakia was not altogether a sturdy growth. It was real enough for some time after the Peace Treaty, but became more and more precarious during the economic depression of the nineteen-thirties.

Bohemia's economic vigour, and the high cultural level of the better-educated classes among the Czechs, tended to make the Prague government fall into a slightly narrow outlook; the national interests of Slovakia were ignored.

'Czechoslovakism', or the theory of the 'unitary Czechoslovak nation', tended to regard Slovakia not so much as an equal partner in a new state as a passive appendage under process of assimilation. Despite the revival of the Matica Slovenska in 1919, the creation of the Šafařik Society in 1926, and a proliferation of educational institutions of one kind and another, in which Slovakian was used as the officially recognized language, Slovakia was rather pushed on one side. The death, between 1916 and 1928, of the great Slovakian writers of the early part of the century, and the attraction of Prague for the young, accentuated the impression of a certain efface-ment which the importance of Bratislava – a provincial capital of too slight and marginal a kind – was insufficient to camouflage. Nor was the situation affected much by the fact that Slovakia participated in the literary and artistic life of the *entre-deux-guerres* through her novelists(e.g.P.Jilemnicky, d.1949), poets (e.g. Jan Smrek), musicians (A.Moyzes, E.Suchon and others) and painters (e.g.G.Mally), and the Slovakian National Theatre, founded in Bratislava in 1920.

Her economy benefited along with that of the country as a whole, which was going ahead strongly. But any passing whisper of recession was imme-diately exploited by the proponents of Slovakian autonomy, who were led by the clergy and encouraged by Nazi Germany. The economic crisis of the 'thirties, which hit the export industries, ensured popular support for a separatism which, after Munich and the subjugation of Bohemia, ex-pressed itself in the proclamation of an independent state of Slovakia (14 March 1939).

Bohemia's unity was threatened by her substantial German minority whose members, like everyone else, were affected by the crisis of 1932–7, and who were egged on by Nazi propaganda; organized as the 'Sudeten German Party', they emerged as the most powerful factor in the 1935 elections and took their stand on a demand for political autonomy. The democratic elements in the country rallied round Dr Beneš, who had suc-ceeded Masaryk in 1935, but although help was guaranteed by treaties with the West it never came, and the Czechs were unable to prevent German intervention; the Munich partition (29 September 1938), which tore the state apart, was quickly followed by the occupation of central Bohemia and Moravia, which were converted into 'protectorates' of the Greater Reich (figure 46).

Socialist Czechoslovakia

Seven years later, after the harsh ordeals of occupation and war, Czechoslovakia rose again, though with different frontiers and demo-graphic structures and a new political régime. The road to liberation was paved from both London and Moscow: by the Beneš government in exile, and by the Czechoslovak Communist Party. Meanwhile the resistance movement had undergone the savage suppression of the Slovak rising of 29 August 1944 and of the Prague rising of 5 May 1944. Liberation itself came from the east: Soviet troops entered Prague on 9 May 1945, at which time a National Front government of Czechs and Slovaks was being formed at Košice and was working out a democratic and anti-fascist programme. The latter was put into action without delay, and was subsequently adopted by a Constituent Assembly which met for the first time in 1946. The Communist Party, which received 38 per cent of the votes cast in the legislative elections of that year, became the leading party in the republic.

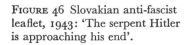

FIGURE 46 Slovakian anti-fascist leaflet, 1943: 'The serpent Hitler is approaching his end'.

In two years, by the elimination of the bourgeois parties on 25 February 1948, Czechoslovakia became a people's democracy, defined by the Constitution of 9 June 1948. The temporary harmony between the proletariat and the property-owning classes had proved too frail to withstand the proposals for socialization put forward by the National Front. The Soviet presence, combined with the action of the organized masses in support of the Communist Party, accounts for the rapidity of this slide towards a socialist régime in a country where the numerical strength of the middle class would have appeared to guarantee a conservative outcome.

In practice, the Košice programme and the policy of the National Front entailed immediate nationalization of banks, insurance companies, collieries and major industrial concerns, and also an agrarian reform which put 4,200,790 acres into the hands of 170,000 farmworkers. A Two-Year Plan for 1947–8, followed by a programme presented in March 1948 by the new National Front government under K. Gottwald (who became president on 7 June, after Beneš's resignation), set in motion the complete transformation of the country's economic and social structures. The foundations of the new régime were a planned economy (carried out under five-year plans from 1949 onwards), elimination of the capitalist sector in industry, the break-up of all estates of more than 124 acres and the organization of agricultural co-operatives, and democratization of the educational system.

Geopolitically, the bastion of Bohemia was as important as ever, but in the opposite direction now, towards the West; which is why the régime was harsher and less accommodating than in neighbouring Poland. Another reason is to be found in the character and temperament of the Czech people, serious, thoughtful, and inclined by its historical traditions to an austere view of life and a somewhat rigorous conception of duty and obedience.

Meanwhile the country was recovering from the misfortunes of war. Its geographical position and industrial importance had preserved it from the Nazi policy of extermination, which had threatened the continued existence of the Poles. The occupation had been harsh – the martyrdom of Lidice remains a memorial to that; but it had left much of the nation's vital forces intact. Material devastation was limited in scale. Bohemia and Slovakia began to look like their old selves; the delighted stroller in the ancient streets of Prague, and the summer visitor to the big Slovakian hotels of Tatranska Lomnica, could taste their pre-war pleasures over again.

But a peaceful revolution had caused the country's destiny to switch tracks; in this time-hallowed setting, where, even between the World Wars, modernity had begun stamping its image on the suburbs of the big cities, a new society was coming to birth.

Ethnically, this society is more homogeneous than the one it has replaced: Czechoslovakia has suffered the loss, by amputation, of Subcarpathian Russia and its Ukrainian population; and the mass departure of the Sudeten Germans has been followed by the partial re-population of the fringes of Bohemia by Czechs. In an area of 49,367 square miles, the Czechs (9,567,000 in Bohemia-Moravia) and the Slovaks (4,175,000) represent 95 per cent of a densely distributed population (41·3 inhabitants to the square mile in 1961), a population which is highly urbanized, but whose low birthrate constitutes a serious handicap for the future. Co-operatives and nationalized organizations employ very nearly the whole of the labour force, two thirds of which are accounted for by industry. Between 1948 and 1960 a process of socialization has been carried through which justifies the state's new name, the Socialist Republic of Czechoslovakia (ČSR).

In a country which had already reached a high pitch of economic development during its earlier experience as an independent republic, the creative dynamism proper to a revolutionary régime could hardly be expected to produce spectacular results. There was a lengthy phase during which the difficulties encountered in setting up the new structures diverted attention from the profound changes which were in fact taking place, but whose advantages could as yet be only anticipated, not enjoyed. Czechoslovakia's advanced society, with its high degree of differentiation, a society where differences of income were small but opportunities for betterment great, made it certain that the revolution would be a peaceful one. Its consequences were none the less both far-reaching and exacting.

In none of the other countries of popular democracy, except east Germany, was such a large proportion of the population affected by the reforms; and in none did the introduction of socialism meet with fewer opponents. The levelling-down of the rich bourgeoisie and the middle classes prompted only a small fraction of them to emigrate. National pride and an exceptionally high standard of public spirit took the sting out of the sacrifices involved. The Czech people, in spite of the burdens incurred by their entering the Soviet sphere of influence, lost none of their gratitude towards the Great Slav power on their eastern flank, with which they had no major source of disagreement (figure 47). The memory of Munich was still very much alive.

FIGURE 47 Slovakian satirical poster by A. Hajdučík, extolling high productivity and the struggle against war criminals.

There were a good many fields in which the tragic phase preceding the outbreak of war had prepared men's minds for radical changes. During the 'thirties, Czech writing had been marked by strong socialist tendencies combined with a patriotism intensified by the German danger. Occupation condemned the writers to silence; the return of peace found them all the readier to throw their energies into the expression of contemporary reality. The Marxist literary critic Bedřich Vaclavek (1897–1943), and Joseph Hora (1891–1945), had lost their lives; so too had Julius Fučik (1903–43), who had been executed by the Germans – not, however, before writing his admirable *Report from the Foot of the Gallows* (which by 1957 had

15*

been translated into seventy-one languages). But the originator of Czech socialist realism, Ivan Olbracht (1882–1952), was still writing. Others were Maria Majerová; Karel Novy (b.1890); Kark Biebl (1898–1951); Maria Pujmanova (1893–1958), whose trilogy of novels covers the period 1930–45; František Kubka (b.1894), the author of a *Family Chronicle* which presents a tapestry of Bohemian life and history from 1848 to 1945; the poet Nezval (1900–58), with his *Song of Peace*; Jarmila Glazarová (b.1901), who eulogized the resistance of Leningrad; and Vaclav Rezać (1901–56), who cast a critical eye over pre-war society. A younger generation of writers have since gained a firm footing; others yet younger are rising, taking as their subject-matter the ordeals endured by their country, or chronicling the immediate past, or analysing social conflicts, and striving to reconcile the natural aristocracy of art with the duty of participating in socialist construction. Names to note include Jan Drda (b.1911), short-story writer; Jan Otčenašek (b.1924) and Karel Ptačnik (b.1921), novelists; and the playwright Pavel Kohout (b.1928).

THE CZECHOSLOVAK REPUBLIC IN 1959: GENERAL STATISTICAL PICTURE

Area	48,981 sq. m.	
Population	13,602,613	
Compositon (in %)	Czechs	66·2
	Slovaks	28·2
	Hungarians	3·1
	Germans	1·2
	Poles	0·6
	Various	0·7
Principal cities *(population)*	Prague	999,000
	Brno	315,000
	Bratislava	259,000
	Ostrava	237,000
	Plzen	139,000
Contributions to national income in 1958 (in %):	Socialized production 93 (State enterprise 85%, co-operatives 8%) Individual production 4 Private firms 3	

The tradition of the puppet theatre has been carried on by the films of Jiři Trnka (b.1912), which have added new lustre to the Czech cinema by employing the animated cartoons – realistic or baroque, as occasion demands – of Karel Zeman to put across old legends, both Czech and foreign, and humorous stories (*The Adventures of the Good Soldier Schwejk*). Other aspects of Czech film-making, relying mainly on history (*Jan Hus*) or contemporary political events, have not displayed comparable progress.

The Czechoslovakia of 1960 has become a more evenly developed country. Slovakia (which is responsible for one third of the total agricultural production) has benefited from a remarkable programme of industrialization (the new steelworks at Huko). The training of future technicians and managers has been ensured by the laws of 1948 and 1955, which have reorganized education on a democratic footing. Agriculture is extremely up-to-date, largely in public ownership (70 per cent of cultivated land is in the hands of socialist-type co-operatives), and represents only 13 per cent of the national income, as compared with 20 per cent in 1948.

No other popular democracy is so highly industrialized. The mechanization characteristic of the economy has been carried further by the revolution, though the demands of the country's adherence to the Communist bloc have so far prevented the benefits from being passed on to the people in the form of higher living-standards. The revolution has also cemented the country's unity, though it has not quite succeeded in curing the Slovaks of a certain cautious reserve in their attitude to the Czechs. And a further shadow hanging over the destinies of Czechoslovakia is her low birthrate, combined with the fact that geography makes her the forward position of the Slav peoples in their resistance to any future external danger.

17

The Slav Peoples of the Balkans: Bulgaria and Yugoslavia

TWICE in the last thirty years Yugoslavia and Bulgaria have collided in nationalistic war; and Yugoslavia has won both times. They are now to some extent linked by socialism, though their régimes differ greatly. Bulgaria came off unluckily in the territorial as well as the military sense; the most that can be said is that the federal solution adopted by Yugoslavia does something to mitigate the injustice imposed on her neighbour by the fortunes of war.

I BULGARIA UNDER THE SOVIET UNION'S WING

After her defeat in the First World War, Bulgaria found her frontiers contracted, by the Treaty of Neuilly, to an oppressively small size (43,039 square miles). She underwent several years of social unrest, culminating in the suppression of the attempted Communist *coup d'état* in September 1923. The October Revolution had caused considerable stirrings in an essentially peasant people whose destinies during the preceding fifty years had been closely linked with Russia.

The defeat of the revolutionary movement in no way reduced the adhesion of a section of the intellectuals to a social ideal which aroused proletarian leanings in the poets: the enthusiastic socialist Christo Smirnenski (1898–1923) was succeeded by Arsen Raztsvetnikov (1897–1951), who commemorated the events of 1923, and Nicolas Vaptsorov (1909–42), who wrote of a world in which human values and technical progress would be harmoniously united. In the years before the Second World War there arose a new generation of writers, such as Pavel Veginov (b.1914), who threw in their lot with socialist realism.

A social preoccupation in a more general sense is characteristic of most modern Bulgarian writing, whether the accent be on the glories of the past or the difficulties of the present. Writers of the period of transition from an archaic to a modern Bulgaria included Elin-Pelin (1878–1949), whose stories and tales describe the peasant *milieu* with a certain nostalgia for the old, patriarchal way of life threatened by modernity, and Yordan Yovkov

(1880–1937), the 'great master of Bulgarian prose' (Bernard), whose inspiration was his love for his home country, the Dobrudja, from which so many refugees poured into Bulgaria after 1918. George Stamatov (1869–1942), a sombre writer, depicted bourgeois and military circles. Meanwhile poetry was dominated by the symbolist trend, represented by (among others) the patriotic Todor Trianov (1882–1945).

Socialist realism has dominated writing since 1945. Industrialization, the modernization of agriculture, and the moulding of a new type of man, supply most writers with their themes. The struggle for social justice and for freedom waged by Macedonians and Bulgars in the nineteenth century inspired Dimitar Talev (b.1899), one of the best contemporary Bulgarian novelists. A similar repertory of themes is used by figurative painters and sculptors, who, like many of the writers, display a realism which, if elementary, is at any rate vigorous.

AGRICULTURE AND INDUSTRY IN BULGARIA 1939–63				
YEAR	AGRICULTURE		INDUSTRY	
	Gross national product	% of the active population employed	Gross national product	% of the active population employed
1939	75	80	25	50
1963	30	20	70	50

Bulgaria has been completely transformed in a space of less than twenty years. The country has remained primarily agricultural and still exports tobacco, rose-attar and vegetables, but it has built up an industrial structure no longer based exclusively on a modernized agriculture. It possesses abundant resources in coal (annual production 22,000,000 tons); and heavy industry is growing. Its membership of COMECON, from which it has received considerable financial support and technical aid (particularly from the USSR but also from Czechoslovakia and East Germany), has enabled it to build numerous factories; electrical fitments have become a speciality. A quarter of its export trade (four fifths of which goes to the other socialist countries) consists of capital equipment. This rapid industralization is creating new towns and making both them and the old ones grow larger; buildings are going up fast – half of them are less than twenty years old; and the rising tide of savings, encouraged by the foundation of the State Savings Bank in 1951, bears witness to the increase in the national income.

The economy has been brought over almost exclusively to socialism: 72·2 per cent of agricultural production is carried out by co-operative farms, 5·6 per cent by government establishments, and 21·8 per cent by members of co-operatives on their personal holdings. The considerable increase in the country's productive capacity is evident in the development of irrigation schemes (88,958 acres irrigated in 1950, 2,223,948 acres in 1964), the expansion of horticulture and industrial agriculture, and the contribution of new activities, such as tourism. Bulgaria had 80,000 visitors from abroad in 1958, and 324,000 in 1962; the Black Sea beaches (notably the Golden Sands) are becoming as familiar to westerners as those of the Adriatic. The imposition of a popular-democratic régime has subjected the country to an acceleration of development whose result, at present, is a condition of creativeness and tension which makes it impossible to gauge how far this material progress has been matched by a corresponding change in the people's mentality and outlook. Eighty years of life as an independent nation, after many centuries of foreign domination, make a precarious basis on which to lay the foundations of socialism.

Every side of the state's organization of life is orientated towards the socialist ideal, starting from education, which is based on compulsory primary schooling over an eight-year period (age-group 7–16 years), followed by polytechnic secondary education for four years; in recent times,

BULGARIA: GENERAL STATISTICAL PICTURE	
Area	3,861 sq. m.
Population	1956 7,613,000 1962 8,062,000
Distribution of population (%)	Urban, in 1920, 19·9; in 1946, 25·9; in 1961, 38·8 Rural, in 1920, 80·1; in 1946, 74·1; in 1961, 61·2
Growth of industrialization:	Contribution to national income Agriculture in 1950, 65%; in 1961, 15% Industry in 1950, 22%; in 1961, 49%
Principal cities	Sofia (1961) 700,000 Plovdiv 300,000 Varna 200,000 Burgas 100,000 Dimitrovgrad 80,000

namely since the law of 3 July 1959, the latter has involved an admixture of vocational with academic work: the secondary school leaving certificate is usually accompanied by a certificate of vocational aptitude (this applied to 90 per cent of the cases in 1961). In higher education, one third of the total number of hours of study is allocated to some form of work connected with production. The country, which had 1,380,000 illiterates in 1944, now has a higher proportion of schoolchildren and university students than any other in the world.

Uniform schooling is levelling out class-differences and religious divisions; and harmony has been attained between the Marxism of the state and the Orthodoxy of the clergy, whose national feelings remain as strong as ever.

II ORIGINALITY: YUGOSLAVIA

Dictatorship and Assimilation

A new chapter in the history of the Yugoslav peoples was initiated by the *de facto* creation, in 1918, of a kingdom of the Serbs, Croats and Slovenes. The new state was officially established on 28 June 1921; its frontiers were recognized by the Treaty of Versailles (May 1919), and the following further Treaties: Saint-Germain, with Austria (10 September 1919); Neuilly, with Bulgaria (27 November 1919); Trianon, with Hungary (4 June 1920); and Rapallo, with Italy (12 November 1920). Under a parliamentary monarchy, an Assembly (the *Skupshtina*) elected by universal suffrage enabled such party groupings to take shape as expressed the national and social desires at work in the country. The government, based on the two largest parties (Radicals and Democrats), embarked on a policy of conservatism and centralism.

But the 'national' union of Serbs, Croats and Slovenes was largely unreal, though strengthened by the wave of democratic feeling which followed the War. The union had been aimed against Austria-Hungary: it proved inadequate to survive the rise of petty nationalisms and the Belgrade government's policy of Serbianization. The ideal of Yugoslav solidarity, by which the union was cemented in the minds of a handful of intellectuals, could have carried weight only in a context of social democracy which was quite alien to the vast majority of the people. The government in Belgrade was powerless to reconcile the unity of the whole with respect for minority national rights.

Only Serbia, under the liberal King Peter, had had any experience of life in a genuine democracy. Though there was no difficulty in securing the attachment of Montenegro (whose authoritarian monarchy had commanded little popular support), Bosnia-Herzegovina (which had risen against Austria-Hungary), and the Voivodina (which had defended Serbian nationality against Hungary in a long and painful struggle), the jumble of nationalities along the Adriatic coast, in Dalmatia and Istria, soon began to cause difficulties. But it was Croatia which was the real stumbling-block. Nominally at least, the Croats had been autonomous, in a state framework of their own, until 1918; both they and the Slovenes were now quick to claim real autonomy, and to jeopardize the unity of the state. Meanwhile in Macedonia, which since 1912 had suffered from the competitive greed of Bulgaria, Greece and Serbia, all bent on assimilation, a national consciousness was developing which was incompatible with the policy of Serbianization.

There was the burden of the past: the country was made up of historic provinces which had preserved, along with their separate languages and cultures, a sense of regional and even national reality, and this sense had been strengthened by foreign overlordship. And there was the burden of religion: a heterogeneity in which the worst rivalry was not that between the Muslims and Orthodox in Bosnia, but between the Orthodox Serbs

RELIGIOUS GROUPS IN YUGOSLAVIA IN 1931

PRINCIPAL GROUPS	ORTHODOX	ROMAN CATHOLICS	PROTESTANT SECTS	MUSLIMS	JEWS
Serbo-Croats	6,577,398 (Serbia, Bosnia-Herzegovina, Montenegro, Macedonia)	3,186,295		908,167 (Bosnia-Herzegovina)	
Slovenes		1,110,063			
Germans		383,674 (Voivodina)	102,698 (Voivodina)		
Hungarians		410,350 (Voivodina)			
Rumanians	134,795 (Voivodina)				
Albanians				481,770 (Kosmet)	
Turks				132,781	
Jews					
Gipsies	20,688 (Macedonia)				
TOTAL	6,785,501	5,217,847	254,713	1,561,166	68,405

and the Catholic Croats. These two burdens made unification harder. And failure to unite was the outstanding characteristic of Yugoslavia's history between the World Wars.

Within the preconditions determined by the centralistic constitution of 1921, the predominance of the Serbian Radical Party, backed in its policy of hegemony by the Democratic Party (which was more amenable to the demands of the minority nationalities but none the less Serbian for that), led the state into a blind alley. The fact that the Croatian Diet in Zagreb had been elected by some two or three per cent of the population had left room for uncertainty about what the Croatian people in general really felt; the Croatian Peasants' Party, adopting under Raditch's leadership a hostile attitude to the state, rendered the fiction of unity untenable. The strength of the Communist Party (which was founded in August 1919 at the initiative of the Serbian social democrats) was derived less from its adherents among the small class of industrial workers, than from a general longing for social and political reform. Reforms had indeed been set on foot by the would-be national government, but were quickly dropped.

Partial agrarian reform, and temporary liberties (of association and public assembly), were the only concessions granted by a monarchy which pursued a policy of conservatism and centralization at home, and displayed a predominantly Serbian façade abroad. The outlawing of the Communist Party, and the denial of the claims of the Croatian Peasants' Party (though the latter collaborated with the Radical Party until the assassination of Raditch on 20 June 1928), characterized Yugoslavia's political life in the early years, during which a pretence of parliamentary government was still in being.

In 1929 a royal dictatorship was declared and remained in power until 1941. The Constitution was suspended, to be replaced by that of 3 September 1931. The administration was reorganized, overriding the country's time-honoured ethnic anatomy. The Communist Party had gone underground; the police campaign against it was stepped up and its membership melted away (by 1932 they numbered a few hundred). A similar campaign was carried out against the Ustashis, the Croatian national resistance movement; an armed rising which nearly broke out in the Velebit region in 1932, and the assassination of King Alexander in Marseilles on 9 October 1934, were among the consequences. Close links were established with the Axis powers after 1936. An autonomous state of Croatia was formed, with foreign help, in 1939. All these developments were so many steps on the road to fascism, a process not only determined by the internal logic of the régime but also hastened by contagious example: surrounded by states which had joined the Tripartite Pact one after another in 1940 and 1941, Yugoslavia followed suit on 25 March of the latter year.

The patriotic reaction of the Serbs and the *coup d'état* of 27 March 1941 caused German and Italian intervention. The state of the Serbs, Croats and Slovenes collapsed. Autonomous Croatia became an independent nation, and, under the leadership of Ante Pavelitch, conducted a war of extermination against the Serbs and also against anti-fascists. A partisan struggle, carried on by Mikhailovitch's *chetniks* and later, from July 1941, by the Yugoslav Communist Party under the leadership of Tito, developed in the countryside. The former soon compromised themselves by collaborating with the forces of occupation and the pseudo-government of Belgrade. The Communist Party was the spirit and backbone of the national liberation movement.

In the early part of its history that Party had scarcely ventured to deviate from reformism. But subsequent experience underground had rejuvenated and toughened it. Out of touch with the masses, but having acquired military experience by service in the volunteer forces despatched to the civil war in Spain, and political experience in the internment camps for ex-fighters in that war in France, and also in the prisons of their own country, an army of three thousand hardened fighters was ready and able, in 1941, to impose on Yugoslavia a policy of revolutionary and national resistance very different from the wavering, conciliatory attitude of the *chetniks*, who were recognized by the Yugoslav government in exile in London as the 'Royal Army of the Fatherland'.

As early as 1942 Tito showed his independence of the orders of Stalin. The latter, looking at things from the standpoint of a European war and of world strategy, regarded the increasingly acute conflict between Tito and Mikhailovitch with distrust and expressed his hostility to the formation, in 1943, of a government drawn from the Communist resistance movement. As the partisan war proceeded, Tito set up people's committees and anti-fascist councils, bringing the Croats and Serbs together in a single democratic framework, and gradually constructing the political cadres of a federal Communist state. This state came into being on the defeat of Italy and Germany.

From a Federal to a Socialist Republic
Twenty eventful years have passed since a Federal Republic of the People was created by the enactment of the Constitution of 29 November 1945. The later Constitution, that of 7 April 1963, defines the state of Yugoslavia as a 'federal socialist republic ... of the peoples, freely united and equal before the law', and as a 'socialist democratic community based on the power of the working people and the principle of self-management' (Article 1).

Alone among the people's democracies, the Yugoslav state is trying, not without grave difficulties and a good many inconsistencies, to reconcile effective government from the centre with a system of communal autonomies which, at all administrative and economic levels, is intended to give to both groups and individuals a sense of genuine, first-hand participation in the nation's affairs. Economic decentralization and the diffusion of authority – in constant conformity, however, with the Communist ideal, which remains the government's lodestar – have received special emphasis under the new Constitution: Article 108 declares that 'the working people

... exercises within the Republic all the social functions which concern its [the people's] life and economic, cultural and social development, except those which are reserved by the present Constitution to the rights and duties of the Federation.'

The Federal Solution

The Yugoslav federal system reconciles the unity of the state with the diversity of nationalities of which the state consists (the expression 'national minority' is regarded as a slur, and is no longer used). The Yugoslav citizen is allowed to have dual nationality if he likes. This is typical: it implies that the official policy is no mere empty federalism, a simulacrum, but is based on the real needs of the federated peoples and removes any pretext for separatism.

Yugoslavia suffered grievously in the war; her total loss of a million lives wiped out a decade of population growth. Montenegro and northern Serbia were hit the hardest, losing respectively 16 and 11 per cent of their population. But recovery has been rapid because the birthrate, particularly in the south, is high. In 1950, over half the population was under twenty-five years of age.

On the basis of the new federalism, the Yugoslav economy began by treading the path of centralization and bureaucracy exemplified by the Soviet Union. From 1946 to 1949 a tyrannical policy of rural collectivization in the form of production co-operatives, a process stubbornly resisted by the peasants, and a similar policy applied to small industrial and business firms, was enforced in a poor country depleted by war and, in spite of external aid, experiencing great difficulty in rising from its own ruins.

In 1945, all peasant indebtedness was declared void and an agrarian law was passed limiting individual agricultural holdings to 61·8 acres; simultaneously there was a drive towards collectivization which ended in fiasco. The economic situation became so grave that the Communist Party abandoned compulsion and, by an order enacted on 23 March 1953, left the peasants free to choose whichever system they preferred. Most of the agricultural production co-operatives thereupon broke up; meanwhile the maximum permitted size for private holdings was reduced from 61·8 to 24·7 acres. By 1963, four fifths of the arable land was in private ownership; half the peasants were farming properties of between 9·9 and 12·4 acres. Yugoslavia's agricultural system is characterized by the consolidation of peasant smallholdings and the fact that the country's available resources in cultivable land are not large, and are considered not as state but social property – a significant distinction – entrusted to collective management (plate 26).

In contrast to this, the whole of industry and 70 per cent of craft manufacture have been nationalized. But here again, direct state management and rigid control from the top have been replaced by social self-management, in which an essential part is played by the workers' councils created in 1950. By a further innovation, introduced in April 1964, these councils, half of whose members are changed every year, elect factory managers, a short list of entrants being obtained by holding an open competition beforehand.

AREA AND POPULATION OF YUGOSLAVIA AND ITS REGIONS ON 31 MARCH 1953

REPUBLIC	CAPITAL	AREA Sq. miles	POPULATION			
			%[1]	Total	%[2]	Per sq. mile
Serbia	Beograd	34,079	34·3	6,983,544	41·3	204·9
Old Serbia	—	21,516	21·7	4,460,405	26·4	207·2
Voivodina	Novi Sad	8,505	8·7	1,713,905	10·0	199·7
Kossovo-Metohija	Pritina	3,986	4·0	809,234	4·9	203·0
Croatia	Zagreb	21,725	22·0	3,913,753	23·1	180·0
Slovenia	Ljubljana	7,707	7·8	1,462,961	8·6	189·6
Bosnia-Herzegovina	Sarajevo	20,179	20·1	2,843,486	16·0	142·7
Macedonia	Skoplje	10,230	10·3	1,303,906	7·7	127·4
Montenegro	Titograd	5,169	5·4	419,625	2·4	78·5
Yugoslavia	Beograd	99,089	100·0	16,927,275	100·0	170·8

[1] Percentage of total area of the country
[2] Percentage of total population

Federalism has triggered intense regional development, turned provincial centres into capitals and created new cities (Titograd). Architecture in the most modern styles is appearing in the new quarters ('New Belgrade'). Serbia has perhaps benefited less than the other republics from the general stimulus. But everywhere a campaign for industrialization and cultural development is gradually changing the face of the country, though the everyday details of life remain as custom-bound as ever. Traditional costume and its regional variations have not disappeared, particularly outside Serbia. Religious customs (rather than religion) have kept their force. Offerings of fruit are still placed on graves in Macedonia; Communist atheism, professed and practised, co-exists comfortably with prayers in front of icons. Official reconciliation between the state authorities and religious leaders has created a climate of tolerance, not unassisted by a certain degree of underlying indifference on the part of the ostensibly devout. National peculiarities are perpetuated by language, folk customs and popular beliefs; the Oriental streak in Yugoslav folklore is specially noticeable in the south. These autochthonous features have even been accentuated in some cases, such as the Croatian village of Hlebin, a centre of peasant art (painting, woodcuts and sculpture).

Of all the Slav countries, Yugoslavia is the one which presents the greatest degree of variety. As economic development proceeds life inevitably becomes more uniform, more standardized, but this sameness is nowhere less marked than in Yugoslavia. A strange country if ever there was one, Yugoslavia is a zone formed by the overlapping of two worlds and is a part of both of them; a country whose mixed inheritance, Byzantine and Greek, Turkish, Austrian, Latin, seems not so much superimposed on the Slav foundation as integrated into it, not only in the most obviously colourful aspects of folk life but in the very minds of the population. The unifying factor is a sense of togetherness, a Yugoslav concord with a Serbian overtone.

Literary and artistic activity in Yugoslavia over the last fifty years reflect both the strength of regional attachments and that of influences from abroad – Vienna, Paris and, more recently, Moscow. Before World War One, Slovenian writers were prominent, particularly Ivan Cankar (1876–1918) and Oton Župančič (1879–1949), who is regarded as 'the greatest lyrical poet since Prešren'. The 'twenties produced the same phenomena as elsewhere: an explosion of *avant-garde* writing, an expressionistic revolt corresponding to simultaneous unrest on the social plane. A certain number of lasting works appeared, however, and each of Yugoslavia's peoples can lay claim to its own share of them; a high proportion of them are impregnated with a sharply particularist feeling and draw their material from history remote or recent, peasant life, and social conflicts. The lyricism of a poet like Miroslav Krleža (b.1893), and the narrative talent of Ivo Andrič (b.1892), who was to win a Nobel Prize for his historical novels after the Second World War, were not involved in the contemporary problems which preoccupied most of the writers of the 'thirties: a decade marked by the rise of a social trend which, though stamped with regionalism, showed no hankering after folklore and rusticity. Subsequent literary generations have been attracted towards Marxism, a tendency already visible in the work of Djordje Ivanović (d.1943). With the end of the Second World War came a transition to social realism which, however, is finding plenty of room for the psychology of the individual and his warring conscience – in other words, for those inner crises which the militant socialist must of necessity undergo in achieving his precarious victories over the frailties of flesh and blood, and in overcoming the difficulties and growing-pains inherent in the transformation of human society.

Conclusion:
Diversity and Unity: A New World
in the Making

THE SLAV peoples today – and Yugoslavia is no exception – find themselves, by virtue of their political régime, on the brink of an entirely new destiny. The dynamic principles they have applied to their own development are tending to differentiate them more sharply than ever before from the peoples of the West. The function of the State; the new economic framework of society; the spirit of collectivization, the drive for justice in the distribution of wealth; the attempted abolition of class distinctions; faith in the human species, in man's effort to master the material world while remaining indifferent to the possibility of an afterlife – all this adds up to the practical application of Marxism in every department of existence, and represents an attempt to transform the nature of human life. The aim of communism, a noble and legitimate aim, is to create a new man and, through him, a new civilization. The foundations of that civilization, which is intended to have universal validity, have been laid in the Soviet Union, that is to say in a setting which is essentially something more than just the homeland of the largest Slav group; so it must be conceded that these foundations have nothing specifically Slav about them. And in any case the new structures are so young, so recent, with only a half-century of life behind them – a tiny span in relation to the time-scale of human history – that it would be vain to expect them to engender the promised new civilization here and now. So heavy is the burden of the past that their effect on men's minds is still very limited.

Rapid industrialization is the keynote – for the present, at least, and on the material plane – of the transformations initiated in eastern and south-eastern Europe as a result of the October Revolution. Towns have increased in size and number and there has been an upsurge of the urban spirit. Despite all the differences in political and social structure, this development has not driven a wedge between East and West but has brought them closer together, rapidly making daily life in eastern society indistinguishable from that in western: life as experienced at the factory and in public transport, in blocks of flats and architectural residential complexes (functional or otherwise) for the workers; a life in which leisure is controlled by direction or suggestion, imposed by regulation or made inevitable by circumstances; a life scrutinized by authority, recorded in card-indexes and statistical records, and digested into the official documents and permits which swell the wallet of the individual in Moscow as in Paris, in Uzbekistan as in Belgium. In ever fewer cases does the Russian peasant settle down for the night on a bench alongside the tiled stove which warms his cottage; he sleeps in a bed from a department store. The same forest of television aerials, visible from miles away, rises over the town of Vjazniki (district of Vladimir) as over Paris (Illinois). Queues at bus stops are more orderly in London than in Moscow, but otherwise identical. Soviet Russia and the other popular democracies – in spite of their form of government and very largely because of it – are moving towards that 'general destiny of mankind' in which Guizot, in a vast visionary perspective, foresaw the gradual coalescence of all the 'families of peoples'.

None of this, however, should lead us to minimize the new spirit pulsing in the transformations now going on in eastern and south-eastern Europe. Marxism involves a complete revolution in man's conception of the world. It directs and defines the actions of the governing cadre in every sector of life and is progressively establishing its hold on people's minds. 'Communist man' is a creature who will doubtless not appear on earth just yet; but the conditions necessary for his existence are being created and the cherished dreams of the nineteenth century socialists no longer seem entirely utopian. The fact that, where Europe is concerned, this new experiment by mankind is being conducted predominantly by the Slav peoples must give us cause for reflection; since in history – minor details apart – there is no such thing as chance. That the father of Marxism was a German matters little; its first practical application, its translation into living reality, is Russian, and it is highly significant that the new régime has been effectively challenged and forced into partial compromise only on the western fringe of the Slav world. The past explains both the successes and the difficulties of the present. The respective characteristics of the various Slav civilizations enable us to understand the adaptations and resistances which, in different regions, a single set of socio-political imperatives has called into being. Acceptance of these imperatives presupposes profound psychological and intellectual changes, changes which have yet to take place.

Bibliography

The bibliography of the subject is immense and is in very many languages – much of it in the Slav languages, and therefore inaccessible to most western readers. What is given here is a modicum of works in French, English, German and Italian, with a few in the Slav languages; those in the latter category contain illustrations or statistics and can be profitably consulted by any reader with the bare minimum of linguistic equipment.

More detailed bibliographical information, extremely wide in scope, will be found in the series 'Clio' (Paris: Presses Universitaires de France, first edition, 1934 ...); and 'La nouvelle Clio' (same publisher, 1963 ...), which is still in course of publication.

A handy list, mostly of works in English, is:

Epstein K.T., 'A Short Bibliography on the Slavs', in *The Slavonic and East European Review*, October 1944.

Also worth noting is:

Malclès, L.N., *Les Sources du travail bibliographique* (Geneva, 1950–8). No specialist should be without this. The chapters on Soviet Russia: general and specialized bibliographies (language, literature and history), are by David Dzhaparidze.

A current bibliography is published early by the *Revue des Etudes slaves* (Paris: Institut d'Études Slaves).

I HISTORICAL SERIES

'Peuples et Civilisations', Paris: Alcan, 1927 ...; new edition by PUF, 1950 ...
'Histoire générale des civilisations', Paris: PUF, 1953 ...
The interest of this series lies in the treatment: the Slav peoples are studied in the setting of European and world history.
'Encyclopédie de la Pléiade' (*Histoire universelle*, vols. 2 and 3, chapters on the Slav world), Paris: Gallimard, 1957–8
The studies published by the Institut d'Études slaves, Paris, covering every part of the field.

A brief selection of illustrated works in Slav languages:

USSR

Ocherki istorii SSSR (General history of the USSR [to 1800], Moscow, 1953–7
SSSR (USSR), a large volume of excerpts from the *Bolshaya sovietskaya Entsiklopediya* (Great Soviet Encyclopaedia); 2nd edition, 1957.

Poland

Historia Polski (to 1864), vols I and II, Warsaw, 1959 ...

Czechoslovakia

HUSA, Valcav, *Dejiny Ceskoslovenska* (History of Czechoslovakia), Prague: Orbis, 1961

Yugoslavia

Historija naroda Jugoslavije (History of the Yugoslav Peoples), vols. I and II, Belgrade, 1953 . . .

Bulgaria

Istorija Bolgarii, vols. I and II (Sofia, 1954–5)

2 REVIEWS

Many articles on the Slav peoples (studies and accounts of important works) will be found in the major French reviews, such as *Annales* (*Economies, Sociétés, Civilisations*), *Revue historique, Revue d'histoire moderne et contemporaine* (and the collections of articles which preceded it: *Etudes d'histoire moderne et contemporaine*). More specialized are *Le Monde slave* (which appeared from 1924 to 1938) and the *Cahiers du monde russe et soviétique* (since 1959); in English: *The Slavic Review, Oxford, Slavonic Papers* and *The Slavonic and East European Review* (the last-mentioned being American); in German: *Jahrbücher für Geschichte Osteuropas*, Wiesbaden.

A few studies of institutions will be found in the *Recueils de la Société Jean Bodin* (Brussels, 1936 . . .)

This seems the most appropriate place in which to mention such of the reports of the International Congresses of the Historical Sciences (held from 1900 to 1960) as are devoted to the Slav countries; particularly the *Transactions of the VIIth Congress* (Warsaw, 1933) and *Poland at the Xth International Congress of the Historical Sciences* (held in Rome in 1955); also the series of historical booklets published for that Congress by the Soviet, Czechoslovak, Yugoslav and Bulgarian Academies of Sciences.

Finally, historical articles and fine illustrations (of monuments and the arts) will be found in the periodicals published in French, for distribution in France, from Czechoslovakia (*La Vie tchécoslovaque*), Poland (*La Pologne*) and Bulgaria (*La Bulgarie*). The Yugoslavs bring out, at irregular intervals, a magnificent journal of the arts, *Jugoslavija*.

3 INDIVIDUAL WORKS

On the Slav countries considered as a whole (origins, history, literature and art):
CROSS, S.H., *Les Civilisations slaves à travers les siècles*, Paris: Payot, 1963
DVORNIK, F., *The Slavs in European History and Civilization*, New Brunswick, New Jersey: Rutgers University Press, 1962
Histoire générale des Littératures (*Histoire universelle*), 3 vols., Paris: A. Quillet, 1961
KOVALEVSKY, P., *Atlas historique et culturel de la Russie et du monde slave*, Paris: Elzevier, 1961. Much illustrated.

The chapters on Slav music in various musical encyclopaedias, especially:
COMBARIEU, J., and DUMESNIL, R., *Histoire de la Musique*, vols. 3, 4 and 5, Paris: Armand Colin, 1955, 1958 and 1960
La Musique, des origines à nos jours, Paris: Larousse; new edition 1954

Russia and the Soviet Union

General Histories

CARR, E.H., *A History of Soviet Russia* (publication commenced in 1950. The period so far covered is 1917–26.)
CLARKSON, J.D., *A History of Russia from the Ninth Century*, London: Longmans, 1962
GITERMANN, V., *Geschichte Russlands*, 3 vols., Zurich, 1944–9
History of the USSR, 3 vols., Moscow: Foreign Languages Publishing House, 1948
MAZOUR, A.G., *Russia Tsarist and Communist*, Princeton, New Jersey: Van Nostrand, 1962 – 995 pp.
MILYUKOV, P., SEIGNOBOS, Ch., and EISEMANN, L., *Histoire de Russie*, 3 vols., Paris: Leroux; new edition 1935
SUMNER, B.H., *Survey of Russian History*, London: Duckworth, 1944
VERNADSKY, G., *A History of Russia*, New Haven: Yale University Press, 1943–59. Includes four volumes on the Middle Ages in Russia

Collected Studies on Most of the Major Problems of Russian History

Readings in Russian History, I: From Ancient Times to the Abolition of Serfdom; II: The Modern Period, New York: Sidney Harcave Harpur College, 1962
Le Statut des paysans libérés du servage (1861–1961), Paris: Mouton, 1963
The Russian Intelligentsia, New York: Columbia University Press, 1961
Continuity and Change in Russian and Soviet Thought, Cambridge, Mass.: Harvard University Press, 1955
The Transformation of Russian Society (since 1861), idem, 1961

Specialized Studies

AMMAN, A.M., *Ostslawische Kirchengeschichte*, Vienna: Thomas Morus Press, 1943
BLUM, J., *Lord and Peasant in Russia, from the Ninth to the Nineteenth Century*, Princeton University Press, 1961
CONFINO, M., *Domaines et seigneurs en Russie vers la fin du XVIIIe siècle*, Paris: Institut d'Etudes slaves, 1963
DANZAS, J.N., *L'Itinéraire religieux de la conscience russe*, Paris: Grün, 1961
DUCHARTRE, P.C., *L'imagerie populaire russe (1629–1825)*, Paris: Grün, 1961
ECK, A., *Le Moyen âge russe*, Paris: Maison du livre étranger, 1933
ECK, A., 'Le Grand Domaine dans la Russie du moyen âge', *Revue historique du Sud-Est européen*, 1944
GILLE, B., *Histoire économique et sociale de la Russie, du moyen âge au XXe siècle*, Paris: Payot, 1949
GEORGE, P., *L'U.R.S.S.*, Paris: PUF, 1962, 'Orbis' series. Geographical description
GREKOV, B., *La Culture de la Russie de Kiev*, Moscow: Foreign Languages Publishing House, 1947

HAUMANT, E., *La Russie au XVIIIe siècle*, Paris: L.H. May, 1957

HOFMANN, Rostislav, *La Musique en Russie, des origines à nos jours*, Paris: L.H. May, 1904

JOHNSON, W.H.E., *Russia's Educational Heritage*, Pittsburg, Penn.: Carnegie Press, 1940

KERNER, R., *The Urge to the Sea. The Course of Russian History*, Berkeley, 1942

KHROMOV, P.A., *Ekonomitcheskoe razvitie rossii v XIX–XXe vekakh* (Economic development of Russia in the nineteenth and twentieth centuries), Moscow, 1950. Includes statistical tables

KLUTCHEVSKY, V.O., *Histoire de Russie, I: Des origines au XIXe siècle*, Paris: Gallimard, 1956. Translated from the Russian

KLUTCHEVSKY, V.O., *Pierre le Grand et son oeuvre*, Paris: Payot, 1953

KOHN, H., *Pan-slavism. Its History and Ideology*, Notre Dame University Press, 1953

KOYRÉ, A., *La Philosophie et le problème national en Russie au début du XIXe siècle*, Paris: Honoré Champion, 1929

LENIN, *The Development of Capitalism in Russia*, London: Lawrence and Wishart, 1957

LEROY-BEAULIEU, A., *L'Empire des Tzars et les Russes*, 3 vols., Paris: Hachette, 1883

LO GATTO, E.O., *Storia della literatura russa*, 2 vols, Florence: Sansoni, 5th edition, 1964. French translation, Paris: Desclée de Brouwer, 1965

LO GATTO, E.O., *Storia del teatro russo*, 2 vols., Florence: Sansoni, 1952

LYASHCHENKO, P., *History of the National Economy of Russia to the 1917 Revolution*, New York: Macmillan, 1949. Translated from the Russian

LEGRAS, J., *La Litterature en Russie*, Paris: Armand Colin, 1929

LUCIANI, G., *La Société des Slaves unis (1823–1825)*, University of Bordeaux, 1963

MALIA, Martin, *Alexandr Herzen and the Birth of Russian Socialism (1812–1835)*, Cambridge University, Mass., 1961

NOLDE, B., *La Formation de l'Empire russe*, vols I and II, Paris: IES, 1952–3

PASCAL, P., *Avvakoum et les débuts du raskol*, Paris: new edition, Mouton, 1959

PIPES, P., *The Formation of the Soviet Union*, Cambridge, Mass.: Harvard University Press, 1954

PORTAL, R., *Pierre le Grand*, Paris: Club français du livre, 1961

PROKOPOWICZ, S.N., *Histoire économique de l'U.R.S.S.*, Paris: Flammarion, 1952

SMITH, R.E., *The Origins of Farming Russia*, Paris and The Hague: Mouton, 1959

SOKOLOV, J., *Le Folklore russe*, Paris: Payot, 1945

SORLIN, P., *La Société soviétique (1917–1964)*, Paris: Armand Colin, 1964

SORLIN, L., 'Les Traités de Byzance avec la Russie au Xe Siècle', in *Cahiers du monde russe et soviétique*, Nos. 3 and 4, 1961

STREMOUKHOFF, D., 'Moscow the Third Rome. Sources of the Doctrine', *Speculum*, 1953

RASHIN, A.G., *Naselenie Rossii za 100 let* (The Population of Russia, from 1800 to 1900), Moscow, 1956 (statistics)

RAEFF, Marc, *Michael Speransky, Statesman of Imperial Russia (1772–1839)*, The Hague: Martinus Nijhoff, 1957

RAEFF, M., *Siberia and the Reforms of 1822*, Seattle: University of Washington Press, 1956

RÉAU, L., *L'Art russe*, 2 vols., Paris: Laurens, 1922–3

STRUVE, N., *Les Chrétiens en U.R.S.S.*, Paris: Le Seuil, 1963

TREADGOLD, D.W., *The Great Siberian Migration. Government and Peasant in Re-settlement from Emancipation to the First World War*, Princeton, New Jersey: Princeton University Press, 1957

TREADGOLD, D.W., *Lenin and his Rivals. The Struggle for Russia's Future (1898–1906)*, London: Methuen, 1955

TROYAT, H., *La Vie quotidienne en Russie au temps du dernier tsar*, Paris: Hachette, 1959

VENTURI, F., *Il populismo russo*, 2 vols., Turin: Giulio Einaudi, 1952

WALISZEWSKI, K., a series of works arranged according to reigns, and covering Russian history from the Time of Troubles to the death of Alexander I

WEIDLE, W., *La Russie absente et présente*, Paris: Gallimard, 1949

Poland

General Works

Cambridge History of Poland, vols. I and II, Cambridge University Press, 1950–1

Encyclopédie polonaise and *Atlas*, Lausanne and Paris: Payot, 1916–20

GIEYSZTOR, A., HERBST, S., and LESNODORSKI B., *Mille ans de l'histoire polonaise*, Warsaw: Editions Polonia, 1959

HERMAN M., *Histoire de la littérature polonaise*, Paris: Nizet, 1963

La Pologne de 1944 à 1964, Warsaw: Editions Polonia, 1964

Polen (Osteuropa-Handbuch) (contemporary Poland), Cologne and Graz: Böhlau, 1959

Among the various short histories of Poland (such as those by O. HALECKI, H. GRAPPIN and E. KRAKOWSKI), special note should be taken of the excellent *Histoire de la Pologne* by A. JOBERT (Paris: PUF, 1953, series 'Que sais-je?').

Essential Studies

FABRE, J., *Stanislas-Auguste Poniatowski et l'Europe des Lumières*, Paris: Institut d'Etudes slaves, 1952

FRANCASTEL, P. (ed.), *L'Origine des villes polonaises* (collected essays), Paris: Ecole Pratique des Hautes Etudes, VIe Section, 1960

HENSEL, W., *Les Origines de l'Etat polonais*, Warsaw: Editions Polonia, 1960

JOBERT, A., 'L'Etat polonais, la liberté religieuse et l'Eglise orthodoxe au XVIIe siècle', in *Revue internationale d'histoire politique et constitutionelle*, Paris, Nos. 19 and 20, 1955

JOBERT, A., *La Commission d'éducation nationale en Pologne (1773–1794)*, Paris: Les Belles Lettres, 1941

KONOPCZYNSKI, L., *Le 'Liberum Veto'. Etude sur le développement du principe majoritaire*, Paris: Champion, 1930

KOSTRZEWSKI, J., *Les Origines de la civilisation polonaise. Préhistoire. Protohistoire*, Paris: PUF, 1949

KULA, W., *Les Débuts du capitalisme en Pologne dans la perspective de l'Histoire comparée*, Rome: Signorelli, 1960

LESNODORSKI, B., *Les Institutions polonaises au Siècle des Lumières*, Paris: Centre d'Etudes polonaises, 1963

LESNODORSKI, B., *Le Nouvel Etat polonais du XVIIIe siècle*, in *Utopie et institutions au XVIIIe siècle*, Paris: Mouton, 1963

RUTKOWSKI, J., *Histoire économique de la Pologne*, Paris: Institut d'Etudes slaves, 1937

TAYLOR, J., *The Economic Development of Poland (1919–1950)*, Ithaca, N.Y.: Cornell University Press, 1952

WOJCIECHOWSKI, Z., *L'Etat polonais au moyen âge. Histoire des institutions*, Paris: Recueil Sirey, 1949

Czechoslovakia

DENIS, E., *La Bohême depuis la Montagne Blanche*, 2 vols., Paris: Leroux, 1903

GEORGE, P., *Le Problème allemand en Tchécoslovaquie (1919–1946)*, Paris: Institut d'Etudes slaves, 1947

JIRECEK, C., *La Civilisation tchèque au moyen âge*, Paris: IES, 1920

KOZIK, K., *La Vie douloureuse et héroïque de Jean Amos Comenius*, Prague, 1959

MACEK, J., *Le Mouvement hussite en Bohême*, Prague, 1958

POLISENSKY, J.V., *History of Czechoslovakia in Outline*, Prague 1948

PROKÈS, J., *Histoire tchécoslovaque*, Prague, 1927

SETON-WATSON, *A History of the Czechs and Slovaks*, 1943

Yugoslavia, Bulgaria

ANCEL, J., *Peuples et nations des Balkans*, Paris: Armand Colin, 2nd edition, 1930

BLANC, A., *La Croatie occidentale. Etude de géographie humaine*, Paris: IES, 1957

Enciklopedija Jugoslavije, 5 vols. (more to come), Zagreb: Leksik. Zavod. (Many illustrations)

Jugoslawien (Osteuropa-Handbuch) (contemporary Yugoslavia), Cologne and Graz: Böhlau, 1954

HAUMANT, E., *La Formation de la Yougoslavie*, Paris: IES, 1930

MOUSSET, J., *La Serbie et son Eglise*, Paris: IES, 1938

SAMIC, M., *Les Voyageurs francais en Bosnie à la fin du XVIIIe siècle*, Paris: Didier, 1960

STOYANOVIC, *L'Agriculture au XVIIIe siècle dans les Balkans*, Paris, 1954

VAILLANT, A., 'Les Chants épiques des Slaves du Sud', in *Revue des cours et conférences*, 1932

Glossary

Alphabet, Cyrillic (after Cyril, its creator): one of the two alphabets of Old Slavonic (cf. Glagolitic); the ancestor of the modern Russian, Ukrainian, Byelorussian, Serbian and Bulgarian alphabets.

Alphabet, Glagolitic (etym. *glagol* = word, speech): one of the two alphabets of Old Slavonic, with letter-forms differing from those of Cyrillic. It survived for some time in Dalmatia and Croatia.

Artel: A kind of production co-operative of village workers; the customary, traditional form of work organization in Russia.

Ban, Banat: the title of *ban* was borne from the twelfth century onwards by the local rulers of the Hungarian marches. After the middle of the nineteenth century it survived only in Croatia. As a proper name, 'the Banat' means the banat of Temesvar.

Bartshina (from the Russian *barin*, lord): the unpaid work owed by a serf to his lord.

Bogomilism, Bogomils: a heresy which was widespread in the Balkans from the tenth to the seventeenth century. The Bogomils disapproved of formal worship and the ecclesiastical hierarchy and fought against established authority and the rich. Bogomilism has much in common with the heresy of the Cathars.

Boyars: the uppermost stratum of the ancient Russian nobility. The boyars bore arms in defence of the sovereign prince.

Bolsheviks, Mensheviks: respectively, those who, at the Second Congress of the Russian Social Democrats in 1903, sided with Lenin and formed the majority on the question of the conception of the Party; and those who formed the minority.

Bund: a Jewish working-class organization set up in Russia in 1897. It seceded from the Social Democratic movement in 1903, adopted the Menshevik programme and ceased from all activity in Russia in 1921.

Burlaki: barge or boat hauliers on the Russian rivers.

Burnt clearings, cultivation on: nomadic cultivation in forest clearings; after the necessary trees had been felled, the underbush was destroyed by burning.

Bylin: folk poem of an epic nature, celebrating the real or legendary heroes of Russia between the eleventh and sixteenth centuries.

Chin: administrative and aristocratic hierarchy created by Peter the Great.

Compacta: agreement between the Hussites and the Council of Bâle (1433), permitting the Hussites to celebrate communion in both kinds.

Dekabrists (Decembrists), revolt of the: a revolt by members of the Russian nobility, mostly officers, who took advantage of the death of Alexander I, on 14 December 1825, to attempt the overthrow of tsarism. The ensuing repression was frightful; some of the conspirators were hanged and the rest were deported to Siberia.

Desiatin: Russian unit of area, equivalent to 2·7 acres or 1·092 hectare.

Diet: national assembly. The term was used in Germany, Poland and Hungary.

Domostroi: a sixteenth-century Russian handbook of household management, which gives us a picture of Russian daily life at that time.

Druzhina: personal retinue of a sovereign, and the basis of his army.

Duma: (etym. [assembly of individuals who] think): a representative assembly authorized to advise the sovereign (Duma of the Boyars) or exercise administrative powers (Duma of the Towns) or political powers (State Duma, after 1905).

Exarch, exarchate: the title of exarch, normally applicable to military leaders, also occurs in the ecclesiastical hierarchy. In 1870, for example, the Bulgarian Church, previously subject to the authority of the Greek Patriarch of Constantinople, attained autonomy by the establishment of a Bulgarian Exarchate.

Gorod, grad: originally meaning a stockade, this word subsequently denoted a fortified town and finally any town. It occurs in the name of many Slav towns or cities: Novgorod, 'New town', Beograd, 'White town', etc.

Gosti: 'hosts', the rich Russian merchants of the seventeenth and eighteenth centuries.

Great Russia: the northern and central portion of Russia, inhabited by the principal branch of the East Slavs (Great Russians), differentiated by linguistic features from the Byelorussians (White Russians) and the Ukrainians (Little Russians).

Guild: (1) in a general sense, an association of merchants or craftsmen; (2) in a particular sense, in Russia, an association of merchants, these associations being hierarchically graded by the state in accordance with differences in personal fortune (eighteenth and nineteenth centuries).

Guzla: a one-stringed musical instrument, played with a bow. It is very popular in Montenegro and is used for accompanying epic songs.

Haiduks: the heroes of Serbia and Bulgaria, half brigand, half patriot, whose feats are celebrated in the epic folksongs of those countries.

Hansa: association of the great German trading cities, from the thirteenth century to the eighteenth. The Hansa had a post at Novgorod.

Holy Synod: a council created by Peter the Great to exercise authority over the Russian church, through the Procurator of the Holy Synod.

Horde, the Golden: state founded in the twelfth century by the Tatar Mongols, on the Lower Volga. Though their power was shaken by the Battle of Kulikovo in 1380, it was not until the sixteenth century that they were brought under control by Ivan the Terrible.

Iconostasis: a large partition which, in churches of the eastern rite, separates the sanctuary from the nave, and is covered with icons.

Intelligentsia: educated people in whose outlook and social position the accent was on education and not on the class to which their parents belonged. The intelligentsia were the backbone of the revolutionary opposition in the nineteenth century.

Isba: wooden house in rural Russia.

Islam: religion of the Muslims.

Janissary: Turkish infantry soldier.

Jassak: tribute levied in the form of furs.

K.D. or Cadets: Constitutional Democratic Party (Russia).

Kasha: a kind of gruel which is one of Russia's national dishes.

Khanate, khan: a khan is a ruler of Tatar birth, ruling over a khanate.

Khata: Ukrainian house, usually timber-built and whitewashed.

Kisel: fruit jelly made with starch.

Knez: prince of the Serbian or Croatian nobility.

Knights of the Sword, Order of the: a religious military order founded in Livonia in 1202, and amalgamated with that of the Teutonic Knights in 1237. It remained very active until the mid-sixteenth century.

Knights, Teutonic, Order of: a religious military order founded in the early twelfth century. Recruited from the German nobility, it was very active in Germany and the surrounding countries. Its power was broken at the battle of Grünwald (Tannenberg) in 1910.

Kokochniki: a kind of tiara worn by Russian ladies; in architecture, a set of superimposed arches.

Kolkhoz: an agricultural production co-operative, a collective farm.

Kreml (kremlin): 'At mention of the Kreml' (writes Louis Réau) 'people commonly assume there is only one, that of Moscow; as if in antiquity there had been only one Acropolis, that of Athens. In fact, however, just as most Greek cities, Corinth, for example, had their acropolis, kremls towered over most of the Russian cities: over Novgorod and Nijni Novgorod, Pskov and Tula, Vladimir and Rostov. The distinction is exactly the same as that between the *ville haute* and the *ville basse* in feudal France [the upper town and lower town].' The Kreml was at once a fortress, an administrative hub and a sanctuary. That of Moscow was originally constructed of timber, but was rebuilt in stone by Ivan III with the aid of Italian architects.

Kulak (etym. a fist, i.e. a fist closed over money acquired): a peasant who was thought to be wealthy.

Kurgan: in southern Russia, a tumulus containing ancient graves.

Kustary: rural craftsmen working for the merchants.

Kvass: an alcoholic beverage whose ingredients vary; the basis is rye-flour.

Lapti: crude footgear made of birch bark.

Laura (Gk. *Lavra):* a large monastery of the first class, with several churches. There were four in Russia in 1917.

Liberum veto: the right of veto which every member of the Polish Diet possessed, and which was regarded as a safeguard of existing liberties.

Limes: a system of fortified frontier defences. The word is borrowed from the history of the Roman empire.

Little Russia: from the sixteenth century onwards, this expression means the central Ukraine (provinces of Kiev, Poltava, Chernigov, later Kharkov), in contradistinction to Great Russia (q.v.).

Lubki: a term of Russian folk-art, a simple kind of picture, comparable to the French *images d'Epinal.*

Manifesto, October: The Tsar's declaration of October 1905.

Marxism and Marxism-Leninism: theory of the development-laws of nature and society, a theory whose foundations were laid by K. Marx (1818–83) and F. Engels (1820–95) and adapted to historical conditions by Lenin (1870–1924).

Meshchanstvo: the various classes of the urban population, inferior in rank to the nobles and bourgeoisie, but not including the workers and peasants.

Mir: a form of village organization, led by the largest cultivators in the rural community (cf. *obshchina*). The *mir*'s functions were administrative and economic.

Moujik: Russian peasant. Originally, the word was a mildly unfavourable diminutive from *muzh,* man.

Nadiel: in Russia, before the agrarian reforms of 1861, a piece of community land set aside for individual cultivation. After 1861, plot of land which the peasant acquired by purchase.

Nagaika: Cossack whip.

Namestniki: lieutenants of the kingdom, nominated in Old Russia by the Grand Prince (and later by the tsar).

NEP: the New Economic Policy of the Bolshevik Government after 1921, the sequel to the period of War Communism.

Nihilism, Nihilists (Lat. *nihil,* nothing): a special kind of Russian radicalism. 'Nihilism is simply the Russian form of the negative, revolutionary spirit of the [nineteenth] century' (Leroy-Beaulieu). The word was used for the first time in Turgenev's novel, *Fathers and Sons* (1862).

Oblomovshchina: the weak, passive, negligent mentality of many Russian noblemen. (Oblomov is the chief character of a novel by Ivan Goncharov.)

Obrok: a tithe payable by the serf to his owner, in kind or, as was more often the case, in cash.

Obchtchina: agrarian community; the land owned by a village and periodically shared between its families, either to be individually cultivated (arable land) or left in communal use (pastures).

Old Slavonic: the first written Slav language, of which the earliest texts were the translations made by Cyril and Methodius in the ninth century from Greek ecclesiastical writings.

Oprichnina: the administrative measures enacted by Ivan the Terrible between 1565 and 1584. They were intended to diminish the power of the aristocracy, and were accompanied by a reign of terror.

Otrezki ('strips of land'): in Russia, bits of land lopped from the property of the serfs liberated under the Statute of 1861.

Perelog: land left fallow; part of the three-year crop rotation system.

Pesme: Serbian folksongs.

Pirogi: small Russian sweetmeats or cakes.

Plug: generic term for a plough (cf. *sokha*), usually reserved for modern ploughs making a deep furrow (two feet or even deeper).

Pomaks: Bulgars who were converted to Islam in the sixteenth century. There are about 100,000 of them surviving today.

Pomestie: an estate granted temporarily by the sovereign in return for services rendered in war. The *pomestie* could be neither sold nor bequeathed. The owner (*pomeshchik*) gradually came to wield the same rights on his estate as the owner of a *votchina* (q.v.). By the eighteenth century there was no difference between the two.

Populism: a movement 'to the people' (especially the peasants) on the part of young Russian nobles, eager for reform and social justice, in the period 1860–90. It was a revolutionary trend with socialistic tendencies, but embodied a conviction that revolution in Russia meant revolution by the peasantry.

Posad: in Russia, an urban quarter inhabited by craftsmen and traders, which grew up round the fortress (*Kreml*). The *posad* is the archetypal nucleus of the city.

Prikaz: an administrative department (the forerunner of a ministry in the modern sense) in early tsarist Russia.

Pud: former Russian unit of weight; about 36 lb.

Pugachevshchina: a peasant rising led by Emelian Pugachev in the time of Catherine II of Russia.

Rascie: the Serbian state in the twelfth century.

Raskol: (etym. 'separation'): schism. The name given to the heretical movement of the Old Believers in seventeenth century Russia.

Raznochintsy ('from all estates of life, all classes'): educated people who had opted out of the traditional class distinctions. In the nineteenth century they constituted an enlightened opposition to the tsarist régime.

Riady ('drawn up in lines'): rows of craftsmen's shops and workshops which, in market villages, constituted the nucleus of a future town (sixteenth and seventeenth-century Russia).

Russkaya Pravda: 'Russian Law', a collection of juridical rules put together in Kievan Russia during the first half of the eleventh century, under Yaroslav the Wise.

Russalka: water-sprite of the Russian rivers.

Sarafan: part of the clothing of peasant women in Great Russia: a pinafore generally worn over a blouse with puffed sleeves.

Shaman: a tribal priest and sorcerer, especially in eastern Siberia.

Skupshtina: elected representative assembly in Serbia, and later in Yugoslavia.

Slavonic: Old Slavonic (q.v.) as developed differently in different countries (Russian Slavonic, Croatian Slavonic, etc.).

Slavophils: the representatives of one section of Russian opinion in the nineteenth century (Khomiakov, Aksakov, etc.), who considered that Russia had been diverted from her true path by the reforms of Peter the Great and his successors. The Slavophils endeavoured to prove the superiority of such typically Russian institutions as the rural community, the Russian national church, and so on. (Cf. Westernizers).

Slobod: village agglomeration inhabited by free peasants; later, the word came to mean a suburb or urban quarter housing a specific trade or occupation (e.g. the *slobod* of the coachmen).

Sobor: in old-time Russia, either an assembly of elected representatives, or an important church at which the patriarch and bishops officiated.

Social democracy: a general term for the revolutionary parties which grew up on a Marxist basis in most European countries in the latter part of the nineteenth century.

Sokha: a crude form of plough much used in forested regions of eastern Europe, the Urals and Siberia, with an iron ploughshare penetrating the soil to a depth of four or five inches.

Sokols ('Falcons'): gymnastic clubs inaugurated in Bohemia in 1862. They were encouraged in the Slav countries as a youth movement and an instrument of national struggle.

Soviet ('council'): a term mainly applied to a mass political organization which appeared for the first time in Russia in 1905. Originating as committees for directing strikes, and subsequently insurrections, the soviets seized power in 1917.

Sovkhoz: state farm.

Starosta ('old man'): in Russia, elected village mayor.

Steppe: grassy plain in Russia and southern Siberia; in the south the steppe becomes a salt-marsh.

Strieltsy: archers; they constituted a kind of Russian militia. They mutinied under Peter the Great.

Sudebnik: Russian legal code. The first *Sudebnik* was adopted by Ivan III in 1497.

Szlachta: minor Polish nobility.

Taiga: the Siberian forest.

Telega: four-wheeled cart used by Russian peasants.

'*Time of Troubles*': the early part of the seventeenth century in Russia, marked by the Swedish and Polish invasions and the peasant war of 1606-7. The Time of Troubles terminated at the accession of the Romanovs (1613).

Troika: three horses harnessed to a vehicle.

Tundra: typical vegetation of northern Russia and northern Siberia, where the ground is marshy, with moss, lichen and occasional shrubs.

Ukase: edict, order.

Utraquism: doctrine of the moderate Hussites, who demanded communion in both kinds (i.e. wine as well as bread).

Veche: municipal assembly in Russian towns, before the sixteenth century.

Vlachs (*Wallachians*): mountain-dwelling elements of Greco-Illyrian origin, strongly affected by Roman influence, and later gradually Slavicised. Stock-raising is their characteristic occupation.

Vodka: Russian spirit distilled from grain (diminutive of *voda*, water).

Voisko: army.

Votchina: estate whose owner wielded absolute proprietary rights.

Westernizers (*Occidentalists*): the name given in nineteenth-century Russia to a certain number of intellectuals (Byelinsky, Herzen and others) who approved of Peter the Great's reforms, and held that the way to overcome Russia's backwardness was to adopt the best that the West had to offer. In this they differed from the Slavophils (q.v.).

Zadruga: ancient patriarchal organization of village life in north-western Yugoslavia.

Zemstvo: local assemblies established under the reforms of 1864, with various responsibilities (road construction and maintenance, statistical studies, hospitals, elementary schools, etc.).

Zeta: the first Serbian state, set up in the ninth century, in what is now Montenegro.

Župa: former administrative divisions in Croatia.

Chronological Tables

	Russia	Poland
7th cent.		
9th–10th cent.	9th–10th cent. The Varangians in Russia.	
860	860 Cyril and Methodius among the Khazars (Crimea).	
863		
893		
894		
911	911–945. Treaties with the Byzantines.	
921		
924		
929		
965		
973		
980	980. Kiev becomes the royal capital.	963–992. First Polish state, under Mieszko.
992	980–1015. Vladimir's reign; kingdom of Kiev becomes Christian	10th–12th cent. Poland is won to Christianity.
		11th cent. Cracow becomes the capital.
1015		
1025	1025–37. St Sophia of Kiev built.	
1037		
1039		1039. Feudal lords of Great and Little Poland united under the Piasts.
1045	1045–52. St Sophia of Novgorod built.	
1051	Monastery of the Crypts (Kiev).	
1052		
1054	1054–1203. Wars with the Polovtsy.	
1085		
1098	9th–13th cent. First legal code (*Russkaya Pravda*).	Early 12th cent. Earliest chronicle (anon., in Latin).
1147	1147. Foundation of Moscow.	
1169	Unified Kievan state disintegrates.	
1180		12th cent. Drive to the East by the Teutons. Spread of the Romanesque style.
1185		
1187	Late 12th and early 13th cent. Church of St Dmitri under construction at Vladimir.	
1200	1200. Foundation of Riga.	13th cent. Spread of 'Magdeburg Law'.
1211	13th–15th cent. 'Mongol peace'.	Earliest texts in Polish.
1220	1200. Foundation of Nijni Novgorod.	
1236	1236. Moscow becomes the political and religious capital.	
1240	1240. Capture of Kiev by the Mongols.	
1241	1240–2. Alexander Nevsky's victories over the Knights of the Sword.	1241. The Mongols halted at Cracow.
1242		
1249		Second half of 13th cent. Gothic architecture predominant.

Czechoslovakia	Yugoslavia, Bulgaria	
624–659. Empire of Samo.		7th cent.
		9th–10th cent.
		860
863. Cyril and Methodius in Moravia.		863
	893–927. Bulgarian empire, under Simeon.	893
	894. Magyar invasion.	894
		911
		921
921–929. First Czech state, under Wenceslas.	924. Kingdom of Croatia, under Tomislav.	924
		929
		965
973. See of Prague. Slovakia annexed to Hungary.		973
		980
		992
		1015
		1025
		1037
		1039
		1045
		1051
		1052
		1054
1085. Wratislaw II king of Bohemia.		1085
	1098. Croatia subjugated by the Hungarians.	1098
		1147
		1169
Mid-12th cent. First stone bridge over the Vltava.		1180
1185. Cosmas' *Chronica Bohemorum.*	1185. Nemanovitch dynasty in Serbia.	1185
	1187–1396. Second Bulgarian state.	1187
		1200
	1211. Council of Tirnovo (conflict with the Bogomils).	1211
		1220
		1236
		1240
		1241
		1242
1249. Mining law of Jihlava.		1249

16*

	Russia	Poland
1278		
1286	1286. The Hansa begins trading at Novgorod.	
1289		1289. Warsaw receives its municipal charter.
1300	14th cent. Formation of Great Lithuania.	
1306		
1344		
1346		
1348		
1352		
1355		
1364		1364–1400. University of Cracow founded.
1371		
1372		
1380	1380. Dmitri, grand prince of Moscow, defeats the Mongols at Kulikovo.	
1386		1386. Marriage of Hedwig of Poland to Ladislas, grand duke of Lithuania.
1389		1386–1572. Polish dynasty of the
1391	1391. Death of St Sergius.	Jagellons.
1396		Conversion of Lithuania to Christianity.
1410		1410. The Germans defeated at Grünewald (Tannenberg).
1420		
1434	15th cent. Subjection of Pskov and Novgorod to Moscow.	
1457		
1468		
1472	1472. Marriage of Ivan III and Sophia Paleologou.	
1480	1480. Liberation from the Mongol yoke.	Cira 1480. Altar-table by Wit Stowsz.
1490	Late 15th cent. Rebuilding of the Kremlin.	
1492		1492–1648. Poland's 'Golden Century'.
1496		1496–1532. Laws reducing the peasants to a state of servitude.
1497	1497. The peasants' liberty restricted.	
1502	1502. End of the Golden Horde.	
1505		1505. Statute Nihil Novi.
1515		
1520		
1524		
1526		1526. Lutheran rising in Dantzig.

Czechoslovakia	Yugoslavia, Bulgaria	
	1278. The Slovenes conquered by the Hapsburgs.	1278
		1286
		1289
1300. Monetary reform; the groat of Prague.		1300
1306. Premysl dynasty comes to an end.		1306
1344. Prague becomes an archbishopric.		1344
1346–78. Charles I emperor (Charles IV).		1346
1348. Foundation of university of Prague.		1348
	1352. First Turkish victories in the Balkans.	1352
	1355. Death of Dushan, prince of Serbia.	1355
		1364
1371–1415. Jan Hus.		1371
	1372. The Serbs crushed by the Turks on the Maritza.	1372
		1380
		1386
	1389. Turkish victory at Kossovo.	1389
	1391. Death of Tvrtko, prince of Bosnia.	1391
	1396. Beginning of Turkish overlordship in Bulgaria.	1396
		1410
1420. Tabor founded.		1420
1434. Hussite defeat at Lipany.		1434
1457. The Bohemian Brethren.		1457
1468. First book printed in Czech.		1468
		1472
	1480–90. Serbianization of southern Hungary.	1480
		1490
		1492
		1496
		1497
		1502
		1505
1515. First Czech newspapers.		1515
	1520–66. Suleyman I 'the Magnificent'.	1520
	1524. Montenegro conquered by the Turks.	1524
1526–1918. Hapsburg dynasty.	1526. Turkish victory at Mohacz.	1526

	Russia	Poland
1533	1533–84. Ivan the Terrible.	
1543		1543. Copernicus brings out the *De revolutionibus orbium caelestium.*
1547		
1549	1549. First meeting of the Zemsky Sobor.	
1550	1550. The Stoglav.	
1552	1552. Conquest of Kazan.	
1553	1553. Chancellor in Russia.	
1554	1554. Conquest of Astrakhan.	
1555	1555. The Muscovy Company founded in London.	
1556		
1558	1558. The Russians capture Narva.	
1564	1564. First book (*incunabulum*) printed in Moscow.	
1565	1565. Administrative reorganization: the *opritschnina.*	
1569		1569. Union of Lublin (Polish-Lithuanian state).
1571	1571. Tatar raid on Moscow.	
1572		1572. Confederation of Warsaw, Treaty of Toleration.
1574		
1580	1580. Creation of the port of Arkhangelsk.	
1581	1581. First steps towards legalizing serfdom.	
1582	1582. Ermak in Siberia.	
1584	1584–1613. The 'Time of Troubles'.	
1589	1589. Patriarchate of Moscow established.	
1592		
1596		1596. Assembly of Brześć; ecclesiastical union.
1598		
1599	1599–1605. Boris Godunov.	
1606		
1607		
1609		1609. Warsaw becomes the capital.
1610	1610. The Poles in Moscow.	
1613	1613. Romanov dynasty ascends the throne.	
1618		
1620		1620. College of Mohila founded at Kiev.
1627		
1632	1632–1640. Russia's first blast furnaces, at Tula.	
1640		
1647	1647. First engraving on copper.	
1648	1648. Dezhnev discovers the Bering Strait.	1648. Revolt of Bogdan Khmelnicki.

Czechoslovakia	Yugoslavia, Bulgaria	
		1533
		1543
1547. Subordination of the Czech towns.		1547
		1549
		1550
		1552
		1553
		1554
	1555. Foundation of the Patriarchate of Pec.	1555
1556. *De re metallica* (Agricola).		1556
		1558
		1564
		1565
		1569
	1571. Battle of Lepanto.	1571
		1572
1574. First literary text in Slovakian.		1574
		1580
		1581
		1582
		1584
		1589
1592–1670. Jan Amos Komensky (Comenius).		1592
		1596
	1598. First Bulgarian revolt against the Turks, at Tirnovo.	1598
		599
		1606
		1607
1609. 'Letters of Majesty'.		1609
		1610
		1613
1618–48. Thirty Years War.		1618
1620. The Czechs defeated at the Battle of the White Mountain.		1620
1627. New Constitution. Emigration of Czech nobles.		1627
		1632
		1640
		1647
1648. Treaties of Westphalia.		1648

	Russia	Poland
1649	1649. Legal code of Alexis Mikhailovitch. The Russians reach the Amur.	
1654	1654. The Ukraine embodied in the Russian state.	
1657		
1600		1600. Treaty of Oliva.
1662	1662. Riots in Moscow.	
1667	1667. Schism of the Old Believers. 1667–71. Stenka Razin's revolt.	
1673	1673. First theatrical performance in Moscow.	
1680		
1683		1683. Jan Sobieski's defeat of the Turks before Vienna.
1686		
1687	1687–92. Great stone bridge over the Moskva.	
1688		
1689	1689. Treaty of Nerchinsk with China. Peter the Great's reign begins.	
1690		
1699		1699. Treaty of Carlovitz (Karlovci).
1700	1700. Abolition of the Patriarchate. Calendar reformed. First paved street in Moscow.	1700–21. War of the North.
1703	1703. St Petersburg founded. First newspaper printed.	
1708	1708. Reform of the alphabet. Bulavin's rising.	
1711	1711. Inauguration of the Senate.	
1718		
1719	1719. The first census is undertaken.	
1721	1721. Peace of Nystadt concluded with Sweden. Peter I emperor. The Holy Synod created.	
1722	1722. The 'Table of Ranks'. Foundation of Ekaterinburg.	
1725	1725. Foundation of the Academy of Sciences.	
1730	1730. First oil-fired street lamps.	
1733		1733–8. War of Polish Succession.
1739		
1740		1740–8. War of Austrian Succession. 1740–60. Career of Father Stanislas Konarski; the Piarist schools.
1755	1755. University of Moscow founded.	
1760	1760. The Russians in Berlin.	

Czechoslovakia	Yugoslavia, Bulgaria	
		1649
1654. First government land-survey.		1654
1657. Bohemia recaptured by Catholicism.		1657
		1660
		1662
		1667
		1673
1680. Revolt of the Czech peasants.		1680
	1683. The Turks halted before Vienna.	1683
	1686. Second rising against the Turks at Tirnovo.	1686
		1687
	1688–9. Risings in Bulgaria and Macedonia.	1688
		1689
	1690. Large-scale emigration of Serbs to Hungary.	1690
		1699
		1700
		1703
		1708
		1711
	1718. Treaty of Passarowitz (further withdrawal by the Turks).	1718
		1719
		1721
		1722
		1725
		1730
		1733
	1739. Treaty of Belgrade (partial withdrawal by the Austrians).	1739
		1740
		1755
		1760

	Russia	Poland
1764		1764–95. Stanislas Poniatowski's reign.
1765	1765. Foundation of the Free Society of Economic Studies.	
1767		
1768		1768. Confederation of Bar.
1770	1770. The Russians in the Mediterranean (Battle of Chesme).	
1771		
1772		1772. First Partition of Poland.
1774	1774. Treaty of Kutchuk-Kainardji.	
1775	1775. Pugachev's rising.	
1780		
1781		
1783	1783. Annexation of the Crimea. First dictionary in Russian.	
1784		1784. University of Lwów founded.
1785	1785. Charter of Nobility. The merchant guilds organized.	
1788		1788–92. The 'Great Diet'.
1791		1791. Constitution of 3 May.
1793		1793. Second Partition.
1794		1794. Nation-wide insurrection.
1795		1795. Third Partition. Dissolution of Polish state.
1796	1796. Death of Catherine II.	
1797		1797. Formation of the Polish Legions.
1798	1798. First cotton-mill in St Petersburg.	
1799	1799. Suvorov's army in the Alps.	
1800	1800. Odessa established.	1800. Foundation of the Warsaw Society of Friends of the Sciences.
1801	1801. Georgia brought into the Empire.	
1802		1802. Foundation of the Imperial University of Vilno.
1804		
1806		
1807	1807. Treaty of Tilsit.	
1808		
1809		1809–12. Period of the 'Grand Duchy' of Warsaw.
1810	1810. Administrative reform.	
1811		
1812	1812. The French in Moscow.	
1813	1813. Treaty of Gulistan (acquisition of Transcaucasia).	
1814	1814. The Russians in Paris.	
1815	1815. Congress of Vienna.	1815. 'Kingdom of the Congress'.
1816	1816–64. Conquest of the Caucasus.	

Czechoslovakia	Yugoslavia, Bulgaria	
		1764
		1765
	1767. Patriarchate of Peć abolished.	1767
		1768
		1770
		1771
		1772
		1774
1775. Great revolt of the Czech peasants. Balbin's 'Defence of the Czech Language'.		1775
		1780
1781–5. Partial abolition of serfdom in Bohemia and Slovakia.		1781
		1783
1784. Foundation of the Royal Academy of Sciences of Bohemia.		1784
		1785
	1788–90. Serbian insurrection.	1788
		1791
1793. Lectures on Czech literature at the University of Prague.		1793
		1794
		1795
		1796
		1797
		1798
		1799
		1800
		1801
		1802
	1804. Serbian rising in Shumadija.	1804
	1806–11. Marmont governor-general of the Illyrian provinces.	1806
		1807
	1808. The 'Great School' of Belgrade.	1808
		1809
		1810
	1811. Death of Dositej Obradović	1811
		1812
		1813
		1814
	1815. Serbia attains autonomy.	1815
		1816

	Russia	Poland (*i.e. Polish territories*)
1818		1818. Foundation of the University of Warsaw.
1819	1819–21. Lazarev's expedition to the Antarctic.	
1823		1823. Agrarian law.
1824	1824. The Little Theatre, Moscow, inaugurated.	
1825	1825. The Great Theatre inaugurated. Decembrist rising.	
1826		
1828		1828. Bank of Poland founded.
1829	1829. The Black Sea opened for trade.	1829. Steam navigation on the Vistula.
1830		1830. 'November insurrection'. Girard begins building textile mills at Zyrardów.
1831		
1832	1832. Complete codification of Russian laws.	
1835	1835. Law concerning the Jews.	
1836		
1837	1837. Death of Pushkin. Puddling introduced into steel manufacture.	
1839		
1841		
1842		1842. School of Fine Arts, Warsaw
1844		
1846		1846. Cracow revolt.
1847		
1848		1848. Warsaw-Vienna railway.
1850		
1851	1851. Moscow-St. Petersburg railway.	
1853	1853–6. Crimean War.	
1856		
1857	1857–67. Herzen in exile, publishes *Kolokol*.	
1858	1858. Telegraph service starts at St Petersburg.	
1860	1860. First state bank. Vladivostok founded.	
1861	1861. Statute of the peasants freed from serfdom.	
1862	1862–5. The great administrative reforms.	
1863		1863. 'January insurrection'.

Czechoslovakia	Yugoslavia, Bulgaria	
		1818
		1819
		1823
		1824
		1825
	1826. Foundation of the Matica Srpska.	1826
		1828
	1829. Milos Obrenovic becomes hereditary ruler of Serbia.	1829
	1830. Gaj's 'Croato-Slavic' alphabet.	1830
1831. Foundation of the Matice Ceska.		1831
		1832
		1835
1836. Railway from Vienna to Brno.		1836
		1837
	1839. Foundation of the Matica ilirska.	1839
	1841. Illyrian Agricultural Society, Zagreb.	1841
		1842
1844. Workers rioting in Prague and Liberec.	1844. Serbian legal code.	1844
	1846. First Bulgarian newspaper. First opera in Serbo-Croatian.	1846
1847. Magyar the sole official language of the Hungarian state.		1847
1848. Abolition of the corvée. Slav Congress in Prague.	1848–9. Fighting between Serbs and Magyars.	1848
	1850. Formal agreement on Serbo-Croatian language.	1850
	1851. State of Montenegro freed from ecclesiastical control.	1851
		1853
1856. Death of Havlicek.		1856
		1857
	1858. First Bulgarian printing company, at Samokov and Salonika.	1858
		1860
		1861
1862. The Sokols founded.		1862
	1863. Sokols formed in Slovenia. Death of Vuk Karadzic. Matica slovenska.	1863

	Russia	Poland
1865	1865–76. Conquest of Central Asia.	
1867	1867. Alaska sold to USA.	
1868	1868. Initial activities of Putilov works, St Petersburg.	
1869		1869. University of Warsaw Russianized.
1870	1870. Urban statute. Russian section of First International set up.	1870–4. University of Lwów Polonized.
1873		
1874	1874. Military law.	
1875		
1877	1877–8. Russo-Turkish War. Treaty of Berlin.	
1878		
1879	1879. Electric light in St Petersburg. 'The People's Will' (secret society).	
1880		
1881	1881. Assassination of Alexander II.	1881. Telephone service starts in Warsaw.
1882		
1885	1885. Strike in the Morozov factories at Orekhovo-Zuievo.	
1886		1886. Prussia sets up a colonization commission.
1888	1888. Railway from the Caspian to Samarkand.	1888. Polish land bank, Poznan.
1890		
1891	1891. Severe famine on the Volga.	
1892	1891–1901. Trans-Siberian Railway.	1892. Polish Socialist Party.
1893	1893–5. Franco-Russian alliance.	
1894		
1896	1896. Universal exhibition of Nijni Novgorod.	
1897	1897. First comprehensive census. Gold rouble.	1897. Polish Social-Democratic Party.
1898	1898. Russian Social-Democratic Party.	
1899		
1900	1900–3. Economic crisis.	
1902		1902. University of Lwów sacked by its Ukrainian students.
1903		
1904	1904–6. Russo-Japanese war.	
1905	1905. 'Red Sunday' (22 January).	

Czechoslovakia	*Yugoslavia, Bulgaria*	
		1865
	1867. Austro-Hungarian Compromise.	1867
	1868. 'Nagodba' (agreement with the Croats).	1868
1869. First Czech bank (Zinovbanka).		1869
	1870. Bulgarian Exarchate founded.	1870
		1873
		1874
	1875. Revolt of Bosnia-Herzegovina.	1875
	1877. Russian army in Bulgarian territory.	1877
1878. Czechoslovak Social-Democratic Party.	1878. Treaty of Berlin. Serbia becomes a kingdom. Bulgaria becomes autonomous. The Austrians occupy Bosnia-Herzegovina.	1878
		1879
		1880
1881. National Theatre, Prague.		1881
1882. Prague University divided into two sections, Czech and German.		1882
	1885. Bulgaria unified. Hostilities between Serbs and Bulgars.	1885
1886. Foundation of Skoda works.		1886
	1888. University of Sofia founded.	1888
1890. 1 May, great workers' demonstration. Czech Academy of Arts and Sciences.		1890
	1891. Bulgarian Social-Democratic Party.	1891
		1892
		1893
	1894. Foundation of IMRO (Bulgaro-Macedonian Revolutionary Organization).	1894
		1896
		1897
		1898
1899. Manufacture of motor-bicycles begins.		1899
		1900
		1902
	1903. Serbian Social-Democratic Party. July: St Elias' Day rising.	1903
		1904
1905–7. Universal suffrage. Slovakian Social-Democratic Party.		1905

	Russia	Poland
1906	1906. Stolypin's agrarian laws. First Duma.	
1908		1908. Prussian law of expropriation.
1912		
1914	1914–18. First World War.	
1917	1917. February Revolution. October Revolution.	
1918	1918. Treaty of Brest-Litovsk. Third Congress of Soviets. First Soviet Constitution. 1918–26. Construction of the Volkhov electric power station.	1918. President Wilson's message on Polish independence.
1919		
1920		1920. Agrarian law.
1921	1921. New Economic Policy.	1921. Treaty of Riga. Work begins on the port of Gdynia. Universities of Poznan and Wilno founded.
1922	1922. Foundation of the USSR. First Congress of the Soviets of the USSR.	
1924	2 January 1924. Death of Lenin. First motor-car manufactured in USSR. First Constitution of the USSR.	
1925		
1926		1926. Pilsudski's *coup d'état*.
1927	1927–31. Construction of Turksib railway. 1927–32. Construction of Dnieprostroi.	
1928	1928–33. First Five-Year Plan.	
1929		
1930	1930. First cinemas equipped for sound.	
1932		
1933	1933. Trolleybuses. Colour films.	
1934	1934. USSR admitted to League of Nations. Academy of Sciences transferred to Moscow. 1934–9. Second Five-Year Plan. Moskva-Volga canal.	
1935	1935. Cheliuskin's Polar expedition.	1935–9. 'Dictatorship of the colonels'.
1936	1936. USSR's new Constitution.	
1938	1938–9. Icebreaker *Sedov*'s expedition.	
1939	1939. Inception of the Third Five-Year Plan.	1939. Partition of Poland by Germany and USSR.
1941	1941. German invasion. 1941–3. Siege of Leningrad.	
1942		

Czechoslovakia	Yugoslavia, Bulgaria	
1906. Mass production of cars.		1906
	1908. Austria annexes Bosnia-Herzegovina. Bulgaria an independent monarchy.	1908
	1912–3. Balkans War. Albania becomes a state. Treaty of Bucharest.	1912
		1914
		1917
1918. General strike. 28 October: Birth of the Czechoslovak Republic.	31 October 1918. National Council of Agram (Zagreb). Foundation of the kingdom of the Serbs, Croats and Slovenes.	1918
	1919–20. Treaties of Saint-Germain, Neuilly and Trianon.	1919
1920. General strike.		1920
1921. Foundation of Communist Party.		1921
	1922. Centralized rule decreed in Yugoslavia.	1922
	1922–5. Measures against the Democrats.	1924
1925. Mutual assistance pact with France.	1925. Bomb outrage in Sofia cathedral.	1925
		1926
		1927
	1928. Trial of Croatian terrorists.	1928
	1929–41. Dictatorial rule by monarchy in Belgrade.	1929
		1930
	1932. Ustashi rising.	1932
		1933
	1934. Assassination of King Alexander in Marseilles	1934
1935. Mutual assistance pact with USSR. Benes succeeds Marsaryk.	1935. Concordat (Yugoslavia).	1935
		1936
29 September 1938. Munich.	1938. Industrial undertaking 'Yugoslav Steel founded at Sarajevo.	1938
1939. Tiso's 'Slovakian State'. 'Protectorate of Bohemia-Moravia'.	1939. 'Yugoslav Cellulose' founded at Sarajevo.	1939
	1941. Yugoslavia joins the Tripartite Pact. German invasion.	1941
1942. Destruction of Lidice.		1942

	Russia	Poland
1943	Stalingrad.	April 1943. Destruction of the Warsaw ghetto.
1944	1944. Red Army in Bucharest (August) and Belgrade (October).	1944. 22 July: Formation of the Lublin Council of Liberation. 1 August–3 October: Warsaw rising.
1945	1945. Red Army in Warsaw (January), Vienna (April) and Berlin (2 May). Yalta and Potsdam Agreements.	
1946		1946. Nationalization of industry.
1947		
1948		
1949		
1950	Gold rouble.	1950. Building begins at Nowa Huta. Agreement concluded with the episcopate.
1952		1952. New Constitution.
1953	1953. Death of Stalin.	
1954		
1955		
1956	1956. Construction of the Lenin Stadium, Moscow.	
1960	1960. The Great Moscow.	

Czechoslovakia	Yugoslavia, Bulgaria	
	1943. Anti-fascist Council of Jajce (Yugoslavia).	1943
1944. Slovakian national insurrection.	1944. Liberation of Belgrade. Anti-fascist rising in Bulgaria.	1944
1945. Liberation of Prague (9 May). 'Kosice programme'. Beginning of nationalization.	29 November 1945. Yugoslav Republic proclaimed.	1945
1946. Slovakia acquires autonomous status.	1946. Yugoslav Federal Constitution. Bulgarian People's Republic.	1946
1947. Czechoslovakia joins COMECON.	1947. New Constitution, and beginning of nationalization, in Bulgaria.	1947
1948. People's democracy instituted.		1948
1949–53. First Five-Year Plan.	1949–53. First Bulgarian Five-Year Plan.	1949
		1950
		1952
	1953. Tito president of the Federated Peoples' Republic of Yugoslavia.	1953
		1954
1965. Czechoslovakia signs the Warsaw Pact.		1955
1956. Second Five-Year Plan.		1956
1960. New Socialist Constitution.		1960

Index

Numbers in italics refer to pages on which tables, figures or maps appear or to entries in the glossary.